PRICEWATERHOUSE COOPERS 🏦

Manual of Accounting – Financial instruments 2011

Global Accounting Consulting Services
PricewaterhouseCoopers LLP

Published by

CCH

a Wolters Kluwer business

Wolters Kluwer
145 London Road
Kingston upon Thames
KT2 6SR
Telephone: 0844 561 8166
Facsimile: +44 (0) 208 547 2638
E-mail: cch@wolterskluwer.co.uk
Website: www.cch.co.uk

This book has been prepared for general guidance on matters of interest only and does not constitute professional advice. You should not act upon the information contained in this book without obtaining specific professional advice. Accordingly, to the extent permitted by law, PricewaterhouseCoopers LLP (and its members, employees and agents) and publisher accept no liability, and disclaim all responsibility, for the consequences of you or anyone else acting, or refraining from acting, in reliance on the information contained in this document or for any decision based on it, or for any consequential, special or similar damages even if advised of the possibility of such damages.

ISBN 978-1-84798-342-8

Printed and bound in Italy by Legoprint
Typeset by YHT Limited, London

British Library Cataloguing-in-Publication Data.
A catalogue record for this book is available from the British Library.

© 2010 PricewaterhouseCoopers

Foreword

By Sir David Tweedie
Chairman
International Accounting Standards Board

Much of the work of practising accountants and standard-setters today is concerned with the global harmonisation of accounting. Since 2005, large parts of the world have used IFRS and a number of other major countries are likely to adopt IFRS around 2011. The credit crunch and associated economic difficulties have, in the last two years, put increased spotlight on accounting standards, especially those dealing with financial instruments. Politicians have interested themselves in accounting like never before. Difficult though these issues have been, they have at the same time underlined the immense need for and importance of truly global accounting standards. Developing and improving these is one of our main priorities.

Given the importance of global harmonisation, it is important that the interpretation and application of IFRS is consistent from country to country. IFRSs are based partly on the application of rules and partly on principles and judgement. Judgement is, of course, most likely to be sound when it is based on experience. In today's rapidly changing environment, I commend this Manual of Accounting – Financial instruments, which gives preparers and practitioners the benefits of the extensive experience and professional judgement of PricewaterhouseCoopers.

October 2010

Authors

The Manual of Accounting is written by the Global Accounting Consulting Services team of PricewaterhouseCoopers LLP. This book was originally written by Jyoti Ghosh.

Writing team led by
Barry Johnson
Peter Holgate

Authors, contributors and reviewers

John Althoff	Judith Gehrer	Helen McCann	Laura Taylor
Michelle Amjad	Jyoti Ghosh	Jill McCormack	Liza ThÕrache
Ariane Amiot	Rob Glasgow	John McDonnell	Sandra Thompson
Wayne Andrews	Angela Green	Malcolm J Millar	Steve Todd
Jan Backhuijs	Julian Griffiths	Marc Minet	Giovanni Andrea Toselli
Gábor Balázs	Imre Guba	Tasos Nolas	Frank Traczewski
Rod Balding	Rodney Hamill	Renshia van Noordwyk	Folker Trepte
Scott Bandura	Maarten Hartman	Michelle Orozco	Sarah Troughton
Andrea Bardens	Frank G. Hauser	Kristin Orrell	Gail Tucker
Dieter Baumann	Margaret Heneghan	Florence Ortega	Ago Vilu
Erin Bennett	Holger Meurer	Sebastian di Paola	Zubair Wadee
Daniel Blight	Peter Hogarth	John Patterson	Dave Walters
Andreas Bödecker	Sue Horlin	Moshe Peress	Wolfgang Weigel
Dasa Brynjolffssen	Claire Howells	Monica Peters	Simon Whitehead
Elizabeth Buckley	Lyn Hunt	Jennifer L Peterson	Barbara Willis
Gillian Burrows	Agnes Hussherr	Tom Quinn	Michelle Winarto
Francoise Bussac	Doug Isaac	Niranjan Raman	Katie Woods
Holger Busack	Claes Janzon	Bernd Roese	Caroline Woodward
Beate Butollo	Wendy Jessup	Meina Rose	Simon Wray
Lisa Casciaro	Eric Kahrl	James Saloman	Elza Yuen
Tracy YH Chen	Udo Kalk-Griesan	Darsen Samaroo	Milan Zeleny
Voon Hoe Chen	Yvonne Kam	Guilaine Saroul	Reto Zemp
Sophie Cren	Hannah King	Olivier Scherer	Per-Ove Zetterlund
Tony de Bell	Marie Kling	Iain Selfridge	Karen Zhang
Adrian Dadd	Matthias Kroner	Rich Sharko	
Jens Otto Damgaard	Sabine Koch	Paul Shepherd	
Lisa Dang	Margot Le Bars	Leila Sijelmassi	
Richard Davis	Liina Link	Ada Siu	
Anita Dietrich	Mark Lohmann	Cody Smith	
Lawrence Dodyk	Claude Lopater	Shelley So	
Mary Dolson	Marian Lovelace	Jennifer Spang	
Peter Eberli	Elizabeth Lynn	Lihor Spazzoli	
Michele Embling	Gesa Mannigel	Dusty Stallings	
Ian Farrar	Marie-Jeanne Morvan	Henrik Steffensen	
Peter Feige	Joanna Malvern	Tue Stensgård Sørensen	
Yulia Feygina	David Mason	Bjørn Einar Strandberg	
Peter Flick	Avni Mashru	Dennis Svensson	
Michael Gaull	Jan McCahey	Jessica Taurae	

Preface

Manual of Accounting – Financial instruments is a practical guide to IAS 32, 'Financial instruments: Presentation', IAS 39, 'Financial instruments: Recognition and measurement', and IFRS 7, 'Financial instruments: Disclosures'.

This Manual covers the complex accounting requirements of financial instruments. This aspect of accounting has become increasingly complicated in recent years and this book includes a wealth of practical examples and illustrations to help explain this difficult subject. It also includes a new chapter on IFRS 9, 'Financial instruments', which will eventually replace IAS 39.

The views expressed in this Manual are based on the experience of the PricewaterhouseCoopers' UK Accounting Consulting Services team. The views expressed are a guide to applying IFRS rather than a set of definitive interpretations. The application of IFRS to a specific company is a matter of judgement given its particular facts and circumstances. Moreover, the application of IFRS might be influenced by the views of regulators.

The chapters in this Manual form an integral part of the IFRS Manual of Accounting, but are reproduced in a separate volume. Even in a work of the size of the Manual of Accounting it is not possible to cover every aspect of company reporting. For example, this Manual does not deal with the issues faced by specific industries, such as banks and insurance companies, although much of the advice given in the text will assist them.

We hope that finance directors, accountants, legal practitioners, company administrators, financial advisors and auditors will find this Manual useful.

Barry Johnson, Peter Holgate
PricewaterhouseCoopers LLP
October 2010

Contents

IFRS Manual of Accounting

This separate book is part of this Manual of Accounting and includes the following chapters.

Contents

Abbreviations and terms used

AAPA	Association of Authorised Public Accountants
Accounts	financial statements
ADR	american depositary receipts
AESOP	all employee share ownership plan
ACT	advance corporation tax
AFS	available-for-sale
AG	Application Guidance
AGM	Annual General Meeting
AMPS	auction market preferred shares
App	Appendix
ARC	Accounting Regulatory Committee
ARSs	auction rate securities
BC	Basis for Conclusions (to an accounting standard)
C	currency unit
CCA	current cost accounting
CEO	chief executive officer
CESR	Committee of European Securities Regulators
CGAA	Co-ordinating Group on Audit and Accounting Issues
CGU	cash-generating unit
Chp	Chapter
chapter (1)	'PricewaterhouseCoopers' Manual of accounting' – chapter (1)
CIF	cost, insurance, freight
CBO	collateralised bond obligation
CDO	collateralised debt obligation
CLO	collateralised loan obligation
CMO	collateralised mortgage obligation
COSO	Committee of Sponsoring Organisations of the Treadway Commission
CPP	current purchasing power
CSR	corporate social responsibility
CTD	cumulative translation difference
CUV	continuing use value
DG XV	Directorate General XV
DP	discussion paper
DRC	depreciated replacement cost
EASDAQ	European Association of Securities Dealers Automated Quotation
EBIT	earnings before interest and tax
EBITDA	earnings before interest, tax, depreciation and amortisation
EC	European Community
ECU	european currency unit

ED	exposure draft
EEE	electrical and electronic equipment
EFRAG	European Financial Reporting Advisory Group
EITF	Emerging Issues Task Force (US)
EPS	earnings per share
ESOP	employee share ownership plan
ESOT	employee share ownership trust
EU	European Union
EU 2005 Regulation	Regulation (EC) No 1606/2002 on the application of International Accounting Standards
EUV	existing use value
FASB	Financial Accounting Standards Board (US)
FEE	The European Federation of Accountants
FIFO	first-in, first-out
financial statements	Accounts
FM	facilities management
FOB	free on board
FPI	foreign private investors (US-listed)
Framework	Framework for the preparation and presentation of financial statements
FRA	forward rate agreement
FRN	floating rate note
FVTPL	at fair value through profit or loss
GAAP	generally accepted accounting principles (and practices)
GAAS	generally accepted auditing standards
GB	Great Britain
GRI guidelines	Global Reporting Initiative guidelines
HP	hire purchase
IAASB	International Auditing and Assurance Standards Board
IAS	International Accounting Standard (see also IFRS)
IASB	International Accounting Standards Board
IASC	International Accounting Standards Committee
IBNR	incurred but not reported
IFAC	International Federation of Accountants
IFRIC	International Financial Reporting Interpretations Committee
IFRS	International Financial Reporting Standard (see also IAS)
IG	Implementation Guidance (to an accounting standard)
IGU	income-generating unit
IOSCO	International Organisation of Securities Commissions
IPO	initial public offering
IPR&D	in-process research and development
ISA	International Standard on Auditing
ISDA	International Swap Dealers Association
ISP	internet service provider
IVSC	International Valuation Standards Committee
LIFO	last-in, first-out

MBO	management buy-out
MD&A	management's discussion and analysis
NASDAQ	National Association of Securities Dealers Automated Quotations
NCU	national currency unit
OIAC	Oil Industry Accounting Committee
OTC	over-the-counter market
PA	preliminary announcement
para(s)	paragraph(s) of IFRSs or IASs or EDs, or DPs, or text
PCAOB	Public Company Accounting Oversight Board (US)
PE	price-earnings
PPE	property, plant and equipment
QUEST	qualifying employee share ownership trust
R&D	research and development
SAC	the Standards Advisory Council
SDC	Standards Development Committee
SEC	Securities and Exchange Commission (US)
SEE	social, environmental and ethical
SFAC	Statement of Financial Accounting Concepts issued in the US
SFAS	Statement of Financial Accounting Standards issued in the US
SIC	Standing Interpretation Committee of the IASC (see IFRIC)
SIPs	share incentive plans
SMEs	small and medium-sized entities
SOI	Statement of Intent
SORIE	statement of recognised income and expense
SPE	special purpose entity
SPV	special purpose vehicle
UK	United Kingdom
US	United States of America
VIE	variable interest entity
WACC	weighted average cost of capital
WEEE	Waste electrical and electronic equipment

Chapter 1

Overview

Overview

Introduction

1.1 Current requirements for financial instruments are included in IAS 32, 'Financial instruments: Presentation', IAS 39, 'Financial instruments: Recognition and measurement', IFRS 9, 'Financial instruments', and IFRS 7, 'Financial instruments: Disclosures'.

1.2 To apply in the EU, IFRSs must be endorsed by an EU 'endorsement mechanism'. In November 2004, the European Commission adopted a 'carve-out' version of IAS 39, which deleted a limited number of words and paragraphs from IAS 39 relating to the use of the 'fair value option' for financial liabilities and certain aspects of hedge accounting. Since that time, the IASB has published an amendment to IAS 39 incorporating a revised 'fair value option' and this has been adopted for use within the EU. However, differences between the IASB's 'full IAS 39' and the EU's 'carve-out' version of the standard still remain. The IASB issued IFRS 9 in November 2009. The EU has not yet endorsed IFRS 9. The Board intends that IFRS 9 will ultimately replace IAS 39 in its entirety. However, in response to requests from interested parties that the accounting for financial instruments should be improved quickly, the Board divided its project to replace IAS 39 into three main phases. As the Board completes each phase it will delete the relevant portions of IAS 39 and create chapters in IFRS 9 that replace the requirements in IAS 39. Further discussion of the development of the financial instruments standards and of their adoption for use within the EU is provided in chapter 2.

Objectives and scope of IAS 32, IAS 39 and IFRS 7

1.3 IAS 32 establishes principles for presenting financial instruments as liabilities or equity and for offsetting financial assets and liabilities. It applies to classification of financial instruments into financial assets, financial liabilities and equity instruments from the issuer's perspective; the classification of related interest, dividends, losses and gains; and the circumstances in which financial assets and liabilities can be offset.

1.4 IAS 39 is an extremely long and complex standard that establishes principles for recognising and measuring financial assets, financial liabilities and some contracts to buy or sell non-financial items. IAS 39 also deals with derecognition of financial assets and liabilities and hedge accounting.

1.5   IFRS 7 requires entities to provide disclosures that enable users to evaluate:

■   the significance of financial instruments for the entity's financial position and performance; and

■   the nature and extent of risks arising from financial instruments to which the entity is exposed and how the entity manages them.

1.6   The scope of the three standards is very wide ranging. The definition of a financial instrument under IFRS is *"any contract that gives rise to a financial asset of one entity and a financial liability or equity instrument of another entity"*. This definition encompasses cash, debt and equity investments, trade receivables and payables, debt, certain provisions, net cash-settled commodity contracts and derivatives (including embedded derivatives). However, certain financial instruments are excluded from the scope of one or all of the standards, as summarised in the table below.

Within scope of IAS 32, IAS 39 and IFRS 7		Within scope of IAS 32 and IFRS 7 only	Out of scope
Debt and equity investments			
Contingent consideration in a business combination that is a financial instrument (Note 1).			Investments in subsidiaries, associates and joint ventures accounted for under IAS 27, IAS 28 or IAS 31. Any forward contract between an acquirer and a selling shareholder to buy or sell an acquiree that will result in a business combination at a future acquisition date (Note 2).
Loans and receivables		Lease receivables (Note 3)	
Gross amount due from customers for construction contract work			
Own debt		Lease payables (Note 3) Own equity	Employee benefits Share-based payments
Cash and cash equivalents			
Derivatives – for example:		Derivatives on own shares settled only by delivery of a fixed number of shares for a fixed amount of cash	Own use commodity contracts (Note 4)
■	Interest rate swaps		
■	Currency forwards/swaps		
■	Purchased/written options		
■	Commodity contracts (Note 4)		
■	Collars/caps		
■	Credit derivatives		
■	Cash or net share settleable derivatives on own shares		

Derivatives on subsidiaries, associates and joint ventures		
Embedded derivatives		
Weather derivatives		
Loan commitments held for trading (Note 5)	Other loan commitments	
Financial guarantees (Note 6)		Insurance contracts

Note 1 – IFRS 3 has removed the scope exemption for contingent consideration in a business combination. On adoption of IFRS 3 contingent consideration from both the acquiree and acquiror's perspective is in the scope of IAS 32, IAS 39 and IFRS 7.

Note 2 – The term of the forward contract should not exceed a reasonable period normally necessary to obtain any required approvals and to complete the transaction. Any forward contract between an acquirer and a selling shareholder to buy or sell an acquiree that will result in a business combination at a future acquisition date is within IFRS 7's scope.

Note 3 – Lease receivables are included in IAS 39's scope for derecognition and impairment purposes only. Finance lease payables are subject to the derecognition provisions. Any derivatives embedded in lease contracts are also within IAS 39's scope.

Note 4 – Contracts to buy or sell non-financial items are within IAS 32's scope, IAS 39 and IFRS 7 if they can be settled net in cash or another financial asset and they do not meet the test of being entered into and continuing to be held for the purpose of receipt or delivery of non-financial items to meet the entity's expected purchase, sale or usage requirements (known as "own use commodity contracts"). Settling net includes taking delivery of the underlying and selling it within a short period after delivery to generate a profit from short-term fluctuations in price.

Note 5 – Loan commitments are outside IAS 39's scope if they cannot be settled net in cash or by some other financial instrument unless: they are held for trading or to generate assets of a class which the entity has a past practice of selling; or the entity chooses to include them with other derivatives under IAS 39.

Note 6 – From the issuer's perspective, financial guarantee contracts are within IAS 39's scope, unless the issuer has previously asserted explicitly that it regards such contracts as insurance contracts and has used accounting applicable to insurance contracts, in which case either IAS 39 or IFRS 4, 'Insurance contracts' may be applied.

1.7   The objectives and scope of IAS 32, IAS 39 and IFRS 7 is explained in greater detail in chapter 3.

Nature and characteristics of financial instruments

1.8   The definition of a financial instrument is set out in paragraph 1.6 above. One of the key components of the definition is that all financial instruments are defined by contracts. It follows that non-contractual obligations, such as taxation, are not financial instruments.

1.9   A financial asset is any asset that is:

■   Cash.

■   An equity instrument of another entity.

- A contractual right:

  - to receive cash or another financial asset from another entity; or

  - to exchange financial assets or financial liabilities with another entity under conditions that are potentially favourable to the entity.

- A contract that will or may be settled in the entity's own equity instruments and is:

  - a non-derivative for which the entity is or may be obliged to receive a variable number of the entity's own equity instruments; or

  - a derivative that will or may be settled other than by the exchange of a fixed amount of cash or another financial asset for a fixed number of the entity's own equity instruments. For this purpose the entity's own equity instruments do not include puttable financial instruments, instruments that impose on the entity an obligation to deliver to another party a *pro rata* share of the entity's net assets on liquidation and are classified as equity instruments, or instruments that are contracts for the future receipt or delivery of the entity's own equity instruments.

1.10   A financial liability is any liability that is:

- A contractual obligation:

  - to deliver cash or another financial asset from another entity; or

  - to exchange financial assets or financial liabilities with another entity under conditions that are potentially unfavourable to the entity.

- A contract that will or may be settled in the entity's own equity instruments and is:

  - a non-derivative for which the entity is or may be obliged to deliver a variable number of the entity's own equity instruments; or

  - a derivative that will or may be settled other than by the exchange of a fixed amount of cash or another financial asset for a fixed number of the entity's own equity instruments. For this purpose the entity's own equity instruments do not include puttable financial instruments, instruments that impose on the entity an obligation to deliver to another party a *pro rata* share of the entity's net assets on liquidation and are classified as equity instruments, or instruments that are contracts for the future receipt or delivery of the entity's own equity instruments.

1.10.1   The above definitions were amended to require certain puttable instruments and obligations arising on liquidation to be classified as equity, despite the contractual requirement to deliver cash or another financial asset.

1.10.2 For accounting period beginning on or after 1 February 2010, the above definition was amended to classify rights, options or warrants to acquire a fixed number of the entity's own equity instruments for a fixed amount of any currency as equity instruments. This only applies where the entity offers the rights, options or warrants *pro rata* to all of its existing owners of the same class of its own non-derivative equity instruments.

1.11 An equity instrument is any contract that evidences a residual interest in the assets of an entity after deducting all of its liabilities. Examples of equity instruments include non-puttable ordinary shares, some types of preference shares, share warrants or written call options that allow the holder to subscribe for or purchase a fixed number of non-puttable ordinary shares in the issuing entity in exchange for a fixed amount of cash or another financial asset.

1.12 Derivatives are financial instruments that derive their value from an underlying price or index, such as an interest rate, a foreign exchange rate or commodity price. IAS 39 defines a derivative as a financial instrument or other contract with all of the following characteristics:

- Its value changes in response to the change in a specified interest rate, financial instrument price, commodity price, foreign exchange rate, index of prices or rates, credit rating or credit index, or other variable, provided in the case of a non-financial variable that the variable is not specific to a party to the contract (sometimes called the 'underlying').

- It requires no initial net investment or an initial net investment that is smaller than would be required for other types of contracts that would be expected to have a similar response to changes in market factors.

- It is settled at a future date.

1.13 The nature and characteristics of financial instruments are considered further in chapter 4.

Embedded derivatives

1.14 A derivative instrument that falls within IAS 39's scope need not be free-standing. Terms and conditions may also be embedded within another financial instrument or non-financial contract (referred to as the 'host' contract) that behave like a free standing derivative. These 'embedded derivatives' should be recognised at their fair value, separately from the non-derivative host contract, when they have economic characteristics and risks that are not closely related to those of the host contract. However, an entity may designate a contract that contains one or more embedded derivative as a financial asset or financial liability at fair value through profit or loss, unless the embedded derivative does not significantly modify the cash flows required by the contract or it is clear that separation of the embedded derivative is prohibited.

1.15 Analysing non-derivative financial instruments and executory contracts for potential embedded derivatives is one of the more challenging aspects of IAS 39. This subject is considered further in chapter 5.

Classification of financial instruments

1.16 IAS 39 is a partial rather than a full fair value model. Financial assets and liabilities are measured at fair value or amortised cost depending on which defined category they fall into under the standard.

1.17 IAS 39 has four clearly defined categories of financial assets:

- A financial asset is 'at fair value through profit or loss' if it is either:
    - Held-for-trading, that is:
        - it was acquired or incurred principally for the purpose of selling or repurchasing it in the near term;
        - it forms part of a portfolio of identified financial instruments that are managed together and for which there is evidence of a recent actual pattern of short-term profit-taking; or
        - it is a derivative (except for a derivative that is a designated and effective hedging instrument).
    - Designated on initial recognition as 'at fair value through profit or loss'. The conditions that are required to be met in order to designate a financial asset (or a financial liability) as 'at fair value through profit or loss' are any of the following:
    - Where the designation eliminates or significantly reduces an accounting mismatch.
    - When a group of financial assets, financial liabilities or both are managed and their performance is evaluated on a fair value basis in accordance with a documented risk management or investment strategy and information about this group is provided on that basis to the entity's key management personnel.
    - When a contract contains an embedded derivative that meets particular conditions.

        The designation is irrevocable.

- Loans and receivables are non-derivative financial assets with fixed or determinable payments that are not quoted in an active market, with the following exceptions:
    - Those that are to be sold immediately or in the near future (held-for-trading) and any others that are designated as 'at fair value through profit or loss' on initial recognition.

- Those that are designated as available-for-sale on initial recognition.

- Those where the entity may not recover substantially all of its original investment, other than because of credit deterioration. Such assets should be classified as available-for-sale.

- Held-to-maturity investments are non-derivative financial assets with fixed or determinable payments and fixed maturity (for example, debt securities, quoted loans and mandatory redeemable preferred shares) that an entity has the positive intention and ability to hold to maturity. Exceptions are those investments that an entity designates on initial recognition as 'at fair value through profit or loss' or as 'available-for-sale' and those that meet the definition of 'loans and receivables'. Held-to-maturity instruments must have a maturity date, so investments in equity shares cannot fall into this category. There are a number of conditions set out in IAS 39 that restrict an entity's ability to categorise investments as held-to-maturity. For example, an entity may not classify any financial assets as held-to-maturity if during the current or preceding two financial years it has sold or reclassified more than an insignificant amount of held-to maturity investments, except in certain very narrowly defined circumstances.

- Available-for-sale financial assets are non-derivative financial assets that are designated as such on initial recognition or that are not classified in any other category.

1.18 IAS 39 defines two categories of financial liabilities:

- A financial liability is 'at fair value through profit or loss' if it is either held-for-trading or designated at initial recognition as 'at fair value through profit or loss' (see the first major bullet point in para 1.17).

- All other financial liabilities fall into the other liabilities category.

1.19 The classification of financial assets and financial liabilities is considered further in chapter 6.

Financial liabilities and equity

1.20 The classification of a financial instrument as either a financial liability (debt) or equity is governed by the contractual arrangements' substance rather than its legal form. An instrument is debt when the issuer is or can be required to deliver either cash or another financial asset to the holder. This is the critical feature that distinguishes debt from equity. An instrument is classified as equity when it represents a residual interest in the issuer's net assets.

1.21 All relevant features need to be considered when classifying a financial instrument. The following are some basic examples of where an instrument will be classified as a financial liability disregarding, for the moment, the requirements for certain puttable instruments and obligations arising on liquidation:

- If the issuer can or will be forced to redeem the instrument, classification as debt is appropriate.

- If the choice of settling a financial instrument in cash or otherwise is contingent on the outcome of genuine circumstances beyond the control of both the issuer and the holder, the instrument is debt as the issuer does not have an unconditional right to avoid settlement.

- An instrument that includes an option for the holder to put the rights inherent in that instrument back to the issuer for cash or another financial instrument is debt.

1.21.1 Applying the requirements for certain puttable instruments and obligations arising on liquidation, some of the instruments in the first and third bullet points above that give the holder an equity-like return will be classified as equity, provided that all of the strict criteria in the amendment are met.

1.22 The treatment of interest, dividends, losses and gains in the income statement follows the classification of the related instrument. So, if a preference share is classified as debt, its coupon is shown as interest. But the coupon on an instrument that is treated as equity is shown as a distribution.

1.23 Not all instruments are either debt or equity. Some, known as compound instruments, contain elements of both in a single contact. Such instruments, such as bonds that are convertible into equity shares either mandatorily or at the holder's option, must be split into debt and equity components. Each is then accounted for separately. The debt element is determined first by fair valuing the cash flows excluding any equity component and the residual is assigned to equity.

1.24 Derivative contracts that only result in the delivery of a fixed amount of cash or other financial assets for a fixed number of an entity's own equity instruments are classified as equity instruments. All other derivatives on own equity are treated as derivatives and accounted for as such. This includes any that:

- can or must be settled on a net basis in cash (or other financial assets) or in shares;

- may be settled gross by delivery of a variable number of own shares; or

- may be settled by delivery of a fixed number of own shares for a variable amount of cash (or other financial assets).

Any derivative on own equity that gives either party a choice over how it is settled is a financial asset or liability, unless all of the settlement alternatives would result in equity classification.

1.25 The classification of financial instruments as either debt or equity and the treatment of contracts that may be settled in an entity's own shares are considered further in chapter 7.

Recognition and derecognition

1.26 A financial asset or liability is recognised on the balance sheet when an entity becomes a party to the contract. IAS 39's rules for removing or 'derecognising' a financial asset or liability are far more complex.

1.27 IAS 39 includes a flow chart that summarises the criteria for derecognising a financial asset and this is reproduced below.

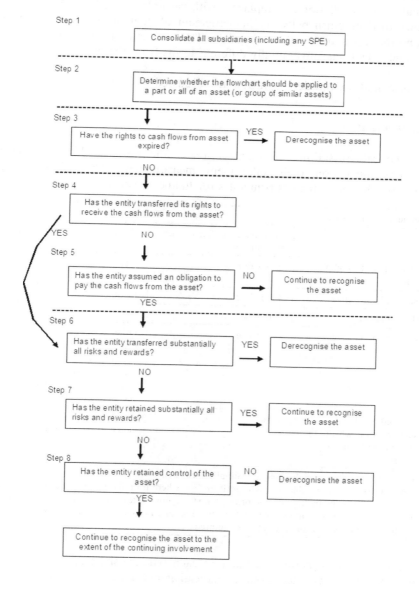

1.28   A financial liability is derecognised when it is extinguished, that is when the obligation is discharged, cancelled or expired. This condition is met when the liability is settled by paying the creditor or when the debtor is released from primary responsibility for the liability, either by process of law or by the creditor.

1.29   Entities frequently negotiate with bankers or bond-holders to cancel existing debt and replace it with new debt on different terms. For example, an entity may decide to cancel its exposure to high-interest fixed-rate debt, pay a fee or penalty on cancellation and replace it with variable-rate debt. IAS 39 provides guidance to distinguish between the settlement of debt that is replaced by new debt and the restructuring of existing debt. The distinction is based on whether or not the new debt has substantially different terms from the old debt.

1.30   Recognition and derecognition are discussed in detail in chapter 8.

Measurement

1.31   The categorisations of financial assets and financial liabilities have a significant impact on their subsequent measurement. The following table summarises the measurement principles for financial assets.

Measurement of assets		
	Measurement after initial recognition*	Changes in carrying amount
At fair value through profit or loss	Fair value	Income statement
Loans and receivables	Amortised cost	Income statement
Held-to-maturity	Amortised cost	Income statement
Available-for-sale	Fair value	Other comprehensive income (but interest, dividends, foreign exchange differences on monetary assets and changes due to impairment are taken to income statement)
Unquoted equity investments for which fair value cannot be reliably measured	Cost	Yields and impairments are taken to income statement
* All categories of financial assets are initially measured at fair value plus transaction costs, except for assets 'at fair value through profit or loss' where transaction costs are not included. Fair value is normally the transaction price (that is, the fair value of the consideration given for the asset), but the transaction price may have to be adjusted to fair value where, for example, a non-interest bearing loan or receivable is acquired.		

1.32   An assessment should be made at each balance sheet date as to whether there is any objective evidence that a financial asset (or a group of financial assets) is impaired. IAS 39 sets out rules for accounting for impairment losses on financial assets carried at amortised cost, at cost and for available-for-sale assets.

1.33 The following table summarises the measurement principles for financial liabilities.

Measurement of liabilities		
	Measurement after initial recognition*	Changes in carrying amount
At fair value through profit or loss	Fair value	Income statement
Other liabilities	Amortised cost	Income statement
* Liabilities 'at fair value through profit or loss' are initially measured at fair value (transaction costs are not included). Other liabilities are initially measured at fair value less transaction costs. Fair value is generally the transaction price, but the transaction price may have to be adjusted to fair value where, for example, convertible debt is issued and it is necessary to separate out the element of proceeds that relates to the conversion right, which is an equity instrument.		

1.34 The carrying amount of a financial instrument measured at amortised cost is computed as the amount to be paid/re-paid at maturity (usually the principal amount or par/face value), plus or minus any unamortised original premium or discount, net of any origination fees and transaction costs and less principal repayments. The amortisation is calculated using the effective interest method, which calculates the rate of interest that is necessary to discount the estimated stream of principal and interest cash flows (excluding any impact of credit losses) through the expected life of the financial instrument or, when appropriate, a shorter period to equal the amount at initial recognition. That rate is then applied to the carrying amount at each reporting date to determine the interest income (assets) or interest expense (liabilities) for the period. In this way, interest income or expense is recognised on a level yield to maturity basis.

1.35 Fair value is the amount for which an asset could be exchanged, or a liability settled, between knowledgeable, willing parties in an arm's length transaction. There is a general presumption that fair value can be reliably measured for all financial instruments. In looking for a reliable measure of fair value, IAS 39 provides a hierarchy to be used in determining an instrument's fair value.

■ Active market – quoted market price. The existence of published price quotations in an active market is the best evidence of fair value and they must be used to measure the financial instrument. The price can be taken from the most favourable market readily available to the entity, even if that was not the market in which the transaction actually occurred. The quoted market price cannot be adjusted for 'blockage' or 'liquidity' factors. The fair value of a portfolio of financial instruments is the product of the number of units of the instrument and its quoted market prices.

■ No active market – valuation technique. If the market for a financial instrument is not active, fair value is established by using a valuation technique. Valuation techniques that are well established in financial markets include recent market transactions, reference to a transaction that is substantially the same, discounted cash flows and option pricing models. An acceptable valuation technique incorporates all factors that market participants would consider in setting a price and should be consistent with accepted economic methodologies for pricing financial instruments. Normally the amount paid or received for a financial instrument is the best estimate of fair value at inception. However, where all data inputs to a valuation model are obtained from observable market transactions, the resulting calculation of fair value can be used for initial recognition.

■ No active market – equity instruments. Normally it is possible to estimate the fair value of an equity instrument that an entity has acquired from an outside party. However, if the range of reasonable fair value estimates is significant, and no reliable estimate can be made, an entity is permitted to measure the equity instrument at cost less impairment as a last resort. A similar dispensation applies to derivative financial instruments that can only be settled by physical delivery of such unquoted equity instruments.

1.36 The principles for measuring financial assets and liabilities are considered further in chapter 9.

Hedge accounting

1.37 In simple terms, 'hedge accounting' is a technique that modifies the normal basis for recognising gains and losses (or income and expenses) on associated hedging instruments and hedged items so that both are recognised in earnings in the same accounting period.

1.38 A hedged item is an asset, liability, firm commitment, highly probable forecast transaction or net investment in a foreign operation that exposes the entity to risk of changes in fair value or future cash flows that could affect profit or loss. In particular, a hedged item could be:

■ A single asset, liability, firm commitment or highly probable forecast transaction.

■ A group of assets, liabilities, firm commitments or highly probable forecast transactions with similar risk characteristics.

■ A portion of the risk or cash flows of a financial asset or liability.

■ A non-financial asset or liability (such as inventory) for either foreign currency risk or the risk of changes in the fair value of the entire item.

■ A held-to-maturity investment for either foreign currency risk or credit risk (but not interest rate risk).

■ A net investment in a foreign operation.

1.39 Generally, only assets, liabilities, firm commitments or highly probable forecast transactions that involve a party external to the entity can be designated as hedged items. However, there are exceptions to this rule for certain foreign currency intra-group transactions.

Hedging instruments

1.40 Derivatives that involve an external party may be designated as hedging instruments, except for some written options. An external non-derivative financial asset or liability may not be designated as a hedging instrument, except as a hedge of foreign currency risk.

1.41 A proportion of the entire hedging instrument, such as 50 per cent of the notional amount, may be designated as the hedging instrument. However, a hedging relationship may not be designated for only a portion of the time period during which a hedging instrument remains outstanding.

Hedge accounting criteria

1.42 In order to qualify for hedge accounting, an entity should formally designate and document the hedging relationship. This includes identifying the hedging instrument, the hedged item or transaction, the nature of the risk being hedged and how the entity will assess hedge effectiveness, together with the entity's risk management objective and strategy for undertaking the hedge.

1.43 The entity must also be able to measure and track the hedging instrument's effectiveness at the start and on an ongoing basis. IAS 39 does not require a hedge to be perfectly effective, although it is expected to be 'highly effective'. A hedge is regarded as highly effective if both of the following conditions are met:

- At the inception of the hedge and in subsequent periods, the hedge is expected to be highly effective in achieving offsetting changes in fair value or cash flows attributable to the hedged risk during the period for which the hedge is designated.

- The actual results of the hedge are within a range of 80-125 per cent.

Hedge accounting rules

1.44 In order to apply hedge accounting the above criteria must be met and the hedging relationship must fall into one of three defined categories.

1.45 A 'fair value hedge' is a hedge of the exposure to changes in fair value of a recognised asset, liability or unrecognised firm commitment, or identified portion thereof, that is attributable to a particular risk and could affect profit or loss. An example is an interest rate swap hedging a fixed rate borrowing. A fair value hedge is accounted for as follows:

- The hedging instrument is measured at fair value if it is a derivative. Non-derivatives may only be designated as hedging instruments for hedges of a foreign currency risk and in that case it is only the foreign currency element of the non-derivative that is remeasured in accordance with IAS 21, 'The effects of changes in foreign exchange rates'.

■ The carrying value of the hedged item is adjusted for the hedged risk only. If it is normally carried at cost, the hedged item is not adjusted to its full fair value. For example, a fixed rate borrowing is still basically measured at amortised cost and is adjusted only for the hedged risk (for example, foreign currency risk).

■ All gains and losses are taken to the income statement so the result is that there is no net profit and loss effect, other than any hedge ineffectiveness. Where the hedged item is an available-for-sale financial asset, the gain or loss attributable to the hedged risk is recognised in profit or loss, rather than equity, although the remainder of any fair value gain or loss is recognised in equity.

1.46   A 'cash flow hedge' is a hedge of the exposure to variability in cash flows that is attributable to a particular risk associated with a recognised asset or liability or a highly probable forecast transaction and could affect profit or loss. An example is an interest rate swap hedging a variable rate borrowing. A cash flow hedge is accounted for as follows:

■ The hedging instrument is measured at fair value.

■ The portion of the gain or loss on the hedging instrument that is determined to be an effective hedge is recognised directly in equity. The ineffective portion of the gain or loss on the hedging instrument is recognised in profit or loss.

■ The gain or loss deferred in equity is recycled to the income statement when the hedged cash flows affect income. If the hedged cash flows result in the recognition of a non-financial asset or liability on the balance sheet, the entity can choose to adjust the basis of the asset or liability by the amount deferred in equity. This choice has to be applied consistently to all such hedges.

1.47   A 'hedge of a net investment' in a foreign operation is a hedge of the reporting entity's interest in the net assets of that operation. For this purpose, net investment includes any monetary items that are accounted for as part of the net investment under IAS 21. In the consolidated financial statements, the foreign operation's net assets are retranslated with gains and losses being recognised in equity. The hedging instrument (whether a derivative or a non-derivative) is accounted for similarly to a cash flow hedge with the portion of the gain or loss on the hedging instrument that is determined to be an effective hedge being recognised directly in equity. The ineffective portion is recognised in profit or loss. The gain or loss that has been recognised in equity is recycled to profit or loss on the foreign operation's disposal.

Discontinuing hedge accounting

1.48 Hedge accounting is discontinued prospectively if any of the following occur:

- The hedge fails the effectiveness tests.
- The hedging instrument is sold, terminated or exercised.
- The hedged item is settled.
- The entity decides to revoke the hedge relationship.
- In a cash flow hedge, the forecast transaction that is hedged is no longer expected to occur.

1.49 When a non-derivative liability has been adjusted for changes in fair value under a hedging relationship, the adjusted carrying amount becomes amortised cost. Any 'premium' or 'discount' is then amortised through the income statement over the remaining period to the liability's maturity.

1.50 If a cash flow hedge relationship ceases, the amounts accumulated in equity will be maintained in equity until the hedged item affects profit or loss. However, if the hedge accounting ceases because the forecast transaction that was hedged is no longer expected to occur, gains and losses deferred in equity are recognised in profit or loss immediately. Similarly, any amounts accumulated in equity while a hedge of net investment was effective remain in equity until the disposal of the related net investment.

1.51 Hedge accounting is considered in greater detail in chapter 10.

Presentation and disclosure

1.52 The offset principle for financial instruments is set out in IAS 32. A financial asset and a financial liability should be offset when, and only when, an entity currently has a legally enforceable right to offset the recognised amounts and intends either to settle on a net basis or to realise the asset and settle the liability simultaneously.

1.53 IFRS 7 sets out the disclosure requirements for financial instruments. The standard was developed as a response to the need for more relevant information and greater transparency about an entity's exposure arising from financial instruments, and how those risks are managed.

1.53.1 In 2008 IFRS 7 was amended effective for annual periods on or after 1 January 2009. The amendment was in response to criticisms around the quality of disclosure of financial risk and particularly around financial instruments measured at fair value. This was due in part to the fact that IFRS 7 did not cover some of the disclosures that have been key as a result of the financial crisis and due to teething problems with the new standard.

1.54   IFRS 7's disclosure requirements and IAS 32's requirements for presenting financial instruments are described in chapter 11.

IFRS 9, 'Financial instruments'

1.55   IFRS 9 replaces the multiple classification and measurement models for financial assets in IAS 39 with a single model which has reduced the classification categories to amortised cost and fair value. Classification under IFRS 9 is driven by the entity's business model for managing the financial assets and the contractual characteristics of the financial assets. A financial asset is measured at amortised cost if two criteria are met: (1) the objective of the business model is to hold the financial asset for the collection of the contractual cash flows; and (2) the contractual cash flows under the instrument solely represent payments of principal and interest.

1.56   The new standard removes the requirement to separate embedded derivatives from financial asset hosts. It requires a hybrid contract to be classified in its entirety as either amortised cost or fair value. Most embedded derivatives introduce variability to cash flows, which is inconsistent with the notion that the instrument's contractual cash flows solely represent the payment of principal and interest. Most hybrid contracts with financial asset hosts are, therefore, measured at fair value in their entirety.

1.57   Two of the three fair value option criteria become obsolete under IFRS 9, as a fair value driven business model requires fair value accounting, and hybrid contracts are classified in their entity. The remaining fair value option condition in IAS 39 is carried forward to IFRS 9 – that is, management may still designate a financial asset as at fair value through profit or loss on initial recognition if this significantly reduces an accounting mismatch. The designation at fair value through profit or loss continues to be irrevocable.

1.58   IFRS 9 prohibits reclassifications except in rare circumstances when the entity's business model changes. In this case, the entity is required to reclassify affected financial assets prospectively.

1.59   There is specific guidance for contractually linked instruments that create concentrations of credit risk, which is often the case with investment tranches in a securitisation. In addition to assessing the instrument itself against the IFRS 9 classification criteria, management should also 'look through' to the underlying pool of instruments that generate cash flows to assess their characteristics. To qualify for amortised cost, the investment must have equal or lower credit risk than the weighted-average credit risk in the underlying pool of instruments, and those instruments must meet certain criteria. If 'a look through' is impracticable, the tranche is classified at fair value through profit or loss.

1.60   The IFRS 9 classification principles indicate that all equity investments should be measured at fair value. However, management has an option to present in other comprehensive income unrealised and realised fair value gains and losses on equity investments that are not held for trading. Such designation is available on initial recognition on an instrument-by-instrument basis and is irrevocable. There is no subsequent recycling of fair value gains and losses to profit or loss; however, dividends from such investments continue to be recognised in profit or loss.

1.61   IFRS 9 removes the cost exemption for unquoted equities and derivatives on unquoted equities although it provides guidance on when cost may be an appropriate estimate of fair value.

1.62   The principles for IFRS 9's classification and measurement of financial assets are considered further in chapter 12.

Chapter 2

Introduction

Chapter 2

Introduction

Accounting for financial instruments

2.1 Financial markets have experienced, and continue to experience, significant developments since the 1980s. As foreign exchange rates, interest rates and commodity prices became increasingly volatile, a need arose to manage the commercial risks arising from the instability of these markets. Primary financial instruments, such as bonds and shares, that comprised much of the traditional financing and risk management activities, gave way to derivative products, such as futures, options, forward contracts and swaps, in managing risks. Entities were able to change substantially their financial risk profile, virtually instantaneously, by entering into foreign exchange or interest rate swaps, or by acquiring options or forward contracts to hedge or take positions on future price movements. With the globalisation of financial markets, growth in international commerce, advancement in financial risk management and information technology, the development and use of cost effective innovative derivative products and complex financial instruments for managing risk and improving return on assets became commonplace.

2.2 However, it became apparent that this growth in the use of financial instruments had outstripped the development of guidance for their accounting. Traditional realisation and cost-based measurement concepts were no longer adequate to portray effectively their impact and risks, as some derivatives (for example, forward contracts and swaps) with no initial cost were simply not recognised until settlement, although some instruments with negative fair values were recorded as liabilities in the financial statements. Deficiencies in current accounting practices, inconsistent treatment of economically similar transactions and the lack of visibility in the financial statements caused difficulty for both preparers and users of financial statements. This resulted in an atmosphere of uncertainty, which many people believed might discourage the legitimate use of derivative instruments. Concern about inadequate accounting for derivatives was also heightened by the publicity surrounding large derivative-instrument losses at several companies. As a result, a pervasive need to develop a single, comprehensive standard for accounting and disclosure of financial instruments and hedging activities became a necessity.

Development of financial instruments standards

2.3 In 1988, the International Accounting Standards Committee (IASC), the predecessor body of the IASB, started work developing a comprehensive standard on the recognition, measurement and disclosure of financial instruments. The first standard, IAS 32, 'Financial instruments: Presentation and disclosure,' was issued in 1995 followed by IAS 39, 'Financial instruments: Recognition and measurement', in March 1999. However, when the IASB was formed in 2001, it undertook a project to improve international standards inherited from the IASC. As a result, revised versions of IAS 32 and IAS 39 were issued in December 2003. Since then further amendments have been made to these standards, the principal one being the issue of a new standard IFRS 7, 'Financial instruments: Disclosures', in August 2005. As IFRS 7 includes all the disclosure requirements relating to financial instruments, the title of IAS 32 was amended to 'Financial instruments – Presentation'.

2.3.1 The credit crisis of 2008 highlighted the complexity of both financial instruments and the accounting for them. There was pressure from the public, politicians and regulators, to re-think and simplify the accounting for financial instruments. IFRS 9, 'Financial instruments', represents the first milestone in the IASB's planned replacement of IAS 39. IFRS 9 was issued in November 2009 and replaces the multiple classification and measurement models for financial assets. The IASB continues to work on further stages of this standard as described below. IFRS 9 has been available for adoption since November 2009 but is not mandatory until periods commencing on or after 1 January 2013. The scope of the financial instrument standards is considered in chapter 3.

EU adoption

2.4 The EU Regulation required listed groups to prepare their consolidated financial statements using IFRS for periods commencing on or after 1 January 2005. For this to happen, IFRSs had to be brought into EU law through a complex endorsement mechanism. Although most of the IASB standards were endorsed, IAS 39 was not endorsed in full. Some aspects of IAS 39, namely the option to fair value all liabilities and certain aspects of hedge accounting that troubled banks and regulators, did not find favour with the EU and were removed. This 'carved out' version was endorsed by the EU in November 2004. The 'carve out' relating to the fair value option was removed as a result of a subsequent amendment to IAS 39 and endorsement by the EU in November 2005, but the one relating to hedge accounting remains with the result that there is still a difference between full IAS 39 and EU endorsed IAS 39. The EU has not yet endorsed IFRS 9.

The way forward

2.5 IAS 39 has been in place for over 11 years and during this time it has been amended several times. In 2008, certain clarifications and improvements were made to the standard as part of the IASB annual improvements project. However, many prepares and users of financial statements still find the requirements of IAS 39 complex. The IASB is keen to find a better accounting solution for financial instruments that will produce meaningful results without undue complexity and dependence on detailed rules.

2.6 As a first step in that process, the IASB and FASB identified three long-term projects relating to financial instruments being: derecognition; financial instruments with characteristics of equity; and replacement of IAS 39. These projects from part of the memorandum of understanding, which sets out a roadmap for convergence between IFRS and US GAAP.

2.6.1 As a result of the recent global financial crisis, the IASB has been reviewing accounting issues that have emerged, including those identified by the G20 and other international bodies such as the Financial Stability Forum. The IASB is working closely with the FASB with the aim of ensuring a globally consistent and appropriate response to the crisis. As part of this it has accelerated its project to replace IAS 39 and sub-divided it into three phases. IFRS 9, 'Financial instruments', which deals with accounting for financial assets, is part of the first stage of the project and has been finalised. The IASB is planning to finalise the remainder of the project by the second quarter of 2011 (see below). The table below summarises the large number of current projects relating to IAS 32, IAS 39 and IFRS 7 on the Boards' agenda with anticipated publication dates.

Project	Final standard publication date	Notes	Further details
IASB			
Exposure draft: Derecognition – disclosures	Q3 2010	1,2,3	8.4.1
Discussion paper: Financial instruments with characteristics of equity (exposure draft expected Q1 2011)	H2 2011	1,2	
Financial instruments (IAS 39 replacement)		1,2,3	
– Exposure draft: Fair value option for financial liabilities	Q2 2011		2.7.3-2.7.5
– Exposure draft: Amortised cost and impairment	Q2 2011		2.7.6-2.7.9
– Hedging (exposure draft expected Q3 2010)	Q2 2011		
– Asset and liability offsetting (exposure draft expected Q4 2010)	Q2 2011		
Exposure draft: Fair value measurement guidance	Q1 2011	1,2,3	
Exposure draft: Fair value measurement – measurement uncertainty analysis disclosure for fair value	Q1 2011		

Notes:
1 Part of the memorandum of understanding.
2 Joint project with the FASB.
3 Financial crisis related project.

2.6.2 The IASB issued IFRS 9, 'Financial instruments', in November 2009 as part of phase 1 of its accelerated project to replace IAS 39. The standard reduces the many financial asset classifications and measurement categories and their associated impairment models in IAS 39. The classification and measurement requirements under IFRS 9 are considered further in chapter 12.

2.6.3 The IASB published the exposure draft 'Fair value option for financial liabilities' in May 2010. Except for the proposal below, the IASB intends to retain the existing guidance in IAS 39 regarding the classification and measurement of financial liabilities. The IASB decided not to change the accounting for liabilities substantially, as the existing requirements for liabilities generally work well. However, the main concern regarding liabilities is the impact of 'own credit' for liabilities recognised at fair value.

2.6.4   Under the proposals, entities with financial liabilities designated at FVTPL follow a two-step measurement approach. First, all changes in fair value of the financial liability are recognised in the profit or loss. Secondly, the change in value due to changes in the liability's credit risk is recognised in other comprehensive income (OCI) with an offsetting entry to profit or loss. There is no subsequent recycling of the amounts in OCI to profit or loss and the entity may transfer the cumulative gain or loss within equity.

2.6.5   Financial liabilities that are required to be measured at FVTPL (as distinct from those that the entity has designated at FVTPL) continue to have all fair value movements recognised in profit or loss, with no transfer to OCI. Derivatives (including embedded derivatives), such as foreign currency forwards and interest rate swaps, or instruments held in a trading portfolio continue to have all fair value movements recognised in profit or loss.

2.6.6   The IASB issued the exposure draft 'Financial instruments: Amortised cost and impairment' in November 2009. The IASB is proposing fundamental changes to the impairment guidance for financial assets accounted for at amortised cost. This is the second stage of the IAS 39 replacement project. The exposure draft proposes an 'effective return' approach to amortised cost measurement. For financial assets, this implies an 'expected cash flow' (ECF) impairment model.

2.6.7   The proposed approach is built on the premise that interest charged on financial instruments includes a premium for expected losses, which should not be included as part of interest revenue/income, and results in an allocation of the initial estimate of expected credit losses over the expected life of the financial asset. The lender is required to identify the 'effective interest rate' (EIR) component at the inception of an instrument that represents compensation for the expected losses. Interest income is recognised over the instrument's life at the EIR, net of the expected loss component identified at inception. The premium associated with the expected losses is reflected each period as a reduction in the carrying value of the receivable (effectively a provision for bad debts).

2.6.8   Unlike the incurred loss model currently used under IAS 39, the ECF approach does not wait for evidence that an impairment has occurred; instead it requires a continuous assessment of the expected cash flows over the instrument's life. No impairment losses are recognised if the original expectations of the expected losses prove accurate. The premium associated with the initial estimate of expected losses will have reduced the receivable balance to the amount expected to be collected. However, if more losses are expected than originally estimated, an impairment charge is recognised for the decrease in the expected cash flows. If favourable changes to loss expectations occur, a credit to income is recognised for the increase in expected cash flows. The approach requires the use of an allowance account for credit losses and no direct write-offs are permitted. The exposure draft makes allowance for practical expedients in calculating amortised cost if the overall effect is immaterial. An example would be short-term trade receivables.

2.6.9 The exposure draft sets out robust presentation and disclosure requirements to ensure that users can evaluate the financial effect of interest revenue and interest expense, and the credit quality of financial assets held by the entity.

Structure of the chapters

2.7 Detailed discussion of accounting for financial instruments is structured around the following chapters:

- Objectives and scope of IAS 32, IFRS 7 and IAS 39.

- Nature and characteristics of financial instruments.

- Embedded derivatives in host contracts.

- Classification of financial instruments.

- Financial liabilities and equity.

- Recognition and derecognition of financial instruments.

- Measurement of financial instruments.

- Hedging and hedge accounting.

- Presentation and disclosure of financial instruments.

- IFRS 9, 'Financial instruments'.

2.8 The above chapters address the requirements of IAS 32, IFRS 7, IAS 39 and IFRS 9 extant as at 31 August 2010. All four standards are supplemented by application guidance that is an integral part of the standards and, where relevant, by illustrative examples that accompany them, but that are not part of the standards. In addition, IAS 39 and IFRS 7 are also supplemented by implementation guidance that is not part of the standards. Furthermore, as IAS 39 is largely based on the US standard FAS 133, 'Accounting for derivative instruments and hedging activities', the chapters that follow draw on the guidance of that standard where it is considered appropriate and necessary to do so.

Chapter 3

Objectives and scope of IAS 32, IAS 39 and IFRS 7

Objectives and scope of IAS 32, IAS 39 and IFRS 7

Objectives

3.1 IAS 32's objective is to establish principles for presenting financial instruments as financial liabilities or equity and for offsetting financial assets and financial liabilities. It applies to the classification of financial instruments into financial assets, financial liabilities and equity instruments from the perspective of the issuer. Furthermore, it deals with the classification of related interest, dividends, losses and gains; and the circumstances in which financial assets and liabilities should be offset. [IAS 32 para 2].

3.2 IAS 39's objective is to establish principles for recognising and measuring financial assets, financial liabilities and some contracts to buy or sell non-financial items. [IAS 39 para 1]. IAS 39 also deals with derecognition of financial assets and financial liabilities and hedge accounting. Requirements for presenting and disclosing information about financial instruments set out in IAS 32 and IFRS 7 are designed to complement those principles.

3.3 IFRS 7's objective is to require entities to provide disclosures that enable users to evaluate:

■ The significance of financial instruments for the entity's financial position and performance.

■ The nature and extent of risks arising from financial instruments to which the entity is exposed during the period at the reporting date and how the entity manages these risks.

[IFRS 7 para 1].

Scope

3.4 Generally, IAS 32, IAS 39 and IFRS 7 have to be applied by all entities preparing their financial statements in accordance with IFRS and to all types of financial instruments, except for those specifically excluded from their scope [IAS 32 para 4; IAS 39 para 2; IFRS 7 para 3]. The definition of a financial instrument is broad and is discussed in chapter 4.

3.5 The scope of the three standards is very wide-ranging, but not identical. While IAS 32 and IAS 39 only deal with recognised financial instruments, IFRS 7 applies to both recognised as well as unrecognised financial instruments. Recognised financial instruments include financial assets and financial liabilities that are within IAS 39's scope. Unrecognised financial instruments include some financial instruments, for example, loan commitments that, although scoped out of IAS 39, are within IFRS 7's scope. [IFRS 7 para 4]. In other words, all financial instruments that are scoped out of IFRS 7 are also scoped out of IAS 39, but IAS 39 contains additional scope exclusions that go beyond IFRS 7 and IAS 32. [IAS 32 para 4; IFRS 7 para 3; IAS 39 para 2]. In general, items are scoped out of all the three standards if another standard is more prescriptive.

Interests in subsidiaries, associates and joint ventures

3.6   Interests in subsidiaries, associates and joint ventures that are accounted for using the cost method prescribed in IAS 27, 'Consolidated and separate financial statements', IAS 28, 'Investment in associates', and IAS 31, 'Interest in joint ventures', or that are accounted for in accordance with IFRS 5, 'Non-current assets held-for-sale and discontinued operations,' [IAS 27 para 38; IAS 28 para 14; IAS 31 para 2(a)] are outside the scope of IAS 32, IFRS 7 and IAS 39.

3.7   However, such interests fall within the scope of the financial instrument standards in either of the following circumstances:

■   The parent or the investor accounts for such interests in its separate financial statements in accordance with IAS 39 either as at fair value through profit or loss or as available for sale. [IAS 27 para 38]. In that situation, the interest in a subsidiary, associate or joint venture falls within IAS 32's and IFRS 7's scope. [IAS 32 para 4(a); IFRS 7 para 3(a)]. In addition, the disclosure requirements of IAS 27, IAS 28 and IAS 31 continue to apply.

■   An interest in an associate or a joint venture that is scoped out of IAS 28 or IAS 31, because it is held by a venture capital organisation, mutual fund, unit trust and similar entity including an investment-linked insurance fund that upon initial recognition is designated as at fair value through profit or loss (so called fair value option) or categorised as held for trading. [IAS 28 para 1, IAS 31 para 1]. In that situation, the investment is accounted for in accordance with IAS 39 and the disclosure requirements of IFRS 7, as well as of paragraph 37(f) of IAS 28 and of paragraphs 55 and 56 of IAS 31, apply.

3.8   Derivatives linked to interests in subsidiaries, associates and joint ventures fall within the scope of IAS 32, IFRS 7 and IAS 39, except where the derivative meets the definition of an equity instrument of the entity in IAS 32. In that situation, it is scoped out of IAS 39 and accounted for as equity in accordance with IAS 32. [IAS 32 para 4(a); IFRS 7 para 3(a); IAS 39 para 2(a)].

3.9   An investor may, in addition to having a present ownership interest, hold share options in an investee (that is not presently a subsidiary) that, if exercised, give the investor voting power or reduce another party's voting power over the financial and operating policies of the investee (potential voting rights). Such potential voting rights that are currently exercisable and give access to the economic benefits would have been taken into account in establishing not only whether the investor has control, significant influence or joint control, but also in determining the share of the investment (economic interest) to be accounted for by consolidation, equity method or proportional consolidation. [IAS 27 paras 14, IG 4-5; IAS 28 para 8]. When instruments containing potential voting rights in substance currently give access to the economic benefits associated with an ownership interest and so affect the share of profits the investee accounts for when consolidating, proportionately consolidating or applying the equity method, the instrument is scoped out of IAS 39. [IAS 27 para IG 7]. This exclusion makes sense as it avoids double counting the same instrument twice, first by inclusion in the economic interest calculation and, secondly, by fair valuing the derivative through profit or loss. Therefore, in this situation, IAS 32 and IFRS 7 apply, but not IAS 39.

Employee benefit plans and share-based payments

3.10 Employee rights and obligations under employee benefit plans are financial instruments, because they are contractual rights or obligations that will result in the flow of cash to the past and present employees. However, as they are specifically accounted for under IAS 19, 'Employee benefits', they are outside the scope of IAS 32, IFRS 7 and IAS 39. [IAS 32 para 4(b); IFRS 7 para 3(b); IAS 39 para 2(c)].

3.11 Similarly, share-based payment transactions to which IFRS 2, 'Share-based payment', applies are outside the scope of IAS 32, IFRS 7 and IAS 39. However, IAS 32, IFRS 7 and IAS 39 apply to contracts to buy or sell non-financial items in share based payment transactions that can be settled net, unless they fall within the own use purchase and sale exception (see para 3.34 below). For example, if an entity enters into a contract to purchase a fixed quantity of a particular commodity in exchange for issuing a fixed number of own equity instruments that could be settled net in cash, the contract would fall within IAS 39's scope, unless it qualifies for the own use exception. [IAS 32 para 4(f)(i); IFRS 7 para 3(e); IAS 39 para 2(i)].

3.12 Furthermore, IAS 32 applies to treasury shares that are purchased, sold, issued or cancelled in connection with employee share option plans, employee share purchase plans and all other share-based payment arrangements. [IAS 32 paras 4(f)(ii), 33, 34].

Business combinations

3.13 In accordance with IFRS 3 'Business combinations', contracts for contingent consideration usually fall within the scope of IAS 32, IAS 39 and IFRS 7, provided they do not meet the definition of an equity instrument. [IFRS 3 paras 40 and 58]. However, from an acquirer's perspective only, contracts for contingent consideration in a business combination that occurred under IFRS 3 (superceded) – that is, those that occurred in annual periods starting prior to 1 July 2009, are still scoped out of IAS 32, IFRS 7 and IAS 39. From the perspective of the seller, all contracts for contingent consideration normally fall within the scope of IAS 39 and IFRS as a financial asset (see also IFRS Manual of Accounting chapter 26).

3.14   Forward contracts between an acquirer and a vendor in a business combination to buy or sell an acquiree at a future date are scoped out of IAS 39, but not IFRS 7. [IAS 39 para 2(g)]. The scope exemption applies to both the acquirer and the seller. The Board amended paragraph 2(g) of IAS 39 in the 2009 'Improvements to IFRSs' to clarify that:

■   The scope exemption applies only to forward contracts entered into before the acquisition date (that is, before the date the acquirer obtains control of the acquiree).

■   The term of the forward contract should not exceed a reasonable period normally necessary to obtain any required approvals and to complete the transaction.

■   The exemption in paragraph 2(g) should not be applied by analogy to investments in associates and other similar transactions.

The amendment was effective prospectively to all unexpired contracts for annual periods beginning on or after 1 January 2010.

3.14.1   Prior to the amendment, it was unclear as to whether the paragraph 2(g) scope exemption only applied to forward contracts or also to other instruments (such as options) that, if exercised or converted, would give control of an entity to an acquirer. Significant diversity had arisen in practice as a result. The two main interpretations of the scope exemption prior to the amendment were:

■   A 'narrow' interpretation under which only forward contracts between the purchaser and seller would be outside the scope of IAS 39.

■   A 'broad' interpretation under which all kinds of contracts between the purchaser and seller would be outside the scope of IAS 39. This would include options (both purchased and written) that, if exercised, would give control of an entity to an acquirer.

3.14.2   If the 'broad' interpretation, referred to above, had been applied to options, these would have been remeasured from cost to fair value when the amendment was first applied. There were no 'grandfathering' rules in the amendment. We believe that the transition guidance in the amendment suggests that the adjustment from cost to fair value that arises when the amendment is first applied should be recorded in the income statement in the year of adoption. However, the wording of the transition requirements is not clear; as a result, the adjustment could also be taken to opening retained earnings in the period of adoption (that is, no prior-year restatement).

Own equity instruments

3.15 Financial instruments issued by an entity, including options and warrants that meet the definition of an equity instrument in IAS 32 or are required to be classified as equity in accordance with paragraphs 16A, 16B, 16C and 16D of IAS 32, are outside IAS 39's but inside IAS 32's scope. Such instruments, along with other equity accounts including retained earnings, represent the residual interest of the reporting entity and are, therefore, subject to different measurement considerations to those relevant to financial assets and financial liabilities. However, the holder (but not issuer) of such an instrument should apply IAS 39 unless it meets the exceptions discussed in paragraphs 3.6 to 3.9 above. [IAS 39 para 2(d)]. IFRS 7 deals with disclosures of financial instruments in general and doesn't scope out issuers' own equity instruments, for example, disclosure about compound financial instruments in IFRS 7 para 17.

Rights and obligations under lease contracts

3.16 Finance lease contracts that give rise to financial assets for lessors and financial liabilities for lessees are financial instruments that are specially dealt within IAS 17, 'Leases'. Therefore, they fall within the scope of IAS 32 and IFRS 7, but outside of IAS 39's scope, except as follows:

■ Lease receivables are included in IAS 39's scope for derecognition and impairment purposes only.

■ Finance lease payables are subject to IAS 39's derecognition provisions.

■ Any derivatives embedded in lease contracts are also within IAS 39's scope. [IAS 39 para 2(b)].

Rights and obligations under insurance contracts

3.17 An insurance contract is a contract under which one party (the insurer) accepts significant insurance risk from another party (the policyholder) by agreeing to compensate the policyholder if a specified uncertain future event (the insured event) adversely affects the policyholder. [IFRS 4 App A]. Principally, rights and obligations under insurance contracts are scoped out of IAS 32, IFRS 7 and IAS 39 and are accounted for under IFRS 4, because the policyholder transfers to the insurer significant insurance rather than financial risk. [IAS 32 para 4(d); IAS 39 para 2(e)]. Financial risk is the risk of a possible future change in one or more of a specified interest rate, financial instrument price, commodity price, foreign exchange rate, index of prices or rates, credit rating or credit index or other variable, provided in the case of a non-financial variable that the variable is not specific to a party to the contract. [IFRS 4 App A]. If a financial instrument takes the form of an insurance contract, but involves the transfer of financial risks, as opposed to insurance risk, the contract would fall within the financial instrument standards. The distinction between insurance risk and other risks are set out in Appendix B to IFRS 4. [IFRS 4 App B paras 8-17]. IFRS 4 contains numerous examples of insurance contracts that fall within IFRS 4's scope and those that are not insurance contracts and may fall within the scope of IAS 32, IFRS 7 and IAS 39. [IFRS 4 App B paras 18-19] IFRS 7 provides disclosure only for those rights and obligations under insurance contracts that are also in IAS 39's scope. [IFRS 7 para 3(d)].

Contracts with discretionary participating features

3.18   Financial instruments that are within IFRS 4's scope, because they contain a discretionary participation feature are also scoped out of IAS 39. A discretionary participation feature is a contractual right to receive significant additional benefits, as a supplement to guaranteed benefits, whose amount and timing is at the issuer's discretion and that are contractually based on the performance of a specified pool of contracts, investment returns or profit or loss of the company, fund or other entity that issues the contract. [IFRS 4 App A]. However, these instruments are in IFRS 7's scope and subject to the requirements of IAS 32 except for those with respect to the distinction between financial liabilities and equity instruments. [IAS 32 para 4(e); IAS 39 para 2(e)].

Derivatives embedded in insurance contracts

3.19   Derivatives embedded in insurance contracts or in contracts containing discretionary participating features as discussed above are within the scope of IAS 32, IFRS 7 and IAS 39 if they require separation in accordance with IAS 39. [IAS 39 para 2(e); IFRS 4 para 34(d)]. For example, separate accounting would be required in circumstances where contractual payments embedded in a host insurance contract that is indexed to the value of equity instruments are not related to the host instrument, because the risks inherent in the host and the embedded derivative are dissimilar. [IAS 39 para AG 30(d)]. However, no separation is required if the embedded derivative itself is an insurance contract. [IAS 39 para 2(e); IFRS 4 para 7].

Financial guarantee contracts

3.20   Financial guarantee contracts (sometimes known as 'credit insurance') require the issuer to make specified payments to reimburse the holder for a loss it incurs if a specified debtor fails to make payment when due under a debt instrument's original or modified terms. [IAS 39 para 9]. That is, the holder is exposed to and has incurred a loss on the failure of the debtor to make payments. These contracts are often written by financial guarantee insurers in the form of insurance contracts, or they may be written by banks and entities that do not operate as insurance entities in other forms (for example, letter of credit, credit default contracts).

3.21   A contract that compensates the holder for more than the loss incurred does not meet the definition of a financial guarantee contract. For the definition to be met, the amount of reimbursement must be either less than the amount of the loss incurred or equal to the amount incurred in order to reimburse some or all of the loss the holder suffered because the debtor defaulted.

3.22 Contracts that provide compensation if another party fails to perform a contractual obligation, such as an obligation to construct a building, are performance guarantees. They do not transfer credit risk and, therefore, do not meet the definition of a financial guarantee contract. These type of guarantees are accounted for under IFRS 4 as insurance contracts.

[The next paragraph is 3.25.]

3.25 The accounting treatment of a financial guarantee contract does not depend on its legal form nor whether it is issued by a bank, insurance company or other entity. Rather, all contracts that meet the definition of a financial guarantee fall within IAS 39's scope and are accounted for by the issuer as financial liabilities. However, an option is available to insurers to continue to account for these contracts under IFRS 4 if they had met two conditions before IAS 39 was amended to include financial guarantees in its scope. These are that the issuer has:

- previously *asserted* explicitly that it regards such contracts as insurance contracts; and

- used accounting applicable to insurance contracts.

If these two conditions are met, the issuer may elect to apply either IFRS 4 or IAS 39 to such financial guarantee contracts. The issuer can make the election on a contract by contract basis, but the election for each contract is irrevocable. [IAS 39 paras 2(e), AG4]. Assertions that the issuer regards contracts as insurance can typically be found in business documentation, contracts, accounting policies, financial statements and communication with customers and regulators. [IAS 39 para AG 4A].

3.25.1 In contrast, some credit related guarantees do not, as a precondition for payment, require that the holder is exposed to, and has incurred a loss on, the failure of the debtor to make payments on the guaranteed asset when due. Such guarantees are not financial guarantee contracts as defined in paragraph 3.20 above and are not insurance contracts as defined in IFRS 4. Such guarantees are derivatives that must be accounted for as such under IAS 39. [IAS 39 para AG 4(b)]. However, a contract that requires an entity to make payments when the counterparty to a derivative contract fails to make a payment when due, is considered to meet the definition of a financial guarantee contract. This is because it is not the risk inherent in the derivative that is being guaranteed; it is the counterparty's credit risk that is being guaranteed in the event the counterparty defaults.

Example 1 – Credit related guarantee

A bank issues a credit-related guarantee contract (sometimes referred to as credit derivative) that provides for payment if the credit rating of a debtor falls below a particular level.

In this situation, the credit related contract will be accounted for as a derivative financial instrument under IAS 39, because the contract holder is not required to suffer a loss on a specified debt instrument – the bank will pay for the decrease in the credit worthiness of the debtor even if the debtor does not actually default. However, if the contract provides for payment only in the event that the entity suffers loss as a result of non-payment by the debtor, the contract would be a financial guarantee contract. Holders and issuers of credit derivatives will always account for them under IAS 39.

Example 2 – Residual value guarantee

An insurer is required to make payments to the insured party based on the fair value of a non-financial asset at a future date under a residual value guarantee contract.

In this situation, the risk of changes in the fair value of the non-financial asset is not a financial risk because the fair value reflects not only changes in market prices for such assets (a financial variable), but also the condition of the specific asset held (a non-financial variable). As the change in fair value of the non-financial asset is specific to the owner, it is not a derivative instrument and, therefore, the contract will be accounted for as an insurance contract in accordance with IFRS 4. However, if the contract compensates the insured party only for changes in market prices and not for changes in the condition of the specific non-financial asset held, the contract is a derivative and within IAS 39's scope. [IFRS 4, IG example 1.15, IAS 39 para AG 12A].

3.26 There is no exemption under IAS 39 for financial guarantee contracts issued between members of a group or entities under common control similar to those under US GAAP FIN 45, 'Guarantor's accounting and disclosure requirements for guarantees, including direct guarantees of indebtedness to others'. Such guarantees are inter-company transactions that are eliminated on consolidation. However, in the individual financial statements of the group member issuing the guarantee, the guarantee contract will need to be accounted for in accordance with IAS 39. This is considered further in chapter 9.

Example – Parent provides a comfort letter to a subsidiary

A subsidiary of a group takes out a loan with a bank. The parent provides a comfort letter to the subsidiary such that if the subsidiary fails to repay the loan to the bank when due, the parent will pay on its behalf.

The comfort letter simply constitutes an undertaking given by the parent to its subsidiary that, in the event the subsidiary fails to repay the loan to the bank when due, the parent will step in and discharge the subsidiary's debt. This is not a financial guarantee contract as the parent has not provided any guarantee to the bank (nor would the bank be able to enforce payment under what is effectively a private arrangement between the parent and its subsidiary) to repay the loan if the subsidiary defaults.

3.27 Intra-group guarantees also frequently cover other obligations, such as pension plan contributions, lease rentals and taxes. The issue is whether, in the group members' individual financial statements, such obligations are financial guarantee contracts or insurance contracts. As noted in paragraph 3.17 above, if a financial instrument takes the form of an insurance contract, but involves the transfer of financial risks, as opposed to insurance risk, the contract would fall within the scope of the financial instrument standards. It is, therefore, necessary to determine whether the risk transferred represents insurance risk or financial risk. The risk transferred in a guarantee of pension plan contributions, operating lease rentals and taxes is the risk that the subsidiary (or joint venture or associate) will not make a payment when due. The reasons for non-payment could vary widely and, whilst they might include some financial risk variables, it is likely that a significant part of the risk transferred will be operational (for example, cash flow difficulties or, at the extreme, bankruptcy). Hence, it appears that the significant risk transferred in a typical guarantee of pension plan contributions, operating lease rentals and taxes will be insurance risk. It is arguable, therefore, that guarantees of pension plan contributions, operating lease rentals and taxes should be treated as insurance contracts and accounted for accordingly.

3.28 Notwithstanding that guarantees of pension plan contributions, operating lease rentals and taxes are insurance contracts within IFRS 4's scope, it is still necessary to consider whether they meet the definition of financial guarantee contracts within IAS 39's scope. The definition of a financial guarantee contract refers specifically to the terms of a debt instrument. Although the term 'debt instrument' is not specifically defined in IFRS, it is clear from the various references made in IAS 32 that a debt instrument is a type of loan, involving a borrower and a lender. It can be concluded, therefore, that pension plan contributions and tax liabilities are not debt instruments. As regards leases, paragraph AG9 of IAS 32 states that *"a finance lease is regarded as primarily an entitlement of the lessor to receive, and an obligation of the lessee to pay, a stream of payments that are substantially the same as blended payments of principal and interest under a loan agreement. ... An operating lease, on the other hand, is regarded as primarily an uncompleted contract committing the lessor to provide the use of an asset in future periods in exchange for consideration similar to a fee for a service"*. This analysis suggests that a finance lease resembles a debt instrument, while an operating lease does not. Even where operating leases do fall within the definition of a financial instrument (that is, in respect of individual payments currently due and payable), the amounts represent short-term payables, which Appendix A of IFRS 7 suggests are something other than a loan payable. Accordingly, guarantees of finance leases, but not operating leases, should be included within IAS 39's definition of a financial guarantee contract. We note that the IASB published its discussion paper 'Leases' in March 2009, which proposes to remove the distinction between operating and finance leases. If this proposal is progressed to a standard, additional guarantee contracts will be brought into IAS 39's scope.

3.29 Financial guarantee contracts fall within the scope of IAS 32 and IFRS 7 if they are accounted for in accordance with IAS 39. However, if the issuer elects to apply IFRS 4 to those contracts, the disclosure requirements of IFRS 4 and not IFRS 7 apply. [IAS 32 para 4(d); IFRS 7 para 3(d)]. The accounting treatment of financial guarantee contracts is considered further in chapter 9.

Weather derivatives

3.30   Some contracts require a payment based on climatic variables (sometimes described as weather derivatives) or on geological or other physical variables. For such contracts, payments are sometimes made on the amount of loss suffered by the entity and sometimes not. Prior to IAS 39's revision, all such contracts were scoped out of IAS 39 and treated as insurance contracts. However, following IFRS 4's publication, such contracts are accounted for as follows:

■   Contracts that require a payment only if a particular level of the underlying climatic, geological, or other physical variables adversely affects the contract holder.

These are insurance contracts as payment is contingent on changes in a physical variable that is specific to a party to the contract.

■   Contracts that require a payment based on a specified level of the underlying variable regardless of whether there is an adverse effect on the contract holder.

These are derivatives and are within IAS 39's scope.

[IAS 39 para AG 1, IFRS 4 para BC 55].

Example – Weather derivatives

A farming entity in Punjab, a State in India, relies on the prospect of a good monsoon that would favourably impact its earnings for the season. A good monsoon in Punjab involves an average rainfall of about 400mm during the months of June, July and August. The entity enters into a contract with a counterparty that would pay a fixed sum of Rs1m if the entity suffers loss due to poor production caused by below average rainfall during the monsoon months. The premium paid on the contract is Rs50,000.

This is an example of a highly tailored or customised policy that provides the entity protection against an adverse impact on earnings due to poor production caused by poor monsoon in Punjab, irrespective of whether the rest of India has a good monsoon or not. Hence, the contract is an insurance contract and is scoped out of IAS 39. It should be noted that even if the farming entity's loss due to poor production is less than Rs1m, the entity would receive Rs1m as stipulated in the contract. The definition of an insurance contract does not limit the payment by the insurer to an amount equal to the financial impact of the adverse event. [IFRS 4 App para B13].

If, on the other hand the sum of Rs1m was paid if the average rain fall was below 400mm during the months of June, July and August and it would be payable irrespective of fact that the farming entity in Punjab had suffered any damage, then the contract would be accounted for as a derivative instrument. This is because payment is made following the change in average rainfall which is a non-financial variable that is not specific to the holder of the contract and hence one of the variables considered in the definition of financial risk.

Loan commitments

3.31 Loan commitments are firm commitments to provide credit under pre-specified terms and conditions. [IAS 39 BC15]. They are usually entered into by financial institutions such as banks for providing loans to third parties at a specified rate of interest during a fixed period of time. Such a commitment is a derivative, since it has no initial net investment, it has an underlying variable (interest rate) and it will be settled at a future date. In effect, the lender has written an option that allows the potential borrower to obtain a loan at a specified rate.

3.32 The following loan commitments are within IAS 39's scope:

- Loan commitments that the entity designates as financial liabilities at fair value through profit or loss. This may be appropriate, for example, if the entity manages risk exposures related to loan commitments on a fair value basis. [IAS 39 para 4(a)].

- An entity that has a past practice of selling the assets resulting from its loan commitments shortly after origination should apply IAS 39 to all its loan commitments in the *same class*. The term 'same class' is not explained in the standard, but we believe that a commitment to provide borrowing facilities to a corporate entity is not in the same class as a commitment to provide residential mortgage loans, because of differing risk return profiles. [IAS 39 para 4(a)].

- Loan commitments that can be settled net in cash or by delivering or issuing another financial instrument. These loan commitments are derivatives. A loan commitment is not regarded as settled net merely because the loan is paid out in instalments (for example, a mortgage construction loan that is paid out in instalments in line with the progress of construction). [IAS 39 para 4(b)].

- Commitments to provide a loan at a below-market interest rate (see chapter 9). [IAS 39 para 4(c)].

3.33 Loan commitments that are not within IAS 39's scope should be accounted for in accordance with IAS 37. Where events make such a loan commitment an onerous contract, the contract falls within IAS 37's scope and a liability exists that should be recognised. However, all loan commitments, whether scoped in or out of IAS 39, are subject to IAS 39's derecognition provisions and to IFRS 7's disclosure requirements. [IAS 39 para 2(h); IFRS 7 para 4].

Contracts to buy or sell non-financial assets

3.34 Contracts to buy or sell non-financial items are, in general, not financial instruments. Many commodity contracts are of this type. However, if such contracts can be settled net in cash or by exchanging another financial instrument, they fall within the scope of IAS 32, IFRS 7 and IAS 39 as if they were financial instruments (derivatives). This is so, unless the contracts were entered into and continue to be held for the purpose of receipt or delivery of non-financial items to meet the entity's expected purchase, sale or usage requirements (often referred to as 'own use' purchase or sale exception). [IAS 32 paras 8-10; IFRS 7 para 5; IAS 39 para 5]. In other words, if the own use exception is met, the contract must not be accounted for as a derivative (that is, the application of the own use exception is not a choice).

Contracts that can be settled net

3.35   There are various ways in which a contract to buy or sell a non-financial asset can be settled net in cash, including when:

■   The terms of the contract permit either party to settle net in cash or another financial instrument or by exchanging financial instruments. Net settlement means that the entity will pay or receive cash (or an equivalent value in other financial assets) to and from the counterparty, equal to the net gain or loss on the contract on exercise or settlement.

■   The ability to settle the contract net is not explicitly stated in the contract, but the entity has a practice of settling similar contracts net in cash (whether with the counterparty, by entering into offsetting contracts or by selling the contract before its exercise or lapse). For example, a futures exchange permits an entity to enter into offsetting contracts that relieves the entity of its obligation to make or receive delivery of the non-financial asset.

■   For similar contracts, the entity has a practice of taking delivery of the underlying and selling it within a short period after delivery to generate a profit from short-term fluctuations in price or dealer's margin. An example is an exchange that offers a ready opportunity to sell the contract.

■   The non-financial asset that is the subject of the contract is readily convertible into cash.

[IAS 32 para 9; IAS 39 para 6].

3.36   Where the second and third bullet points above apply, the entity's activities make it clear that the contracts cannot qualify for 'normal' purchase or sale exception. Accordingly, such contracts are within the scope of the financial instrument standards. Other contracts that can be settled net should be evaluated to determine whether they qualify for the exception. For example, to qualify for the exception, a contract's terms must be consistent with the terms of an entity's normal purchases or sales; that is, the quantity specified in the contract must be expected to be used or sold by the entity over a reasonable period in the normal course of business. Other factors that may be relevant in determining whether or not the contract qualifies for the exception may include the locations to which delivery of the items will be made, the period of time between entering into the contract and delivery and the entity's prior practices with regard to such contracts.

Example – Forward contract to purchase a commodity

Entity XYZ enters into a fixed price forward contract to purchase one million kilograms of copper in accordance with its expected usage requirements. The contract permits XYZ to take physical delivery of the copper at the end of 12 months or to pay or receive a net settlement in cash, based on the change in fair value of copper.

The above contract needs to be evaluated to determine whether it falls within the scope of the financial instruments standards. The contract is a derivative instrument because there is no initial net investment, the contract is based on the price of copper and it is to be settled at a future date. However, if XYZ intends to settle the contract by taking delivery and has no history for similar contracts of settling net in cash, or of taking delivery of the copper and selling it within a short period after delivery for the purpose of generating a profit from short-term fluctuations in price or dealer's margin, the contract is not accounted for as a derivative under IAS 39. Instead, it is accounted for as an executory contract. [IAS 39 IG A1].

In the above example, it is possible for entity XYZ and the counterparty to reach different conclusions about whether the contract falls within IAS 39's scope. For example, a 'normal' sale by the counterparty may not be a 'normal' purchase by entity XYZ that would treat the contract as a derivative. This is one of the few areas of IAS 39 where a contract may be treated as a derivative by one party, but not be treated as a derivative by the other party.

Written options

3.37 A written option to buy or sell a non-financial item that can be settled net in accordance with paragraph 3.34 above cannot be considered to be entered into for the purpose of the receipt or delivery of the non-financial item in accordance with the entity's expected purchase, sale or usage requirements. This is because an option written by the entity is outside its control as to whether the holder will exercise or not. Such contracts are, therefore, always within the scope of IAS 32 and IAS 39. [IAS 32 para 10; IAS 39 para 7]. Volume adjustment features are also common, particularly within commodity and energy contracts and are discussed within chapter 5.

Royalty agreements

3.38 Although not specifically mentioned in IAS 39's scope section, the standard does not change the accounting treatment of royalty agreements which are based on the volume of sales or service revenues and that are accounted for in accordance with IAS 18, 'Revenue'. [IAS 39 para AG 2]. However, derivative contracts that are based on both sales volume and a financial variable (such as an exchange rate) are not excluded from IAS 39's scope, as set out in the example in chapter 4.

Chapter 4

Nature and characteristics of financial instruments

Chapter 4

Nature and characteristics of financial instruments

Introduction

4.1   Financial instruments embrace a broad range of assets and liabilities. They include both primary financial instruments – financial assets such as cash, receivables and equity securities of another entity and financial liabilities such as debt – and derivative financial instruments such as financial options, forwards, swaps and futures. Derivative financial instruments are considered separately from paragraph 4.23 below.

Definitions relating to financial instruments

4.2   The definitions relating to financial instruments that appear in paragraph 11 of IAS 32 are common to three financial instrument standards, that is, IAS 32, IAS 39 and IFRS 7. The definitions are noted below.

4.3   A financial instrument is any contract that gives rise to a financial asset of one entity and a financial liability or equity instrument of another entity. The definitions of a financial asset and financial liability stated below include some derivative and non-derivative contracts that will or may be settled in the entity's own equity instruments. This is because a contract is not necessarily an equity instrument just because it may result in the receipt or delivery of the entity's own equity instruments, as discussed in chapter 7. [IAS 32 para 21].

4.4   A financial asset is any asset that is:

■   Cash.

■   An equity instrument of another entity.

■   A contractual right:

■   to receive cash or another financial asset from another entity; or

■   to exchange financial assets or financial liabilities with another entity under conditions that are potentially favourable to the entity.

■   A contract that will or may be settled in the entity's own equity instruments and is:

■   a non-derivative for which the entity is or may be obliged to receive a variable number of the entity's own equity instruments; or

■   a derivative that will or may be settled other than by the exchange of a fixed amount of cash or another financial asset for a fixed number of the entity's own equity instruments. For this purpose the entity's own equity instruments do not include puttable instruments and obligations arising on liquidation that are classified as equity or instruments that are contracts for the future receipt or delivery of the entity's own equity instruments.

4.5   A financial liability is any liability that is:

■   A contractual obligation:

   ■   to deliver cash or another financial asset to another entity; or

   ■   to exchange financial assets or financial liabilities with another entity under conditions that are potentially unfavourable to the entity.

■   A contract that will or may be settled in the entity's own equity instruments and is:

   ■   a non-derivative for which the entity is or may be obliged to deliver a variable number of the entity's own equity instruments; or

   ■   a derivative that will or may be settled other than by the exchange of a fixed amount of cash or another financial asset for a fixed number of the entity's own equity instruments. For this purpose the entity's own equity instruments do not include puttable instruments and obligations arising on liquidation that are classified as equity or instruments that are themselves contracts for the future receipt or delivery of the entity's own equity instruments.

4.5.1   As an exception to the above, an instrument that meets the definition of a financial liability is classified as an equity instrument if it meets certain criteria set out in the February 2008 amendment to IAS 32, 'Puttable financial instruments and obligations arising on liquidation'. This amendment came into effect for accounting periods beginning on or after 1 January 2009, with earlier application permitted, and is discussed in detail in chapter 7.

4.5.2   As mentioned in chapter 7, the IASB issued an amendment to IAS 39 on the classification of rights issues. This amendment further revises the definition of a financial liability to treat certain rights issues (including rights, options and warrants), that are denominated in a currency other than the functional currency of the issuer, as equity. This amendment is mandatory for accounting periods beginning on or after 1 February 2010.

4.6   An equity instrument is any contract that evidences a residual interest in an entity's assets after deducting all of its liabilities. [IAS 32 para 11]. The term 'entity' includes individuals, partnerships, incorporated bodies and government agencies. [IAS 32 para 14]. Examples of equity instruments include non-puttable ordinary shares, some types of preference shares and share warrants or written call options that allow the holder to subscribe for or purchase a fixed number of non-puttable ordinary shares in the issuing entity in exchange for a fixed amount of cash or another financial asset.

Key features of the definitions

4.7 Some of the important concepts associated with the various terms that are included in the above definitions are considered below. An understanding of these concepts is particularly important and relevant in evaluating instruments that might qualify as financial instruments including derivatives.

Contractual basis

4.8 All financial instruments are defined by contracts. The rights or obligations that comprise financial assets or financial liabilities are derived from the contractual provisions that underlie them. The terms 'contract' and 'contractual' refer to an agreement between two or more parties that has clear economic consequences that the parties have little, if any, discretion to avoid, usually because the agreement is enforceable by law. Contracts defining financial instruments may take a variety of forms and need not be in writing. [IAS 32 para 13]. An example of an item that would not meet the definition of a financial instrument is an entity's tax liability, as it is not based on a contract between the entity and the tax authority, but arising through statute. Similarly, constructive obligations, as defined in IAS 37, 'Provisions, contingent liabilities and contingent assets', do not arise from contracts and are not financial liabilities. [IAS 32 para AG 12]. On the other hand, a provision for an onerous contract (for example, provision for vacant leasehold property that is being sublet) is a financial liability as it arises from the unavoidable cost of meeting the obligations under the contract. Nevertheless, such provisions are scoped out of IAS 39 and are accounted for in accordance with IAS 37. [IAS 37 para 66].

4.9 A contractual right or contractual obligation to receive, deliver or exchange financial instruments is itself a financial instrument. This is evident from the definitions of financial assets and liabilities that include the terms financial assets and financial instruments within them. However, the terms are not circular. They envisage the possibility that a chain of contractual rights or contractual obligations may be established, but this chain must end ultimately with the receipt or payment of cash or to the acquisition or issue of an equity instrument. [IAS 32 para AG 7].

4.10 As the IAS 32 definitions require all financial instruments to be contracts, some question whether cash can be considered to be a contract. However, this concern is overcome because the definition of a financial asset stated in paragraph 4.4 above specifically states that cash is a financial instrument. IAS 32 application guidance also clarifies that currency (cash) is a financial asset because it represents the medium of exchange and is, therefore, the basis on which all transactions are measured and recognised in financial statements. A deposit of cash with a bank or similar financial institution is a financial asset because it represents the contractual right of the depositor to obtain cash from the institution or to draw a cheque or similar instrument against the balance in favour of a creditor in payment of a financial liability. [IAS 32 para AG 3]. On the other hand gold bullion is not a financial instrument like cash. It is a commodity.

Although the bullion market is highly liquid, there is no contractual right to receive cash or another financial instrument inherent in bullion. [IAS 39 para IG B1].

4.11   Some common examples of financial instruments that give rise to financial assets representing a contractual right to receive cash in the future for the holder and corresponding financial liabilities representing a contractual obligation to deliver cash in the future for the issuer are as follows:

■   Trade accounts receivable and payable.

■   Notes receivable and payable.

■   Loans receivable and payable.

■   Bonds receivable and payable.

In each case, one party's contractual right to receive (or obligation to pay) cash is matched by the other party's corresponding obligation to pay (or right to receive). [IAS 32 para AG 4].

4.12   Another type of financial instrument is one for which the economic benefit to be received or given up is a financial asset other than cash. For example, a note payable in government bonds gives the holder the contractual right to receive and the issuer the contractual obligation to deliver government bonds, not cash. The bonds are financial assets because they represent obligations of the issuing government to pay cash. The note is, therefore, a financial asset of the note holder and a financial liability of the note issuer. [IAS 32 para AG 5].

Conditional (contingent) rights and obligations

4.13   The ability to exercise a contractual right or the requirement to satisfy a contractual obligation may be absolute, or it may be contingent on the occurrence of a future event. A note receivable or payable is an unconditional promise to pay, but a financial guarantee is a conditional financial instrument as it results in a contractual right of the lender to receive cash from the guarantor and a corresponding contractual obligation of the guarantor to pay the lender, if the borrower defaults. The contractual right and obligation exist because of a past transaction or event (assumption of the guarantee), even though the lender's ability to exercise its right and the requirement for the guarantor to perform under its obligation are both contingent on a future act of default by the borrower. [IAS 32 para AG 8].

4.14   Even though a contingent right and obligation can meet the definition of a financial asset and a financial liability, they are not always recognised in the financial statements. Some of these contingent rights and obligations may be insurance contracts within IFRS 4's scope, whilst others may be excluded from the standards' scope. [IAS 32 para AG 8].

4.15 Other contingencies that may require the payment of cash but do not as yet arise from a contract, such as a contingent receivable or payable for a court judgment, are not financial instruments. However, when those judgments become enforceable by a government or a court of law, and are thereby contractually reduced to fixed payment schedules, the judgment would be a financial instrument. When the parties agree to payment terms and those payment terms are reduced to a contract, then a financial instrument exists. Contrast this with a fine, which is not contractual.

Exchange under potentially favourable or unfavourable terms

4.16 The definitions of financial assets and financial liabilities make references to exchanges under conditions that are 'potentially favourable' or 'potentially unfavourable'. The meaning of these terms and the way they work in practice are best explained by means of an example.

> **Example – Exchange under potentially favourable or unfavourable terms**
>
> Entity A holds an option to purchase equity shares in a listed entity B for C5 per share at the end of a 90 day period.
>
> The above call option gives entity A a contractual right to exchange cash of C5 for an equity share in another entity and will be exercised if the market value of the share exceeds C5 at the end of the 90 day period. This is because as the terms will be favourable to entity A at the end of term, it will exercise the call option. Since entity A stands to gain if the call option is exercised, the exchange is potentially favourable to the entity. Therefore, the option is a derivative financial asset from the time the entity becomes a party to the option contract.
>
> On the other hand, if entity A writes an option under which the counterparty can force the entity to sell equity shares in the listed entity B for C5 per share at any time in the next 90 days, entity A has a contractual obligation to exchange equity shares in another entity for cash of C5 per share on potentially unfavourable terms if the holder exercises the option, because the market price per share exceeds the exercise price of C5 per share at the end of the 90 day period. Since entity A stands to lose if the option is exercised, the exchange is potentially unfavourable and the option is a derivative financial liability from the time the entity becomes a party to the option contract.

Comparison with non-financial assets and liabilities

4.17 As discussed above, financial instruments represent contractual rights or obligations to receive or pay cash or other financial assets. Non-financial items have a more indirect, non-contractual relationship to future cash flows.

4.18 The non-financial assets of a business (such as inventories, property, plant and equipment and intangibles) are inputs to some productive process. They are expected to contribute, along with other inputs, to the production and sale of goods or services. They must be used in a productive activity, and effectively transformed into goods or service, which must be sold, before there is any right to receive cash. Control of such physical and intangible assets creates an opportunity to generate an inflow of cash or another financial asset, but it does not give rise to a present right to receive cash or another financial asset. [IAS 32 para AG 10]. Even where physical assets, such as properties, are held as investments rather than as inventories, they are not financial instruments.

4.19   A contract to acquire or sell a non-financial asset at a specified price at a future date is not a financial instrument, because the contractual right of one party to receive a non-financial asset and the corresponding obligation of the other party do not establish a present right or obligation of either party to receive, deliver or exchange a financial asset. For example, contracts that provide for settlement only by the receipt or delivery of a non-financial item (for example, an option or forward contract on silver) are not financial instruments. Many commodity contracts are of this type. However, as stated in paragraph 3.33 above, contracts to buy or sell non-financial items that can be settled net or by exchanging financial instruments, or in which the non-financial item is readily convertible to cash, are treated as if they are financial instruments. [IAS 32 para AG 20]. For the same reasons as stated above, a firm commitment that involves the receipt or delivery of a physical asset is not a financial instrument. [IAS 32 para AG 21].

4.20   Another example is an operating lease to rent an office building. Under the lease, the lessor has committed to provide office space in future periods for consideration similar to a fee for a service. The contractual right of the lessee to receive the service and the corresponding obligation of the lessor do not establish a present right or obligation of either party to receive, deliver or exchange a financial asset. On the other hand, a finance lease is regarded as primarily an entitlement of the lessor to receive, and an obligation of the lessee to pay, a stream of payments that are substantially the same as a loan agreement. The lessor accounts for its investment in the amount receivable under the lease contract rather than the leased asset itself. [IAS 32 para AG 9]. Accordingly, an operating lease is not regarded as a financial instrument (except as regards individual payments currently due and payable), but a finance lease is regarded as one.

4.21   Assets (such as pre-paid expenses) for which the future economic benefit is the receipt of goods or services, rather than the right to receive cash or another financial asset, are not financial assets. Similarly, items such as deferred revenue and most warranty obligations are not financial liabilities, because the outflow of economic benefits associated with them is the delivery of goods and services, rather than a contractual obligation to pay cash or another financial asset. [IAS 32 para AG 11].

Identification of financial instruments

4.22   Paragraphs 4.8 to 4.21 considered some of the important concepts associated with the definitions relating to financial instruments supplemented, where necessary, with examples. For ease of understanding and as a practical aid, the table below provides a list of common balance sheet items and applies the concepts discussed above to determine whether the items meet the definition of a financial instrument. Paragraph references are included where applicable. The list is by no means exhaustive, but provides an aide-mémoire to help in identifying primary financial instruments. For the sake of completeness, the last two columns also establish whether the instruments so identified fall within or outside the scope of IAS 32, IFRS 7 or IAS 39 discussed in detail from paragraph 3.4 above.

Balance sheet item	Financial instrument? Yes = √ No = X	Included within the scope of IAS 32 and IFRS 7 Yes = √ No = X	Included within the scope of IAS 39 Yes = √ No = X
Intangible assets	X – para 4.18	n/a	n/a
Property, plant and equipment	X – para 4.18	n/a	n/a
Investment property	X – para 4.18	n/a	n/a
Interests in subsidiaries, associates and joint ventures – accounted for under IAS 27, IAS 28 or IAS 31 respectively	√ – para 3.6	X – para 3.6	X – para 3.6
Interests in subsidiaries, associates and joint ventures held for sale under IFRS 5	√ – para 3.6	X – para 3.6	X – para 3.6
Interests in subsidiaries, associates and joint ventures – accounted for under IAS 39 (in accordance with IAS 27 para 37(b))	√ – para 3.6	√ – para 3.7	√ – para 3.7
Inter-company trading balances with subsidiaries, associates and joint ventures	√ – para 4.11	√	√
Investments in other entities (available-for-sale and held for trading)	√ – para 4.4	√	√
Inventories	X – para 4.18	n/a	n/a
Gross amount due from customers for construction contract work	√ – para 11.30.2	√	√
Finance lease receivables (recognised by a lessor)	√ – para 4.20	√ – para 3.16	X – para 3.16
Trade receivables	√ – para 4.11	√	√
Pre-payments – goods and services	X – para 4.21	n/a	n/a
Cash and cash equivalents	√ – para 4.4	√	√
Trade payables	√ – para 4.11	√	√
Contingent consideration in a business combination	√ – para 3.13	√ – para 3.13	√ – para 3.13
Accruals – goods and services (settlement in cash)	√ – para 4.11	√	√
Deferred income	X – para 4.21	n/a	n/a
Debt instruments	√ – para 4.5	√	√
Derivative instruments	√ – para 4.1	√	√
Net settled commodity-based contracts	√ – para 3.34	√ – para 3.34	√ – para 3.34

Retirement benefit obligations	v – para 3.10	X – para 3.10	X – para 3.10
Provisions for constructive obligations (as defined in IAS 37)	X – para 4.8	n/a	n/a
Vacant leasehold property provision	√ – para 4.8	√	X – para 4.8
Warranty obligations (settled by delivery of goods or service)	X – para 4.21	n/a	n/a
Warranty obligations (settled by delivery of cash or other financial asset)	√ – para 4.5	√	√
Financial guarantee contracts	√ – para 4.13	√ – para 3.25 (unless IFRS 4 applied)	√ – para 3.25 (unless IFRS 4 applied)
Operating lease	X – para 4.20	n/a	n/a
Finance lease obligations	√ – para 4.20	√ – para 3.16	X – para 3.16
Dividend payable	note 1	note 1	note 1
Current and deferred tax	X – para 4.8	n/a	n/a
Redeemable preference shares (debt)	√ – para 4.5	√	√
Entity's own equity shares	√ – para 4.6	√ – para 3.15	X – para 3.15
Employee share options	√ – para 4.6	X – para 3.11	X – para 3.11
Other equity options over own equity shares	√ – para 4.6	√ – para 3.15	X – para 3.15
Non-controlling interest	√ – note 2	√ – note 2	note 2

Notes:

1 Dividend payable on the balance sheet is a financial liability when the dividend has been formally declared by the members in a general meeting and becomes a legal obligation of the entity to deliver cash to shareholders for the amount of the declared dividend. [IAS 32 para AG 13].

2 The non-controlling interest that may arise on consolidating a subsidiary is presented in the consolidated balance sheet within equity, separately from the equity of the owners of the parent. [IAS 27 (revised) para 27; IAS 32 para AG 29]. However, where the parent or any fellow subsidiary undertaking has an obligation to deliver cash or another financial asset in respect of a subsidiary's shares (for example, by virtue of a written put option), they are treated as financial liabilities in consolidated financial statements under IAS 32 and are in the scope of IAS 39. [IAS 32 para AG 29].

Derivative financial instruments

Introduction

4.23 Derivatives are financial instruments that derive their value from an underlying price or index, which could be for example, an interest rate, a foreign exchange rate or commodity price. Their primary purpose is to create rights and obligations that have the effect of transferring between the parties to the instrument one or more of the financial risks inherent in an underlying primary instrument. Consequently, they may be used for trading purposes to generate profits from risk transfers or they may be used as a hedging instrument for managing risks. Generally, there is no transfer of the underlying instrument between the parties either at inception or at maturity, but there are some exceptions.

4.24   A derivative instrument gives one party a contractual right to exchange financial assets or financial liabilities with another party under conditions that are potentially favourable, or a contractual obligation to exchange financial assets or financial liabilities with another party under conditions that are potentially unfavourable. Because the terms of the exchange are determined at inception, as prices in the financial markets change, those terms may become favourable or unfavourable (see para 4.16 above). Derivative instruments may either be free-standing or embedded in a financial instrument or in a non-financial contract.

Definition

4.25   IAS 39 defines a derivative as a financial instrument or other contract with all of the following characteristics:

- its value changes in response to the change in a specified interest rate, financial instrument price, commodity price, foreign exchange rate, index of prices or rates, credit rating or credit index, or other variable, provided in the case of a non-financial variable that the variable is not specific to a party to the contract (sometimes called the 'underlying');

- it requires no initial net investment or an initial net investment that is smaller than would be required for other types of contracts that would be expected to have a similar response to changes in market factors; and

- it is settled at a future date.

[IAS 39 para 9].

Key features of the definition

4.26   The characteristics referred to above make the definition of a derivative not only complex but fairly wide. For example, many contracts such as loan commitments (see para 3.31 above), certain contracts to buy or sell a non-financial item (see para 3.34 above) and regular way trades (see para 4.41 below) meet the definition of a derivative, in addition to the more commonly used and typical derivative instruments such as forwards, swaps, futures and options. Therefore, an understanding of these characteristics is particularly important and relevant in evaluating instruments that might qualify as, or contain, a derivative instrument. The paragraphs that follow examine some of the important concepts associated with these characteristics.

Underlying

4.27   As evident from the first characteristic stated in paragraph 4.25 above, an underlying is a variable, such as:

- An interest rate (for example, LIBOR).

- A security price (for example, the price of an XYZ entity equity share listed on a regulated market).

- A commodity price (for example, the price of a bushel of wheat).

- A foreign exchange rate (for example, /$ spot rate).

- An index (for example, FTSE 100, a retail price index).

- A credit rating or a credit index (for example, Moody's credit rating).

- An insurance index or catastrophe-loss index.

- Other variable (for example, sales volume indices specifically created for settlement of derivatives).

- Non financial variable (for example, a climatic or geological condition such as temperature, rainfall, or earthquake severity).

4.28   Generally, an underlying may be any variable whose changes are observable or otherwise objectively verifiable. It may be the price or rate of an asset or liability that changes in response to changes in the market factors, but it is not the asset or the liability itself in most instances. Accordingly, the underlying will generally be the referenced index that determines whether or not the derivative instrument has a positive or a negative value.

4.29   If the underlying is a non-financial variable as referred to in the last bullet point in paragraph 4.27 above, it must not be specific to a party to the contract in order for the derivative definition to be met. In other words, the terms of the contract must be sufficiently generic in nature to qualify as a derivative. For example, such variables might include an index of earthquake losses in a particular region or an index of temperatures in a particular city. On the other hand, non-financial variables that are specific to a party to the contract can include the occurrence or non-occurrence of a fire that damages or destroys an asset of a party to the contract, or EBITDA or revenue. A change in the fair value of a non-financial asset is specific to the owner if the fair value reflects not only changes in market prices for such assets (a financial variable) but also the condition of the specific non-financial asset held (a non-financial variable). [IAS 39 para AG 12A]. Such contracts may fall to be treated as insurance contracts (see para 3.25 example 2 above).

4.30   A derivative instrument may have more than one underlying or variable. A typical example is a cross-currency interest rate swap that has one underlying based on a foreign exchange rate and another underlying based on an interest rate. A complex option may have two such variables, one based on an interest rate and the other based on the price of a commodity such as oil. Another example based on IAS 39's implementation guidance is given below.

> **Example – Foreign currency contract based on sales volume**
>
> Entity XYZ, whose functional currency is the US dollar, sells products in France denominated in euro. XYZ enters into a contract with an investment bank to convert euro to US dollars at a fixed exchange rate. The contract requires XYZ to remit euro based on its sales volume in France in exchange for US dollars at a fixed exchange rate of 1.20.
>
> The contract has two underlying variables (the foreign exchange rate and the volume of sales), no initial net investment or an initial net investment that is smaller than would be required for other types of contracts that would be expected to have a similar response to changes in market factors and a payment provision. If a contract has two or more underlyings, and at least one of those underlyings is not a non-financial variable specific to a party to a contract, the entire contract is accounted for as a derivative (assuming the rest of the definition of a derivative is met).
>
> Therefore, the contact is a derivative even though one of the variables (sales volume) is a non-financial variable that is specific to a party to the contract. IAS 39 does not exclude from its scope derivatives that are based on sales volume. [IAS 39 para IG B8].

Notional amounts and payment provisions

4.31 A derivative usually has a notional amount, which is an amount of currency, a number of shares, a number of units of weight or volume or other units specified in the contract. However, a derivative instrument does not require the holder or writer to invest or receive the notional amount at the inception of the contract. The interaction of the notional amount and the underlying determines the settlement amount under a derivative instrument. The interaction may consist of a simple multiplication (for example, price × number of shares), or it may involve a formula that has leverage factors or other constants (for example, notional amount × interest rate where interest rate = 2.5 × LIBOR; the effect of any change in LIBOR is magnified by two and a half times).

4.32 Alternatively, a derivative could contain a 'payment provision' specifying a fixed payment or payment of an amount that can change (but not proportionally with a change in the underlying) as a result of some future event that is unrelated to a notional amount. For example, a contract may require a fixed payment of C1,000 if six month LIBOR increases by 100 basis points. Such a contract is a derivative even though a notional amount is not specified. [IAS 39 para AG 9]. Another example is where an entity receives C10 million if the share price of another entity decreases by more than five per cent during a six month period, but pays C10 million if the share price increases by more than five per cent during the same six month period. No payment is made if the share price is less than five per cent up or down. This is a derivative contract where there is no notional amount to determine the settlement amount. Instead, there is a payment provision that is based on changes in the underlying.

Initial net investment

4.33   The second characteristic of a derivative instrument is that it has no initial net investment, or one that is *smaller* than would be required for other types of contracts that would be expected to have a similar response to changes in market factors. Professional judgement is required in interpreting the term in italic as it does not necessarily mean insignificant in relation to the overall investment. It is a relative measure and needs to be interpreted with care. This reflects the inherent leverage features typical of derivative instruments compared to the underlying instruments.

4.34   The following examples illustrate how initial net investment is determined in various circumstances:

Example 1 – No initial net investment of the notional amount

Forward based derivative contracts such as forward foreign exchange contracts and interest rate swaps are typical derivative instruments that do not require an initial net investment. This is because they are priced at-the-money at inception, which means that the fair value of the contracts is zero. If the fair value of the contract is not zero at inception, the contract is recognised as an asset or liability.

Under a forward foreign exchange contract the two parties agree to purchase or sell a foreign currency at a specified price, with delivery or settlement at a specified future date. Although the forward contract has a notional amount equal to the amount of the foreign currency, it does not require the holder or the writer to invest or receive the notional amount at the inception of the contract. Indeed, forward contracts do not have cash flows during the contract term. Settlement takes place at maturity of the contract.

Similarly, an interest rate swap may be viewed as a variation of a forward contract in which the two parties agree to exchange one set of interest cash flows calculated with reference to a fixed interest rate for another set of interest cash flows calculated with reference to a floating interest rate. No exchange of principal takes place. Typically, the rates are set so that the fair values of the fixed and floating legs are equal and opposite at inception with the result that the fair value of the swap on initial recognition is nil. As no money changes hands at inception, there is no initial net investment. Swap cash flows occur at regular intervals over the life of the swap contract based on a notional principal amount and fixed and floating rates specified in the swap.

Example 2 – Initial net investment less than the notional amount

Option contracts are derivative instruments that do require an initial net investment. An option is a contractual agreement that gives the buyer of the option the right, but not the obligation, to purchase (call) or sell (put) a specified security, currency or commodity (the underlying) at a specified price (exercise price) during a specified period of time (or on a specified date). For this right, the buyer pays a premium, which is the amount the seller requires to take on the risk involved in writing the option. Although this premium can be significant, it is often less than the amount that would be required to buy the underlying financial instrument to which the contract is linked. As such, the option fulfils the initial net investment criterion. [IAS 39 para AG 11].

On the other hand, if the option premium is so deep in-the-money that the premium paid is close to making an investment in the underlying, then the option contract will fail the initial net investment criterion. In that situation, the instrument would not be accounted for as a derivative under IAS 39, but rather as an investment in the underlying asset itself.

Example 3 – Exchange of currencies

Some contracts may require a mutual exchange of currencies or other assets, in which case the net investment is the difference between the fair values of the assets exchanged. An example is a currency swap that requires the exchange of currencies at both inception and at maturity. The initial exchange of currencies at fair values in those arrangements (zero net investment) is not seen as an initial net investment. Instead, it is an exchange of one kind of cash for another kind of cash. [IAS 39 para AG 11].

Example 4 – Margin accounts

Many derivative instruments, such as futures contracts and exchange traded written options, require a margin payment – an initial amount that must be deposited before trading begins and which approximately equals the daily price fluctuation permitted for the contract being traded. Such payments are not part of the initial net investment. Rather, they are a form of collateral for the counterparty or clearing house to ensure that traders will perform on their contractual obligations. The initial margin may take the form of cash, securities or other specified assets, typically liquid assets. These are separate assets that are accounted for separately. [IAS 39 para IG B10]. Any variation in margin payments would be adjusted against the asset.

Example 5 – Pre-paid interest rate swap (fixed leg pre-paid)

Entity S enters into a C100m notional amount five-year pay-fixed, receive-variable interest rate swap. The interest rate of the variable part of the swap is reset on a quarterly basis to three month LIBOR. The interest rate of the fixed leg of the swap is 10% per year. At inception of the swap, Entity S pre-pays its fixed obligation of C50m (C100m × 10% × 5 years) discounted using market interest rates, while retaining the right to receive interest payments on the C100m reset quarterly based on three-month LIBOR over the life of the swap.

As stated in example 1 above at the money interest rate swap has a zero fair value at inception. Since entity S has pre-paid the fixed leg of the swap at inception at its fair value, the amount pre-paid is also equal to the fair value of the variable leg of the swap. This amount is however significantly less than the notional amount (C100m) on which the variable payments under the variable leg will be calculated. In other words, the initial net investment (the amount pre-paid) is still smaller than investing in a similar primary instrument, such as a variable rate bond, that responds equally to changes in the underlying interest rate. Therefore, a pre-paid fixed leg swap fulfils the initial net investment criterion of IAS 39. Even though entity S has no future performance obligation, the ultimate settlement of the contract is at a future date and the value of the contract changes in response to changes in the LIBOR index. Accordingly, the contract is a derivative instrument.

On the other hand, if the fixed rate payment obligation is pre-paid subsequent to initial recognition, that is, during the term of the swap, then that would be regarded as a termination of the old swap and an origination of a new instrument that is evaluated under IAS 39. [IAS 39 para IG B4]. There is no explanation in the implementation guidance as to why this is so. Presumably this is because a significant fall in LIBOR between inception date and pre-payment date would cause the amount pre-paid (that is, the fair value of the fixed leg at the date of the pre-payment) to be significantly higher than the fair value of the fixed leg at date of inception. Therefore, the entity receiving the variable payments may not recover substantially all of its pre-paid investment under the contractual terms resulting in the termination of the old swap and the creation of a new instrument.

Example 6 – Pre-paid interest rate swap (floating leg pre-paid)

Entity S enters into a C100m notional amount five-year pay-variable, receive-fixed interest rate swap. The variable leg of the swap is reset on a quarterly basis to three-month LIBOR. The fixed interest payments under the swap are calculated as 10% times the swap's notional amount, that is, C10m per year. Entity S pre-pays its obligation under the variable leg of the swap at inception at current market rates, while retaining the right to receive fixed interest payments of 10% on C100m per year.

As stated in the previous example, the fair value of the fixed leg and the fair value of a floating leg are equal and offsetting so that the fair value of the interest rate swap at inception is zero. Since entity S has pre-paid the variable leg of the swap at inception at its fair value, the amount pre-paid, all else being equal, is also equal to the fair value of the fixed leg of the swap. That is, the initial net investment (the amount pre-paid) is equal to the present value of a fixed annuity of C10m per year over the swap's life. Thus, the initial net investment is equal to the investment required in a non-derivative contract that has a similar response to changes in market conditions. In other words, the amount pre-paid provides a return that is the same as that of an amortising fixed rate debt instrument of the amount of the pre-paid. For this reason, the instrument fails the initial net investment criterion of IAS 39. Therefore, the contract is not accounted for as a derivative. By discharging the obligation to pay variable interest rate payments, entity S in effect provides a loan to the counterparty. [IAS 39 para IG B5].

Example 7 – Pre-paid forward

Entity XYZ enters into a forward contract to purchase 1m entity T ordinary shares in one year. The current market price of entity T's shares is C50 per share; the one-year forward price of entity T's shares is C55 per share. XYZ is required to pre-pay the forward contract at inception with a C50m payment.

The initial investment in the forward contract of C50m is less than the notional amount applied to the underlying, 1m shares at the forward price of C55 per share, that is, C55m. However, the initial net investment *approximates* the investment that would be required for other types of contracts that would be expected to have a similar response to changes in market factors because entity T's shares could be purchased at inception for the same price of C50m. Accordingly, the pre-paid forward contract does not meet the initial net investment criterion of a derivative instrument. In this situation, the entity would record the investment itself as a non-derivative financial asset. [IAS 39 para IG B9].

It is not clear why the example in the implementation guidance uses the term 'approximate' when the initial net investment of C50m is equal to the amount that would be exchanged to acquire the asset relating to the underlying (market price of the share). Presumably the term is used to emphasise the point that the initial net investment test is a relative measure as indicated in paragraph 4.33 above and that a pre-payment amount of, for example, C42.5m (15% smaller than the original amount) may still meet the initial net investment criterion.

Settlement at a future date

4.35   The final part of the definition relates to settlement at a future date. All derivatives are settled at a future date. As explained in example 1 above, forward contracts are settled at a specified date in the future, whilst for an interest rate swap settlement occurs at regular intervals over the swap's life. An option is settled upon exercise or at maturity. Therefore, even if an option is expected not to be exercised, for example, because it is out-of-the-money and no additional exchange of consideration is expected to take place, the option still meets the settlement criterion, because expiry at maturity is a form of settlement. [IAS 39 para IG B7].

4.36   A derivative can be settled net in cash (that is, the entity has the right to receive or the obligation to pay a single net amount) or gross in cash/other financial asset (exchange of cash/other financial asset). Consider the following example:

Example – Interest rate swap with net or gross settlement

Entity ABC enters into an interest rate swap with a counterparty (XYZ) that requires ABC to pay a fixed rate of 8% and receive a variable amount based on three month LIBOR, reset on a quarterly basis. The fixed and variable amounts are determined based on a C100m notional amount. ABC and XYZ do not exchange the notional amount. ABC pays or receives a net cash amount each quarter based on the difference between 8% and three-month LIBOR. Alternatively, settlement may be on a gross basis.

As the swap contract is settled on a periodical basis, each interest payment can be viewed as a series of forward contracts to exchange and receive cash on potentially favourable or unfavourable terms. The contract meets the definition of a derivative regardless of whether each interest payment is settled net or gross, because its value changes in response to changes in an underlying variable (LIBOR). There is no initial net investment and settlements occur at future dates. In other words, it makes no difference whether ABC and XYZ actually make the interest payment to each other (gross settlement). [IAS 39 para IG B3].

4.37 Settlement may also occur gross through physical delivery of the underlying financial item. An example is a forward contract to purchase C100 million of five per cent fixed rate bond at a specified fixed date in the future. In this situation, at settlement date the entity would exchange cash for physical delivery of the bond (the underlying financial item) whose nominal value is equal to the notional amount of the contract and the market interest rate is the underlying. [IAS 39 para AG10].

Specific examples of derivative instruments

4.38 The key characteristics of a derivative contract were explained and illustrated above, where relevant, with examples. The following table provides typical examples of contracts that normally qualify as derivatives together with the relevant underlying, notional and settlement amounts.

Derivative	Underlying	Notional amount	Settlement amount
Stock options	Market price of share	Number of shares	(Market price at settlement – Strike Price) × Number of shares
Currency forward	Currency rate	Number of currency units	(Spot rate at settlement – Forward rate) × number of currency units
Commodity future	Commodity price per unit	Number of commodity units	Net settlement occurs daily and is determined by the change in the futures price and discounted to reflect the time to maturity
Interest rate swap	Interest rate index (receive 5% fixed and pay LIBOR)	Amounts in C's	Net settlement occurs periodically throughout the contract's term based on the formula: (Current interest rate index – fixed rate specified in the contract) × Amounts in C's
Fixed payment contract	6 month LIBOR increases by 100 points	Not specified	Settlement amount based on payment provision in the contract.

Contracts to buy or sell non-financial items

4.39 An entity may also have a contract to buy or sell a non-financial item that can be settled net in cash or another financial instrument, or by exchanging financial instruments. Such contracts may fall within the definition of a derivative if they meet certain criteria (see further para 3.34 of chapter 3). [IAS 39 para AG 10].

Contracts that are in substance derivatives

4.40 It is generally inappropriate to treat two or more separate financial instruments, such as an investment in a floating rate debt instrument and a floating to fixed interest rate swap with different counter parties, as a single combined instrument ('synthetic instrument' accounting), as discussed in chapter 11. [IAS 39 para IG C6]. However, as an exception to this, non-derivative transactions should be aggregated and treated as a derivative when, in substance, the transactions result in a derivative instrument. Indicators of this would include circumstances where the transactions:

■   Are entered into at the same time and in contemplation of one another.

■   Have the same counterparty.

■   Relate to the same risk.

■   Have no substantive business purpose or there is no apparent economic need for structuring the transactions separately that could not also have been accomplished in a single transaction.

[IAS 39 para IG B6].

> **Example – In substance derivatives**
>
> Entity A makes a five-year fixed rate loan to entity B, while entity B at the same time makes a five-year variable rate loan for the same amount to entity A. There are no transfers of principal at inception of the two loans, since entities A and B have a netting agreement.
>
> The contractual effect is that the loans are, in substance, equivalent to an interest rate swap arrangement that meets the definition of a derivative – there is an underlying variable, no initial net investment and future settlement. The same answer would apply if entity A and entity B did not have a netting agreement, because the definition of a derivative instrument does not require net settlement. [IAS 39 para IG B6].

Regular way contracts

4.41 A regular way purchase or sale is a purchase or sale of a financial asset under a contract whose terms require delivery of the asset within the time frame established generally by regulation or convention in the marketplace concerned. [IAS 39 para 9]. Such contracts give rise to a fixed price commitment between trade date and settlement date that meets the definition of a derivative. However, because of the commitment's short duration, it is not recognised as a derivative financial instrument. Rather, IAS 39 provides for special accounting for such regular way contracts which is dealt with in chapter 8. [IAS 39 para AG 12].

Accounting for derivatives

4.42 The measurement requirements of IAS 39 require all derivatives to be measured at fair value on the balance sheet, with changes in fair value being accounted through profit or loss, except for derivatives that qualify as effective hedging instruments and derivatives that are linked to and must be settled by delivery of unquoted equity instruments whose fair value cannot be reliably measured. Measurement and hedging requirements are dealt with further in chapters 9 and 10 respectively.

Chapter 5

Embedded derivatives in host contracts

Chapter 5

Embedded derivatives in host contracts

Introduction

5.1   A derivative instrument that falls within IAS 39's scope need not be free-standing. Terms and conditions may also be embedded in a financial instrument or in a non-financial contract (referred to as the 'host' contract) that behave like a free standing derivative. These terms and conditions are referred to as embedded derivatives. The combination of the host contract and the embedded derivative is referred to as a 'hybrid instrument'.

5.2   An embedded derivative can arise from deliberate financial engineering, for example to make low interest-rate debt more attractive by including an equity-linked return. However, in other cases, they arise inadvertently through market practices and common contractual arrangements, such as leases and insurance contracts. Even purchase and sale contracts that qualify as executory contracts may contain embedded derivatives. In fact, they may occur in all sorts of contracts and instruments – the objective being to change the nature of cash flows that otherwise would be required by the host contract and effectively shift financial risks between the parties.

5.3   Analysing non-derivative financial instruments and executory contracts for potential embedded derivatives is one of the more challenging aspects of IAS 39. However, the challenge does not end there. As will be apparent later, a derivative identified in a host contract needs further evaluation to determine whether it should be accounted for separately as a stand alone derivative at fair value. Not all embedded derivatives would fall to be accounted for separately from the host contract in which they reside.

Definition and key characteristics

5.4   An embedded derivative is a component of a hybrid instrument that also includes a non-derivative host contract – with the effect that some of the cash flows of the hybrid instrument vary in a way similar to a stand-alone derivative (see para 5.1). An embedded derivative causes some or all of the cash flows that otherwise would be required by the contract to be modified according to a specified interest rate, financial instrument price, commodity price, foreign exchange rate, index of prices or rates, credit rating or credit index, or other variable, provided in the case of a non-financial variable that the variable is not specific to a party to the contract. [IAS 39 para 10]. Variation of the cash flows over the contract's term is a critical indicator of the presence of one or more embedded derivatives. An example of a hybrid instrument is a loan that pays interest based on changes in the FTSE 100 index. The component of the contract that is to repay the principal amount is the host contract – this is the 'base state' with a pre-determined term and pre-determined cash flows. The component of the contract that is to pay interest based on changes in the FTSE 100 index is the embedded derivative – this component causes some or all of the cash flows of the host contract to change. A diagrammatic representation explaining the above terms is given below:

Hybrid (combined) instrument

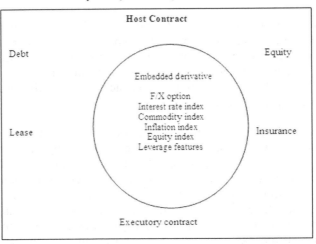

5.5 A derivative that is attached to a financial instrument but is contractually transferable independently of that instrument, or has a different counterparty from that instrument, is not an embedded derivative, but a separate financial instrument [IAS 39 para 10]. An example is a bond with a detachable warrant where the owner of the bond-warrant package can exercise the warrant and buy shares for cash but keep the bond. This is unlike an owner of a convertible bond where the owner has to give up the bond in order to exercise the option.

Conditions for separation

5.6 Paragraph 11 of IAS 39 states that an embedded derivative should be separated from the host contract and accounted for as a derivative if all of the following three conditions are met:

■ the economic characteristics and risks of the embedded derivative are not closely related to the economic characteristics and risks of the host contract;

■ a separate instrument with the same terms as the embedded derivative would meet the definition of a derivative; and

■ the hybrid instrument is not measured at fair value with changes in fair value recognised in profit or loss.

5.7   In relation to the third bullet point above, paragraph 11A of IAS 39 states that if a contract contains one or more embedded derivatives, an entity may designate the entire hybrid contract as a financial asset or financial liability at fair value through profit or loss unless:

■   the embedded derivative(s) does not significantly modify the cash flows that otherwise would be required by the contract; or

■   it is clear with little or no analysis when a similar hybrid instrument is first considered that separation of the embedded derivative(s) is prohibited, such as a pre-payment option embedded in a loan that permits the holder to pre-pay the loan for approximately its amortised cost.

5.8   The above requirements are summarised in the diagram below.

Questions that need to be asked

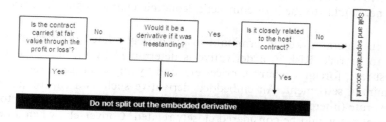

5.9   The rationale for the above requirements is to ensure that all the underlying risks in an instrument are properly accounted for, which would not otherwise be apparent from the accounting. For instance, a debt host contract may contain an embedded derivative that exposes the contract to risks that are non-interest related. If there were no requirement to separate the non-interest related exposure from the host debt instrument, entities would be able to achieve an accounting result different from the accounting result that it would have achieved if it had issued two separate contracts with the same combined economic effect. Therefore, separation of the embedded derivative not only ensures that the accounting faithfully represents the contract's underlying nature and its exposure to various risks, but also achieves consistency in accounting with freestanding derivatives. However, measuring an embedded derivative separately from its host contract requires judgement, and sometimes such measurements may be difficult. Therefore, practical expedient IAS 39 provides that an embedded derivative need not be separated if it is regarded as closely related to its host contract.

5.10   Although the requirement to separate an embedded derivative from a host contract applies to both parties to a contract (that is, both the issuer and the holder of a hybrid instrument), the two parties to the contract might reach different accounting treatments when applying the decision tree in paragraph 5.8 above. For example, an equity conversion feature embedded in a convertible debt instrument denominated in the functional currency of the issuer is not closely related to the host debt instrument from the perspective of the holder of the instrument. However, from the issuer's perspective, the equity conversion option is an equity instrument and excluded from IAS 39's scope, provided it meets the conditions for that classification under IAS 32.

Interpretation of 'closely related'

5.11   Once an embedded derivative is identified, it is necessary to consider whether its economic characteristics and risks (that is, the factors that cause the derivative to fluctuate in value) are closely related to the economic characteristics and risks of the host contract. IAS 39 does not provide a definition of 'closely related'. Instead, the application guidance to the standard provides examples of situations where the embedded derivative is, or is not, closely related to the host contract. Those examples have an underlying theme. They tend to focus attention on the question of whether the underlying economic characteristics and risks of an embedded derivative (that is, the factors that cause a derivative to fluctuate in value) behave in a manner similar to the host contract's economic characteristics and risks.

5.12   In general, a key determinant in the closely related assessment process is likely to be risk. Risk in a derivative is determined by the underlying such as interest rate, foreign exchange, prices etc, and by any leverage in the formula for determining settlement. An embedded derivative such as a cap or floor on the interest rate (interest rate risk) that bears a close economic relationship to its host debt contract would be considered closely related. Conversely, when a derivative that is embedded in a debt instrument embodies an equity instrument's economic characteristics (for example, the derivative has a rate of return that is tied to the DAX 30 index), the economic characteristics of the derivative (equity-price risk) and host contract (interest rate risk) are different. In this situation, the embedded derivative would not be considered closely related to the host contract.

5.12.1   The following example illustrates how quantitative as well as qualitative factors should be taken into account in determining whether the economic characteristics and risks of an embedded derivative are closely related to those of the host contract.

> **Example – Electricity contract linked to coal prices**
>
> Entity A, an electricity provider, operates in a country where electricity is not traded on a market, and has a number of electricity contracts that have prices linked to coal prices. Management believes that, from a qualitative perspective, the electricity price is linked to the price of coal, as coal is a major input to the electricity generation process. A quantitative analysis reveals that electricity prices are not directly correlated with coal prices.
>
> A qualitative approach should be supported by quantitative analysis when determining whether the economic characteristics and risks of an embedded derivative are closely related to those of the host contract (that is in this case, when determining whether the coal price is closely related to the electricity price).

Whilst coal is an important input in the production of electricity, the price of electricity is driven by many other factors and, therefore, it is important to assess the extent to which the economic characteristics and risks of coal are in practice closely related to those of electricity. A quantitative assessment of correlation may be relevant to this determination.

Leverage embedded features in host contracts

5.13 Leverage embedded features can significantly modify some or all of the cash flows that otherwise would be required by the host contract. IAS 39 does not define the term 'leverage', although the term appears in several examples in paragraph AG33. In general, a hybrid instrument is said to contain embedded leverage features if some or all of its contractually required cash flows, determined by reference to changes in one or more underlyings, are modified in a manner that multiply or otherwise exacerbate the effect of those changes. An example of this would be a lease with payments linked to an inflation index multiplied by a factor of 2.5. It follows that the effect of leverage is only relevant for those embedded derivatives that would otherwise be 'closely-related' to the non-derivative host contract. This is because embedded derivatives that are not 'closely-related' would have to be separated out from the host contract in any event, irrespective of whether they are considered to be leveraged.

5.14 Although, in general, leverage has a multiplying effect, the standard does not quantify a numerical measure of leverage for closely related embedded derivatives although it does include the notion of at least doubling the holders interest rate of return in relation to embedded derivatives in which the underlying is an interest rate or an interest rate index (see para 5.27 below). In other words, although it may be clear that any embedded feature that leverages the exposure of the host contract to more than an insignificant amount would require separation, no guidance is given as to what would constitute an acceptable threshold. An example of this would be a contract for delivery of paper where the price is linked to a pulp index, transportation index and relevant inflation index where the indices are multiplied by percentages that reflect relative weighting of the cost factor in the production of paper. Such percentages would normally add up to 100 per cent. To support the closely related assertion it has to be demonstrated that it was the normal way to price commercial contract in the market for paper at the time when the contract entered into. That could be done, for example, by reference to web sites of relevant industry associations, commodity or goods exchanges, etc. Therefore, judgement should be exercised after considering all relevant facts and circumstances that are specific to the situation.

Identifying the terms of embedded derivative and host contracts

5.15 Because an assessment of whether an embedded derivative is 'closely related' to the host contract requires an understanding of the economic characteristics and risks of both the host contract and the derivative, it is necessary to consider the general principles that may be helpful in identifying the hosts and any derivatives that may be embedded in them.

5.16 Determining the type of host should not cause undue difficulty in practice as its economic characteristics and risks are readily transparent. In practice, there are generally a few common types of host contracts that have derivatives embedded in them and these are stated below.

- Debt instruments.

- Equity instruments.

- Leases.

- Executory contracts such as purchase and sales contracts.

- Insurance contracts.

The economic characteristics and risks of each of these contracts are considered in the application section below. Other hosts may exist, but as these are likely to be rare they are not considered in this chapter.

5.17 Difficulties begin to surface and become challenging when searching for derivatives that may be embedded in the above hosts. Because few hybrid contracts actually use the term 'derivative', a thorough evaluation of a contract's terms must be performed to determine whether the contract contains an embedded derivative. Certain terms and phrases, however, may indicate the presence of an embedded derivative in a contract. Such terms and phrases may include:

- Pricing based on a formula.

- The right to purchase/sell additional units.

- Exchange/exchangeable into.

- Indexed to/adjusted by/referenced to.

- Premium/strike/limits.

- The right to cancel/extend/repurchase/return.

5.18 Another method of determining whether a contract has an embedded derivative is to compare the terms of a contract (such as interest rate, maturity date(s), cancellation provisions, etc) with the corresponding terms of a similar, non-complex contract. In other words, an entity should ascertain whether there are differences between typical market terms and the terms of the contract that is being evaluated. An investigation of differences may uncover an embedded derivative.

5.18.1 The following list illustrates how the nature of a host contract and embedded derivative may be determined:

Instrument	Host contract	Embedded derivative
Convertible bond	Debt instrument	Purchased call option on equity securities
Debt paying interest quarterly based on an equity index	Debt instrument	Four forward contracts p.a. on equity index
A two-year fixed-quantity sales contract including maximum and minimum pricing limits	Purchase contract	Commodity price collar
A two-year fixed-quantity sale contract of mobile phones denominated in GBP between a French seller and German buyer both with Euro functional currencies	Purchase contract	Foreign currency forward contract

Assessment of closely related criterion

5.19   It is clear that the assessment of the closely related criterion should be made when the contract is initially recognised, which is usually at inception of the contract. The question arises as to whether this initial assessment should be revisited during the contract's life. For example, an entity may determine, based on market conditions existing at the date of inception, that an embedded derivative in a host contract is closely related. Subsequently, market conditions change and the entity concludes that the embedded derivative is not closely related and, therefore, separate accounting may be required. The converse situation can also arise. The issue is whether in these circumstances the entity should make this reassessment, and if so, with what frequency.

5.20   The above issue is addressed in IFRIC 9, 'Reassessment of embedded derivatives'. IFRIC 9 reconfirms the treatment in IAS 39 that an entity should assess whether an embedded derivative is required to be separated from the host contract and accounted for as a derivative when the entity first becomes a party to the contract. This initial assessment is not revised, unless the contractual terms change and the change significantly modifies the expected future cash flows associated with the embedded derivative, the host contract or both relative to the previously expected cash flows on the contract. [IFRIC 9 para 7]. It follows that if the market conditions change and the market was the principal factor in determining whether the host contract and the embedded derivative are closely related, no reassessment is required, unless the terms of the contracts are changed and the changes result in the revised expected cash flows being significantly different from the previously expected cash flows.

5.20.1   Furthermore, the IASB issued 'Amendments to International Accounting Standard 39 Financial instruments: Recognition and measurement – Embedded derivatives' in March 2009, which requires financial assets reclassified out of the fair value through profit or loss category (see chapter 6) to be assessed for embedded derivatives. The assessment is based on the circumstances that existed on the later date of (a) when the entity first became a party to the contract and (b) when a change in the terms of the contract significantly modifying the cash flows that otherwise would have been required under the contract. In the basis for conclusions to the amendment the board noted that, upon reclassification, the terms of any embedded derivative recognised, should not be different to those that would have been recognised at the relevant date for assessment of embedded derivatives. The effective date for the amendment is for annual periods ending on or after 30 June 2009.

5.21 Similarly, a first time adopter of IFRS should assess whether an embedded derivative is required to be separated from the host contract and accounted for as a derivative on the basis of the conditions that existed at the later of the date it first became a party to the contract and the date a reassessment is required by the above paragraph. [IFRIC 9 para 8]. It follows that as the conditions existing at the date the entity first adopts IFRS are of no relevance to the assessment of whether the embedded derivative is closely related or not, there is no difference in treatment between a continuing IFRS reporter and a first time adopter of IFRS. [IFRS 1 para IG 55].

5.21.1 Paragraph 16 of IFRS 3, 'Business combinations', requires a company that acquires another company (the 'acquirer') to re-assess all contracts of the acquired entity for embedded derivatives at the acquisition date of. The rationale for this approach is that all such contracts (to which the acquirer becomes a party as a result of the acquisition) should be accounted for in the same way as if the acquirer had taken them out individually at the time of acquisition. Generally this will result in more embedded derivatives being separated from host contracts in the group's consolidated financial statements, as compared with the acquired entity's stand-alone financial statements. This is because the embedded derivative guidance links some of the criteria for separating embedded derivatives to market conditions existing at initial recognition of the host contract. These embedded derivatives will be accounted for at fair value through profit or loss separately from their host contracts in the consolidated financial statements, after the acquisition (unless they are designated in a valid hedge relationship in accordance with IAS 39).

Example – Re-assessment of embedded derivative

A UK entity entered into an 'own use' long-term electricity purchase contract in the late 1980s. At that time, there was no market for electricity. However, prices for gas and electricity were linked and, there was high correlation between the two prices. Hence, the price of the electricity contract was linked to gas prices. However, following deregulation of the energy market in the UK in the mid 1990s, the prices of gas and electricity are no longer correlated. On transition to IFRS, the contract has a remaining maturity of two years.

When considered at the date of transition to IFRS the price adjustment feature would have been regarded as closely related, reflecting market conditions prevailing at the date the contract was entered into. Given that there were no amendments to the terms of the contract, in accordance with paragraph 5.20 above, the initial assessment is not updated even though over time market conditions have changed and prices of gas and electricity are no longer correlated at the date of transition to IFRS.

On the other hand, if the entity entered into a similar contract after deregulation of the energy market, but before transition to IFRS, the price adjustment feature (electricity price in the contract is linked to gas prices and not market price of electricity) would not be regarded as closely related. Therefore, the embedded derivative would have to be separated and accounted for as a derivative at the date of transition to IFRS in accordance with paragraph 5.21 above.

Application of closely related criterion to different types of hosts

5.22   As stated in paragraph 5.11 above, the application guidance to IAS 39 provides examples of situations where the embedded derivative is, or is not, closely related to the host contract. [IAS 39 paras AG30-AG33]. This guidance is not an exhaustive list of contract features or embedded derivatives. It contains many of the common features found in typical host contracts. Therefore, a considerable degree of judgement will be required to analyse situations that are not included in the standard's examples. However, as determining what is closely related can prove very challenging in practice, we have supplemented the standard's examples by providing additional examples where relevant. The following paragraphs deal with the application of the closely related criterion to different types of hosts and embedded derivatives.

Embedded derivatives in debt host contracts

5.23   The most common host for an embedded derivative is a debt contract. However, it is first necessary to identify the host debt in the hybrid instrument. The implementation guidance states that the terms of the host debt instrument should reflect the stated or implied substantive terms of the hybrid instrument. [IAS 39 para IG C1]. For example, if the terms indicate that the host instrument has a stated or predetermined maturity and pays a fixed, floating or zero-coupon rate of interest, then its economic characteristics and risks are those of a debt instrument.

5.24   In the absence of implied or stated terms, the entity makes its own judgement of the terms. However, in exercising such judgement, the entity should not endeavour to seek out a component that is not specified in the contract. Nor should it endeavour to establish terms of the host debt instrument in a manner that would result in the separation of an embedded derivative that is not already clearly present in the hybrid instrument, that is to say, it cannot create a cash flow that does not exist. For example, if a five-year debt instrument has fixed interest payments of C40,000 annually and a principal payment at maturity of C1 million multiplied by the change in an equity price index, it would be inappropriate to identify a floating rate host contract and an embedded equity swap that has an offsetting floating rate leg in lieu of identifying a fixed rate host. In that example, the host contract is a fixed rate debt instrument that pays C40,000 annually, because there are no floating interest rate cash flows in the hybrid instrument. [IAS 39 para IG C1].

5.25   The value of a debt instrument is determined by the interest rate that is associated with the contract. The interest rate stipulated in the debt instrument is usually a function of the following factors:

- Risk free interest rate.
- Credit risk.
- Expected maturity.
- Liquidity risk.

Thus, embedded derivatives that affect the yield on debt instruments because of any of the above factors would be considered to be closely related (unless they are leveraged or do not change in the same direction as interest rates and fail the test described in para 5.27 below, such as the inverse floater in example 3 of para 5.30 below). On the other hand, if the economic characteristics and risks of the embedded derivatives have features that are unrelated to interest rates (such as equity or commodity features), they would not be considered to be closely related to the debt host. Examples relating to the application of closely related criterion to a debt host and different types of derivatives embedded in it are considered in the paragraphs that follow.

Index linked interest payments

5.26   It is not uncommon for debt instruments to contain embedded interest rate indices that can change the amount of interest that would otherwise be paid or received. Typical interest rate indices are LIBOR and the prime rate index. More complex ones include leveraged interest rate indices, such as levered inverse floaters, range floaters, etc.

5.27   An embedded derivative in which the underlying is an interest rate or interest rate index that can change the amount of interest that would otherwise be paid or received on an interest-bearing host debt contract (or insurance contract) is closely related to the host contract unless:

- the combined instrument can be settled in such a way that the holder would not recover *substantially all* of its recognised investment; or
- the embedded derivative *could* at least double the holder's initial rate of return on the host contract *and could* result in a rate of return that is at least twice what the market return would be for a contract with the same terms as the host contract.

[IAS 39 para AG 33(a)].

Note that this assessment is made when the entity becomes party to the contract and on the basis of market conditions existing then (see para 5.20).

5.28 An example of an instrument meeting the first condition would be a bond callable by the issuer at an amount significantly lower than its issue price. Should the issuer decide to exercise the call option (that is, repurchase the bond) the holder would be required to sell it and, therefore, not recover substantially all of its recognised investment. The first condition that *"the holder would not recover substantially all of its recognised investment"* is not satisfied if the terms of the combined instrument permit, but do not require, the investor to settle the combined instrument in a manner that causes it not to recover substantially all of its recognised investment and the issuer has no such right (for example, a puttable debt instrument). An embedded interest rate derivative with such terms is regarded as closely related to the interest-bearing host contract. The condition that *"the holder would not recover substantially all of its recognised investment"* applies to situations in which the holder can be forced to accept settlement at an amount that causes the holder not to recover substantially all of its recognised investment. [IAS 39 para IG C10]. The term 'substantially all' is not defined in IAS 39 and, therefore, judgement should be exercised after considering all the relevant facts and circumstances that are specific to the situation.

5.29 The second condition has two parts and, therefore, both these parts should be met for the embedded derivative not to be considered closely related. So, for example, if the embedded derivative feature results in doubling the initial return under a possible future interest rate scenario no matter how remote, but, at the same time, that interest rate scenario would not result in a rate of return that is at least twice what the then-current market return would be for a contract that has the same terms as the host, then only one part of the condition would have been met and the embedded derivative would be regarded as closely related to the host.

5.30 The above provisions are intended to 'scope in' those embedded derivatives that cause the hybrid instrument to perform less like a debt instrument and more like a derivative (for example, hybrid instruments that are highly leveraged). The following examples illustrate the application of the above guidance to various interest rate index linked debt instruments.

Example 1 – Floating rate debt

Entity A takes out a floating rate loan with a bank. The contractually determined interest rate on the debt is six-month LIBOR plus two percentage points (assuming credit spread is two percentage points).

A plain vanilla floating rate instrument with a normal credit spread whose risk free interest rate component (for example, LIBOR) is periodically reset to market interest rate cannot contain an embedded derivative.

Example 2 – Floating rate debt with investor payment provision

Entity A issues a floating rate debt instrument with a face value of C50m. The contractually determined interest rate on the debt is six-month LIBOR. However, there is a provision that if six-month LIBOR increases by 200 basis points, the investor will pay C2m to the issuing company.

In this situation, the embedded derivative consists of a contingent payment provision that depends on LIBOR increasing by 200 basis points. The embedded derivative is not separated, because the investor will receive C50m and the C2m payment is not considered to reduce its initial investment substantially. Therefore, the first condition in paragraph 5.27 above is not met. Furthermore, there is no provision in the contract that causes the investor's yield to increase to at least twice the initial rate. Therefore, the second condition is not met. Accordingly, the embedded derivative is closely related to the debt host and no separation is necessary. The fact that LIBOR may increase by 200 basis points in a year is simply a condition that triggers the payment and is not relevant to determining whether the embedded derivative is closely related.

Example 3 – Leveraged inverse floater

Entity A takes out a loan with a bank. The contractually determined interest rate on the debt is calculated as 14.5% – 2.5 × three-month LIBOR (sometimes referred to as a leveraged inverse floater).

Three-month LIBOR at inception = 4% giving an initial yield of 4.5%.

The embedded derivative has an underlying that is highly leveraged such that there is the possibility of either a negative yield or a significantly higher than market yield. This is because, if under a future interest rate scenario three-month LIBOR increases to 8%, the yield would be negative, that is, -9.5% (14.5% – 24%) and the investor would not be able to recover substantially all of its recognised investment. Therefore, as the first condition in paragraph 5.27 above is satisfied, the embedded derivative is not closely related to the host contract and will be accounted for separately. In practice sometimes the yield will not be allowed to go negative. To prevent this happening, a floor is often imposed on the coupon rate.

Note that in this example there is no need to evaluate the second condition in paragraph 5.27 above. But if this condition were to be evaluated the result would be the same, that is, the embedded derivative would not be considered closely related to the host debt contract. This is because, for example, if under a future interest rate scenario, three-month LIBOR falls to 2%, the yield would be 9% which is twice the initial yield of 4.5%. Furthermore, the yield of 9% is also likely to be twice the then market yield for a contract with the same terms as the host.

Example 4 – Forward starting interest rate swap

Entity A issues a 8% fixed rate debt instrument that matures at the end of year 5. The entity has an option to convert the loan into a variable rate debt at LIBOR + 3% after two years. LIBOR at inception is 5%.

The embedded derivative included in the above debt host is an option on a forward starting interest rate swap that changes the fixed rate interest payments to floating rate after two years. In order to determine whether the option on the forward starting swap should be accounted for as a separate derivative, it is necessary to apply the second condition in paragraph 5.27 above.

Accordingly, if, under a future interest rate scenario (however remote), LIBOR increases to 14%, the increase would have the effect of more than doubling the initial return on the investment from 8% to 17% (14% + 3%). However, that interest rate scenario of 14% does not result in a market rate of interest that is twice the current market rate for a contract with the same terms as the host contract, which is only 17% assuming no change in credit rating. Therefore, as only one part of the second condition in paragraph 5.27 is satisfied, the embedded option on the forward starting interest rate swap is closely related to the debt host and no separation is permitted.

Inflation-linked interest and principal payments

5.31   There is often a close relationship between interest rates and inflation in an economy. The nominal rate of interest is often thought of as the real interest rate (the amount earned on a sum loaned or deposited in a bank) plus the rate of inflation. The more precise version that allows for the compounding effect is given by the following relationship know as the Fisher equation:

$$1 + n = (1 + r)(1 + i)$$

where:

n = nominal interest rate
r = real rate of interest
i = expected inflation rate

5.32   The above equation illustrates that the nominal interest rate reflects compensation to the lender for expected decreases, due to inflation, in the purchasing power of the principal and interest during the course of the loan. In other words, the nominal interest rate will vary directly with the expected rate of inflation, indicating that, in general, there is a strong correlation between the two.

5.33   A strong correlation is particularly true for a country whose interest and inflation rates are managed together as part of the country's monetary policy decisions. For example, the Bank of England in the UK, like the Federal reserve system in the US, is responsible for setting interest rates that are aimed at accommodating economic growth in an environment of stable prices. Consider, however, countries in the Eurozone where the interest rate is set by the European Central Bank (ECB). Although the ECB sets short-term interest rates aimed at maintaining inflation rates in the Eurozone below, but close to, two per cent (measured by year-on-year increase in the Harmonised Index of Consumer Prices) over the medium term, the inflation rate in a particular country within the Eurozone may be different from overall Eurozone inflation due to, for example, differences in national rates of growth, local market regulation, etc.

5.34   Therefore, where a company issues a debt instrument where the amount of interest or the principal to be repaid or both is linked to an inflation index, it would be necessary to perform both a qualitative and quantitative analysis to determine whether the underlying inflation index is closely related. This analysis should be performed on a case by case basis and would include at least the following considerations:

■   Demonstration via a regression analysis to support the contention that there is a long run statistically significant relationship between the interest rate for the maturity specified in the debt instrument and the inflation measure to which that debt's coupon is linked.

- The inflation index is the one that is a recognised measure of inflation in the economic environment in which the loan originates. If the inflation index relates to a different economy or is not one that is commonly used for the purpose of lending and borrowing, the underlying inflation index will not be regarded as closely related to the debt host. In the UK, inflation indices that are most commonly used are the retail price index and the consumer price index. Therefore, no other inflation indices will be appropriate where the bond is linked to UK inflation rate indices.

- The inflation adjustment is related to the same period that the coupon payments relate.

- The resulting real rate of return delivered by the inflation linked debt is itself a rate that would not be considered an embedded derivative under IAS 39 and is not dissimilar to market estimates of real rates at the time when the debt is issued.

- The inflation index is not leveraged in any way (see example in para 5.65 below).

- A judgemental qualitative analysis supports the view that any short term deviations from the defined relationship are not indicative that the two measures are no longer closely related. For example, it is likely that short-term deviations between the two measures may indicate a disparity in a country whose interest and inflation rates are not managed together as part of the country's monetary policy decisions aimed at maintaining price stability.

- A quantitative analysis demonstrates that the inflation index would not result in the rate of return on the debt instrument that would at least double the holder's initial rate of return on the instrument or at any point would not exceed twice what the market rate would be a contract with the same terms as the host debt instrument.

5.35   An entity issuing an inflation linked bond would need to perform the above analysis at inception to determine whether the inflation index is closely related to the host debt instrument. If the above conditions are not met, the embedded derivative would have to be separated from the host contract and accounted for as a derivative.

Example – Inflation-linked bond

A UK entity issues an inflation-linked sterling bond that pays a fixed interest of 5% per annum. The return of the principal amount is linked to UK Retail Price Index (RPI), which is a recognised headline measure of inflation in the economic environment in which the entity operates.

As the coupon on the bond is 5%, and the underlying principal of the bond is £100, the bond pays £5 interest per annum. If the inflation index increases to 10%, the principal of the bond would then increase to £110 and the interest payment increases to £5.50 (5% × C110).

In this example, as the principal payment is not leveraged and it is indexed to the headline measure of inflation in the economic environment in which the entity operates and, assuming all the other conditions in the above paragraph are met, the inflation index is regarded as closely related to the host debt instrument.

Equity and commodity linked interest and principal payments

5.36 Equity-indexed interest or principal payments embedded in a host debt instrument or insurance contract – by which the amount of interest or principal is indexed to the value of equity instruments – are not closely related to the host instrument, because the risks inherent in the host and the embedded derivative are dissimilar. [IAS 39 para AG 30(d)]. Similarly, commodity-indexed interest or principal payments embedded in a host debt instrument or insurance contract – by which the amount of interest or principal is indexed to the price of a commodity (such as gold) – are not closely related to the host instrument, because the risks inherent in the host and the embedded derivative are dissimilar. [IAS 39 para AG 30(e)]. Therefore, where interest and principal payments in a debt instrument are indexed to an equity-index that is not specific to the entity, a commodity index or any other non-financial index, the embedded derivative must be accounted for separately.

Example 1 – Cash settled put option in a convertible bond

Entity A issues convertible bonds to entity H. The term of the bonds is 3 years and the par value is C2m. Each bond pays fixed interest annually at 6% a year and is convertible at any time by entity H until maturity into a fixed number of entity A's ordinary shares. Entity H also has the option to put the convertible bond back to entity A for cash at par.

Entity A has determined that the market rate for a loan with comparable credit status and providing substantially the same cash flows on the same terms, but without the conversion option, is 7%.

Entity A's management should separate the convertible bond's equity and liability elements. [IAS 32 para 28]. The conversion option is an equity instrument of entity A provided it can only be settled by physical delivery of a fixed number of shares for a fixed amount of cash or other financial assets. It is not accounted for as a derivative. [IAS 39 para 2(d)].

The option to put the convertible bond back to entity A for cash at par is an embedded derivative. This option is closely related to the host debt instrument, as the exercise price is approximately equal to the bond's amortised cost before separating the equity element under IAS 32. [IAS 39 para AG30(g)].

Paragraph 49 of IAS 39 states that the fair value of a liability with a demand feature is not less than the amount payable on demand, discounted from the first date that the amount can be required to be paid. Hence entity A would record the liability at its nominal value with any residual consideration received being attributed to the equity component.

Example 2 – Call option linked to an equity index

An entity issues a debt instrument at par with a term of five years. The debt is callable by the issuer 3 years after issue. If the debt is called, the holder will receive a sum that is the greater of the par value of the debt or the par value as adjusted by the percentage increase in the FTSE 100 index.

The embedded call option that is exercisable 3 years after the issue of the debt instrument is not closely related to the debt host as the payoff is indexed to an equity index. The equity linked feature provides an upside to the investor, which is linked to an index representing different risks from those of the ordinary debt instrument. Hence, the option should be separated from the host debt instrument and accounted for separately.

Example 3 – Payments linked to the price of a listed share

An entity issues a debt instrument at par with a term of five years. The debt is also redeemable at par. However, the loan agreement provides that during the term of the loan the entity will either receive or pay an amount based on the changes in the share price of an unrelated listed company A plc, the reference point being the market price of A plc at the date of issue of the debt instrument.

As the interest payments are based on the changes in the price of an equity instrument (equity risk), they are not closely related to the host debt instrument (characterised mainly by interest rate and credit risk). Therefore, the embedded equity linked amounts should be separated by both the issuer and the holder of the debt instrument and recorded on the balance sheet at fair value, with subsequent changes in fair value recognised in the income statement.

The answer would be the same if the interest or principal payments were linked to the movement in an equity index, such as S&P500 and even if they were linked to the market price of the entity's own shares as explained above.

Example 4 – Equity linked bond with repayment floor

Entity A purchases a one-year debt instrument issued by bank B for its principal amount of C1,000 on the issue date. Bank B will make no interest payments during the life of the instrument. At maturity the holder will receive the principal amount plus any increase in the S&P 500 index since the issue date. The fair value of an at-the-money European option maturing in one year is C48 at issuance date.

Entity A classifies the debt instrument as held-to-maturity.

Management should recognise the hybrid instrument as a combination of a call option and a zero-coupon debt instrument. Entity A should first determine the option contract's fair value and strike price. [IAS 39 para AG 28].

Since the holder only receives increases in the value of the index since the issue date, the embedded option is at the money at the date of issue and its fair value consists only of its time value and no intrinsic value. Consequently, its fair value at the issue date is C48 and the balance of the consideration given (C1000 – C48 = C952) is attributed to the carrying amount of the zero-coupon debt instrument.

The zero-coupon host contract should be recognised at amortised cost with interest accreted at the original effective interest rate of 5% to reach C1,000 at maturity. The option should be recognised at fair value against the benchmark of C1,000, with gains or losses recognised in the income statement.

Example 5 – Commodity linked bond

A gold mining company issues a debt instrument with a face value of C10m and contingent interest payments in addition to a guaranteed minimum interest payment of 4% per annum. The contingent payments are linked to the price of gold such that an additional interest payment of 0.5% would be paid for every US$25 increase in gold price above US$260. The price of gold at issue date was US$310 per ounce. The market rate for a fixed interest loan is 5%.

A commodity linked bond such as the one described above enables the issuer to reduce its financing cost by offering contingent payments to investors, whilst the investor is assured of a guaranteed minimum, but able to participate in any increase in the price of gold.

In this situation, the issuer would be viewed as having (a) issued a host debt instrument at a market rate of interest of 5%; and (b) purchased a swap contract to receive 1% fixed interest and pay a variable amount equal to the movement in the gold price above US$260. The swap contract is not closely related to the debt instrument as the factors that cause the swap to change in value (commodity price risk) are not the same as the factors that cause the debt host to change in value (interest rate risk).

Accordingly, the embedded swap contract should be separated from the host contract by both the issuer and the holder and recorded on the balance sheet at fair value, with subsequent changes in fair value recognised in the income statement.

5.37 Example 2 in the previous paragraph dealt with call options held by the issuer. A similar treatment arises in circumstances where the holder has the right to put the debt instrument back to the issuer in exchange for an amount of cash or other financial assets that varies on the basis of the change in an equity or commodity index that may increase or decrease. These instruments are commonly referred to as 'puttable instruments'. Unless the issuer on initial recognition designates the puttable instrument as a financial liability at fair value through profit or loss, it is required to separate an embedded derivative (that is, the indexed payment). [IAS 39 paras AG30(a), AG31].

Interest rate caps, floors and collars

5.38 Floating rate securities may have a maximum coupon that is paid at any reset date. The maximum coupon rate is called a cap. For example, suppose for a floating rate note with a coupon of three-month LIBOR + 50 basis points, there is a cap of eight per cent. If the three-month LIBOR at the coupon reset date is eight per cent, then the coupon rate would be eight and a half per cent. However, the cap would restrict the coupon rate to eight per cent. Therefore, a cap can be attractive to the issuing company as a protection against rises in interest rates. A cap can be thought of as an embedded option requiring no action by the issuer to be protected from a rise in interest rates. Effectively, the bondholder has granted to the issuer the right not to pay more interest than the cap. For the grant of this privilege, the issuer of the bond (the cap buyer) will have to pay a premium that will increase the overall cost of funds. If the relevant/market interest rate rises above the cap strike rate, then in effect payments are made by the cap seller to the cap buyer to compensate for the excess. This means that the cap is in-the-money whenever the strike rate is the lower than the relevant/market rate of interest. It is out-of-the-money whenever the strike rate is above the relevant/market rate of interest.

5.39   In contrast, there could be a minimum coupon rate specified for a floating rate security. The minimum coupon rate is called a floor. If the coupon formula provides a coupon rate that is below the floor, the floor rate is paid instead. A floor is the mirror image of a cap. While a cap benefits the issuer if interest rates rise, a floor benefits the bondholder if interest rate falls. As with other options, the buyer must pay a premium to the issuer of the bond (the floor seller) that will reduce the issuer's overall cost of funds. If the coupon rate falls below the floor strike rate then payments are made by the seller to the buyer to compensate for the shortfall. This means that the floor is in-the-money whenever the strike rate is the above the relevant/market rate of interest. It is out-of-the-money whenever the strike rate is lower than the relevant/market rate of interest.

5.40   A floating rate security can have a cap and a floor. This feature is referred to as a collar. The buyer of a collar limits the maximum rate that he will pay and sets a minimum rate that he will pay and, therefore, will be exposed to interest rate movements within a range. Hence, as long as interest rates are within this band the buyer of the collar pays floating interest, no compensating payment is made or received by the buyer under the terms of the collar and the collar is said to be out-of-the-money.

5.41   An embedded floor or cap on the interest rate on a debt contract is closely related to the host contract, provided when the instrument is issued:

■   the floor is at or below the market rate of interest (out-of-the-money); or

■   the cap is at or above the market rate of interest (out-of-the-money); and

■   the cap or floor is not leveraged in relation to the host contract.

[IAS 39 para AG 33(b)].

5.42   The assessment of whether the cap or floor is closely related to the host is made when the entity becomes party to the contract and is not subsequently revised, unless the terms of the debt instrument are changed significantly (see para 5.20 above). An entity would become party to the contract when the debt is issued at inception, bought in the secondary market or on the date of the business combination in which the debt was acquired. It follows from the above that only in-the-money caps and floors when the entity becomes party to the contract or leverage provision would fail the closely related test. Therefore, an interest floor embedded in a variable rate debt instrument that was out-of-the-money when the debt instrument was initially recognised would not be separated from the host debt even if interest rates subsequently fall so that the floor becomes in-the-money. Similar considerations apply to caps.

> **Example – Debt subject to an interest rate collar**
>
> Entity A has borrowed cash from a bank. The debt is interest-bearing at a variable rate, but within a collar. The variable rate on the date of inception of the loan was 7%, the floor was 5% and the cap was 9%.
>
> In this situation, the embedded derivative is a collar that modifies the cash flows of variable rate debt if the variable rate moves outside the range of the collar. IAS 39 does not specifically deal with collars in this context, although the guidance relating to caps and floors can be extended to collars. Since at the time when the variable rate debt instrument is issued, the interest rate is 7%, which is within the collar range, the collar is out-of-the-money. Hence, based on the guidance in paragraph 5.41 above, the embedded collar is regarded as closely related and separate accounting for the embedded derivative is prohibited.

Calls, puts and pre-payment options

5.43   The terms of a debt instrument may include an issuer call option (a callable bond), that is, a right of the issuer (but not the investor) to redeem the instrument early and pay a fixed price (generally at a premium over the par value). There may also be other pre-payment features that cause the whole or part of the outstanding principal to be repaid early. Adding call options and/or other pre-payment options should make it less attractive to buyers, since it reduces the potential upside on the bond. As interest rates go down and the bond price increases, the bonds are likely to be called back. Alternatively, the investor may have a put option to force early redemption of the outstanding principal. Such call option, put option and pre-payment features that are embedded in the debt host are derivatives.

5.44   The application guidance explains that these embedded derivatives are not closely related to the host debt contract, unless the option's exercise price is approximately equal on each exercise date to the host debt instrument's amortised cost. [IAS 39 para AG 30(g)].

> **Example 1 – Calls and puts in debt instruments**
>
> An entity issues the following debt instruments:
>
> - 5 year zero coupon debt for proceeds of C7m with a face value of C10m; issue costs are insignificant. The debt is callable by the issuer at its amortised cost calculated on the basis of the effective interest rate method in the event of a

change in tax legislation adversely affecting the tax deductions available to the issuer.

■ 5 year zero coupon debt for proceeds of C7m with a face value of C10m; issue costs are insignificant. The debt is puttable at its face value in the event of a change of control of the issuer.

In both scenarios above, the zero coupon debt will be recorded initially at its fair value of C7m, which is the consideration received. The debt will accrete to its final value of C10m at maturity in year 5. Therefore, between inception and maturity the debt's amortised cost will not be the same as its face value, except in the period close to maturity.

In the first scenario, if the debt is called by the issuer at its amortised cost, the call option does not accelerate the repayment of principal as the option's exercise price is the same as the debt's amortised cost (the exercise price is not fixed but variable), even though the debt was initially issued at a substantial discount. Therefore, in accordance with paragraph AG 30(g) of IAS 39, the call option is closely related to the debt host and would not be accounted for separately.

In the second scenario, if the debt is put back by the holder at its face value before maturity, the put option's exercise price of C10m (fixed at the outset) would not be the same as the debt's amortised cost at exercise date. Therefore, in accordance with paragraph AG 30(g) of IAS 39, the put option is not closely related to the debt host. This means that the put option must be separately accounted for.

Both debt instruments contain terms that allow the debts to be called or put back on the occurrence of a contingent event (adverse change in tax legislation or change in control). These terms (relating to factors other than interest rate risk and credit risk of the issuer) are not closely related to the debt hosts. However, determining whether the call or the put option is closely related to the host contract is based solely on the difference between the option's exercise price and the debt's amortised cost.

Example 2 – Pre-payment option in debt instruments

Entity A takes out a fixed rate loan with a bank for C1m. The loan is repayable in quarterly instalments. The debt contains a pre-payment option that may be exercised by entity A on the first day of each quarter. The exercise price is the remaining capital amount outstanding on the debt plus a penalty of C100,000.

At inception, entity A would record the financial liability at its fair value of C1m. As entity A makes repayments of capital to the bank, the amortised cost of the debt will change.

The exercise price of the pre-payment option at inception is C1m plus the penalty of C100,000. Whether the entity will exercise its option to pre-pay the loan early may depend on a number of reasons, but the level of interest rates is a critical variable. If there is a significant decline in interest rates, any potential gain from early pre-payment may well be more that the cost of the pre-payment (the penalty payable).

Therefore, given the penalty payable is fixed, the option's exercise price (outstanding principal + penalty) will always exceed the debt's amortised cost at each option exercise date as the loan is paid off in instalments. Hence, the pre-payment option is not closely related to the debt host and should be separately accounted for. The fair value of the option would need to be calculated and this will be a positive value to the entity as the value of the pre-payable bond = value of straight bond – value of pre-payment feature. If interest rates decline, the option's value will increase making it more attractive to the entity to repay the debt early.

Sometimes the pre-payment option's exercise price is a 'market adjusted value'. A market adjusted value is calculated by discounting the contractual guaranteed amount payable at the end of the specified term to present value using the current market rate that would be offered on a new loan having a maturity period equal to the remaining maturity period of the current loan. As a result, the adjustment necessary to arrive at the market adjusted value may be positive or negative, depending upon market interest rates at each option exercise date. In that situation, the pre-payment option enables the holder simply to cash out of the instrument at fair value at the date of pre-payment. Since the holder receives only the market adjusted value, which is equal to the fair value of the loan at the date of pre-payment, the pre-payment option has a fair value of zero at all times. Infact, on a stand-alone basis, the pre-payment option with a strike price equal to market value would not meet the definition of a derivative, so it cannot be an embedded derivative per IAS 39 paragraph 11.

5.44.1 In the April 2009 'Improvements to IFRSs', the IASB added another example of a prepayment option into paragraph AG30(g) of IAS 39 which would be deemed to be closely related to the host contract. This states that if the prepayment option reimburses the lender for an amount up to the approximate present value of lost interest for the host contract's remaining term it is closely related to the host contract. Lost interest is the product of the principal amount multiplied by the interest differential. The interest differential is the difference between the effective interest rate on the host contract less the effective interest rate that could be obtained by the lender if it invests the principal at the repayment date for the host contract's remaining term in a similar contract.

5.45 An embedded pre-payment option in an interest-only or principal-only strip (that is, an interest or principal cash flow stream that has been separated and payable at different dates) is closely related to the host contract provided the host contract:

- initially resulted from separating the right to receive contractual cash flows of a financial instrument that, in and of itself, did not contain an embedded derivative; and

- does not contain any terms not present in the original host debt contract.

[IAS 39 para AG 33(e)].

Term-extending options

5.46 Sometimes clauses are included in debt instruments that allow the issuer to extend the debt's term beyond its original maturity. An option or automatic provision to extend the remaining term to maturity of a debt instrument is not closely related to the host debt instrument, unless there is a concurrent adjustment to the approximate current market rate of interest at the time of the extension. [IAS 39 para AG 30(c)]. Thus, if there is no reset of interest rates at the time of the extension, the embedded derivative is not closely related to the debt host.

5.46.1   An alternative view is that the option to extend the term of the debt may be considered a loan commitment. Not all loan commitments fall within the scope of IAS 39, as set out in paragraphs 2(h) and 4 of IAS 39. In particular, only the following loan commitments are within the scope of IAS 39:

- Instruments that the entity designates as financial liabilities at fair value through profit or loss.

- Loan commitments that can be settled net in cash or by delivering or issuing another financial instrument.

- Commitments to provide a loan at a below-market interest rate.

Loan commitments that are not in the scope of IAS 39 do not meet the definition of a derivative, as all derivatives must be financial instruments within the scope of IAS 39. [IAS 39 paras 9, 11]. Hence, an option to extend the term of a debt instrument that is considered to be a loan commitment, that is, out of the scope of IAS 39 could not be an embedded derivative that needs to be assessed for separation (see para 5.6). The approach adopted (that is, whether to treat an option to extend the term of a debt instrument as only within the embedded derivatives requirements or as also within the requirements for loan commitments) is an accounting policy choice that should be applied consistently.

Example 1 – Term-extending options not reset to market rates

An entity issues 6% fixed rate debt that has a fixed term of 3 years. The entity is able to extend the debt before its maturity for an additional 2 year period at the same 6% interest.

In this example, as the entity is able to extend the debt's term at the same interest rate and there is no reset to current market rates, the term extending option is not considered to be closely related to the debt host.

Such term-extending options could be valuable to the entity as it allows the issuer to refinance the debt at the same interest rate when market rates are rising. Conversely, if market rates are falling, the entity would not exercise its options to extend. Therefore, the option is a derivative that would need to be separated from the debt host and accounted for separately, even though its value is closely related to interest rates that also affect the value of the underlying debt host.

The above treatment regarding term-extending options is justified, because otherwise such options could be used to circumvent the requirement to bifurcate a derivative in circumstances where the investor might not recover substantially all its initial recorded investment (see further para 5.27 above). Term-extending options in host debt typically involve postponement of the repayment of the principal and, even though such postponement does not cause the failure to recover substantially all of its initial recorded investment, it can significantly reduce the fair value of the recovery of that investment.

Alternatively, if the term-extending option was considered to be a loan commitment out of IAS 39's scope, it would not be separated from the host debt instrument.

Example 2 – Term-extending option reset to market rates

An entity issues a 6% fixed rate debt that has a fixed term of 3 years. The company is able to extend the debt before its maturity for an additional 2 year period, but the rate for the period of extension is the market rate at the time of the extension.

In this example, as the option to extend the term causes the interest rate to reset to current market rates, the option is regarded as closely related to the host debt. Common sense would also suggest such an option has no real value to the entity other than providing liquidity. This is because if the market interest rate at the time of extension is 8%, the entity cannot extend the term without paying an additional 2% interest anyway. On the other hand, if the market interest rate drops to 4%, the extension is equivalent to taking out a new loan at 4%.

5.47 If an entity issues a debt instrument and the holder of that debt instrument writes a call option on the debt instrument to a third party, the issuer regards the call option as extending the term to maturity of the debt instrument provided the issuer can be required to participate in or facilitate the remarketing of the debt instrument as a result of the call option being exercised. [IAS 39 para AG 30 (c)].

5.48 It is interesting to note that a bond that has a put option is economically no different to one that has a term-extending option, yet IAS 39 prescribes a different treatment for the derivatives embedded in them. Consider the following example:

Example – Comparison of put and extension option

An entity purchasers two bonds A and B with the following terms:

- Bond A has a stated maturity of 10 years, but the entity can put it back to the issuer at par after 3 years.

- Bond B has a stated maturity of 3 years, but after 3 years the entity can extend the maturity to 10 years (that is, 7 more years) at the same initial rate (that is, the interest rate is not reset to the interest rate at the date of extension).

Both bonds are issued by the same issuer at par and have a coupon rate of 6%.

Assume also that the following two scenarios exist at the end of year 3:

Scenario 1: For the issuer, the interest rate for 7 year debt is at 8%.

- The holder will put bond A back to the issuer and reinvest the par amount of the bond at 8%.

- The holder will not extend the maturity of bond B and, instead, will reinvest the principal at 8%.

Scenario 2: For the issuer, the interest rate for 7 year debt is at 4%.

- The holder will not put bond A back to the issuer and, instead, will continue to receive 6% for the next 7 years.

- The holder will extend the term of bond B and continue to receive 6% for the next 7 years.

As can be seen from the above, the entity is in the same position with respect to either Bond A or Bond B. However, IAS 39 prescribes a different treatment for the put and the term extension options embedded in Bond A and Bond B respectively.

As discussed in paragraph 5.44 above, the embedded put option derivative in Bond A is regarded as closely related to the Bond as the bond's amortised cost based on the effective interest rate at the end of three years is the same as par, which is also the put option's exercise price. This is because the expected cash flows would take into account the possibility of the debt being pre-paid early for the purposes of calculating the effective interest rate. [IAS 39 para 9]. Therefore, the embedded put option would not be recognised separately and fair valued.

On the other hand, the embedded term extension option is not regarded as closely related to the host debt, because under Bond B's terms the interest rates are not reset when the option is exercised. Therefore, the option would be separated and fair valued. Alternatively, if the embedded term extension option was considered to be a loan commitment outside IAS 39's scope, the option would not be separated, as it would not meet the definition of a derivative.

The above example illustrates that two instruments that are economically similar, but different in form by virtue of the way in which the terms of the embedded options are expressed, can lead to different accounting treatments for the embedded options.

To be able to rationalise the apparent conflict in accounting treatment between these two economically identical situations, it is necessary to consider the issuer's expectation of the instrument's life for the purposes of the effective interest rate calculation. Thus the issuer will not follow the legal form of the terms, but the economics in determining whether the instrument has a put option or a term extending option and thus the appropriate accounting treatment.

Credit sensitive payments and credit derivatives

5.49 IAS 39 does not deal specifically with payments based on the creditworthiness of the issuer of an instrument. However, as the stated in paragraph 5.25 above, the creditworthiness of the issuer is a key factor in setting the level of interest rate on the debt instrument. Thus, for debt instruments that provide for the interest rate to be reset in the event of a change in the issuer's published credit rating (say down from A to BBB) or a change in the issuer's creditworthiness, the embedded derivative would be closely related to the debt host, and so would not be separated from the host contract.

Example – Credit sensitive payments

Entity A issues a bond with a coupon step-up feature that requires the issuer to pay an additional coupon to bondholders in the event of deterioration in the issuer's credit rating below a specified level. The coupon payable on the bond will return to the initial fixed rate in the event that the issuer's credit rating returns to the specified level.

The coupon step-up clause meets the definition of a derivative as the value fluctuates in response to an underlying (in this case the credit rating); it requires no initial net investment and it is settled at a future date.

The economic characteristics and risks of the embedded derivatives in both cases are closely related to the economic characteristics and risks of the host bond because:

- both the embedded derivative and the host contract are driven by changes in the indications of the issuer's credit risk; and

- such clauses do not transfer the credit risk to another party external to the original contractual relationships created by the debt instrument (see para 5.50 below).

The embedded derivative is not accounted for separately from the host debt contract.

5.50   IAS 39 does, however, deal with credit derivatives that are embedded in host debt instruments. A credit derivative is a financial instrument designed to transfer credit risk from the person exposed to that risk to a person willing to take on that risk. The derivative derives its economic value by reference to a specified debt obligation, often described as the 'reference asset'.

5.51   Credit derivatives that are embedded in a host debt instrument and allow one party (the 'beneficiary') to transfer the credit risk of a particular reference asset, which it may not own, to another party (the 'guarantor') are not closely related to the host debt instrument. Such credit derivatives allow the guarantor to assume the credit risk associated with the reference asset without directly owning it. [IAS 39 AG30(h)].

Example – Credit-linked note

An investment bank issues a credit-linked note to another party (the investor) in return for a consideration equal to the par value of the note. The coupon on the note is linked to the credit risk of a portfolio of third party bonds (the reference assets). In economic terms, the credit-linked note comprises a fixed income instrument with an embedded credit derivative.

The embedded credit derivative must be accounted for separately as it is linked to credit risks of debt instruments issued by third parties and not to the credit risk of the host debt instrument issued by the investment bank. The notion of an embedded derivative in a hybrid instrument refers to provisions incorporated into a single contract and not to provisions in separate contracts between different counterparties.

Equity conversion features

5.52 When an investor holds debt securities that are convertible into the issuer's equity shares at the investor's option, the equity conversion feature represents an embedded option written by the issuer on its equity shares. The embedded derivative is not closely related to the host debt instrument from the investor's perspective. [IAS 39 para IG C3]. From the issuer's perspective, the written equity conversion option is an equity instrument and excluded from IAS 39's scope provided it meets the conditions for that classification under IAS 32. [IAS 39 para AG 30(f)]. If, on the other hand, the debt instrument is convertible (or exchangeable) into shares of another entity, both the issuer and the holder would have to separate the embedded derivative from the host contract.

5.53 If the holder of a convertible bond is required to separate the embedded derivative, the holder is generally precluded from accounting for the debt host contract as a held-to-maturity investment. This is because classification as a held-to-maturity investment would be inconsistent with paying for the conversion feature – the right to convert into equity shares before maturity. However, the investor will be able to classify the bond as an available-for-sale financial asset provided it is not purchased for trading purposes. If the bond is classified as available-for-sale (that is, fair value changes are recognised directly in equity until the bond is sold or impaired), the equity conversion option (the embedded derivative) is separated. The accounting for the holder, which is significantly different from the issuer and considered in chapter 7, is as follows:

■ The embedded derivative's fair value (the equity conversion option from the issuer's perspective) is calculated first and this becomes the embedded derivative's fair value. The option's fair value comprises its time value and its intrinsic value, if any. The option has value on initial recognition even when it is out of the money.

  After initial recognition, the embedded derivative is constantly remeasured at fair value at each balance sheet date and changes in the fair value are recognised in profit or loss, unless the option is part of a cash flow hedging relationship.

■ The carrying value of the host contract (the liability component from the issuer's perspective) is assigned the residual amount after deducting from the fair value of the instrument as a whole (the consideration paid to acquire the hybrid instrument) the amount separately determined for the embedded derivative.

If the convertible bond is measured at fair value with changes in fair value recognised in profit or loss, separating the embedded derivative from the host bond as illustrated above is not permitted. [IAS 39 para IG C3].

5.54 Another type of embedded derivative that is often found in practice relates to a type of funding provided by venture capital entities as illustrated in the example below.

Example – Equity kicker

A venture capital entity provides a subordinated loan that, in addition to interest and repayment of principal, contains terms that entitles the venture capital company to receive shares of the borrower free of charge or at a very low price (an 'equity kicker') in the event the borrower undergoes an IPO. As a result of this feature, the interest on the subordinated loan is lower than it would otherwise be.

The 'equity kicker' meets the definition of a derivative even though the right to receive shares is contingent upon the future listing of the borrower. IAS 39 paragraph AG 9 states that a derivative could require a payment as a result of some future event that is unrelated to a notional amount. An 'equity kicker' feature is similar to such a derivative except that it does not give a right to a fixed payment, but an option right, if the future event occurs. Therefore, as the economic characteristics and risks of an equity return are not closely related to the economic characteristics and risks of a host debt instrument, the embedded derivative would be accounted for separately by the venture capital entity. [IAS 39 para IG C4].

Foreign currency features

5.55   An entity may issue debt in a currency other than its functional currency. Such a foreign currency loan is accounted for under IAS 21, 'The effects of changes in foreign exchange rates', which requires foreign currency gains and losses on monetary items to be recognised in profit or loss. Therefore, a foreign currency derivative that may be embedded in such a host debt instrument is considered closely related and is not separated. This also applies to an embedded foreign currency derivative that provides a stream of principal or interest payments that are denominated in a foreign currency and embedded in a host debt instrument (for example, a dual currency bond). [IAS 39 para AG 33(c)].

Example – Dual currency bond

An entity with pound sterling as a functional currency issues a £10m debt instrument that provides for the annual payment of interest in euros and the repayment of principal in pound sterling.

This dual currency bond can be viewed as containing a foreign currency swap that converts the pound sterling interest payments to euro interest payments. As discussed above, this embedded swap is not accounted for separately as under IAS 21, any exchange gains and losses arising on the annual euro interest payments due to exchange rate changes are themselves reported in profit or loss. [IAS 21 para 28]. See also the example of the measurement of a dual currency bond in chapter 9.

5.56   Although many embedded foreign currency derivatives will not have to be separated from a foreign currency host debt instrument, certain embedded foreign currency features may require separation. For example, an entity would be required to separate the embedded foreign currency derivative involving a loan with a foreign currency option. Consider the following examples:

Example 1 – Loan with foreign currency option

An entity issues a C10m loan at an above average market rate. The entity has the option to repay the loan at par for C10m or a fixed amount in a foreign currency, say €15m.

The debt instrument can be viewed as combining a loan at prevailing market interest rates and a foreign currency option. In effect, the issuer has purchased a foreign currency option that allows it to take advantage of changes in foreign currency exchange rates during the outstanding period of the loan. The premium for the option is paid as part of the higher interest cost. Similarly, the lender has written an option that exposes it to foreign currency risk. Because the borrower has the option of repaying the loan in its functional currency or in a foreign currency, the option is not closely related to the debt instrument (that is, it is not directly related to the currency of the loan or the interest rate that applies to that currency). Therefore, the principle discussed in paragraph 5.55 above does not apply since application of IAS 21 rules for revaluing of monetary items would not lead to revaluation of the foreign currency option. Accordingly, the embedded foreign currency option should be separated from the host contract and accounted for separately by both parties to the contract. In contrast, if both the principal and the interest payments were made in a foreign currency (that is, if no optionality was involved), there would be no embedded derivative.

Example 2 – Interest payments linked to foreign currency exchange rates

An entity issues a £10m debt security at par. Quarterly interest payments, which are payable in pound sterling, are computed based on a formula that is linked to the £/€ exchange rate.

In this example, the quarterly interest is not denominated in foreign currency and, therefore, the principle discussed in paragraph 5.55 above does not apply. Since the formula for computing the interest payable on a sterling bond is linked to the £/€ exchange rate and not based on an interest rate or an index based on interest rates, an inflation index or the creditworthiness of the debtor, it is an embedded derivative that is not closely related to the sterling bond. Hence, it should be accounted for separately. The embedded derivative is a forward foreign exchange contract.

Embedded derivatives in equity host contracts

5.57   For embedded derivatives in an equity host contract, an analysis should first be performed to determine whether the host contract is an equity host. In carrying out this analysis, it is necessary to determine whether the host contract has any stated or pre-determined maturity and, if not, whether the residual interest represents a residual interest in the entity's net assets (see section 7 of this financial instruments chapter for more detail on the definition of equity). Generally, when a host contract encompasses a residual interest that involves the rights of ownership, it is an equity host. The value of an equity instrument is a function of the underlying equity price or index. Therefore, an embedded derivative would need to possess equity characteristics related to the same entity to be regarded as closely related. [IAS 39 para AG 27].

Calls and puts

5.58 A call option embedded in an equity instrument that enables the issuer to re-acquire that equity instrument at a specified price is not closely related to the host equity instrument from the holder's perspective. From the issuer's perspective, on the other hand, the call option is an equity instrument provided it meets the conditions for that classification under IAS 32, in which case it is excluded from IAS 39's scope. [IAS 39 para AG 30(b)].

5.59 A put option that requires the issuer to re-acquire an equity instrument at a specified price is similarly not closely related to the host equity instrument from the holder's perspective. From the issuer's perspective, the put option is a written option that gives the counterparty the right to sell the issuer's own equity instrument to the entity for a fixed price. Under paragraph 23 of IAS 32, the issuer recognises a financial liability equal to the present value of the redemption amount (that is, the present value of the option's exercise price). See further chapter 7.

5.60 In the case of a puttable instrument that can be put back at any time for cash equal to a proportionate share of the entity's net asset value (such as units of an open-ended mutual fund or some unit-linked investment products), the effect of separating an embedded derivative and accounting for each component is to measure the combined instrument at the redemption amount that is payable at the balance sheet date if the holder exercised its right to put the instrument back to the issuer. [IAS 39 para AG 32]. This will apply to both the issuer and the investor in such an instrument, but for the issuer it is only relevant if the instrument is classified as a debt instrument in accordance with an amendment to IAS 32 and IAS 1, 'Puttable financial instruments and obligations arising on liquidation'.

5.61 The treatment of call and put options embedded in preference shares require careful consideration. This is because the terms of the preference share must be analysed first to determine whether the preference shares are more akin to an equity instrument or a debt instrument. Consider the following examples:

Example 1 – Puttable preference shares

An entity issues C50m mandatorily redeemable preference shares at par with a fixed dividend of 8% per annum. The preference shares are puttable to the company for cash at par if market interest rate exceeds 12%.

The mandatorily redeemable preference shares are a financial liability of the issuer and akin to a debt instrument. Furthermore, the embedded put option's exercise price, which is par, is approximately equal to the preference's shares amortised cost. Hence, the put option is considered closely related to the debt host.

Example 2 – Convertible preference shares

An entity issues C50m of irredeemable preference shares that give the holders a preferential right to return of capital in a winding up, but which are also convertible into a fixed number of ordinary shares at the holder's option. Any dividends paid in the year are at the discretion of the issuer.

As the preference shares are irredeemable and there is no obligation on the issuer to pay dividends, the shares are equity in nature. The conversion feature represents an embedded written call option on the company's ordinary shares, which on a free-standing basis would be an equity instrument of the entity. As both the embedded call option and the host are equity instruments, the entity does not account for the embedded option separately. Similarly, the investor would not have to account for the embedded option separately.

Embedded derivatives in lease host contracts

5.62 Embedded derivatives may be present in lease host contracts, whether the lease is an operating or a finance lease. The approach for determining whether an embedded derivative is closely related to a lease host is similar to the approach that is used for a debt host.

Inflation indexed rentals

5.63 An embedded derivative in a host lease contract is closely related to the host contract if the embedded derivative is an inflation-related index such as an index of lease payments to a consumer price index provided:

- the lease is not leveraged; and

- the index relates to inflation in the entity's own economic environment.

[IAS 39 para AG 33(f)].

5.64 The first bullet point makes it clear that an embedded inflation adjustment in the lease contract would not be closely related if it is considered to be leveraged. In determining whether inflation features embedded in lease contracts are leveraged, the guidance stated in paragraph 5.13-5.14 above should be followed. Generally, lease contracts often stipulate that the payments will increase in line with inflation, in which case, the indexed linked lease payments would not be considered leveraged. Where this is not the case, an inflationary adjustment of greater than one would be considered sufficiently leveraged for the inflation feature to be accounted for separately. This is because, in practice, the market would expect the prices of goods and services to move in line with inflation, all other factors being equal. Therefore, any inflationary adjustment in a lease contract that has the effect of increasing the indexed cash flows by more than the normal rate of inflation are considered to be leveraged.

5.65 The second bullet point in paragraph 5.63 states that the index should relate to inflation in the entity's own economic environment. IAS 39 is silent as to whether the entity's own economic environment refers to the lessee's or the lessor's economic environment. It is reasonable to assume, however, that the economic environment that is most relevant to the lease contract is the one in which the leased asset is located, as the inflation index of that economic environment is the one that directly affects the lease rentals and, hence, the leased property's value. Consequently, the economic environment in which the lessee or the lessor operates is not relevant to the analysis.

Example 1 – Inflation linked rentals

A UK entity leases a property in France. The rentals are paid in euros and increase each year in line with the increase in the rate of inflation in France. The lessor is located in France.

The future cash flows (the rental payments) will change in response to changes in the inflation index of France. The embedded inflation indexed payments are not leveraged and relate to the economic environment in which the leased asset is located. Therefore, the inflation adjustment is closely related to the lease contract and separation is not required.

Note: this is a lease payable in a currency that is not the functional currency of the UK lessee. Foreign currency features in lease contracts are discussed further from paragraphs 5.72 below.

Example 2 – Inflation linked rentals (leveraged)

A UK entity is the tenant in a 10 year lease of a property in the UK with rental payments in pound sterling that are contractually determined for the first year, but thereafter increasing at a rate of one and a half times the change in UK RPI (Retail Price Index).

The future cash flows (the rental payments) will change in response to changes in the UK RPI. Since the cash flows changes by an amount in excess of one times the change in RPI, such cash flows are considered to be leveraged as discussed in paragraph 5.64 above. Therefore, the embedded inflation indexed payments would be accounted for separately.

A question arises as to whether the embedded derivative should be measured by reference to half times UK RPI or one and a half times UK RPI.

Some would favour the former treatment on the grounds that as the leverage portion of the embedded derivative is the amount over and above the change in the UK inflation index, this portion (half times RPI) should be accounted for separately as a derivative. On this basis, the host contract would contain the non-leveraged portion (one times RPI) that is considered to be closely related.

However, we consider that splitting the change in the fair value of an indexed linked derivative between a leveraged amount and a non-leveraged amount is not appropriate for the following reasons:

■ A derivative has a single value and splitting a portion out in the above manner is not permitted under IAS 39.

■ The leveraged and non-leveraged portions relate to the same risk and, since the inflation is leveraged overall, the entire link to RPI is no longer considered closely related.

■ The separation creates cash flow patterns that are not evident in the lease contract because, in practice, the actual cash flows would consist of the minimum rentals plus amounts relating to the entire change in the inflation adjustment.

Therefore, the leveraged portion of the embedded derivative should be based on the total change in the UK inflation index, that is, one and a half times RPI, whilst the host would consist of a non-inflation linked lease rental contract.

Example 3 – Inflation linked rentals not related to the entity's economic environment

Facts are the same as in example 1 except that the inflation adjustment relates to a specified US annual inflation rate (for example, Retail Price Index, Consumer Price Index etc). The landlord is a US entity.

The future cash flows (the rental payments) will change in response to changes in the US inflation index. The embedded inflation indexed payments, although not leveraged, relate to a different economic environment to that in which the leased asset is located and the UK entity operates. Therefore, the inflation indexed payment is not closely related to the lease host contract and would be accounted for separately.

Example 4 – Upward only inflation-linked rentals

Entity A is a tenant in a 10 year UK property lease agreement. The rent for the first year is contractually determined at C100,000. The rental payments will change in line with an index of UK prices so if, at the end of year 1, the index had increased by 3%, the rent for year 2 would be C103,000. However, the lease provides that the rent may not be decreased. So if, during year 2, the index fell by 1%, the rent for year 3 would remain at C103,000. The index shows that UK prices are generally increasing at the inception of the lease (that is, there is UK inflation).

The rental payments are linked to an index. They follow that index while it is increasing, but do not follow it if it decreases. This feature is often known as 'upward only'. However, this lease contains a floor in the rental payments because of the upward-only feature, so it is necessary to identify whether the floor is in or out-of-the-money at the inception of the lease. Because the upward-only feature of the rent reviews means that the rentals can never fall below the floor, the floor is always out-of-the-money (not influencing the cash flows) both at inception (even where the relevant index is negative at the date of signing) and subsequently. Therefore, its presence does not alter the expected cash flows and so the derivative is closely related.

Contingent rentals based on related sales

5.66 Lease contracts may include contingent rentals that are based on certain related sales of the lessee. Such a contingent rental-related embedded derivative is considered to be closely related to the lease host contract and would not be accounted for separately. [IAS 39 para AG 33(f)].

Example – Lease rentals related to sales

A UK entity leases a property located in the UK. The rentals consist of a base rental of C10,000 plus 5% of the lessee's sales each month.

The rental payments will vary, depending on an underlying, being the entity's sales.

However, as stated above, the portion of the contingent rentals based on related sales is considered to be closely related to the host lease contract. Therefore, the sales related payments should not be separated.

Contingent rentals based on a variable interest rate

5.67 Where lease contracts include contingent rentals that are based on variable interest rates, the contingent rental-related embedded derivative is considered to be closely related to the lease host contract and would not be accounted for separately. [IAS 39 para AG 33(f)]. This is because a lease contract is akin to a debt instrument and, therefore, the obligation to make future payments for the use of the asset and the adjustment of those payments to reflect changes in a variable interest rate index such as the LIBOR are considered to be closely related.

Example – Lease rentals indexed to LIBOR

A UK entity leases a property located in the UK. The lease rentals are indexed to the UK LIBOR rate. The contract does not contain any leverage feature.

The embedded derivative does not need to be separated as the rentals are based on a variable interest rate index of the UK economy.

On the other hand, if the rentals were indexed to a variable interest rate of an economic environment that is different from the economic environment in which the leased asset is located, the related embedded derivative would not be regarded as closely related in the same way that a similarly indexed inflation payment would not be regarded as closely related (see para 5.63 above).

Purchase options in lease agreements

5.68 Often lease contracts may include an option that allows the lessee to purchase the asset at the end of the lease term. Such a purchase option would not qualify as an embedded derivative for a number of reasons. First, the purchase option is based on a non-financial variable (the underlying price of the leased asset) that is specific to a party to the contract and, hence, currently fails the definition of a derivative. [IAS 39 para AG12A]. Secondly, in order to exercise the option, the lessee must pay the purchase price in cash and the lessor must physically deliver the leased asset (a non-financial asset). This constitutes a gross settlement and, therefore, the option is not a financial instrument. However, if the terms in the contract allow either party to settle net in cash (considered unlikely) or the leased asset is readily convertible into cash (because an active trading market exists for the asset in question and, therefore, it is not specific to a party to the contract), the purchase option could qualify as a derivative (see chapter 3). [IAS 39 para 6].

Term extension or renewal options

5.69   A finance lease is viewed as being equivalent to debt for accounting and disclosure purposes. However, the right to extend the lease term is different from the right to extend the term of a debt instrument. The right to extend the lease is not a right to borrow funds for a further period as would be the case with a debt instrument; rather, the right to extend the lease is a right to use a non-financial asset for an additional period. Furthermore, under IAS 17 the extension term would either be included in the calculation of the minimum lease term if it is reasonably certain that, at the inception of the lease, the lessee will exercise the option; or the renewal would constitute a new lease because the leased asset and the corresponding liability (if either exists) would have been amortised to nil by the end of the original lease term. In either case, the renewal or the extension option would not meet the definition of a derivative, for it does not contain a net settlement provision.

Residual value guarantee in lease agreements

5.70   Where a lease includes a residual value guarantee, the lessee undertakes to make a payment if the residual value of the asset at the end of the lease falls below a pre-determined amount. A residual value guarantee does not meet the definition of a derivative because it has an underlying (price of the leased asset) that is specific to a party to the contract. Furthermore, under IAS 17, the gross value amount of any residual value guarantee is treated as part of the minimum lease payments and is accounted for as such. Therefore, it is not accounted for under IAS 39.

Termination clause in lease agreements

5.71   Lease agreements are generally irrevocable, that is, the lessee is obliged to lease the asset during the non-cancellable period of the lease. However, the lease may contain an early termination clause that allows the lessee to terminate the contract, but only on the payment of a penalty. This penalty payment (sometimes referred to as the 'stipulated loss value') ensures that the lessor will be able to recover its remaining investment in the lease. This situation is similar in substance to a pre-payment option in a debt instrument, which is considered closely related in circumstances where the option's exercise price is approximately equal to the amortised cost of the debt instrument. See example 2 in paragraph 5.44 above where the penalty payment clause resulted in a fair value of zero, until the option was actually exercised.

Lease payments in foreign currencies

5.72   Finance lease contracts that give rise to financial assets in lessors and financial liabilities in lessees are financial instruments. Therefore, as a finance lease denominated in a foreign currency is similar in nature to a foreign currency loan, no separation of the embedded foreign currency derivative is required, because the foreign currency lease receivable and payable are monetary items that are accounted for in accordance with IAS 21. The guidance that applies to foreign currency loans is also applicable to foreign currency finance leases (see para 5.55), that is, the embedded derivative is not separated.

5.73 On the other hand, an operating lease is not regarded as a financial instrument. Therefore, an operating lease agreement that provides for payments in foreign currency may contain foreign currency embedded derivatives that may require separation. Paragraph AG33(d) of IAS 39 contains provisions that deal with embedded foreign currency derivatives in a host contract that is not a financial instrument. These are considered in paragraph 5.84 below. That guidance has been applied to the examples given below.

Example 1 – Operating lease rentals denominated in foreign currency

A UK company enters into an operating lease for a property in France with a European lessor that is denominated in euros. The functional currency of the lessee and the lessor are the pound sterling and the euro respectively.

Paragraph AG33(d) of IAS 39 provides that contracts, other than financial instruments, that specify payments denominated in the functional currency of any substantial party to the contract are closely related to the host contract.

In this example, the lease payments are denominated in the functional currency of the lessor – a substantial party to the contract. Therefore, the embedded derivative is closely related to the host contract and not separated. It is not appropriate to argue that because the payments are in a foreign currency and the UK lessee is exposed to currency risk that there is an embedded foreign currency forward converting sterling payments to euros.

On the other hand, if the lease payments are denominated in a currency that is unrelated to each party's functional currency (for example, US dollars), the embedded foreign currency forward should be separated from the host contract and accounted for as a derivative. This applies to both parties to the contract.

Example 2 – Operating lease rentals denominated in foreign currency

On 1 June 20X2 entity A, a Russian oil refinery, entered into an arrangement with entity S to lease a building in Moscow for a 10-year period. The lease is classified as an operating lease. Entity A's management has determined its functional currency to be the US dollar.

Entity S is a property management and development entity located in Russia. Its management has determined its functional currency to be the Russian Rouble.

Entity S set the monthly lease repayments in Swiss Francs to avoid exposure to any devaluation in the Russian Rouble and to obtain a natural hedge for the repayment of its Swiss Franc denominated bonds.

As the Swiss Franc is neither the functional currency of one of the substantial parties to the lease contract, nor a currency commonly used in Russia, nor the currency in which leases are routinely denominated in the world, the lease contract contains an embedded derivative that is not closely related to the host contract.

From entity S's perspective, the lease contract contains a series of embedded forward contracts to buy Swiss Francs against Russian Roubles. These embedded derivatives are not closely related to the host contract (lease contract denominated in Russian Rouble) and, therefore, should be accounted for separately.

From entity A's perspective, the lease contract contains a series of embedded forward contracts to sell Swiss Francs against US Dollars. These embedded derivatives are not closely related to the host contract (lease contract denominated in USD) and, therefore, should be accounted for separately.

Example 3 – Subsidiary's foreign currency lease payments guaranteed by parent

A major French operating subsidiary of a US parent enters into a lease with a Swiss company that requires lease payments in US dollars. The lease payments are guaranteed by the US parent. The functional currencies of the respective entities are their local currencies.

In this example, the substantial parties to the lease contract are the French lessee and the Swiss lessor. The guarantor is not a substantial party to the contract and, therefore, its functional currency is of no relevance to the analysis (see further para 5.85 below). Since the lease payments are made in US dollars, which is neither the functional currency of the lessee nor the lessor, the embedded foreign currency swap would need to be accounted for separately.

Embedded derivatives in executory contracts

5.74   Contracts to buy or sell a non-financial asset that qualify as executory contracts, including commitments (for example, take or pay contracts) that are entered into to meet the entity's expected purchase, sale or usage requirements and are expected to be settled by physical delivery, are not financial instruments. Accordingly, they are scoped out of IAS 39 under the own use purchase or sale exception. [IAS 39 para 5]. However, even though such contracts are not financial instruments, they may contain embedded derivatives. Embedded derivatives may also be present in some service contracts.

5.75   IAS 39 contains little specific guidance relating to derivatives embedded in such contracts, except for features involving foreign currency. Therefore, it would be necessary to consider carefully the economic characteristics and risks of such contracts in assessing whether embedded derivatives are present and, if so, whether they should be separately accounted for. In doing so, it would be necessary to consider both quantitative and qualitative factors. Sometimes it may be possible to draw on the guidance discussed above for other host contracts. Indeed, it would not be unreasonable to do so, particularly for features such as pricing adjustments, inflation adjustments and caps, floors and collars on prices and quantities.

Price adjustment features

5.76 Normal purchase and sale contracts may contain price clauses that modify the contract's cash flows. In assessing the closely related criterion for the embedded derivative, it would be necessary to establish whether the underlying in a price adjustment feature incorporated into such a contract is related or unrelated to the cost or fair value of the goods or services being sold or purchased.

Example 1 – Price adjustment linked to market prices of goods purchased

An entity (whose functional currency is pound sterling) contracts to purchase 200 tonnes of aluminium from a UK supplier in 12 months' time. The aluminium is intended for use in the course of entity's business. The purchase price will be the market price at the contract date plus an amount determined by a specified index of aluminium prices. The contract does not contain any leverage feature.

The future cash outflows are linked to movements in the market price for aluminium. The purpose of the embedded derivative is to ensure that the price paid for the aluminium is the market price at the date of purchase/supply rather than the date the two parties entered into the supply contract. This ensures that the seller passes any price risk to the entity. As the underlying is related to the price of the aluminium purchased, the derivative is closely related to the aluminium supply contract (host) and would not be accounted for separately.

Example 2 – Coal purchase contract linked to changes in the price of electricity

An entity enters into a coal purchase contract that includes a clause that links the price of coal to a pricing formula based on the prevailing electricity price at the date of delivery. The entity purchases the coal for its own use and there are no provisions to settle the contract net.

The coal purchase contract is the host contract. The pricing formula that changes the price risk from coal price to electricity price is the embedded derivative. Although coal may be used for the production of electricity, the underlying based on electricity prices is not pertinent to both the changes in the cost and the changes in the fair value of coal. Therefore, the embedded derivative (the electricity price adjustment) is not closely related to the host contract and should be accounted for separately.

Example 3 – Supply contract subject to multiple pricing adjustments

An entity has entered into a contract with a customer to sell 10,000 wooden chairs for a period of five years. The price per chair is contractually determined at C100 per chair for the first year and thereafter increases in line with changes in certain indices. 50% of the price of each chair is linked to an index of timber prices, 30% is linked to the UK wage inflation index. So if the timber index rises by 10% and the wage inflation index increases by 5%, the price for each chair will be C106.50 (being C50 × 1.1 + C30 × 1.05 + C20). The sales contract in its entirety does not meet the definition of a derivative as it will be settled by physical delivery in the normal course of business.

There are two embedded derivatives contained in this contract, because the price of chairs over the contract term is linked to the two indices (timber and wage inflation).

The purpose of these embedded derivatives is to protect the entity's profit margin over the contract term by ensuring that changes in the prices of inputs are passed on to the end customer.

Although both indices are considered to be relevant and pertinent to the cost or fair value of the chairs being sold, they would be considered to be closely related to the host contract if, and only if, the entity can reliably demonstrate that the standard mix of direct material and direct labour for each chair produced is maintained.

If, however, the entity is unable to demonstrate reliably the clear linkage, then the embedded derivatives *may* be leveraged (because the percentage of the price linked to each index may not accurately reflect the cost structure). In other words, the magnitude of the price adjustment may cause the price of the host contract to increase by more than an insignificant amount (see para 5.14 above). In that situation, the indexed linked price adjustments would not be considered to be closely related.

5.77   Where a contract to buy or sell non-financial assets does not qualify for the own use purchase or sale exception, the entire contract would fall to be treated as if it were a financial instrument (and in most cases a derivative). In that situation, as the entire derivative contract would be accounted for at fair value through profit or loss, any derivatives embedded in such contracts would no longer need to be accounted for separately.

Example – Contract not qualifying for 'normal' purchase or sale exception

An entity enters into a forward contract to purchase 10,000 tonnes of coal. The contract does not qualify for the 'normal' purchase or sale exception as there is a provision in the contract for net settlement and the entity's past practice indicates that it will settle the contract net. Settlement is based on changes in the fair value of coal during the contract's term plus a payment provision based on a formula linked to prevailing electricity prices.

Given that the own use exception does not apply, the entire forward contract to purchase coal will be accounted for as a derivative in accordance with IAS 39 with gains and losses on the entire contract reported in the profit and loss account. Therefore, there is no need to identify separately the leverage payment provision as an embedded derivative.

Volume adjustment features

5.78   Many contracts for the supply of goods usually give the buyer the right to take either a minimum quantity of goods or any amount based on the buyer's requirements. A minimum annual commitment does not create a derivative as long as the entity expects to purchase all the guaranteed volume for its 'own use'. However, if it becomes likely that the entity will not take physical delivery of the product and, instead pay a penalty under the contract based on the market value of the product or some other variable, a derivative or an embedded derivative may well arise. In this situation, since physical delivery is no longer probable, the derivative would be recorded at the amount of the penalty payable. Changes in market price will affect the penalty's carrying value until the penalty is paid. On the other hand, if the amount of the penalty payable is fixed or pre-determined, there is no derivative as the penalty's value remains fixed irrespective of changes in the market value of the product. In other words, the entity will need to provide for the penalty payable once it becomes clear that non-performance is likely.

5.79   On the other hand, if the quantity specified in the contract is more than the entity's normal usage requirement and the entity intends to net settle part of the contract that it does not need in the normal course of the business, the contract will fail the 'own use' exemption. Chapter 3 sets out a number of ways in which the entity can settle the contract net. For example, the entity could take all the quantities specified in the contract and sell on the excess or it could enter into an offsetting contract for the excess quantity. In such situations, the entire contract falls within IAS 39's scope and should be marked-to-market.

5.80   From the supplier's perspective, however, the volume flexibility feature in the contract can be viewed in two ways. The first is to view the contract as a whole. The contract includes a written option for the element of volume flexibility. The whole contract should be viewed as one instrument and, if the item being supplied (electricity) is readily convertible to cash, entity A would be prevented from classifying the contract as 'own use' by paragraph 7 of IAS 39. This states that a written option on a non-financial item that is readily convertible to cash cannot be entered into for the purpose of the receipt or delivery of a non-financial item in accordance with the entity's expected purchase, sale or usage requirements. A second view is that the contract has two components, an 'own use' fixed volume host contract outside of IAS 39's scope for any contractually fixed volume element and an embedded written option within IAS 39's scope for the volume flexibility element. The latter would be in IAS 39's scope if the item being supplied (electricity) is readily convertible to cash for the same reason as under the first view. In March 2010, IFRIC discussed the issue of volume flexibility and recognised that significant diversity exists in practice. However, IFRIC decided not to add the issue to its agenda because of the Board's project to develop a replacement for IAS 39.

5.80.1   As explained in section 3 of this financial instrument chapter, such written options have to be accounted for in accordance with IAS 39 if they can be 'settled net in cash'. 'Settled net in cash' in this context means either that the contract allows net settlement or the item that is the subject of the contract is readily convertible into cash.

5.81   Therefore, it is necessary to consider whether the contract contains a written option. A contract will not contain a true written option if the buyer did not pay any premium to receive the option. Receipt of a premium to compensate the supplier for the risk that the buyer may not take the optional quantities specified in the contract is one of the distinguishing features of a written option. [IAS 39 IG F1.3(a)(b)]. Therefore, it would be necessary to consider whether a net premium is received either at inception or over the contract's life in order to determine the accounting treatment. Any penalty payable for non-performance by the buyer may well amount to the receipt of a premium. If no premium can be identified, other terms of the contract may need to be examined to determine whether it contains a written option, in particular, whether the buyer is able to secure economic value from the option's presence. Contracts need to be considered on a case-by-case basis in order to determine whether they contain written options.

Example 1 – Contract with a volume adjustment feature that still qualifies for the oen-use exemption

Entity A, a car manufacturer enters into a contract to sell cars to entity B that is engaged in renting cars. The contracts provide for entity A to supply 50 cars of a specific model at a specified future date at a fixed price. Entity B has the option to take between 90% and 110% of the contract quantity. Available market information indicates that a similar contract for 50 cars but without volume flexibility would also be priced at the same fixed price specified in the contract. Entity B cannot monetise the value of the contract by selling on any excess cars in the market.

The supply contract would not be considered a written option, as the pricing of the contract is the same as that for a similar contract with no volume flexibility. There is, therefore, no premium associated with the contract. Entity B cannot exercise any value from the option's presence; the contract is, therefore, not a written option and qualifies for the own-use exemption.

Example 2 – Contract with a volume adjustment feature that fails the own-use exemption

Entity A, an electricity producer in the United Kingdom where there is an active electricity market, enters into a contract to sell electricity to entity B. The contracts provide for entity A to supply 100 units of electricity at a specified future date to entity B at a fixed price per unit. Entity B has the option to take between 90% and 110% of the contract quantity. The total quantity taken will be priced at C0.21 per unit. Available market information indicates that a similar contract for 100 units of electricity but without volume flexibility would be priced at C0.20 per unit. Entity B is also a supplier of electricity and can, therefore, monetise the contract's value by selling on any excess power into the market, that is, it can readily convert the electricity contract to cash.

The pricing of the contract is not the same as that for a similar contract without volume flexibility. The price per cubic meter includes a premium for the additional risk accepted by entity A in offering volume flexibility. The contract is, therefore, a written option and entity A cannot claim the own-use exemption. In that situation, the contract will be marked-to-market in accordance with IAS 39. As noted above entity A can viewed the contract in two ways:

■ as a written option in its entirety and hence entity A cannot claim the own-use exemption. In that situation, the contract will be marked-to-market in accordance with IAS 39; or

■ as a fixed volume contract for 90 units of electricity for C0.20 per unit for which the own use exemption could be claimed and a written option for 20 units at C0.21 per unit, which would be accounted for within IAS 39's scope.

Inflation related features

5.82 It is not uncommon for purchase, sale or long-term service contracts to contain terms that are linked to an inflation index, particularly in periods of rising inflation. Inflation escalator clauses are included in such long-term contracts to protect the seller's margin in real terms. Although IAS 39 is silent on the treatment of inflationary adjustments in such executory contracts, there is no reason, in principle, as to why the guidance relating to inflation adjustment features in lease host contracts would not be appropriate for such contracts. That guidance states that an embedded inflation-related index is closely related to the lease host contract if the index is not leveraged and the index relates to inflation in the entity's own economic environment. [IAS 39 para AG 33(f)]. The application of this principle to lease contracts is considered from paragraphs 5.63 above. We believe similar considerations can be applied also to purchase, sale and service contracts.

> **Example – Purchase contract linked to inflation**
>
> A UK entity contracts to purchase a fixed quantity of certain raw material from a UK supplier in 12 months' time. The raw materials are intended for use in the entity's business. The purchase price will be the market price at the contract date plus an adjustment for UK RPI from the beginning of the contract. The contract does not contain any leverage feature.
>
> The future cash flows are linked to an inflation index that is not leveraged and the index is in the local economic environment. Therefore, the embedded derivative is closely related to the host purchase contract.
>
> If, on the other hand, the entity is unable to demonstrate that these goods are to be used in the course of its business, that is, the own use exception does not apply, the entire contract would be treated as a forward purchase contract that would fall to be settled net. In that situation, the forward purchase contract meets the definition of a derivative and, is itself, accounted for at fair value through profit or loss. So there is no need to account separately for any derivatives that may be embedded in it.

Caps, floors and collars

5.83 Contracts to buy or sell a non-financial asset may contain provisions that provide for payments to be made at the market price at the time of payment, but set an upper or lower limit or both on the final price to be paid or received. Such caps, floors or collars included in contracts are embedded derivatives. IAS 39 states that provisions included in a contract to purchase or sell an asset (for example, a commodity) that establish a cap and a floor on the price to be paid or received for the asset are closely related to the host contract if both the cap and floor were out-of-the-money and are not leveraged. [IAS 39 para AG 33(b)]. This guidance can be extended to a collar that would be closely related if it was out-of-the-money at inception (see para 5.40 above).

Example – Purchase contract with selling price subject to a cap and a floor

A manufacturer enters into a long-term contract to purchase a specified quantity of certain raw materials from a supplier. Under the contract, the supplier will provide the raw materials at the list price prevailing at the delivery date, but within a specified range. For example, the purchase price may not exceed C20 per kg or fall below C15 per kg. The current list price at inception of the contract is C18 per kg.

From the manufacturer's perspective, the embedded derivatives contained in the purchase contracts are two options; a purchased call option with a strike price of C20 per kg and a written put with a strike price of C15 per kg. These options would each meet the definition of a derivative if they were free standing, because they have a notional amount (the fixed quantity to be purchased), have an underlying (the price per kg), require no initial net investment and will be settled in the future.

The economic characteristics and risks of the two options are closely related to the purchase contract, because the options are indexed to the asset's purchase price that is the subject of the contract and both the embedded cap (cap price of C20 is greater than current list price of C18) and the floor (floor price of C15 is lower than current list price of C18) are out-of-the-money at inception of the contract. Hence, the embedded derivatives are closely related and the host contract can be considered to be a purchase contract that requires delivery of the specified quantity of raw materials at a price equal to the current list price.

Foreign currency features

5.84   IAS 39 provides specific guidance for an embedded foreign currency derivative in a host contract that is not a financial instrument. An embedded foreign currency derivative in a host contract that is not a financial instrument (such as a contract for the purchase or sale of a non-financial item where the price is denominated in a foreign currency) is closely related to the host contract provided it is not leveraged, does not contain an option feature and requires payments denominated in one of the following currencies:

■   The functional currency of any substantial party to that contract.

■   The currency in which the price of the related goods or service that is acquired or delivered is routinely denominated in commercial transactions around the world (such as the US dollar for crude oil transactions).

■   A currency that is commonly used in contracts to purchase or sell non-financial items in the economic environment in which the transaction takes place (for example, a relatively stable and liquid currency that is commonly used in local business transactions or external trade).

[IAS 39 para AG 33(d)].

5.85   The term 'substantial party' to the contract referred to in the first bullet point above is not explained in IAS 39. Generally, it is taken to mean a party that is acting as principal to the contract, that is, the buyer/seller. A bank that provides a guarantee on behalf of a local importer to a foreign supplier that the buyer will meet its payment obligations in foreign currency under the contract's terms is not a substantial party to the contract. Furthermore, the guarantor's functional currency is of no relevance in determining whether the payments denominated in the foreign currency are closely related to the contract.

5.86 A question also arises in practice as to the efforts one party to a contract needs to employ to determine the functional currency of its counterparty. Generally, there would be a rebuttable presumption that the local currencies of the economic environment in which the counterparties operate would be their functional currencies. In addition, the local currency is always presumed to be commonly used. Therefore, if the contract requires payment in either one of the two local currencies of the counterparties, the condition in the first bullet point above would be met. The position is less clear if payments are denominated in a third currency that is not the local currency of either party to the contract. In that situation, the contracting parties would need to determine whether that third currency is the functional currency of their counterparty. In practice, this determination should be made on the basis of all available evidence and reasonable assumptions about the counterparty. Furthermore, the guidance for determining functional currency in IAS 21 would need to be considered in determining the functional currency. An entity should not necessarily rely on a single indicator such as the currency in which the counterparty's sales are denominated. Rather, the entity should consider all relevant available information in determining the counterpary's functional currency.

Example 1 – Payments denominated in the functional currency of a party to the contract

A UK entity (whose functional currency is pound sterling) contracts to sell goods to a French purchaser whose functional currency is the euro. The contract will be fulfilled by the physical delivery of goods and payments by the French buyer would be made in euros.

In this example, the payment in euros exposes the UK entity to currency risk as the cash flows under the contract will vary with the £/€ exchange rate. The contract can be viewed as a host contract that is denominated in sterling containing an embedded foreign currency swap that converts payments in pound sterling to euros or an embedded foreign currency forward contract to sell pound sterling and buy euros. However, the embedded swap or the forward contract is not separated as the payments are denominated in the functional currency of the French buyer who is a substantial party to the contract.

Example 2 – Payments denominated in a third currency

A UK entity (whose functional currency is pounds sterling) contracts to sell goods to a Swiss purchaser whose functional currency is the Swiss francs. The contract will be fulfilled by the physical delivery of goods and payments by the Swiss buyer would be made in euros. The goods are not commonly priced in euros.

In this example, the payment and the receipt in euros exposes both the substantial parties to the contract to exchange risk. Since the contract requires that payments be denominated in euros, which is not the functional currency of either party to the transaction, the embedded derivative is not closely related and should be accounted for separately at fair value by both the Swiss buyer and the UK seller. From the UK seller's point of view the embedded derivative would be to buy euros and sell sterling. In the books of the Swiss buyer the embedded derivative would be to sell euros and buy Swiss francs. The nominal amount of the embedded forwards will be equal to the amount specified under the terms of the supply contract.

A particular issue arises in connection with the nature of the foreign currency embedded derivative in a foreign currency purchase/sale contracts when the embedded derivative is required to be separated under AG 33(d). The issue is whether the embedded derivative is a forward contract that matures on the date on which goods are physically delivered, or on the date when cash settlement takes place.

Assume that the UK entity enters into the contract with the Swiss buyer to sell goods amounting to €100 on 1 March 20X6 for delivery on 30 June 20X6 and settlement on 31 July 20X6. The goods are not commonly priced in €. The UK entity's year end is 31 March 20X6. The following data is relevant.

Date	Event	Spot €/£	Forward €/£ (maturity June 20X6)	Forward €/£ (maturity July 20X6)
1 Mar 20X6	UK entity enters into a contract to sell goods for €100	0.70	0.725	0.72
31 Mar 20X6	UK entity's year end. Embedded derivative revalued	0.73	0.745	0.74
30 Jun 20X6	Goods delivered	0.75	0.77	
31 Jul 20X6	Invoice amounting to €100 settled	0.78		

In this example, from the perspective of the UK seller, the firm commitment to sell goods is separated into two contracts – a host contact that is a firm commitment to sell goods in pound sterling and an embedded forward contract to buy euro and sell pound sterling with an inception date of 1 March 20X6. However, as stated above there is some debate regarding the deemed date of settlement/maturity of the embedded derivative.

Some take the view that the embedded derivative's settlement/maturity date is 30 June 20X6 when the goods are delivered. This is because the derivative that is embedded in the host firm commitment can no longer exist after that date as there is no host contract – the seller having fulfilled its commitment by delivering the goods to the customer. Following performance by the seller, the seller has an unconditional right to receive consideration from the customer. In other words, the embedded derivative is in the sales contract not in the receivable; the derivative being effectively settled by creation of a financial asset (receivable). Under this view, the accounting entries would be as follows:

Accounting for sale and embedded derivative

				Dr (Cr)		
		Sales	Debtors	Cash	Derivative	Profit and loss
Date	Transaction	£	£	£	£	£
1 Mar 20X6	Embedded derivative – nil fair value					
31 Mar 20X6	Change in fair value of embedded derivative – €100 @ (0.745 – 0.725) – ignoring discounting – there is a gain as using the forward rate at the balance sheet date to buy €100 would cost £74.5 as compared to a cost of £72.5 using the contracted forward rate				2.0	(2.0)
30 Jun 20X6	Change in fair value of embedded derivative – €100 @ (0.75 – 0.745)				0.5	(0.5)
30 Jun 20X6	Recording sales at forward rate – 100 @ 0.725	(72.5)	72.5			
30 Jun 20X6	Embedded derivative settled against debtors		2.5		(2.5)	
31 Jul 20X6	Debtor carried at spot rate at 30 June 20X6 settled by receipt of €100 at spot rate – €100 @ 0.78		(75.0)	78		(3.0)
	Effect on profit or loss and balance sheet	(72.5)	–	78	–	(5.5)

Others take the view that the embedded derivative being a forward foreign exchange contract matures at the date of cash settlement on the grounds that the cash leg of the firm commitment is settled at that date. Under this view, the sale and the corresponding receivable are recognised in local currency using the forward rate when the goods are delivered, that is (C72). The embedded derivative and the debtor is settled when cash is received at 30 June 20X6 with any gain or loss arising on settlement recorded in profit or loss. Under this view, the accounting treatment would be as follows:

Accounting for sale and embedded derivative

				Dr (Cr)		
		Sales	Debtors	Cash	Derivative	Proft and loss
Date	Transaction	£	£	£	£	£
1 Mar 20X6	Embedded derivative – nil fair value					
31 Mar 20X6	Change in fair value of embedded derivative – €100 @ (0.74 – 0.72) – ignoring discounting – there is a gain as using the forward rate at the balance sheet date, to buy €100 would cost £74 as compared to a cost of £72 using the contracted forward rate				2.0	(2.0)
30 Jun 20X6	Change in fair value of embedded derivative – €100 @ (0.77 – 0.74)				3.0	(3.0)
30 Jun 20X	Recording sales at forward rate – 100 @ 0.72	(72.0)	72.0			
31 Jul 20X6	Settlement date – receipt of €100 at spot rate – €100 @ 0.78		(72.0)	78	(5.0)	(1.0)
	Effect on profit and loss and balance sheet	(72.0)	–	78	–	(6.0)

Although both views can be sustained, in practice, entities generally tend to adopt the first treatment as they view these types of contract as inherent in future sales.

Example 3 – Payments denominated in the functional currency of a party to the contract, but the functional currency changes subsequently

A UK entity (whose functional currency is pound sterling) contracts to sell goods to a Japanese purchaser whose functional currency is the yen. The contract will be fulfilled by the physical delivery of goods and payments by the Japanese buyer would be made in yen. Subsequently, because of changes in economic circumstances, the Japanese buyer changes its functional currency to US dollars.

The UK entity is required to assess whether the embedded derivative should be separated from the host sales contract and accounted for as a derivative when it first becomes a party to the contract. At the time the UK entity entered into the contract, the functional currency of the Japanese buyer was the yen. Therefore, no separation of the embedded derivative is required as yen is the functional currency of a substantial party to the contract. The issue is whether this initial assessment should be revisited following the change in the functional currency of the Japanese buyer.

As explained in paragraph 5.20 above, IFRIC 9 prohibits reassessment unless there is a change in the contract's terms that meet certain criteria. In such an instance, reassessment is required. In this situation, the contract terms remain unchanged, that is, the UK entity will still make payments in yen irrespective of the fact that the functional currency of the Japanese supplier has subsequently changed to US dollars. Therefore, the contract continues to be accounted for in the same manner as before, irrespective of the fact that the factors that led to the initial assessment have changed. However, any yen denominated contracts entered into with the Japanese buyer after it has changed its functional currency to US dollar would fail the closely related criterion, as they would not be in the functional currency of either party to the contract.

The above treatment also applies to the Japanese buyer even though it will be exposed to Yen/dollar currency risk when it makes payments under the contract. Such exchange gains and losses will fall to be accounted for in accordance with IAS 21. In other words, as long as the contract terms remain unchanged, the Japanese buyer cannot create an embedded currency exposure that did not exist at the date it became a party to the contract.

Example 4 – Option to make payments in alternative currencies

Facts are the same as in example 1 except that the contract contains an option to make payment in either euros or in Swiss francs.

In this example, the UK seller has written an option to receive payments in a currency that is not its functional currency and, therefore, exposes it to £/€ or £/Swiss Fr currency risk. Although euro is the functional currency of the other substantial party to the contract, there is no certainty at inception of the contract that settlement will be in euros. Hence, the foreign currency option is not closely related to the host.

Similarly, the French buyer has effectively purchased an option to make payments in its own functional currency (euros) or in a foreign currency (Swiss Fr) that exposes it to euros/Swiss Fr currency risk. Although the French buyer has the option to settle the contract in its own currency and eliminate any exchange risk, there is no certainty at inception of the contract that it would eventually exercise that option. Since the contract could also be settled in Swiss francs, the settlement can either be potentially favourable or unfavourable and is not closely related to the purchase contract.

Accordingly, the embedded option should be separated from the host contract and accounted for separately by both parties to the contract.

5.87   In relation to the second bullet point in paragraph 5.84 above, the currency in which the price of the related goods or services is routinely denominated in commercial transactions around the world is a currency that is used for similar transactions *all around the world*, not just in one local area. For example, if cross-border transactions in natural gas in North America are routinely denominated in US dollars and such transactions are routinely denominated in euros in Europe, neither the US dollar nor the euro is a currency in which natural gas is routinely denominated in commercial transactions around the world. [IAS 39 para IG C9]. Accordingly, apart from crude oil and some metals which are routinely denominated in US dollar in international commerce, very few items, if any, are likely to meet this requirement. To date, our research has resulted in a list of commodities that are routinely denominated in US dollars. These are:

- Oil.
- Gold.
- Silver.
- Platinum.
- Aluminium (and alumina).
- Copper (refined and concentrate).
- Coal (thermal and coking).
- Iron ore (fines, lump and pellet).
- Rough diamonds.
- Titanium.
- Uranium.

5.87.1   We also determined that there is evidence that the following commodities are not routinely denominated in a single currency in commercial transactions around the world:

- Borates.
- Salt.
- Talc.

5.87.2   'Shipping costs' are also not routinely denominated in US dollars, because a substantial number of transactions are undertaken in other currencies, such as euro.

5.87.3   In addition, our research indicated that sales of wide-bodied aircraft as well as transactions in components supplied by 1st and 2nd tier suppliers to manufacturers of wide-bodied aircraft are routinely denominated in US dollars around the world. This covers only components that are specific and certified to a certain type of wide-bodied aircraft (such as landing gear, wings, flaps, etc.). The exemption is not applicable to components that could be used on a variety of aircraft (for example seats).

Example – Leveraged foreign currency provision

Entity A, whose functional currency is the euro, enters into a contract with entity B, whose functional currency is the Norwegian krone, to purchase oil in six months for US$10m. The host oil contract is not within IAS 39's scope, because it was entered into and continues to be for the purpose of delivery of a non-financial item in accordance with the entity's expected purchase, sale or usage requirements. The oil contract includes a leveraged foreign exchange provision that states that the parties, in addition to the provision of, and payment for, oil will exchange an amount equal to the fluctuation in the exchange rate of the US dollar and Norwegian krone applied to a notional amount of US$100,000.

In the example above, the payment provision under the host oil contract of US$10m can be viewed as a foreign currency derivative because the US dollar is neither entity A's nor entity B's functional currency. This foreign currency derivative would not be separated, however, because it follows from the second bullet point of paragraph 5.84 above that a crude oil contract that requires payment in US dollars is not regarded as a host contract with a foreign currency derivative.

However, the leveraged foreign exchange provision that states that the parties will exchange an amount equal to the fluctuation in the exchange rate of the US dollar and Norwegian krone applied to a notional amount of US$10m is in addition to the required payment for the oil transaction. It is unrelated to the host oil contract and, therefore, should be separated from the host oil contract, and accounted for as an embedded derivative. [IAS 39 para IG C8].

5.88 The third bullet point in paragraph 5.84 refers to a currency that is *commonly used* in contracts to purchase or sell non-financial items in the economic environment in which the transaction takes place (for example, a relatively stable and liquid currency that is commonly used in local business transactions or external trade). This flexibility was added when IAS 39 was revised so that entities domiciled in small or developing economies may find it more convenient to denominate business contracts with entities from other small or developing economies in an internationally liquid currency (such as the US dollar or the euro) rather than the local currency of any parties to the contract.

5.89 The standard uses the term 'commonly used' to mean a currency that is relatively stable or liquid and that is commonly used in local business transactions or external trade. A currency is commonly used in local business transactions when monetary amounts are viewed by the general population not in terms of the local currency, but in terms of a relatively stable foreign currency and prices may be quoted in that foreign currency. [IAS 39 para BC40]. Indeed, undertaking business transactions in a stable or hard currency is fairly common for entities operating in a hyperinflationary economy as a protection against inflation. [IAS 29 para 3(b)]. It follows that the currency must be commonly used within the country, not just commonly used within a particular industry or particular market. This is an exemption to the general rule that foreign currency embedded derivative derivatives need to be separated. The exemption's application should be supported by an appropriate analysis specific to the respective country.

5.90 Many countries around the world use more than one stable or liquid currency in undertaking local business transactions or external trade. Therefore, where such countries undertake transactions in those stable or liquid currencies rather than in their local currencies, the foreign currency derivative would be viewed as closely related to the host contract and would not be accounted for separately. Based on our research there is evidence to support the common use of another currency/other currencies than the local currency in the following countries:

Countries	International stable currency commonly used
Europe: Azerbaijan, Bulgaria, Georgia, Hungary, Kazakstan, Latvia, Lithuania, Macedonia, Poland, Serbia, Russia, Turkey, Ukriane, Uzbekistan Albania, Bosnia and Hercegovina, Croatia, Czech Republic, Estonia, Montenegro.	US$ and €
Middle East: Saudi Arabia, Qatar, UAE, Bahrain Oman, Kuwait.	US$
Caribbean: Bermuda, Turks & Caicos, Antigua & Bermuda, Cayman Islands, Jamaica.	US$
Asia: China (excluding Hong Kong), India, Vietnam, Cambodia, Indonesia, Malaysia, Laos, Thailand.	US$
Africa: South Africa, Tanzania, Uganda.	US$
South America: Brazil, Peru	US$
Research has also indicated a list of countries where no other currency other than local currency is 'commonly used': Hong Kong. Singapore. Philippines.	

This list is not neccesarily complete, and countries may be added to it, if supporting evidence is obtained and validated to determine the common use of a particular currency in a given country. As circumstances develop, it is also possible that some countries or currencies might be removed from the list.

> **Example – Contract denominated in a currency commonly used in local business transactions**
>
> An entity located in a country with a hyper-inflationary economy contracts to purchase raw materials for use in its manufacturing process. The contract is denominated in US$, a stable currency, and not in the local currency, as most local transactions and external trade are undertaken in US$.
>
> The embedded foreign currency derivative (denominated in a currency other than the local currency) does not need to be separated as the contract is denominated in a currency that is commonly used in the local economic environment.

If, however, the contract was priced in another international stable currency say the euro rather than the US$, and euro is not a currency that is commonly used in local business transactions, the embedded derivative (euro *versus* the entity's functional currency) would have to be separated.

Flow chart for identifying embedded derivatives in executory contracts

5.91   As stated previously, IAS 39 provides little or no guidance on derivatives that may be embedded in purchase, sale or service contracts. As identification of such embedded derivatives can be complex, the flow charts given below are to aid in the identification process. It should be noted that the flow chart has been constructed from the discussions undertaken above and is based on a simple executory contract to buy or sell a good i.e. does not need to be assessed for an embedded lease under IFRIC 4. In practice, such contracts may contain other terms and conditions whose interaction with the host is not obvious. Options that allow early termination of a contract by paying a penalty, options to change the quantities to be delivered and options to defer delivery are some examples of terms and condition that can be problematic and would require careful consideration.

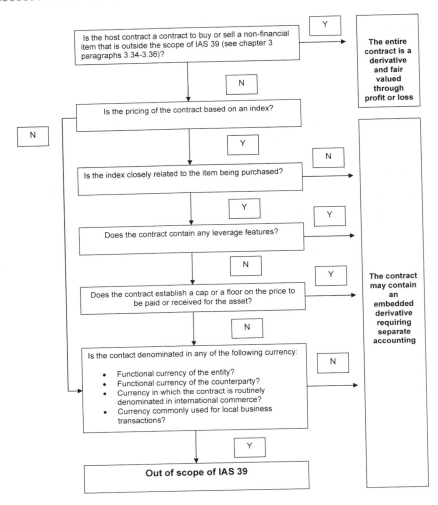

Embedded derivatives in insurance contracts

5.92   In recent years, a growing number of complex insurance products have been developed and many of them may contain embedded derivatives. As stated in chapter 3, derivatives embedded in insurance contracts or in contracts containing discretionary participation features are within IAS 39's scope. A derivative embedded in an insurance contract is closely related to the host insurance contract if the embedded derivative and host insurance contract are so interdependent that an entity cannot measure the embedded derivative separately (that is, without considering the host contract). [IAS 39 para AG 33(h)]. However, if a policy combines a derivative instrument with an insurance contract thereby creating a hybrid instrument, the embedded derivative may have to be separated from the insurance contract in accordance with IAS 39, unless the embedded derivative itself is an insurance contract. [IFRS 4 para 7].

5.93   Contracts such as equity indexed annuities, equity indexed life insurance and embedded guarantees of minimum returns may contain embedded derivatives that are not closely related to the host insurance contract and will have to be separated and accounted for under IAS 39. Much of the guidance discussed above also applies to embedded derivatives in insurance contracts as it does to any other contract. However, IFRS 4 paragraph 8 introduces a major exception to the principle of separation of embedded derivatives that are not closely related to the host contract. IFRS 4 permits an insurer to not separate a policyholder's embedded put option (also known as a cash surrender option) embedded in a host insurance contract when the option price is a fixed amount or a fixed amount and an interest rate. This exemption applies at all times even when the exercise price differs from the host insurance liability's carrying amount. The requirement to separate does, however, apply when the surrender value varies in response to a change in an equity or commodity price or index or a similar variable. [IFRS 4 para 8]. IFRS 4 paragraph 9 specifies that the same exemption applies to issuers of financial instruments with a discretionary participation feature. This area of accounting for embedded derivatives should always be considered in conjunction with IFRS 4. The implementation guidance to IFRS 4 contains many examples that illustrate the treatment of embedded derivatives contained in insurance contracts. [IFRS 4 paras IG 3, 4].

Accounting for embedded derivatives

5.94   On initial recognition, similar to all financial assets and liabilities, a financial instrument containing an embedded derivative is recognised at its fair value, that is, the fair value of the entire instrument. If the consideration paid / transaction price is not equal to the fair value of the instrument as a whole, then a day 1 gain or loss may arise. Whether such a gain or loss is recognised immediately within profit or loss depends on whether the conditions in paragraph AG76 of IAS 39 are met (as discussed in further detail in chapter 9). In summary, a day 1 gain or loss is recognised only when the fair value of the entire instrument is evidenced by either other observable current market transactions in the same instrument (without modification or packaging) or it is based on a valuation technique whose variables include only data from observable markets.

5.94.1   When an embedded derivative is required to be separated from a host contract, the derivative element must be measured at fair value on the balance sheet, consistent with the accounting for a freestanding derivative. At initial recognition of the embedded derivative, the embedded derivative's fair value must be determined before that of the host contract. Paragraph AG28 of IAS 39 states that *"The initial carrying amount of the host instrument is the residual after separating the embedded derivative"*. The host contract's carrying value at initial recognition is the difference between the fair value of the hybrid contract as a whole and the embedded derivative's fair value.

5.94.2   While a day 1 gain or loss may arise on the initial recognition of the entire instrument, if the criteria in paragraph AG76 of IAS 39 are met (see para 5.94), a day 1 gain or loss will not arise as a result of separating the embedded derivative from the host contract.

5.95 Published price quotations in an active market are normally the best evidence of fair value. Valuation techniques are used to determine the derivative's fair value if there is no active market for the embedded derivative. Valuing a derivative usually involves the exercise of judgement by management in making certain estimates such as the discount rate, extrapolation of future interest rates, foreign exchange rates and so on. The use of estimates for certain valuation parameters could be subjective, especially for long-term contracts that are common in the energy industry. Furthermore, certain embedded derivatives, in particular those arising from complex structured products, may contain several underlying variables making the valuation process complex.

5.96 If an entity is unable to determine reliably the fair value of an embedded derivative on the basis of its terms and conditions (for example, because the embedded derivative is based on an unquoted equity instrument), the embedded derivative's fair value is the difference between the fair value of the hybrid (combined) instrument and the host contract's fair value, if those can be determined reliably. [IAS 39 para 13]. If the entity is unable to determine the embedded derivative's fair value using this method either at initial recognition or at a subsequent financial reporting date, the entity should fair value the hybrid (combined) instrument and designate it as at fair value through profit or loss. [IAS 39 paras 12, 13]. Designation of financial instruments is discussed in chapter 6.

> **Example – Debt instrument that is exchangeable into shares of an unlisted entity**
>
> An entity issues a debt instrument that is exchangeable into shares of an unlisted entity whose fair value cannot be reliably measured. If the debt instrument is converted the unlisted equity investment would be recorded on the balance sheet at cost in accordance with paragraph 46(c) of IAS 39.
>
> In this situation, the equity exchangeable feature is not closely related to the debt host and should be separated. However, although the equity instrument's fair value cannot be measured reliably, it would not be appropriate to measure the embedded derivative at cost. Instead, the entire combined contract is designated as a financial instrument at fair value through profit or loss. [IAS 39 para 12]. This presumes that the combined contract's fair value can be measured reliably.
>
> However, the entity might conclude that the combined instrument's equity component may be sufficiently significant to preclude it from obtaining a reliable estimate of the fair value of the entire instrument. In that case, the combined instrument is measured at cost less impairment. [IAS 39 para IG C.11].
>
> It should be noted that as embedded derivative's fair value that is linked to, and must be settled by delivery of, the above unlisted equity instrument cannot be measured, the embedded derivative cannot be designated as a hedging instrument. [IAS 39 para AG 96].

5.97   The requirement to identify an embedded derivative in a hybrid instrument, assess whether it is required to be separated from the host contract and, for those that are required to be separated, measure the derivatives at fair value at initial recognition and subsequently, can be complex or may result in less reliable measures than measuring the entire instrument at fair value through profit or loss. For that reason, the standard permits the entire instrument to be designated as at fair value through profit or loss. The option would be particularly helpful to banks and other entities that issue structured products containing several embedded derivatives.

5.98   Therefore, if a contract contains one or more embedded derivatives, an entity may designate the entire hybrid (combined) contract as a financial asset or financial liability at fair value through profit or loss, unless:

- the embedded derivative(s) does not significantly modify the cash flows that otherwise would be required by the contract; or

- it is clear with little or no analysis when a similar hybrid (combined) instrument is first considered that separation of the embedded derivative(s) is prohibited, such as a pre-payment option embedded in a loan that permits the holder to pre-pay the loan for approximately its amortised cost.

[IAS 39 para 11A].

Note that at the December 2007 meeting the IASB decided to replace the term 'contract' with the term 'financial instrument in the scope of IAS 39' to clarify that paragraph 11A applies only to financial instruments in IAS 39's scope that contain embedded derivatives. However, the IASB has not yet incorporated this amendment into IAS 39 and it is unclear when or whether it will (see para 5.7.1 above).

5.99   If an embedded derivative is separated, the host contract should be accounted for in accordance with IAS 39 if it is a financial instrument and in accordance with other appropriate standards if it is not a financial instrument. IAS 39 does not address whether an embedded derivative should be presented separately on the face of the balance sheet. [IAS 39 para 11].

Separating a non-option-based embedded derivative

5.100   When separating a non-option-based embedded derivative, such as an embedded forward or swap, the standard requires the embedded derivative to be separated from its host contract on the basis of its stated or implied substantive terms, so as to result in it having a fair value of zero at initial recognition. [IAS 39 para AG 28]. If it were permitted to separate embedded non-option derivatives on other terms, a single hybrid instrument could be decomposed into an infinite variety of combinations of host instruments and embedded derivatives. However, as already explained in paragraph 5.24 above, an embedded derivative that is not already clearly present should not be separated, that is a cash flow that does not exist cannot be created (with exception of, for example, assuming a functional currency cash flow in an embedded FX forward contract). If the terms of an embedded forward contract were determined so as to result in a fair value other than zero at the inception of the hybrid instrument, that amount would essentially represent a borrowing or lending. Therefore, it is inappropriate to separate an embedded non-option derivative on terms that result in a fair value other than zero at the inception of the hybrid instrument. [IAS 39 paras IG C1, C2]. This means that the forward price assumed in the embedded derivative should generally be at market rates observed when the embedded derivative is separated.

> **Example – Separation of a non-option-based derivative to produce zero fair value at inception**
>
> Entity X advances C900 to entity Y for one year at 6% interest rate and concurrently enters into an equity-based derivative in which it will receive any increase or pay any decrease in the current market price (C100) of entity Z's equity shares. The current forward price for one year for entity Z's equity shares is C200. These two transactions (the loan and the derivative) can be bundled into a structured note that could have almost an infinite variety of terms. Three possible contractual terms for the structured note that would be purchased by entity X for C900 are shown below.
>
> ■ Entity X to receive at the end of the year C954 plus any excess (minus any shortfall) in the current market price of entity Z's equity shares over (or under) C200.
>
> ■ Entity X to receive at the end of the year C1,054 plus any excess (minus any shortfall) in the current market price of entity Z's equity shares over (or under) C300.
>
> ■ Entity X to receive at the end of the year C755 plus any excess (minus any shortfall) in the current market price of entity Z's equity shares over (or under) C1.
>
> All the above terms of the structured note will provide the same cash flows, given a specified market price of entity Z's shares. If the market price of entity Z's shares remains at C200 at the end of year 1, entity A will receive C954 under all the three options. Similarly, if the market price of entity Z's shares increases to C306, entity A will receive C1,060 under all the options.
>
> As is apparent, the difference in terms under the above three options are totally arbitrary, because those differences have no impact on the ultimate cash flows under the structured note. Thus those differences are not substantive and should have no influence on how the terms of the embedded derivatives are identified. Therefore, the hybrid instrument's separation into an embedded derivative and a host debt instrument should be the same for all the three options described above for the structured note.
>
> That separation would generally result in the structured note being accounted for as a debt host contract with an initial carrying amount of C900 and a fixed annual interest rate of 6% and an embedded forward contract with C200 forward price, which results in an initial fair value of zero.

Separating an option-based embedded derivative

5.101 An embedded option-based derivative (such as an embedded put, call, cap, floor or swaption) is separated from its host contract on the basis of the option feature's stated terms. The initial host instrument's carrying amount is the residual amount after separating the embedded derivative. [IAS 39 para AG 28].

5.102 The implementation guidance explains that the economic behaviour of a hybrid instrument with an option-based embedded is fundamentally different from a non-option based derivative and depends critically on the strike price (or strike rate) specified for the option feature in the hybrid instrument.

5.103 If an entity were required to identify the terms of an embedded option-based derivative so as to achieve a fair value of the embedded derivative of zero, the strike price (or strike rate) generally would have to be determined so as to result in the option being infinitely out-of-the-money. This would imply a zero probability of the option feature being exercised. However, since the probability of the option feature in a hybrid instrument being exercised generally is not zero, it would be inconsistent with the likely economic behaviour of the hybrid instrument to assume an initial fair value of zero for the embedded derivative. Similarly, if an entity were required to identify the terms of an embedded option-based derivative so as to achieve an intrinsic value of zero for the embedded derivative, the strike price (or strike rate) would have to be assumed to equal the price (or rate) of the underlying variable at the initial recognition of the hybrid instrument. In this case, the option's fair value would consist only of time value. However, such an assumption would not be consistent with the likely economic behaviour of the hybrid instrument, including the probability of the option feature being exercised, unless the agreed strike price was indeed equal to the price (or rate) of the underlying variable at the initial recognition of the hybrid instrument. [IAS 39 para IG C.2].

5.104 Adjusting the strike price of an option-based embedded derivative, therefore, alters the nature of the hybrid instrument, whereas adjusting the strike price of a forward based embedded derivative does not necessarily alter the nature of the hybrid instrument. For example, if an option based embedded derivative is in-the-money, that intrinsic value does not represent a lending activity since the option may never be exercised (that is, it may expire out-of-the money due to a change in the underlying). Therefore, the separation of an option-based embedded derivative (including any embedded put, call, cap, floor, caption, floortion or swaption feature in a hybrid instrument) should be based on the stated terms of the option feature documented in the hybrid instrument. As a result, the embedded derivative would not necessarily have a fair value or intrinsic value equal to zero at the initial recognition of the hybrid instrument. [IAS 39 para IG C.2].

Multiple embedded derivatives

5.105 A host contract may contain more than one embedded derivative. Each individual derivative must be identified and assessed to see whether they warrant separate accounting. Separate accounting is required in circumstances where the derivatives relate to different risk exposures and are readily separable and independent of each other. [IAS 39 para AG 29].

5.106 Where, however, it is not possible to value each embedded derivative separately because of inter-dependencies, they should be bundled together and treated as a single compound embedded derivative. [IAS 39 para AG 29]. In that situation, the single compound derivative should be valued in accordance with the guidance discussed from paragraph 5.94 above.

> **Example 1 – Callable convertible bond**
>
> An entity issues 20,000 callable convertible bonds at a total par value of C2 million. Each bond pays fixed interest and is convertible, at the holder's option, at any time up to maturity into the entity's ordinary shares. Each bond also contains an embedded call option that gives the bond's issuer the right to call and redeem the bond at any time before maturity.
>
> The bond has two embedded options that are held by different parties. The bond's holder has the option to convert the bond into a specified number of shares. The issuer has the option to call back the bond and pay an amount generally at a premium over par value.
>
> From the issuer's perspective, the equity conversion option is an equity instrument of the issuer and, therefore, it is outside IAS 39's scope. Under IAS 32, the issuer must separate the equity and the liability elements of the compound instrument. As far as the issuer's call option (the right to call and redeem the bond) is concerned, this must be valued separately (using an option pricing model) as it is distinct in character and risk from the written equity conversion option. This value is then included in the liability component before separating the equity component under IAS 32. The call option may need to be accounted for separately unless the option exercise price is approximately equal on each exercise date to the amortised cost of the host debt instrument. [IAS 39 para AG 30(g); IAS 32 paras 31, IE 37].
>
> From the holders' perspective, the purchased call option (to convert) and the written call (to redeem) are interlinked. This is because as the share price increases the issuer is likely to call the bond, thereby depriving the holder of the opportunity to make further returns on the bond. Although the optimal policy is to call the bond when its conversion price is equal to the call price, in practice, companies can establish a variety of call policies such as calling the instant the market value of the convertibles rises above the call price or waiting until the market value is well in excess of the call price. This interaction between the two options implies that they have to be valued together using an option pricing model. The single compound derivative is then accounted for separately from the host plain vanilla bond. Alternatively, the holder can designate the entire bond as at fair value through profit or loss as discussed in paragraph 5.98 above.

Example 2 – Bond with embedded forward and option features

An entity issues a debt instrument at par with a term of 5 years. The debt is callable 3 years after the issue. If the debt is called, the holder will receive an amount that is adjusted by the percentage change in the FTSE 100 index and that amount doubles if the FTSE 100 index exceeds a certain level.

In the above instrument, there are two embedded derivatives – a forward contract that pays double if the FTSE 100 index exceeds a certain level and an option that is linked to changes in the FTSE 100 index. It is not appropriate to separate both a forward and an option on the equity index, because those derivative features relate to the same risk exposure. Instead the forward and option elements are treated as a single compound, embedded derivative.

Embedded derivatives as hedging instruments

5.107   IAS 39 does not restrict the circumstances in which a derivative may be designated as a hedging instrument provided the hedge accounting criteria are met (subject to some limitations on written options). [IAS 39 para 72]. Therefore, embedded derivatives that are accounted for separately can be designated as hedging instruments, like any free standing derivatives, as long as the hedge accounting criteria are met. Hedge accounting is considered in chapter 10.

Chapter 6

Classification of financial instruments

Classification of financial instruments

Introduction

6.1 IAS 39 classifies all financial assets and financial liabilities into specific categories. The need to classify financial instruments into specific categories arises from the mixed measurement model in IAS 39, under which some financial instruments are carried at amortised cost whilst others are carried at fair value. Consequently, a particular financial instrument's classification that is carried out at initial recognition drives the subsequent accounting treatment. IAS 39 prescribes four categories for financial assets and two categories for financial liabilities.

6.1.1 In November 2009, the IASB published the first part of IFRS 9, 'Financial Instruments', relating to classification and measurement of financial instruments. The new requirements are a fundamentally new approach to the classification and measurement of financial assets. Further proposals have been exposed regarding classification and measurement of financial liabilities. IFRS 9 applies a consistent approach to classifying financial assets based on the entity's business model for managing the financial assets and the contractual cash flow characteristics of the financial assets, and replaces the numerous categories of financial assets in IAS 39 as shown in para 6.2 below, each of which has its own classification criteria. It is the IASB's intention that IFRS 9 will ultimately replace IAS 39 in its entirety. IFRS 9 is dealt with in chapter 12.

Classification of financial assets

6.2 IAS 39 has four clearly defined categories of financial assets, as follows:

- Financial assets 'at fair value through profit or loss' (FVTPL).
- Held-to-maturity investments (HTM).
- Loans and receivables.
- Available-for-sale financial assets (AFS).

[IAS 39 para 9].

As stated above, the classification is important as it dictates how the financial assets and liabilities are subsequently measured in the financial statements. This classification is also relevant when looking at whether embedded derivatives need to be bifurcated (split). In the above list, the first and the last items are measured at fair value whilst the remaining two are measured at amortised cost.

6001

Financial assets at fair value through profit or loss

Definition

6.3   A financial asset can be classified as at fair value through profit or loss only if it meets of the following conditions:

■   Upon initial recognition, it is designated by the entity as at fair value through profit or loss.

■   It is classified as held-for-trading.

[IAS 39 para 9].

6.4   The fair value through profit or loss category incorporates items that are 'held-for-trading'. More significantly, it also gives entities the option to classify any financial instruments at fair value with all gains and losses taken to profit and loss in restricted circumstances (see further para 6.5 (assets) and 6.80 (liabilities)).

Designation at fair value through profit or loss on initial recognition

6.5   An entity *may* designate a financial asset at fair value through profit or loss on initial recognition only in the following three circumstances:

■   The designation eliminates or significantly reduces a measurement or recognition inconsistency (sometimes referred to as an 'accounting mismatch') that would otherwise arise (see para 6.8).

■   A group of financial assets, financial liabilities or both is managed and its performance is evaluated on a fair value basis, in accordance with a documented risk management or investment strategy (see para 6.17).

■   The item proposed to be designated at fair value through profit or loss is a hybrid contract that contains one or more embedded derivatives unless:

    ■   the embedded derivative(s) does not significantly modify the cash flows that otherwise would be required by the contract; or

    ■   it is clear with little or no analysis when a similar hybrid (combined) instrument is first considered that separation of the embedded derivative(s) is prohibited, such as a pre-payment option embedded in a loan that permits the holder to pre-pay the loan for approximately its amortised cost. [IAS 39 para 11A]. See further chapter 5.

[IAS 39 para 9].

6.6   The decision to designate a financial asset at fair value through profit or loss in the above situations is similar to an accounting policy choice where the policy selected is one that provides more relevant information. However, unlike an accounting policy choice, the above designation need not be applied consistently to all similar transactions. [IAS 39 para AG 4C]. In other words, the designation can be applied on an asset-by-asset or a liability-by-liability basis, with the result that different holdings of the same type of asset or liability may be accounted for differently, some using the fair value option and others not. For example, assume an entity expects to issue a number of similar financial liabilities amounting to C100 and expects to acquire a number of similar financial assets amounting to C50 that will be carried at fair value. Provided the criteria are satisfied, the entity may significantly reduce the measurement inconsistency by designating at initial recognition all of the assets but only some of the liabilities (for example, individual liabilities with a combined total of C45) as at fair value through profit or loss. The remaining liabilities amounting to C55 can still be carried at amortised cost.

6.7   The option can be applied only to whole instruments and not to portions, such as component of a debt instrument (that is, changes in value attributable to one risk such as interest rate risk and not credit risk); or proportions (that is, percentages). [IAS 39 para AG 4G]. This is because it may be difficult to isolate and measure the portion of a financial instrument if the portion is affected by more than one risk; the amount recognised in the balance sheet for that portion would be neither fair value nor cost; and the fair value adjustment for the portion may move the carrying amount of an instrument away from its fair value.

Accounting mismatch

6.8   IAS 39 imposes a mixed measurement model under which some financial instruments are measured at fair value and others at amortised cost; some gains and losses are recognised in profit or loss and others initially in other comprehensive income. This combination of measurement and recognition requirements can result in inconsistencies (sometimes referred to as an 'accounting mismatch') between the accounting for an asset (or group of assets) and a liability (or group of liabilities). An accounting mismatch occurs when assets and liabilities that are economically related (that is, share a risk) are treated inconsistently. This could occur where, in the absence of the fair value option, a financial asset is classified as available-for-sale (with most changes in fair value recognised directly in other comprehensive income), while a related liability is measured at amortised cost (with changes in fair value not recognised). In such circumstances, an entity may conclude that its financial statements would provide more relevant information if both the asset and the liability were classified as at fair value through profit or loss. [IAS 39 para AG 4D].

6.9   As explained above, the use of the fair value option may eliminate measurement anomalies for financial assets and liabilities that provide a natural offset of each other because they share the same risk, but where hedge accounting cannot be used because none of the instruments is a derivative. More importantly, even if some of the instruments are derivatives that could qualify for fair value hedge accounting, classification of both items at fair value through profit or loss achieves the same accounting result whilst avoiding the designation, tracking and assessing of hedge effectiveness that hedge accounting entails. It follows that the use of the fair value option as an alternative to hedge accounting can be of significant benefit to entities. However, such advantage also has a cost. Under the fair value option the entire change in fair value of the asset or liability would fall to be recognised in profit or loss, not simply the change in fair value attributable to the risk that is hedged by an offsetting derivative. As a result, the amount reported in profit or loss under the fair value option is unlikely to be the same as the change in fair value of the hedging derivative. This may lead to greater profit or loss volatility. Furthermore, hedge accounting can be revoked at any time, but the fair value option is irrevocable.

6.10   The IASB has not established a percentage, or a 'bright line', for interpreting 'significant' in the context of an accounting mismatch. However, the Basis for Conclusion makes it clear that an effectiveness test similar to that used for hedge accounting is not required to demonstrate that a reduction in an accounting mismatch is significant. [IAS 39 BC para 75B]. This means judgement is required to determine when the fair value option should be applied. In this regard, management should look at the objective of the proposed designation as 'at fair value through profit or loss'. Comparing the accounting impact – that is, the measurement basis and the recognition of gains and losses – of all relevant items (including, for example, any funding that it is not proposed to be designated at fair value through profit or loss) before and after the designation will give an indication of whether an accounting mismatch has been eliminated or significantly reduced.

6.11   Although it is necessary to demonstrate that there is an accounting mismatch, the extent of evidence needed to identify the accounting mismatch for which the fair value option is to be used need not be extensive. It may be possible to use the same evidence for a number of similar transactions, depending on the circumstances – for example, by identifying a particular kind of accounting mismatch that arises from one of the entity's chosen risk management strategies. It is not necessary to have the extensive documentation required for hedge accounting, but the entity does need to provide evidence that the fair value option was designated at inception. Also, IFRS 7 require disclosure of the carrying amounts of assets and, separately, liabilities designated as 'at fair value through profit or loss'. The evidence must, therefore, include precise identification of the assets and liabilities to which the fair value option has been applied.

Example 1 – Fixed rate assets financed by fixed rate debentures

An entity is about to purchase a portfolio of fixed rate assets that will be financed by fixed rate debentures. Both financial assets and financial liabilities are subject to the same interest rate risk that gives rise to opposite changes in fair value that tend to offset each other.

In the absence of the fair value option, the entity may have classified the fixed-rate assets as available-for-sale with gains and losses on changes in fair value recognised in other comprehensive income and the fixed-rate debentures at amortised cost. Reporting both the assets and the liabilities at fair value through profit and loss corrects the measurement inconsistency and produces more relevant information. [IAS 39 para AG 4E(d)(i)].

Example 2 – Fixed rate bond converted to floating rate

An entity purchases a fixed rate bond and immediately enters into an interest rate swap to convert the fixed rate to floating rate.

Instead of claiming hedge accounting, the entity could designate the bond at fair value through profit or loss. Since both the bond and the swap will be measured at fair value through profit or loss, the entity achieves a similar accounting result to if fair value hedge accounting has been applied, but without the added burden of designating, assessing and measuring hedge effectiveness that hedge accounting entails.

It should be noted that the bond is fully fair valued for all risks and not just for the hedged interest rate risk that hedge accounting would require. Furthermore, the fair value option is irrevocable. Hedge accounting is revocable (see chapter 9).

Example 3 – Fixed rate loan offset by derivative liabilities

An entity is about to originate a 10-year fixed rate loan that, if not designated as at fair value through profit or loss, will be measured at amortised cost. The entity also has a nine-year derivative that it regards as related to, and shares the same risk as, the loan. The entity wishes to designate the asset as at fair value through profit or loss to eliminate the measurement and recognition inconsistency with the derivative.

Although, in this example, the relationship does not completely eliminate the economic exposure, the entity can still designate the asset at fair value through profit or loss. The difference in maturities does not prevent the entity from designating the asset at fair value through profit or loss, provided there is a perceived economic relationship between the asset and the derivative. The fair value option does not require the elimination of economic volatility; it requires the elimination or significant reduction of an accounting mismatch. In the above example, the asset is measured at amortised cost and the derivative is measured at fair value, hence the accounting mismatch. Secondly, there is a perceived economic relationship between the asset and liability – for example, they share a risk that gives rise to opposite changes in fair value that tend to offset.

Example 4 – Financing a group of loans with traded bonds

An entity is about to originate a specified group of loans to be financed by issuing traded bonds whose changes in fair value tend to offset each other. The entity expects to regularly buy and sell the bonds but rarely, if ever, to buy and sell the loans.

Reporting both the loans and the bonds at fair value through profit or loss eliminates the inconsistency in the timing of recognition of gains and losses that would otherwise result from measuring them both at amortised cost and recognising a gain or loss each time a bond is repurchased. [IAS 39 para AG 4E(d)(ii)].

Example 5 – Subsidiary's debt offset by interest rate swap with parent

A subsidiary is about to issue a liability to a third party and enter into a related interest rate swap with its parent. An accounting mismatch exists in the subsidiary's stand alone financial statements, and it intends to designate the liability as at fair value through profit or loss.

Although it is appropriate for the subsidiary to designate the liability as at fair value through profit or loss in its individual financial statements, such designation is not possible in the consolidated financial statements. This is because the inter-company swap will be eliminated, and the 'mismatch' will not exist in the consolidated financial statements. However, if the parent can identify an external swap or other instrument that gives rise to an accounting mismatch on a consolidated basis, this may justify designating the liability as at fair value through profit or loss in the consolidated financial statements.

6.12   An accounting mismatch need not occur only between related financial assets and financial liabilities. It could also occur between a financial asset and a related non-financial liability or between a non-financial asset and a related financial liability. In both situations, the entity may use the fair value option, provided it concludes that the changes in fair value of both items are subject to the same risk and an accounting mismatch will be eliminated or significantly reduced by the designation.

> **Example – Financial assets offsetting non-financial liabilities**
>
> An insurer holds financial assets whose fair value exposure offsets that of non-financial liabilities under insurance contracts that are measured using techniques that incorporate current market information, but are not measured at fair values.
>
> Reporting both the insurance liability at fair value (as permitted by para 24 of IFRS 4) and the financial asset at fair value through profit or loss eliminates the inconsistency that would otherwise result from measuring the insurance liability at cost and the financial asset as available-for-sale or at amortised cost. [IAS 39 para AG 4E(b)].

6.13   Designations as at fair value through profit or loss should be made at initial recognition and once made are irrevocable. For practical purposes, the entity need not enter into all of the assets and liabilities giving rise to measurement or recognition inconsistency at exactly the same time. A reasonable delay is permitted provided that each transaction is designated as at fair value through profit or loss at its initial recognition and, at that time, any remaining transactions are expected to occur. [IAS 39 para AG 4F].

6.14   'Reasonable delay' should be assessed on a case-by-case basis, based as to what is reasonable in the circumstances. For example, a 'reasonable delay' could be a fairly short period in the case of entering into a derivative to offset some of the risks of an asset. A longer period could be justified if the delay arises from the need to assemble a portfolio of similar assets and arrange their funding. However, all financial assets and liabilities designated as at fair value through profit or loss must be accounted for on this basis from their initial recognition (and not only from the time any offsetting position is entered into).

6.15   It should be noted that if, for some reason, one of the offsetting instruments is derecognised, for instance, the fixed rate assets in example 1 or the interest rate swap in example 2 in paragraph 6.11 above, the other offsetting instrument – the fixed rate debentures in example 1 or the fixed rate bond in example 2 – would continue to be carried at fair value with gains and losses reported in profit or loss. This is because the designation at fair value through profit or loss at initial recognition is irrevocable, irrespective of whether the initial conditions that permitted the use of the option (to correct an accounting mismatch) still hold.

6.16   IFRS 7 also requires the entity to provide disclosures about financial assets and financial liabilities it has designated as at fair value through profit or loss, including how it has satisfied those conditions. For instruments that qualify for designation as at fair value through profit or loss in accordance with paragraph 6.8 above, the disclosure should include a narrative description of the circumstances underlying the measurement or recognition inconsistency that would arise. [IAS 39 para 9(b); IFRS 7 para B(5)]. See further chapter 11.

Group of financial assets and liabilities managed on a fair value basis

6.17   An entity may manage and evaluate the performance of a group of financial assets, financial liabilities or both in such a way that measuring that group at fair value through profit or loss results in more relevant information. Therefore, in order to designate financial instruments at fair value through profit or loss under the second criterion in paragraph 6.5 above, the designation should be based on the manner in which the entity manages and evaluates performance, rather than on the nature of those financial instruments. [IAS 39 para AG 4H]. An entity should designate all eligible financial instruments that are managed and evaluated together. [IAS 39 para AG 4J]. However, designation under this criterion must meet the following two requirements:

■   The financial instruments are managed and performance evaluated on a fair value basis in accordance with a documented risk management or investment strategy.

■   Information about the group is provided internally on that basis to the entity's key management as defined in IAS 24, 'Related party disclosures', (for example, the entity's board of directors and chief executive officer).

[IAS 39 para 9(b)(ii)].

6.18   The requirement that a group of financial assets and liabilities should be managed and performance evaluated on a fair value basis means that management should evaluate the portfolio on a full fair value basis and not on a risk-by-risk basis. For example, an entity that originates fixed interest rate loans and manages the interest rate risk of this portfolio based on the fair value attributable only to interest rate changes will be unable to use the fair value option. This is because the fair value concept is a broader notion than hedge accounting, such that evaluating the portfolio's performance for only some risks is not sufficient. Therefore, an entity's risk management policy and the resulting management information should look at the entire change in fair value and not for only some risks to justify the fair value option's use.

6.19   The required documentation of the entity's strategy need not be on an item-by-item basis, nor need it be in the level of detail required for hedge accounting. Documentation may be on a portfolio or group basis as long as it clearly identifies the items for which the fair value option is to be used. If the documentation relies on several other pre-existing documents, there needs to be an overall document that references these other documents and clearly demonstrates that the entity manages and evaluates the relevant financial assets or financial liabilities on a fair value basis. The documentation also needs to be sufficient to demonstrate that using the fair value option is consistent with the entity's risk management or investment strategy. In many cases, the entity's existing documentation, as approved by key management personnel, should be sufficient for this purpose. For example, if the performance management system for a group – as approved by the entity's key management personnel – clearly demonstrates that its performance is evaluated on a total return basis, no further documentation is required to demonstrate compliance with the above requirements. [IAS 39 para AG 4K].

6.20   As stated in paragraph 6.16 above, IFRS 7 requires the entity to provide disclosures about financial assets and financial liabilities it has designated as at fair value through profit or loss, including how it has satisfied those conditions. For instruments that qualify for designation as at fair value through profit or loss as a group of financial assets on liabilities, in accordance with paragraph 6.17 above, the disclosure should include a narrative description of how designation as at fair value through profit or loss is consistent with the entity's documented risk management or investment strategy. [IAS 39 para 9(b); IFRS 7 para B(5)]. See further chapter 11.

> **Example 1 – Portfolio of financial assets held by venture capital firms**
>
> A venture capital organisation invests in a portfolio of financial assets with a view to profiting from their total return in the form of interest or dividends and changes in fair value and evaluates its performance on that basis. Some investments meet the definition of associates and joint ventures, while others do not.
>
> IAS 28, 'Investments in associates', and IAS 31, 'Interests in joint ventures', allow such investments to be measured at fair value through profit or loss rather than using equity accounting.
>
> The fair value option allows the other investments, which are also managed and evaluated on a total return basis, but which fall outside the scope of IAS 28 and IAS 31 to be measured at fair value through profit or loss if that is consistent with the manner in which the entity manages and evaluates the performance of these investments. [IAS 39 para AG 4I(a)].
>
> In other words, the entire portfolio can be measured at fair value through profit or loss provided the two requirements of paragraph 6.17 above are met.

Example 2 – Portfolio of financial assets held to back specific liabilities

An entity holds a portfolio of financial assets. The entity manages the portfolio so as to maximise its total return (that is, interest or dividends and changes in fair value) and evaluates its performance on that basis. The portfolio is held to back specific liabilities.

In this situation, the entity may designate the portfolio at fair value through profit or loss, because it is likely that the entity's strategy to maximise total return would be set by, and information about performance of the portfolio would be provided to, key management on a timely basis. This is so regardless of whether the entity also manages and evaluates the liabilities on a fair value basis. [IAS 39 para AG 4I(c)].

Exception

6.21   The fair value option is not available for investments in equity instruments that do not have a quoted market price in an active market and whose fair value cannot be reliably measured. [IAS 39 para 9]. Therefore, in the absence of a quoted market price in an active market, if the fair value of an equity investment is not reliably measurable, because the range of reasonable fair value estimates is significant and the probabilities of the various estimates within the range cannot be reasonably assessed, an entity is precluded from measuring the instrument at fair value. [IAS 39 paras AG 80, AG 81].

Held-for-trading

6.22   A financial asset is held-for-trading if it is:

■   acquired or incurred principally for the purpose of selling or repurchasing it in the near-term;

■   on initial recognition, part of a portfolio of identified financial instruments that are managed together and for which there is evidence of a recent actual pattern of short-term profit taking; or

■   a derivative (except for a derivative that is a financial guarantee contract or a designated and effective hedging instrument).

[IAS 39 para 9].

6.23   Financial assets held-for-trading include:

■   Debt and equity securities that are actively traded by the entity.

■   Loans and receivables acquired by the entity with the intention of making a short-term profit from price or dealer's margin.

■   Securities held under repurchase agreements.

Derivatives are always categorised as held-for-trading, unless they are accounted for as effective hedging instruments.

6.24 Trading generally reflects active and frequent buying and selling and financial instruments held-for-trading generally are used with the objective of generating a profit from short-term fluctuations in price or dealer's margin. [IAS 39 para AG 14]. Whether an entity holds financial assets to generate profit on short-term differences in prices must be assessed on the basis of the facts and circumstances surrounding the trading activity rather than on the individual transaction's terms. Evidence of this is based on the frequency of buying and selling, the turnover rate or average holding period of the financial assets included in the portfolio (portfolio churning). All available evidence should be considered to determine whether the entity is involved in trading activities.

6.25 Financial assets that are brought and held principally in a portfolio for the purpose of selling them in the near-term (thus held for only a short period of time) should be classified as trading at acquisition date. Although the term 'portfolio' is not explicitly defined in IAS 39, the context in which it is used suggests that a portfolio is a group of financial assets or financial liabilities that are managed together. Also the phrases 'selling them in the near-term' and 'held for only a short period of time' are not explained in IAS 39. Therefore, in practice, an entity should adopt a suitable definition of these phrases and apply them on a consistent basis to avoid any ambiguity. For example, it is likely that if a security was acquired with the intent of selling it within a few weeks or months, the security would be classified as held-for-trading. After being designated as held-for-trading, a single instrument in a portfolio may in fact be held for a longer period of time, as long as there is evidence of a recent actual pattern of short-term profit taking on financial instruments included in such a portfolio.

Example – Shares held-for-trading

An entity purchased quoted equity shares from the market with the intention of profiting from short-term price fluctuations. The entity held the shares for three years due to a large unexpected downturn in the stock market after which it sold the shares in a more buoyant market.

Since management's intention at acquisition was to profit from short-term price fluctuations, the entity would have classified the shares as held-for-trading. The fact that after designation the shares were in fact held for a longer term, because the entity was unable to sell the shares at a loss in a bear market, would not frustrate the held-to-trading classification. Indeed, IAS 39 does not limit the period for which such an instrument can be held as long as the principal purpose at acquisition was to sell them in the near-term. Furthermore, as there is no definition of 'near-term' it is important for the entity to adopt a suitable definition and apply it consistently as explained in paragraph 6.24 above.

Held-to-maturity investments

Definition

6.26 Held-to-maturity investments are non-derivative financial assets with fixed or determinable payments and fixed maturity that an entity has the positive intention and ability to hold to maturity other than:

- Those that the entity upon initial recognition designates as at fair value through profit or loss.

- Those that the entity designates as available-for-sale.

- Those that meet the definition of loans and receivables.

[IAS 39 para 9].

6.27 For most financial assets, the standard regards fair value as a more appropriate measure than amortised cost. Classifying a security as held-to-maturity means that the enterprise is indifferent to future opportunities to profit from changes in the security's fair value and intends to accept the debt security's stipulated contractual cash flows, including the repayment of principal at maturity. The held-to-maturity category is, therefore, an exception. Consequently, its use is restricted to instruments that have specific terms and characteristics and by a number of detailed conditions, largely designed to test whether the entity has genuine intention and ability to hold those instruments to maturity. Also, significant penalties exist for entities that classify an instrument as held-to-maturity, but which is sold before maturity. These issues are considered below.

Fixed or determinable payments and fixed maturity

6.28 Instruments classified as held-to-maturity must have fixed or determinable payments and fixed maturity, which means that a contractual arrangement defines the amounts and dates of payments to the holder, such as interest and principal payments. Investments in equity shares have indefinite lives and, therefore, cannot be held-to-maturity financial assets. Other equity instruments, such as share options and warrants, cannot be classified as held-to-maturity because the amounts the holder receives may vary in a manner that is not predetermined. [IAS 39 para AG 17]. It follows that since held-to-maturity financial assets must have fixed maturity, it is mainly debt instruments that fall within this category. A mandatorily redeemable preference share is also, in substance, a debt instrument that may fall within this category.

6.29 The amount of determinable payment of principal or interest is normally established by reference to a source other than the financial instrument, and may involve a calculation. For example, floating rate interest on a financial instrument that is calculated from a reference interest rate such as the LIBOR or a bank's prime, and a principal amount that is linked to a price index such as the market price of a commodity like oil, are examples of determinable cash flows.

Example 1 – Floating rate note

Entity A purchases a note with variable interest rate and a fixed payment at maturity.

The floating rate note could qualify as a held-to-maturity investment since its payments are fixed (the principal) and the interest payments are specified by reference to a market or bench mark rate such as the LIBOR, which is determinable. A held-to-maturity classification for floating rate notes is, however, of little benefit, since its fair value will not change significantly in response to changes in interest rates.

Example 2 – Indexed linked principal payments

Entity A purchases a five-year equity-index-linked note with an original issue price of C10 at a market price of C12 at the time of purchase. The note requires no interest payments before maturity. At maturity, the note requires payment of the original issue price of C10 plus a supplemental redemption amount that depends on whether a specified share price index exceeds a predetermined level at the maturity date. If the share index does not exceed or is equal to the predetermined level, no supplemental redemption amount is paid. If the share index exceeds the predetermined level, the supplemental redemption amount equals the product of 1.15 and the difference between the level of the share index at maturity and the level of the share index when the note was issued divided by the level of the share index at the time of issue. Entity A has the positive intention and ability to hold the note to maturity.

The embedded equity feature is not closely related to the debt host and must be separated. Once the embedded derivative is fair valued and separated, the debt host can be classified as a held-to-maturity investment because it has a fixed payment of C10 and fixed maturity and entity A has the positive intention and ability to hold it to maturity. [IAS 39 para IG B13].

In this example, the purchase price of C12 is allocated between the host debt instrument and the embedded derivative. If, for instance, the fair value of the embedded equity feature at acquisition is C4, the host debt instrument is measured at C8 on initial recognition. In this case, the discount of C2 that is implicit in the host bond (principal of C10 minus the original carrying amount of C8) is amortised to profit or loss over the term to maturity of the note using the effective interest method.

Example 3 – Indexed linked interest

Entity A purchases a bond with a fixed payment at maturity and a fixed maturity date. The interest payments on the bond are indexed to the price of a commodity or equity and the entity has the positive intention and ability to hold the bond to maturity.

The commodity-indexed or equity-indexed interest payments result in an embedded derivative that is not closely related to the bond. Hence, it is necessary to separate the host debt investment (the fixed payment at maturity) from the embedded derivative (the index-linked interest payments).

Once the embedded derivative has been separated, the debt host can be classified as held-to-maturity as it has a fixed payment and a fixed maturity and entity A has the positive intention and ability to hold the bond to maturity. [IAS 39 para IG B14].

Example 4 – Perpetual debt instrument

Entity A purchases two perpetual debt instruments X and Y as follows:

- Instrument X pays an interest rate of 10% per annum for an indefinite period.

- Instrument Y pays an interest rate of 16% for the first 10 years and zero per cent in subsequent periods.

Entity A cannot classify instrument X that provides for interest payments for an indefinite period as held-to-maturity, because there is no maturity date. [IAS 39 para AG 17].

As far as instrument Y is concerned, it may be possible to argue from an economic perspective, that the instrument has a fixed maturity of 10 years. This is because the initial amount is amortised to zero over the first ten years using the effective interest method, since a portion of the interest payments represents repayments of the principal amount. The amortised cost is zero after year 10, because the present value of the stream of future cash payments in subsequent periods is zero (there are no further cash payments of either principal or interest in subsequent periods). Since the only cash flows under the terms are fixed interest payments over a period of 10 years, there is a strong argument to support held-to-maturity classification on the grounds that entity A has recovered all of its initial investment and the rights in the event of a liquidation has no value, notwithstanding that the terms do not specify a maturity date.

Intent to hold to maturity

6.30 A positive intent to hold financial assets to maturity is a much higher hurdle than simply having no present intention to sell. An entity does not have a positive intention to hold to maturity an investment in a financial asset with a fixed maturity if:

- The entity intends to hold the financial asset for an undefined period. In other words, as the entity has not actually defined a period, the positive intent to hold-to-maturity does not exist.

- The entity stands ready to sell the financial asset (other than if a situation arises that is non-recurring and could not have been reasonably anticipated by the entity) in response to changes in market interest rates or risks, liquidity needs, changes in the availability of and the yield on alternative investments, changes in financing sources and terms or changes in foreign currency risk. All these situations are indicative that the entity intends to profit from changes in the asset's fair value and has no intention of holding the financial asset to maturity.

■ The issuer has a right to settle the financial asset at an amount significantly below its amortised cost. Where this is the case and the issuer is expected to exercise that right, the entity cannot demonstrate a positive intent to hold the financial asset to maturity. See further paragraph 6.32 below.

[IAS 39 para AG 16].

6.31 An entity's intention to hold a financial asset to maturity is not negated by unusual and unlikely events that could not be anticipated at the time of the original classification. For example, a disaster scenario that is only remotely possible, such as a run on a bank or a similar situation affecting an insurer, is not something that is assessed by an entity in deciding whether it has the positive intention and ability to hold an investment to maturity. [IAS 39 para AG 21].

6.32 A financial asset that is callable by the issuer would satisfy the criteria for classification as a held-to-maturity investment if the holder intends and is able to hold it until it is called or until maturity and the holder would recover substantially all of its carrying amount. This means that if the issuer can call the instrument at or above its carrying amount, the holder's original classification of the instrument as held-to-maturity is not invalidated because the call option, if exercised, would simply accelerate the asset's maturity. However, if the financial asset is callable on a basis that would result in the holder not recovering substantially all of its carrying amount, the financial asset cannot be classified as a held-to-maturity investment. Any premium paid and capitalised transaction costs should be considered in determining whether the carrying amount would be substantially recovered. [IAS 39 para AG 18]. If the issuer can call the instrument for an amount substantially different from its carrying amount, potentially, the embedded derivative should be separated (see chapter 5).

6.33 On the other hand, a financial asset that is puttable (that is, the holder has the right to require that the issuer repay or redeem the financial asset before maturity) cannot be classified as a held-to-maturity investment, because paying for a put feature in a financial asset is inconsistent with the positive intent to hold the financial asset until maturity. [IAS 39 para AG 19].

6.34 Similarly, an investment in a convertible bond that is convertible before maturity generally cannot be classified as a held-to-maturity investment, because that would be inconsistent with paying for the conversion feature – the right to convert into equity shares before maturity. [IAS 39 para IG C3]. By paying for the conversion feature in terms of a lower interest rate, the investor hopes to benefit from appreciation in value of the option embedded in the debt security. Therefore, in general, it is unlikely that the investor will be able to assert the positive intent and ability to hold a convertible debt security to maturity and forego the opportunity to profit by exercising the conversion option. Even if the convertible debt is separated into an equity option and a host debt instrument (see chapter 7), it generally still would be contradictory to assert the positive intent and ability to hold the debt host contract to maturity and forego the opportunity to exercise the conversion option. On the other hand, if the conversion option can only be exercised at maturity, it may be possible for the holder to demonstrate positive intent to hold the bond to maturity.

Ability to hold to maturity

6.35 It is not sufficient for the entity to demonstrate a positive intent to hold a financial asset to maturity; the entity must also demonstrate its ability to hold such an asset to maturity. An entity cannot demonstrate that ability if:

■ it does not have the financial resources available to continue to finance the investment until maturity; or

■ it is subject to an existing legal or other constraint that could frustrate its intention to hold the financial asset to maturity (although as noted in para 6.32 above, an issuer's call option does not necessarily frustrate this intention).

[IAS 39 para AG 23].

For example, it is unlikely that an open ended fund would be able to classify any financial asset as held-to maturity. Management might intend to hold the investments to maturity, but calls for redemption of shares or units could constrain the fund's ability to hold its investments to maturity.

6.36 An entity's intention and ability to hold debt instruments to maturity is not necessarily constrained if those instruments have been pledged as collateral or are subject to a repurchase agreement or securities lending agreement. However, an entity does not have the positive intention and ability to hold the debt instruments until maturity if it does not expect to be able to maintain or recover access to the instruments. [IAS 39 para IG B18].

Example 1 – Pledge of held-to-maturity assets as security

Entity A requires C18m of cash for its operating activities in 20X7. The entity's latest cash flow forecast indicates a C2m shortfall. The entity intends to raise the funds required by pledging its investments in bonds, which are classified as held-to-maturity, to a bank to obtain a banking facility.

The bonds can continue to be classified as held-to-maturity provided that the entity is able to fulfil the conditions of the banking facility such that the bank will not exercise the pledge. Short-term liquidity problems do not necessarily undermine the entity's ability to hold the investments until maturity.

Assessment of held-to-maturity classification

6.37 An entity should assess its intention and ability to hold its held-to-maturity investments to maturity not only when those financial assets are initially recognised, but also at each subsequent balance sheet date. [IAS 39 para AG 25]. Because an entity is expected not to change its *intent* about a held-to-maturity security, the requirement to reassess the appropriateness of a security's classification would necessarily focus on the entity's *ability* to hold a security to maturity. Facts and circumstances may change that may cause the entity to lose its ability to hold a debt security to maturity. Unless those facts and circumstances fall within one of the exceptions discussed in paragraph 6.41 below, the entity would be forced to reclassify its held-to-maturity investments to available-for-sale.

The tainting rules

6.38   Because management should assert that the criteria for a held-to-maturity investment have been met for each investment, the sale, reclassification or exercise of a put option of certain held-to-maturity securities will call into question ('taint') management's intent to hold all securities in the held-to-maturity category. An entity should not classify any financial assets as held-to-maturity if the entity has, during the current financial year or during the two preceding financial years, sold or reclassified more than an insignificant amount of held-to-maturity investments before maturity. In other words, where an entity during the current financial year has sold or reclassified more than an insignificant amount of held-to-maturity investments before maturity (more than insignificant in relation to the total amount of held-to-maturity investments), it is prohibited from classifying any financial asset as held-to-maturity for a period of two years after the occurrence of this event. Furthermore, all the entity's held-to-maturity investments, not just investments of a similar type, should be reclassified into the available-for-sale category and measured at fair value (see para 6.77). In a sense, a penalty is imposed for a change in management's intention. When the prohibition ends (at the end of the second financial year following the tainting), the portfolio becomes 'cleansed', and the entity is once more able to assert that it has the intent and ability to hold debt securities to maturity. [IAS 39 paras 9, 54].

6.39   The tainting rules do not apply if only an insignificant amount of held-to-maturity investments is sold or reclassified. The standard does not define what an insignificant amount means, except that it should be measured by reference to the total amount of held-to-maturity investments. Therefore, judgement is needed to assess what is insignificant in each particular situation.

Example 1 – Application of the tainting rules

An entity's held-to-maturity portfolio consists of a mixture of sterling corporate bonds, treasury bonds and eurodollar bonds. The entity prepares its financial statements to 31 December 20X5. During September 20X5, the entity sold a certain eurodollar bond to realise a large gain.

The fact that the entity has sold one eurodollar investment (not considered insignificant in relation to the total held-to-maturity portfolio) does not mean that only the eurodollar sub-category has been tainted. The tainting rule is very clear. If an entity has sold or reclassified more than an insignificant amount of held-to-maturity investments, the entire portfolio and all remaining investments must be reclassified to the available-for-sale category. [IAS 39 para IG B20]. It follows that sub-classification of securities for the purpose of limiting the impact of sales or transfers of held-to-maturity securities is not acceptable practice.

The reclassification is recorded in the reporting period in which the sales occurred (that is, the year to 31 December 20X5). Furthermore, as explained in paragraph 6.38 above, the entity is prohibited from reclassifying any investments in the held-to-maturity category for two full financial years after 31 December 20X5. This means that any fixed interest securities acquired during 20X6 and 20X7, which could qualify for held-to-maturity classification, cannot be classified as such in those years. The earliest date that the entity is able to classify investments as held-to-maturity is 1 January 20X8 as shown in the diagram below:

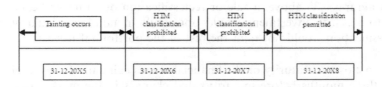

At 1 January 20X8 when the portfolio becomes cleansed, and it once again becomes appropriate to carry securities at held-to-maturity, the fair value of the affected securities on 1 January 20X8 becomes the new amortised cost. Furthermore, as tainting occurs in the year to 31 December 20X5, the held-to-maturity classification for the comparative period to 31 December 20X4 is not affected.

Example 2 – Regular disposal of small amounts of held-to-maturity securities

Entity X has a portfolio of financial investments that is classified as held-to-maturity. In the current period, it sold small amounts of investments from time to time.

Regular or systematic sales or transfers of immaterial amounts are indicative of management's intention not to hold financial assets to maturity. The tainting rules would apply and the entity should reclassify all its held-to-maturity investments as available-for-sale and measure them at fair value.

In addition, the entity may not create a sub-category of held-to-maturity in which to hold these investments. (The aim of this sub-categorisation would have been so that the sale of investments prior to maturity from that sub-category did not taint the entire held-to-maturity portfolio.)

Tainting in group situations

6.40 The tainting rules are designed to test an entity's assertion that it has the positive intent and ability to hold each security to maturity. The rules apply to all entities within a group. Therefore, if a subsidiary operating in a different legal or economic environment sells more than an insignificant amount of held-to-maturity investments, it would preclude the entire group from using the held-to-maturity category. This means that the entity would have to reclassify all its held-to-maturity investments in its consolidated financial statements, unless the sale qualifies for one of the exceptions noted in paragraph 6.41 below.

[IAS 39 para IG IB21]. Furthermore, at least two full financial years must pass before the entity can again classify financial assets as held-to-maturity in its consolidated financial statements. Sales between group entities generally would not taint the held-to-maturity classification at the group level, but may do so at the individual entity level. As the consequences of breaching the conditions are harsh, entities should carefully consider any plans to sell or transfer before classifying any asset to this category.

Exceptions to the tainting rules

6.41   There are a number of exceptions to the tainting rules. As already discussed in paragraph 6.38 above, a sale or reclassification of an insignificant amount of held-to-maturity investment would not result in tainting. Similarly, a sale or reclassification would not taint the rest of the portfolio if it was:

■   so close to maturity or the financial asset's call date (for example, less than three months before maturity) that changes in the market rate of interest would not have a significant effect on the financial asset's fair value;

■   made after the entity has collected substantially all of the financial asset's original principal through scheduled payments or pre-payments; or

■   due to an isolated event that is beyond the entity's control, is non-recurring and could not have been reasonably anticipated by the entity.

[IAS 39 para 9].

6.42   The conditions referred to in the first and second bullet points above relate to situations in which an entity can be expected to be indifferent whether to hold or sell a financial asset, because movements in interest rates after substantially all of the original principal has been collected or when the instrument is close to maturity will not have a significant impact on its fair value. Accordingly, in such situations, a sale would not affect reported net profit or loss and no price volatility would be expected during the remaining period to maturity. For example, if an entity sells a financial asset less than three months prior to maturity, that would generally qualify for use of this exception because the impact on the fair value of the instrument for a difference between the stated interest rate and the market rate generally would be small for an instrument that matures in three months relative to an instrument that matures in several years.

6.43   The term 'substantially all' in the second bullet point of paragraph 6.41 is not defined in IAS 39. The guidance to the previous version of IAS 39 stated that if an entity sells a financial asset after it has collected 90 per cent or more of the financial asset's original principal through scheduled payments or pre-payments, this would generally qualify for this exception. However, if the entity has collected, say, only 10 per cent of the original principal, that condition clearly is not met. Although the previous guidance has not been carried forward in the revised version, we believe that applying a 90 per cent threshold as a rule of thumb to test whether 'substantially all' of the original principal has been collected is acceptable. Clearly, though, it cannot be applied as a hard-and-fast rule and cannot be applied to the derecognition criteria of IAS 39 (see chapter 8).

6.44   In relation to the last bullet point in paragraph 6.41 above, very few events would qualify as isolated events beyond the entity's control, that are non-recurring or reasonably unanticipated. A disaster scenario that is only remotely possible, such as a run on a bank or a similar situation affecting an insurer, would qualify as it is not something that would be assessed by an entity in deciding whether it has the positive intention and ability to hold an investment to maturity. [IAS 39 para AG 21]. The corollary is that if the sale or reclassification resulted from an event that is not isolated but within the entity's control or is potentially recurring or could have been anticipated at the date the held-to-maturity classification was made, this inevitably will cast doubt on the entity's intent and ability to hold a security to maturity. Consider the following example:

Example – Permitted sales

Entity X has a portfolio of financial assets that is classified as held-to-maturity. In the current period, at the direction of the board of directors, the senior management team has been replaced. The new management wishes to sell a portion of the held-to-maturity financial assets in order to carry out an expansion strategy designated and approved by the board.

A change in management is not identified under the standard as an instance where sales or transfers from held-to-maturity do not compromise the classification as held-to-maturity (see para 6.41 above).

Although the previous management team had been in place since the entity's inception and entity X had never before undergone a major restructuring, sales in response to a change in management would, nevertheless call into question entity X's intention to hold remaining held-to-maturity financial assets to maturity. [IAS 39 IG B16].

6.45   In addition to the above, the standard identifies some specific circumstances that may not have been anticipated at the time of the initial held-to-maturity classification and, therefore, would justify the sale of a security classified as held-to-maturity without calling into question management's intent to hold other debt securities to maturity in the future. Thus a sale or transfer of a held-to-maturity security due to one of the following circumstances would not result in tainting of a held-to-maturity portfolio.

- A significant deterioration in the issuer's credit worthiness (see para 6.46).
- Changes in tax laws (see para 6.49).
- Major business combination or disposition, such as a sale of a segment (see para 6.50).
- Changes in statutory or regulatory requirements (see para 6.53).

[IAS 39 para AG 22].

A significant deterioration in the issuer's creditworthiness

6.46 A sale due to a significant deterioration in the issuer's creditworthiness (evident by a downgrade in the issuer's credit rating by an external rating agency) might not raise a question about the entity's intention to hold other investments to maturity. However, the deterioration in creditworthiness must be significant judged by reference to the credit rating at initial recognition. If the rating downgrade in combination with other information provides evidence of impairment (for example, if it becomes probable that all amounts due (principal and interest) will not be collected), the deterioration in creditworthiness often would be regarded as significant. Also, the significant deterioration must not have been reasonably anticipated when the entity classified the investment as held-to-maturity in order to meet the condition in IAS 39. A credit downgrade of a notch within a class or from one rating class to the immediately lower rating class could often be regarded as reasonably anticipated. Therefore, a sale triggered by such a downgrade would result in tainting of the held-to-maturity portfolio. Similarly, a sale as a result of the issuer's bankruptcy would be regarded as a permitted sale, but not one where the bankruptcy was anticipated at the acquisition date and the investor was, therefore, able to control the outcome. [IAS 39 para IG B15].

6.47 Where a credit rating is not available from an external rating agency to assess a decline in the issuer's creditworthiness, the entity is permitted to use its internal credit rating system to support the demonstration of significant deterioration in the issuer's creditworthiness. However, the internal credit rating system must be sufficiently robust to provide a reliable and objective measure of the issuer's credit rating and changes in those ratings on a consistent basis.

6.48 A sale following a significant deterioration in the issuer's creditworthiness should normally take place as soon as the entity becomes aware of the credit downgrade and not left until a later date. This is because if the sale or reclassification out of held-to-maturity category is not made immediately or shortly afterwards following the credit downgrade, it provides evidence that the entity is indifferent to the loss incurred in its held-to-maturity portfolio and intends to hold those investments to maturity. If, then a sale occurs many months after the credit downgrade, it is likely to be for reasons other than a credit downgrade.

Changes in tax laws

6.49 A sale following a change in tax law that eliminates or significantly reduces the tax-exempt status of interest on the held-to-maturity investment (but not a change in tax law that revises the marginal tax rates applicable to interest income) would not compromise the classification of held-to-maturity. This is because such a change was not contemplated at the time of the initial classification. On the other hand, if an entity undertakes a sale in anticipation of a change in the tax law that was not substantively enacted at the time of sale or reclassification, the entire held-to-maturity portfolio may well be tainted. Similarly, a sale as a result of change in tax law that revises the marginal tax rates for interest income will taint the entire held-to-maturity portfolio, since the change is likely to affect all debt instruments not simply the ones sold.

Major business combination or disposition

6.50 Following a business combination or disposal of a business segment, it may be necessary for the entity to sell or reclassify some of its own held-to-maturity securities in order to maintain the entity's existing interest rate risk position or credit risk policy that predated the business combination or disposal. In a business combination, it may also be necessary to sell some of the acquired entity's held-to-maturity securities, even though all of the acquired securities would be classified anew following such an acquisition. Although a business combination is an event that is within the entity's control, sales or reclassifications that are necessary to maintain the entity's existing interest rate risk position or credit risk policy arises as a direct consequence of the business combination or disposition and are not anticipated. Hence, such sales or reclassifications would not taint the entity's held-to-maturity portfolio.

6.51 On the other hand, sales of held-to-maturity securities to fund an acquisition that is within the entity's control would taint the portfolio. This is because such sales are not a consequence of the acquisition. Rather, as they have been made to fund the acquisition, they call into question the entity's intent and ability to hold the investment to maturity. Similarly, a sale in response to an unsolicited tender offer or a sale due to a change in the entity's business strategy would also taint the held-to-maturity portfolio. This is because such events are unlikely to fall into the category of isolated events that are beyond the entity's control, are non-recurring events and could not have been reasonably anticipated by the entity.

[The next paragraph is 6.53.]

Changes in statutory or regulatory requirements

6.53 IAS 39 identifies the following situations where sale or reclassification out of the held-to-maturity category necessitated by changes in statutory or regulatory requirements would not call into question the entity's intent and ability to hold other investments to maturity.

■ A change in statutory or regulatory requirements significantly modifying either what constitutes a permissible investment or the maximum level of particular types of investments, thereby causing an entity to dispose of a held-to-maturity investment.

■ A significant increase in the risk weights of held-to-maturity investments used for regulatory risk-based capital purposes.

■   A significant increase in the industry's regulatory capital requirements that causes the entity to downsize by selling held-to-maturity investments.

[IAS 39 para AG22(d-f)].

6.54   Sales of held-to-maturity securities resulting from statutory or regulatory requirements that affect the whole regulated industry as set out above are clearly isolated events beyond the entity's control, are non-recurring and could not have been reasonably anticipated by the entity.

6.55   In relation to the last situation in paragraph 6.53 above, if an entity is forced to downsize to comply with a significant increase in the industry's capital requirements, the sale of one or more held-to-maturity securities in connection with that downsizing would not call into question the classification of other held-to-maturity securities. Sometimes downsizing may be required to comply with a significant increase in *entity-specific* capital requirements imposed by regulators. In that situation, it may be difficult for the entity to demonstrate that the regulator's action could not have been reasonably anticipated at the time of the initial classification. Therefore, in this situation, the entity can avoid tainting only if it can demonstrate that the downsizing results from an increase in capital requirements, which is an isolated event that is beyond its control, is non-recurring and could not have been reasonably anticipated. [IAS 39 para IG B17].

6.56   It follows that blanket sales of held-to-maturity investments made as a matter of course to comply with regulatory capital requirements are not consistent with held-to-maturity accounting. For example, a sale of a held-to-maturity investment to realise gains to replenish regulatory capital depleted by a loan loss provision would taint the entire held-to-maturity portfolio, because realising such a gain is inconsistent with the held-to-maturity classification.

Decision tree for classifying financial assets as held-to-maturity

6.57   A decision tree for classifying financial assets as held-to-maturity is shown below.

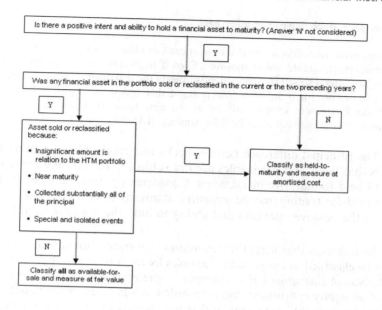

Loans and receivables

6.58   Loans and receivables are non-derivative financial assets with fixed or determinable payments that are not quoted in an active market other than:

- Those that the entity intends to sell immediately or in the near term, which should be classified as held-for-trading, and those that the entity upon initial recognition designates as at fair value through profit or loss.

- Those that the entity upon initial recognition designates as available-for-sale.

- Those for which the holder may not recover substantially all of its initial investment, other than because of credit deterioration, which should be classified as available-for-sale.

[IAS 39 para 9].

6.59   Loans and receivables typically arise when an entity provides money, goods or services directly to a debtor with no intention of trading the receivable. Examples include trade receivables, bank deposits and loan assets originated by the entity either directly or by way of syndication/participation arrangements. It also includes loans that are *purchased* in a secondary market that is not active and the loans are not quoted. Investments in debt securities that are quoted in a non-active market can also be classified as loans and receivables.

> **Example – Bank deposits in other banks**
>
> Banks make term deposits with a central bank or other banks. Sometimes, the proof of deposit is negotiable, sometimes not. Even if negotiable, the depositor bank may or may not intend to sell it. Such a deposit meets the definition of loans and receivables, whether or not the proof of deposit is negotiable, unless the depositor bank intends to sell the instrument immediately or in the near term, in which case the deposit is classified as a financial asset held-for-trading. [IAS 39 para IG B23].

6.60 The principal difference between loans and receivables and other financial assets is that loans and receivables are not subject to the tainting provisions that apply to held-to-maturity investments. Consequently, loans and receivables that are not held-for-trading may be measured at amortised cost even if an entity does not have the positive intention and ability to hold the loan asset until maturity.

6.61 Instruments that meet the definition of an equity instrument under IAS 32 cannot be classified as loans and receivables by the holder. On the other hand, if a non-derivative instrument (for example, a preference share) that has the legal form of an equity instrument, but is recorded as a liability by the issuer and it has fixed or determinable payments and is not quoted in an active market, can be classified within loans and receivables by the holder, provided the definition is otherwise met. [IAS 39 para IG B22].

6.62 An interest acquired in a pool of assets that are not loans or receivables (for example, an interest in a mutual fund or a similar fund) cannot be classified as a loan or receivable. [IAS 39 para 9]. The corollary is that a purchase of a securitised asset that consists of a pool of loans and receivables that meets the definition of loans and receivables can be classified as loan and receivables by the holder. However, where an entity securitises its own portfolio of loans and receivables that were classified as loans and receivables before the securitisation and the derecognition provisions of IAS 39 apply, the securitisation may give rise to a new financial asset that is classified in accordance with the four categories of financial assets.

[The next paragraph is 6.65]

Purchased loans

Debt instruments quoted in an active market

6.65 As stated in paragraph 6.58 above, an entity is not permitted to classify as a loan or receivable an investment in a debt instrument that is quoted in an active market. The IASB considered that the ability to measure a financial asset at amortised cost (as in the case of loans and receivables) is most appropriate when there is no liquid market for the asset. It is less appropriate to extend the category to debt instruments traded in liquid markets. Accordingly, for such investments an amortised cost basis of measurement is only permitted if the entity can demonstrate its positive intention and ability to hold the investments until maturity (see para 6.26 above). It is likely, therefore, that many originated and purchased investments in quoted bonds would be classified as available-for-sale.

Available-for-sale financial assets

6.66   Available-for-sale (AFS) financial assets are those non-derivative financial assets that are designated as available-for-sale or are not classified as:

■   Loans and receivables.

■   Held-to-maturity investments.

■   Financial assets at fair value through profit or loss.

[IAS 39 para 9].

6.67   Under the previous version of IAS 39, available-for-sale was a residual category for all those financial assets that did not properly belong in one of the three other categories – originated loans and receivables, trading or held-to-maturity. The revision introduces a degree of choice, on initial recognition to classify any non-derivative financial asset, except those held-for-trading or designated at fair value through profit or loss, as available-for-sale and, therefore, to measure it at fair value with changes in fair value recognised directly in other comprehensive income. In other words, only assets that would otherwise be classified as loans and receivables can be designated as available-for-sale at initial recognition. (An asset that is classified as held-to-maturity cannot by definition at the same time be regarded as available-for-sale.)

6.68   Examples of available-for-sale financial assets that are likely to be included in this category are:

■   Equity investments that are not designated on initial recognition as at fair value through profit and loss.

■   Financial assets that could have been classified as loans and receivables on initial recognition, but the holder chooses to designate on initial recognition as available-for-sale.

■   Financial assets where the holder is unable to recover substantially all its initial investment, except through credit deterioration of the issuer.

■   Puttable quoted debt securities that cannot be classified either as held-to-maturity because they are puttable (see para 6.33 above) or any quoted debt instrument that fails the held-to-maturity criteria (because they may be sold in response to liquidity needs (see para 6.38) or loans and receivables because they are quoted (see para 6.58)).

The main issue is, therefore, likely to focus on whether investments quoted in an active market should be classified as fair value through profit or loss or designated as available-for-sale on initial recognition.

6025

> **Example – Balancing a portfolio**
>
> Entity A has an investment portfolio of debt and equity instruments. The documented portfolio management guidelines specify that the portfolio's equity exposure should be limited to between 30 and 50% of total portfolio value. The portfolio's investment manager is authorised to balance the portfolio within the designated guidelines by buying and selling equity and debt instruments.
>
> Whether entity A is permitted to classify the instruments as available-for-sale would depend on entity A's intentions and past practice. If the portfolio manager is authorised to buy and sell instruments to balance the risks in a portfolio, but there is no intention to trade and there is no past practice of trading for short-term profit, the instruments can be classified as available-for-sale. If the portfolio manager actively buys and sells instruments to generate short-term profits, the financial instruments in the portfolio are classified as held-for-trading. [IAS 39 para IG B12].

Reclassification of assets between categories

6.69 Once a financial asset has been classified into a particular category on initial recognition, IAS 39 restricts the circumstances in which it is permissible or necessary to transfer that asset into another category. However, these rules were eased somewhat in October 2008 when the IASB amended IAS 39 to allow reclassification of certain financial assets out of a category requiring fair value measurement (that is, held-for-trading or available-for-sale) and into another category under limited circumstances (see paras 6.73 and 6.78). However, derivatives and financial assets designated as at fair value through profit or loss, as described in paragraph 6.5, are not eligible for this reclassification.

Transfer into and out of fair value through profit or loss

6.70 As explained in paragraph 6.5, entities are permitted to designate on initial recognition any financial asset at fair value through profit and loss if it meets the criteria of paragraph 9 of IAS 39. However, to impose discipline on this approach, a financial asset that has been voluntary designated cannot be transferred into or out of this category while it is held. [IAS 39 para 50]. Such irrevocable designation at inception prevents 'cherry picking', as it is not known at initial recognition whether the asset's fair value will increase or decrease.

Transfer into and out of held-for-trading

6.71 After initial recognition, a financial asset may not be reclassified into the sub-category held-for-trading from another category. [IAS 39 para 50]. However, as mentioned in paragraph 6.69, from 1 July 2008, this requirement has been relaxed: a non-derivative financial asset can be reclassified out of the sub-category held-for-trading and into another category in the following circumstances:

■ If the financial asset meets the definition of loans and receivables at the date of reclassification and the entity at that date has the intent and ability to hold it for the foreseeable future or to maturity. [IAS 39 para 50D]. Note that a financial asset cannot meet the definition of loans and receivables if it is quoted in an active market (see para 6.65) or if it represents an interest in a pool of assets that are not themselves loans and receivables (see para 6.62).

- For other financial assets (that is, those that do not meet the definition of loans and receivables) only in rare circumstances, provided that these financial assets are no longer held for the purpose of selling or repurchasing in the near term and meet the definition of the target category. [IAS 39 para 50B].

6.71.1 Paragraph BC104D of the Basis for Conclusions of the amendment to IAS 39 defines a rare circumstance as arising *"from a single event that is unusual and highly unlikely to recur in the near-term"*. In its press release announcing the publication of this amendment to IAS 39, the IASB indicated that the deterioration of the world's financial markets that occurred during the third quarter of 2008 was a possible example of 'a rare circumstance'.

6.71.2 At the date of reclassification, the fair value of any financial asset reclassified under these provisions becomes its new cost or amortised cost as applicable. Any gain or loss already recognised in profit or loss is not reversed. [IAS 39 paras 50C, 50F]. Further guidance on measurement is provided in chapter 9.

6.71.3 Reclassification is not permissible for derivative financial assets. [IAS 39 para 50(a)]. However, this prohibition does not prevent a derivative that was initially classified as held-for-trading from being designated as a hedging instrument while it is held. Nor does it prevent a derivative that was designated as a hedging instrument from being classified as held-for-trading following revocation of the hedge. [IAS 39 para 50A].

6.71.4 Although reclassification does not imply any change to the financial instrument's terms, an amendment to IFRIC 9, 'Reassessment of embedded derivatives', issued in March 2009 introduces a requirement for an entity to assess whether a contract contains an embedded derivative when it reclassifies a financial asset out of the sub-category of held-for-trading. [IFRIC 9 para 7]. The amendment to IFRIC 9 is effective for accounting period ending on or after 30 June 2009, further guidance is provided in chapter 5.

Transfer into and out of loans and receivables

6.71.5 As explained in paragraphs 6.71 and 6.74.1, a non-derivative financial asset may be reclassified out of held-for-trading or available-for-sale and into loans and receivables if it meets the definition of loans and receivables and the entity has the ability and intention to hold it for the foreseeable future or until maturity.

6.72 Additionally, an entity can choose to designate a financial asset that satisfies the loans and receivables definition as available-for-sale only on initial recognition or on the date of transition to IFRS. If an asset is initially designated as a loan and receivable or has been reclassified as a loan and receivable per paragraph 6.71, it may not subsequently be re-designated as available-for-sale or held-for-trading.

6.72.1 However, different considerations apply if an asset that was initially classified as a loan and receivable becomes quoted in an active market such that the definition of loans and receivables is no longer met. This case is not specifically covered by IAS 39 and accordingly an entity has an accounting policy choice of reclassifying or not. The chosen policy should be applied consistently. So if an entity chooses reclassification as its accounting policy, it will need to reclassify all loans and receivables that become quoted in an active market as available-for-sale.

Transfer out of held-to-maturity into available-for-sale

6.73 Where, as a result of a change in intention or ability, it is no longer appropriate to classify an investment as held-to-maturity, it is reclassified as available-for-sale and remeasured at fair value. [IAS 39 para 51]. As explained in paragraph 6.38, a sale or reclassification calls into question management's intent and ability to hold financial assets to maturity and 'taints' the entire portfolio. Therefore, whenever sales or reclassification of more than an insignificant amount of held-to-maturity investments that do not meet any of the conditions of permitted sales set out in paragraph 6.41 occur, any remaining held-to-maturity investments are be reclassified as available-for-sale. In such circumstances, the assets are remeasured to fair value, with any difference recognised in other comprehensive income. [IAS 39 para 52]. Accounting for reclassifications is addressed in chapter 9.

Transfer out of available-for-sale into held-to-maturity

6.74 An entity is allowed to reclassify a financial asset from available-for-sale to held-to-maturity, except in periods where the held-to-maturity category is tainted. For example, a quoted loan in an active market that was initially classified as available-for-sale may subsequently be reclassified to held-to-maturity category if the entity intends and has the ability to hold the loan to maturity. An instrument may be reclassified into the held-to-maturity category when the tainted held-to-maturity portfolio has been 'cleansed' at the end of the second financial year following the tainting (see para 6.38). In this case, the financial asset's carrying value, that is, its fair value at the date of reclassification, becomes the asset's new amortised cost. [IAS 39 para 54(a)]. Accounting for reclassifications is dealt with in chapter 9.

Transfer out of available-for-sale to loans and receivables

6.74.1 As mentioned in paragraph 6.69, an entity may reclassify a non-derivative financial asset from available-for-sale to loans and receivables if:

■ the entity has the intention and ability to hold the asset for the foreseeable future or until maturity; and

■ the asset meets the definition of loans and receivables. Note that a financial asset cannot meet the definition of loans and receivables if it is quoted in an active market (see para 6.65), if it represents an interest in a pool of assets that are not themselves loans and receivables (see para 6.62), or if the holder does not substantially recover all of its investment (see para 6.42).

[IAS 39 para 50C, 50E].

6.74.2   At the date of reclassification, the fair value of any financial asset reclassified under these provisions becomes its new cost or amortised cost as applicable. The treatment of any gain or loss already recognised in other comprehensive income depends on whether the asset has a fixed maturity. [IAS 39 paras 50C and 50F]. Further guidance on measurement is provided in chapter 9.

Summary

6.74.3   The reclassification requirements for financial assets described above are summarised in the following table:

From category	To category				
	Held-for-trading	Designated at fair value	Loans and receivables	Held-to-maturity	Available-for-sale
Held-for-trading		No	Yes (see paras 6.71-71.3)	Yes (see paras 6.71-71.3)	Yes (see paras 6.71-71.3)
Designated at fair value	No		No	No	No
Loans and receivables	No	No		No	Yes (see para 6.72.1)
Held-to-maturity	No	No	No		Yes (see para 6.73)
Available-for-sale	No	No	Yes (see para 6.74.1)	Yes (see para 6.74)	

Classification of financial liabilities

6.75   IAS 39 has two defined categories of financial liabilities, as follows:

■ Financial liabilities 'at fair value through profit or loss'.

■ Other financial liabilities (measured at amortised cost).

6.76 Like financial assets, a financial liability can be classified as at fair value through profit or loss only if it meets either of the following conditions:

■ Upon initial recognition, it is designated by the entity at fair value through profit or loss.

■ It is classified as held-for-trading.

[IAS 39 para 9].

Designation at fair value through profit or loss on initial recognition

6.77 An entity may designate a financial liability at fair value through profit or loss on initial recognition only in the following circumstances:

■ The designation eliminates or significantly reduces a measurement or recognition inconsistency (sometimes referred to as an 'accounting mismatch') that would otherwise arise.

■ A group of financial assets, financial liabilities or both is managed and its performance is evaluated on a fair value basis, in accordance with a documented risk management or investment strategy.

■ The item proposed to be designated at fair value through profit or loss is a hybrid contract that contains one or more embedded derivatives unless:

    ■ The embedded derivative(s) does not significantly modify the cash flows that otherwise would be required by the contract; or

    ■ It is clear with little or no analysis when a similar hybrid (combined) instrument is first considered that separation of the embedded derivative(s) is prohibited, such as a pre-payment option embedded in a loan that permits the holder to pre-pay the loan for approximately its amortised cost. [IAS 39 para 11A].

[IAS 39 para 9].

6.78 The entity's ability to designate a financial instrument at fair value through profit or loss is an option. It does not restrict an entity's ability to measure a financial liability at amortised cost. Furthermore, as the above three conditions for designating a financial liability at fair value through profit or loss on initial recognition also apply to financial assets, similar considerations that apply to financial assets and dealt with in paragraphs 6.5 to 6.21 also apply to financial liabilities.

6.79 However, the above situations effectively reduce the possibility of measuring an entity's own debt instruments at fair value and thereby recognising income as a result of deteriorating credit quality (and an expense as a result of improving credit quality) that was possible under the unrestricted fair value option in the 2003 revision of IAS 39 and that caused a significant amount of controversy. However, where an entity takes the fair value option and measures its own debt at fair value because it falls within one of the first two situations mentioned in paragraph 6.77, changes in the entity's creditworthiness should be reflected in the fair value measurement of own debt instruments. This issue is addressed in chapter 9.

Held-for-trading

6.80 A financial liability is held-for-trading if it is:

- acquired or incurred principally for the purpose of selling or repurchasing it in the near-term;

- part of a portfolio of identified financial instruments that are managed together and for which there is evidence of a recent actual pattern of short-term profit taking; or

- a derivative (except for a derivative that is a designated and effective hedging instrument).

[IAS 39 para 9].

6.81 Financial liabilities held-for-trading include:

- Derivative liabilities that are not accounted for as hedging instruments. For example, it will include derivatives with a negative fair value.

- Obligations to deliver financial assets borrowed by a short seller. A short sale is a transaction in which an entity sells securities it does not own, with the intention of buying securities at an agreed price on a future date to cover the sale. Securities borrowed are not recognised on the balance sheet, unless they are sold to third parties, in which case the obligation to return the securities is recorded as a trading liability and measured at fair value and any gains or losses are included in the income statement.

- Financial liabilities that are incurred with an intention to repurchase them in the near-term. For example, a quoted debt instrument that the issuer may buy back in the near-term depending on changes in its fair value.

- Financial liabilities that are part of a portfolio of identified financial instruments that are managed together and for which there is evidence of a recent pattern of short-term profit-taking.

The fact that a liability is incurred and used to fund trading activities does not mean that the liability is classified as held-for-trading.

[IAS 39 para AG 15].

Other financial liabilities

6.82   Financial liabilities that are not classified as at fair value through profit or loss would automatically fall into this category and are measured at amortised cost. Common examples are trade payables, borrowings and customer deposits.

Reclassification between categories

6.83   Reclassification of financial liabilities into or out of fair value through profit or loss is prohibited. However, as explained in paragraph 6.73, this prohibition does not apply to derivative financial liabilities that are designated or re-designated as hedging instruments.

Financial guarantee contracts

6.84   Financial guarantee contracts do not fit clearly into any category above if they were not initially classified as at fair value through profit or loss. They seem to form a separate category of their own. This is because subsequent measurement of these contracts, unless designated at inception as at fair value through profit or loss, is not consistent with that of the categories described above. Measurement of financial guarantee contracts is considered further in chapter 9.

Chapter 7

Financial liabilities and equity

Chapter 7

Financial liabilities and equity

Introduction

7.1   IAS 32, 'Financial instruments: presentation', contains the principles for distinguishing between liabilities and equity issued by an entity. The substance of the contractual arrangement of a financial instrument, rather than its legal form, governs its classification. The overriding criterion is that if an entity does not have an unconditional right to avoid delivering cash or another financial asset to settle a contractual obligation, the contract is not an equity instrument.

7.1.1   IAS 32 should be applied by all entities to all types of financial instruments except those outside the standard's scope. The scope exemptions to IAS 32 are discussed in chapter 3. In practice one of the more common and complex scope exemptions relates to contracts that fall within the scope of IFRS 2, 'Share-based payment', IAS 19, 'Employee benefits', or IFRS 4, 'Insurance contracts'. Where the holder is an employee, director or provider of service to the entity, the contract should be carefully analysed to determine whether it is within the scope of IFRS 2, (see chapter 12 of the IFRS Manual of Accounting) or IAS 19 (see chapter 11 of the IFRS Manual of Accounting) or IAS 32.

7.2   The IASB published an amendment to IAS 32 on the classification of rights issues on 8 October 2009. The amendment addresses the accounting for rights issues (including rights, options and warrants) that are denominated in a currency other than the functional currency of the issuer (see para 7.40). The amendment is effective for annual periods beginning on or after 1 February 2010, with early adoption permitted.

7.2.1   The IASB published IFRIC 19, 'Extinguishing financial liabilities with equity instruments', in November 2009. This interpretation clarifies the accounting when an entity renegotiates the terms of its debt with the result that the liability is extinguished by the debtor issuing its own equity instruments to the creditor. The interpretation is effective for annual periods beginning on or after 1 July 2010, with early adoption permitted. Refer to chapter 8 for further guidance on IFRIC 19.

7.3   Classifying liability and equity instruments in accordance with IAS 32's rules is complex and requires the assessment of each component of an instrument's contractual terms. The impact of an incorrect classification on such issues as borrowings and other ratios (including debt covenants) and reported earnings can be highly significant to investors and other users of financial statements.

[The next paragraph is 7.6.]

Principles for classifying financial liabilities and equity instruments

7.6   Before considering IAS 32's general principles for classifying a financial instrument as a financial liability or equity, it is appropriate to set out the standard's basic definitions of a financial liability and an equity instrument.

7.7   IAS 32 defines a financial liability as any liability that is:

- A contractual obligation
    - to deliver cash or another financial asset to another entity; or
    - to exchange financial assets or financial liabilities with another entity under conditions that are potentially unfavourable to the entity.

- A contract that will or may be settled in the entity's own equity instruments and is:
    - a non-derivative for which the entity is or may be obliged to deliver a variable number of the entity's own equity instruments; or
    - a derivative that will or may be settled other than by the exchange of a fixed amount of cash or another financial asset for a fixed number of the entity's own equity instruments. For this purpose the entity's own equity instruments do not include puttable instruments and obligations arising on liquidation that are classified as equity (as explained in para 7.7.1), rights issues denominated in a currency other than the functional currency of the issuer if they meet certain conditions (as explained in para.7.40) or instruments that are contracts for the future receipt or delivery of the entity's own equity instruments.

[IAS 32 para 11].

7.7.1   An exception is built in to the above general definition to the effect that an instrument that meets the definition of a financial liability is classified as an equity instrument if it has all the features and meets the conditions in the February 2008 amendment to IAS 32, 'Puttable financial instruments and obligations arising on liquidation' (see para 7.24.5). This amendment came into effect for accounting periods beginning on or after 1 January 2009.

7.8   IAS 32 defines an equity instrument as any contract that evidences a residual interest in an entity's assets after deducting all of its liabilities. [IAS 32 para 11]. A residual interest is not necessarily a proportionate interest ranking *pari passu* with all other residual interests, for example, it may be an interest in a fixed amount of the entity's shares that may rank first in preference. For the purposes of determining whether a financial instrument is an equity instrument rather than a financial liability, the standard requires an issuer to apply the following expanded definition of an equity instrument that is essentially a converse of the above definition of a financial liability. Accordingly, an instrument is an equity instrument if, and only if, both of the conditions below are met:

- The instrument includes no contractual obligation:

    - to deliver cash or another financial asset to another entity; or

    - to exchange financial assets or financial liabilities with another entity under conditions that are potentially unfavourable to the entity.

- If the instrument will or may be settled in the issuer's own equity instruments, it is:

    - a non-derivative that includes no contractual obligation for the issuer to deliver a variable number of its own equity instruments; or

    - a derivative that will be settled only by the issuer exchanging a fixed amount of cash or another financial asset for a fixed number of its own equity instruments. For this purpose the issuer's own equity instruments do not include puttable instruments and obligations arising on liquidation that are classified as equity or instruments that are contracts for the future receipt or delivery of the issuer's own equity instruments.

A contractual obligation, including one arising from a derivative financial instrument, that will or may result in the future receipt or delivery of the issuer's own equity instruments, but does not meet both conditions above, is not an equity instrument. As an exception, an instrument that meets the definition of a financial liability is classified as an equity instrument if it has all the features and meets the conditions in the February 2008 amendment to IAS 32, 'Puttable financial instruments and obligations arising on liquidation' (see para 7.24.5). [IAS 32 para 16].

7.9   IAS 32 is a contract-based standard. 'Contract' or 'contractual' refers to an agreement between two or more parties that has clear economic consequences that the parties have little, if any, discretion to avoid, usually because the agreement is enforceable by law. Contracts, and thus financial instruments, may take a variety of forms and need not be in writing. [IAS 32 para 13]. Liabilities or assets that are not contractual (for example obligations established from local law or statute, such as income taxes) are not financial liabilities or financial assets. Similarly, constructive obligations, as defined in IAS 37, do not arise from contracts and are not financial liabilities. [IAS 32 para AG 12].

7.10   IAS 32 states that an issuer of a financial instrument should classify a financial instrument, or *its component parts,* on initial recognition as a financial liability, a financial asset or an equity instrument in accordance with the contractual arrangement's substance and the definitions of a financial liability, a financial asset and an equity instrument. [IAS 32 para 15]. The role of 'substance' in the classification of financial instrument should be restricted to considering the instrument's contractual terms. Anything that falls outside the contractual terms should not be considered for the purpose of assessing whether an instrument should be classified as a liability under IAS 32. Furthermore, in assessing the substance of the terms and conditions of a financial instrument, the impact of relevant local laws, regulations and the entity's governing charter in effect at the date of classification on those terms should also be considered as noted in paragraph 7.21, but not expected future amendments to those laws, regulations and charter. [IFRIC 2 para 5].

7.11 A contractual financial obligation is necessary to classify a financial instrument as a liability. Such a contractual obligation could be established explicitly or could be indirectly established (see para 7.27). However, the obligation must be established through the terms and conditions of the financial instrument. As the IFRIC agreed in March 2006, economic compulsion, by itself, does not result in a financial instrument being classified as a liability.

Example 1 – 'Step-up' instrument

An entity issues a non-redeemable callable bond where the fixed dividend of 5% can be deferred at the issuer's option. The instrument includes a 'step-up' dividend clause that would increase the dividend to 25% at a pre-determined date in the future unless the instrument had previously been called by the issuer.

This instrument includes no contractual obligation to pay the dividends or to call the instrument. Although there is an economic compulsion for the issuer to call the instrument on the date the dividend payment 'steps-up', there is no contractual obligation to do so. Therefore, the instrument would be classified as an equity instrument.

Example 2 – Discretionary dividends that have historically been paid each year.

An entity issues a non-redeemable callable subordinated bond with a fixed 6% coupon. The coupon can be deferred in perpetuity at the issuer's option. The issuer has a history of paying the coupon each year and the current bond price is predicated on the holders expectation that the coupon will continue to be paid each year. In addition the stated policy of the issuer is that the coupon will be paid each year, which has been publicly communicated.

Although there is both pressure on the issuer to pay the coupon, to maintain the bond price, and a constructive obligation to pay the coupon, there is no contractual obligation to do so. Therefore the bond is classified as an equity instrument.

7.12 Examining a financial instrument's component parts is key to correct classification. This is because debt instruments and shares come in many forms. They may be redeemable or non-redeemable. The returns may be mandatory or discretionary or may combine elements of both. Sometimes they may contain features (such as put and call options) that may or may not oblige the issuer to settle the instrument in cash or other financial assets. Consequently, it is necessary to examine the contractual terms of each component carefully, bearing in mind the definitions of a financial liability and an equity instrument, to determine whether they exhibit characteristics of a financial liability or equity. Once the characteristics of the individual components are determined, they can be combined to arrive at the overall assessment of whether the entire instrument is classified as a financial liability, or an equity instrument, or a compound instrument containing both liability and equity components.

[The next paragraph is 7.14.]

7.14   Where an entity issues two or more instruments at (or nearly at) the same time to the same counterparty, the indicators outlined in IAS 39 must be considered when determining whether the contracts are linked and viewed as a single arrangement or as two separate contracts. Indicators that contracts are linked include:

- they are entered into at the same time and in contemplation of one another;

- they have the same counterparty;

- they relate to the same risk;

- there is no apparent economic need or substantive business purpose for structuring the transaction separately that would not also have been accomplished in a single transaction; and

- they cannot be transferred or redeemed separately.

[IAS 39 paras AG 51(e) and IG B.6].

7.14.1   The general classification principles described above appear to be relatively simple, but the application in practice often presents difficulties. The contractual arrangement's substance and its legal form are commonly consistent, but not always. Since the contractual arrangement's substance rather than its legal form takes precedence, there could be situations where instruments that qualify as equity for regulatory or legal purposes are, on closer examination, liabilities for financial reporting purposes.

Reclassifications

7.15   Equity or liability classification is made by the entity on initial recognition in accordance with paragraph 15 of IAS 32. However, if the contractual terms and conditions are subsequently changed, it may result in derecognising the original instrument (equity or liability) and the recognising of a new instrument (liability or equity). The accounting treatment for modifications of the contractual terms of financial liabilities, that may result in derecognising the liability and recognition of an equity instrument is dealt with in chapter 8.

7.15.1   The IFRIC issued rejection wording in November 2006 that clarified the accounting treatment for transfers from equity to liability when the transfer is a result of a change in the instrument's contractual terms. This might be, for example a change in the contractual terms to require a coupon, which was previously at the discretion of the issuer, to be paid on the occurrence of a genuine contingent settlement event. The IFRIC clarified that a financial liability is initially recognised at the time when the contractual terms are changed, irrespective of whether the change affects the contractual cash flows. The new liability is measured at fair value in accordance with paragraph 43 of IAS 39.

7.15.2   The IFRIC also observed that the change in the instrument's terms gives rise to derecognising the original equity instrument. Paragraph 33 of IAS 32 states that no gain or loss is recognised in profit and loss on the purchase, sale, issue or cancellation of an entity's own equity instruments. The difference between the carrying amount of the equity instrument and the fair value of the newly-recognised financial liability is recorded in equity at the time the terms are changed. This applies even if the change in terms has no impact on the instrument's expected cash flows.

7.15.3   As far as reclassifications from financial liability to equity are concerned absent any modifications to the instrument's contractual terms and conditions, the guidance where the instrument's contractual terms and conditions have not changed is less clear than the case where the instrument's contractual terms and conditions have changed . IAS 32 is silent on whether a re-assessment is required after initial recognition as paragraph 15 of IAS 32 only prescribes that an entity should classify the instrument, or its component parts, on initial recognition. Therefore, it is possible to argue that an instrument should not be reclassified after inception. On the other hand, paragraph 39 of IAS 39 states that an entity should remove a financial liability (or a part of a financial liability) from its balance sheet when, and only when, it is extinguished; that is when the obligation specified in the contract is discharged or cancelled or expires. Therefore, one could argue that if the contractual obligation that triggered liability classification terminates, then reclassification is appropriate because the obligation has been discharged or cancelled. Because of the lack of clarity in the literature, we believe that both treatments can be supported, and as a result an entity should determine an appropriate accounting policy and apply it consistently.

7.15.4   Consider the following example: An entity issues a 5 year convertible bond where the holder has the option to convert it into the issuers's equity shares after the first year, but where the conversion ratio is only fixed at the end of the first year at the lower of CU5 and 130 per cent of the equity share price. As the number of shares the bond could be converted into is variable, on initial recognition the conversion option is recognised as a separate embedded derivative liability. However, at the end of year one, under the contract's original terms, the conversion ratio is fixed and, therefore, no longer meets the definition of a financial liability. In considering the guidance in IAS 32 above, the change in the conversion ratio from variable to fixed at the end of year 1 would not result in reclassification because the assessment would be based only on the terms at inception of the contract. Alternatively, in considering the guidance in IAS 39, the conversion option would be reclassified from a derivative liability to equity, because the obligation to deliver a variable number of shares upon conversion expires and the obligation to then deliver a fixed number of shares meets the definition of equity.

7.15.5 Reclassifications of puttable instruments and obligations arising on liquidation are dealt with from paragraph 7.24.8.

The next paragraph is 7.17.]

Contracts that are settled in cash or another financial assets

Contractual obligation to settle in cash or another financial assets

7.17 It is apparent from the above IAS 32 definitions of liability and equity instrument that the critical feature that distinguishes a liability from an equity instrument is the existence of a contractual obligation to deliver cash or another financial asset to the holder or to exchange a financial asset or financial liability with the holder under conditions that are potentially unfavourable to the issuer. In other words, if the issuer does not have an unconditional right to avoid delivering cash or another financial asset to settle a contractual obligation, the obligation meets the definition of a liability, with the limited exception of puttable instruments and obligations arising on liquidation that meet the strict criteria set out from paragraph 7.23.

7.18 An instrument that an issuer may be obliged to settle in cash or another financial instrument is a liability regardless of the manner in which it otherwise could be settled. For example, the obligation to deliver cash may cover the basic obligation either to repay the principal or interest/dividends or both. Also, the obligation need not be discharged in cash or another financial asset; it could be discharged by transfer of other kinds of assets in certain circumstances (for example, a property) as illustrated in paragraph 7.27 below. Indeed, in some circumstances it can even be settled by the issuer's own equity instruments. As long as the instrument involves a contractual unconditional obligation to deliver cash or another financial asset, that instrument (or component of the instrument) should be classified and accounted for as a liability (with the exception of certain puttable instruments and obligations arising on liquidation). Some examples of instruments that contain an obligation to transfer cash are considered below:

> **Example 1 – 6% mandatorily redeemable preference shares with mandatory fixed dividends**
>
> Preference share is the name given to any share that has some preferential rights in relation to other classes of shares, particularly in relation to ordinary shares. These preferential rights are of great variety, but refer normally to the right to a *fixed dividend*, although they could also refer to the right on winding up to receive a fixed part of the *capital* or otherwise to participate in the distribution of the company's assets (shares with such rights are often known as participating preference shares).
>
> In determining whether a mandatorily redeemable preference share is a financial liability or an equity instrument, it is necessary to examine the particular contractual rights attaching to the instrument's principal and return components.

The instrument, in this example, provides for mandatory periodic fixed dividend payments and mandatory redemption by the issuer for a fixed amount at a fixed future date. Since there is a contractual obligation to deliver cash (for both dividends and repayment of principal) to the shareholder that cannot be avoided, the instrument is a financial liability in its entirety.

Example 2 – Non-redeemable preference shares with mandatory fixed dividends

When preference shares are non-redeemable, the appropriate classification is determined by the other rights that attach to them. Classification is based on an assessment of the contractual arrangement's substance and the definitions of a financial liability and an equity instrument. [IAS 32 para AG 26].

It is necessary to examine the particular contractual rights attaching to the instrument's principal and return components. In this example, the shares are non-redeemable and thus the amount of the principal has equity characteristics, but the entity has a contractual obligation to pay dividends that provides the shareholders with a lender's return. This obligation is not negated if the entity is unable to pay the dividends because of lack of funds or insufficient distributable profits. Therefore, the obligation to pay the dividends meets the definition of a financial liability. The overall classification is that the shares may be a compound instrument, which may require each component to be accounted for separately (see further para 7.65 below). It would be a compound instrument if the coupon was initially set at a rate other than the prevailing market rate (an 'off-market' rate) or the terms specified payment of discretionary dividends in addition to the fixed coupon. If the coupon on the preference shares was set at market rates at the date of issue and there were no provisions for the payment of discretionary dividends, the entire instrument would be classified as a financial liability, because the stream of cash flows is in perpetuity.

Example 3 – Perpetual debt

'Perpetual' debt instruments (such as 'perpetual' bonds, debentures and capital notes) normally provide the holder with the contractual right to receive payments on account of interest at fixed dates extending into the indefinite future. The holder either has no right to receive a return of principal or a right to a return of principal under terms that make it very unlikely or very far in the future.

In this example, the instrument is perpetual and non-redeemable, but the entity has a contractual obligation to deliver cash in the form of interest payments to perpetuity. The obligation to pay interest meets the definition of a financial liability. For example, an entity may issue a financial instrument requiring it to make annual payments in perpetuity equal to a stated interest rate of 8% applied to a stated par or principal amount of C1m. Assuming 8% to be the market rate of interest for the instrument when issued, the instrument is classified as a liability in its entirety at the net present value of the interest payments. In this situation, the instrument's holder and issuer have a financial asset and a financial liability, respectively. [IAS 32 para AG 6].

Example 4 – Zero coupon bond

A zero coupon bond is an instrument where no interest is payable during the instrument's life and that is normally issued at a deep discount to the value at which it will be redeemed. Although there are no mandatory periodic interest payments, the instrument provides for mandatory redemption by the issuer for a determinable amount at a fixed or determinable future date. Since there is a contractual obligation to deliver cash for the value at which the bond will be redeemed, the instrument is classified as a financial liability.

7.18.1 Paragraph 19 of IAS 32 states that a contractual obligation does not give rise to a financial liability if the entity has an unconditional right to avoid delivering cash or another financial asset in settlement of that obligation. Shareholders as a collective body make key decisions affecting an entity's financial position and performance over its life (for example regarding the distribution of dividends). Hence, their decisions have to be analysed from an accounting perspective. Shareholders can make decisions as part of the entity (as members of the entity's corporate governance structure) or they can be separate and distinct from the entity itself when making these decisions (as holders of a particular instrument). In light of the accounting principles under IAS 32, the role of shareholders – that is whether they are viewed as 'part of the entity' or as 'separate and distinct from the entity' – is critical in determining the classification of financial instruments where the entity's shareholders decide whether the entity delivers cash or another financial asset under those instruments.

7.18.2 Shares usually have voting rights leading to a two-fold role for a shareholder: (1) a holder of a financial instrument issued by the entity and (2) a member of the corporate governance structure of the entity. In other words, in addition to the contractual rights to cash flows (for example, dividends), the shareholder has a contractual right to participate in the decision-making process of the entity's governing body. Shareholder rights in relation to the entity's decision making process are generally exercised collectively in a general shareholder meeting (GSM). In many jurisdictions, corporate law stipulates that the GSM is one of the governing bodies of the entity and prescribes a specific process regarding how a GSM is to be held, who is entitled to propose an agenda item and how decisions are to be taken. In order to determine whether collective decisions of shareholders are decisions of the entity, it is necessary to determine whether these decisions are made as part of the entity's normal decision making process for similar transactions.

7.18.3 If the decisions are made as part of the entity's normal decision-making process for similar transactions, the shareholders are considered to be part of the entity. For example, if an entity's equity instruments embody a contractual obligation to pay cash, but the shareholders can as part of their normal decision making process for this type of transaction refuse to make such a cash payment, the shares would be classified as equity. The entity in this case has an unconditional right to avoid the payment of cash. [IAS 32 para 19].

7.18.4 If the decisions are not made as part of the entity's normal decision making process for similar transactions (for example, one shareholder or a class of shareholders can make the decision and this is not the process the entity generally follows to make financial decisions), the shareholders are viewed as separate and distinct from the entity. For example, if a single shareholder can make a decision that creates a contractual obligation for the issuer to pay cash for the entity's shares and such decisions normally require a majority of the shareholder votes, these shares would be classified as a liability. The entity in this case does not have an unconditional right to avoid payment of cash. See paragraph 7.51 for more examples.

Restriction on the ability to satisfy contractual obligations

7.19   A restriction on the ability of an entity to satisfy a contractual obligation, such as lack of access to foreign currency or the need to obtain approval for payment from a regulatory authority, does not negate the entity's contractual obligation or the holder's contractual right under the instrument. [IAS 32 para 19(a)]. For example, an obligation is not negated even if the instrument's terms are such that the amount payable on redemption is dependent on the company having sufficient distributable profits or reserves. A type of income bond where the bond is not redeemable by the issuer, but interest is payable only in the event that the issuer has sufficient distributable profits, is such an instrument. The bond would be classified as a liability because of the obligation to pay interest. The fact that the obligation to pay is dependent on the existence of profits makes the obligation contingent, but it does not remove the obligation (see further chapter 4).

Puttable instruments and obligations arising on liquidation

7.20   Other than those instruments that meet the criteria set out from paragraph 7.24.5 below, financial instruments that give the holder the right to put them back to the issuer for cash or another financial asset (a 'puttable instrument') are financial liabilities. For example, an entity that issues a preference share that is puttable by the holder at some future date would recognise a financial liability. The holder has a put option that requires the issuer to redeem the instrument for cash or another financial asset at some future date. Since the existence of an option for the holder to put the instrument back to the issuer for cash or another financial asset means that the issuer does not have an unconditional right to avoid delivering cash or cash equivalent, the puttable instrument meets the definition of a financial liability. This is so whether or not the amount of cash or other financial assets to be delivered to the holder is fixed. For example it may be determined on the basis of an index or other item that has the potential to increase or decrease the final amount payable. [IAS 32 para 18(b)]. In these situations, from the issuer's perspective, the embedded put option is a written option that may need to be separated from the host contract, unless the whole instrument is accounted for at fair value through profit or loss. Embedded derivatives are discussed in chapter 5. Puttable instruments can also arise in finite life entities, as noted in the example below.

Example – Obligation arising on the liquidation of the issuer

A limited partnership has a finite life of 25 years. The partnership's equity will be redeemed at the end of its term.

In this situation, unless the criteria in paragraph 7.24.5 are met, the partnership's equity will be presented as a liability because the amount is payable only on liquidation and liquidation is certain (that is, not contingent) as the entity has a finite life.

Even where a partnership has an indefinite life, if a partner's equity interest is redeemable upon a partner's death, that partner's equity interest should be classified as a liability, unless the criteria applicable to puttable financial instruments in paragraph 7.24.5 are met. This is because the redemption is based on an event that is certain to occur, although the partnership itself is not being liquidated.

7.21 Financial instruments that would be classified as equity if the holders did not have the right to request redemption are equity if the entity has the unconditional right to refuse redemption of the instrument. This is the case even if, in practice, the entity rarely does refuse a holder's request for redemption or if the unconditional right to refuse redemption arises from local law, regulation or the entity's governing charter rather than the terms of the instrument itself. Sometimes redemption is prohibited only if conditions, such as liquidity constraints, are met (or not met). In such cases, the entity still has an obligation in respect of the holder's redemption rights, as the conditions merely defer the payment of a liability already incurred. Alternatively, an unconditional prohibition may be partial. For example, a co-operative entity may be prohibited from redeeming its members' shares if redemption would cause the number of shares to fall below a specified level. In such circumstances, only members' shares in excess of the prohibition against redemption are liabilities. The number of shares or the amount of paid-in capital subject to a redemption prohibition may change over time. Such a change in the redemption prohibition leads to a transfer between financial liabilities and equity. The amount, timing and reason for the transfer should be separately disclosed. [IFRIC 2 paras 5-13].

[The next paragraph is 7.23.]

7.23 In February 2008 the IASB published 'Amendments to IAS 32 and IAS 1, 'Puttable financial instruments and obligations arising on liquidation' (the amendment). Some financial instruments, commonly issued by open-ended mutual funds, unit trusts, partnerships and some co-operative entities, allow the holder to 'put' the instrument – that is, require the issuer to redeem the instrument for cash or another financial asset – on terms that give the holder an equity-like return. Before the amendment, such financial instruments were classified as financial liabilities rather than equity, because of the contractual obligation for the issuer to deliver cash if the put is exercised by the holder, as discussed above.

7.24 The amendment introduces a limited exception to this rule. It requires financial instruments that would otherwise meet the definition of a financial liability to be classified as equity where certain strict criteria are met, as set out in paragraph 7.24.5. Those instruments addressed by the amendment are:

- Puttable financial instruments. A puttable instrument is defined as a financial instrument that gives the holder the right to put the instrument back to the issuer for cash or another financial asset or is automatically put back to the issuer on the occurrence of an uncertain future event or the death or retirement of the instrument holder. [IAS 32 para 11].

■ Instruments, or components of instruments, that impose on the entity an obligation to deliver to another party a *pro rata* share of the entity's net assets only on liquidation. The obligation arises because liquidation is either certain to occur (such as in limited life entities) or is uncertain to occur but is at the option of the instrument holder. [IAS 32 para 16C].

7.24.1 The amendment's scope is limited to non-derivative contracts. Derivative contracts (such as warrants) to be settled by the issue of a fixed number of financial instruments classified as equity under the amendment for a fixed amount of cash or other financial asset cannot be equity themselves. [IAS 32 para 11].

7.24.2 The amendment should not be used by analogy. [IAS 32 para 96B]. Furthermore, the classification of instruments under this exception should be restricted to the accounting for such an instrument under IAS 32, IAS 39, IFRS 7 and IAS 1. The instruments should not be considered an equity instrument under other guidance, in particular IFRS 2, 'Share-based payments'. [IAS 32 para 96C].

7.24.3 Entities should apply the amendment for accounting periods beginning on or after 1 January 2009. The amendment is applied retrospectively if applicable.

7.24.4 The concurrent amendment to IAS 1 requires disclosures about financial instruments classified as equity as a result of the amendment to IAS 32. Detail about these disclosures is given in chapter 23 of the IFRS Manual of Accounting.

Criteria to be classified as equity

7.24.5 A non-derivative puttable instrument or obligation on liquidation (for example, arising in a limited life entity) is classified as equity only if all of the following criteria are met:

Criteria	Comment
1 The financial instrument is in the most subordinated class of instruments. That is, it: ■ has no priority over other claims to the entity's assets on liquidation; and ■ does not need to be converted to another instrument before it is in the most subordinated class. [IAS 32 paras 16A(b) and 16C(b)].	The instrument's claim on liquidation is assessed as if the entity were to liquidate on the date of classification. [IAS 32 para AG14B]. If an entity has two equally subordinated classes of instrument with different terms, neither can be classified as equity under the amendment. Additionally, if an open-ended investment fund has a small class of non-redeemable voting management shares that are the most subordinated, and a large class of non-voting investor shares that are puttable at fair value at the option of the holder, the investor shares are not the most subordinated class of instrument. Therefore, the non-voting investor shares cannot be classified as equity, regardless of the value or number of the management shares.
2 For puttable instruments, all instruments in its class should have identical features. [IAS 32 para 16A(c)]. For obligations arising on liquidation, only the obligation on liquidation should be identical for all instruments in that class. [IAS 32 para 16C(c)].	To be identical, all puttable instruments in a class should: ■ have the same formula or other method to calculate the redemption price; ■ rank equally on liquidation; ■ have identical voting rights; and ■ have all other features identical (for example, calls, management fees, currency of denomination). For example, an open-ended fund has two sub-funds – sub-fund A and sub-fund B – and two classes of puttable share – A shares and B shares – whose returns are based on the performance of sub-funds A and B respectively. The A and B shares are both the most subordinated class of shares in the fund's consolidated financial statements. However, neither are equity, as they do not have identical features because they carry rights to different sub-funds.

3   The instrument should entitle the holder to a *pro rata* share of the entity's net assets on liquidation. [IAS 32 paras 16A(a) and 16C(a)].

An instrument with a preferential right on liquidation is not an instrument with an entitlement to a *pro rata* share of the entity's net assets. So if a puttable instrument has a right to a fixed dividend on liquidation in addition to a share of the entity's net assets, but the other instruments in the class do not have the same right on liquidation, none of the shares in that class are equity. [IAS 32 para AG14C].

4   For puttable instruments only, the total expected cash flows attributable to the instrument over the instrument's life should be based substantially on the profit or loss, the change in recognised net assets, or the change in the fair value of entity over the instrument's life (excluding any effects of the instrument). [IAS 32 para 16A(e)].

Profit or loss and the change in recognised net assets should be measured in accordance with the relevant IFRSs and not any other GAAP. [IAS 32 para AG14E].

Cash flows attributable to the instrument over its life should be based on the profit or loss or change in the entity's net assets as a whole, not just part of the entity's business.

This condition would be met where the put is for cash equivalent to the entity's:
- fair value;
- IFRS book value of assets; or
- approximation to fair value using a formula based on net profit, for example, multiples of EBITDA, provided that the formula (for example, the multiple used) is reviewed regularly to ensure that it results in an approximate of fair value.

5   There are no other instruments that:
- substantially restrict or fix the return earned by the instrument holder; and
- have cash flows based substantially on profit or loss; the change in recognised net assets; or the change in the fair value of the entity over the instrument's life (excluding any effects of the instrument). [IAS 32 paras 16B and 16D].

If an instrument provides a fixed or limited return because of the interaction with other instruments issued by the entity (for example, another instrument is participating in the share of net assets), it is not equity.

Non-financial contracts with the holder of the instrument should be ignored if those contracts have similar terms and conditions to an equivalent contract that might occur between a non-instrument holder and the entity. However, if the entity cannot determine that the non-financial contract with the puttable instrument holder is similar to an equivalent contract that might occur between a non-instrument holder and the issuing entity, it should not classify the puttable instrument as an equity instrument.

Examples of contracts entered into on normal commercial terms with unrelated parties that are unlikely to prevent puttable instruments from being classified as equity include:
- Instruments with cash flows substantially based on individual assets of the entity or on a percentage of revenue, such as commission arrangements.
- Employee profit-related performance bonuses.
- Contracts requiring the payment of an insignificant percentage of profit for services rendered or goods provided.

[IAS 32 para AG14J].

6   For puttable instruments only, the instrument should not contain any liability features, other than the put itself. [IAS 32 para 16A(d)].

For instruments containing obligations arising on liquidation there is no requirement for there to be no other contractual obligations, so the instrument may be compound (for example, a compound instrument where the liability component is extinguished over the instrument's life).

However, a puttable instrument cannot have another contractual obligation apart from the put itself and, hence, can never be a compound instrument.

For example, a puttable financial instrument that contains an obligation to either:

- distribute current period profits on the demand of each holder based on a *pro rata* share of the entity's profits; or
- distribute all taxable income as a requirement of the entity's constitution

cannot be classed as an equity instrument.

Transactions entered into by an instrument holder other than as owner of the entity

7.24.6   In certain situations the holder of a puttable instrument may enter into transactions with the entity in a role other than that of an owner. For example, a partner in a partnership may also provide management services to the entity or be remunerated for providing a financial guarantee for the partnership's debts. In other cases, rebates are given to the instrument holders based on their services rendered or business generated during the current and previous years. Such cash flows and contractual terms and conditions should be disregarded for the purposes of determining the classification of an instrument under all the criteria above, as long as they are similar to an equivalent transaction that might occur between a non-instrument holder and the issuing entity, that is, at arm's length. [IAS 32 para AG14I]. This is because such cash flows and contractual features are separate and distinct from the cash flows and contractual features of the puttable financial instrument.

Impact on consolidation

7.24.7   Instruments issued by a subsidiary that meet the criteria outlined above, and are, therefore, within the scope of the amendment at a separate or individual financial statements level, are not considered to be the most subordinated class from the group's perspective. [IAS 32 para BC 68]. Furthermore, the total expected cash flows over the life of a puttable financial instrument issued by a subsidiary will not be substantially based on the profit or loss or change in net assets of the whole group, but rather will be a subset of that group, being that of the subsidiary. Consequently, a puttable non-controlling interest is always classified as a liability on consolidation, even if it is classified as an equity interest in the subsidiary's own financial statements [IAS 32 para AG 29A].

7.24.7.1   Instruments issued by the parent that meet the criteria outlined above, and are, therefore, within the scope of the amendment at a separate financial statements level, in most cases will continue to be classified as equity at a consolidated financial statements level. Any non-controlling interest reflected at the group level does not generally meet the conditions in paragraph 16B of IAS 32 and, therefore, will generally not prevent such parent puttable instruments from being classified as equity on consolidation. This is because:

■ cash flows attributable to the non-controlling interest are based on a subset of the consolidated net assets, that is, net assets of the respective subsidiary, rather than consolidated net assets; and

■ in most cases the non-controlling interest will not have the effect of substantially restricting or fixing the residual return attributable to holders of the parent's puttable instruments.

[IAS 32 paras 16B, AG14J(a)].

7.24.7.2 If, however, the non-controlling interest meets the conditions in paragraph 16B of IAS 32 the parent's puttable instruments that meet the conditions for equity classification at a separate financial statements level are classified as a liability on consolidation. This will be the case when:

■ the subsidiary's net assets represent substantially all of the consolidated net assets such that the cash flows attributable to the non-controlling interest are substantially based on consolidated net assets; and

■ the non-controlling interest in the respective subsidiary is so significant that combined with the condition above it has the effect of substantially restricting or fixing the residual return attributable to holders of the parent's puttable instruments.

Judgement is applied to determine whether the subsidiary's net assets and the non-controlling interest in the respective subsidiary are so significant that the parent's puttable instruments classified as equity at a separate financial statements level are classified as a liability on consolidation.

7.24.7.3 The evaluation of instruments, or components of instruments, that impose on the entity an obligation to deliver to another party a *pro rata* share of the net assets of the entity only on liquidation will follow the criteria above as the requirements of paragraph 16D of IAS 32 are consistent with paragraph 16B.

Reclassification of puttable instruments and obligations arising on liquidation

7.24.8 Instruments will be in the scope of the amendment from the date when the instrument has all the features and meets the criteria set out above. This may not occur at the date of issue of the instrument, so it is necessary to reassess the classification if there is a change in relevant circumstances. For example, an entity may issue or redeem other instruments that change the most subordinated class of shares, which may require reclassification of some financial instruments from debt to equity or vice versa. [IAS 32 para 16E]. See chapter 23 of the IFRS Manual of Accounting for specific disclosure requirements on such a reclassification.

7.24.9 An entity should reclassify a financial instrument when appropriate, as follows:

■ Reclassify an equity instrument to a financial liability from the date the instrument ceases to have all the features required by the amendment. The financial liability is measured at the instrument's fair value at the date of reclassification. Any difference between the carrying value of the equity instrument and liability's fair value on the date of reclassification is recognised in equity.

■ Reclassify a financial liability as equity from the date the instrument has all the features required by the amendment. The equity instrument should be measured at the carrying value of the financial liability at the date of reclassification. [IAS 32 para 16F].

Own share buy-back programmes

7.25 During certain times of the year (for example, before an entity releases its results), listed companies are prohibited by certain local listing rules from buying their own shares in the market. The local listing rules may permit other arrangements to be entered into with independent third parties that result in the listed entity's shares being purchased on behalf of the listed entity, for example, by a bank. The contract requires the company to buy the shares the bank has purchased immediately after the prohibition period. For further details on own share buy-back programmes see chapter 23 of the IFRS Manual of Accounting.

7.26 Own share buy-back programmes contain an obligation for an entity to purchase its own equity instruments for cash or another financial asset from the third party. This, therefore, gives rise to a financial liability for the present value of the redemption amount (for example, the present value of the forward repurchase price, option exercise price or other redemption amount). [IAS 32 para 23].

Absence of explicit obligations

7.27 IAS 32 states that the obligation to deliver cash or another financial asset need not be explicitly stated in the instrument. It may be established indirectly. However, the indirect obligation must be established through the terms and conditions of the financial instrument. [IAS 32 para 20]. IAS 32 clarifies the notion that an instrument may establish an obligation indirectly through its terms and conditions in two specific situations that are considered below.

7.28 First, a financial instrument may contain a non-financial obligation that must be settled if, and only if, the entity fails to make distributions or to redeem the instrument. If the entity can avoid a transfer of cash or another financial asset only by settling the non-financial obligation, the financial instrument is a financial liability. [IAS 32 para 20(a)].

Example – Settlement of obligation by transfer of non-cash asset

A property company raises C150m for constructing a number of properties. The loan has a maturity period of 5 years. The loan agreement stipulates that the property company must transfer to the lender one of its investment properties if it is unable to settle the loan for cash at maturity.

In this agreement, if the property company is unable to settle the loan at maturity for cash, it is obliged to settle the obligation by transferring to the lender one of its other investment properties that, at the time of the settlement, may well be in excess of C150m. Therefore, an indirect financial obligation arises as the agreement contains a non-financial obligation that can be avoided only by making a transfer of cash. Hence, it is a financial liability.

7.29   The second situation is where a financial instrument is a financial liability if it provides that on settlement the entity will deliver either:

- cash or another financial asset; or
- its own shares whose value is determined to exceed substantially the value of the cash or other financial asset.

Although the entity does not have an explicit contractual obligation to deliver cash or another financial asset, the value of the share settlement alternative is such that the entity will have little choice but to redeem the obligation in cash. In any event, the holder has been guaranteed, in substance, receipt of an amount that is at least equal to the cash settlement option. Hence, the instrument is a financial liability.

[IAS 32 para 20(b)].

7.30   The IFRIC clarified in March 2006 that where an instrument (the 'base' instrument) contains a clause that requires cash or other financial assets to be delivered on that base instrument if there is a contractual obligation to make payment on another (the 'linked') instrument, then the inclusion of this linker clause would establish an indirect obligation to deliver cash or another financial assets on the base instrument. As a result the IFRIC agreed that the base instrument would be classified as a financial liability.

Example – Financial instrument ('base' instrument) linked to another (the 'linked') instrument

An entity issues non-redeemable callable preference shares (the 'base' instrument) with dividends that must be paid if interest is paid on another (the 'linked') instrument. The issuer must pay the interest on the 'linked' instrument that is also perpetual.

In this example, the linkage to the linked instrument, on which there is a contractual obligation to pay interest, results in an indirect contractual obligation to pay dividends on the base instrument. If the linked instrument is callable by the issuer at any time, the issuer could avoid paying the dividends on the base instrument. Therefore, until the linked instrument is called, a contractual obligation to pay dividends on the base instrument exists. If the present value of the expected dividend stream to perpetuity is equal to the whole principal of the financial instrument, the entire instrument would be classified as a liability. On the other hand, if the present value of the expected dividend stream is not equal to the whole principal of the financial instrument, the residual amount is attributable to the equity component.

7.30.1 Indirect obligations are considered part of the terms and conditions of a contract. A change to the indirect obligations of an instrument, which would include the repurchase by the entity of the 'linked' instrument in the above example, is, therefore, considered a change to the contract's contractual terms and conditions.

7.30.2 Whether changes to the terms of a 'base' liability that remove any contractual obligation to pay cash or transfer another financial asset result in extinguishment accounting is a matter of accounting policy choice as such changes are not specifically addressed in IAS 32 and such a transaction is not within IFRIC 19's scope. An entity can apply the same accounting treatment as when convertible debt is converted into shares (see para 7.70) where the existing debt's carrying value is transferred to equity and no gain or loss arises on conversion. Alternatively, the entity applies the extinguishment principles in chapter 8 where the existing instrument is derecognised and the new equity instruments issued are recognised at fair value. The difference would be recognised in profit or loss. [IAS 39 para 41].

Contracts settled in cash or other financial asset that are discretionary or at the option of the issuer

7.31 An equity instrument is any contract that evidences a residual interest in an entity's assets after deducting all of its liabilities. Therefore, only those instruments (or components of instruments) that do not meet the definition of a liability will be classified as equity. In other words, the entity must have an unconditional right to avoid delivery of cash or another financial asset. A typical example is an entity's non-puttable ordinary shares. The exception to this principle is when a puttable instrument or an obligation arising on liquidation meets the strict criteria in the February 2008 amendment to IAS 32 to be classified as equity (see para 7.24.5).

Payments that are discretionary or at the option of the issuer

7.32 If an instrument does not have a contractual (including contingent) obligation to deliver cash or another financial asset, it is classified as an equity instrument. Therefore, where payments of interest/dividends or the principal amount or both are discretionary in nature, equity treatment is appropriate for some or all of the instrument. For example, dividends payable on non-puttable ordinary shares depend on the entity's profitability. However, there is no compulsion on the directors to declare a dividend even though a past pattern of dividend payments may have created an expectation on the shareholders that a dividend will be declared and payable. Such discretionary payments do not create contractual obligations, because the directors cannot be required to deliver cash or another financial asset to the shareholders. Nevertheless, a liability must be recognised in respect of such non-puttable ordinary shares where the directors formally act to make a distribution and become legally obligated to the shareholders to do so. This may be the case following the declaration of a dividend, or when the entity is being wound up and any assets remaining after the satisfaction of liabilities become distributable to shareholders. [IAS 32 para AG 13]. Chapter 23 of the IFRS Manual of Accounting provides further guidance on the accounting for dividends.

> **Example – Non-redeemable preference shares with dividend payments linked to ordinary shares**
>
> An entity issues an non-redeemable preference shares on which dividends are payable only if the entity also pays a dividend on its ordinary shares ('dividend pusher').
>
> In this example, the dividend payments on the preference shares are discretionary and not contractual, because no dividends can be paid if no dividends are paid on the ordinary shares, which are an equity instrument. As the perpetual preference shares contain no contractual obligation ever to pay dividends and there is no obligation to repay the principal, they should be classified as equity in their entirety.
>
> Where the dividend payments are also cumulative, that is, if no dividends are paid on the ordinary shares, the preference dividends are deferred, the perpetual shares will be classified as equity only if the dividends can be deferred indefinitely and the entity does not have any contractual obligations whatsoever to pay those dividends.
>
> A liability for the dividend payable would be recognised once the dividend is declared.

7.33 The classification of a preference share as an equity instrument or a financial liability would not be impacted by, for example:

- A history of making distributions.

- An intention to make distributions in the future.

- A possible negative impact on price of the issuer's ordinary shares if distributions are not made (because of restrictions on paying dividends on the ordinary shares if dividends are not paid on the preference shares).

- The amount of the issuer's reserves.

- An issuer's expectation of a profit or loss for a period.

- An ability or inability of the issuer to influence the amount of its profit or loss for the period.

[IAS 32 para AG 26].

7.34 As explained in paragraph 7.20 unless, exceptionally, the criteria to be treated as equity in the February 2008 amendment to IAS 32 are met, where the holder has a put option that requires the issuer to redeem equity shares at some future date, the instrument (that is the equity shares and the put) is treated as a liability; the issuer cannot avoid settling the principal in cash. On the other hand, as discussed in chapter 5, if the issuer has an option to call or redeem what would be otherwise equity shares for cash at some future date, the instrument does not satisfy the definition of a financial liability as the issuer can avoid settling the principal in cash. This is because the issuer does not have a present obligation to transfer financial assets to the shareholders. In this case, redemption of the shares is solely at the issuer's discretion. An obligation may arise, however, when the issuer of the shares exercises its option, usually by formally notifying the shareholders of an intention to redeem the shares. [IAS 32 para AG 25].

7.34.1   The accounting treatment becomes more complex when the issuer has the option to avoid settling an instrument in cash through exercising an option to convert the instrument into a fixed number of equity shares, as illustrated below.

Example – Instrument convertible only at the option of issuer

An entity issues an instrument with the following terms

■   The instrument has a stated 5% coupon that is mandatory.

■   The issuer has an option to convert the instrument into a fixed number of its own shares at any time. The holder has no conversion option.

■   The issuer has an option to redeem the instrument in cash at any time. The redemption price is the fair value of the fixed number of shares into which the instrument would have converted if it had been converted. The holder has no redemption option.

■   The instrument has a 30 year stated maturity and, if not converted or redeemed previously, will be repaid in cash at maturity for its par value plus accrued but unpaid interest.

There are two valid views regarding the classification of the instrument by the issuer depending on analysis of the host contract (that is, liability host versus equity host). Therefore, we consider that an issuer has a policy choice between the following two treatments

(1)   The host contract can be viewed as an equity instrument, as the issuer has the ability to convert the instrument into a fixed number of its own shares at any time. It, therefore, has the ability to avoid making a cash payment or settling the instrument in a variable number of its own shares. Any feature that may have been considered to be an embedded derivative would not meet the definition of a derivative on a stand-alone basis given the ability to avoid payment. Hence, the issuer's conversion and redemption options would not be separated and the entire instrument would be classified as equity.

(2)   The issuer can classify this instrument as a liability, being a hybrid instrument comprised of:

(a)   a host liability component for the obligation to pay the mandatory coupons and to repay the instrument at maturity; and

(b)   an embedded derivative component for the entity's option to settle the instrument early in either a fixed number of its own shares or cash of an equivalent value. As these two early settlement mechanisms are interdependent, they are viewed as part of a single embedded derivative rather than as two separate embedded derivatives.

If option 2 is taken as a policy choice then the issuer has a second decision to make with regards measurement. On initial recognition either the fair value option can be taken in accordance with IAS 39 (as there is a significant embedded derivative) and the entire contract will be measured at fair value through profit or loss, or the issuer can value the host liability contract at amortised cost and separate the embedded derivative.

7.35   Where a financial instrument only results in a contractual obligation for the issuer to deliver cash or other financial assets upon the occurrence of an uncertain future event, the instrument may still need to be classified as a financial liability from initial recognition if it meets the definition of a contingent settlement event. See paragraph 7.50 for more details.

Contracts that will or may be settled in an entity's own equity instruments

7.36   A contract is not an equity instrument solely because it may result in the receipt or delivery of the entity's own equity instruments. [IAS 32 para 21]. The classification of contracts that will or may be settled in the entity's own equity instruments is dependent on whether there is variability in either the number of own equity instruments delivered and/or variability in the amount of cash or other financial assets received, or whether both are fixed.

7.37   A contract that will be settled by the entity receiving (or delivering) a fixed number of its own equity instruments in exchange for a fixed amount of cash or another financial asset is an equity instrument [IAS 32 para 22]. This is commonly referred to as the 'fixed for fixed' requirement. For example, an entity receives C100 upfront from the holder to issue 100 of the entity's own equity in three years time. This would meet the 'fixed for fixed' requirement as both the number of own equity shares delivered and the cash received is fixed when the financial instrument is initially recognised. The instrument would meet the definition of an equity instrument as the holder gets a residual interest in the entity. By fixing upfront the amount paid and the number of shares received the holder benefits from any upside and suffers the loss from any fall in the residual value of the entity.

7.38   However, an entity may have a contractual right or obligation to receive or deliver a number of its own shares or other equity instruments that varies so that the fair value of the entity's own equity instrument to be received or delivered equals the amount of the contractual right or obligation. Such a contract may be for a fixed amount or an amount that fluctuates in part or in full in response to changes in a variable. [IAS 32 para 21]. It would be inappropriate to account for such contracts as an equity instrument when an entity's own equity instruments are used 'as currency' as such a contract represents a right or obligation for a specified amount rather than a specified residual equity interest. Therefore, such a contract would be classified as a financial liability. The underlying variable can include the entity's own share price. [IAS 32 para AG 27(d)].

Financial liabilities and equity

> **Example 1 – Own shares to the value of C1 million**
>
> An entity receives C1m in exchange for its promise that it will deliver its own equity shares in an amount sufficient to equal a value of C1m at a future date. If the share price at the date on delivery of the contract is C5, the entity would be required to issue 200,000 shares ie a total value of C1m.
>
> On the day the issuer delivers its own equity, the holder would be indifferent whether it received cash of C1m or shares to the value of C1m which it could sell and receive C1m in cash. Therefore, the entity is using its own equity as currency and as such the holder does not get a full residual interest. Hence the financial instrument is a liability.
>
> **Example 2 – Bermudan option with fixed but different strike prices**
>
> An entity issues an option to sell a fixed number of its own equity shares at a specified exercise price. The terms of the option state that the specified exercise price varies with the share price of the entity such that:
>
> | Share price | Conversion ratio |
> |---|---|
> | 0-10C | 10 shares at 1C per share |
> | 11-20C | 10 shares at 1.5C per share |
>
> The variability in the exercise price, as a function of share price of the entity, results in a variable amount of cash for a fixed number of shares. The 'fixed for fixed' requirement is therefore violated. The option is, therefore, classified as a derivative financial liability and not as an equity instrument.
>
> **Example 3 – Call options where the underlying is an exchange ratio**
>
> Entities A, B and X are all listed companies. Entity A purchases an option to buy 5% of the share capital of entity X from entity B in return for entity A delivering its own equity shares to entity B. The exchange ratio is fixed when the option is written (for example, entity A pays 0.8 of entity A's own shares for the purchase of an option over 1 share of entity X).
>
> This exchange ratio will violate the 'fixed for fixed' requirement. The fixed number of entity A's shares that entity A may issue is not equal to a fixed amount of cash, as the value of each share acquired in exchange can vary. Therefore, entity A must treat its purchased option as a derivative instrument under IAS 39.

7.39 The IASB was concerned that restricting the definition of an underlying variable could lead to structuring opportunities and abuse. Therefore, the standard requires that all forms of variability in either the own shares received or delivered, or the cash or another financial asset delivered or received, would result in financial asset or financial liability classification.

7.40 A contract that will be settled by an entity delivering a fixed number of its own equity instruments in exchange for a fixed amount of foreign currency (that is a currency other than the functional currency of the entity) is a financial liability. The exception to this rule, in relation to rights issues, applicable to accounting periods beginning on or after 1 February 2010 is discussed in paragraph 7.41. This is a liability because an obligation denominated in a foreign currency represents a variable amount of cash in the entity's functional currency. A foreign currency convertible bond (see example at para 7.79) is, therefore, a financial liability made up of two components. These components are: (1) a host bond denominated in the foreign currency (whose foreign exchange risk is accounted for under IAS 21, 'The effects of changes in foreign exchange rates') and (2) an embedded derivative which is a written option for the holder to exchange the foreign currency bond for a fixed number of functional currency denominated shares.

7.41 The IASB published an amendment to IAS 32, 'Financial instruments: Presentation' on the classification of rights issues on 8 October 2009. The amendment addresses the accounting for rights issues (including rights, options and warrants) that are denominated in a currency other than the functional currency of the issuer. The amendment states that, if such rights are issued pro rata to an entity's existing shareholders for a fixed amount of any currency, they should be classified as equity, regardless of the currency in which the exercise price is denominated. This is a narrow amendment and should not be extended to other instruments by analogy (for example, warrants or rights issues on other than a *pro rata* basis and foreign currency denominated convertible bonds – see paragraph 7.79). The amendment is effective for annual periods beginning on or after 1 February 2010, with early adoption permitted. If an entity applies the amendment to an earlier period it shall disclose that fact. An example of an entity that has applied the amendment is shown in Table 7.1 below.

Table 7.1 – classification of rights issues

HSBC Holdings plc – Annual report – 31 December 2009

1 Basis of preparation (extract)

(a) Compliance with International Financial Reporting Standards (extract)

During 2009, HSBC adopted the following significant standards and amendments to standards:
• 'Classification of Rights Issues – Amendment to IAS 32', ('the amendment') which is effective for annual periods beginning on or after 1 February 2010, with early adoption permitted. HSBC has elected to adopt the amendment in advance of the effective date and, as required by IAS 8, has applied the amendment retrospectively. The amendment requires that rights issues, options or warrants to acquire a fixed number of the entity's own equity instruments for a fixed amount of any currency are equity instruments if the entity offers the rights issues, options or warrants pro rata to all of its existing owners of the same class of its own non-derivative equity instruments. The offer of rights by HSBC Holdings plc to its shareholders on 20 March 2009 was accounted for as an equity instrument, as required by the amendment, in the consolidated financial statements of HSBC and the separate financial statements of HSBC Holdings.

2 Summary of significant accounting policies (extract)
(ac) Rights issues

Rights issues to acquire a fixed number of the entity's own equity instruments for a fixed amount of any currency are equity instruments if the entity offers the rights issues pro rata to all of its existing owners of the same class of its own non-derivative equity instruments. On initial recognition, these rights are recognised in shareholders' equity and are not subsequently re-measured during the offer period. Following the exercise of the rights and the allotment of new shares, the cash proceeds of the rights issue are recognised in shareholders' equity. Incremental costs directly attributable to the rights issue are shown as a deduction from the proceeds, net of tax.

---

41 Rights issue (extract)

On 2 March 2009, HSBC Holdings announced its proposal to raise £12.5 billion (US$17.8 billion), net of expenses, by way of a fully underwritten rights issue. Under the proposal, HSBC offered its shareholders the opportunity to acquire 5 new ordinary shares for every 12 ordinary shares at a price of 254 pence per new ordinary share. For shareholders on the Hong Kong and Bermuda Overseas Branch Registers this offer was expressed in Hong Kong dollars and US dollars, respectively, fixed at published exchange rates on 27 February 2009. The proposal was subject to authorisation by the shareholders which was obtained at a general meeting held on 19 March 2009. The offer period commenced on 20 March 2009 and closed for acceptance on 3 April 2009. Dealing in the new shares began on 6 April 2009.

For details of called-up share capital and other equity instruments see Note 37.

7.42   Some financial instruments (denominated in the same currency as the issuer's functional currency) may be settled in a variable number of own equity instruments but also include a cap or floor or both (that is, a collar) that limits that variability. The existence of the cap, floor or collar does not change the instruments classification from being a financial liability, as it is settled in a variable number of shares. However, it is necessary to determine whether the cap, floor or collar represents an embedded derivative and, if so, whether it is required to be separated out from the host instrument, as discussed in the examples below.

Example 1 – Instruments that are settled in a variable number of shares but subject to a cap

An entity issues an instrument that is settled at the end of the year by delivering equity shares to the value of C100. The fair value of the shares at the date of issue is C10. The instrument also contains a cap that limits the number of shares that the entity is required to deliver to 20 shares in order to prevent excessive dilution of the existing shareholders through the issue of new shares.

There are two acceptable views on how the cap should be accounted for. Therefore, the issuer has an accounting policy choice between the following two treatments.

View 1 – The contract is a non-derivative liability for a fixed monetary amount

The host contract is an obligation to issue a variable number of shares whose *value equals 100* (that is, a fixed monetary amount). The entire instrument is a liability on the grounds that the 'fixed for fixed' requirement in paragraph 16(b)(ii) of IAS 32 is not met for the instrument as a whole (that is, the instrument is settled in a variable number of shares).

The cap itself is scoped out of IAS 39 because it meets the definition of equity under IAS 32 since it results in the exchange of a fixed amount of cash (that is, the fixed monetary amount of 100) for a fixed number of shares of 20. However, it is not recognised separately as an equity component under IAS 32 because paragraph 16(b)(i) is applied to the whole instrument (rather than only the cap), and the whole instrument results in the delivery of a variable number of shares. Paragraph 25 of IAS 32 further supports this view because the movement in share price that determines the number of shares to be delivered under the contract (that is, to the fixed monetary amount of 100) is outside the control of the issuer and the holder.

View 2 – Contract contains a debt host with a purchased put

The host instrument is an obligation to deliver a *variable number of shares* which is a liability. The instrument also contains an embedded derivative whose effect is to cap the amount of shares the entity will have to deliver according to the debt host, so that, overall, the issuer does not deliver shares in excess of the cap. This embedded derivative can be viewed as a purchased put that will be net share settled (that is, the number of shares to be delivered under the put will vary depending on the share price so that the overall contract results in the delivery of the capped number of shares).

As the cap is not closely related to the debt host (it is linked to movements in the share price), the embedded cap would need to be bifurcated and accounted for at fair value through profit and loss (assuming the fair value option is not used for the entire contract).

Example 2 – Instruments that are settled in a variable number of shares but subject to a cap and floor (that is, a collar)

An entity issues an instrument that is settled at the end of the year by delivering equity shares to the value of C100. The fair value of the shares at the date of issue is C10. The instrument also contains:

■ A cap that limits the number of shares that the entity is required to deliver to 20 shares.

■ A floor that requires the entity to deliver a minimum of 5 shares.

The host instrument can be viewed as an obligation to deliver a variable number of shares to the value of C100 which is a liability. The instrument also contains two embedded derivatives: a cap and a floor. Because the cap and floor are linked to the same risk exposure (that is, the share price) and are interdependent, they cannot be analysed as two separate instruments. The cap and floor need to be bundled together and treated as a single compound embedded derivative [IAS 39 para AG 29]. This compound embedded derivative is within IAS 39's scope because it does not result in the delivery of a fixed amount of cash for a fixed number of shares and, therefore, needs to be assessed for bifurcation. However, note that even if was considered that the cap and floor were individually scoped out of IAS 39 as described in view 1 of example 1 for the instrument with a cap only the instrument as a whole would still be a liability on the basis that paragraph 16(b)(i) of IAS 32 results in the delivery of a variable number of shares. Assuming that the fair value option is not used for the entire contract, the cap and floor should be bifurcated as a single compound derivative that is not closely related to the debt host (the underlying of the compound derivative is the share price).

Alternatively if the instrument is viewed as a host instrument with an obligation to deliver a *variable number of shares* (as described in view 2 of example 1 for the instrument with a cap only), this debt host would contain both a purchased put for the cap that is net share settled as well as a written call for the floor that is net share settled. The cap and floor need to be bundled together and treated as a single embedded derivative as noted above. [IAS 32 para AG29].

As a result, under both approaches the instrument would be accounted for as a debt host with a compound embedded derivative that should be accounted for separately.

7.43 A single instrument should not be separated into a number of different instruments in order to satisfy the 'fixed for fixed' requirement where otherwise it would result in variability in either own equity, cash or another financial asset, if accounted for as a single instrument. For example, variability resulting from interdependent profit levels.

Example – Contingent consideration varies with time and performance conditions

Entity A acquires entity B and the contingent consideration payable to the seller is based on the following terms:

- If a performance target of profits of C100m is achieved by entity B in year 1, 100 additional shares will be issued to the seller.

- If a performance target of profits of C200m is achieved by entity B by the end of year 2 (cumulative of year 1 and year 2), 150 more shares will be issued to the seller.

- Entity B must meet the performance target in year 1 in order to be eligible to earn the additional shares in year 2 (that is, it is not possible to only receive 150 shares)

Where there are multiple contingent events it must be determined whether the unit of account is the overall contract or separate contracts within that overall contract. In order to be assessed as separate contracts they must be readily separable and independent of each other and relate to different risk exposures. In this example the periods are not readily separable or independent of each other as the delivery of shares in year 2 depends on the profits and delivery of shares in year 1. This is considered as one overall contract that results in a variable number of shares. It fails the 'fixed for fixed' requirement and is classified as a liability not equity.

7.43.1 In November 2009 the IFRIC discussed whether a type of instrument where the exercise price is pre-determined at inception and only varies over time met the fixed for fixed condition and would, therefore, be classified as equity. The IFRIC acknowledged there is diversity in practice in accounting for such instruments, but rejected issuing interpretive guidance due to the longer term debt-equity project (Financial instruments with characteristics of equity – 'FICE') that is in progress.

7.43.2 In the light of the IFRIC discussions and diversity in practice, our view is that an entity may determine that such an instrument, where the exercise price is pre-determined at inception and only varies over time, meets the fixed for fixed condition and is classified as equity. If the strike price is not pre-determined at inception but determinable based on variables, such as the share price for example, the fixed for fixed condition would not be met. An entity may also determine that such an instrument where the exercise price is pre-determined at inception and only varies over time is a financial liability on the basis that the predetermination of the exercise price introduces some variability that fails the fixed for fixed criterion.

7.43.3 An entity's decision as to whether the fixed for fixed condition is met when the strike price is pre-determined at inception and only varies over time is an accounting policy decision that should be applied consistently and disclosed appropriately.

7.43.4 An entity that previously considered that the fixed for fixed condition was not met may continue with its existing policy or may change its policy by following the guidance for changes in accounting policy as discussed in chapter 5 of the IFRS Manual of Accounting.

> **Example – Variation in the cash received due to step-up adjustments**
>
> Entity A (US dollar functional currency) writes an option to entity B (not an employee) that enables entity B to buy 1 share of entity A on the following terms:
>
> ■ If the option is exercised in year 1 the strike price is $1.
>
> ■ If the option is exercised in year 2 the strike price is $2.
>
> ■ If the option is exercised in year 3 the strike price is $3.
>
> Entity A has a policy choice, which should be applied consistently.
>
> Entity may consider that the instrument is an equity instrument, because the exercise price is pre-determined and varies only with time. It, therefore, can be considered as meeting the condition that a fixed number of equity instruments will be issued for a fixed price.
>
> On the other hand, entity A may consider that the instrument is a derivative financial liability. Entity A may consider that the different strike prices introduce variability such that a fixed number of shares will not be issued for a fixed amount of cash.

7.44 Complexity arises in practice when applying the principles for settlement in an entity's own equity instruments. Although IAS 32 states that variability in either the entity's own equity delivered or cash or another financial asset received results in a financial liability, not all forms of variability do in fact violate the 'fixed for fixed' requirement, including the example of a pre-determined price that only varies over time in paragraph 7.43.4 above. Another example is an adjustment to the conversion ratio of a convertible bond triggered by a stock split. For example the original conversion ratio is 1 share for every £1 (with a notional value of £2), however, upon a stock split each share now has a notional value of £1. It would, therefore, be necessary to adjust the conversion ratio to 2 shares for every £1 in order to maintain the relative economic rights of the shareholders and bondholders. Although the adjustment results in variability in the number of own equity delivered, the fact that this variability serves to maintain the relative economic rights of the shareholders and bondholders results in no violation of the 'fixed for fixed' requirement.

7.45 Where variability is caused by the inclusion of an anti-dilution clause, such as the stock split clause outlined above, this will not result in a violation of the 'fixed for fixed' requirement provided, firstly the relative rights of the shareholders and bondholders are maintained, and secondly the instrument would otherwise meet the 'fixed for fixed' requirement. Other examples of anti-dilutive clauses are adjustments made for the payment of dividends and bonus issues, where new shares are issued to the entity's shareholders for no additional consideration though a capitalisation of reserves.

7.46 A common adjustment in convertible bonds is the inclusion of a change of control clause. The clause adjusts the otherwise fixed for fixed conversion ratio upon a change of control event. The purpose of the adjustment is to compensate the bondholder for the loss of optionality either through a stated compensation amount or via a formula. As this change in control adjustment is not compensation that relates to the issuance of the equity shares but rather is compensation for the loss of optionality, it does not affect the relative rights of the shareholders and bondholders and does not result in a violation of the 'fixed for fixed' requirement.

7.47 The table below sets out the classification in various scenarios where a fixed or variable monetary obligation (not indexed to the entity's own share price) is settled in a fixed number or variable number of the entity's own shares. Instruments classified as financial liabilities under IAS 32, will require further analysis under IAS 39 to determine whether any embedded derivatives require to be bifurcated.

Contract settled in the equity's own shares	Monetary value of consideration[1]	Number of equity shares	Classification
Scenario 1	Fixed	Variable	Financial liability
Scenario 2	Variable	Variable	Financial liability
Scenario 3	Variable	Fixed	Financial liability
Scenario 4	Fixed in a currency other than the entity's functional currency[2]	Fixed	Financial liability
Scenario 5	Fixed	Fixed	Equity

1 in the functional currency of the issuer.
2 subject to the exception discussed from paragraph 7.41.

7.48 IAS 32 does not deal with the option to exchange a fixed number of one kind of the entity's own equity for a fixed number of a different kind of equity. An example is an option for a minority shareholder to exchange its holding of shares in a subsidiary for a fixed number of equity shares in the parent. Both legs of the contract are a fixed number of shares and in both cases the shares are a residual interest in some or all of the entity, that is equity. The contract does not violate the part of the definition of a financial liability in paragraph 11(b)(i) of IAS 32 because, although it is a non-derivative contract, it does not oblige the entity to deliver a variable number of its own equity instruments and hence the entity is not using its own equity instruments as 'currency'. From the perspective of the parent in preparing its separate financial statements, the contract is a derivative as it is over an asset (investment in its subsidiary), rather than an equity instrument.

7.49 A contract that will be settled in cash or another financial asset as opposed to the delivery of shares is a financial asset or financial liability even if the amount of cash or another financial asset that will be received or delivered is based on changes in the market price of the entity's own equity. An example is a net cash-settled share option. [IAS 32 para AG 27(c)]. Derivatives on own shares are considered further from paragraph 7.89 below.

Contingent settlement provisions

7.50 The obligation to deliver cash or financial assets need not be certain of occurring, it may be contingent on the occurrence or non-occurrence of uncertain future events (or on the outcome of uncertain circumstances) that are beyond the control of both the issuer or the holder of the instrument. Examples of such uncertain future events may include, but are not limited to:

- Changes in stock market index or consumer price index.
- Changes in interest rates or exchange rates.
- Changes in tax laws or other regulatory requirements.
- Changes in the issuer's key performance indicators such as revenue, net income or debt-to-equity ratios.

7.51 In accordance with IAS 32 paragraph 25, the instrument is a financial liability in the circumstances specified above. This is because at the time of the initial recognition, the issuer does not have an unconditional right to avoid delivering cash or another financial asset (or otherwise to settle it in such a way that it would be a financial liability) as it does not control the final outcome. A transfer of economic benefits as a result of a past event (the issue of the instrument) cannot be avoided depending on the outcome of the future event. Such financial instruments should, therefore, be classified as a financial liability.

Example 1 – Change of control events

A contract between entity A and a third party contains a requirement for entity A to make payments to the third party on a change of control of entity A. For example, where entity A may be taken over by entity B and where entity B is not connected to entity A.

The change of control event is outside the control of both the entity and the third party provided that it does not need to be agreed by the entity at a general meeting, as discussed in paragraphs 7.18.1-7.18.4. This will be the case if a purchaser could approach individual shareholders and buy their shares. Payments to a third party that are contingent on a change of control event are, therefore, financial liabilities when no agreement by a general meeting is required.

Example 2 – Shares with an obligation to pay out a percentage of profits

A bond includes an obligation to pay out a fixed 10% of profits each year and is mandatorily redeemable at par after 20 years.

The instrument has two liability components, a contractual obligation to redeem the instrument at par after 20 years and a contractual obligation to pay 10% of profits until redemption. The latter is a financial liability because, although the payment depends on the entity making profits (an uncertain future event), the future profits are outside the control of both the issuer and holder, but if profits are made the issuer cannot avoid making the payment, hence it meets the definition of a contingent settlement event. The 10% obligation does not meet the definition of an embedded derivative as the entity's profit is a non-financial variable that is specific to a party to the contract. [IAS 39 para 9].

Example 3 – mandatorily redeemable where an IPO does not occur

An undated cumulative bond, whose interest payments are at the discretion of the entity absent an IPO, contains a clause that states that the instrument (including all unpaid cumulative interest) will become mandatorily payable if there is not an IPO by the end of three years from the instrument's issuance date. Although it may be within the entity's control to determine whether the IPO is attempted, market and regulatory forces determine whether any attempt is successful (that is, whether the market will accept an IPO and whether all regulatory approvals will be obtained). These forces are beyond the control of the entity, therefore redemption upon an IPO event not occurring meets the definition of a contingent settlement event and results in the bond being classified as a financial liability from inception.

7.52   Where the event is within the control of the issuer but not the holder, it is possible for the issuer to avoid the event occurring and hence avoid settling the instrument, hence the event would not meet the definition of a contingent settlement event. For example an undated cumulative bond whose interest payments are at the discretion of the entity that contains a clause that states that the instrument (including all unpaid cumulative interest) will become mandatorily payable if a successful IPO occurs. As outlined in example 3 above, it is within an entity's control to determine whether an IPO is attempted and, hence, the entity can avoid a successful IPO taking place. Therefore, the clause does not meet the definition of a contingent settlement provision and results in the bond being classified as an equity instrument from inception.

7.52.1   Contingent settlement provisions sometimes exist within the terms of convertible loan instruments. If a convertible instrument must be settled in cash on the occurrence of a contingent settlement event (for example, a change in tax law; default on the instrument) that is, outside the control of both issuer and holder, the whole instrument, including the option to convert, is treated as a financial liability.

7.52.2   Cash settlement of one financial instrument can be contingent upon the default of another financial instrument as discussed below.

Example – Instruments that are redeemable on default on another instrument ('cross default clauses')

An entity has issued two instruments. The first instrument is mandatorily redeemable and pays a mandatory fixed coupon and is therefore classified as a financial liability in accordance with IAS 32. The second instrument has no mandatory payments other than it is mandatorily redeemable if there is an event of default on the first instrument.

The event of default on the first instrument is a contingent settlement provision that makes the second instrument a financial liability of the issuer under paragraph 25 of IAS 32. Whether or not an entity defaults on the payment related to an instrument depends, in part, on whether it has adequate resources to make the payments when contractually due. The availability of adequate resources depends primarily on the future revenue and income of the entity. Paragraph 25 of IAS 32 is clear that revenues and net income are not within the entity's control. Therefore, mandatory redemption in the event of default meets the definition of a genuine contingent settlement provision, which results in the second instrument being classified as a financial liability.

7.53   There are three exceptions where uncertain events outside the control of the issuer would not meet the definition of a contingent settlement event. These are where:

- The part of the contingent settlement provision that could require settlement in cash or another financial asset (or otherwise in such a way that it would be a financial liability) is not *genuine* (see para 7.54). [IAS 32 para 25].

- The issuer can be required to settle the obligation in cash or another financial asset (or otherwise to settle it in such a way that it would be a financial liability) only in the event of liquidation of the issuer (see para 7.56). [IAS 32 para 25].

- A third exception is introduced by the amendment to IAS 32 for puttable instruments and obligations arising on liquidation, as discussed from paragraph 7.2. This is effective for accounting periods beginning on or after 1 January 2009.

Settlement terms that are not genuine

7.54   The standard explains that a contingent settlement provision in a contract is not genuine if it requires settlement in cash only on the occurrence of an event that is extremely rare, highly abnormal and very unlikely to occur. In that situation, the contingent settlement provisions are not taken into account in the instrument's classification. Thus, a contract that requires settlement in cash or a variable number of the entity's own shares only on the occurrence of an event that is extremely rare, highly abnormal and very unlikely to occur is an equity instrument. Similarly, if settlement in a fixed number of an entity's own shares may be contractually precluded in circumstances that are outside the control of the entity, those circumstances can be ignored if there is no genuine possibility that they will occur. In that situation, the instrument continues to be classified as an equity instrument and not as a financial liability. [IAS 32 para AG 28].

7.55 In practice, terms are included in a contract for a purpose that is likely to have commercial effect. Therefore, it would be unusual to include settlement terms in a contract that are contingent on an event that is extremely rare, highly abnormal and very unlikely to occur. If such ineffective terms are included, it should be concluded that the terms are not genuine and should be ignored in determining the instrument's classification. However, 'not genuine' should not be equated to 'remote'. The IASB makes it clear in the Basis for conclusions to IAS 32 that it is not appropriate to disregard events that are merely 'remote'. The specific facts and circumstances would need to be considered.

Example 1 – Settlement terms based on increase in an index

An entity issues an instrument that is redeemable in cash if the FTSE 100 triples within a two month period.

In general, it is not for the entity to speculate whether an index will behave in a certain manner that may or may not trigger redemption of the instrument. As the entity will be unable to avoid a settlement in cash if the index reaches that level, the instrument should be treated as a financial liability.

However, in this situation, the tripling of the FTSE 100 within such a short period of time is extremely rare, highly abnormal and unlikely to occur. Furthermore, in practice, an investor is highly unlikely to advance funds on such redemption terms. Clearly the terms are artificial and not genuine and should be ignored for classification purposes.

Example 2 – Settlement terms based on changes in regulation

A bank issues an instrument that is redeemable in cash if the banking regulator changes the instrument's current classification from tier 1 capital to tier 2 capital in the future.

Whether the contingency in this example is genuine would depend upon the specific facts and circumstances. In some jurisdictions, the industry regulator has a history of applying such changes always prospectively and grandfathering existing instruments under their original classification. In that situation, a regulatory change would not affect the classification of an instrument that is currently outstanding and, consequently, the contingency would be regarded as not genuine.

Settlements that arise only on liquidation

7.56 Obligations to deliver cash or other financial assets that are contingent only on the issuer's liquidation should be ignored. This is rather obvious because different rights and obligations associated with the instruments come into effect at liquidation that would not otherwise be triggered during the ordinary course of business and, hence, would be inconsistent with the going concern assumption. A contingent settlement provision that provides for payment in cash or another financial asset only on the entity's liquidation is similar to an equity instrument that has priority in liquidation. Such a provision should, therefore, be ignored in classifying the instrument. However, if the instrument is redeemable on the occurrence of an event that may ultimately lead to eventual liquidation (for example, the entity becomes insolvent, goes into receivership or administration which is beyond the control of the entity), the instrument should still be classified as a financial liability.

Derivative financial instruments with settlement options

7.57 Sometimes a derivative contract may contain settlement options that give either party a choice over how it is settled (for example, the issuer or the holder can choose to settle the contract net in cash, or by exchanging shares for cash). IAS 32 states that when a derivative financial instrument gives one party a choice over how it is settled, it is a financial asset or a financial liability, unless all of the settlement alternatives would result in it being an equity instrument. [IAS 32 para 26].

7.58 An example of a derivative financial instrument with a settlement option that is a financial liability is an option for an entity to buy its own shares from a third party that the entity can decide to settle net in cash or by exchanging its own shares for cash. Forward and option contracts to buy or sell an entity's own equity instruments that contain settlement options are discussed in paragraph 7.97 below. Also, some contracts to buy or sell a non-financial item (not for 'own use') in exchange for the entity's own equity instruments are financial assets or financial liabilities and not equity instruments, if they can be settled either by delivery of the non financial item or net in cash or another financial instrument. [IAS 32 para 27]. Where the settlement option is contingent on a future event occurring, it will still fall under the settlement option accounting in accordance with paragraph 26 of IAS 32 from initial recognition, as discussed in paragraph 7.76.

Shares issued by subsidiaries

7.59 Normally equity shares issued by subsidiaries to persons outside the group are classified as non-controlling interests in the consolidated financial statements in accordance with IAS 1, 'Presentation of financial instruments', and IAS 27, 'Consolidated and separate financial statements'. When classifying a financial instrument (or a component of it) in consolidated financial statements, an entity should consider all the terms and conditions agreed between group members and the instrument holders in determining whether the group as a whole has an obligation to deliver cash or another financial asset in respect of the instrument, or to settle it in a manner that results in liability classification.

7.60 For example, a member of the group might give a guarantee to pay amounts in respect of those shares, such as dividends or amounts due on their redemption; or another group member might undertake to purchase the shares in the event that the subsidiary issuing them fails to make the expected payments.

Where this is so, the outside shareholders will look to the guarantor if the subsidiary has defaulted.

7.61   Consequently, in such a situation, the subsidiary may appropriately classify the instrument without regard to these additional terms in its separate financial statements. However, in the consolidated financial statements, the effect of other agreements between group members and the instrument holders means that the group as a whole is unable to avoid the transfer of economic benefits. Therefore, where such an obligation or settlement provision exists from the perspective of the group, the instrument (or the component of it that is subject to the obligation) is classified as a financial liability in the consolidated financial statements. [IAS 32 para AG 29].

[The next paragraph is 7.63.]

Compound financial instruments

Introduction

7.63   Not all financial instruments are either liability or equity. Some, known as compound instruments contain elements of both in a single contract. A compound financial instrument is a non-derivative financial instrument that, from the issuer's perspective, contains both a liability and an equity component. [IAS 32 paras 28, AG 30]. Typical examples of such instruments are:

■   A bond that is convertible into a fixed number of equity shares at the holder's option. From the issuer's perspective, such an instrument comprises two components: a financial liability (issuer's contractual obligation to deliver cash or another financial asset for payment of interest and principal, if not converted) and an equity instrument (a written call option granting the holder the right, for a specified period of time, to convert it into a fixed number of the entity's ordinary shares). The economic effect of issuing such an instrument is substantially the same as issuing simultaneously a debt instrument with an early settlement provision and warrants to purchase ordinary shares, or issuing a debt instrument with detachable share purchase warrants. [IAS 32 para 29]. If the issuer call option is contingent on a future event, it should still be for accounted for as a call option from initial recognition. For example:

Example 1 – Provisional issuer call option to redeem at par

Company A issues a convertible bond that, if converted, converts into a fixed number of equity shares. The bond also contains a provisional call option that gives the issuer the option to redeem the bond at par if the share price is 130% of the conversion price for at least 20 days.

The convertible bond is a compound financial instrument with a debt host and equity conversion option. As the issuer call option is to redeem the bonds at par, it does not result in the conversion option having a cash settlement alternative. The conversion option is not, therefore, accounted for as an embedded derivative in accordance with paragraph 26 of IAS 32.

In respect of the issuer call option, the value of any derivative feature (such as a call option) embedded in a compound financial instrument, (other than the equity component) is included in the liability component. [IAS 32 para 31]. The call option is, therefore, considered part of the liability and not the equity component. The assessment of whether the call or put option is closely related to the host debt contract from the issuer's perspective is made before separating the equity element under IAS 32. [IAS 39 para AG 30(g)].

■ A mandatorily redeemable preference shares with dividend payments made at the issuer's discretion before the redemption date. Such an instrument contains a liability component (issuer's contractual obligation to deliver cash or another financial asset for payment of the redemption amount) and an equity component (the holder's right to receive dividends, if declared). [IAS 32 para AG 37].

Separation of a compound financial instrument on initial recognition

7.64 The issuer of a non-derivative financial instrument should first evaluate the financial instrument's terms to determine whether it contains both a liability and an equity component. This evaluation should be done in accordance with the contractual arrangement's substance and the definition of a financial liability, financial asset and an equity component. If such components are identified, the issuer should account for the components separately as financial liabilities, financial assets or equity instruments. [IAS 32 para 28]. The liability and the equity components must be presented separately on the balance sheet. [IAS 32 para 29].

7.65 The above approach is often described as 'split accounting'. Split accounting is applied by the issuer of the financial statement to measure the liability and the equity components upon initial recognition of the instrument. The method, illustrated by reference to a convertible bond that is a most common form of a compound financial instrument, but which is equally applicable to other forms of compound financial instruments, allocates the fair value of the consideration for the compound instrument into its liability and equity components, as follows:

■ The fair value of the consideration in respect of the liability component is measured first, at the fair value of a similar liability (including any embedded non-equity derivative features such as an issuer's call option to redeem the bond early) that does not have any associated equity conversion option. This becomes the liability component's carrying amount at initial recognition.

In practice, the liability component's initial carrying value is determined by discounting the contractual stream of future cash flows (interest and principal) to the present value at the current rate of interest applicable to instruments of comparable credit status and providing substantially the same cash flows on the same terms, but without the equity component (the equity conversion option).

The value of any embedded non-equity derivative features is separately determined and included in the liability component.

■ The equity component (the equity conversion option) is assigned the residual amount after deducting from the fair value of the instrument as a whole the amount separately determined for the liability component.

The equity component is excluded from IAS 39's scope and is never remeasured after initial recognition.

Since the sum of the carrying amounts assigned to the liability and equity components on initial recognition is always equal to the consideration received, which, in most circumstances is equal to the fair value of the instrument as a whole, no gain or loss arises from initially recognising the instrument's components separately in the above manner.

[IAS 32 paras 31, AG 31].

7.66 The requirement to separate the liability and the equity components of a single compound financial instrument in the above manner is consistent with the requirements for initial measurement of a financial liability in IAS 39 and the definitions in IAS 32 and the Framework of an equity instrument as a residual interest. Furthermore, the approach removes the need to estimate inputs to, and apply, complex option pricing models to measure the equity component of some compound financial instruments. [IAS 32 paras BC 29-30].

7.67 Once a compound financial instrument has been separated into its liability and equity components on initial recognition, the classification of the liability and equity components is not revised as a result of a change in the likelihood that a conversion option will be exercised, even when the option's exercise may appear to have become economically advantageous to some holders. This is because the entity's contractual obligation to make future payments remains outstanding until it is extinguished through conversion, the instrument's maturity or some other transaction. [IAS 32 para 30].

Example – Separation of a convertible bond

An entity issues 600,000 convertible bonds at the start of year 1. The bonds have a 3-year term, and are issued at par with a face value of C100 per bond, resulting in total proceeds of C60m, which is also the fair value of the bonds. Interest is payable annually in arrears at a nominal annual interest rate of 6%. Each C100 nominal bond is convertible at any time up to maturity into 25 ordinary shares. When the bonds are issued, the prevailing market interest rate for similar debt without conversion options is 9%. The entity incurs an issue cost of 1% on the nominal value of the bond amounting to C600,000.

As explained in paragraph 7.65 above, the liability component is measured first by discounting the contractually determined stream of future cash flows (interest and principal) to present value using a discount rate of 9%, the market interest rate for similar bonds having no conversion rights, as shown below.

	C
PV of interest payable at the end of year 1 – 3,600,000/1.09	3,302,752
PV of interest payable at the end of year 2 – $3,600,000/(1.09)^2$	3,030,048
PV of interest payable at the end of year 3 – $3,600,000/(1.09)^3$	2,779,861
PV of principal of C60,000,000 payable at the end of three years – $60,000,000/(1.09)^3$	46,331,009
Total liability component	55,443,670
Total equity component (residual)*	4,556,330
Fair value of bonds	60,000,000

* The equity component is a written call option that allows the holder to call for the shares on exercise of the conversion option at any time before maturity (American option). Since equity is a residual, application of complex option pricing models are not necessary to determine the equity component. Instead, the difference between the bond's proceeds and the liability component's fair value of the liability component as computed above – the residual – is assigned to the equity component.

In accordance with IAS 32, the issue cost of C600,000 will need to be allocated between the liability and the equity components in proportion to the allocation of the proceeds as shown below:

	Equity component C	Liability component C	Total C
Gross proceeds allocated as above	4,556,330	55,443,670	60,000,000
Issue cost	(45,563)	(554,437)	(600,000)
Net proceeds	4,510,767	54,889,233	59,400,000

The amount credited to equity of C4,510,767 is not subsequently remeasured.

The liability component will be classified under IAS 39 either as a financial liability at fair value through profit or loss or as another liability measured at amortised cost using the effective interest rate method. If classified as a financial liability at fair value through profit or loss, the liability component will be initially recognised at C55,443,670 and the issue cost of C554,437 allocated to the liability component will be immediately expensed to the income statement. However, under the latter classification, the liability component will be initially recognised net of issue cost at C54,889,233. [IAS 39 para 43]. It will accrete to its final redemption amount of C60,000,000 at the end of year 3 at an effective interest rate of 9.38837% as shown below:

Year	Opening liability	Interest @ 9.38837%	Cash paid	Closing liability
	C	C	C	C
1	54,889,233	5,153,205	(3,600,000)	56,442,438
2	56,442,438	5,299,025	(3,600,000)	58,141,464
3	58,141,464	5,458,536	(63,600,000)	–
Total finance cost		15,910,767		

Total finance cost consists of:

Interest payments	10,800,000
Issue cost allocated to liability component	554,437
Discount (representing gross proceeds allocated to equity component)	4,556,330
	15,910,767

Separation of a compound instrument containing non-equity derivatives

7.68   As explained above, a non-derivative compound financial instrument must be separated into its equity and liability components. In a convertible bond, the equity component arises from the embedded option to convert the liability into the issuer's equity. However, a convertible bond may also contain other non-equity derivative features such as a call, put or pre-payment option. The way in which a compound financial instrument with multiple derivative features is separated into its constituent parts is indicated below:

- First, the value of non-equity derivatives must be included in the liability component. [IAS 32 para 31]. This means that the liability component is established by measuring a bond's fair value with similar terms, credit status and containing similar non-equity derivative features, but without the equity conversion feature.

- Secondly, the equity component is then arrived at by deducting the fair value attributable to the bond as determined above from the compound instrument's fair value.

- Thirdly, given that the liability component contains the non-equity derivative features, it is necessary to assess whether such embedded derivative features are closely related to the host debt contract. This assessment is made before separating the equity element as determined above (see chapter 5). [IAS 39 para AG 30(g)]. In a convertible bond, that assessment will involve determining whether the call option's exercise price is approximately equal to the sum of the debt and the equity components, which is equal to the convertible bond's par value. If the bond is callable at par, the embedded call option is closely related to the host debt instrument. The embedded call option is not bifurcated (split out) and the liability component is determined as indicated above. If, on the other hand, the bond is callable at the carrying value of the liability component, the embedded call option is not closely related to the debt host. In that situation, the embedded call option is separated out of the liability component and accounted for separately. Separating the embedded derivative from the liability component does not affect the amount determined for the equity component as noted in bullet point two above.

Example – Convertible debt with embedded puts and calls

A company issues a convertible debt instrument that contains both an equity conversion option and embedded written puts and purchased calls. The debt component is initially measured at the fair value of a plain vanilla debt with the same contractual maturity plus the value of the written puts less value of the purchased calls, in accordance with paragraph 31 of IAS 32 and as illustrated in paragraphs IE 37 and IE 38 (example 10) of IAS 32.

Where the puts and calls are not required to be separated from the debt host, the debt component is measured at amortised cost using the effective interest rate method as defined in paragraph 9 of IAS 39 and discussed in chapter 9. The puts and calls are considered in determining the expected future life of the instrument and, therefore, the expected interest rate.

- Finally, the sum of the carrying amounts assigned to the various components as indicated above on initial recognition must always be equal to the compound instrument's fair value as a whole. No gain or loss should arise from initially recognising the instrument's components separately. [IAS 32 para 31].

7.69   The ability to convert the host instrument into own equity of the entity may be contingent on an uncertain future event. Where the uncertain future event meets the definition of a contingent settlement event as defined as in paragraph 7.50, the classification of the conversion option on initial recognition would depend on whether the conversion option meets or violates the 'fixed for fixed' requirement if the uncertain future event occurs.

Example 1 – Contingently convertible bond

Entity A issues a contingently convertible bond; the debt host becomes convertible into common shares of entity A at a fixed ratio of 1:1.25 only if the contingent event occurs. The contingent event meets the definition of a contingent settlement event in accordance with paragraph 25 of IAS 32 and is 'genuine' – for example, a change in control event. There are no adjustments to the conversion ratio upon the contingent event occurring, and there are no other put or call options.

The instrument is first separated into its component parts, namely a debt host and equity conversion option. The fact that the option is only contingently convertible will not cause liability classification of the conversion option under paragraph 25 of IAS 32 provided that, upon occurrence of the contingent event, it would be settled in such a way as to require classification as equity. If the contingent event were to occur in the example above, the conversion to own shares would still satisfy the 'fixed for fixed' requirement in paragraph 16(b)(ii) of IAS 32. The conversion option would be classified as an equity component, resulting in a compound financial instrument.

Example 2 – Separation of a callable convertible bond

An entity issues 600,000 callable convertible bonds at the beginning of year 1. The bonds are issued at par with a face value of C100 per bond, giving total proceeds of C60m, which is also the bond's fair value. The bonds are convertible by the holder into a fixed number of shares at any time after the first anniversary of its issue. Furthermore, the bonds do not have a fixed maturity; instead the issuer can call/redeem the bond at any time at the fixed stated principal amount of the bond.

The following information is relevant:

	Cm
Value of a straight bond without a call or equity conversion feature (plain vanilla)	57
Value of issuer call option in a similar bond without an equity conversion option based on an option pricing model (derivative asset)	2

As explained above, the value of the call option (the non-equity derivative) of C2m must be included in the liability component. In this situation, the inclusion results in the value of a callable bond without the equity conversion feature (the liability component) to be less than the value of a plain vanilla bond. This is because the issuer's right to call the bond in the event that interest rates go up and bond price increases makes the value of a callable bond less attractive to the holder than a plain vanilla bond.

Value of callable bond (the liability component)	55
Value of equity component (the conversion option) = residual	5
Fair value of bond = consideration received	60

As the liability component contains the call option, it is now necessary to assess whether the call option is closely related to the host debt instrument. In this situation, the call option's exercise price is set at C60m, the fixed stated principal of the bond. Therefore, at each exercise date, the option's exercise price of C60m is likely to be approximately equal to the amortised carrying amount of the bond plus the equity conversion option. Therefore, the call option is closely related to the host debt instrument. As a result, the call option is not separately accounted for, but remains part of the liability component. [IAS 39 AG 30(g)(i)].

The liability component of C55m will be subsequently measured in accordance with its classification under IAS 39 either as a financial liability at fair value through profit or loss or as another liability measured at amortised cost using the effective interest rate method. Although, in this situation, the bond can be called by the issuer at any time or converted by the holder at any time after the first anniversary of its issue, the liability component of C55m is not automatically accreted to its redemption amount of C60m by the end of year 1. This is because the effective interest rate method requires the entity to discount the cash flows over the instrument's expected life, taking into account all the financial instrument's contractual terms including pre-payment, call and similar options [IAS 39 para 9]. This period may well be a period greater than one year.

On the other hand, if the call option's exercise price were set at an amount that is not approximately equal to the debt instrument's amortised carrying amount or not set to reimburse the lender for the approximate present value of lost interest for the remaining terms of the host contract, the call option would fall to be accounted for separately [IAS 39 AG30(g). In that situation, the proceeds of the converted bond would be allocated as follows:

	Dr Cm	Cr Cm
Cash	60	
Derivative asset (issuer call option)	2	
Host debt instrument		57
Equity component (written equity call option)		5

As can be seen from the above, the separation of the call option asset affects the value of the liability and not the equity component. The derivative asset will be fair valued at each subsequent balance sheet date until the option is exercised. The liability component would be amortised over its expected life (determined without reference to the call option to avoid double counting) under the effective interest method as stated above.

Conversion at or before maturity

7.70 The terms of a convertible instrument may require the instrument to be converted into the entity's ordinary shares either at or any time before maturity. IAS 32 states that on conversion of a convertible instrument at maturity, the entity derecognises the liability component and recognises it as equity. The original equity component remains in equity. There is no gain or loss on conversion at maturity. [IAS 32 para AG 32].

Example – Conversion at maturity

The facts are the same as the example in paragraph 7.67 above, except that the bond is converted at the end of its three-year term.

The amortised cost of the bond will be stated at C60m at maturity after the last payment of interest has been made. As the bond is converted, the entity will issue 15m (600,000 × 25) of C1 nominal value. The liability component will be derecognised and transferred to equity. The accounting entries would be as follows:

	Dr Cm	Cr Cm
Liability	60	
Share capital		15
Reserves (a component of equity)		45

The amount that was previously recognised in equity, that is, C5 remains in equity.

7.71 The guidance included in paragraph AG 32 of IAS 32 as discussed above deals with conversion at maturity. However, the contractual terms of some convertible instruments allow for the conversion before the instrument's final maturity date. There is no specific guidance in IAS 32 as to what should be the accounting treatment if the holder elects to convert the bond early. However, as the instrument 'matures' on the date that the holder converts in accordance with the instrument's contractual terms, the guidance in IAS 32 paragraph AG 32 is relevant. Therefore, where a convertible debt is converted before maturity, the amount recognised in equity in respect of the shares issued should be the amount at which the liability for the debt is stated as at the date of conversion.

> **Example – Before maturity conversion of a convertible bond with an American conversion option**
>
> Convertible bonds with American options (those that give the holder the right to exercise the option at any time) are regularly converted before the loan's original maturity. To the extent that the carrying amount at the conversion date is not equal to the principal amount converted this should be accounted for in accordance with paragraph AG 32 of IAS 32, as the word 'maturity' means any date when the holder converts in accordance with the instrument's contractual terms. As an American option allows for conversion at any time before the expiry date, the conversion date will be the maturity date. As such, there is no gain or loss on conversion with American options. During the life of the host bond, expectations about early conversion should not be taken into account when estimating the cash flows used to apply the effective interest rate. The early conversion option is a characteristic of the equity component (the conversion option) not of the host liability. The estimated cash flows used to apply the effective interest rate method are, therefore, the contractual cash flows based on the contractual final maturity of the host liability (assuming there are no other puts or calls).

Mandatorily convertible instruments

7.72 A convertible bond may contain terms that *compel* the holder to convert the bond rather than being at the holder's option. Depending on the terms, the number of shares issued on conversion may be either variable or fixed. To the extent that the mandatorily convertible bond can only be settled by the issue of a variable amount of ordinary shares calculated to equal a fixed amount in the issuer's functional currency (that is, there is a repayment of principal), the instrument is a liability. To the extent that the mandatorily convertible bond can only be settled by the issue of a fixed number of ordinary shares, that part of the instrument is an equity component. Some mandatorily convertible instruments pay no interest or pay interest only if an ordinary dividend is paid (discretionary). This type of instrument has no liability component. Others pay interest until the bond is converted, in which case the issuer allocates part of the consideration received equal to the liability component. This is measured at the present value of the interest payments, discounted at the market rate of interest for a similar instrument with a similar credit status that has no conversion option. The balance of the consideration is allocated to the equity component as illustrated below.

Example – Mandatorily convertible bonds

An entity issues 600,000 convertible bonds at the start of year 1. The bonds have a 3-year term, and are issued at par with a face value of C100 per bond, resulting in total proceeds of C60m, which is also the bond's fair value. Interest is payable annually in arrears at a nominal annual interest rate of 6%. Each C100 nominal bond is mandatorily convertible at the end of the 3 year term into 25 ordinary shares. When the bonds are issued, the prevailing market interest rate for similar debt without conversion options is 9%. The entity incurs issue cost of 1% on the nominal value of the bond amounting to C600,000.

As explained in the above paragraph, the liability component is measured first by discounting the contractually determined stream of future cash flows (interest only) to present value using a discount rate of 9%, the market interest rate for similar bonds having no conversion rights, as shown below.

	C
PV of interest payable at the end of year 1 – C3,600,000/1.09	3,302,752
PV of interest payable at the end of year 2 – C3,600,000/$(1.09)^2$	3,030,048
PV of interest payable at the end of year 3 – C3,600,000/$(1.09)^3$	2,779,860
Total liability component	9,112,660
Total equity component (residual)*	50,887,340
Total proceeds of the bond issue	60,000,000

* The difference between the proceeds of the bond and the fair value of the liability component as computed above (the residual) is assigned to the equity component.

In accordance with IAS 32, the issue cost of C600,000 will need to be allocated between the liability and the equity components in proportion to the allocation of the proceeds as shown below:

	Equity component	Liability component	Total
	C	C	C
Gross proceeds allocated as above	50,887,340	9,112,660	60,000,000
Issue cost	(508,873)	(91,127)	(600,000)
Net proceeds	50,378,467	9,021,533	59,400,000

The amount credited to equity of C50,378,467 is not subsequently remeasured.

The liability component of C9,021,533 will be measured subsequently at amortised cost using the effective interest rate method. As the interest payments on the bonds will reduce the liability component to zero, the effective interest rate in this situation is that rate of interest which discounts the three interest payments of C3,600,000 per year to its present value of C9,021,533. This rate amounts to 9.5659% as shown below:

Financial liabilities and equity

Year	Opening liability	Interest @ 9.5659%	Cash paid	Closing liability
	C	C	C	C
1	9,021,533	862,990	(3,600,000)	6,284,523
2	6,284,523	601,171	(3,600,000)	3,285,694
3	3,285,694	314,306	(3,600,000)	–
Total finance cost		1,778,467		

When the bond is converted, the entity issues 15 million shares of C1 each. The original equity component of C50,378,467 effectively becomes the consideration for these shares where relevant, this amount would be allocated between share capital and share premium as follows:

	C
Share capital – 15 million shares of C1 each	15,000,000
Share premium	35,378,467
Original equity component	50,378,467

In other words, a mandatorily convertible instrument issued in the functional currency of the issuer is effectively a forward contract to issue or to deliver a fixed number of shares for which the consideration has been received in advance. Contrast this with the situation of an instrument that is convertible at any time before maturity (a written call option) discussed in paragraph 7.67 above.

Early redemption or repurchase

7.73   An entity may redeem or repurchase a convertible instrument before maturity, for example through negotiations with the bondholders, without affecting the conversion rights. When an entity extinguishes a convertible instrument before maturity through an early redemption or repurchase in which the original conversion privileges are unchanged, the entity should allocate the redemption consideration paid (including any transaction costs) to the instrument's liability and equity components at the date of repurchase or redemption. In making this allocation, the entity should use the same methodology (using current market data) that was used in the original allocation of proceeds received from the convertible instrument's issue between the separate components on initial recognition. [IAS 32 para AG 33].

7.74   Once the allocation of the consideration has been made, any resulting gain or loss is treated in accordance with accounting principles applicable to the related component, as follows:

- The difference between the consideration allocated to the liability component and its carrying value is recognised in profit or loss.

- The amount of consideration relating to the equity component is recognised in equity.

[IAS 32 para AG 34].

Example – Early redemption of a convertible bond

The facts are the same as the example in paragraph 7.67 above, except that on the first day of year 2, the entity makes a tender offer to the bondholders to repurchase the bond for its fair value at that date of C63m, which the bondholders accept. At the date of repurchase, the entity could have issued a non-convertible bond with a two-year term bearing an interest rate of 7%. The transaction cost of redeeming the bonds amounted to C200,000.

The carrying value of the liability component prior to redemption at the end of year 1 as calculated previously amounts to C56,442,438. The original equity component amounts to C4,510,767.

As explained above, the repurchase price is allocated between the liability component and the equity component on the same basis used in the original allocation process. This means the fair value of the liability component is measured first by discounting the remaining stream of future cash flows (interest and principal) to present value at the beginning of year 2, using a discount rate of 7%, the market interest rate for similar bonds having no conversion rights, as shown below.

	C
PV of interest payable at the end of year 2 – C3,600,000/1.07	3,364,486
PV of interest payable at the end of year 3 – C3,600,000/(1.07)^2	3,144,379
PV of principal of C60,000,000 payable at the end year 3 – C60,000,000 / (1.07)^2	52,406,324
Total liability component	58,915,189
Total equity component (residual)*	4,084,811
Total consideration payable on repurchase of bonds	63,000,000

* The difference between the consideration payable and the liability component's fair value as computed above is assigned to the equity component.

In accordance with IAS 32, the redemption cost of C200,000 will need to be allocated between the liability and the equity components in proportion to the allocation of the consideration as shown below:

	Equity component	Liability component	Total
	C	C	C
Consideration allocated as above	4,084,811	58,915,189	63,000,000
Redemption cost	12,968	187,032	200,000
Total	4,097,779	59,102,221	63,200,000

Difference arising on repurchase is as follows:

Consideration inclusive of costs as above	4,097,779	59,102,221	63,200,000
Carrying value prior to redemption as stated above	4,510,767	56,442,438	60,953,205
	412,988	(2,659,783)	(2,246,795)

The accounting entries in respect of the repurchase of the bond are as follows:

	Dr C	Cr C
Bond Liability	56,442,438	
Debt Settlement expense (income statement)	2,659,783	
Cash		59,102,221

To record the repurchase of the liability component and the loss arising thereon

	Dr C	Cr C
Equity	4,097,779	
Cash		4,097,779

To record the cash paid on the repurchase of the equity component

The resulting balance of C412,988 relating to the equity component can be transferred to a different line item in equity, for example, retained earnings.

Modification of terms to induce early conversion

7.75   An entity may amend the terms of a convertible instrument to induce early conversion, for example by offering a more favourable conversion ratio or paying other additional consideration in the event of conversion before a specified date. In that situation, the entity should recognise a loss, at the date the terms are amended, calculated as the difference between:

■   the fair value of the consideration the holder receives on the instrument's conversion under the revised terms; and

■   the fair value of the consideration the holder would have received under the original terms.

[IAS 32 para AG 35].

Example – Early conversion of a convertible bond

The facts are the same as the example in paragraph 7.67 above, except that on the first day of year 2, the entity modifies the convertible instrument's terms to induce the bondholders to convert the bond within 60 days. Each C100 nominal bond is now convertible into 30 ordinary shares rather than the 25 ordinary shares under the original terms. The market value of the entity's shares at the date of the amendment is C5 per share.

As explained above, the loss arising on increasing the conversion ratio is calculated as follow:

	Cm
Fair value of consideration receivable under the new terms:	
Number of bonds (600,000) x Conversion ratio (30) x C5	90
Fair value of consideration receivable under the original terms:	
Number of bonds (600,000) x Conversion ratio (25) x C5	75
Value of additional shares issuable on conversion recognised in profit or loss	15

On the date of conversion, the entity issues 18m shares instead of 15m under the original conversion terms. Therefore, the consideration received for the 18m shares comprises the carrying value of the bond of C56,442,438 plus C15m (the market value of 3m shares @ C5 per share).

The accounting entries to record the early conversion are as follows:

	Dr	Cr
Bond liability	56,442,438	
Profit or loss (fair value of 3m shares @ C5 per share)	15,000,000	
Equity (issue of 18m shares)		71,442,438

Settlement options

7.76 In some instances, a convertible instrument may contain a settlement option that allows the issuer either to deliver a fixed number of shares when the bondholders exercise their rights to convert or deliver cash equal to the fair value of those shares at the date of conversion. Consistent with paragraph 7.57, where a convertible instrument contains such a cash settlement option, the conversion option is not an equity instrument, even though it is indexed to the market price of the entity's shares. Rather, it is an embedded derivative (effectively a written call option issued by the entity over its own shares) that is not closely related to the debt host. This means that instead of accounting for the conversion right as an equity instrument, the entity would account for the conversion right as a financial liability (a derivative) at fair value, with changes in fair value recognised in profit or loss. The effect of fair valuing the derivative means that gains and losses based on the entity's own share price would be reported in the profit or loss. This is also the case where the cash settlement option is contingent on a future event happening.

Example – Contingent settlement options

An entity has issued convertible bonds whose terms include a clause giving the issuer the option to redeem in cash the bonds at their fair market value in the event of the occurrence of an uncertain future event instead of issuing a fixed number of equity shares.

The conversion option is a derivative. The terms of the convertible bond give the issuer the option to redeem the bonds for cash at their fair market value contingent upon a future event. On the occurrence of the uncertain future event there is a settlement alternative for the equity conversion option, as it can be settled at fair value, either in shares or in cash – that is, there is a net cash settlement option. An equity conversion option for which either party has a choice of settlement in cash or shares is a financial liability. [IAS 32 para 26]. Paragraph 26 of IAS 32 overturns the usual principle that something that is in the control of an issuer is not an obligation. This right of choice of settlement is contingent upon a future event in the example above, but the equity conversion option must still be accounted for as an embedded derivative in accordance with paragraph 26 of IAS 32.

7.77 When the holder exercises its right to convert and the entity chooses to settle its obligation by issuing a fixed number of shares, then the liability's carrying value together with the derivative's fair value would be derecognised and transferred to equity as the share issue is treated as an equity transaction. Alternatively, the entity may record the shares at fair value and the difference between the fair value of the shares and the carrying value of the liability plus the fair value of the derivative is recognised in profit or loss. The same accounting treatment is achieved if the entity chooses the cash alternative as the amount of the cash consideration that is equal to the fair value of the shares at the date of conversion will be applied to extinguish the liability and the derivative instruments with any difference taken to profit or loss. Either method is acceptable, but it is an accounting policy choice that should be disclosed and applied consistently.

Convertible bond denominated in a foreign currency

7.78   It is not uncommon for an entity to issue a convertible bond that is denominated in a currency other than its functional currency, as discussed in paragraph 7.40. For example, an entity whose functional currency is the Swiss franc may issue a euro denominated convertible bond that can be converted into a fixed number of its own Swiss franc denominated equity instruments. In this case, the instrument comprises a host debt instrument denominated in a foreign currency and a written option to exchange a fixed number of the entity's own equity instruments for a fixed amount of cash that is denominated in a foreign currency.

7.79   In April 2005, the IFRIC considered the accounting for a foreign currency convertible bond and stated that a fixed amount of foreign currency constitutes a variable amount of cash in the entity's functional currency. This position has not changed as a result of the IAS 32 amendment for the classification of rights issues discussed in paragraph 7.41. Therefore, foreign-currency-denominated-convertible bonds that will be settled by an entity delivering a fixed number of its own equity instruments in exchange for a fixed amount of foreign currency fail the 'fixed for fixed' requirement. The whole of the convertible bond is classified as a financial liability under IAS 32 and is subject to IAS 39 for recognition and measurement. The embedded written option's value changes in response to changes in the values of entity's equity and foreign exchange movements. Therefore, it is not a closely related embedded derivative, because the risks inherent in the derivative (equity risk) and in the debt host are dissimilar. [IAS 39 para AG 30(d)]. If the host debt is carried at amortised cost it will be subject to the translation rules of IAS 21, 'The effect of changes in foreign exchange rates', and the embedded derivative liability will be separated and fair valued through profit or loss.

Example – Convertible debt denominated in a foreign currency

On 1 January 20X5 a company with C functional currency issued 36,000 convertible bonds at par with a face value of US$1,000 per bond, giving total proceeds of US$36m. The bonds carry a coupon rate of 4% per annum payable in arrears. Each $1,000 bond is convertible, at the holder's discretion, at any time prior to maturity on 31 December 20X9, into 100 ordinary shares of C1 nominal.

The following information is relevant:

	Spot rate	Fair value of embedded derivative*
1 January 20X5	C1 = US$1.80	C3m
31 December 20X5	C1 = US$1.75	C4m
Average rate for the year	C1 = US$1.775	

* In accordance with paragraph AG 28 of IAS 39, the embedded derivative's fair value (the written option) must be determined first at inception of the contract. In this instance, the embedded derivative is indexed to both the share price denominated in C and the C/US$ exchange rate. Generally, where the derivatives relate to different risk exposures and are readily separable and independent of each other, they should be valued and accounted for separately. [IAS 39 para AG 29]. However, in this case, the exercise price of the equity conversion option is denominated in US$, but the underlying share is traded in C. Therefore, it is not possible to separate the equity price risk from the foreign currency risk and value each component separately, because the two are interdependent. In that situation, they should be bundled together and treated as a single compound derivative. [IAS 39 para AG 29]. On this basis, the fair value of the embedded derivative at initial recognition, calculated using an option pricing model, amounted to C3m and C4m respectively at 1 January 20X5 and 31 December 20X5.

As explained above, as the issuer's functional currency is C and the convertible bonds are denominated in US dollars, the conversion option is not an equity instrument, but an embedded derivative that is not closely related to the host debt instrument, because the risks inherent in the derivative (equity risk) and the host are dissimilar. Therefore, the conversion option should be separated and classified as a derivative liability.

The carrying value of the host contract at initial recognition is the difference between the consideration received of C20m ((US$36m @ 1.8) and the fair value of the embedded derivative of C3m, that is, C17m or US$30.6m (C17m @1.8).

The host foreign currency debt of US$30.6m will be measured subsequently at amortised cost using the effective interest rate method and then retranslated at each subsequent reporting date at the closing US$/C exchange rate. The company will pay 4% interest per annum on US$36m, that is, US$1.44m each year for the next 4 years and a principal amount of US$36m at the end of year 4, if the debt is not converted. The effective interest rate that discounts the interest and principal payments to its present value of US$30.6m is 8.5883% as shown below:

	Opening liability	Interest @ 8.5883%	Cash paid	Closing liability
	$'000	$'000	$'000	$'000
Year 1	30,600	2,628	(1,440)	31,788
Year 2	31,788	2,730	(1,440)	33,078
Year 3	33,078	2,841	(1,440)	34,479
Year 4	34,479	2,961	(37,440)	0

The interest payable in US$ would be recorded in profit or loss at the average rate ruling during the year. The closing liability would be translated at the spot rate at the balance sheet. Any exchange difference arising is recognised in profit or loss as part of finance cost. Therefore, the amortised cost of the host foreign currency debt instrument at 31 December 20X5 would be calculated as follows:

		C'000
Opening liability	US$30,600,000 @ 1.8	17,000
Interest cost (profit or loss)	US$2,628,000 @ 1.775	1,481
Cash paid	US$1,440,000 @ 1.75	(823)
Exchange difference (profit or loss)*		507
Closing liability	US$31,788 @ 1.75	18,165

* The exchange difference comprises the exchange difference on the opening liability of C486 (US$30,600 @ [1.75-1.8]) and the exchange difference on the interest cost between closing rate and average rate of C21 (US$2,628 @ [1.775-1.8]).

At 31 December 20X5, the fair value of the embedded derivative liability is C4m. The increase in fair value results in a loss of C1m, which is recognised in profit or loss.

The foreign currency convertible bond would be reported and presented in the financial statements as follows:

Income statement for the year ended 31 December 20X5	C'000
Other gains and (losses)	
Derivative instrument	(1,000)
Finance cost	
Interest expense	(1,481)
Foreign exchange difference	(507)
	(1,988)

Balance sheet	31 Dec 20X5	1 Jan 20X5
	C'000	C'000
Current liabilities		
Borrowings	18,165	17,000
Derivative on convertible bond	4,000	3,000
	22,165	20,000

Alternatively, the foreign exchange difference may be presented in other gains and (losses). Similarly, the bond and the derivative can be presented as a single number on the balance sheet. The convertible bond is classified as a current liability because it can be converted at any time prior to maturity as settlement of a liability is not confined to delivery of cash or other assets.

7.79.1   If a subsidiary issues a convertible bond that (if converted) converts into the parent's shares, the currency that should be looked to in determining whether the 'fixed for fixed' requirement in IAS 32 is met depends on the specific circumstances. For the purposes of the group's consolidated financial statements, a group should look to either the functional currency of the parent (whose shares the bond is convertible into), or that of the subsidiary (whose liability will be extinguished if the bond is converted). The choice to look to the functional currency of the subsidiary or the parent is a policy choice and should be applied on a consistent basis to all similar instruments. The IFRIC decided to give no guidance on this issue. In the subsidiary's individual financial statements, the convertible is classified as a financial liability in its entirety, as the conversion option relates to the parent's shares and not the subsidiary's equity. In the subsidiary's individual financial statements, under IAS 39 the conversion option is an embedded derivative, which should be separated, as it is not closely related to the debt host.

Preference shares with various rights

7.80 Preference shares come with various rights. They may be redeemable at the option of the holder or the issuer, mandatorily redeemable or non-redeemable. Dividends on such shares may be either fixed or payable at the issuer's discretion or their payments may be linked to payments on another instrument. IAS 32 requires the classification of preference shares to be based on an assessment of the contractual arrangement's substance and the definitions of a financial liability and an equity instrument. [IAS 32 paras AG 25, AG 26].

7.81 Because preference shares are relatively common, we summarise below, for ease of understanding and as a practical aid, the appropriate classification of preference shares for various combinations of redemption and dividend rights. It is assumed that the criteria for equity classification in the 2008 amendment to IAS 32 for puttable financial instruments and obligations arising on liquidation summarised in paragraph 7.24.5 have not been met.

Classification of preference shares

Terms		Classification	
Redemption of principal	Payment of dividends (assume all at market rates)	Type of Instrument	Reasons
Non-redeemable	Discretionary	Equity	There is no contractual obligation to pay cash. Any dividends paid would be recognised in equity (see para 7.56).
	Non-discretionary	Liability	Liability component is equal to the present value of the dividend payments to perpetuity. As the dividends are set at market rates, the proceeds will be equivalent to the fair value (at the date of issue) of the dividends payable to perpetuity. Therefore, the

			entire proceeds would be classified as a liability.
Redeemable at the issuer's option at some future date.	Discretionary	Equity	There is no contractual obligation to pay cash. An option to redeem the shares for cash does not satisfy the definition of a financial liability. Any dividends paid would be recognised in equity (see para 7.33).
	Non-discretionary	Liability with an embedded call option derivative	Liability component equal to the present value of the dividend payments to perpetuity. As the dividends are set at market rates, the proceeds will be equivalent to the fair value (at the date of issue) of the dividends payable to perpetuity. Therefore, the entire proceeds would be classified as a liability. In addition, because the entire instrument is classified as a liability, the issuer call option to redeem the shares for cash is an embedded derivative (an asset). The embedded derivative may have to be accounted for separately, unless the option's exercise price is approximately equal on each exercise date to the instrument's amortised cost (see para 7.65).
Mandatorily redeemable at a fixed or determinable amount at a fixed or future date	Discretionary	Compound	Liability component equal to the present value of the redemption amount. Equity component is equal to proceeds less liability component. Any dividends paid are related to the equity component and would be recognised in equity (see para 7.103). It should be noted, however, that if any unpaid dividends are added to the redemption amount, then the whole instrument is a financial liability. [IAS 32 para AG 37].

	Non-discretionary	Liability	The entity has an obligation to pay cash in respect of both principal and dividends.
Redeemable at the holder's option at some future date.	Discretionary	Compound	Liability component equal to the present value of the redemption amount (on the basis that the criteria in the 2008 amendment to IAS 32 have not been met (see para 7.24.5)). Equity component is equal to proceeds less liability component (see para 7.53). Any dividends paid are related to the equity component and would be recognised in equity (see para 7.103). It should be noted, however, that if any unpaid dividends are added to the redemption amount, then the whole instrument is a financial liability. [IAS 32 para AG 37].
	Non-discretionary	Liability with an embedded put option derivative	There is a contractual obligation to pay cash in respect of both the principal and dividend. In addition, because the entire instrument is classified as a liability, the embedded put option to redeem the shares for cash is an embedded derivative. The embedded derivative may have to be accounted for separately unless the option's exercise price is approximately equal on each exercise date to the instrument's amortised cost (see chapter 5).

7.82   In the above table, dividend payments need not be a fixed percentage of the preference shares' nominal value. In some circumstances, the payment of dividends may be based on a fixed percentage of profits, for example, ten per cent of profits made each year. Such dividends would not be an embedded derivative because they are based on a non-financial variable that is specific to one party to the contract (see further chapter 4). To the extent that the distribution based on a percentage of profits, is non-discretionary and cannot be avoided, such payments would give rise to a liability treatment, even though the payments are contingent on the issuer making profits (see para 7.50 above).

[The next paragraph is 7.89.]

Derivatives over own equity instruments

7.89 An entity may enter into a derivative contract for the purchase or sale of its own equity instruments. Depending upon the nature of the contract (forward based or option based) and the settlement terms (for example, gross or net in cash) in particular, such contracts may be accounted for as equity instruments, financial liabilities or as derivative assets and liabilities.

Contracts accounted for as equity instruments

7.90 A derivative contract that will be settled by the entity receiving or delivering a fixed number of its own equity instruments in exchange for a fixed amount of cash or another financial asset is an equity instrument. [IAS 32 paras 22, AG 27(a)]. An example is an issued share option that gives the counterparty a right to buy a fixed number of the entity's shares for a fixed price. The contract's fair value may change due to variation in the share price and market interest rates. However, provided that such changes in the contract's fair value do not affect the amount of cash or other financial assets to be paid or received, or the number of equity instruments to be received or delivered, on the contract's settlement, the contract is treated as an equity instrument. [IAS 32 para 22].

7.91 Any consideration received (such as the premium received for a written option or warrant on the entity's own shares) on a derivative contract that is an equity instrument is added directly to equity. Any consideration paid (such as the premium paid for a purchased option) is deducted directly from equity. Changes in an equity instrument's fair value are not recognised in the financial statements. [IAS 32 para 22].

7.92 The following examples illustrate the accounting treatment discussed above where an entity enters into derivative contracts to receive or deliver a fixed amount of its own shares in exchange for a fixed amount of cash at some future date.

> **Example 1 – Purchased call option to receive a fixed number of own shares for a fixed sum** [IAS 32 para IE 15]
>
> On 1 February 20X5, an entity purchases a call option for C5,000 under which it has the right but not the obligation to acquire 1,000 of its own shares for cash at the option's exercise of C102 per share. The option will be gross settled in that the entity will take delivery of the shares and pay the exercise price of C102,000 (C102 × 1,000) on the fixed maturity date of 31 January 20X6.

The following information is given:

	Market price per share	Fair value of option
	C	C
At 1 February 20X5	100	5,000
At 31 December 20X5	104	3,000
At 31 January 20X6	104	2,000

The accounting entries from inception to settlement of the contract are as follows:

At 1 February 20X5

	Dr	Cr
Equity	C5,000	
Cash		C5,000

At inception of the contract, the entity would record the premium paid for the right to receive a fixed amount of its own shares in one year for a fixed price. As the contract meets the definition of an equity instrument, the premium is charged directly to equity as discussed above.

At 31 December 20X5

No entry is made on 31 December because no cash is paid or received. As the option contract meets the definition of an equity instrument, it is not subsequently re-measured as explained in paragraph 7.91. Therefore, the option's fair value is not relevant.

At 31 January 20X6

	Dr	Cr
Equity	C102,000	
Cash		C102,000

The entity exercises the call option on the exercise date as it is in the money (exercise price of C102 per share < market price of C104 per share). As the contract is settled gross, the entity takes delivery of 1,000 of its own shares and pays a fixed amount of C102,000 to the counterparty that is recognised directly in equity. Hence, the total amount debited to equity in relation to the purchase is C107,000.

Example 2 – Written call option to deliver a fixed number of own shares for a fixed sum
[IAS 32 para IE 20]

On 1 February 20X5, an entity writes a call option for C5,000 under which it has an obligation to sell 1,000 of its own shares for cash at a fixed price of C102 per share, if the counterparty exercises the option. The option will be gross settled in shares in that the entity will deliver its own shares and receive the exercise price of C102,000 (C102 × 1,000) on the fixed maturity date of 31 January 20X6.

The following information is given:

	Market price per share	Fair value of option
	C	C
At 1 February 20X5	100	5,000
At 31 December 20X5	104	3,000
At 31 January 20X6	104	2,000

The accounting entries from inception to settlement of the contract are as follows:

At 1 February 20X5

	Dr	Cr
Cash	C5,000	
Equity		C5,000

At inception of the contract, the entity would record the premium received in exchange for the obligation to deliver a fixed amount of its own shares in one year for a fixed price. As the contract meets the definition of an equity instrument, the premium is credited directly to equity as discussed above.

At 31 December 20X5

No entry is made on 31 December because no cash is paid or received. As the option contract meets the definition of an equity instrument, it is not subsequently re-measured as explained in paragraph 7.69. Therefore, the option's fair value is not relevant.

At 31 January 20X6

	Dr	Cr
Cash	C102,000	
Equity		C102,000

The counterparty exercises the call option on the exercise date as it is in the money (exercise price of C102 per share < market price of C104 per share). Therefore, the entity is obliged to deliver 1,000 of its own shares in exchange for C102,000 in cash. Hence, the total amount credited to equity in relation to the sale is C107,000.

Example 3 – Purchased put option to deliver a fixed number of own shares for a fixed sum [IAS 32 para IE 25]

On 1 February 20X5, an entity purchases a put option for C5,000 under which it has the right to sell 1,000 of its own shares for cash at a fixed price of C98 per share, if the entity exercises the put option. The option will be gross settled in that the entity will deliver its own shares and receive the exercise price of C98,000 (C98 × 1,000) on the fixed maturity date of 31 January 20X6.

The following information is given:

	Market price per share	Fair value of option
	C	C
At 1 February 20X5	100	5,000
At 31 December 20X5	95	4,000
At 31 January 20X6	95	3,000

The accounting entries from inception to settlement of the contract are as follows:

At 1 February 20X5

	Dr	Cr
Equity	C5,000	
Cash		C5,000

At inception of the contract, the entity would record the premium paid received in exchange for the obligation to deliver a fixed amount of its own shares in one year for a fixed price. As the contract meets the definition of an equity instrument, the premium is credited directly to equity as discussed above.

At 31 December 20X5

No entry is made on 31 December because no cash is paid or received. As the option contract meets the definition of an equity instrument, it is not subsequently re-measured as explained in paragraph 7.91. Therefore, the option's fair value is not relevant.

At 31 January 20X6

	Dr	Cr
Cash	C98,000	
Equity		C98,000

The entity exercises the put option on the exercise date as it is in the money (exercise price of C98 per share > market price of C95 per share). Therefore, the counterparty is obliged to deliver C98,000 in cash to the entity in exchange for 1,000 shares. Hence, the total amount credited to equity is C93,000.

Example 4 – Forward contract to sell a fixed number of own shares for a fixed sum [IAS 32 para IE 10]

On 1 February 20X5, an entity enters into a forward sale contract under which it has an obligation to sell 1,000 of its own shares for cash at a fixed price of C104 per share on 31 January 20X6.

For simplicity, it is assumed that no dividends are paid on the underlying shares (that is the 'carry return' is zero) so that the present value of the forward price equals the spot price when the fair value of the forward contract is zero. The fair value of the forward has been computed as the difference between the market share price and the present value of the fixed forward price.

The following information is given:

	Market price per share	Fair value of forward
	C	C
At 1 February 20X5	100	Nil
At 31 December 20X5	110	(6,300)
At 31 January 20X6	106	(2,000)

The present value of the forward price on 1 February 20X5 is C100 per share.

The accounting entries from inception to settlement of the contract are as follows:

At 1 February 20X5

At inception of the contract, no entries are made as no cash is paid or received for the forward contract – it has an initial fair value of zero. As the entity enters into a forward contract to deliver a fixed number of its own shares in exchange for a fixed amount of cash or another financial asset, the forward contract meets the definition of an equity instrument because it cannot be settled otherwise than through the delivery of shares in exchange for cash.

At 31 December 20X5

No entry is made on 31 December because no cash is paid or received. As the forward contract meets the definition of an equity instrument, it is not subsequently re-measured as explained in paragraph 7.91. Therefore, the contract's fair value is not relevant.

At 31 January 20X6	Dr	Cr
Cash	C104,000	
Equity		C104,000

The entity settles the forward contract by delivery of 1,000 of its own shares and receives cash of C104,000 in exchange.

Contracts accounted for as financial liabilities

7.93 The above circumstances deal with derivative contracts that require gross physical settlement in shares for a fixed amount of cash at some future date. These physically settled contracts are treated as equity instruments. However, a contract that contains an obligation for an entity to purchase its own equity instruments for cash or another financial asset gives rise to a financial liability for the present value of the redemption amount (for example, for the present value of the forward repurchase price, option exercise price or other redemption amount). This is the case even if the contract itself is an equity instrument. When the financial liability is recognised initially under IAS 39, its fair value (the present value of the redemption amount) is reclassified from equity. Subsequently, the financial liability is measured in accordance with IAS 39. If the contract expires without delivery, the carrying amount of the financial liability is reclassified to equity. [IAS 32 para 23].

> **Example 1 – Forward contract to purchase a fixed number of own shares for a fixed sum** [IAS 32 para IE 5]
>
> On 1 February 20X5, an entity enters into a forward purchase contract under which it has the obligation to acquire 1,000 of its own shares for cash at a fixed price of C104 per share on 31 January 20X6.
>
> For simplicity, it is assumed that no dividends are paid on the underlying shares (that is the 'carry return' is zero) so that the present value of the forward price equals the spot price of the entity's shares when the fair value of the forward contract is zero. The fair value of the forward has been computed as the difference between the market share price and the present value of the fixed forward price.
>
> The following information is given:
>
> | | Market price per share | Fair value of forward |
> |---|---|---|
> | | C | C |
> | At 1 February 20X5 | 100 | Nil |
> | At 31 December 20X5 | 110 | 6,300 |
> | At 31 January 20X6 | 106 | 2,000 |
>
> The present value of the forward price on 1 February 20X5 is C100 per share.
>
> The accounting entries from inception to settlement of the contract are as follows:
>
> | At 1 February 20X5 | Dr | Cr |
> |---|---|---|
> | Equity | C100,000 | |
> | Liability | | C100,000 |

As the entity enters into a forward contract to purchase a fixed number of its own shares in exchange for a fixed amount of cash or another financial asset, the forward contract meets the definition of an equity instrument, because it cannot be settled otherwise than through the delivery of shares in exchange for cash. Furthermore, at inception of the contract the entity has an obligation to pay C104,000 in cash in one year's time. Therefore, in accordance with paragraph 7.93, the entity recognises a liability for the redemption amount of C104,000 payable in one year at its present value of C100,000.

At 31 December 20X5

	Dr	Cr
Interest expense	C3,660	
Liability		C3,660

As the liability needs to be accreted to its final redemption amount of C104,000, the entity recognises interest expense to 31 December in accordance with the effective interest rate method.

At 31 January 20X6

	Dr	Cr
Interest expense	C340	
Liability		C340

The entity recognises interest expense to 31 January with the result that the liability is stated at its redemption amount.

	Dr	Cr
Liability		C104,000
Cash		C104,000

The entity settles its obligation under the forward contract to purchase its own shares for cash of C104,000.

It should be noted that whilst an entity is required to recognise a liability at inception for a forward purchase of its own shares, there is no equivalent requirement to recognise an asset for a forward sale of its own shares, even though the two contracts are economically the 'mirror image' of each other (see example 4 in para 7.92 above). This is because in the former situation the shares that are the subject of a forward purchase cease to be equity until acquired as the entity has an obligation to pay cash. In a forward sale, the equity shares continue to be equity until sold.

7.94   An entity's contractual obligation to purchase its own equity instruments gives rise to a financial liability for the present value of the redemption amount even if the obligation to purchase is conditional on the counterparty exercising a right to redeem. An example is a written put option that gives the counterparty the right to sell an entity's own equity instruments to the entity for a fixed or variable price. See also chapter 24 of the IFRS Manual of Accounting concerning obligations to acquire a minority interest.

Example 2 – Written put option to purchase a fixed number of own shares for a fixed sum
[IAS 32 para IE 30]

On 1 February 20X5, an entity writes a put option for C5,000 under which it has the obligation to purchase 1,000 of its own shares for cash at a fixed price of C98 per share, if the counterparty exercises the put option. The option will be gross settled in that the entity will purchase its own shares and pay the exercise price of C98,000 (C98 × 1,000) on the fixed maturity date of 31 January 20X6.

The following information is given:

	Market price per share	Fair value of option
	C	C
At 1 February 20X5	100	5,000
At 31 December 20X5	95	4,000
At 31 January 20X6	95	3,000

The present value of the option's exercise price on 1 February 20X5 is C95 per share

The accounting entries from inception to settlement of the contract are as follows:

At 1 February 20X5	**Dr**	**Cr**
Cash	C5,000	
Equity		C5,000

At inception of the contract, the entity would record the premium received in exchange for the obligation to deliver a fixed amount of its own shares in one year for a fixed price. As the contract meets the definition of an equity instrument, the premium is credited directly to equity.

	Dr	**Cr**
Equity	C95,000	
Liability		C95,000

Furthermore, at inception of the contract the entity has an obligation to pay C98,000 in cash in one year's time. Therefore, as stated in the above paragraph, the entity recognises the obligation's present value to pay C98,000 in one year's time, that is, C95,000 as a liability.

At 31 December 20X5	**Dr**	**Cr**
Interest expense	C2,750	
Liability		C2,750

As the liability needs to be accreted to its final redemption amount of C98,000, the entity recognises interest expense to 31 December in accordance with the effective interest rate method.

At 31 January 20X6	**Dr**	**Cr**
Interest expense	C250	
Liability		C250

The entity recognises interest expense to 31 January with the result that the liability is stated at its redemption amount of C98,000.

	Dr	Cr
Liability	C98,000	
Cash		C98,000

On the same date, the counterparty exercises the put option as it is in the money (exercise price of C98 per share > market price of C95 per share). The entity settles its obligation under the put option by taking delivery of 1,000 of its own shares and paying cash of C98,000 to the counterparty.

If, on the other hand, the contract expires unexercised, the liability of C98,000 is reclassified to equity.

Contracts accounted for as derivative assets or liabilities

7.95   All other contracts on own equity that are not physically settled gross in shares for a fixed sum are treated as derivatives and accounted for as derivative assets or liabilities in accordance with IAS 39. These include contracts that are:

■   Settled net in cash (or other financial assets). [IAS 32 para AG 27(c)]. Settled net in cash means that the party with a loss delivers to the party with a gain a cash payment equal to the gain and no shares are exchanged.

■   Settled net in the entity's own shares. [IAS 32 para AG 27(c)]. Settled net in shares means that the party with a loss delivers to the party with a gain shares with a current fair value equal to the gain. In other words, the entity's own shares are used as a settlement currency.

■   Settled net in cash or net in shares at the option of the entity or the counterparty (see para 7.57).

7.96   The following examples illustrate the accounting treatment discussed above where an entity enters into derivative contracts on an entity's own equity instruments that require settlement either net in cash or net in shares.

Example 1 – Forward purchase contract on own shares settled net in cash or net in shares [IAS 32 paras IE 3, IE 4]

On 1 February 20X5, an entity enters into a forward purchase contract under which it has the obligation to acquire 1,000 of its own shares at a fixed price of C104 per share on 31 January 20X6.

In scenario 1, the contract can only be settled net in cash (no choice by either party).

In scenario 2, the contract can only be settled net in shares (no choice by either party).

For simplicity, it is assumed that no dividends are paid on the underlying shares (that is the 'carry return' is zero) so that the present value of the forward price equals the spot price of the entity's shares when the fair value of the forward contract is zero. The fair value of the forward has been computed as the difference between the market share price and the present value of the fixed forward price.

The following information is given:

	Market price per share	Fair value of forward
	C	C
At 1 February 20X5	100	Nil
At 31 December 20X5	110	6,300
At 31 January 20X6	106	2,000

The present value of the forward price on 1 February 20X5 is C100 per share.

The accounting entries from inception to settlement of the contract in the two scenarios (settled net in cash or net in shares) are as follows:

At 1 February 20X5

The price per share when the contract is agreed on 1 February 20X5 is C100, which is also the market price of the shares at that date. No entry is required, because the derivative's fair value is zero and no cash is paid or received. This applies whether the forward purchase contract is settled net in cash or net in shares.

At 31 December 20X5	Dr	Cr
Forward asset	C6,300	
Gain in profit or loss		C6,300

On 31 December 20X5, the market price per share has increased to C110 and, as a result, the forward contract's fair value has increased to C6,300. The increase in the contract's fair value is recognised in profit or loss.

At 31 January 20X6	Dr	Cr
Loss in profit or loss	C4,300	
Forward asset		C4,300

On 31 January 20X6, the market price per share has decreased to C106. The fair value of the forward contract is C2,000 [1,000 * (C106-C104)]. The decrease in the fair value on the forward contract from C6,300 to C2,000 is recognised in profit or loss.

Scenario 1 – Settled net in cash	Dr	Cr
Cash	C2,000	
Forward asset		C2,000

On the same day, the contract is settled net in cash. The entity has an obligation to deliver C104,000 in cash, being the settlement amount of the contract, to the counterparty. The counterparty has an obligation to deliver cash equal to the fair value of 1,000 shares at the date, that is C106,000 (1,000 × C106) to the entity. So the counterparty pays the net amount of C2,000 to the entity.

Scenario 2 – Settled net in shares	Dr	Cr
Equity	C2,000	
Forward asset		C2,000

If the contract is settled net in shares, the entity has an obligation to deliver C104,000 worth of its own shares to the counterparty. The counterparty has an obligation to deliver C106,000 (1,000 × C106) worth of the entity's shares to the entity. So the counterparty delivers the net amount of C2,000 worth of the entity's shares to the entity, that is, 18.9 shares (C2,000/C106). The settlement in shares is accounted for as an equity transaction.

Example 2 – Written call option on own shares settled net in cash or net in shares [IAS 32 paras IE 18, IE 19]

On 1 February 20X5, an entity writes a call option for C5,000 under which it has an obligation to sell 1,000 of its own shares at a fixed price of C102 per share, if the counterparty exercises the call option. The option will be settled on the fixed maturity date of 31 January 20X6.

In scenario 1, the contract can only be settled net in cash (no choice by either party).

In scenario 2, the contract can only be settled net in shares (no choice by either party).

The following information is given:

	Market price per share C	Fair value of option C
At 1 February 20X5	100	5,000
At 31 December 20X5	104	3,000
At 31 January 20X6	104	2,000

The accounting entries from inception to settlement of the contract in the two scenarios (settled net in cash or net in shares) are as follows:

At 1 February 20X5

	Dr	Cr
Cash	C5,000	
Call option obligation		C5,000

At inception of the contract, the entity would record the premium received under the contract in both scenarios.

At 31 December 20X5

	Dr	Cr
Call option obligation	C2,000	
Gain in profit or loss		C2,000

On 31 December 20X5, the fair value of the call option obligation has fall to C3,000. The decrease in the fair value of the obligation is recognised as a gain in profit or loss.

At 31 January 20X6

	Dr	Cr
Call option obligation	C1,000	
Gain in profit or loss		C1,000

On 31 January 20X6, the fair value of the call option obligation has fallen further to C2,000. The decrease in the fair value is recognised as a gain in profit or loss.

Scenario 1 – Settled net in cash

	Dr	Cr
Call option obligation	C2,000	
Cash		C2,000

If the contract is settled net in cash, the entity has an obligation to deliver C104,000 in cash, being the fair value of the 1,000 shares on 31 January 20X6, to the counterparty. The counterparty has an obligation to deliver cash equal to the option's exercise price of C102,000 to the entity. So the entity pays the net amount of C2,000 to the counterparty.

Scenario 2 – Settled net in shares	**Dr**	**Cr**
Call option obligation	C2,000	
Equity		C2,000

If, the contract is settled net in shares, the entity has an obligation to deliver C104,000 worth of its own shares to the counterparty. The counterparty has an obligation to deliver C102,000 worth of the entity's shares to the entity. So the entity delivers the net amount of C2,000 worth of its own shares to the counterparty, that is, 19.2 shares (C2,000/C104). The settlement in shares is accounted for as an equity transaction.

Issuer or holder's settlement options

7.97 The examples above deal with situations where the settlement of the derivative contracts on own equity, either net in cash or net in shares, was dictated by the contractual terms (no choice). Sometimes such derivative contracts may contain settlement options that give either party a choice over how it is settled (for example, the issuer or the holder can choose to settle the contract net in cash, or net in shares or by exchanging shares for cash). As explained in paragraph 7.57 above, when a derivative financial instrument gives one party a choice over how it is settled, it is a financial asset or a financial liability unless all of the settlement alternatives would result in it being an equity instrument. [IAS 32 para 26].

[The next paragraph is 7.99.]

Treatment of interest, dividends, gains and losses

7.99 The general principle of IAS 32 is that the treatment of interest, dividends, losses and gains follows the classification of the related instrument. Therefore, where such items relate to equity instruments, they are included in equity. On the other hand, if they relate to instruments that are classified as financial liabilities, they are included in profit or loss. IAS 32, therefore, requires that:

■ Interest, dividends, losses and gains relating to a financial instrument or a component that is a financial liability should be recognised as income or expense in profit or loss.

■ Distributions to holders of an equity instrument should be debited by the entity directly to equity, net of any related income tax benefit.

[IAS 32 para 35].

7.100 It follows from the above requirement that dividend payments on preference shares that are classified wholly as liabilities are included in calculating amortised cost and, hence, recognised as expenses in the same way as interest on a bond. They may be presented in the income statement either with interest on other liabilities or as a separate item. The standard notes that in some circumstances, it may be desirable to disclose interest and dividends separately in the income statement, because of the differences between interest and dividends with respect to matters such as tax deductibility. Disclosure of interest and dividends is subject to the requirements of IAS 1, 'Presentation of financial statements', and IFRS 7, 'Financial instruments: Disclosures'. Disclosures of the tax effects should be made in accordance with IAS 12, 'Income taxes'. [IAS 32 para 40].

7.101 Gains and losses associated with redemptions or refinancings of financial liabilities are recognised in profit or loss. Similarly, gains and losses related to changes in the carrying amount of a financial liability are recognised in profit or loss. This is so even when they relate to an instrument that includes a right to the residual interest in the entity's assets in exchange for cash or another financial asset (for example, units in mutual funds that are puttable – see para 7.19 above). Under IAS 1, the entity presents any gain or loss arising from remeasurement of such an instrument separately on the face of the income statement when it is relevant in explaining the entity's performance. [IAS 32 para 41]. IAS 32 contains examples of income statement presentation where an entity has little or no equity. [IAS 32 paras IE 32-IE 33].

7.102 Redemptions or refinancings of equity instruments are recognised in equity. Changes in the fair value of an equity instrument are not recognised in the financial statements. [IAS 32 para 36].

7.103 The application of the principle in paragraph 7.99 above to compound financial instruments would require any payments relating to the liability component to be reported in profit or loss and any payments relating to the equity component to be reported in equity. A classic example is mandatorily redeemable preference shares with discretionary dividend payments. Such an instrument is a compound financial instrument, with the liability component being the present value of the redemption amount. The unwinding of the discount on this component is recognised in profit or loss and classified as interest expense. Any dividends paid relate to the equity component and are recognised as a distribution of profit or loss. A similar treatment would apply if the redemption was not mandatory but at the option of the holder, or if the preference shares were mandatorily convertible into a variable number of ordinary shares calculated to equal a fixed amount or an amount based on changes in an underlying variable (for example, a commodity). However, if any unpaid dividends are added to the redemption amount, the entire instrument is a liability. In such a case, any dividends are classified as interest expense that will be accounted for in accordance with the effective interest method. [IAS 32 para AG 37].

Example – Premium payable on the cancellation of the conversion option in a convertible bond

An entity has issued a convertible bond, which is classified as a compound instrument (liability host bond and an equity conversion option). The entity decides after issue to cancel the conversion option in order to remove the dilution effect on its share capital. The issuer will have to pay the bondholder a premium to compensate for giving up its conversion rights, which is likely to be greater than the fair value of the conversion option to incentivise the bondholder to accept the change in terms. Provided that the terms of the liability component of the bond remain unchanged, the premium paid to cancel the equity conversion option is a payment for an own equity instrument. The premium paid is, therefore, debited to equity, as for any repurchase of an entity's own equity instruments.

Treatment of transaction costs of equity instruments

7.104　An entity typically incurs various costs in issuing or acquiring its own equity instruments. Those costs might include registration and other regulatory fees, underwriting costs and brokerage fees, amounts paid to lawyers, accountants, investment bankers and other professional advisers, fees and commissions paid to agents, brokers, and dealers, printing costs and stamp duties. Most such costs are transaction costs, that is, incremental costs that are directly attributable to the equity transaction that otherwise would have been avoided had the equity instruments not been issued. Transaction costs arising on the issue of equity instruments, however, do not include indirect costs, such as the costs of management time and administrative overheads, or allocations of internal costs that would have been incurred had the equity instruments not been issued. Nor do they include costs of researching different types of equity instruments or of ascertaining the suitability or feasibility of particular equity instruments. Generally, costs for marketing an IPO, including the 'road show', do not meet the definition of a transaction cost. Marketing costs primarily relate to the marketing of the entity itself. Therefore in most situations marketing costs for an IPO do not meet the definition of directly attributable and therefore are expensed through profit or loss.

7.105　IAS 32 requires that transaction costs of an equity transaction should be accounted for as a deduction from equity, net of any related income tax benefit. [IAS 32 para 35]. This treatment is based on the view that the transaction costs incurred are a necessary part of completing the equity transaction and form an integral part of it. Linking the equity transaction and costs of the transaction reflects the net proceeds received from the transaction in equity. This approach achieves a result which is consistent with paragraph 7.99 above, which states that a financial instrument's classification in the balance sheet determines whether interest, dividends, losses and gains relating to that instrument are reported in the income statement. As a result, losses relating to a financial instrument classified as the issuer's equity are reported by the issuer as movements in equity.

7.106　Transaction costs that relate to the issue of a compound financial instrument are allocated to the instrument's liability and equity components in proportion to the allocation of proceeds (see example in para 7.67). See Chapter 9 for more discussion on transaction costs.

7.107　Transaction costs that relate jointly to more than one transaction (for example, costs of a concurrent offering of some shares and a stock exchange listing of other shares) are allocated to those transactions using a basis of allocation that is rational and consistent with similar transactions. [IAS 32 para 38]. This situation often arises when an entity undertakes an initial public offering (IPO) of its shares. As a result of the IPO, new shares are issued to investors to raise additional capital and, along with existing shares, subsequently become listed on a stock exchange. Costs incurred in listing existing shares on a stock exchange are not transaction costs relating to the issue of an equity instrument. This is because these costs are simply incurred to make the existing shares more marketable and are not related to the equity instrument's issue. In some situations, the existing shares may be included in a 'secondary offering' (that is, a sale of shares by existing shareholders as opposed to the company itself). As the cash generated from the sale of secondary shares is given to the selling shareholders, rather than the company, any costs incurred are not equity transaction costs. Therefore, these costs should be charged to the income statement. On the other hand, costs incurred in issuing new shares to raise capital ('primary offering') in an IPO are transaction costs of equity instrument and, as explained above, fall to be charged to equity. In practice, entities would need to identify the costs that are specifically attributable to the issue of new shares. All other costs of the IPO that would not have been incurred had the IPO not taken place should be allocated between the new shares and old shares on some reasonable basis, for example, in the ratio of old to new shares. It follows from the above that any costs incurred by the company in a 'secondary offering' of its own shares are not equity transaction costs. Accordingly, those costs should be charged to profit or loss.

7.108   The amount of transaction costs accounted for as a deduction from equity in the period is disclosed separately under IAS 1. The related amount of income taxes recognised directly in equity is included in the aggregate amount of current and deferred income tax credited or charged to equity that is disclosed under IAS 12. [IAS 32 para 39; IAS 12 para 81(a)].

Treasury shares

7.109   When an entity purchases its own shares and holds them in treasury ('treasury shares'), IAS 32 requires the following:

■   The amount paid for the treasury shares is deducted from equity. This is because an entity's own equity instruments are not recognised as a financial asset regardless of the reason for which they are acquired. However, where an entity holds its own equity on behalf of others, for example, a financial institution holding its own equity on behalf of a client, there is an agency relationship and as a result those holdings are not included in the entity's balance sheet.

■   No gain or loss should be recognised in profit or loss on the purchase, sale, issue or cancellation of an entity's own equity instruments. This is because the acquisition and subsequent resale of treasury shares are transactions with entity's owners rather than a gain or loss to the entity.

■   Consideration paid or received for the purchase or sale of an entity's own equity instruments should be recognised directly in equity.

[IAS 32 paras 33, AG 36].

7.110   IAS 32 notes that own equity instruments may be acquired and held by the entity or by other members of the consolidated group (that is, the parent and its subsidiaries, but excluding the group's associates and joint ventures). [IAS 32 para 33]. Therefore, the above accounting applies to all interests in own equity instruments held by a company and, in consolidated financial statements, the parent's shares held by subsidiaries. In the latter case, this applies to all such shareholdings, including those held by subsidiaries that carry on a business of dealing in securities. However, in the individual financial statements of a subsidiary that holds shares in its parent, such shares are treated as an asset; that is, 'treasury shares' accounting does not apply as these are not 'own shares' for the subsidiary itself.

> **UK.7.111** In the UK, certain public listed companies that have 'qualifying shares' may hold them as treasury shares under sections 724 to 732 of the 2006 Act, as discussed in chapter 23 of the Manual of Accounting – IFRS for the UK.

Example – Purchase of own shares held in treasury

Entity A (a listed company) has in issue 1,000,000 C1 ordinary shares originally issued at a premium of C9. It buys back 20,000 shares when their market value is C40 per share. The purchase is made out of retained profits and the entity holds the shares in treasury. In this situation, the entity does not reduce its issued share capital, but instead will reduce its retained profits by the consideration paid for the shares (that is, 20,000 × C40 = C800,000), as shown below.

It should be noted that this treatment only applies in the UK and the treatment in other jurisdictions may be different.

	Before purchase C'000	Purchase C'000	After purchase C'000
Net assets other than cash	20,000	20,000	
Cash	5,000	(800)	4,200
	25,000	(800)	24,200
Share capital	1,000	1,000	
Share premium	9,000	9,000	
Capital	10,000	10,000	
Retained profits	15,000	(800)	14,200
	25,000	(800)	24,200

As can be seen from the above example, the entire consideration paid for the purchase is recognised directly in equity (retained profits).

In the notes to the financial statements, entity A should explain that 20,000 C1 ordinary shares with an aggregate nominal value of C20,000 were purchased during

Chapter 8

Recognition and derecognition

Recognition and derecognition

Introduction

8.1 Previous chapters have dealt with what qualifies as financial assets and financial liabilities. The next step in the accounting is to determine when financial assets and financial liabilities should be recognised, that is, included in an entity's balance sheet. Conversely, it is also necessary to know when a financial asset or financial liability should be derecognised, that is, when a previously recognised financial asset or financial liability should be removed from an entity's balance sheet.

8.2 As explained in chapter 3, the rights or obligations that comprise financial assets or financial liabilities are derived from the contractual provisions that underlie them. As a result, an entity only recognises a financial asset or a financial liability at the time it becomes a party to a contract. [IAS 39 para 14]. That is the point at which it has the contractual rights or contractual obligations. As the above discussion suggests, recognition issues for financial assets and financial liabilities tend to be straightforward. They are dealt with in paragraphs 8.5 to 8.23 below.

8.3 Conversely, when considering whether to cease recognising (derecognise) a financial asset or a financial liability, an entity needs to consider whether it still has that asset or liability. In other words, the entity needs to determine whether the rights or obligations contained in the original asset or liability cease to be contractual rights or obligations.

8.4 Derecognition issues for financial instruments are generally far from straightforward, except where relatively simple financial instruments and transactions are involved. The derecognition requirements in IAS 39 are complex as a result. These issues for financial instruments are discussed from paragraph 8.24 for financial assets and paragraph 8.143 for financial liabilities respectively.

8.4.1 In March 2009, the IASB issued the exposure draft 'Derecognition: Proposed amendments to IAS 39 and IFRS 7'. The exposure draft proposed an approach intended to reduce the complexity of the current requirements, and the resulting difficulty in applying them in practice, but did not attract significant support. Derecognition is a joint project with the US FASB. In June 2010, the FASB and IASB decided to defer work on a new standard to concentrate on other more urgent projects. However, the IASB is proposing to issue a new standard on disclosures in 2010, while keeping the existing derecognition requirements in IAS 39.

Initial recognition

General principles

8.5 Under IAS 39 an entity is required to recognise a financial asset or liability on its balance sheet when, and only when, it becomes a party to the instrument's contractual provisions. [IAS 39 para 14].

Application of the general principles

8.6 Examples of situations where an entity becomes a party to the contractual provisions of a financial instrument are many and varied. Some of these situations are considered in the paragraphs that follow.

Unconditional receivables and payables

8.7 Unconditional receivables and payables are recognised as assets or liabilities when the entity becomes a party to the contract and, as a consequence, has a legal right to receive or a legal obligation to pay cash. [IAS 39 para AG 35(a)].

Forwards and options

8.8 When an entity becomes a party to a forward contract that falls within IAS 39's scope, it becomes exposed to risks and benefits at the contract commitment date, rather than on the date on which settlement takes place. At the commitment date, the fair values of the right and obligation are often equal, so that the net fair value of the forward contract is zero. If the net fair value of the right and obligation is not zero at inception, the contract is recognised as an asset or liability. [IAS 39 para AG 35(c)]. A forward contract that has a zero fair value at inception may become a net asset or liability in the future depending on the value of the underlying instrument or commodity that is the subject of the forward.

8.9 Similarly, option contracts that fall within IAS 39's scope are recognised as assets or liabilities when the holder or writer become a party to the contract. [IAS 39 para AG 35(d)]. Evidence that a recognisable event arises when the entities become parties to the contract lies in the fact that the option holder usually pays, and the option writer usually receives, a premium for the contract, which indicates that the rights and obligations undertaken by each party have value at that date.

Firm commitments to buy or sell non-financial assets

8.10 When an entity enters into a firm commitment to purchase a non-financial asset in the future, it does not have the contractual rights that comprise the asset. This means that the entity cannot use that asset, or sell it, or pledge it as collateral until the contract matures and the underlying asset is acquired. Therefore, assets to be acquired and liabilities to be incurred as a result of a firm commitment to purchase or sell goods or services are generally not recognised as assets or liabilities until at least one of the parties has performed under the agreement. For example, an entity that receives a firm order does not generally recognise an asset for the consideration to be received (and the entity that places the order does not recognise a liability for the consideration to be paid) at the time of the commitment but, rather, delays recognition until the ordered goods or services have been shipped, delivered or rendered. Another example is given in paragraph 8.89.1.

8.11 However, as stated in chapter 3 above, contracts to buy or sell non-financial assets that can be settled net or by exchanging financial instruments are treated as if they are financial instruments, that is, derivatives unless they were entered into and continued to be held to meet the entity's normal purchase, sale or usage requirements. Therefore, the net fair value of the contract itself is recognised as an asset or liability at the commitment date.

8.12 Also, if a previously unrecognised firm commitment is designated as a hedged item in a fair value hedge, IAS 39 requires that any change in the net fair value attributable to the hedged risk is recognised as an asset or liability after the inception of the hedge (see chapter 10). Some argue that it is conceptually incorrect to recognise an asset or liability for a firm commitment because it has been hedged. The IASB explains in the Basis of Conclusions that the only difference between a firm commitment that is not hedged and a one that is hedged is that the latter is re-measured for changes in the hedged fair value while the former is measured at its historical cost of zero. Accordingly, there is no fundamental difference in concept as far as recognition is concerned. [IAS 39 paras AG35(b), BC152].

Planned future transactions

8.13 As stated in paragraph 8.5 above, a financial asset or a liability should not be recognised before an entity becomes a party to the contract. It follows that planned future transactions, no matter how likely, cannot give rise to financial assets and liabilities because the entity has not become a party to a contract. [IAS 39 para AG 35(e)]. Such future transactions are future events to be recognised in the future periods when contractual rights are acquired or obligations incurred.

Regular way transactions

8.14 A regular way purchase or sale is a purchase or sale of a financial asset under a contract whose terms require delivery of the asset within the *time frame* established generally by regulation or convention in the *marketplace* concerned. [IAS 39 para 9]. Marketplace is not limited to a formal stock exchange or organised over-the-counter market. Rather, it means the environment in which the financial asset is customarily exchanged. An acceptable time frame in such a marketplace would be the period reasonably and customarily required for the parties to complete the transaction, prepare, and execute closing documents. [IAS 39 para IG B28].

8.15 In many regulated financial markets, a settlement mechanism will exist under which transactions in financial instruments (particularly quoted equities and bonds) entered into on a particular date are settled a few days after this transaction date. The date on which the transaction is entered into is called the 'trade date'. It is the date on which the entity commits to purchase or sell an asset. The date on which the transaction is settled by delivery of the underlying asset is called the 'settlement date'. For example, the standard settlement periods on the London Stock Exchange for equity market securities and wholesale gilts are trade date plus 3 business days (T + 3) and trade date plus 1 business day (T + 1) respectively. A contract with an individual or through a broker to buy or sell a financial asset that is normally traded on a regulated financial market, but with a settlement period that differs from that established by regulation in that financial marketplace, does not qualify as a regular way transaction. [IAS 39 para IG B29, B30].

8.16 A regular way purchase or sale that gives rise to a fixed price commitment between trade date and settlement date is a derivative – a forward contract. Therefore, in accordance with the principle explained in paragraph 8.8, a regular way purchase or sale would fall to be recognised as a forward contract at the commitment date (that is, trade date). However, because of the short duration of the commitment, such contracts are not recognised as derivative financial instruments under IAS 39. Instead, IAS 39 provides for special accounting for such regular way contracts, as discussed from paragraph 8.18 below. [IAS 39 para AG12]. This exception is a practical expedient to prevent the recognition of derivatives for short periods where the marketplace mechanism prevents settlement at the trade or commitment date. Furthermore, the exception also removes a potential distortion that would occur by recognising changes in fair value of the asset between trade and settlement date through profit or loss, when such changes in fair value after settlement date would either not be recognised at all (where the financial asset is classified as a held-to-maturity asset), or recognised in other comprehensive income (where the financial asset is classified as available-for-sale).

8.17 The regular way exception requires that the transaction will be settled by physical delivery of the financial instrument within the normal market time frame. Therefore, where a contract permits net settlement in cash or other financial assets equivalent to the change in the contract's fair value, it does not qualify as a regular way transaction. Such a contract is accounted for as a derivative in the period between trade and settlement date. [IAS 39 para AG 54]. Contracts that are settled outside the normal market time frame, whether settled net in cash or gross, will always be accounted for as derivatives.

Trade date versus settlement date accounting

8.18   IAS 39 provides that a regular way purchase or sale of financial assets should be recognised and derecognised, as applicable, using trade date accounting or settlement date accounting. Either method is acceptable, but it is an accounting policy choice that should be disclosed and applied consistently for all purchases and sales that belong to the same category of financial assets as set out in chapter 6. For this purpose assets that are held for trading form a separate category from assets designated at fair value through profit and loss. [IAS 39 para AG 53].

8.19   Where an entity adopts trade date accounting (the date on which an entity commits itself to purchase or sell an asset), the accounting treatment is as follows:

■   In respect of a purchase of a financial asset, the asset received and the liability to pay for it are recognised on the trade date. After initial recognition, the financial asset is subsequently measured either at amortised cost or at fair value depending on its initial classification as explained in chapter 9.

■   In respect of a sale of a financial asset, the asset is derecognised and the receivable from the buyer for the payment together with any gain or loss on disposal are recognised on the trade date.

IAS 39 notes that, generally, interest does not start to accrue on the asset and corresponding liability until settlement date when title passes.

[IAS 39 para AG 55].

8.20   Where an entity adopts settlement date accounting (the date that an asset is delivered to or by an entity), the accounting treatment is as follows:

■   In respect of a purchase of a financial asset, the asset is recognised on the day it is received by the entity. Any change in the asset's fair value to be received during the period between the trade date and the settlement date is accounted for in the same way as the acquired asset. In other words:

    ■   for assets carried at cost or amortised cost, the change in value is not recognised;

    ■   for assets classified as financial assets at fair value through profit or loss, the change in value is recognised in profit or loss; and

    ■   for available-for-sale assets, the change in value is recognised in other comprehensive income.

■   In respect of a sale of a financial asset, the asset is derecognised and the receivable from the buyer for the payment together with any gain or loss on disposal are recognised on the day that it is delivered by the entity. Any change in the fair value of the asset between trade date and settlement date is not recognised, as there is an agreed upon sale price at the trade date, making subsequent changes in fair value irrelevant from the seller's perspective. In other words, the seller's right to changes in the fair value ceases on the trade date.

[IAS 39 para AG 56].

8.21   The following examples illustrate the application of trade date and settlement date accounting to the various categories of financial asset identified by IAS 39. These examples are based on those included in IAS 39's implementation guidance. [IAS 39 paras IG D2.1, D2.2].

Example 1 – Regular way purchase of a financial asset

On 29 December 20X5, an entity commits to purchase a financial asset for C1,000, which is its fair value on commitment (trade) date. Transaction costs are immaterial. On 31 December 20X5 (financial year-end) and on 4 January 20X6 (settlement date) the fair value of the asset is C1,002 and C1,003, respectively.

The amounts to be recorded for the asset will depend on how it is classified and whether trade date or settlement date accounting is used, as shown in the two tables below.

Trade date accounting

Details	Held-to-maturity investments – carried at amortised cost	Available-for-sale assets – remeasured to fair value with changes in other comprehensive income	Assets at fair value through profit or loss – remeasured to fair value with changes in profit or loss
29 December 20X5	C	C	C
Dr Financial asset	1,000	1,000	1,000
Cr Liability for payment	(1,000)	(1,000)	(1,000)
To record asset and liability for payment			
31 December 20X5			
Dr Financial asset	–	2	2
Cr Other comprehensive income	–	(2)	–
Cr Income statement	–	–	(2)
To recognise change in fair value			
4 January 20X6			
Dr Financial asset	–	1	1
Cr Other comprehensive income	–	(1)	–
Cr Income statement	–	–	(1)
To recognise change in fair value			

4 January 20X6			
Dr Liability for payment	1,000	1,000	1,000
Cr Cash	(1,000)	(1,000)	(1,000)
To record settlement of liability			
Asset's carrying value at 4 January 20X6	1000	1003	1003

Settlement date accounting

29 December 20X5			
No entries are recorded at the commitment date	–	–	–
31 December 20X5			
Dr Financial asset	–	2	2
Cr Other comprehensive income	–	(2)	–
Cr Income statement	–	–	(2)
To recognise change in fair value			
4 January 20X6			
Dr Financial asset	–	1	1
Cr Other comprehensive income	–	(1)	–
Cr Income statement	–	–	(1)
To recognise change in fair value			
4 January 20X6			
Dr Financial asset	1,000	1,000	1,000
Cr Cash	–	(1,000)	(1,000)

To record the asset's purchase at the contracted cash amount plus changes in fair value since trade date.

Asset's carrying value at 4 January 20X6	1000	1003	1003

Example 2 – Regular way sale of a financial asset

On 29 December 20X5 (trade date) an entity enters into a contract to sell a financial asset for its current fair value of C1,010. The asset was acquired one year earlier for C1,000 and its amortised cost is C1,000. On 31 December 20X5 (financial year-end), the fair value of the asset is C1,012. On 4 January 20X6 (settlement date), the fair value is C1,013.

The amounts to be recorded will depend on how the asset is classified and whether trade date or settlement date accounting is used as shown in the two tables below (any interest that might have accrued on the asset is disregarded).

Trade date accounting			
Date	Held-to-maturity investments - carried at amortised cost	Available- for-sale assets – remeasured to fair value with changes in other comprehensive income	Assets at fair value through profit or loss – remeasured to fair value with changes in profit or loss
	C	C	C
Carrying value prior to 29 December 20X5	1,000	1,010	1,010
29 December 20X5			
Dr Receivable	1,010	1,010	1,010
Cr Asset	(1,000)	(1,010)	(1,010)
Dr Other comprehensive income		10	
Cr Profit or loss	(10)	(10)	–

To record disposal of the asset and 'recycling' of cumulative gain from other comprehensive income to profit or loss on disposal of the available-for-sale asset on trade date.

31 December 20X5
A change in the fair value of a financial asset that is sold on a regular way basis is not recorded in the financial statements between trade date and settlement date because the seller's right to changes in the fair value ceases on the trade date.

4 January 20X6			
Dr Cash	1,010	1,010	1,010
Cr Receivable	(1,010)	(1,010)	(1,010)

To record settlement of sales contract

Settlement date accounting

29 December 20X5			
Carrying value prior to 29 December 20X5	1,000	1,010	1,010

31 December 20X5

A change in the fair value of a financial asset that is sold on a regular way basis is not recorded in the financial statements between trade date and settlement date, even if the entity applies settlement date accounting, because the seller's right to changes in the fair value ceases on the trade date.

4 January 20X6

Dr Cash	1,010	1,010	1,010
Cr Asset	(1,000)	(1,010)	(1,010)
Dr Other comprehensive income		10	–
Cr Profit or loss	(10)	(10)	–

To record the disposal of the asset and 'recycling' of cumulative gain on the available-for-sale asset recognised in other comprehensive income to profit or loss on settlement date.

In summary, regular way sale is accounted for as a sale on trade date if trade date accounting is used and on settlement date if settlement date accounting is used.

8.22   It should be noted that the above requirements apply only to transactions in financial assets. IAS 39 does not contain any specific requirements about trade date accounting and settlement date accounting for transactions in financial instruments that are classified as financial liabilities. This means that the general recognition and derecognition requirements for financial liabilities in IAS 39 apply. [IAS 39 para IG B32]. Under IAS 39, liabilities are recognised on the date the entity 'becomes a party to the contractual provisions of the instrument' (see para 8.5 above). Financial liabilities are derecognised only when they are extinguished, that is, when the obligation specified in the contract is discharged or cancelled or expires (see further para 8.144 below).

Exchange of non-cash financial assets

8.23   Sometimes an entity may enter into a regular way transaction to sell a non-cash financial asset not for cash, but in exchange for another non-cash financial asset. In this situation, a question arises as to whether any change in fair value of the financial asset to be received should be recognised between trade and settlement date in circumstances where the entity adopts settlement date accounting for the financial asset to be disposed of. The answer depends on the classification of the asset to be received in exchange and whether the entity uses trade date or settlement date accounting for purchases or sales of assets in that category. Consider the following example:

Example – Regular way sale of a financial asset for non-cash consideration

On 29 December 20X5 (trade date) entity A enters into a contract to sell note receivable A, which is carried at amortised cost, in exchange for bond B, which will be classified as held for trading and measured at fair value. Both assets have a fair value of C1,010 on 29 December, while the amortised cost of note receivable A is C1,000. Entity A uses settlement date accounting for loans and receivables and trade date accounting for assets held for trading.

On 31 December 20X5 (financial year-end), the fair value of note receivable A is C1,012 and the fair value of bond B is C1,009. On 4 January 20X6, the fair value of note receivable A is C1,013 and the fair value of bond B is C1,007.

The following entries are made:

	Dr C	Cr C
29 December 20X5		
Bond B	1,010	
Liability for payment		1,010

To record the purchase of bond B on the trade date as per entity's policy of using trade date accounting for assets held for trading.

	Dr	Cr
31 December 20X5		
Profit or loss	1	
Bond B		1

To record the change in fair value of bond B from C1,010 to C1,009.

	Dr	Cr
4 January 20X6		
Liability for payment	1,010	
Note receivable A		1,000
Profit or loss		10

To record the disposal of note receivable A and the resultant gain on sale in exchange for bond B on settlement date.

	Dr	Cr
Profit or loss	2	
Bond B		2

To record the change in fair value of bond B from C1,009 to C1,007.

Derecognition of financial assets

Introduction

8.24   It is fairly common for entities to raise finance by selling financial assets, such as portfolios of trade receivables, loans, etc. No special problem arises where a transferor sells financial assets for cash or other assets, with no continuing involvement with the asset sold or with the transferee. The accounting for such transactions as sales with corresponding derecognition of the asset is well established. At the other extreme is a transfer of a financial asset where the buyer has an unconditional right and obligation to return the asset at the original price, usually with interest as in a repurchase transaction. Again, the accounting in this situation is fairly straightforward. The transaction is treated as a financing, with both the asset and the liability on balance sheet, because the risk and rewards of ownership of the asset have not been transferred.

8.25 Problems begin to surface, however, when transfers are undertaken between the above two extremes in circumstances where the seller retains certain interests in the assets transferred. Examples include transfers that are subject to recourse and agreements to acquire the transferred asset or make additional payments that reflect the performance of the transferred asset.

[The next paragraph is 8.30.]

Requirements in IAS 39 for derecognition

8.30 IAS 39 contains one set of requirements that apply to the derecognition of all financial assets, from the simple maturity of an instrument to the more complex securitisation transactions. The standard provides a flowchart (below) that summarises IAS 39's requirements for evaluating whether, and to what extent, a financial asset is derecognised. Every transaction should be analysed using the strict sequence set out in the flowchart. Most importantly, there are two separate approaches to derecognition under IFRS: the 'risks and rewards' approach and the 'control' approach. The control approach is only used where the risks and rewards approach does not provide a clear answer. Hence the risks and rewards approach should be evaluated first. A detailed explanation of these two approaches and each step of the flow chart follows.

8.30.1 For analysis purposes and ease of reference, each step has a number and refers to a particular step in the diagram. For example, if step 6 = Yes, this means that the entity has transferred substantially all the risks and rewards of ownership. Similarly, if step 6 = No and step 7 = No, this means that the entity has neither transferred nor retained substantially all of the risks and rewards of ownership. This notation is used throughout the remainder of the chapter.

Recognition and derecognition

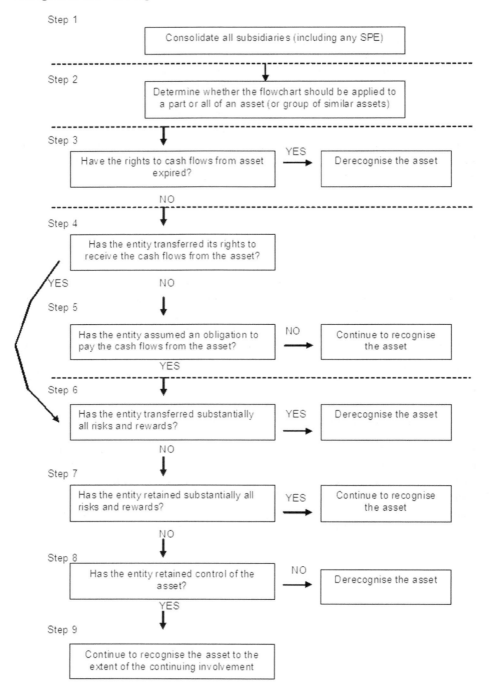

Step 1
Consolidate all subsidiaries (including any SPE)

Step 2
Determine whether the flowchart should be applied to a part or all of an asset (or group of similar assets)

Step 3
Have the rights to cash flows from asset expired?
YES → Derecognise the asset
NO

Step 4
Has the entity transferred its rights to receive the cash flows from the asset?
YES
NO

Step 5
Has the entity assumed an obligation to pay the cash flows from the asset?
NO → Continue to recognise the asset
YES

Step 6
Has the entity transferred substantially all risks and rewards?
YES → Derecognise the asset
NO

Step 7
Has the entity retained substantially all risks and rewards?
YES → Continue to recognise the asset
NO

Step 8
Has the entity retained control of the asset?
NO → Derecognise the asset
YES

Step 9
Continue to recognise the asset to the extent of the continuing involvement

Consolidate all subsidiaries including any SPEs (step 1)

8.31   Many entities establish special purpose entities (SPEs), trusts, partnerships, etc. to acquire financial assets before these financial assets, or a portion thereof, are transferred to third-party investors. The transfer of financial assets to such an entity might qualify as a legal sale. However, if the substance of the relationship between the transferor and the SPE indicates that the transferor controls the SPE, the transferor should consolidate the SPE. The first step is to determine what is the reporting entity that is considering whether to derecognise the financial asset – that is, whether it is the consolidated or the individual entity. If it is the consolidated entity, the entity should first consolidate all subsidiaries, including any special purpose entities, in accordance with IAS 27, 'Consolidated and separate financial statements', and SIC 12, 'Consolidation – Special purpose entities'. It should then apply the derecognition analysis to the resulting group. (Note that an entity preparing separate financial statements will not need to consider this step.) [IAS 39 para 14].

8.32   Step 1, therefore, ensures that the derecognition analysis produces the same answer regardless of whether the entity transfers financial assets, or a portion thereof, directly to third party investors or through a consolidated SPE or trust that obtains the transferred assets and, in turn, transfers them directly to third party investors. [IAS 39 para BC64].

8.32.1   A variety of factors needs to be evaluated to determine whether the substance of the relationship between an entity and an SPE indicates the entity controls the SPE such that the SPE is consolidated. Indicators of control provided in SIC 12 paragraph 10 are:

■   In substance, the activities of the SPE are being conducted on the entity's behalf according to its specific business needs, so that the entity obtains benefits from the SPE's operation;

■   In substance, the entity has the decision-making powers to obtain the majority of the benefits of the SPE's activities or, by setting up an 'autopilot' mechanism, the entity has delegated these decision-making powers;

■   In substance, the entity has rights to obtain the majority of the SPE's benefits and, therefore, may be exposed to risks incidental to the SPE's activities; or

■   In substance, the entity retains the majority of the residual or ownership risks related to the SPE or its assets in order to obtain benefits from its activities.

8.32.2   The decision to consolidate an SPE always depends on specific facts and circumstances; if those change, entities will need to re-assess their consolidation decisions. This is especially relevant in difficult market conditions where companies might need to step in to support SPEs when there was previously no contractual obligation to do so. These issues are considered further in chapter 24 of the IFRS Manual of Accounting.

Determine whether the flow chart applies to all or part of an asset (step 2)

8.33   The next step (step 2 in the diagram in para 8.30 above) is to determine whether the analysis should be applied to a part of a financial asset (or part of a group of similar financial assets) or to a financial asset in its entirety (or a group of similar assets in their entirety). The standard stipulates that the derecognition rules should be applied to a part of a financial asset (or part of a group of similar financial assets) if, and only if, the part being considered for derecognition meets one of the following three conditions:

■   The part comprises only specifically identified cash flows from a financial asset (or a group of similar financial assets).

■   The part comprises only a fully proportionate (*pro rata*) share of the cash flows from a financial asset (or a group of similar financial assets).

■   The part comprises only a fully proportionate (*pro rata*) share of specifically identified cash flows from a financial asset (or a group of similar financial assets). For example, if an entity enters into an arrangement in which the counterparty obtains the rights to a 90 per cent share of interest cash flows from a financial asset (the specifically identified part), the derecognition rules are applied to that 90 per cent of those interest cash flows. If there is more than one counterparty, it is not necessary for each counterparty to have a proportionate share of the specifically identified cash flows provided that the transferring entity retains a fully proportionate share.

[IAS 39 para 16(a)].

8.34   The above criteria must be applied strictly to determine whether the derecognition rules should be applied either to the whole asset, or to only a part of the asset. The meaning of 'a group of similar assets' is considered further from paragraph 8.52 below.

8.35   If it is not possible to identify a part, the derecognition rules must be applied to the financial asset in its entirety (or to the group of similar financial assets in their entirety). [IAS 39 para 16(b)]. Consider the examples below.

> **Example 1 – Sale of the first or the last specified amount of cash flows from a financial asset**
>
> An entity originates a portfolio of similar five-year interest-bearing loans of C1m. It then enters into an agreement with a counterparty. It agrees to pay the counterparty the first C0.9m of cash collected from the portfolio plus interest, in exchange for an upfront cash payment from the counterparty. The entity retains the rights to the last C0.1m plus interest, representing a subordinated interest in the portfolio. In this situation, the entity (transferor) cannot apply the derecognition requirements to part of the asset. This is because:
>
> ■   the first C0.9m of cash flow represents neither a specifically identifiable cash flow nor a fully proportionate (*pro rata*) share of all or part of the cash flows from the

asset (it is not possible to identify which loans in the portfolio the first C0.9m cash flows will arise from); and

- any credit losses are borne in the first instance by the entity (transferor) and are not shared proportionally between the parties.

As a result, the derecognition rules must be applied to the whole asset. On the other hand, if the arrangement resulted in the transfer of 90% of all cash flows from the asset, the derecognition rules would have been applied only to the proportion transferred, that is, 90%.

Example 2 – Sale of an asset subject to a guarantee

An entity enters into an arrangement to transfer the rights to 90% of the cash flows of a group of receivables, but provides a guarantee to compensate the buyer for any credit losses up to 8% of the principal amount of the receivables.

In this situation, although the transferor has transferred 90% of all cash flows from the asset, the existence of the guarantee means that the transferor has an obligation that could involve it in repaying some of the consideration received. Therefore, the derecognition requirements must be applied to the asset in its entirety and not just to the proportion of cash flows transferred.

Example 3 – Sale of an asset for part of its life

An entity enters into an arrangement to transfer the rights to 100% of the cash flows (interest and principal) arising in the last four years of a fixed rate loan receivable with an original maturity of 10 years. The principal is payable in a lump sum in year 10. In other words, the entity retains the right to interest cash flows for the first six years.

In this situation, it is clear that the entity has transferred the rights to the last 4 years of cash flows that represent specifically identifiable cash flows (the last 4 years of interest cash flows + principal cash flow). Therefore, in accordance with paragraph 8.33 above, the derecognition rules should be applied to this identifiable portion.

Example 4 – Sale of a right to receive dividends or sale of shares but retained rights to dividends

Entity A has a holding of shares in entity X (an available for sale financial asset). Entity A transfers to entity B the right to receive dividends paid on those shares in the next year.

In this situation, the dividends for the next year are specifically identifiable cash flows and the derecognition rules should be applied to the dividend strip.

Similarly, if entity A had transferred its holding of shares to entity B and retained the right to receive dividends for the next year, the cash flows arising on the transferred asset from the second year to perpetuity are also specifically identifiable cash flows. Therefore, the derecognition rules would be applied to only that part of the asset.

8.36 Once it has been established that the derecognition rules should be applied to the whole asset (or a group of similar assets) or to the qualifying part or portion identified in step 2 above, the remaining steps of the flow chart should be applied to that whole or part identified. This is referred to as 'the financial asset' in the paragraphs that follow. [IAS 39 para 16(b)].

Determine whether the rights to the cash flows from the asset have expired (step 3)

8.37 Once the entity has determined at what level (entity or consolidated) it is applying the derecognition requirements and to what identified asset (individual, group or component) those requirements apply, it can start assessing whether derecognition of the asset is appropriate. Step 3 considers whether the contractual rights to the financial asset have expired. If they have, the financial asset is derecognised. [IAS 39 para 17(a)]. This would be the case, for example, when a loan is extinguished, in the normal course, by payment of the entire amount due, thereby discharging the debtor from any further obligation. Another example is where a right from a purchased financial option is extinguished as a result of the contractual terms expiring without the holder requiring the writer to deliver or purchase the underlying financial asset. Derecognition at this step is usually obvious and requires little or no analysis, however, the situation can be more complex when the contractual terms of an instrument are changed.

> **Example – Derecognition of financial asset due to modification of cash flows**
>
> Bank A has entered into a 10 year loan arrangement with borrower B (classified either as AFS debt or L&R). The loan accrues interest at four per cent.
>
> At the end of year 8, as a result of an arm's-length renegotiation, the remaining maturity has been modified from two years to 12 years and the coupon revised to six per cent to maturity. Borrower B is not in any financial difficulty and there is no objective evidence of impairment.
>
> Substantive changes of contractual terms arising from the renegotiation are not revisions to estimated cash flows and, hence, IAS 39 paragraph AG 8 does not apply.
>
> In this situation, bank A has surrendered its rights to the four per cent coupon for the next two years and the principal repayment in two year's time; the rights to these cash flows have expired and, hence, should be derecognised. A new 12 year loan and receivable should be recognised at fair value upon renegotiation, comprising a new principal payment in 12 years and six per cent interest coupons for the next 12 years.
>
> Judgment is required in assessing whether a change in the contractual terms (such as a change in the currency or the remaining term of the loan, etc) is significant enough to represent an expiry of the original instrument (or a part thereof).

Determine whether the entity has transferred the cash flows from the asset or assumed an obligation to pay the cash flows from the asset (steps 4 and 5)

8.38 If the contractual rights to the cash flows have not expired, an entity derecognises the financial asset only when, amongst other criteria, it 'transfers' the cash flows from the asset. IAS 39 identifies two ways in which a transfer can be achieved. An entity 'transfers' a financial asset if, and only if, it either:

- transfers the contractual rights to receive the financial asset's cash flows. [IAS 39 para 18(a)]. See step 4 in the diagram in paragraph 8.30 and paragraph 8.39 below; or

- retains the contractual rights to receive the financial asset's cash flows, but assumes a contractual obligation to pay the cash flows to one or more recipients, in what is often referred to as a 'pass-through arrangement'. [IAS 39 para 18(b)]. See step 5 in the diagram in paragraph 8.30 and paragraph 8.43 below.

Transfer of contractual rights to receive cash flows

8.39 IAS 39 does not explain what is meant by the phrase *"transfers the contractual rights to receive the cash flows of the financial asset"*. A literal reading of the words would suggest that the phrase would apply to an asset's legal sale or a legal assignment of the rights to the cash flows from the asset. For example, an entity that has sold a financial asset (such as a legal sale of a bond) has transferred its rights to receive the cash flows from the asset. In this situation, the transferee has unconditional, presently exercisable rights to all the future cash flows. The transfer then has to be assessed in Step 6 in the diagram in paragraph 8.30 to determine whether it meets the derecognition criteria (see para 8.56 below).

8.39.1 On the other hand, consider an entity that enters into an arrangement with a bank whereby the bank manages the entity's securities. The entity transfers the securities into a safe custody account of the bank. The bank receives a management fee for its service, with the entity still making the decisions as to which securities will be sold and when. Such a transfer of securities to a custodian is not a transfer under paragraph 18(a) of IAS 39. The bank does not have the rights to the cash flows of the transferred securities and simply acts as the entity's agent.

8.40 Some types of financial asset (for example, a receivable or a portfolio of receivables), cannot be 'sold' in the same way as other types (for example, a bond), but they can be transferred by means of a novation or an assignment as explained in paragraph 8.96 below. Both novation and assignment will generally result in the transfer of contractual rights to receive the financial asset's cash flows. However, any further conditions or obligations placed upon the transferor in an assignment need to be considered and may impact this assessment.

8.41 Sometimes transfers of financial assets are made subject to certain conditions. Conditions attached to a transfer could include provisions relating to the existence and value of transferred cash flows at the date of transfer or conditions relating to the asset's future performance. Examples of such provisions include warranties relating to a transferred loan (for example, that the borrower met the specified lending criteria when the loan was advanced and is not in arrears at the date of transfer) or to its future performance (for example, that all repayments will be made when due). In our view, such conditions would not affect whether the entity has transferred the contractual rights to receive cash flows (under IAS 39 para 18(a)). Consider the various examples in 8.42.2. However, the existence of conditions relating to the asset's future performance might affect the conclusion related to the transfer of risks and rewards (see para 8.60), as well as the extent of any continuing involvement by the transferor in the transferred asset (see para 8.73).

8.42   In some instances, following the transfer of the contractual rights to receive a financial asset's cash flows, the transferor may continue to administer or provide servicing on the transferred asset. For example, a transferor may transfer all rights to cash flows, but continues to collect cash flows on behalf of the transferee in a capacity as an agent, rather than for its own benefit. This could occur where the original asset counterparties are notified that their obligation has been legally transferred to the transferee and are requested to pay the cash flows into a bank account for the transferee's benefit. In this case, the transferor continues to act purely as an agent in managing the collection of the transferee's cash flows. Determining whether the contractual rights to cash flows have been transferred is not affected by the transferor retaining the role of an agent to administer collection and distribution of cash flows. Therefore, retention of servicing rights by the entity transferring the financial asset does not in itself cause the transfer to fail the requirements in paragraph 18(a) of IAS 39. This would also apply in a scenario where the servicer co-mingled cash collections from the transferred assets with its own assets.

8.42.1   Where a receivable is transferred, in some instances, the original debtor may have the right to offset amounts that it owes to the transferor against any receivables due from the transferor. For example, entities Q and R owe each other amounts that are subject to a legal right of set off. Entity R sells its receivables from entity Q to entity S and agrees with entity S that if entity Q exercises its right of set off on the transferred receivable, entity R will make an equivalent payment to entity S. Such an arrangement (two-party offset) would not cause a transfer of the receivable to fail the requirements in paragraph 18(a) of IAS 39. The payment made by the transferor to the transferee if the right of offset is exercised, merely transfers to the transferee the value the transferor obtained when its liability to the original debtor was extinguished. Such rights of offset would also not impact the risks and rewards test (see further para 8.56 below). However, some offset arrangements involve three parties. In such an arrangement, a third party (for example, a sub-contractor who performed some of the services that gave rise to the receivable) has a right to offset amounts it is owed by the transferor against the transferred receivable. As a result, the third party has the unilateral ability to extinguish the contractual rights to receive cash flows from the original debtor. In our view, such an arrangement precludes the transfer from meeting the requirements of paragraph 18(a).

8.42.2   An entity may transfer receivables in respect of which it may subsequently issue credit notes. An example includes a situation where an entity's customer qualifies for a volume discount that is included in the general sales conditions between the entity and its customer. Such credit notes may be used against any existing or future invoice. Contractual credit notes issued by a transferor do not preclude a transfer of contractual rights to receive cash flows from an asset (that is, the original receivable). Such credit notes relate to the relationship between the transferor and its customer and not to the contract that is the receivable. They would, therefore, not preclude a transfer of the original receivable (for example, if the receivable was subsequently part of a debt factor arrangement) from meeting the criterion in paragraph 18(a). In a similar manner, normal warranties (a warranty provided on sale of goods that allows the customer to return the goods if faulty in a stated time period for a full refund) would also not preclude a transfer of the receivable from meeting the criterion in paragraph 18(a), because they relate to the business risk of the underlying transaction, which affects the existence of the receivable, rather than the financial risks associated with the receivable. For the same reasons, these conditions are also not taken into account for the risks and rewards test (see further from para 8.56).

8.42.3   Some transfers may include an option or a commitment for the transferor to repurchase the assets. These are often included for good business reasons, such as to enable the transferor to repurchase a receivable in a change of circumstances, for example, a change in tax laws. Such options do not prevent a transfer of the contractual rights to receive the cash flows from an asset, but do need to be considered when applying the risks and rewards test (see further from para 8.56 and the examples in IAS 39 para AG 51).

Assumption of obligations to pay cash flows to others (pass-through arrangements)

8.43   If there is no transfer of contractual rights under paragraph 18(a) of IAS 39 an entity should determine if there is an obligation to pass on the cash flows of the financial asset under a pass-through arrangement. (see step 5 in the diagram in para 8.30). Such pass-through arrangements arise where the entity continues to collect cash receipts from a financial asset (or more typically a pool of financial assets), but assumes an obligation to pass on those receipts to another party that has provided finance in connection with the financial asset. They are common in securitisations and sub-participation arrangements (see further para 8.90 below). The entity could be the financial asset's originator, or it could be a group that includes a consolidated special purpose entity that has acquired the financial asset from the originator and passes on cash flows to unrelated third party investors. For example, a transferor that is a trust or SPE may issue beneficial interests in the underlying financial assets to investors but continue to own those financial assets.

8.44   Under IAS 39, all of the following conditions have to be met by the entity (transferor) to conclude that such pass-through arrangements meet the criteria for a transfer. (Note that an eventual recipient is any party that may receive cash flows from the assets, excluding the transferor. Most often, they are the noteholders that have invested in a group of securitised assets, but they can also be swap counterparties or credit insurers that have an interest in the assets.)

- The entity has no obligation to pay amounts to the eventual recipients, unless it collects equivalent amounts from the original asset. Short-term advances by the entity to the eventual recipients with the right of full recovery of the amount lent plus accrued interest from the amounts eventually payable to the eventual recipients at market rates do not violate this condition.

- The entity is prohibited by the transfer contract's terms from selling or pledging the original asset other than as security to the eventual recipients for the obligation to pay them cash flows.

- The entity has an obligation to remit any cash flows it collects on behalf of the eventual recipients without material delay. In addition, the transferor is not entitled to reinvest such cash flows, except in cash or cash equivalents as defined in IAS 7, 'Cash flow statements', during the short settlement period from the collection date to the date of required remittance to the eventual recipients, with any interest earned on such investments being passed to the eventual recipients.

[IAS 39 paras 19(a)-(c)].

The financial assets remain on the balance sheet if any one of these conditions is not met. If a transfer meets the pass-through requirements, the transferor is deemed to have transferred the asset. However, the transferor will still then need to assess whether it has transferred sufficient risks and rewards associated with the asset to achieve derecognition. These pass-through conditions follow from the Framework's definitions of assets and liabilities.

8.45   The first condition ensures that the transferor is not obliged to transfer funds to the transferee that it has not collected, that is, it is not required to fund payments to the eventual recipients. This means that the transferee must bear the late payment risk. However, short-term advances made by the transferor in periods where there are shortfalls in collection due to late payments from the asset or differences in the dates of collection from the assets and payments to the eventual recipients will not prevent the transaction from being treated as a transfer provided:

- the short-term advances are made at market rates; and

- those advances plus any accrued interest are recoverable by deduction from the amounts eventually payable to the eventual recipients, or otherwise recoverable in full in the event that cash flows from the assets are insufficient.

8.46   The above conditions are necessary to ensure that derecognition is not prevented simply because a short-term cash flow is provided to the transferee. This would not be the case and derecognition would be prevented if the transferor was obliged to provide short-term loans at below market rates of interest or interest free loans because in such a case, the transferor, and not the transferee, would bear the slow-payment risk. Consider the examples below.

Example 1 – Fixed payments

Manufacturer D offers a financing scheme for the sale of its office furnishing products. A customer has the option to pay the purchase price and accrued interest in fixed monthly instalments over a maximum period of 24 months. Entity D agrees to pay to bank E every month a pre-determined amount of cash equal to the instalments due from its customers in exchange for an upfront cash payment. The payment of a fixed amount of cash does not qualify as a pass-through arrangement, because the amounts entity D is obliged to pay to bank E are not dependent on actual cash collections from its customers/receivables. Entity D is obliged to pay a pre-determined amount of cash calculated at the outset of the contract even if it has not collected the cash from its customers.

Example 2 – One party assumes a contractual obligation to pay cash flows from a financial asset to another party

Entity F enters into an arrangement with factor G. Entity F agrees to pass on the cash flows it collects from specified trade receivables to entity G for an upfront payment. Entity F has to transfer the collected cash flows within two working days. Entity F has no obligation to transfer cash to entity G, unless it collects equivalent amounts from the trade receivables; and it is prohibited by the arrangement's terms with entity F from selling or pledging the trade receivables to a third party. The three conditions for a pass-through arrangement are met in this scenario, because entity F:

■ retains the contractual rights to receive the financial asset's cash flows, but assumes an obligation to pass on the cash flows from the underlying assets without material delay;

■ cannot sell or pledge the asset; and

■ has no obligation to make payments, unless it collects equivalent amounts from the asset.

Example 3 – Credit enhancements

Entity H sells C10,000 of receivables to a consolidated SPE for an up-front cash payment of C9,000 and a deferred payment of C1,000. The SPE issues notes of C9,000 to investors. Entity H will only receive the deferred payment of C1,000 if sufficient cash flows from the receivables remain after paying amounts due to investors. This provides credit enhancement to the noteholders in the form of over-collateralisation – that is, entity H suffers the first loss on the transferred assets up to a specified amount. Such a transaction that provides credit enhancement *via* over-collateralisation may result in the entity meeting the pass-though requirements, provided these requirements are not failed due to other features in the arrangement.

Example 4 – Loan sub-participations

Bank I originates a large loan for a corporate client. Bank I agrees with other banks that in return for an upfront cash payment, bank I will pass on a percentage of all payments of principal and interest collected on the original loan to the participating banks as soon as they are received from the corporate client. The arrangement is non-recourse – that is, bank I has no obligation to pay the other banks, unless it collects equivalent amounts from the corporate loan. Bank I also cannot sell or pledge the loan. The transaction meets the requirements for a pass-through arrangement for the same reasons as discussed in example 3 above.

Example 5 – Pre-funded liquidity reserve

In a securitisation transaction, the SPE (a consolidated subsidiary of the transferor) is required to maintain a liquidity reserve to enable timely payments to be made to noteholders in the event of delayed receipts from the original assets. The transferor (entity A) has pre-funded this reserve by contributing cash or other assets to the SPE when establishing the SPE. If used, the reserve can be recovered only *via* the retention of future cash flows from the transferred assets.

By establishing a pre-funded liquidity reserve, entity A now has an obligation to pay amounts to eventual recipients that were not collected from the original asset. The transaction does not meet the pass-through requirement in paragraph 19(a) of IAS 39, because the amounts paid do not represent allowable short-term advances with a full right of recovery, they may be outstanding for some time and there is no right of recovery in the event of insufficient cash flows from the original asset. Similarly, the transaction would also fail the pass-through requirements if entity A had provided a firm commitment to advance cash to the SPE when required (rather than pre-funding the reserve), which can be recovered only *via* retention of future cash flows from the transferred assets. In this case, entity A can be obliged to pay amounts to eventual recipients that were not collected from the original asset, and those amounts are not short-term advances with a full right of recovery.

On the other hand, consider a situation where the liquidity reserve in the SPE was not pre-funded or committed to by entity A, but is created out of 'excess' cash flows collected from the transferred assets over and above those required to pay noteholders or other eventual recipients. It is contractually specified which cash flows are considered to be 'excess' cash flows. When the notes issued by the SPE are fully repaid at the end of the arrangement, entity A is entitled to the remaining balance of the reserve fund. Such a transaction may meet the pass-through requirements. This is because entity A is not paying the eventual recipients any amounts other than those collected from the original asset, because the fund is created through the cash flows from the transferred assets. Therefore, this meets the requirements of paragraph 19(a). In addition, as any amounts due to entity A (transferor) that are held in this reserve fund are not 'collected on behalf of eventual recipients', and therefore are not subject to the 'material delay' requirement of paragraph 19(c) of IAS 39. The purpose of setting up the fund is to make sure the cash is passed to eventual recipients without material delay once amounts become due to those eventual recipients. Also note that in this example, even though the pass-through requirements are met, the risks and rewards analysis should be applied to the transferred financial asset in its entirety, as there is not a transfer of a fully proportionate share of the cash flows; the transferor retains the most residual interest in cash flows from the asset in this arrangement, which affects the risks and rewards analysis.

Example 6 – Revolving structure

An entity sets up a programme to sell specified short-term receivables (such as trade receivables or credit card receivables) originated over five years to a consolidated special purpose entity (SPE). The SPE issues long-term notes to investors. As cash flows are collected on the receivables, those amounts are used by the SPE to purchase new receivables from the entity. At the end of five years, collections from the receivables are used to repay the principal of the long-term notes rather than being invested in new receivables.

Such an arrangement will fail the third condition in paragraph 8.44 because the arrangement involves a material delay before the original collection of cash is remitted. Furthermore, the nature of the new assets typically acquired means that most revolving arrangements involve reinvestment in assets that would not qualify as cash or cash equivalents.

8.47   The second condition regarding the transferor's ability to sell or pledge the financial assets highlights that the transferor does not control access to the future economic benefits associated with the transferred cash flows and, therefore, may not have an asset.

8.48   The third condition ensures that the transferor does not have use of, or benefit from, the cash it collects on the transferee's behalf and is required to remit them 'without material delay'. Again, this condition helps ensure the transferor has no asset. Immaterial delay is permitted for practical reasons. 'Without material delay' is not defined in the standard so judgment is required in making this assessment. The underlying facts and circumstances need to be reviewed carefully to assess whether the time interval between collection of the cash flows and their remittance to eventual recipients is reasonable in relation to the timing of payments on the underlying assets and market practices. For example, in some pass-through arrangements, such as securitisation of a portfolio of a large number of receivables (for example, credit card balances where customers often pay off the outstanding balance on a range of days each month), it is often not practical for the entity to transfer the relatively small amount of cash collected from individual accounts as and when they arise. Instead, for administrative convenience, the contractual arrangement may provide for their remittance to be made in bulk on a weekly, monthly or quarterly basis. In such situations, a remittance period of three months or less is generally acceptable, as in most securitisations interest is paid on a quarterly basis.

8.49   The third condition not only prohibits the transferor from reinvesting the cash flows received in the short settlement period between collection and remittance, but also restricts any investment made for the transferee's benefit to cash or cash equivalents as defined in IAS 7. This means that the transferor is not allowed to invest the funds in other high yielding medium-term investments for the benefit of the transferee or utilise the funds in generating further assets for securitisations (see below). Furthermore, the transferor is not permitted to retain any interest from such short-term highly liquid investments. All such interest received (but no more) must be remitted to the transferee as they arise. In practice, the funds are often paid into a trustee bank account for the transferee's benefit.

8.50   These pass-through tests are strict and some securitisation arrangements may well fail them.

8.51 The effect of meeting all the three pass-through conditions in paragraph 8.44 above is that the entity does not have an asset or a liability as defined in the Framework. The entity does not have an asset because it does not have the rights to control or benefit from the cash flows arising from the asset (second and third conditions). It follows that it also does not have a liability. Rather, in these situations, the entity acts more as an agent of the eventual recipient, merely collecting cash on its behalf, rather than as the asset's owner. Accordingly, if the conditions are met, the arrangement is treated as a transfer and considered for derecognition (that is, subject to the risk and rewards and control tests – see below). Conversely, if the conditions are not met, the entity acts more as the asset's owner with the result that the asset should continue to be recognised.

8.52 In the above discussions reference was made to the cash flows from the 'original asset'. An issue that arises in practice is what may be included in the 'original asset'? For example, it is not uncommon for an entity that originates loans and receivables to enter into contracts with third parties to mitigate some of the risks of the underlying assets, such as credit insurance, interest rate swaps etc. If those loans/receivables are later transferred together with the third party contracts to a buyer, the question arises as to what should be regarded as the 'original asset'. Consider the example below.

> **Example – Original assets (contracts between the vendor and a consolidated special purpose entity (SPE))**
>
> Entity A (the transferor) sells assets (for example, loans) to a consolidated SPE. The SPE issues notes to investors that are secured on those assets. Entity A then enters into derivatives (for example, interest rate swaps) and guarantees with the SPE to mitigate some of the risk on the assets for the noteholders. Cash flows to the noteholders that come from the transferor in relation to the derivatives or guarantees are not considered to be cash flows from the original asset. Therefore the arrangement does not meet the requirements of paragraph 19(a).
>
> The situation would have been different if entity A above had entered into derivatives or guarantees with a third party to mitigate the risks relating to the loans. Entity A then transfers the loans and the related third party contracts to a consolidated SPE. The SPE issues notes to investors that are secured on those loans. In such a case, our view is that the original asset can be interpreted to mean:
>
> - all related contracts, including insurance contracts, guarantees and derivatives (for example, purchased options and swaps), transferred with the loans/ receivables in a single transaction that share and mitigate some of the risks on the loans because those are the cash flows that will be paid to eventual recipients. Under this view, the related contracts would still meet the requirements of paragraph 19(a) above; or
>
> - only the transferred loans/receivables themselves, in which case the arrangement would not meet the requirements of paragraph 19(a) as described above.

An entity should choose one of these two approaches as its accounting policy and apply it consistently. Furthermore, when performing a risks and rewards analysis (see para 8.56 below), the net cash flows of the transferred asset should be determined consistently with the policy chosen for determining the original asset.

[The next paragraph is 8.56.]

Perform risk and rewards analysis (steps 6 and 7)

8.56   Once an entity has established that it has transferred a financial asset, either by transferring the contractual rights to receive the cash flows or under a qualifying pass-through arrangement, it carries out the risks and rewards test. This test begins in Step 6 in the diagram in paragraph 8.30 and requires the entity to evaluate whether it has:

■   transferred substantially all the financial asset's risks and rewards of ownership (see para 8.57),

■   retained substantially all the risks and rewards of ownership (see para 8.63) or

■   neither transferred nor retained substantially all the risks and rewards of ownership. If this is the case, the entity should perform a control analysis (see Step 8 in the diagram in para 8.30 and para 8.66) to ascertain which party has control of the asset. [IAS 39 para 20].

Determine whether substantially all the risks and rewards of ownership have been transferred

8.57   If the entity transfers substantially all the risks and rewards of ownership of the asset, the entity must derecognise the financial asset as shown in step 6 in the diagram in paragraph 8.30 above. It may also have to recognise separately as assets and liabilities any rights and obligations created or retained in the transfer (see also para 8.106 below). [IAS 39 para 20(a)].

8.58   Examples of transactions that transfer substantially all the risks and rewards of ownership include:

■   An unconditional sale of a financial asset. This is the most obvious example.

■   A sale of a financial asset, together with an option to repurchase the financial asset at its fair value at the time of repurchase. In this situation, the entity is no longer exposed to any value risk (potential for gain and exposure to loss) on the transferred asset, which is borne by the buyer. The ability for the seller to buy the asset back at its fair value at the date of repurchase is economically no different from buying a new asset.

■   A sale of a financial asset together with a put or call option that is deeply out of the money (that is, an option that is so far out of the money it is highly unlikely to go into the money before expiry). In this situation, the seller has no substantial risks and rewards, because there is no real possibility that the call or put option will be exercised. As the option has little or no value, such a sale is economically little different from an unconditional sale.

■ The sale of a fully proportionate share of the cash flows from a larger financial asset in an arrangement that meets the pass-through conditions addressed in paragraph 8.44 above.

[IAS 39 paras 21, AG39].

8.59 If an entity determines that, as a result of the transfer, it has transferred substantially all the risks and rewards of ownership of the transferred asset, it does not recognise the transferred asset again in a future period, unless it re-acquires the transferred asset in a new transaction. [IAS 39 para AG41]. The risks and rewards to be considered in this derecognition step include interest rate risk, credit risk, foreign exchange risk, equity price risk, late payment risk and prepayment risk; depending on the particular asset that is being considered for derecognition. For example, in the case of short-term trade receivables, the main risks to consider are likely to be credit risk and late payment risk and perhaps foreign currency risk if they have been transacted in a foreign currency. In the case of mortgages, the key risks to consider are likely to be interest rate risk, credit risk and, in the case of fixed rate mortgages, prepayment risk.

8.59.1 In addition, as discussed in paragraph 8.41 above, sometimes transfers of financial assets are made subject to certain conditions. These conditions should be assessed to determine whether they should be taken into account for a risks and rewards analysis. Such conditions could include warranties (for example, the customers can return goods within a certain period if faulty) and credit notes given when customers qualify for volume discounts. In our view, such conditions should not be taken into account for the risks and rewards analysis. This is because warranties relate to the asset's condition at the date of sale and to whether a valid receivable exists rather than to risks and benefits in relation to its future performance. Similarly, contractual credit notes relate to the overall contractual relationship between the seller and its customer and not to the contract that is the receivable.

8.59.2 Two-party offset arrangements are also not factored into the risks and rewards analysis. An example of such an arrangement is when entities Q and R owe each other amounts and these amounts are subject to a legal right of set-off. Entity R sells its receivables due from entity Q to entity S and agrees with entity S that if entity Q exercises its right of set-off on a transferred receivables that entity R will make an equivalent payment to entity S. This is because the payment made by the seller (entity R) to the buyer (entity S), if the right of offset is exercised, merely transfers to the buyer the value the seller obtained when its receivable from the debtor was extinguished.

8.59.3 On the other hand, an option or commitment to repurchase a transferred asset on a change in circumstance (for example, a change in tax law/regulation) is taken into account in the risks and rewards analysis. A common example is where an entity has sold receivables to a factor. Within the terms of the sale agreement, if there is a change in the tax law/regulation, the entity has the option (or is committed) to repurchase the transferred assets from the factor at par. Risks and rewards are measured as an entity's exposure to variability in cash flows from the transferred asset. If the entity may (or may have to) repurchase the transferred asset for other than its fair value, it has retained some of the risks and rewards. The extent of risks and rewards retained depends on how likely the entity is to repurchase the receivables. The implications of options (and commitments) to repurchase at par value for transfers and continuing involvement are discussed in paragraph 8.73 below.

8.60   Determining whether the entity has transferred substantially all the risks and rewards of ownership will often be readily apparent from the terms and conditions of the transfer. Where this is not so obvious, the entity needs to undertake an evaluation. That evaluation requires the entity to compute and compare its exposure to the variability in the present value of the transferred asset's future net cash flows before and after the transfer. The net cash flows of the transferred assets should be determined consistently with the 'original asset', as discussed in the example in paragraph 8.52. If the entity considers the original asset as a combination of the loan portfolio and related derivatives, the post-transfer cash flows will be the seller's residual cash flows, taking into accounts all the payments to and from the recipients (noteholders derivative counterparties, etc.). The computation and comparison should be made using as the discount rate an appropriate current market interest rate. All reasonably possible variability in net cash flows (as to amounts and timing) should be considered, and greater weight should be given to those outcomes that are more likely to occur, that is, the amounts and timing need to be probability weighted. [IAS 39 para 22].

8.61   If, as a result of the contractual arrangements, the entity's exposure to such variability is no longer *significant in relation to the total variability* in the present value of the future net cash flows associated with the financial asset, the entity is regarded as having transferred substantially all the financial asset's risks and rewards of ownership. [IAS 39 para 21]. It should be noted that the computational comparison for derecognition is a relative and not an absolute test. That is, the extent to which the variability in the amounts and timing of the transferred asset's net cash flows is significant is measured in relation to the total variability. In other words, derecognition is not achieved solely if the entity's remaining exposure to an asset's risks and rewards is small in absolute terms, as noted in the example in paragraph 8.65.

8.62   IAS 39 does not provide any guidance as to what is meant by 'significant' as referred to in the above paragraph when comparing the difference between the present value of the cash flows from the financial asset before the transfer with the present value of the cash flow after the transfer. Therefore, judgement is needed to assess what is significant in each particular situation. A numerical computation is not necessarily required – often it will be obvious whether the entity has transferred substantially all the risks and rewards of ownership. [IAS 39 para 22]. In other cases it will be less clear and a computation will be required. There is limited guidance in the standard as to how to perform such a computation of the entity's exposure to the variability in the present value of the future net cash flows before and after the transfer. This can be done in a number of ways, but the example below illustrates one possibility.

Example – Variability in the amounts and timing of cash flows

An entity sells a portfolio of short term 30 day receivables with a nominal value of C1 billion to a third party. The entity guarantees first losses on the portfolio up to 1.25% of the loan volume. The average loss on similar receivables over the last 10 years amounts to 2%.

In this example, the expected losses are C20m and the entity has guaranteed C12.5m. It might, therefore, appear that, as the entity has guaranteed 62.5% of all the expected losses, it has retained substantially all the risks and rewards of ownership. This is not so as the calculation cannot be done in this manner. The test looks to who absorbs variability in the asset's cash flows, rather than who has most of the expected losses. By giving a guarantee the entity has effectively retained a subordinated interest in the receivables. If the subordinated retained interest absorbs all of the likely variability in net cash flows, the entity would retain the risks and rewards of ownership and continue to recognise the receivables in their entirety. However, this is not the case in this example. Therefore, in order to perform a risk and rewards analysis, it is necessary to determine the variability in the amounts and timing of the cash flows both before and after the transfer on a present value basis. One way to determine this is outlined below:

- The first step is to model different scenarios of cash flows from the C1 billion receivables portfolio that reflects the variability in the amounts and timing of cash flows before the transfer as discussed in paragraph 8.58 above.
- For each scenario, the present value of the cash flows is calculated by using an appropriate current market interest rate as stated in paragraph 8.58 above.
- Probabilities are then assigned to each scenario considering all reasonably possible variability in net cash flows, with greater probability weighting given to those outcomes that are more likely to occur.
- An expected variance is then calculated that reflects the cash flows' total variability in the amounts and timing.

The above steps are repeated for cash flows that remain after the transfer.

Finally, the expected variance after the transfer is compared with the variance before the transfer to determine whether there has been a significant change in the amounts and timing of cash flows as a result of the transfer. If the change is not significant, it can be concluded that there has been no substantial transfer of the risks and rewards of ownership. If the change is significant, it can be concluded that the risks and rewards of ownership have been substantially transferred.

An illustration of the modelling discussed above is shown below. For illustrative purposes, only six scenarios are included in this example. In practice, more scenarios may be required in order to adequately model the variability in net cash flows of the asset.

Pre-transfer Scenarios	PV of future cash flows	Probability %	Expected PV	Variability in PV	Probability weighted	Expected Variability
	1	2	3 = 1*2	4 = 1- $\sum$3	5 = 2*4	
Low loss	990,000	15.00	148,500	11,050	1,658	1,658
Normal loss and few pre-payments	985,000	20.00	197,000	6,050	1,210	1,210
Normal loss	980,000	35.00	343,000	1,050	368	368
Normal loss and many pre-payments	970,000	25.00	242,500	-8,950	-2,238	2,238
High loss	960,000	4.50	43,200	-18,950	-853	853
Very high loss	950,000	0.50	4,750	-28,950	-145	145
		100.00	978,950	-38,700	0	6,472

Post-transfer Scenarios	PV of future cash flows	Probability %	Expected PV	Variability in PV	Probability weighted	Expected Variability
	1	2	3 = 1*2	4 = 1- $\sum$3	5 = 2*4	
Low loss	10,000	15.00	1,500	-2,125	-319	319
Normal loss and few pre-payments	12,500	20.00	2,500	375	75	75
Normal loss	12,500	35.00	4,375	375	131	131
Normal loss and many pre-payments	12,500	25.00	3,125	375	94	94
High loss	12,500	4.50	563	375	17	17
Very high loss	12,500	0.50	63	375	2	2
		100.00	12,125	-250	0	638

The relative variability retained after the transfer = 638/6,470 = 9.86%. This implies that the entity has transferred substantially all of the risks and rewards of ownership of the receivables.

It should be noted that, in the above example, the cash flows' present value with their associated probabilities constitutes a discrete random variable, for which it is possible to derive an absolute value for the variability as indicated above. A better measure would be to calculate the standard deviation. However, in this example, that would also produce the same conclusion. In practice, however, the calculation may not be so simple and specialist advice should be taken.

Determine whether substantially all the risks and rewards of ownership have been retained

8.63 If the entity retains substantially all the risks and rewards of ownership of the asset, the entity continues to recognise the asset as shown in step 7 in the diagram in paragraph 8.30. [IAS 39 para 20(b)].

8.64 IAS 39 provides the following examples of transactions where substantially all the risks and rewards of ownership has been retained:

■ A sale and repurchase transaction where the repurchase price is a fixed price or the sale price plus a lender's return (for example, a repo or securities lending agreement).

■ A sale of a financial asset together with a total return swap that transfers the market risk exposure through the swap back to the entity.

- A sale of a financial asset together with a deep in-the-money put or call option (that is an option that is so far in-the-money that it is highly likely to be exercised before expiry).

- A sale of short-term receivables in which the entity guarantees to compensate the transferee for all credit losses which are likely to occur.

[IAS 39 para AG 40].

8.65   In the above examples it is clear that the entity has retained substantially all the risks and rewards of ownership. Where it is unclear whether the entity has retained (or transferred) substantially all the risks and rewards of ownership, it must evaluate the variability of the transferred asset's cash flows before and after the transfer as discussed in paragraph 8.57 above. If this comparison shows that the entity's exposure to the variability in the present value of the future net cash flows (discounted at the appropriate current market interest rate) from the financial asset does not change *significantly* as a result of the transfer, the entity is regarded as having retained substantially all the risks and rewards of the asset's ownership. [IAS 39 para 21]. Sometimes it can be difficult to perform a quantitative analysis of risks and rewards. Consider the following example.

> **Example – Determining a transfer of risks and rewards in a factoring arrangement with recourse**
>
> Entity A transfers a portfolio of trade receivables to a factor. The factor assumes the default risk of the transferred receivables, whereas entity A retains the late payment risk by paying interest on overdue amounts to the factor based on LIBOR plus a margin. The trade receivables transferred have a history of no defaults and no late payment since the start of the business relationship between entity A and the customers.
>
> As noted in paragraph 8.61, the risks and rewards test should consider whether entity A's retained risks and rewards after the transfer (that is, the variability due to late payment risk) is no longer significant in relation to the total risks and rewards associated with the financial asset before the transfer (that is, taking into account both the risk of default and the risk of late payment). It is a relative rather than an absolute test. The lack of observed defaults and late payments does not justify an assumption that there are no risks attached to the receivables transferred to the factor. There are small, as yet unobserved, default and late payment risks attached to the receivables. In the absence of any observable data the risks and rewards test should be performed by looking to both qualitative and quantitative factors. The objective is to gain insight into the economics of the default and the late payment risks so as to be able to assess their relative significance.
>
> Qualitative questions to be addressed could include:
>
> - How are late payment and default risk managed by entity A? The amount of resources entity A devotes to managing a risk might indicate the relative importance it attaches to that risk.
> - If the factor is in general unwilling to assume late payment risk, why is this?

- If the factor is willing to assume the late payment risk as well as the default risk it has actually assumed, what price would/does it charge?

In addition to completing the risks and rewards analysis, entity A should consider quantitative aspects, including using index information of peers or industries to approximate the default risk and the late payment risk inherent in the portfolio of receivables transferred to the factor. Using this information may make the result of the risks and rewards analysis clear.

In other cases, it might be necessary to build a model that encompasses all the data and information gathered and, therefore, come up with a numerical computation of risks and rewards. The modelling of risks and rewards irrespective of any observable data is a challenging task and will be subject to simplifications and assumptions.

To the extent that the qualitative factors indicate that a significant risk has been retained, the entity should be able to demonstrate objectively that the late payment risk is not significant in order to achieve derecognition. Such a quantitative analysis should use data that is relevant to the receivables being factored.

Perform control analysis (steps 8 and 9)

Determine whether control of the asset has been retained

8.66   If the entity (transferor) has neither transferred nor retained substantially all the risks and rewards of ownership of the transferred financial asset – in other words it has retained some risks and rewards but has not substantially all of them – it is in a middle ground in which the risks and rewards analysis does not provide a clear answer. Hence, the transferor has to determine whether it has retained control of the asset (see step 8 in the diagram in para 8.30 above).

- If the transferor has not retained control, it must derecognise the financial asset and recognise separately as assets or liabilities any rights and obligations created or retained in the transfer.

- If the entity has retained control, it must continue to recognise the financial asset to the extent of its continuing involvement in the financial asset (see para 8.73).

[IAS 39 para 20(c)].

8.67   Control, in this context does not have the same meaning as in IAS 27, 'Consolidated and separate financial statements', that is, the power to govern the financial and operating policies of an entity so as to obtain benefits from its activities. In the context of derecognition, control is based on whether the transferee has the *practical ability* to sell the transferred asset. This looks to what the transferee can do with the asset, not what the transferor can do. This is a different concept of control that tries to identify whether the transferor continues to be exposed to the variability in the cash flows of the particular asset that was the subject of the transfer as opposed to having risks of a general nature, similar to a derivative. Therefore, where the transferee has the practical ability to sell the transferred asset, it follows that the transferee has control over the asset and the entity has lost control. On the other hand, if the transferee does not have the practical ability to sell the transferred asset, then the entity has retained control of the transferred asset. [IAS 39 paras 23, AG42].

Practical ability to sell the transferred asset

8.68   IAS 39 explains that the transferee has the 'practical ability' to sell the transferred asset if:

■   the transferee can sell the asset in its entirety to an unrelated third party; and

■   the transferee is able to exercise that ability *unilaterally* and *without imposing additional restrictions*.

The above conditions should be evaluated by considering what the transferee is able to do in practice, not what contractual rights it has with respect to the transferred asset (or indeed what contractual prohibition exists).

[IAS 39 paras 23, AG43].

8.69   In the context of the first condition above, the transferee will have the practical ability to sell the transferred asset if there is an active market in that asset, because the transferee could repurchase the transferred asset in the market if it needs to return the asset to the entity. [IAS 39 para AG42]. For example, the transferor may transfer a security with an option attached that allows the entity to repurchase it from the transferee at some future date. If the security is one in which an active market exists, the transferee may well sell the security to a third party, knowing that it will be easy to obtain a replacement asset and fulfil its obligation if the transferor exercises the option. The concept of control focuses on what the transferee is able to do in practice. Therefore, in this case, it is important that such an active market exists. The fact that the transferee may be unlikely to sell the transferred asset is of no relevance as long as it has the practical ability to do so. Conversely, if there is no market, the transferee is unable to ensure that it can fulfil its obligation to return the asset to the transferor if it sells the asset with no right to repurchase it. Hence in this case, even if the transferee has a contractual right to dispose of the transferred asset, that right will have little practical effect if there is no market for the transferred asset. [IAS 39 para AG43(a)].

8.70   In the context of the second condition above, the transferee should also be able to exercise its ability to transfer the asset independent of the actions of others and without having to impose additional restrictions or 'strings' to the transfer. [IAS 39 para AG43(b)(i)]. If the transferor has imposed obligations on the transferee concerning the servicing of a loan asset, the transferee would need to attach a similar provision to any transfer that it makes to a third party. Such 'additional restrictions' or 'strings' impede the asset's free transfer and fail the 'practical ability' to sell test.

Example – Sale of loan portfolio with credit default guarantee

Entity O sells a portfolio of loans to bank N for cash. The loans have an average historical loss ratio of 5 per cent. Entity O guarantees credit default losses on the transferred assets of up to 4 per cent as part of the arrangement. The terms of the guarantee specify that the holder of the guarantee can only claim under the guarantee if it holds the guaranteed loans. The credit default guarantee means that control has not been transferred. Bank N would lose the value of the credit default protection if it sold the transferred asset without also selling the credit default guarantee to the new buyer. In practice, bank N would only sell the transferred asset if it also sold the credit default protection to the buyer. However, giving such credit default protection is the insertion of an additional feature and, therefore, fails the control test.

8.71 Where the transferor writes a put option or provides a guarantee of the original asset, the transfer will also often fail the control test. In such situations, the transferee has effectively obtained two assets: the original asset that is the subject of the transfer, and the put option or the guarantee. Selling the transferred asset on its own invalidates the remaining asset, as the transferee immediately loses any ability to realise its value. In the absence of an active market, the transferee will only be able to realise the asset's value by selling a similar guarantee or put option with the assets. Put another way, if the put option or guarantee is valuable enough for significant risk to be retained by the transferor, it precludes the transfer of control. That is, it will be so valuable to the transferee that the transferee would not, in practice, sell the transferred asset to a third party without attaching a similar option or guarantee, or otherwise mirroring the conditions attached to the original transfer. As the transferee is constrained from selling the asset without attaching additional restrictions, the 'practical ability' to sell test fails, with the result that control of the transferred asset is retained by the transferor. [IAS 39 para AG44].

8.72 If the transferee has the practical ability to sell the transferred asset, the transferee has control over the asset. Hence the transferor has lost control and derecognises the asset. On the other hand, if the transferee does not have the practical ability to sell the transferred asset, the transferor has retained control of the transferred asset and continues to recognise the asset to the extent of its continuing involvement.

8.72.1 The 'control' concept is important because it helps determine how the transferor's remaining interest in the asset will be presented. If the transferor has retained control, it still has an interest in the specific assets that have been transferred. It should, therefore, continue to show that interest on the balance sheet, gross of any related liability. If control has been lost, the transferor still shows its remaining economic interest on the balance sheet, but presented net. This recognises that the transferor's interest is a net exposure (that is, more akin to a derivative) rather than an interest directly related to the specific assets that have been transferred.

Continuing involvement in transferred asset

8.73 The continuing involvement approach applies if the entity has neither transferred nor retained substantially all the risks and rewards of ownership and control has not passed to the transferee. Under the continuing involvement approach, the entity continues to recognise part of the asset. That part represents the extent of its continuing exposure to the risks and rewards of the financial asset. That is, the continuing involvement includes both obligations to support the risks arising from the asset's cash flows (for example, if a guarantee has been provided) and the right to receive benefits from these cash flows. In these circumstances a related liability is recognised, as well as part of the original asset.

8.73.1 Warranties, contractual credit notes and two-party offset arrangements are not taken into account in measuring an entity's continuing involvement for the reasons discussed in paragraphs 8.42.2, 8.59.1 and 8.59.2. On the other hand, options or commitments to repurchase the transferred assets on a change in circumstances – for example, a change in tax law/regulation – should be taken into account in measuring the entity's continuing involvement. For example, an entity has sold receivables to a factor. Within the terms of the sale agreement, if there is a change in the tax law/regulation, the entity has the option (or commitment) to repurchase the transferred assets from the factor at par. Such right (or commitment) is related specifically to a particular receivable and, therefore, should be taken into account in measuring the entity's continuing involvement. If the option (or commitment) is to repurchase any receivable, the continuing involvement asset would be the entire group of receivables – that is, no derecognition would be achieved. Continuing involvement is addressed further from paragraph 8.127.

Accounting by transferee

8.73.2 Although transferees are required to follow the recognition principles discussed from paragraph 8.5 above, it is important to note that the accounting treatment between the transferor and the transferee is intended to be symmetrical. Therefore, to the extent that a transfer of a financial asset does not qualify for derecognition, the transferee does not recognise the transferred asset as its asset. The transferee derecognises the cash or other consideration paid and recognises a receivable from the transferor. If the transferor has both a right and an obligation to re-acquire control of the entire transferred asset for a fixed amount (such as under a repurchase agreement), the transferee may classify it's receivable as a 'loan and receivable'. [IAS 39 para AG 50]. Similarly, if a transfer of a financial asset qualifies for derecognition, the transferor will treat it as a sale and the transferee will treat it as a purchase.

Disclosure

8.73.3 IFRS 7 sets out specific disclosure requirements for transfers that do not qualify for derecognition; these are addressed in chapter 11. However, paragraph 108 of IAS 1 also requires an entity to disclose the significant accounting policies that are relevant to an understanding of the financial statements. It requires an entity to disclose the judgements that management has made in the process of applying the entity's accounting policies and that have the most significant effect on the amounts recognised in the financial statements. This will include any significant accounting policy choices and judgements it has made in relation to derecognition, for example:

■ What the entity regards as a transfer of contractual rights for the purposes of paragraph 18(a) IAS 39 as discussed in paragraph 8.39.1 above.

■ What the entity regards as the 'original asset' for the purpose of paragraphs 19(a) and 20 of IAS 39 as discussed in paragraph 8.52 above.

For transfers that fail to qualify for derecognition, where relevant, an entity might also disclose that the assets are pledged against the related liability. In addition, the entity will maintain the same classification as it had prior to the failed derecognition. The current or non-current classification of the associated liability depends on the earliest date it is due to be settled. Generally, its classification will be the same as that of the asset. However, in the case of a revolving structure, the receivables that failed the derecognition test might be classified as current, whereas the notes to the investors may be non-current if they are not due to be settled within the next 12 months. In a securitisation of long-term assets funded by short-term commercial paper issuances, the converse could arise.

Practical application of the derecognition criteria

8.74 Having discussed the criteria for derecognition, it is necessary to consider how they can be applied to various types of transfers of financial assets that are often found in practice. Such transfers include repurchase agreements and stock lending agreements, factoring arrangements, securitisation transactions, loan transfers and transfers involving derivatives. Descriptions of these common types of transfers and the consequences of applying the derecognition criteria are considered below. The accounting treatment of transfers that qualify for derecognition, those that fail derecognition and those that continue to be recognised to the extent of the continuing involvement are considered from paragraph 8.99 below.

Repurchase and stock lending agreements

8.75 Repurchase agreements, commonly referred to as 'repos', are transactions involving the legal sale of a financial asset with a simultaneous agreement to repurchase it at a specified price at a fixed future date. In a typical repurchase agreement, an entity might sell a security such as a government bond to a third party in return for a cash consideration that is then reinvested in other assets that earn a return. At the specified date, the transferor repurchases that security. Financial institutions and other entities normally enter into these agreements because they provide liquidity and the opportunity to earn excess returns on the collateral. The main features of such agreements will usually be:

- The sale price – this may be the market value at the date of sale or another agreed price.

- The repurchase price – this may be fixed at the outset, vary with the period for which the asset is held by the buyer, or be the market price at the time of repurchase.

- The nature of the repurchase agreement – this may be an unconditional commitment for both parties, a call option exercisable by the seller, a put option exercisable by the buyer or a combination of put and call options.

- Other provisions – these may include, amongst others, the term of the agreement (overnight, short-term or longer), the buyer's ability to return a similar but not identical security to that which was sold; the buyer's ability to sell the security to a third party, the seller retaining access to any increase in to the asset's value (subject to the buyer receiving a lender's return) from a future sale to a third party and the seller providing any protection against loss through the operation of guarantees.

8.76 Entities may also enter into stock lending (sometimes referred to as securities lending) transactions. These transactions are initiated by broker-dealers and other financial institutions to cover a short sale or a customer's failure to deliver securities sold. In a typical stock lending agreement, the transferor/lender transfers a security to the transferee/borrower for a short period of time. The borrower is generally required to provide 'collateral' to the lender, commonly cash but sometimes other securities or a standby letter of credit, with a value slightly higher than the value of the security borrowed. If the collateral is cash, the lender earns a return and if it is other than cash, the lender receives a fee. At a specified date, the borrower returns the security to the lender.

8.77 Although the motivation to enter into a securities lending transaction is different from a repurchase agreement and the transactions may differ in form and sometimes risk protection, they are similar in substance. IAS 39, therefore, does not distinguish between the two types in determining whether the transferred asset qualifies for derecognition. [IAS 39 para AG 51(a)-(c)].

8.78 The application of the derecognition principles to repurchase and stock lending transactions will obviously depend upon the transaction's nature and specific characteristics. However, some of the typical features that are found in such transactions and how they should be evaluated for derecognition purposes are considered below.

Requirement for a transfer

8.78.1 In repurchase and stock lending agreements there is typically a legal sale of the underlying assets. Hence, the transferor has transferred the contractual rights to receive the cash flows of the financial assets and there is a transfer that meets IAS 39 paragraph 18(a) (step 4 in the diagram in 8.30 = yes).

Repurchase price

8.79 A repurchase agreement will require the transferor to repurchase the transferred asset at a particular price. Such price may be fixed at the outset or be the market price at the time of the repurchase. Depending on the pricing arrangement, the analysis would be as follows:

- If the financial asset is loaned or sold under an agreement to repurchase the transferred asset at fair value at the date of repurchase, the transferred asset is derecognised. This is because the transferor has transferred substantially all the risk and rewards of ownership of the transferred asset (step 6 in the diagram in para 8.30 = Yes). [IAS 39 para AG 51(j)].

- If the financial asset is loaned or sold under an agreement to repurchase the asset at a fixed price or at a price that provides a lender's return on the sale price, the transferred asset is not derecognised. This is because the transferor retains substantially all the risks and rewards of ownership of the transferred asset (step 7 in the diagram in para 8.30 = Yes). [IAS 39 para AG 51(a)].

Agreement to return substantially the same asset

8.80 A repurchase or stock lending agreement may require the transferor to accept back assets that are substantially the same as those initially transferred. The term 'substantially the same' is not defined in the standard. However, it is generally taken to mean that the financial assets returned or repurchased must be identical in form and type and have identical maturities and contractual interest rates, so as to provide the same rights as the asset transferred. As there is no economic difference between the asset initially transferred and the asset to be re-acquired, the analysis would be the same as indicated above.

Agreement to substitute a similar asset with equal fair value

8.81 A repurchase or stock lending agreement may give the transferee the right to substitute a similar asset of equal fair value at the repurchase date. In this case, there is no economic difference in substance between returning the original asset or a similar asset of equal fair value. Depending on the repurchase price, the analysis would be identical to that discussed in the above paragraph. [IAS 39 para AG 51(c)].

Right of first refusal to repurchase at fair value

8.82 If an entity sells a financial asset and retains only a right of first refusal to repurchase the transferred asset at fair value if the transferee subsequently intends to sell it, the entity derecognises the asset because it has transferred substantially all the risks and rewards of ownership (step 6 in the diagram in para 8.30 = Yes). [IAS 39 para AG 51(d)]. This situation is effectively no different in substance to the situation described in the first bullet point in paragraph 8.79 above. Although not dealt with in the standard, if the right of first refusal to repurchase the transferred asset is at a price other than the asset's fair value at the date of repurchase (for example, a price pre-determined at inception), the analysis would be similar to the transferor having a call option. This situation is described in paragraph 8.98.7 below.

Transferee's right to pledge

8.83 A repurchase or securities lending agreement may give the transferee the right to sell or pledge the transferred asset during the term of the repurchase agreement. In this situation, if the transferor continues to recognise the asset, it should reclassify the asset on its balance sheet, for example, as a loaned asset or repurchase receivable. [IAS 39 para AG 51(a)].

8.83.1 Generally, the transferee's right to sell or pledge the transferred asset effectively indicates that the transferee has control of the asset and thus if some significant risks and rewards are transferred, derecognition is appropriate. For control to pass to the transferee, the right to sell or pledge must have economic substance without any 'strings' attached, as explained in paragraphs 8.71 and 8.72 above.

Wash sales

8.84 A 'wash sale' (sometimes referred to as a 'bed and breakfast' transaction) is the repurchase of a financial asset shortly after it has been sold. Such a transaction involves contracting to sell the financial asset to a third party with no express contract to buy it back. Therefore, such a repurchase does not preclude derecognition provided that the original sale transaction met the derecognition requirements. In other words, the sale and the repurchase transactions are viewed as two separate transactions under IAS 39. Since the time interval between sale and repurchase can be very short, it is unlikely that the transferor would benefit or suffer from any changes in asset values. Therefore, such transactions are normally undertaken to crystallise a capital gain or capital loss for taxation purposes or to convert unrealised revaluation gains on investments into realised gains so that they can be used for distribution by way of dividends to shareholders. However, if an agreement to sell a financial asset is entered into concurrently with an agreement to repurchase the same asset at a fixed price or the sale price plus a lender's return, then the asset is not derecognised. [IAS 39 para AG 51(e)].

Security given as collateral

8.85 In the sale and repurchase agreements discussed above, the sale price was assumed to be satisfied in cash. A variant often found in practice is that the sale consideration is satisfied by the transfer of another security rather than in cash. For example, assume that entity A sells security X subject to a repurchase agreement to entity B. The sale consideration is met by entity B transferring security Y. Such a transaction involves two transfers and two transferors so the requirement relating to the accounting treatment relating to transfers of financial assets will need to be applied twice – transfer of security X by entity A and transfer of security Y by entity B.

8.86 Each transferor will first apply the derecognition criteria discussed above to its own security – a risks and rewards approach first followed by the control approach if the risks and rewards approach is found not to be conclusive. It will then apply the derecognition criteria to the asset received as consideration from the point of view of the counterparty. If the counterparty would continue to recognise the asset under IAS 39 it is not recognised by the entity. [IAS 39 para AG50].

Linkage of transactions into a derivative

8.86.1 In some cases, an entity may enter into two or more transactions relating to the same asset at (or about) the same time. The issue arises as to whether these transactions should be accounted for separately, or aggregated and accounted for as a single transaction. As set out in para 4.40, certain linked non-derivative transactions should be aggregated and treated as a derivative when, in substance, the transactions result in a derivative instrument.

> **Example – purchase plus repo**
>
> Entity A purchases a sovereign bond at fair value from entity B. At the same time entity A enters into a sale and repurchase agreement (repo) of the bond with entity B. Under the repo, entity A sells the bond back to entity B and agrees to buy it back from entity B on a specified future date at a specified price. The net effect of the two transactions is that no cash or bonds are exchanged between entity's A and B at inception.
>
> During the term of the transaction, entity A will pay to entity B interest on the notional financing under the repo and entity B will pay to entity A any interest coupons received on the bond (though these amounts may be rolled into the repurchase price and paid at the end of the repo). On maturity of the repo, entity B will deliver the bond to entity A in return for cash equal to the pre-agreed price.
>
> The cash flows of this transaction are consistent with the cash flows of a total return swap with physical settlement at the swap's maturity. If the two interest payments are rolled up and paid at the end of the term of the repo, the cash flows are similar to a forward contract to buy the bond.
>
> The definition of a derivative in IAS 39 paragraph 9 is met as the value of the transaction moves in response to the change in the fair value of the bond, the initial net investment is small and the transaction will be settled at a future date.
>
> The indicators of when non-derivative transactions should be treated as a derivative [IAS 39 para IG B6] are met as the transactions are entered into at the same time and in contemplation of each other, both relate to the same risk as they relate to the same bond and both are with the same counterparty, entity B. There is also no apparent economic need or substantive business purpose for the transactions to be structured separately.
>
> Hence, the above transactions should be accounted for together, as a derivative.

Factoring arrangements

8.87   A factoring transaction involves a transferor transferring its rights to some or all of the cash collected from some financial asset (usually receivables) to a third party (the factor) in exchange for a cash payment. Factoring of receivables is a well established method of obtaining finance, sales ledger administration services or protection from bad debts. Factoring arrangements may take various forms, but some of the principal features are as follows:

- The cash payment – this may be fixed at the outset or vary according to the actual period the receivables remain unpaid (late payment risk). Sometimes the factor may provide a credit facility that allows the seller to draw up to a fixed percentage of the face value of the receivables transferred.

- The nature of the agreement – may be a clean sale without recourse (the transferor has no obligations to make good any shortfall on the transferred assets) or may be more complex with various recourse provisions.

- Other provisions – these may include, amongst others, any representations or warranties provided by the transferor regarding the receivables' quality/ condition at the point of transfer, servicing arrangements (whether the transferor will continue to manage the receivables or management will be taken over by the factor), or any credit protection facility (insurance cover) provided by the factor that may limit or eliminate the extent to which the factor has recourse to the seller.

Factoring without recourse

8.88   In a non-recourse factoring arrangement, the transferor does not provide any guarantee about the receivables' performance. In other words, the transferor assumes no obligations whatsoever to repay any sums received from the factor regardless of the timing or the level of collections from the underlying debts. In that situation, the entity has transferred substantially all the risks and rewards of ownership of the receivables and derecognises the receivables in their entirety (step 6 in the diagram in para 8.30 = yes). The accounting treatment of receivables subject to non-recourse factoring is considered in the second example in paragraph 8.102 below. In some situations, the transferor may continue to service the receivables for which it may receive a fee. The accounting treatment for a sale of receivables with servicing retained that is not subject to recourse and when the transferor has no residual interest in the receivables is considered in paragraph 8.109 below.

Requirement for a transfer

8.88.1   In most factoring arrangements, the factored receivables are assigned to the factor. In most cases, the transferor has transferred the contractual rights to receive the financial asset's cash flows and there is a transfer that meets IAS 39 paragraph 18(a) (step 4 in the diagram in para 8.30 = yes). However, this may not be the case if there are three party offset rights – see paragraph 8.42.1 above.

Factoring with recourse

8.89 In a factoring of receivables with recourse, the transferor provides the factor with full or limited recourse. The transferor is obligated under the terms of the recourse provision to make payments to the factor or to repurchase receivables sold under certain circumstances. These recourse provisions may take the form of guarantees by the seller for non-payment (bad debt credit risk) up to a certain limit or full default amount, a call option by the transferor (for example, to repurchase defaulted receivables), a put option by the factor for any defaulted assets or the seller agreeing to pay interest to the buyer for any overdue receivables (late payment risk). In some cases, they result in the transferor retaining substantially all the risks and rewards of ownership of the receivables with the effect that the entity continues to recognise the factored receivables (step 7 in the diagram in para 8.30 = yes). In other cases, the recourse provisions result in the transferor retaining some, but not substantially all, risks and rewards, in which case the control test must be considered. In most factoring arrangements that are subject to recourse, the transferee is precluded from selling the receivables, which means that the transferor continues to control them (step 8 in the diagram in para 8.30 = yes) and continuing involvement accounting may apply. Examples dealing with the accounting treatment of receivables subject to factoring with recourse can be found under paragraphs 8.120 and 8.133 below.

8.89.1 In some transactions, the contract requires the customer to pay part or all of the consideration before the entity provides any goods or services. The entity may factor the rights to these future cash flows before the goods or services have been provided and the related receivable recognised. For example, an entity may factor a future operating lease receivable. If an entity factors such unrecognised receivables, then the entity should recognise the factoring arrangement as financing, that is, the entity should recognise a liability for the amounts received from the factor, as there is no asset to derecognise.

> **Example – Factor of advance payments**
>
> Consider a five-year maintenance contract with payments to be billed annually in advance or an operating lease contract with rentals due quarterly in advance. Such contracts give rise to the question of when should a financial asset for the amounts due under the contract be recognised, since the entity has a contractual right to receive cash from when the contract is signed even though it has provided no goods or services at that time. In our view, no asset should be recognised until at least one of the parties has performed under the contract (see para 8.10). Such an arrangement comprises two elements. The first element is the sale of goods or services, which is an executory contract and hence is not recognised until the goods or services are delivered. The second element is a loan commitment (being the agreement by the customer to pay in advance, which is outside the scope of IAS 39. [IAS 39 para 2(h)]. Hence, no financial asset is recognised for either of the elements prior to performance or drawdown of the upfront payment.
>
> When the entity receives a payment before it has delivered the goods or services, it should recognise a non-financial liability that is presented in the balance sheet as

revenue received in advance. However, if the entity factors the future cash inflows before recognising the receivable (that is, before the goods and services have been delivered), then the entity should recognise a financial liability for the amounts received from the factor.

Factoring receivables already subject to credit insurance

8.89.2 In some instances an entity may have already obtained credit insurance for a portfolio of receivables prior to factoring them. On factoring the factor becomes the beneficiary of the credit insurance. The question arises as to what is the 'original asset' for the purpose of the derecognition criteria: is it only the receivables or the receivables plus the credit insurance? In the absence of guidance within IAS 39 the term 'original asset' can be interpreted to mean either:

■ all related contracts, including purchased options, swaps and insurance contracts, transferred with the loans/receivables in a single transaction that share and mitigate some of the risks on the loans because those are the cash flows that will be paid to the factor; or

■ only the transferred loans/receivables themselves.

An entity must choose one of these two approaches as its accounting policy and apply it consistently throughout the derecognition assessment. For the above factoring transaction, the latter approach is more likely to result in derecognition. This is because the asset is viewed as uninsured receivables that are likely to have significant credit risk. Since this credit risk is transferred to the factor, it is more likely that the transaction will pass the risks and rewards test (that is, it is more likely that step 6 in the diagram in para 8.30 = yes). Under the first approach, the asset is viewed as credit insured receivables that are likely to have lower credit risk. Thus, any risk retained by the seller (other than that covered by the credit insurance) will be relatively more significant (that is, it is more likely that step 6 in the diagram in para 8.30 = no).

It should be noted that there is a separate question as to whether the credit insurance contract has been transferred, that will depend on the facts and circumstances.

Securitisations

8.90 Securitisation is a method of raising finance, first used by originators of mortgage loans, through a sale of a block or pool of loans, typically to a subsidiary or a thinly capitalised vehicle specially set up for the purpose – a special purpose entity (SPE). The SPE finances the purchase by issuing loan notes or other marketable debt instruments to outside investors that are often secured on the SPE's assets. This process is known as securitisation and is also referred to as asset backed finance. Also other pools of debts, such as credit card receivables, leases, hire purchase loans and trade debtors are securitised in a similar way to mortgages. This kind of SPE structure, that isolates the assets legally from the transferor and its creditors ('ring-fence') to avoid any consequences from bankruptcy, enables the originator to raise funds at competitive rates. The following outlines a typical securitisation transaction:

- The assets to be securitised are transferred by an originator/transferor to an SPE for an immediate cash payment.

- The SPE finances the transfer by issuing loan notes to investors. The SPE's shares or residual beneficial interests, if any, are usually held by a party other than the originator (charitable trusts have often been used for this purpose). In addition, the major financial and operating policies are usually predetermined to a greater or lesser extent by the agreements that establish the securitisation (in other words, the SPE operates on so-called 'autopilot').

- Because the SPE's business activities are constrained and its ability to incur debt is limited, it faces the risk of a shortfall of cash below what it is obligated to pay investors. Arrangements are, therefore, made to protect the investors from losses occurring on the assets by a process termed 'credit enhancement'.

  A commonly used form of credit enhancement occurs *via* the issue of subordinated debt (perhaps to the transferor) and other forms of equity-like claims that have the effect of dividing the risk of loss on the underlying assets ('tranching').

  Credit enhancement may take a variety of other forms, including over-collateralisation (the aggregate value of assets transferred exceeds the consideration provided by the SPE), third party guarantee of the issuer's obligations (securities backed by a letter of credit), or third party credit insurance. All the arrangements provide a cushion against losses up to some limit.

- The transferor is often granted rights to cash remaining from the transferred assets after payment of amounts due on the loan notes and other expenses of the issuer. These rights are generally intended, at least in part, to compensate the transferor for assuming some of the risk of credit or other losses. The mechanisms used to achieve this include servicing or other fees, deferred sale consideration, 'super interest' on amounts owed to the transferor (for example, subordinated debt), dividend payments and swap payments.

- Cash accumulation from the assets (for example, from mortgage redemptions) is either used to redeem the loan notes or reinvested in other more liquid assets until the loan notes are repaid. Any surplus cash usually accrues to the transferor as noted above.

- The transferor may continue to service the assets (for example, collect amounts from the borrower, set interest rates, etc) for which it may receive a 'servicing fee'. Often, the surplus cash mentioned above is extracted by an adjustment to the service fee.

8.91   In many situations, the SPE will be no more than an extension of the originator rather than an economic entity in its own right and, therefore, will be consolidated under SIC 12 (step 1 in the diagram in para 8.30). In that situation, the right to receive the cash flows from the asset will remain with the group (step 4 in the diagram in para 8.30 = no). However, the group may assume an obligation to pass-through the cash flows from the transferred asset to the investors that meets all the three conditions set out in paragraph 8.44 above (step 5 in the diagram in para 8.30 = yes). Nevertheless, the group may retain substantially all the risk and rewards of ownership of the securitised assets, because of credit enhancement measures described above. The IASB recognises that many securitisations may fail to qualify for derecognition either because one or more of the three pass-through conditions are not met, as in securitisation arrangements involving 'revolving structures' (see paragraph 8.50 above) or because the entity has retained substantially all the risks and rewards of ownership. [IAS 39 para BC 63].

Subordinated retained interests and credit guarantees

8.92   As discussed in paragraph 8.90 above, an entity may provide the transferee with credit enhancement by subordinating some or all of its interest retained in the transferred asset. Alternatively, an entity may provide the transferee with credit enhancement in the form of a credit guarantee that could be unlimited or limited to a specified amount. Although such credit enhancement techniques are often used in securitisation transactions, they could also be used in other forms of transfers of financial assets.

8.92.1   The provision of a credit guarantee by the entity will cause the pass-through tests of IAS 39 to be failed (see step 5 in the diagram in para 8.30) and, therefore, will prevent derecognition for transactions in which the pass-through tests are applied. This is because any payments made by the transferor under the guarantee are not cash flows from the original asset and, therefore, the existence of a credit guarantee fails the condition in paragraph 19(a) of IAS 39 (see further para 8.44 above). However, the retention of a subordinated interest in the transferred asset does not, in itself, cause the pass-through tests to be failed as it does not require the entity to make payments other than out of collections on the transferred assets. However, the retention of a subordinated interest is likely to result in the transferor retaining some of the risks and rewards of the asset.

8.92.2   In some securitisation structures an entity may retain an interest in the transferred assets in the form of the right to any 'excess spread'. The excess spread is generally any cash left in the SPE after paying the noteholders their interest and principal and after any costs incurred by the SPE. Again the retention of such an interest does not cause the pass-through test to be failed where the SPE is consolidated, but is likely to result in the transferor retaining at least some of the risks and rewards of the assets.

8.93   If an entity has either transferred the contractual rights of the asset or assumed an obligation to pay the cash flows to others that meets the pass-through tests, but still retains substantially all the risks and rewards of ownership of the transferred asset, the asset continues to be recognised in its entirety (step 7 in the diagram in para 8.30 = yes). However, if the entity retains some, but not substantially all, of the risks and rewards of ownership and has retained control (step 8 in the diagram in para 8.30 = yes), derecognition is precluded to the extent of the amount of cash or other assets that the entity could be required to pay under the subordination or credit guarantee agreement. [IAS 39 para AG 51(n)]. The accounting treatment of continuing involvement through a guarantee is considered in paragraph 8.133 below. The accounting treatment of a subordinated retained interest is considered in paragraph 8.123 below.

Removal of accounts provisions

8.94 Securitisations are sometimes carried out on terms that contain a provision that enables a transferor to call back some of the assets securitised at a subsequent date, subject to some restrictions. Such provisions are referred to as 'removal of accounts' provisions (ROAPs). Some ROAPs may allow the transferor unilaterally to specify the assets that may be removed; others may specify that the identification of assets for removal is done randomly or by the transferee. Such provisions are included for good business reasons. For example, the transferor may wish to protect the credit rating of a securitisation vehicle in the event of default of one of the securitised assets or may desire the ability to repurchase assets associated with operations to be discontinued or exited

8.95 The ROAP described above is effectively a call option enabling the transferor to insist on a return of some of the transferred assets. This means that the transferor has retained control over the transferred assets, provided the transferee does not have the practical ability to sell the assets (which is usually the case in a securitisation). Therefore, if such a provision results in the entity neither retaining nor transferring substantially all the risks and rewards of ownership (step 8 in the diagram in para 8.30 = Yes), derecognition is precluded only to the extent of the amount subject to call/repurchase. For example, if the carrying amount and proceeds from the transfer of loan assets are C100,000 and any individual loan could be called back, but the aggregate amount of loans that could be repurchased could not exceed C10,000, C90,000 of the loans would qualify for derecognition. [IAS 39 para AG 51(l)].

Swaps

8.95.1 In a securitisation involving fixed rate assets, the transferor may enter into an interest rate swap with the SPE. Under the swap's terms, the transferor may undertake to receive the fixed rate interest on the transferred assets and pay a variable rate to the SPE, such that the SPE can pay variable rate interest to noteholders. If the SPE does not fall to be consolidated, then such a swap would not prevent derecognition provided the payments on the swap are not conditional on payments being made on the transferred asset. [IAS 39 para AG 51(p)]. The swap may, however, result in the retention of some risks of the asset's rewards, for example, if the terms cause some late payment risk to be retained.

8.95.2 If, however, the SPE is consolidated and the pass-through tests apply, the swap would prevent derecognition (see step 5 in the diagram in para 8.30). This is because the swap results in the transferor having an obligation to pay amounts to the eventual recipients (investors in the notes) even if it does not collect equivalent amounts from the assets. The swap may require a net payment to the SPE (that is then passed to noteholders) if interest rates rise so that the interest due on the notes exceeds that due on the assets. Hence, the pass-through test in IAS 39 paragraph 19(a) is failed and derecognition is precluded.

Loan transfers

8.96 As explained in paragraph 8.40, some kinds of financial assets cannot be sold in the same way as other assets. However, they can be transferred to third parties in return for an immediate cash payment. The transfer may be of the whole of a single loan, part of a loan, or of all or part of a portfolio of similar loans. The methods by which the benefits and risks of loans can be transferred vary between jurisdictions. As highlighted below and in the examples in paragraphs 8.153 and 8.157, from the issuer's perspective it is necessary to assess whether the loan transfer, regardless of its form, results in the borrower being legally released from its obligations under the existing loan to determine whether the loan has been extinguished. Common loan transfer methods include those described below, although there may be variations across different jurisdictions.

■ Novation

Under a novation, typically the rights and obligations of the original lender (the transferor) under the loan agreement are cancelled and replaced by new ones whose main effect is to change the lender's identity. The transferor is released from its obligations to the borrower.

Such a novation, therefore, will result in the transfer of the contractual rights to receive the financial asset's cash flows. Therefore, in the absence of any side agreements, such as a guarantee or other form of recourse arrangement, a forward purchase arrangement or option, the transferor will derecognise the loan in its entirety.

■ Assignment

Under an assignment, the original lender's (the transferor's) rights to the future cash flows under the loan agreement, but not obligations (for example, warranty obligations to repair faulty goods) are typically transferred to the third party (the assignee). There are generally two types of assignments – assignments where the lender is required to give notice to the borrower (in some jurisdictions these are known as legal or open assignments) and assignments where no notice is required to be given to the borrower (in some jurisdictions these are known as equitable or silent assignments).

Where the lender is required to give notice in writing to the borrower, and in the absence of any side agreements between the transferor and the transferee, the transferee normally acquires a direct legal claim on the future cash flows under the loan agreement.

Where notice is not required to be given to the borrower, as the borrower is not aware that the lender has transferred its rights to the cash flows to another party, there is doubt as to whether the transferee has obtained the unconditional contractual rights to the cash flows of the transferred asset. In general, whether the contractual rights to the cash flows have been unconditionally transferred under such an assignment would depend on the law of the country that governs the assignment..

Both types of assignment are subject to equitable rights arising before notice is received. For example, a right of set-off held by the borrower against the lender will be good against the assignee for any transactions undertaken before the borrower receives notice of the assignment.

Assignments may or may not leave the transferor with continuing involvement in the loans depending on whether there are any residual interests, recourse provisions, buyback provisions, etc. The issues that arise in assignments are very similar to debt factoring and securitisations, most of which involve an assignment.

- Sub-participation

Under a sub-participation, the lender enters into a non-recourse back-to-back arrangement with a third party (the sub-participant) and, in exchange for a cash receipt of an amount equal to the whole or fully proportionate part of the loan, passes on the cash flows (both interest and principal) collected on the loan to the sub-participant. Typically all the contractual rights and obligations legally remain with the transferor.

Like assignments, sub-participation may or may not leave the transferor with continuing involvement in the loans depending on whether there are any residual interests, recourse provisions, buyback provisions, etc. Provided the sub-participation meets all the three pass-through conditions discussed in paragraph 8.44 above, there is no recourse to the transferor and the transferor does not retain any significant risks and rewards of ownership of the loans, derecognition is appropriate.

Loan syndications

8.97 Sometimes, a single lender may not be able to fund a large loan required by a borrower. In those situations, it is quite common for a group of lenders to fund the loan jointly. This is usually accomplished by a syndication under which several lenders share in lending to a single borrower, but each syndicate member lends a specific amount to the borrower and has the right to repayment from the borrower. Such a loan syndication is not a transfer of financial assets. Accordingly, each lender in the syndication should account for the amounts it is owed by the borrower.

8.98   In some loan syndications, the lead lender may advance funds to the borrower and transfer a fully proportionate share of the loan to different lenders. The borrower makes repayments directly to a lead lender who then distributes the collections to the other syndicate lenders in proportion to the amount lent. This situation is no different in substance to a sub-participation discussed above. Derecognition of the loans transferred to the different lenders would be appropriate if the lead lender is simply functioning as an agent, all the syndicate lenders have fully proportionate shares of the total lending and all the pass-through conditions and risks and rewards conditions are met.

Transfers involving derivatives

8.98.1   Transfers of financial assets often include derivatives, either explicitly or implicitly. Common derivatives that are found in transfer arrangements are put and call options, forward sale or repurchase contracts and swap agreements. Derivative instruments normally require exercise by one of the parties to the contract. In some instances, exercise of the derivative may be automatic, for example, where a transferor enters into a forward agreement to repurchase a transferred asset at a pre-determined price. In other instances, the exercise may be conditional on the occurrence of a particular event, for example, where the transferee has the right to put back to the transferor receivables that remain uncollectible.

8.98.2   In some circumstances, the existence of derivatives may not prevent derecognition, for example, if the pre-determined price mentioned in the first example above is set at market price at repurchase date. In other circumstances, derivatives may well prevent a transferor from derecognising a financial asset, thereby precluding sale treatment. Derivatives may also constrain a transferee's practical ability to sell the transferred asset, even if there is no legal constraint, with the result that the transferor retains control over the transferred asset. Any derivative that serves as an impediment to the transferee from realising the economic benefits inherent in the transferred asset should be carefully analysed to determine whether or not the transferor has retained control of the transferred asset.

8.98.3   Where the presence of a derivative prevents a transferor from derecognising a financial asset, the transferor's contractual rights or obligations related to the transfer are not accounted for separately as derivatives if recognising both the derivative and either the transferred asset or the liability arising from the transfer would result in recognising the same rights or obligations twice. [IAS 39 para AG 49].

8.98.4   It follows that the identification and evaluation of such derivatives is crucial to the derecognition analysis. Examples of transfers involving derivatives and the implications of the presence of the derivatives as regards derecognition are considered below. The accounting for transfers including derivatives that result in continued recognition to the extent of the entity's continuing involvement in the transferred asset are considered from paragraph 8.134 below.

Transfers subject to deep out-of-the-money option

8.98.5 A financial asset that is transferred subject only to a deep out-of-the-money put option held by the transferee or a deep out-of-the-money call option held by the transferor is derecognised. As a deep-out-of-the-money option is very unlikely to become in-the-money at the exercise date, the transferor is deemed to have transferred substantially all the risks and rewards of ownership (step 6 in the diagram in para 8.30 = yes). [IAS 39 para AG 51(g)].

8.98.6 If, due to subsequent events or changes in market conditions, it becomes probable that a deep out-of-the-money put or call option is likely to be exercised at the exercise date, the change in the option's probability being exercised would not result in the re-recognition of the financial asset that has previously been derecognised. This is consistent with the requirements in the standard that where an entity determines that, as a result of the transfer, it has transferred substantially all the risks and rewards of ownership, the entity does not recognise the transferred asset again in a future period, unless it re-acquires the transferred asset in a new transaction. [IAS 39 para AG 41]. Instead, the option would be accounted for as a derivative at fair value with the increase in its fair value reflected in profit or loss.

Transfer of readily obtainable assets subject to at-the-money call option

8.98.7 A financial asset that is readily obtainable in the market and transferred subject to the transferor holding a call option that is neither deeply in-the-money nor deeply out-of-the-money is derecognised. This is because the entity has neither retained nor transferred substantially all the risks and rewards of ownership and has not retained control (step 8 in the diagram in para 8.30 = no). [IAS 39 para AG 51(h)]. Although the option's existence means that the transferor has a continuing involvement in the asset, the fact that the asset is readily obtainable in the market means that the call option has no practical effect in creating any constraints on the transferee's practical ability to sell the asset. This is because if the transferred asset has been sold by the transferee and the transferor exercises the call option, the transferee will be able to fulfil its obligation by purchasing a replacement asset from the market. Therefore, the transferor retains no control over the transferred asset and derecognition of the transferred asset is appropriate. The transferor will account for the call option as a derivative at fair value with changes in fair value reflected in profit or loss.

8.98.8 Although not specifically dealt with in the standard, a readily obtainable financial asset that is transferred subject to the transferee holding a put option that is neither deeply in-the-money nor deeply out-of-the-money at the date of transfer is similarly derecognised for the reasons stated above. In this situation, if the transferee decides to exercise its rights under the put, the transferee would be able to meet its obligation by purchasing the asset from the market.

Transfer of assets subject to a fair value put or call option or a forward repurchase agreement

8.98.9   A transfer of a financial asset that is subject only to a put or call option or a forward repurchase agreement that has an exercise or repurchase price equal to the fair value of the financial asset at the time of repurchase results in derecognition, because of the transfer of substantially all the risks and rewards of ownership. [IAS 39 para AG 51(j)].

Transfer of assets subject to interest-rate swaps

8.98.10   An entity may transfer a fixed rate financial asset to a transferee and enter into an interest rate swap with the transferee to receive a fixed interest rate and pay a variable interest rate based on a notional amount that is equal to the principal amount of the transferred financial asset. The interest rate swap does not preclude derecognition of the transferred asset provided the payments on the swap are not conditional on payments being made on the transferred asset. [IAS 39 AG 51(p)].

Call and put options that are deeply in-the-money

8.98.11   If a transferred financial asset can be called back by the transferor and the call option is deeply in-the-money, the transfer does not qualify for derecognition. This is because the transferor has retained substantially all the risks and rewards of the asset's ownership by virtue of the fact that the call option is so valuable that its exercise appears virtually assured at inception. As explained in paragraph 8.98.3, a call option retained by the transferor that prevents the transfer from being accounted for as a sale is not separately recognised as a derivative asset. The accounting treatment is similar to sale and repurchase transactions considered in paragraph 8.119 below. Similarly, if the financial asset can be put back by the transferee and the put option is deeply in-the-money, the transfer does not qualify for derecognition because the transferor has retained substantially all the risks and rewards of ownership. Again the put option is not recognised separately, as to do so would result in double counting the same obligation. [IAS 39 para AG 51(f)].

Total return swaps

8.98.12   An entity may sell a financial asset to a transferee and enter into a total return swap with the transferee, whereby all of the cash flows from the underlying asset plus any increases and less any decreases in the underlying asset's fair value are remitted to the entity in exchange for a fixed or variable rate payment. In such a case, derecognition of all of the asset is prohibited. [IAS 39 para AG 51(o)].

Accounting treatment

8.99 The accounting treatment can be fairly complex, particularly in respect of transfers in which the entity (transferor) has continuing involvement in the transferred asset.

Transfers that qualify for derecognition

8.100 Where an entity determines that a transfer of a financial asset qualifies as a transfer and qualifies for derecognition because either:

■ the entity has transferred substantially all the risks and rewards of ownership of the asset (step 6 in the diagram in para 8.30 = yes); or

■ the entity has neither transferred nor retained substantially all the risks and rewards of ownership of the asset, and no longer retains control of the asset (step 8 in the diagram in para 8.30 = no),

the transferred asset is derecognised in its entirety and any new financial assets obtained, financial liabilities assumed and any servicing obligations are recognised at fair value. [IAS 39 para 25]. It should be noted that the phrase *"in its entirety"* includes part of a financial asset (or part of a group of similar financial assets) to which the derecognition tests have been applied as explained in paragraph 8.33 above.

8.101 On derecognition of a financial asset in its entirety, the difference between the carrying amount and the sum of:

■ the consideration received (including any new assets obtained less any new liabilities assumed); and

■ any cumulative gain or loss that had been recognised in other comprehensive income;

is recognised in profit or loss. The recycling of the cumulative gain or loss that had been recognised in other comprehensive income occurs on the derecognition of an available-for-sale financial asset.

[IAS 39 para 26].

8.102 There may also be instances where, following the financial asset's derecognition, a new financial asset is obtained or a new financial liability is assumed. As noted above, any new asset is part of the proceeds of sale. Any liability assumed, even if it is related to the transferred asset, is a reduction of the sales proceeds.

Example 1 – Derecognition of whole of a financial asset in its entirety

Entity A holds a small number of shares in entity B. The shares are classified as available-for-sale. On 31 March 20X6, the shares' fair value is C120 and the cumulative gain recognised in other comprehensive income is C20. On the same day, entity B is acquired by entity C, a large quoted entity. As a result, entity A receives shares in entity C with a fair value of C130.

In this situation, the transfer of the shares in entity B qualifies for derecognition in their entirety as the entity no longer retains any risk and rewards of ownership. In addition, the transfer results in entity A obtaining a new financial asset, that is, shares in entity C that should be recognised at fair value as stated in paragraph 8.100 above. The gain on disposal, calculated in accordance with paragraph 8.101 above, is as follows:

	C
Proceeds received (fair value of cash or other securities received)	130
+ Fair value of any new financial asset acquired in the transfer	–
- Fair value of any new liability assumed in the transfer	–
Net proceeds	130
Carrying amount of the whole financial asset transferred	(120)
Gain or (loss) arising on derecognition	10
Amount recycled from other comprehensive income	20
Gain or (loss) recognised in profit or loss	30

The accounting entries to record the transfer are shown below:

	Dr C	Cr C
Fair value of shares in entity C acquired	130	
Carrying value of shares in entity B disposed of		120
Other comprehensive income ('recycling' of cumulative gain)	20	
Gain on disposal		30

Example 2 – Factoring without recourse

Entity A (the transferor) holds a portfolio of receivables with a carrying value of C1m. It enters into a factoring arrangement with entity B (the transferee) under which it transfers the portfolio to entity B in exchange for C900,000 of cash. Entity B will service the loans after their transfer and debtors will pay amounts due directly to entity B. Entity A has no obligations whatsoever to repay any sums received from the factor and has no rights to any additional sums regardless of the timing or the level of collection from the underlying debts.

In this example, entity A has transferred its rights to receive the cash flows from the asset *via* an assignment to entity B (step 4 in the diagram in para 8.30 = yes). Furthermore, as entity B has no recourse to entity A for either late payment risk or credit risk, entity A has transferred substantially all the risks and rewards of ownership of the portfolio (step 6 in the diagram in para 8.30 = yes). Hence, entity A derecognises the entire portfolio. The difference between the carrying value of C1m and cash received of C900,000, that is, the entire discount of C100,000 is recognised immediately as a financing cost in profit or loss.

The accounting that would apply if entity A continued to service the receivables is dealt with from paragraph 8.106 below.

Transferred asset is part of a larger asset

8.103   Where an entity transfers an asset that is part of a larger financial asset (for example, when an entity transfers interest only cash flows that are part of a debt instrument), and the part transferred qualifies for derecognition in its entirety, the previous carrying value of the larger financial asset is allocated between the part that continues to be recognised and the part that is derecognised. The allocation is based on the relative fair values of those parts at the date of transfer. For this purpose, a retained servicing asset should be treated as part that continues to be recognised. The difference between the carrying amount allocated to the part derecognised and the sum of:

■   the consideration received for the part derecognised (including any new assets obtained less any new liabilities assumed); and

■   any cumulative gain or loss allocated to it that had been recognised in other comprehensive income;

is recognised in profit or loss. Any cumulative gain or loss that had been recognised in other comprehensive income is allocated between the part that continues to be recognised and the part that is derecognised, based on the relative fair values of those parts. The recycling of the cumulative gain or loss that had been recognised in other comprehensive income arises on derecognition of an available-for-sale financial asset.

[IAS 39 para 27].

8.104   In making an allocation of the previous carrying amount of a larger financial asset between the part transferred and the part that continues to be recognised, it is necessary to determine the fair value of the part that continues to be recognised. When the entity has a history of selling parts similar to the part that continues to be recognised or other market transactions exist for such parts, recent prices of actual transactions provide the best estimate of its fair value. When there are no price quotes or recent market transactions to support the fair value of the part that continues to be recognised, the best estimate of the fair value is the difference between:

■   the fair value of the larger financial asset as a whole; and

■   the consideration received from the transferee for the part that is derecognised.

[IAS 39 para 28].

8.105 In estimating the fair values of the part that continues to be recognised and the part that is derecognised, an entity should apply the fair value measurement requirements discussed in chapter 9. [IAS 39 para AG46].

Example – Derecognition of a part of a financial asset

On 1 April 20X2, an entity acquired corporate bonds at their face value of C5m. The bonds pay interest of 8% per annum in arrears and are redeemable at par at the end of year 10 on 31 March 20Y2.

On 31 March 20X6, when the current market rate of interest was 6%, the fair value of the bonds amounted to C5,491,732, consisting of the present value of the interest only strip of C1,966,930 and principal only strip of C3,524,802. On the same date, the entity unconditionally transferred its right to the principal only strip to a bank under a legal assignment for cash payment equal to its fair value without any recourse whatsoever. The entity retained the interest only strip (right to receive interest income on the bond at C400,000 per annum for the remaining 6 years).

In this example, the entity has transferred its rights to receive the principal cash flows to the bank *via* a legal assignment (step 4 in the diagram in para 8.30 = yes). Furthermore, as the entity has unconditionally sold its right to repayment when the bond matures on 31 March 20Y2 without recourse, it has transferred the risks and rewards attributable to the principal only strip that is part of a larger asset (step 6 in the diagram in para 8.30 = yes). Therefore, the entity can derecognise the principal only strip in its entirety.

In order to calculate the gain or loss on the principal only strip, it is necessary to allocate the carrying amount of C5m between the part sold and the part retained, based on their respective fair values as stated in paragraph 8.103 above. The allocation is shown below:

	Fair value	Percentage of fair value	Allocated carrying amount
	C	%	C
Principal only (PO) strip	3,524,802	64.1838	3,209,190
Interest only (IO) strip	1,966,930	35.8162	1,790,810
Total	5,491,732	100.0000	5,000,000

The accounting entries to record the part derecognised are as follows:

	Dr	Cr
	C	C
Cash received on sale of PO strip	3,524,802	
Carrying amount attributable to PO strip		3,209,190
Gain on sale of PO strip		315,612

If the bond had been classified as an available-for-sale financial asset, the bond would have been recorded at its fair value of C5,491,732 at 31 March 20X6. The amount credited to other comprehensive income would have amounted to C491,732. In that situation, it would be necessary to 'recycle' that portion of the fair value gain that is attributable to the principal only strip to the income statement. As stated in paragraph 8.103 above, this allocation should also be based on the relative fair values of the principal only and interest only strip. Accordingly, the portion of the gain recorded in other comprehensive income that is attributable to the principal only strip and fall to be recycled to the income statement amounts to C315,612 (64.1838% of C491,732).

The accounting treatment would be similar if, instead of unconditionally transferring the principal only strip at its fair value, the entity had transferred the interest only strip (the right to receive future interest income) at its fair value of C1,966,930 and retained the principal only strip. In that situation, a gain of C176,120 (C1,966,930 – C1,790,810) would have arisen on the transfer if the asset was carried at amortised cost. On the other hand, if the asset was carried at fair value as available-for-sale, the 'recycled' gain to profit or loss would have amounted to C176,120 (35.8162% of C491,732).

Servicing assets and liabilities

8.106 Servicing is inherent in all loans and receivables. Servicing of mortgage loans, credit card receivables or other financial assets commonly includes, but is not limited to, collecting payments as they fall due, accounting for and remitting principal and interest payments to the transferee, monitoring non-performing loans/debtors, executing foreclosure if necessary and performing other administrative tasks. The service provider incurs the costs of servicing the assets often in return for a fee for performing the services.

8.107 Servicing rights do not meet the definition of a financial instrument because they represent a commitment to supply a service and can only be settled by the service delivery. However, since such servicing rights are, essentially, an expected stream of cash flows that results from a contractual agreement, they are so similar to financial instruments that they are recognised and initially measured on the same basis as financial assets and liabilities. Accordingly, where an entity transfers a financial asset in a transfer that qualifies for derecognition in its entirety and retains the right to service the financial asset for a fee, IAS 39 requires the entity to recognise either a servicing asset or a servicing liability for that servicing contract as follows:

- If the fee to be received is expected to be more than adequate compensation for the servicing, the entity should recognise a servicing asset for the servicing right. This asset should be recognised at an amount of the determined on the basis of the carrying amount of the larger financial asset as discussed in paragraph 8.103 above.

- If the fee to be received is not expected to compensate the entity adequately for performing the servicing, the entity should recognise a servicing liability for the servicing obligations at its fair value.

[IAS 39 para 24].

8.108 It follows from the above that where the benefits of servicing exactly compensates the service provider for its servicing responsibilities, there is no servicing asset or liability and the service contract's fair value is zero.

8.109 In some arrangements, an entity may retain the right to a part of the interest payments on transferred assets as compensation for servicing those assets. The part of the interest payments that the entity would give up upon termination or transfer of the servicing contract is allocated to the servicing asset or servicing liability. The part of the interest payments that the entity would not give up is an interest-only strip receivable. For example, if the entity would not give up any interest upon termination or transfer of the servicing contract, the entire interest spread is an interest-only strip receivable. For the purposes of applying the requirements of paragraph 8.103 above in respect of a transferred asset that is part of a larger financial asset, the fair values of the servicing asset and interest-only strip receivable are used to allocate the carrying amount of the receivable between the part of the asset that is derecognised and the part that continues to be recognised. If there is no servicing fee specified or the fee to be received is not expected to compensate the entity adequately for performing the servicing, a liability for the servicing obligation is recognised at fair value. [IAS 39 para AG 45].

> **Example 1 – Sale of receivable with servicing retained (servicing fee not specified in the contract)**
>
> Entity A owns a portfolio of loans with a carrying amount of C5m that yield 8% interest income. The loans are accounted for as loans and receivables at amortised cost.
>
> The entity sells the entire portfolio to a bank for C5.25m without any recourse *via* a legal assignment. However, the entity agrees to service the portfolio over the remainder of its life for no additional payment and estimates that the amount that would fairly compensate it for servicing the portfolio is C200,000.
>
> In this situation, as the entity transfers the entire portfolio including its right to receive future interest income on terms that qualify for derecognition under IAS 39, the entity would derecognise the carrying value of the portfolio of C5m. It would also recognise, in the absence of a servicing fee, a servicing liability of C200,000 in accordance with paragraph 8.107 above. The accounting entries to record the transfer are as follows:
>
> | | Dr C | Cr C |
> |---|---|---|
> | Cash | 5,250,000 | |
> | Loans | | 5,000,000 |
> | Servicing liability | | 200,000 |
> | Gain on disposal | | 50,000 |

Example 2 – Sale of receivable with servicing retained (servicing fee specified in the contract)

The facts are the same as in example 1, except that entity A transfers the entire principal amount of the portfolio plus its right to receive interest income of 6% *via* a legal assignment for a consideration of C4,900,000 without any recourse. The entity retains the right to service the portfolio for which it will be compensated through a right to receive one-half of the interest income not sold (that is, 1% of the 2% future interest income retained). The remaining 1% is considered to be an interest-only strip retained by the entity A. At the date of transfer, the fair value of the interest-only strip is C275,000 and the fair value of the servicing asset is C75,000 (calculated as the present value of servicing fee receivable less a market fee for performing the service).

In this example, it is necessary to consider whether the criteria for derecognition should be applied to the portfolio of loans in its entirety or to separate portions (step 2 in the diagram in para 8.30). It is assumed that 75% (6% out of the 8%) of the interest cash flows transferred represents a full proportionate share of all the interest cash flows (see third bullet point of paragraph 8.33). This means that the entity will consider two portions of the whole portfolio, being 100% of the principal cash flows and 75% of the interest cash flows, separately for the purposes of derecognition.

Clearly, in this example, the rights to the cash flows have not expired as the loans still exist (step 3 in the diagram in para 8.30 = No) and so it is necessary to consider whether the entity has transferred its rights to receive the cash flows from the asset (step 4 in the diagram in para 8.30). However, the entity has legally assigned its rights to all of the principal cash flows and 6% of all the interest cash flows from the bond to the bank and, even though it has retained the rights to service the portfolio, this, in itself, does not prevent a transfer under paragraph 18(a) of IAS 39. Therefore (step 4 in the diagram in para 8.30 = Yes). Furthermore, as the transfer was made without any recourse, entity A has transferred substantially all the risks and rewards of those portions (step 6 in the diagram in para 8.30 = Yes). Therefore, entity A would derecognise the transferred portions.

In order to calculate the gain or loss arising on the transfer, the carrying amount of the financial asset (the portfolio of loans) of C5m should be allocated between the part sold and the part retained based on their relative fair values. In this regard, the servicing asset is allocated to the part that continues to be recognised as indicated in paragraph 8.100 above.

	Fair value	Percentage of fair value	Allocated carrying amount
Interest sold/retained	C	%	C
Loan sold (principal and 6% interest)	4,900,000	93.33	4,666,500
Interest-only strip retained	275,000	5.24	262,000
Servicing asset	75,000	1.43	71,500
Total	5,250,000	100.00	5,000,000

The gain arising on sale of the portion derecognised is the difference between the sales proceeds of C4,900,000 and the allocated carrying amount of C4,666,500, that is, C233,500. The retained interest in the transferred asset amounts to C333,500 (consisting of an interest-only-strip of C262,000 + servicing asset of C71,500).

Example 3 – Sale of listed debt securities subject to a call option

On 1 January 20X6, Bank A enters into an agreement to sell a portfolio of held for trading listed debt securities to an investment fund in exchange for a cash payment of C6m. The securities are subject to a call option that allows the bank to repurchase the securities for a price of C6.7m on 31 December 20X6. The securities' fair value at the date of transfer is C6.5m. The option's fair value is C0.5m. The investment fund has the practical ability to sell the securities to a third party.

The presence of the call option means that the bank has a continuing involvement in the transferred asset. However, as the securities are listed and the investment fund has the practical ability to sell the securities to a third party unilaterally and without imposing any conditions, the bank has not retained control of the securities. According the bank will derecognise the securities (step 8 in the diagram in para 8.30 = No), but record its rights under the call option separately.

Given that the call option's strike price (C6.7m) is more than the fair value of the underlying securities (C6.5m), the call option is out-of-the-money. Therefore, the fair value of the call option of C0.5m wholly relates to the time value of the option, which is also the premium paid by the bank.

Therefore, at the date of transfer, the company will record the following entries:

	Dr C	Cr C
Cash	6.0	
Trading portfolio		6.5
Derivative (call option)	0.5	

Bank A will recognise the call option at fair value through profit and loss.

Assume that at 31 December 20X6, the fair value of the shares increases to C7m and the bank exercises the option, Bank A will record the following entries:

	Dr C	Cr C
Derivative		0.2
Profit or loss	0.2	
Trading portfolio	7.0	
Cash		6.7
Derivative		0.3

As 31 December 20X6 is the call's expiry date, its time value at that date will be zero. The decline in the time value is included in the C 0.2 loss recognised in profit or loss.

[The next paragraph is 8.119.]

Transfers that do not qualify for derecognition

8.119 Where a transfer does not result in the transferred asset's derecognition, the entity continues to recognise the transferred asset in its entirety and recognises a financial liability for the consideration received. [IAS 39 para 29]. The asset and the associated liability cannot be offset. In subsequent periods, the entity recognises any income on the transferred asset and any expense incurred on the financial liability. Again the entity cannot offset the income and the expense. [IAS 32 para 42, IAS 39 paras 29, 36]. This reflects the transaction's substance, which is accounted for as a collateralised borrowing.

8.120 It should be noted that the above treatment only applies when a financial asset is precluded from being derecognised in full (step 7 in the diagram in para 8.30 = yes). It does not apply in circumstances where a financial asset is not derecognised, because the entity has a continuing involvement in the financial asset (step 8 in the diagram in para 8.30 = yes). In those circumstances, special provisions apply and these are discussed from paragraph 8.127 below.

> **Example – Factoring with full recourse**
>
> Entity A (the transferor) holds a portfolio of receivables with a carrying value of C1m. It enters into a factoring arrangement with entity B (the transferee) under which it transfers the portfolio *via* an assignment to entity B in exchange for C900,000 of cash. All sums collected from debtors are paid by entity A to a specially nominated bank account opened by entity B (that is, entity A is only servicing the loans and has no right to the cash flows). Entity A agrees to reimburse entity B in cash for any shortfall between the amount collected from the receivable and the consideration of C900,000. Once the receivables have been repaid, any sums collected above C900,000 less interest on the initial payment until the date debtors pay, will be paid to entity A.
>
> In this example, entity A has transferred its rights to receive the cash flows from the asset (step 4 in the diagram in para 8.30 = yes).
>
> The next step is to consider whether entity A has transferred substantially all the risks and rewards of ownership of the receivables. Under the factoring arrangement, entity A's maximum possible exposure to entity B is to repay all of the consideration of C900,000 it has received. Although this situation is unlikely, it means that entity A has given a guarantee to compensate the transferee for all credit losses that are likely to occur. In addition, entity A receives the benefit of sums collected from debtors above C900,000. Consequently, entity A has retained both the credit and late payment risk associated with the receivables. Entity A has therefore retained substantially all the risk and rewards of ownership of the receivables and continues to recognise the receivables (step 7 in the diagram in para 8.30 = yes).
>
> Entity A recognises the consideration received of C900,000 as a secured borrowing. The liability is measured at amortised cost with interest expense recognised over the period to maturity of the receivables in line with the interest rate charged by the factor.

Sale and repurchase agreements

8.121 The essential features of a sale and repurchase transaction are discussed from paragraphs 8.75 above. It is clear from the above discussions that a financial asset that is sold subject to the obligation to repurchase the same or a similar asset at a fixed price should not be derecognised. This is because the entity retains upside as well as downside exposure to gains and losses from the transferred asset. Therefore, the asset continues to be recognised in its entirety and the proceeds received are recognised as a liability. Similarly, the entity continues to recognise any income from the asset along with any expense incurred on the associated liability.

8.122 In some circumstances, a repurchase agreement may contain a provision that may allow the transferor to settle net in cash. That is, instead of taking physical delivery of the asset in consideration for paying the fixed price, the transferor settles the transaction net in cash by paying or receiving the difference between the fair value of the asset at the date of repurchase and the fixed repurchase price. The fact that the transferor is able to settle the transaction net in cash does not automatically mean that the transferor has lost control of the asset. [IAS 39 para AG 51(k)]. Also the transferor must still pass the 'risks and rewards' test (that is, to transfer substantially all risks and rewards), as well as the control test, before the transferor can derecognise the transferred asset. Examples of sale and repurchase transactions that are gross and net settled are considered below.

Example 1 – Sale and repurchase transaction (gross settled)

An entity purchases C10m, 10%, 5 year government bonds on 1 January 20X4 with semi-annual interest payable on 30 June and 31 December for C10.8m that results in a premium of C800,000. The entity classifies the bonds as held-to-maturity investments at amortised cost. The amortisation of the bonds to maturity using the effective interest method (see chapter 9) is shown below.

	Cash received	Interest income @ 4.013%	Carrying amount
1 Jan 20X4			10,800,000
1 Jul 20X4	500,000	433,408	10,733,408
1 Jan 20X5	500,000	430,735	10,664,143
1 Jul 20X5	500,000	427,956	10,592,099
1 Jan 20X6	500,000	425,064	10,517,163
1 Jul 20X6	500,000	422,057	10,439,220
1 Jan 20X7	500,000	418,929	10,358,149
1 Jul 20X7	500,000	415,676	10,273,825
1 Jan 20X8	500,000	412,292	10,186,117
1 Jul 20X8	500,000	408,772	10,094,889
31 Dec 20X8	500,000	405,111	10,000,000
	5,000,000	4,200,000	

On 1 July 20X5, the entity sells the bond at its fair value of C10.6m to a third party with an agreement to repurchase the bond on 1 July 20X6 for C10.65m.

As the repurchase price is fixed at the outset, the entity is precluded from derecognising the bond as discussed in paragraph 8.79 above (step 7 in the diagram in para 8.30 = Yes). The transferee will be entitled to receive the interest due on 1 Jan 20X6 and 1 July 20X6, that is, C1m that, together with the difference between the repurchase price and sale price of C50,000, represents a lender's return of 9.8943% per annum on the sale price. Therefore, the entity will continue to recognise the bond and the interest on it, as if it still held the bonds, as noted in paragraph 8.119 above.

It should be noted that although the repurchase agreement meets the definition of a derivative (it can be viewed as a forward contract), it is not separately recognised as a derivative and measured at fair value, because to do so would result in double counting of the same rights. Therefore, in this situation, the forward contract to repurchase the financial asset at a fixed price is not recorded as an asset (see further para 8.98.3 above).

The entity will also record a liability of C10.6m for the proceeds received. This liability accretes to the amount payable on repurchase of C10.65m at 1 July 20X6, using the effective interest method. The entity will continue to recognise a notional interest income in the periods to 1 Jan 20X6 and 1 July 20X6 and also account for an equal amount of notional interest paid to the third party. On 1 July 20X6 following repurchase of the bond by the entity, the liability of C10.65m will be eliminated as shown below:

	Liability Carrying value
Liability at 1 July 20X5	10,600,000
Interest payable for the half year to 31 December 20X5 @ 9.8943%	524,397
Notional cash paid to third party on 31 December 20X5*	(500,000)
Balance at 31 December 20X5	10,624,397
Interest payable for the half year to 30 June 20X6 @ 9.8943%	525,603
Notional cash paid to third party on 30 June 20X6*	(500,000)
Balance at 30 June 20X6	10,650,000
Liability repaid on 1 July 20X6 at repurchase price	(10,650,000)

* third party will receive interest directly from the bond as legal owner.

It may well be that the transferee is able to pledge or sell the bond during its period of ownership. In that situation, the transferor should reclassify the bond on its balance sheet as a loaned asset or repurchase receivable as explained in paragraph 8.83 above.

Example 2 – Sale and repurchase transaction (net settled in cash)

The facts are the same as in example 1 above, except that the repurchase contract is to be settled net in cash. The fair value of the asset at the date of repurchase amounts to C10.655m. This means that the entity will pay an additional C5,000 to the bank.

As explained in paragraph 8.98.8 above, the fact that the forward repurchase agreement requires net settlement does not automatically lead to derecognition. In this example, it is clear that the entity continues to recognise the asset as the repurchase is at a fixed price. However, as the entity will not physically get the bond back at the repurchase date, the bond will be derecognised following payment of the additional consideration of C5,000 at the repurchase date. Therefore, it would not be appropriate to continue to classify the bond as held-to-maturity at amortised cost as in example 1. Instead, the entity would need to reclassify the bond as an available-for-sale financial asset at fair value at the sale date of 1 July 20X5. (Where an entity during the current financial year has sold or reclassified more than an insignificant amount of held-to-maturity investments before maturity (more than insignificant in relation to the total amount of held-to-maturity investments), it is prohibited from classifying any financial asset as held-to-maturity for a period of two years after the occurrence of this event, see further chapter 6.) The reclassification results in a gain to other comprehensive income as shown below:

Fair value of bond at 1 July 20X5	10,600,000
Amortised cost of bond at 1 July 20X5 as in example 1	10,592,098
Gain transferred to other comprehensive income following reclassification	7,902

Therefore, the entity will record the bond at its fair value of C10,600,000 and a corresponding liability of C10,600,000. The liability accretes to the repurchase price of C10,650,000 as shown in example 1.

At the repurchase date of 1 July 20X6, the repurchase receivable will be fair valued to C10,655,000 and a further gain of C5,000 will be recorded in other comprehensive income. As the repurchase will be net settled in cash, the entity will record the following entries:

	Dr C	Cr C
Liability	10,650,000	
Bond		10,655,000
Cash settlement	5,000	
Other comprehensive income – recycling of cumulative gain (7,902 + 5,000)	12,902	
Gain on disposal		12,902

The above example illustrates the point that although a forward repurchase agreement that requires net settlement in cash is economically equivalent to a deferred sale, the entity cannot derecognise the asset as the risks and rewards of ownership have been retained until settlement.

Subordinated retained interests and credit guarantees

8.123 An entity may provide the transferee with credit enhancement by subordinating some or all of its interest retained in the transferred asset. Alternatively, an entity may provide the transferee with credit enhancement in the form of a credit guarantee that could be unlimited or limited to a specified amount. If the entity retains substantially all the risks and rewards of ownership of the transferred asset, the asset continues to be recognised in its entirety. [IAS 39 para AG 51(n)].

> **Example – subordinated retained interest**
>
> Entity A originates a portfolio of 5 year interest-bearing loans of C10m. Entity A then enters into an agreement with entity B in which, in exchange for a cash payment of C9m, entity A agrees to pay to entity B the first C9m (plus interest) of cash collected from the loan portfolio. Entity A retains rights to the last C1m (plus interest). Expected collections on the loan portfolio are C9.5m and experience suggests that they are unlikely to be less than C9.3m.
>
> Entity A's retained interest in the cash flows from the loans is effectively subordinated. This is because if entity A collects, say, only C8m of its loans of C10m because some debtors default, entity A would have to pass on to entity B all of the C8m collected and keeps nothing for itself. On the other hand, if entity A collects C9.5m, it passes C9m to entity B and retains C0.5m.
>
> In this case, entity A retains substantially all the risks and rewards of ownership of the loans, because the subordinated retained interest absorbs all of the likely variability in net cash flows as discussed in paragraph 8.55. The loans continue to be recognised in their entirety even if the three pass-through conditions discussed in paragraph 8.44 are met, because derecognition is only achieved where, in addition, substantially all the risks and rewards of ownership are transferred. As derecognition is not achieved, the entire proceeds of C9m is recorded as a collateralised borrowing.

[The next paragraph is 8.127.]

Continuing involvement in transferred assets

General

8.127 One of the most difficult derecognition issues relates to transfers of financial assets in which the transferor has some continuing interest in the asset. Examples include full or partial guarantees of the collectability of receivables, conditional or unconditional agreements to re-acquire the transferred assets and written or held options. The accounting treatment for some of these arrangements has been considered before in the context of failed derecognition through retention of risks and rewards. However, the accounting becomes complex when such arrangements give rise to continuing involvement accounting (that is, the transaction falls within the last box in the derecognition flowchart in para 8.30 above).

8.128 Under the derecognition criteria discussed above, when the entity transfers some significant risks and rewards and retains others and derecognition is precluded because the entity retains control of the transferred asset, the entity continues to recognise the asset to the extent of its continuing involvement. This should be measured in such a way that ensures that any changes in value of the transferred asset that are not attributed to the entity's continuing involvement are not recognised by the entity. It follows that the extent of the entity's continuing involvement in the transferred asset is the extent to which it is exposed to changes in the transferred asset's value. [IAS 39 para 30]. Measuring a financial asset in this manner may not be in accordance with the general measurement rules for financial assets, but is necessary to ensure that the accounting properly reflects the transferor's continuing involvement in the asset. IAS 39 contains detailed guidance on how to measure the asset when the continuing involvement takes the form of a guarantee or written or purchased options (including a cash-settled option or similar provision). These issues are considered from paragraphs 8.133 below.

Associated liability

8.129 When an entity continues to recognise an asset to the extent of its continuing involvement, the entity also recognises an associated liability. The associated liability is measured in such a way that the net carrying amount of the transferred asset and the associated liability is:

■ the amortised cost of the rights and obligations retained by the entity, if the transferred asset is measured at amortised cost; or

■ equal to the fair value of the rights and obligations retained by the entity when measured on a stand-alone basis, if the transferred asset is measured at fair value.

[IAS 39 para 31].

8.130 The above measurement basis may often result in a liability amount on initial recognition that is a 'balancing figure' that will not necessarily represent the proceeds received in the transfer. This is in contrast to the treatment for transfers that do not qualify for derecognition through retention of risks and rewards where the entire proceeds are accounted for as collateralised borrowing (see para 8.119 above). However, as explained in paragraph 8.128 above, special rules are necessary to account for transfers involving continuing involvement. The standard makes this clear by providing that *"despite the other measurement requirements in this standard"*, measuring the transferred asset and the associated liability in the manner described above reflects the rights and obligations that the entity has retained. [IAS 39 para 31].

Subsequent measurement

8.131 Subsequent to initial recognition, the fair value of the transferred asset and the associated liability should be accounted for consistently with each other in accordance with the general provisions of IAS 39 for measuring gains and losses. [IAS 39 para 33]. The requirement for consistent measurement means that designation of the associated liability at fair value through profit or loss is not available if the asset is measured at amortised cost. Also, the asset and the associated liability cannot be offset. [IAS 39 para 36].

8.132 The entity should continue to recognise any income arising on the transferred asset to the extent of its continuing involvement. It should also recognise any expense incurred on the associated liability. [IAS 39 para 32]. This requirement is comparable to the requirements for transfers that do not qualify for derecognition through retention of risks and rewards (see para 8.119 above). The income and the expense cannot be offset [IAS 39 para 36].

Continuing involvement through guarantees

8.133 An entity may provide a guarantee to pay for default losses on a transferred asset that prevents the transferred asset from being derecognised to the extent of the entity's continuing involvement. Assuming that the transferred asset was originally measured at amortised cost, the extent of the entity's continued involvement in the transferred asset, that is, the extent to which the entity continues to be exposed to the changes in the value of the transferred asset and the associated liability, is measured as follows:

- The continuing involvement asset at the date of the transfer is measured at the lower of:

  - the carrying amount of the transferred asset; and

  - the maximum amount of the consideration received in the transfer that the entity could be required to repay ('the guarantee amount').

- The associated liability is initially measured at the guarantee amount plus the fair value of the guarantee (which is normally the consideration received for the guarantee).

Subsequently, the initial fair value of the guarantee is recognised in profit or loss on a time proportion basis and the asset's carrying value is reduced by any impairment losses. If the guarantee is subsequently called, the liability is reduced by the cost of settlement. To the extent that the guarantee is not called and the entity is no longer exposed to the changes in the value of the transferred asset, that is the guarantee has lapsed unexercised, both the asset and the liability are reduced. [IAS 39 paras 30(a), AG48(a)].

Example 1 – Factoring with limited recourse (late payment risk retained)

Entity A (the transferor) holds a portfolio of trade receivables with a carrying value of C500m. Entity A enters into a factoring arrangement with entity B (the transferee) under which it transfers the portfolio to entity B in exchange for C490m of cash. Entity A transfers the credit risk, but retains the late payment risk up to a maximum of 180 days. After 180 days, the receivable is deemed to be in default and credit insurance takes effect. A charge is levied on the entity A for these late payments using a current rate of 6%. The fair value of the guarantee of late payment risk is C2m. Apart from late payment risk, entity A does not retain any credit or interest rate risk and does not carry out any servicing of the portfolio. There is no active market for the receivables.

In this example, entity A has transferred some but not all the risks and rewards of ownership – it has retained late payment risks, but has transferred credit risks (step 6 in the diagram in para 8.30 = No and step 7 = No). Furthermore, as there is no active market for the receivables, entity B does not have the practical ability to sell the transferred asset. Therefore, as entity B is constrained from selling the asset, the 'practical ability' test fails with the result that control of the transferred asset is retained by entity A. As a result of the above, entity A determines that it has a continuing involvement in the transferred receivables (step 8 in the diagram in para 8.30 = Yes).

Therefore, in accordance with paragraph 8.133 above, entity A measures the continuing involvement in the transferred asset at the lower of:

■   the carrying amount of the transferred asset, that is, C500m; and

■   the maximum amount of the consideration received in the transfer that entity A could be required to repay, that is, 6% on C500m for 180 days = $6\% \times 500 \times 180/360$ = C15m (the guaranteed amount).

Entity A will, therefore, record the continuing involvement asset at C15m.

Also in accordance with paragraph 8.133 above, entity A will measure the associated liability initially at the guarantee amount (C15m) + the fair value of the guarantee (C2m), a total of C17m. The associated liability is measured in such a way that the net carrying amount of the transferred asset and the associated liability is equal to the fair value of the guarantee.

Therefore, entity A would make the following entries at the date of transfer:

	Dr	Cr
Consideration received in cash	490	
Receivables transferred		500
Continued involvement in transferred asset	15	
Liability		17
Profit or loss – loss*	12	

*Consideration received of C490m – (consideration for guarantee C2m + carrying value of portfolio C500m.) For illustration purposes, the above double entry shows a credit to receivables of C500m and a debit of C15m for the new continuing involvement asset. In practice, these entries would be combined, as the continuing involvement asset is a retained part of the transferred loans, not a new asset.

Entity A would make the following accounting entries subsequent to the date of transfer:

(i) To amortise the consideration for the guarantee over the period to which it relates (180 days):

Liability	2	
Profit or loss		2

(ii) If the guarantee lapsed unexercised, the following entries would be made over the period for which late payment risk is retained as the maximum amount that entity A could be required to repay reduces due to timely payment on the receivables transferred:

Continued involvement in transferred asset		15
Liability	15	

(iii) When late payment occurs, such that a charge is levied by entity B (taking an example charge of C4m), entity A would make the following entries:

Asset (to recognise the impairment of the continuing involvement asset)		4
Profit or loss	4	

(iv) The following entries would be made when a late payment charge is actually paid by entity A (taking an example of a charge of C4m):

Liability	4	
Cash		4

8.133.1 In some factoring transactions, the entity transfers receivables without receiving cash from the factor on the date of transfer and retains late payment risk. However, the entity has a right to draw down cash from the factor of up to a specified amount during the life of the factoring. In such a case, the entity should recognise a continuing involvement asset and liability for the late payment risk retained, calculated as explained in the example above. In addition, the entity should record a receivable from the factor, measured at the sum of the total fair value of the receivables at the date of transfer and the fair value of the late payment guarantee. This will give a similar accounting result as if cash of this amount had been received on the date of transfer.

Continuing involvement through options

8.134   As explained in paragraph 8.98.2 above, derivatives included in the transfer may constrain the transferee's practical ability to sell the transferred asset, even if there is no legal constraint, with the result that the transferor retains control over the transferred asset. In those circumstances, if the entity has neither transferred nor retained substantially all the risks and rewards of ownership of the transferred asset, the entity retains a continuing involvement in the transferred asset. For example, an entity may transfer a financial asset that is not readily obtainable in the market and holds a call option or writes a put option that is neither deeply in nor deeply out-of-the money at the date of transfer. [IAS 39 paras AG51(h)(i)].

8.135   When the entity's continuing involvement takes the form of a written or purchased option (or both) on the transferred asset, the extent of the entity's continuing involvement is the amount of the transferred asset that the entity may repurchase. However, in case of a put option on an asset written by the transferor that is measured by the transferor at fair value, the extent of the entity's continuing involvement is limited to the lower of the fair value of the transferred asset and the option exercise price. [IAS 39 para 30(b)]. This reflects the fact that the entity will not benefit from changes in the fair value above the option's exercise price. The manner in which the options are settled (physical or cash-settled) does not affect the measurement of the continuing involvement asset. [IAS 39 para 30(c)]. Depending on whether the transferred asset is measured at amortised cost or fair value, the associated liability is measured in accordance with paragraph 8.129 above as explained below.

Transfer of assets measured at amortised cost

8.136   Where a put option obligation written by an entity or call option right held by an entity prevents a transferred asset from being derecognised and the entity measures the transferred asset at amortised cost, the associated liability is measured at its cost (that is, the consideration received) adjusted for the amortisation of any difference between that cost and the amortised cost of the transferred asset at the option's expiration date. If the option is exercised, any difference between the associated liability's carrying amount and the exercise price is recognised in profit or loss. [IAS 39 para AG 48(b)].

> **Example – Asset measured at amortised cost subject to call option held by the transferor**
>
> Entity A has a portfolio of high yielding corporate bonds with an amortised carrying value of C102m. The bonds are not traded in the marketplace and are not readily obtainable. On 1 January 20X6, entity A sells the bonds to entity B for a consideration of C100m, but retains a call option to purchase the portfolio for C105m on 31

December 20X6. On that date, the amortised cost of the bonds will be C106m. The fair value of the bonds, at the date of transfer amounted to C104m.

The rights to receive cash flows from the asset have not expired (step 3 in the diagram in para 8.30 = no). However, entity A has transferred its right to receive cash flows (interest and principal on the bonds) to entity B (step 4 in the diagram in para 8.30 = yes). In this situation, the bonds are transferred, subject to a call option that is neither deeply in-the-money nor deeply out-of-the money (the option's exercise price is C105m compared to fair value of asset of C104m). The result is that the entity neither transfers nor retains substantially all the risks and rewards of ownership of the bonds (steps 6 and 7 in the diagram in para 8.30 = no). Furthermore, as the transferee does not have the practical ability to sell the bonds, derecognition of the bonds is precluded to the extent of the amount of the asset that is subject to the call option, because the entity has retained control of the asset (step 8 in the diagram in para 8.30 = yes).

As entity A has an option to buy back all of the bonds, it continues to recognise the bonds at their amortised cost, which will accrete from a carrying value of C102m to C106m at 31 December 20X6 using the effective interest rate method. The initial carrying amount of the liability is recorded at cost, that is, the consideration received of C100m. The liability is then accreted to C106m using the effective-interest rate method, which is the amortised cost of the transferred asset at the expiration date of the option (not the option's exercise price of C105m). As the asset is measured at amortised cost, the liability is also measured in a consistent manner as explained in paragraph 8.135 above.

Therefore, entity A would make the following entries:

	Dr C	Cr C
At 1 January 20X6 (date of transfer)		
Cash	100	
Associated liability		100
For the period to 31 December 20X6		
Bonds carried at amortised cost	4	
Income from bonds (106 – 102)		4
Interest on liability (106 – 100)	6	
Liability carried at amortised cost		6

At 31 December 20X6, entity A will exercise the option if the option exercise price of C105m is less than the fair value of the bonds. In that situation, entity A would record the following entries:

	Dr C	Cr C
Liability	106	
Cash (exercise price of option)		105
Gain on exercise of option		1

On the other hand, for example, if the strike price was 107 and the option lapses unexercised, both the asset and the liability are derecognised.

	Dr C	Cr C
Liability	106	
Carrying value of bond		106

A similar analysis would be carried out if, instead, of purchasing a call option, entity A wrote a put option that gave entity B the right to put the bonds back at 31 December 20X6.

Transfer of assets measured at fair value

8.137   Where a call option right held by the entity prevents a transferred asset from being derecognised and the entity measures the transferred asset at fair value, the transferred asset continues to be measured at fair value. This is because the call option gives the entity access to any increase in the asset's fair value. However, the measurement of the associated liability depends on whether the call option is in or at- the-money or out-of-the money, as described below.

■   If the option is in or at-the-money, the associated liability is measured at the option's exercise price less the option's time value.

■   If the option is out-of-the money, the associated liability is measured at the fair value of the transferred asset less the option's time value.

The effect of the above measurement basis is to ensure that the associated liability is measured in such a way that the net carrying amount of the transferred asset and the associated liability is always equal to the fair value of the call option right. [IAS 39 para AG48(c)].

Example – Asset measured at fair value subject to call option held by the transferor

Entity A has 15% equity holding in entity B that was acquired some years ago for C40m. This holding is treated as an available-for-sale financial asset and the current fair value (and carrying value) is C104m. There is no active market in entity B's shares. On 1 January 20X6, entity A sells its 15% investment in entity B to bank C for a consideration of C100m, but retains a call option to purchase the investment for C105m on 31 December 20X7.

The rights to receive cash flows from the asset have not expired (step 3 in the diagram in para 8.30 = no). However, entity A has transferred its right to receive cash flows (dividends on the shares) from its investment to entity B (step 4 in the diagram in para 8.30 = yes), subject to a call option. The result is that the entity neither transfers nor retains substantially all the risks and rewards of ownership of the transferred asset (steps 6 and 7 in the diagram in para 8.30 = no). This is because:

- entity A can exercise its call option so as to benefit from movements in the asset's fair value above the call option exercise price of C105m; and

- entity A is not exposed to risk from decreases in the asset's market value below the call option exercise price.

With regard to the next question, whether entity A has retained control of its investment in entity B, this will depend upon whether bank C has the practical ability to sell the asset in its entirety to an unrelated third party, unilaterally and without imposing additional restrictions on the transfer. In this situation, there is no active market in entity B's shares, so a 15% stake is not readily obtainable in the market. The call option is neither deeply in-the-money nor deeply out-of-the-money (it is slightly out-of-the-money at inception as the option exercise price of C105m is more than the market value of the shares at C104m), but it is sufficiently valuable to prevent bank C from selling the asset immediately. These facts taken together lead to the conclusion that bank C does not have the practical ability to sell its investment in entity A. Consequently, entity A has retained control and derecognition is precluded to the extent of the amount of the asset that is subject to the call option (step 8 in the diagram in para 8.30 = yes).

Therefore, in accordance with paragraph 8.137, the entity continues to recognise the investment in entity B as an available-for-sale asset at fair value. At the date of transfer, the call option is out-of-the-money (option's exercise price of C105m is greater that the fair value of the asset at C104m). The premium paid on the option (all time value) is C4m (fair value of the asset of C104m less consideration received of C100m). As the option is out-of-the-money, IAS 39 requires the associated liability to be measured at the fair value of the transferred asset less the time value of the option as explained in the above paragraph. Therefore, the associated liability is recorded at C104m – C4m = C100m, which is also equal to the consideration received. This ensures that the net amount of the transferred asset and the associated liability is equal to the fair value of the call option right. Therefore, entity A would make the following entries:

	Dr C	Cr C
At 1 January 20X6 (date of transfer)		
Cash	100	
Associated liability		100

Suppose that the asset's fair value increases to C106m at 31 December 20X6. The option is now in-the-money (exercise price of C105m < C106m) and its time value is C2m.

In accordance with paragraph AG48(c) of IAS 39, the associated liability is measured at the option's exercise price (C105m) less the time value of the option (C2m) = C103m.

This ensures that the net amount of the transferred asset (C106m) and the associated liability (C103m) is equal to the fair value of the call option right of C3m (intrinsic value of C1m + time value of C2m) as explained in paragraph 8.135 above.

	Dr	Cr
	C	**C**
Entity A will record the following entries at 31 December 20X6		
Asset (increase in value from C104m to C106m)	2	
Liability (increase in value from C100m to C103m)		3
Other comprehensive income	1	

As the associated liability should be measured in a manner consistent with the available-for-sale asset in accordance with the general provisions of IAS 39 for measuring gains and losses as explained in paragraph 8.131 above, the movement in the liability is also recognised in other comprehensive income. The net loss of C1m recognised in other comprehensive income represents the fall in the value of the option from C4m to C3m.

It should be noted that to the extent that a transfer of a financial asset does not qualify for derecognition, the transferor's contractual rights or obligations related to the transfer are not accounted for separately as derivatives, since recognising both the derivative and the transferred asset would result in recognising the same rights twice. Therefore, entity A does not recognise the call option separately (see para 8.98.3 above).

Suppose that the fair value of the asset remains unchanged at 31 December 20X7. The entity will exercise the option as it is in-the-money. The accounting entries are as follows:

	Dr	Cr
	C	**C**
Liability derecognised	103	
Other comprehensive income	2	
Cash paid		105

The overall loss of C3m over the two year period recognised in other comprehensive income represents the difference between the amount paid to re-acquire the asset for C105m and the consideration received on the transfer of C100m less the increase in the fair value of the asset of C2m (C106m – C104m) already recognised in other comprehensive income. It forms part of the cumulative net gain in other comprehensive income relating to the 15% equity holding in entity B.

Suppose that the fair value of the asset falls to C103m at 31 December 20X7. In this situation, entity A will not exercise the option and will allow it to lapse. Both the transferred asset and the associated liability will be derecognised as shown below:

	Dr	Cr
	C	**C**
Liability	103	
Asset		106
Other comprehensive income (recycling of cumulative gain C104m – C40m – C1m)	63	
Gain in profit or loss		60

The gain of C60m represents the net cash received of C60m (consideration received of C100m less original cost of C40m).

8.138 Where a put option written by an entity prevents a transferred asset measured at fair value from being derecognised, the transferred asset is measured at the lower of the fair value and the option exercise price. [IAS 39 para 30(b)]. This limitation is placed on the asset value because the entity has no right to the increase in the asset's fair value above the option exercise price. The associated liability is measured at the option's exercise price plus the time value of the option. This ensures that the asset's net carrying amount and the associated liability is always equal to the fair value of the put option obligation. [IAS 39 para AG48(d)]. The treatment is illustrated in the example given below.

> **Example – Asset measured at fair value subject to put option written by the transferor**
>
> Entity A has 15% equity holding in entity B that was acquired some years ago for C40m. This holding is treated as an available-for-sale financial asset and the current fair value at 1 January 20X6 (and carrying value) is C97m. There is no active market in entity B's shares.
>
> On 1 January 20X6, entity A sells its investment in entity B to bank C for a consideration of C102m. However, entity A has granted a put option to bank C. Under the terms of the put option, bank C has the right to sell its investment in entity B back to entity A for C96m if the market value of its investment falls below C96m at any time in the next two years.
>
> Entity A has transferred its right to receive cash flows (dividends on the shares) from its investment to entity B (step 4 in the diagram in para 8.30 = yes). However, in this situation, the investment is transferred, subject to a put option. The result is that the entity neither transfers nor retains substantially all the risks and rewards of ownership of the transferred asset (steps 6 and 7 in the diagram in para 8.30 = no). This is because:
>
> - entity A is still exposed to movements in fair value below C96m, because if the fair value of the investment falls below C96m, bank C will put the investment back to company A for C96m; and
>
> - entity A has not retained any benefit from increases in the market value of entity B.
>
> With regard to the next question, whether entity A has retained control of its investment in entity B, this will depend upon whether bank C has the practical ability to sell the asset in its entirety to an unrelated third party, unilaterally and without imposing additional restrictions on the transfer. In this situation, there is no active market in entity B's shares, so a 15% stake is not readily obtainable in the market. The put option is neither deeply in-the-money nor deeply out-of-the money (it is slightly out-of-the-money at inception as the option exercise price of C96m is less than the market value of the shares at C97m), but it is sufficiently valuable to prevent bank C from selling the asset immediately. There would need to be a significant increase in the share's value to compensate bank C for the premium they have paid for the put option. These facts taken together lead to the conclusion that bank C does not have the practical ability to sell its investment in entity A. Consequently, entity A has retained control and derecognition is precluded to the extent of the amount of the asset that is subject to the put option (step 8 in the diagram in para 8.30 = yes).

Therefore, in accordance with the above paragraph, the entity recognises the investment in entity B at the lower of the fair value of the asset (C97m) and the option exercise price (C96m), that is, C96m, being the option's exercise price.

The premium received by entity A for writing the put option is C5m (consideration received of C102m less fair value of the asset of C97m). As the option is out-of-the-money, the entire premium represents the time value of the option. The associated liability is measured at the option exercise price (C96m) plus the time value of the option (C5m), that is, C101m, as explained in paragraph 8.138 above. This ensures that the net amount of the transferred asset (C96m) and the associated liability (C101m) is equal to the fair value of the put option obligation (C5m). Therefore, entity A would make the following entries:

	Dr C	Cr C
At 1 January 20X6 (date of transfer)		
Cash received	102	
Investment		1
Liability		101

Suppose that the fair value of the asset decreases to C94m at 31 December 20X6. The put option is now in-the-money (exercise price of C96m > C94m) and its time value is C2m.

In accordance with the above paragraph 8.138 above, the asset is measured at the lower of the asset's fair value and the option's exercise price, that is, C94m, being the fair value of the asset. The associated liability is measured at the option's exercise price (C96m) plus the time value of the option (C2m), that is, C98m.

This ensures that the net amount of the transferred asset (C94m) and the associated liability (C98m) is equal to the fair value of the put option obligation of C4m (intrinsic value of C2m + time value of C2m).

	Dr C	Cr C
Entity A will record the following entries at 31 December 20X6		
Asset (fall in value from C96m to C94m)		2
Liability (fall in value from C101m to C98m)	3	
Other comprehensive income		1

As the associated liability should be measured in a manner consistent with the available-for-sale asset in accordance with the general provisions of IAS 39 for measuring gains and losses as explained in paragraph 8.128 above, the movement in the liability is also recognised in other comprehensive income. The net gain of C1m represents the fall in the value of the put option obligation from C5m to C4m.

It should be noted that to the extent that a transfer of a financial asset does not qualify for derecognition, the transferor's contractual rights or obligations related to the transfer are not accounted for separately as derivatives, since recognising both the derivative and the transferred asset would result in recognising the same rights twice. Therefore, entity A does not recognise the put option separately (see para 8.98.3 above).

Suppose that the fair value of the asset remains unchanged at 31 December 20X7. Bank C decides to exercise the option as it is in-the-money. Entity A will have to re-acquire the asset at the put option price. The accounting entries are as follows:

	Dr C	Cr C
Liability derecognised	98	
Cash paid		96
Other comprehensive income		2

The overall gain of C3 recognised in other comprehensive income over the two year period represents the difference of C6m (consideration received of C102m less amount paid to re-acquire the asset for C96m) less C3m (fall in asset value from C97m at inception to C94m at exercise). It forms part of the cumulative net gain in other comprehensive income relating to the 15% equity holding in entity B.

Continuing involvement in a part of a financial asset

8.139 An entity may have a continuing involvement in only a part of a financial asset rather than the entire asset as discussed above. This situation may arise when an entity retains an option to repurchase part of a transferred asset, or retains a residual interest that does not result in the retention of substantially all the risks and rewards of ownership and the entity retains control. Where this is so, the entity allocates the financial asset's previous carrying amount between the part it continues to recognise under continuing involvement and the part it no longer recognises on the basis of the relative fair values of those parts on the date of transfer. [IAS 39 para 34].

8.140 The allocation exercise and the calculation of the gain or loss arising on the part of the asset that is no longer retained are carried out in a similar manner as described in paragraph 8.100 above. That is, the difference between the carrying amount allocated to the part that is no longer recognised and the sum of:

- the consideration received for the part no longer recognised; and
- any cumulative gain or loss allocated to it that had been recognised directly in other comprehensive income;

is recognised in profit or loss. Any cumulative gain or loss that had been recognised in other comprehensive income is allocated between the part that continues to be recognised and the part that is no longer recognised on the basis of the relative fair values of those parts. [IAS 39 para 34]. The recycling of the cumulative gain or loss that had been recognised in other comprehensive income relates to the part no longer recognised of an available-for-sale financial asset. In addition to the part retained, the entity continues to recognise its continuing involvement in the asset and the associated liability. The manner in which the above guidance is applied to continuing involvement in a part of a financial asset is illustrated in paragraph AG52 of IAS 39. Although that example is not presented here, the application illustrated in that example is best understood by reference to a securitisation transaction given below.

> **Example – Continuing involvement in a part of a financial asset**
>
> Entity A enters into a securitisation transaction in which it transfers a pool of receivables amounting to C1,000, but retains a subordinated interest of C100 in that pool.
>
> The terms of the securitisation arrangements show that the transaction is to be accounted for using the continuing involvement approach (which, *inter alia*, requires that the buyer assume significant risks and rewards).
>
> Under the continuing involvement approach, the seller typically recognises an asset of C200 and a liability of C100. This gives a net asset of C100 which might be expected as it represents the retained subordinated interest of C100. However, the gross numbers can be confusing to understand. AG52 analyses the transaction as comprising:
>
> ■ a retention of a non-subordinated 10% interest in the transferred assets; and
>
> ■ the subordination of that interest that is equivalent to the seller providing a credit guarantee.
>
> Both these elements result in continuing involvement and both need to be accounted for. The first element (the retention of a non-subordinated 10% interest) results in a continuing involvement asset of C100. In addition, the second element (the subordination of that interest which is equivalent to the seller providing a guarantee of the first C100 of losses) also results in a continuing involvement asset of C100, and a liability of C100 (being the maximum amount the entity may have to pay by losing the C100 asset recognised for the first element). Therefore, the seller will recognised a total continuing involvement asset of C200 and a liability of C100.
>
> Measuring a financial asset in the above manner may not be in accordance with the general measurement rules for financial assets, but is necessary to ensure that the accounting properly reflects the transferor's continuing involvement in the asset.

Retained servicing

8.140.1   If a transaction is accounted for using continuing involvement and the transferor is required to service the assets without receiving adequate compensation for the service provided, a servicing liability should be recognised to the extent that the asset is derecognised, but no servicing liability should be recognised to the extent of the continuing involvement asset. For example, if the asset pre-transaction was C100 and the continuing involvement in the asset after the transaction was C60, the transferor would recognise a servicing liability for the C40 derecognised, but not for the C60 on the balance sheet. Servicing assets and liabilities are dealt with in detail from paragraph 8.106 above.

Accounting for collateral

8.141 A transfer of financial assets may require the transferor to provide non-cash collateral (such as a debt or equity instruments) to the transferee. If collateral is transferred to the transferee, the custodial arrangement is commonly referred to as a pledge. Transferees sometimes are permitted to sell or repledge (or otherwise transfer) collateral held under a pledge. The accounting for the collateral by the transferor and the transferee depends on whether the transferee has the right to sell or repledge the collateral and on whether the transferor has defaulted as shown in the table below.

Circumstance	Accounting by transferor	Accounting by transferee
Transferee has the right by contract or custom to sell or repledge the collateral.	The transferor reclassifies that asset in its balance sheet (for example, as a loaned asset, pledged equity instruments or repurchase receivable) separately from other assets that are not so encumbered. [IAS 39 para 37(a)]. This is because the transferor retains all the risks and rewards of ownership of the asset pledged as collateral and, therefore, cannot derecognise it under the normal rules for derecognition.	The transferee will not recognise the collateral as an asset. In the event that the transferee sells the collateral pledged to it, it recognises the proceeds from the sale and a liability measured at fair value for its obligation to return the collateral. [IAS 39 para 37(b)].
Transferor defaults under the terms of the contract and is no longer entitled to redeem the collateral.	Transferor derecognises the collateral. [IAS 39 para 37(c)].	Transferee recognises the collateral as its asset initially measured at fair value or, if it has already sold the collateral, derecognise its obligation to return the collateral. [IAS 39 para 37(c)]. This is because the risks and rewards of ownership of the collateral have passed to the transferee.
All other situations not referred to above.	Transferor continues to recognise the collateral as its asset. [IAS 39 para 37(d)].	Transferee does not recognise the collateral as an asset. [IAS 39 para 37(d)].

Accounting by transferee

8.142 Although transferees are required to follow the recognition principles discussed from paragraph 8.5 above, it is important to note that the accounting treatment between the transferor and the transferee is intended to be symmetrical. Therefore, to the extent that a transfer of a financial asset does not qualify for derecognition, the transferee does not recognise the transferred asset as its asset.

The transferee derecognises the cash or other consideration paid and recognises a receivable from the transferor. If the transferor has both a right and an obligation to re-acquire control of the entire transferred asset for a fixed amount (such as under a repurchase agreement), the transferee may account for its receivable as a loan or receivable. [IAS 39 para AG 50]. Similarly, if a transfer of a financial asset qualifies for derecognition, the transferor will treat it as a sale and the transferee will treat it as a purchase.

Derecognition of financial liabilities

8.143 The derecognition rules for financial liabilities are somewhat different from those relating to financial assets. Whereas the derecognition rules for financial assets tend to focus on risks and rewards and may not lead to derecognition even though legal transfer has occurred, the derecognition rules for financial liabilities focus solely on the legal release of the contractual obligations. Consequently, the IAS 39 provisions relating to derecognition of financial liabilities in whole or in part are relatively straight forward and less subjective than those for derecognition of financial assets. The rules in IAS 39 deal with extinguishment of financial liabilities, their modification by lenders and the recognition and measurement of any gains or losses that arise from extinguishment and modification. These issues are considered in detail below.

Extinguishment of a financial liability

General principles

8.144 A financial liability (trading or other) is removed from the balance sheet when it is extinguished, that is when the obligation is discharged, cancelled or expired. [IAS 39 para 39]. This condition is met when the debtor either:

- discharges the liability (or part of it) by paying the creditor, normally with cash, other financial assets, goods or services; or

- is legally released from primary responsibility for the liability (or part of it) either by process of law or by the creditor.

[IAS 39 para AG 57].

8.145 The condition for extinguishment is also met if an entity repurchases a bond that it has previously issued, even if the entity is a market maker or intends to resell it in the near term. [IAS 39 para AG 58]. This is consistent with the treatment of treasury shares re-acquired by an entity, except that in the case of extinguishing a liability, any gain or loss that may arise is recognised (see para 8.148 below).

8.145.1 A financial liability may be converted into an equity instrument (for example, a convertible bond) or become an equity instrument without any change to its contractual terms (for example, through a lapse of certain terms). The treatment of such instruments is discussed in chapter 7.

Legal release by the creditor

8.146 It is clear from the general conditions that a debt is extinguished only if the debtor is legally released from its obligation by the creditor. This condition is met even if a creditor releases a debtor from its present obligation to make payments, but the debtor assumes a guarantee obligation to pay if the party assuming primary responsibility defaults. In this circumstance the debtor:

■ recognises a new financial liability based on the fair value of its obligation for the guarantee; and

■ recognises a gain or loss based on the difference between (i) any proceeds paid and (ii) the carrying amount of the original financial liability less the fair value of the new financial liability.

[IAS 39 para AG 63].

An example illustrating the above treatment is given below. Contrast this with in-substance defeasance discussed below in paragraph 8.145 below.

> **Example – Transfer of debt obligation with legal release**
>
> Entity A transfers C100 million highly liquid government bonds into a trust that is owned by a registered charity. The trust does not fall to be consolidated by entity A. Those bonds will solely be used to repay entity A's issued C100 million fixed rate liability. The holders of the issued C100 million fixed rate liability have released entity A from its obligation to make payments. However, entity A enters into a guarantee arrangement whereby, if the trust does not make payments when due, then entity A will pay the debt holders.
>
> In this situation, derecognition of the fixed rate debt instruments is not precluded by virtue of the guarantee. Entity A has obtained legal release, which is a necessary and sufficient condition for the debt's derecognition, notwithstanding that entity A has given a guarantee to a third party.
>
> Entity A (the debtor) recognises a new financial liability based on the fair value of its obligation for the guarantee and recognises a gain or loss based on the difference between any proceeds paid and the carrying amount of the original financial liability less the fair value of the new financial liability. [IAS 39 para AG 63].

8.147 Sometimes, instead of providing a guarantee, the debtor may pay a third party to assume the obligations under the debt and obtain legal release from its creditor. In that situation, the second condition in paragraph 8.144 above is met and the debt is extinguished. However, if the debtor transfers its obligations under a debt to a third party and obtains legal release from the creditor, but undertakes to make payments to the third party so as to enable it to meet its obligation, the debtor recognises a new debt obligation to the third party. [IAS 39 para AG 60].

Supplier finance and reverse factoring

8.147.1   Some banks offer services to buyers of goods or services in order to facilitate payments of the trade payables arising from purchases from suppliers. Generally, the supplier delivers goods to the buyer and a trade payable is originated. These are commonly referred to as 'supplier finance' or 'reverse factoring arrangements'. The buyer selects payables to the supplier that it wishes to be subject to the reverse factoring or supplier finance arrangement and notifies the bank. Through some mechanism the supplier receives cash for its trade receivable. In some cases, a buyer enters into these contracts to obtain an early payment discount that it would otherwise not be in a position to obtain.

8.147.2   A buyer would not typically present liabilities payable to a financial institution as trade payables. Trade payables are generally understood to arise in the ordinary course of business with suppliers. When the original liability to a supplier has been extinguished in accordance with paragraph 8.144 above, the resulting new liability to the bank should be presented as bank financing or under another suitable heading rather than 'trade payables'. If the latter option is taken, the description of the chosen line item needs to be carefully considered to ensure that the entity's financial position is presented fairly and in a way that faithfully represents the effect of the transaction, as required by IAS 1 (revised) paragraph 15. In particular, similar items should be presented together and should not be presented with dissimilar items, and the overall effect should not be misleading.

[The next paragraph is 8.147.4.]

8.147.4   Another example is where the bank negotiates with the supplier directly, on the buyer's behalf. The bank agrees to pay the supplier before the legal due date to obtain an early payment discount. However, the bank's payment does not result in the legal settlement of the buyer's obligation under its payable to the supplier. Rather, the supplier agrees to receive the amount from the buyer net of the early payment discount at the contractual due date and to reimburse the bank this same amount when it receives the payment from the buyer. Should the supplier fail to reimburse the bank, the buyer agrees to reimburse the bank. The bank charges a fee to the buyer, which effectively results in the bank and supplier sharing the benefit of the early payment discount. In such a case, as the supplier does not legally release the buyer from its original obligation, the buyer continues to recognise the trade payable to the supplier. However, it also recognises a guarantee obligation, initially measured at fair value, for its promise to reimburse the bank if the bank does not receive a reimbursement from the supplier.

8.147.5   In some circumstances, subsequent to the notification of selected receivables by the supplier, the bank offers the supplier a Receivables Purchase Agreement. Under this contract, the rights under the trade receivable are acquired from the supplier by the bank, but there is no legal release for the buyer from the supplier. It is likely the buyer will be involved in some extent in such an arrangement. For example, the buyer agrees on changes in his rights under the original terms of the sale of goods – that is, he may no longer be eligible to offset the payable against credit notes received from the supplier, or the buyer may be restricted from making earlier direct payments to the supplier.

8.147.6   The rights of the trade receivable are transferred to the bank, but the buyer's obligation to the supplier is not legally extinguished. In such a case the buyer would need to consider whether the change to the terms of the trade payable is significant under paragraphs 40 and AG62 of IAS 39. If there is a significant change, the transfer is accounted for as an extinguishment – that is, the previous liability should be derecognised and replaced with a new liability to the bank. The effect of any additional restrictions imposed by the reverse factoring agreement on the buyer's rights will need careful consideration. For example, it may be the case that, as the buyer selects each payable at its sole discretion, it will only select those payables where from the buyer's perspective, the effect of any such restrictions on the rights and obligations is not significant. In contrast, it may be the case that all three, that is the buyer, bank and supplier, have agreed initially on a minimum amount of payables/receivables being refinanced by the bank, whereby the buyer has subsequently no further discretion to avoid the change in his rights even if the change might be significant to an individual payable.

8.147.7   The accounting for supplier finance and reverse factoring arrangements will depend on the exact facts and circumstances relating to them.

In-substance defeasance

8.148   In-substance defeasance is an arrangement whereby an entity makes a lump sum payment relating to its obligations to a third party (typically a trust). The trust then applies those funds and income thereon to discharge the entity's obligation to the lender. The entity has little or no right of access to the funds put in the trust. The trust does not assume any legal responsibility for the obligations and the lender is not a party to the in-substance arrangement. Some argue that as the entity has no right of access to those funds, it has effectively discharged its obligations to the lender. However, this view is inconsistent with the general rule in paragraph 8.144 above that a liability is not extinguished in the absence of a legal release. [IAS 39 para 39]. Therefore, in-substance defeasance arrangements do not result in derecognition of the liability.

Extinguishment through transfer of assets that fails derecognition

8.149   Sometimes an entity may transfer financial assets (other than cash) which the lender accepts as being in full and final settlement and thereby releases the debtor from its obligations. The entity derecognises the liability as the debt has been legally discharged. However, the financial assets transferred may fail the derecognition criteria, because either the entity has retained substantially all the risks and rewards of ownership or the entity has a continuing involvement in the transferred asset by virtue of retaining control. Therefore, where the derecognition criteria are not met, the transferred assets are not derecognised and the entity recognises a new liability relating to the transferred assets. [IAS 39 para AG 61].

Gain or loss arising on extinguishment

8.150   Where a financial liability (or part of a financial liability) is extinguished or transferred to another party, the entity should recognise any difference arising between the carrying amount of the financial liability (or part of the financial liability) extinguished or transferred and the consideration paid, including any non-cash assets transferred or liabilities assumed, in profit or loss. [IAS 39 para 41]. This applies even if the issuer of a debt instrument is a market maker in that instrument or intends to resell it in the near term. [IAS 39 para AG 58].

> **Example – Gain on extinguishment of debt in full**
>
> A bank has loaned C25m to a property investment company that invested the funds in residential properties consisting mainly of high quality apartments. However, as a result of a fall in occupancy rates, the entity is unable to meet its debt obligations. The entity successfully negotiated with the bank whereby the bank agreed to accept a property with a fair market value of C20m in full and final settlement of the C25m obligation. The property's carrying value was C21m.
>
> As a result of the negotiation, the loan is extinguished and the entity recognises a gain on the extinguishment as follows:
>
> | | Cm |
> |--|------|
> | Carrying value of liability | 25 |
> | Fair value of non-cash settlement | 20 |
> | Gain on extinguishment of debt | 5 |
> | Carrying value of property | 21 |
> | Fair value of property transferred | 20 |
> | Loss on disposal | (1) |
>
> The gain on extinguishment of debt typically would be recorded in the income statement under finance income. The loss on disposal of the property would be charged against operating profits. It would not be appropriate to show a net gain of extinguishment of C4m in finance income.

8.151   If an entity repurchases only a part of a financial liability, the entity should allocate the previous carrying amount of the financial liability between the part that continues to be recognised and the part that is derecognised based on the relative fair values of those parts on the date of the repurchase. The difference between the carrying amount allocated to the part derecognised and the consideration paid, including any non-cash assets transferred or liabilities assumed, for the part derecognised is recognised in profit or loss. [IAS 39 para 42]. This means that the consideration paid for the repurchase is not simply set off against the original liability's carrying value, but a gain or loss is calculated based on the part derecognised as set out above.

Example – Derecognition of part of a liability

On 1 January 20X5, an entity issued 1 million 8% C100 nominal 10 year term bonds with interest payable each 30 June and 31 December. The bonds, which are traded in the market, were issued at par. Issue costs of C2m were incurred. Four years after the issue date, the entity repurchases 600,000 bonds at the then market value of C96 per C100 nominal. The amortised cost of the bond at 31 December 20X8 amounted to C98,655,495.

The gain arising on repurchase is calculated as follows:

	C
Carrying value allocated to amount repurchased – 60% of C98,655,495	59,193,297
Amount paid on repurchase of 600,000 @ C96	57,600,000
Gain arising on repurchase	1,593,297

Exchange and modification of debt instrument

8.152 Entities frequently negotiate with lenders to restructure their existing debt obligations. There may be a variety of reasons for doing so, not necessarily when the entity is in financial difficulties. Such restructuring may result in a modification or an exchange of debt instruments with the lender that may be carried out in a number of ways. For instance, an entity may decide to take advantage of falling interest rates by cancelling its exposure to high-interest fixed-rate debt, pay a fee or penalty on cancellation and replace it with debt at a lower interest rate (exchange of old debt with new debt). Alternatively, the entity may seek to roll up the higher interest payments into a single payment that is payable on the loan's redemption or amend the amount payable on redemption (modification). Whether a modification or exchange of debt instruments represents a settlement of the original debt or merely a renegotiation of that debt determines the accounting treatment that should be applied by the borrower.

8.153 IAS 39 requires an exchange between an existing borrower and lender of debt instruments with substantially different terms to be accounted for as an extinguishment of the original financial liability and the recognition of a new financial liability. Similarly, a substantial modification of the terms of an existing financial liability or a part of it (whether or not attributable to the financial difficulty of the debtor) should be accounted for as an extinguishment of the original financial liability and the recognition of a new financial liability. [IAS 39 para 40]. Consider the examples below.

Example – Change in holders and repayment terms

An entity issued a five-year bond that is listed and traded on a stock exchange. In the following year, the entity proposes a modification of the bond's repayment terms, to extend the maturity. The proposed modification becomes effective if it achieves approval of more than 75% of the bondholders, in accordance with the terms set out in the offering circular. The dissenting bondholders are entitled to have their bonds purchased by the entity (or any other party) at fair value, being the market price immediately prior to the proposed modification being put to the bondholders for consideration. The entity appoints an investment bank to stand ready to acquire any bonds from dissenting bondholders and the bank will hold the bonds afterwards as principal. The proposed modification of the repayment terms was accepted by 80% of the bondholders. The dissenting 20% sell their bonds to an investment bank at fair value and 100% of the bonds are then modified

The first step is to determine whether the change in holder of 20% of the bonds to the investment bank from the dissenting bondholders gives rise to a legal release from primary responsibility for the liability. Depending on the legal jurisdiction, if the change in bondholder results in the legal release from primary responsibility for the original liability, those bonds are extinguished and should be derecognised in accordance with paragraph 39 of IAS 39, However, in many cases, a change in the holder of a security such as a bond does not result in the entity being legally released from the primary obligation under the liability. The term sheet for a security usually sets out the trading mechanism; in most cases, there is no new contract signed between the issuer and the new holder upon a transfer. In these circumstances, the acquisition of the bond by the investment bank from the dissenting bondholders is a transfer of an existing bond, not the issue of a new bond to a new lender. The transfer is not, therefore, considered to be a change in 'lender' before and after the transfer of the bonds.

The second step is to determine whether there has been an exchange or modification, under paragraph 40 of IAS 39 , between an existing borrower and lender with substantially different terms. As noted above, the transfer of the bonds does not represent a change in the lender; the modification in the bond's repayment terms is therefore considered to be between an existing borrower and lender for all of the outstanding bonds, rather than merely the 80% that accepted the modification of terms. The entity, therefore, applies paragraphs 40 and AG62 of IAS 39 to assess whether the change in repayment terms amounts to a substantial modification of the terms of an existing liability. Where the change is substantial, it is accounted for as an extinguishment of the original bond and the recognition of a new liability. Where the change in terms is not substantial, it is accounted for as a modification of the original financial liability.

8.154   The terms are substantially different if the discounted present value of the cash flows under the new terms, including any fees paid net of any fees received and discounted using the original effective interest rate, is at least ten per cent different from the discounted present value of the remaining cash flows of the original financial liability. [IAS 39 para AG 62].

8.155   The standard does not clarify whether the quantitative analysis outlined above is an example of a term that is substantially different or whether the analysis is the definition of substantially different. There is an accounting policy choice. Although it is clear that if the discounted cash flows change by at least ten per cent, the original debt should be accounted for as an extinguishment, there is nothing in the standard to suggest that the analysis should be restricted only to cash flow changes. Indeed, in order to meet the spirit of the standard, analysis of any modification of terms that are qualitative in nature may be performed. For example, qualitative changes in risk profile of the newly modified instrument compared to the original instrument may well indicate that the changes in terms are substantially different, as happens for example when the denomination of the original liability is changed to a different currency. In that situation, we believe it is acceptable to account for the substantial modification as an extinguishment, even though the above quantitative analysis may indicate a less than ten per cent cash flow change. Qualitative factors that should be considered include, but are not limited to the following:

- The currency that the debt instrument is denominated in.

- The interest rate (that is fixed *versus* floating rate).

- Conversion features attached to the instrument.

- Changes in covenants.

8.156 Alternatively, since the standard is unclear whether the ten per cent test is the definition of substantially different, a quantitative analysis could be performed to determine whether an exchange or a modification should be accounted for as an extinguishment. Under this alternative view, if the change in discounted cash flows is less than ten per cent, the exchange or modification would not be accounted for as an extinguishment. This alternative view is also acceptable if applied consistently and properly disclosed in the notes.

8.157 There is no guidance in the standard that assists in interpreting the terms 'existing borrower and lender' mentioned in paragraph 8.153 when looking at transactions where lending is *via* a syndicate of banks. In such cases, the borrower should determine in the first instance whether it has borrowed under one loan or under multiple loans. Sometimes syndicated loans are structured with one 'lead lender' signing the loan agreement. The agreement's substance rather than its legal form should dictate the accounting. Presented below are a number of factors that, individually or in combination, would tend to indicate that the borrower has borrowed under multiple loans:

- The borrower has the ability to selectively repay amounts on the loan to different members of the syndicate. In other words any payments made by the borrowers are not always split on a *pro rata* basis amongst all the syndicate members.

- The terms of the loan are not homogenous for various syndicate members.

- The borrower has the ability to selectively renegotiate portions of the loan with individual syndicate members or subsets of all the syndicate members.

■ Individual syndicate members have the ability to negotiate their loan directly with the borrower without the approval of other syndicate members.

This is not an exhaustive list and, in most such arrangements, specific facts and circumstances will be necessary to determine the appropriate accounting. Consider the examples below.

Example 1 – Change of loan terms and change in interests within syndicate (single loan)

An entity signs a loan agreement that was negotiated with a syndicate of 20 banks that each have a 5% interest in the total amount borrowed. The entity has determined that it has borrowed under a single loan.

A year later, the borrower and the syndicate members agree to a change in the contract terms that have an impact of the future cash-flows (such as an extension of the maturity of the loan). In addition three banks sell their interest back to one of the existing syndicate members (bank A), so that bank A now has a 20% stake.

From the borrower's perspective, the loan is a single loan. Accordingly, since the modification is between an existing borrower and lender (the syndicate), the change to the terms of the loan would be evaluated on an aggregate basis to determine if the modification is an extinguishment or not. The transfer between syndicate members has no impact on the accounting by the borrower.

Example 2 – Multiple loans

An entity has a loan agreement signed by 20 banks, which are each determined to have granted separate loans to the borrower. Each of the 20 banks has a 5% stake in the total face amount of the loan. If new creditors join the group they must individually sign a new contract with the borrower. From the borrower's perspective, these are multiple loans and are accounted for as such.

Four of the banks transfer their 20% combined stake to another bank without any other change in the terms of the loan. It is necessary to determine whether the transfer is undertaken in a manner that results in the borrower being legally released from primary responsibility for the liability by the existing bank lender (further guidance on common methods of loan transfer is given in para 8.96). In this example, the new lender has to individually sign a new contract with the borrower and the borrower is legally released by the existing bank lender. The existing liability is therefore extinguished and this transaction is accounted for as an extinguishment of the four individual loans by the borrower and the recognition of a new loan liability. The bank to which the 20% stake is being transferred could be one within the original syndicate or one that was not previously a syndicate member.

However, consider a situation when bank A (a current syndicate member) sells a participation in its loan to bank B. In such a case, there would be no effect on the entity (borrower) unless the entity has been legally released from primary responsibility by bank A. In this example, bank A is still a creditor of the entity and bank B is a creditor of bank A.

On the other hand consider a situation where five of the banks in the above syndicate agree to extend the maturity of their loans. The remaining 15 institutions did not agree to the extension. The loans with the banks that agreed to the modification would be evaluated individually to determine if they were modified or extinguished. The loans to the banks that did not agree to the modification are unchanged and, therefore, do not need to be evaluated for modification or extinguishment.

If all the lenders agree to change terms of the loan that has an impact on its future cash flows, then in principle loans with each lender should be evaluated separately to determine if they have been extinguished or modified. If all the loans have homogenous terms, practically the same answer will be achieved if the loans are evaluated on an aggregate basis.

8.158 The liability being exchanged or modified might be only one component of a financial instrument. Where two or more components of a financial instrument are inter-dependent, a change to the terms of one component is likely to have repercussions on the other components. Each modification will need to be considered based on the specific facts and circumstances. Consider the examples below.

Example 1 – Extension of the term of a convertible bond when the conversion option is accounted for as an embedded derivative

Entity B issues a convertible bond in which the conversion option is accounted for as an embedded derivative (that is, it is part of the liability as it violates the fixed for fixed rule in IAS 32). Some time after issuance, the issuer and the holder renegotiate the terms of the convertible bond and agree to revised terms that include extending the bond's maturity and increasing the conversion ratio (where more ordinary shares of the issuer are to be delivered.)

From the issuer's perspective, the modification to the host contract and the derivative should be assessed together when applying the 10% test in paragraphs 40 and AG62 of IAS 39. This is because, in this case, the cash flows relating to the host debt and embedded derivative are interdependent. This is consistent with paragraph 40 of IAS 39, which states that *"a substantial modification of the terms of an existing financial liability or a part of it. . . . shall be accounted for as extinguishment of the original financial liability"*.

The term 'cash flow' in the 10% test of paragraph AG62 of IAS 39 includes the impact of settlement in a variable number of shares. One possible way of applying paragraph AG62 of IAS 39 is to assess the estimated cash flow as being the higher of the fair value of the share settlement at the date of the modification (using the current market share price) and the present value of cash flows attributable to the host. This approach reflects the optionality from the holder's perspective to choose the more valuable settlement option. Another way of determining the fair value of the share settlement in this approach is to use the forward price(s) of the entity's shares as at the estimated conversion date, and discounting to the modification date. Where the expected conversion date cannot be estimated reliably under this alternative, the contractual maturity date should be used. Other approaches might also be acceptable.

Example 2 – Exchange of a convertible instrument for debt

Entity A has issued two-year convertible debt for C100, in which the conversion option meets the 'fixed for fixed' test in IAS 32. It is, therefore, accounted for as an equity component (with a liability recognised for the debt component). At the end of year 1, the convertible debt has a fair value of C90 and the host debt component has a fair value of C85. Entity A agrees with the convertible debt holders to exchange their instrument for new non-convertible three-year debt with a fair value of C90.

Entity A has a policy choice as to whether a qualitative test is applied in addition to the 10% quantitative test when derecognising financial liabilities (see discussion in paragraphs 8.155 and 8.156). If entity A considers both qualitative factors and the 10% quantitative test, either of the two approaches set out below (approaches A and B) may be applied to determine whether the liability component of the convertible bond should be derecognised. However, if entity A has a policy of only derecognising financial liabilities using the 10% quantitative test, only approach B below is applicable.

Approach A – qualitative assessment: extinguished in its entirety

From a qualitative perspective, provided the original conversion option was substantial (has not insignificant worth to the holder) at the date of the exchange, the new non-convertible debt instrument is substantially different from the convertible debt by virtue of it not being convertible. This is because the risk profile and related returns arising from the original conversion option are effectively terminated. The existing convertible debt should therefore be derecognised and the new debt recognised at its initial fair value of C90. This approach effectively applies the derecognition rules to the whole instrument (debt and equity component together).

A gain or loss is recognised on the extinguishment of the convertible bond in accordance with paragraph AG33 of IAS 32, being the difference between the carrying amount of that debt component and the allocated consideration paid to redeem it. The full consideration paid (in this case the C90 new debt issued) is allocated to the debt and equity components of the existing convertible instrument at the date of the transaction using the same allocation method as on initial recognition (that is, by fair valuing the liability and allocating the residual to the equity component). In this case, the new debt instrument is allocated to the debt and equity components of the convertible instrument using the same method – that is on an 85:5 basis.

The new debt allocated to extinguishing the equity conversion option of C5 (C90 × 5/90) does not result in a gain or loss. Rather, the difference between this amount and the carrying value of the conversion option is taken directly to equity.

Approach B – quantitative assessment: debt component subject to 10% test, equity component extinguished

Under this approach, the derecognition requirements in paragraphs 39 and 40 of IAS 39 are viewed as applying to financial liabilities only. Using the principle in paragraph AG33 of IAS 32, part of the new debt instrument replaces the debt component of the convertible instrument, and part replaces the equity component of the original instrument. The new debt instrument is, therefore, allocated to the debt and equity elements of the convertible instrument for the purpose of their separate derecognition assessments, using the same method as on initial recognition.

The derecognition test (quantitative only, or quantitative and qualitative, depending on entity A's policy) should be applied to the debt component only. In this example, applying the 10% test on this basis results in the entity continuing to recognise the old debt component. Equally, the terms of the debt component are not considered to be substantially modified from a qualitative perspective. The revision of the terms of the debt component is, therefore, treated as a modification in this example. Applying paragraph AG62 of IAS 39 results in spreading the difference due to the change in terms (using the same effective rate) over the remaining life of the new debt.

The remaining part of the new debt instrument extinguishes the conversion option, which does not give rise to a gain or loss. [IAS 32 para 33]. Rather, the difference between the amount of the new debt that extinguishes the conversion option, and the previous carrying value of the conversion option is taken directly to equity.

The combined result of the above two elements has the effect that, at the date of the exchange, part of the new debt is measured at its fair value (being the part that replaces the equity component); where there is no derecognition of the old debt component, part of the debt is measured at the amortised cost of the old debt component (the part that replaces the debt component of the original convertible).

If applying the derecognition criteria to the debt component results in derecognition of the existing old debt component, the gain or loss on derecognition is calculated in the same way as discussed in approach A above.

Debt to equity swaps

8.159 It is not uncommon for companies to replace their existing debt instruments with equity through renegotiations with their debt holders in order to reduce excessive interest burden. Debt for equity swaps are mostly carried out by companies that are in financial distress. Debt holders often agree to swap their loans for equity in the belief that if they take an equity stake in a troubled company, they will ultimately achieve a greater return.

8.160 IFRIC 19, 'Extinguishing financial liabilities with equity instruments', addresses the accounting treatment when an entity renegotiates the terms of its debt, with the result that the liability is extinguished by the debtor issuing its own equity instruments to the creditor (referred to as a 'debt for equity swap'). IFRIC 19 does not affect the investor's accounting. It also does not change the guidance for convertible bonds where extinguishing the liability by issuing equity shares is in accordance with its original terms (see chapter 7). Furthermore, IFRIC 19 does not apply to transactions with shareholders in their capacity as shareholders (see para 8.169) or transactions between entities under common control where there is a capital contribution (see para 8.172).

8.161 IFRIC 19 requires a gain or loss to be recognised in profit or loss when a financial liability is settled through the issuance of the entity's own equity instruments. The interpretation clarifies that the new equity instruments are treated as consideration paid for the extinguishment of a financial liability. The amount of the gain or loss recognised in profit or loss is therefore the difference between the carrying value of the financial liability (or part of a financial liability) extinguished and the fair value of the equity instruments issued, in accordance with paragraph 41 of IAS 39. The equity instruments issued are recognised and measured initially at fair value at the date the financial liability was extinguished.

8.162   If the fair value of the equity instruments cannot be reliably measured, the fair value of the existing financial liability is used to measure the gain or loss. In measuring the fair value of a financial liability extinguished that includes a demand feature (for example a demand deposit), paragraph 49 of IAS 39 is not applied. [IFRIC 19 para 7]. Therefore, for the purposes of IFRIC 19, the fair value of a demand deposit may be determined to be less than the amount payable on demand, discounted from the first date that the amount could be required to be repaid.

8.163   If only part of the financial liability is extinguished, the entity assesses whether some of the consideration paid relates to a modification of the terms of the liability that remains outstanding. If part of the consideration paid does relate to a modification of the terms of the remaining part of the liability, the entity allocates the consideration paid between the part of the liability extinguished and the part of the liability that remains outstanding. The entity should consider all relevant facts and circumstances relating to the transaction in making this allocation. The consideration allocated to the remaining liability should form part of the assessment of whether the terms of the remaining liability have been substantially modified. If the remaining liability has been substantially modified, the entity accounts for the modification as an extinguishment of the original liability and the recognition of a new liability at fair value.

> **Example – Exchange of debt instrument for a modified debt instrument and equity shares**
>
> Entity C owes C500 to a lender, which is not a related party, but is unable to pay this liability in full. It renegotiates the debt with the lender which agrees to waive 80% of the liability (C400) in exchange for equity instruments in entity C with a fair value of C200. In addition, the terms of the remaining debt are modified to reset the interest rate and extend the term of the debt. The debt is carried at C500 prior to the renegotiation and its fair value is C300. The remaining debt has a fair value of C100 after renegotiation. The relative fair values of the instruments after the renegotiation are 33.3% liability (100/300) and 66.7% equity (200/300).
>
> IFRIC 19 applies to 66.7% of the carrying value of the original liability (C500) that is extinguished by equity:
>
> | | Dr Cm | Cr Cm |
> |---|---|---|
> | Liability | 333.3 | |
> | Equity | | 200.0 |
> | Profit or loss | | 133.3 |

The remaining 33.3% of the original liability (C166.7) is compared with the new liability to determine whether there has been a substantial modification of the remaining debt. If there is a substantial modification, additional journal entries are needed to recognise the extinguishment of the remaining debt:

	Dr Cm	Cr Cm
Liability (old)	167.7	
Liability (new)		100.0
Profit or loss		67.7

In a situation where there is a extinguishment of part of a debt by equity and a substantial modification of the remaining part of the debt, the total gain or loss on extinguishment is equal to the difference between the carrying value of the old liability and the total fair value of the new debt and equity (C500 – C300 = C200 in this example).

8.164 The amount of the gain or loss should be separately disclosed in the income statement or in the notes.

8.165 IFRIC 19 is mandatory for accounting periods beginning on or after 1 July 2010. Earlier application is permitted. The interpretation should be applied retrospectively from the beginning of the earliest comparative period presented as application to earlier periods would result only in a reclassification of amounts within equity.

8.166 There are two different views on how to account for debt to equity swaps before IFRIC 19 becomes mandatory. One is the approach in IFRIC 19, which applies the IAS 39 derecognition requirements resulting in a gain or loss, as discussed above. The alternative view is to follow an approach similar to that for the treatment on conversion of convertible debt in IAS 32. In that situation, as explained in chapter 7, the carrying value of the existing debt instrument is simply transferred to equity, and no gain or loss arises on the conversion. That is, the fair value of the new shares is ignored. This treatment is consistent with the usual accounting for the issue of shares that are recorded at the proceeds received rather than the fair value of the shares issued. It does not give rise to a gain or loss, as the exchange is treated as a transaction with owners.

8.167 Either approach is acceptable in accounting periods before the mandatory adoption of IFRIC 19 (that is, for accounting periods beginning on or before 30 June 2010). The choice is a matter of accounting policy. However, early adoption of the IFRIC 19 approach is recommended, as this will be consistent with the required policy in later periods furthermore, for entities with such transactions for the first time, early adoptionb will avoid the need to restate comparatives when IFRIC 19 becomes mandatory. The example below highlights the differences between the two approaches.

Example – Debt to equity swaps

An entity issued a debt instrument amounting to C50m repayable at par in year 10. Four years after issue it became clear that the entity was in financial difficulty and was unable to service its existing debt obligations. It therefore reached an agreement whereby the debt holders agreed to accept 5m equity shares of C1 each in full and final settlement of all amounts due under the debt instrument. The fair value of the equity shares issued in exchange was C25m.

IFRIC 19 approach – Treated as an extinguishment of existing debt and issue of new equity instrument

This approach is mandatory for accounting periods beginning on or after 1 July 2010 and recommended for earlier accounting periods. The new equity instrument is recorded at its fair value of C25m; and a gain is recognised on the extinguishment of the existing debt instrument. The accounting entries are as follows:

	Dr Cm	Cr Cm
Debt instrument	50	
Equity		25
Profit or loss – gain arising on extinguishment of debt		25

Alternative approach – Treated as a conversion of existing debt

This is an acceptable alternative approach for accounting periods beginning on or before 30 June 2010, before IFRIC 19 becomes mandatory. In this situation, the carrying value of the debt of C50m is transferred to equity. No gain or loss arises on conversion. The accounting entries are as follows:

	Dr Cm	Cr Cm
Debt instrument	50	
Equity		50

Transactions involving entities within a group

8.168 Paragraph 3(a) of IFRIC 19 scopes out transactions between an entity and a lender, where the lender is also a direct or indirect shareholder and is acting in that capacity. In addition, IFRIC 19 does not apply to transactions where the lender and the entity are controlled by the same party or parties before and after the transaction and the substance of the transaction includes an equity distribution by, or contribution to, the entity. Transactions between entities within the same group should, therefore, be assessed to determine whether they are in or out of the scope of IFRIC 19.

8.169 An entity should assess the facts and circumstances to determine whether the lender is acting in its capacity as shareholder in the transaction or, for transactions between fellow subsidiaries, whether there is in substance a capital contribution or a distribution given (effectively *via* the parent). This might be the case where the debt for equity swap is structured as a capital contribution or where the subsidiary is, or subsidiaries are, 100 per cent owned and the number of shares issued is not related to the fair value of the liability. In such a circumstance, it may not be appropriate to apply IFRIC 19 and recognise a gain or loss in the income statement based on the fair value of the equity instruments issued. Rather, the transaction could be accounted for either in full or in part as a capital contribution or distribution. In such circumstances, share capital would be measured as applicable under local law, the liability would be derecognised and the difference recorded in the equity of the borrower. The remainder of the transaction could then be accounted for in accordance with IFRIC 19.

8.170 On the other hand, an entity might determine that the transaction between group companies does not, in substance, include an equity distribution by, or contribution to, the entity. This might be the case, for example, when the subsidiary or subsidiaries are not 100 per cent owned, the loan is on commercial terms and the number of shares issued to the other party is based on the fair value of the liability. In such a case, the subsidiary applies IFRIC 19 for accounting periods beginning on or after 1 July 2010 and recognises a gain or loss in the income statement for the difference between the carrying amount of the liability and the fair value of the shares.

Treatment of cost and fees incurred on debt restructuring

8.171 If an exchange of debt instruments or modification of terms is accounted for as an extinguishment, any costs or fees incurred are recognised as part of the gain or loss on the extinguishment. If the exchange or modification is not accounted for as an extinguishment, any costs or fees incurred adjust the liability's carrying amount and are amortised over the modified liability's remaining term. [IAS 39 para AG 62].

8.172 As the above paragraph refers to any cost or fees incurred, it would appear that IAS 39 does not distinguish between costs and fees payable to third parties, such as lawyers and accountants, and those payable directly to the lender. As these costs and fees are properly incurred in connection with the modification of the instrument's terms, it is appropriate to treat them as adjustments to future interest payments rather than costs and fees in the true sense of the term. Accordingly, if the fees paid to third parties are related directly to the modification, they should be recognised as part of the gain or loss if the modification is accounted for as an extinguishment. This is true even if the modification results in the issue of a new debt instrument. Only those costs that the issuer can demonstrate are incremental and directly related to the issue of the new debt instrument should be treated as costs of the new liability, rather than expensed as part of the gain or loss on the extinguishment of the existing instrument.

8.173 Where the modification of a financial liability is not accounted for as an extinguishment, the fees paid to third parties are adjusted against the existing liability's carrying value, together with other payments to the lender.

Example – Renegotiation of debt

A company borrowed C1m on 1 January 20X0 at a fixed rate of 9% per annum for 10 years. The company incurred issue costs of C100,000. Interest on the loan is payable yearly in arrears. As a result of deteriorating financial condition during 20X5, the company approached its bondholders for a modification of the bond's terms. The following terms were agreed with effect from 1 January 20X6 (all interest paid to date):

- The interest rate is reduced to 7.5% payable yearly in arrears.

- The original amount payable on maturity is reduced to C950,000.

- The maturity of the loan is extended by two years to 31 December 20Y1.

- Renegotiation fees of C30,000 are payable on 1 January 20X6.

The loan would be recorded initially at 1 January 20X0 at net proceeds of C900,000 and would be amortised using the effective interest rate (EIR) method discussed in chapter 9. The EIR is 10.6749% as shown below.

	Interest	Payments	Carrying value
	C 10.6749%	C	C
1 Jan 20X0			900,000
31 Dec 20X0	96,074	90,000	906,074
31 Dec 20X1	96,723	90,000	912,797
31 Dec 20X2	97,441	90,000	920,238
31 Dec 20X3	98,235	90,000	928,473
31 Dec 20X4	99,114	90,000	937,587
31 Dec 20X5	100,087	90,000	947,674
31 Dec 20X6	101,164	90,000	958,837
31 Dec 20X7	102,355	90,000	971,192
31 Dec 20X8	103,674	90,000	984,866
31 Dec 20X9	105,134	1,090,000	–

At 1 January 20X6, the remaining cash flows on the old debt comprise four annual interest payments of C90,000 and the C1m of principal payable at redemption. The present value of these remaining cash flows on that date amounts to C947,674 as shown above.

The present value of the cash flows under the revised terms discounted at the original EIR of 10.6749% is shown below:

		Cash Flows	Present value
1 Jan 20X6	Fees	30,000	30,000
31 Dec 20X6	Revised interest	75,000	67,766
31 Dec 20X7	Revised interest	75,000	61,230
31 Dec 20X8	Revised interest	75,000	55,324
31 Dec 20X9	Revised interest	75,000	49,988
31 Dec 20Y0	Revised interest	75,000	45,166
31 Dec 20Y1	Revised interest + principal	1,025,000	557,736
			867,210

The present value of C867,210 represents 91.5% of the present value of the old cash flows. As the difference in present values of C80,464 (947,674 − 867,210) is less than 10% of the present value of the old cash flows, the modification is not accounted for as extinguishment.

The question arises as to how to account for the present value difference of C80,464 arising from the renegotiation. One approach would be to recognise the difference immediately in profit or loss by adjusting the previous carrying value of the liability from C947,674 to C867,210. Another approach would be to recognise the difference over the remaining life of the instrument by adjusting the effective interest rate so that the previous carrying value of C947,674 accretes to the redemption amount of C950,000 by 31 December 20Y1. There is support for both approaches in IAS 39 as explained below.

The first approach is supported by paragraph AG 8 of IAS 39 that states:

> "If the entity revises its estimates of payments or receipts, the entity shall adjust the carrying value of the financial asset or financial liability (or group of financial instruments) to reflect actual and revised estimated cash flows. The entity recalculates the carrying value by computing the present value of estimated future cash flows at the financial instrument's original effective interest rate. The adjustment is recognised as income or expense in profit or loss." [IAS 39 para AG 8].

A renegotiation of an instrument's terms will change its contractual cash flows. This will also result in a change to the expected cash flows in most cases. Paragraph AG 8 can be read to apply to all cases in which cash flows are re-estimated, as there is nothing in that paragraph that limits it to cases when the cash flows are not renegotiated.

The second approach is supported by paragraph AG 62 as discussed in paragraph 8.153 above. As the change in terms is not considered to be a substantial modification and, therefore, does not result in the extinguishment of the original liability, it is a more faithful representation to recognise any net gain or loss over the modified instrument's remaining life. This is further supported by the fact that, in the previous version of IAS 39, IGC 62-1 dealt with this issue and clearly favoured this treatment. There is nothing in the revised IAS 39 that indicates that the IASB intended a change to this treatment. Indeed, the table of concordance between the old and the new standard clearly indicates that IGC 62-1 is mapped into AG 62. Furthermore, it could be argued that paragraph AG 8 is not applicable, as a renegotiation that changes the instrument's terms and, hence, the future cash flows, is not the same as the entity revising its estimates.

The effective interest rate that amortises the old carrying value, as adjusted for fees incurred of C30,000, is 8.6453% as shown below:

	Interest@ 8.6453%	Payments	Carrying value
			947,674
Fees paid			(30,000)
01 Jan 20X0			917,674
31 Dec 20X6	79,336	75,000	922,010
31 Dec 20X7	79,710	75,000	926,720
31 Dec 20X8	80,117	75,000	931,837
31 Dec 20X9	80,560	75,000	937,397
31 Dec 20Y0	81,040	75,000	943,437
31 Dec 20Y1	81,563	1,025,000	–
	482,326	1,400,000	

The treatment applied should be the one that is most appropriate to the particular facts and circumstances of the transaction being accounted for, reflecting the substance of the transaction. For example, if the renegotiation results in an immediate cash payment that includes a repayment of part of the principal, the recognition of a gain or loss would be more appropriate. This is because it would not be appropriate to spread forward a gain or loss that arises on a partial repayment by adjusting the EIR on the portion that continues to be recognised. Conversely, if an entity renegotiates to reduce the future interest payments on a loan in times of falling interest rates and partially compensates the lender by an immediate cash payment, the second method would be the more appropriate. This is because adjusting the EIR would best reflect the effect that the new interest rate environment has had on the remaining cash flows.

Other examples are given below:

Case A
An instalment loan is renegotiated to reduce the payments due in the remaining years of the loan in return for an immediate cash payment. In this case, the cash payment represents a re-payment of part of the liability. The first approach to recognise a gain or loss on the modification is, therefore, the most appropriate. It is not appropriate to spread forwards a gain or loss arising on a partial re-payment by adjusting the EIR on the portion that continues to be recognised.

Case B
An entity is close to breaching a loan covenant on a particular borrowing. It renegotiates the borrowing to remove the covenant in return for an immediate cash payment that reflects the different credit risk now associated with the loan. In this case, the second method to defer the loss over the remaining life of the loan is more appropriate. The removal of the covenant results in a more risky loan that is appropriately reflected in a higher EIR.

Case C

An entity has had a fixed rate borrowing for some years, during which time interest rates have fallen. The entity renegotiates the borrowing to reduce the future interest payments to the current market rate in return for an immediate cash payment. The cash payment does not fully compensate the lender for the lost future interest – that is, in economic terms, the effect of the fall in interest rates is shared between the parties to the loan. In this case, the second method is more appropriate. Adjusting the EIR of the loan reflects the effect that the new interest environment has had on the remaining cash flows

8.174 Transaction costs are also likely to be incurred when an entity extinguishes a liability in exchange for equity instruments. IFRIC 19 does not specify how such costs should be accounted for. However, paragraph 5 of IFRIC 19 states that the issue of equity instruments to extinguish a liability is 'consideration paid' in accordance with IAS 39 paragraph 41 – that is IFRIC 9 considers a 'debt for equity swap' to be a liability extinguishment in accordance with IAS 39. Paragraph AG62 of IAS 39 notes that when an extinguishment of a liability occurs any costs or fees incurred are recognised as part of the gain or loss on extinguishment.

8.175 Paragraph 35 of IAS 32 requires transaction costs arising in respect of an equity transaction to be recognised as a component of equity to the extent they are incremental costs directly attributable to the equity transaction that would otherwise have been avoided. Such transaction costs that can be separately identified as relating solely to the issue of the new equity and not to the debt extinguishment should, therefore, be recognised in equity rather than profit or loss.

Chapter 9

Measurement of financial assets and liabilities

Chapter 9

Measurement of financial assets and liabilities

Introduction

9.1 An entity recognises a financial asset or a financial liability when it first becomes a party to the contractual rights and obligations in the contract. It is, therefore, necessary to measure those contractual rights and obligations on initial recognition. Under IAS 39, all financial instruments are measured initially by reference to their fair value, which is *normally* the transaction price, that is, the fair value of the consideration given or received. However, this will not always be the case.

9.2 Subsequent to initial recognition, IAS 39's measurement approach is best described as a 'mixed attribute' model with certain assets and liabilities measured at cost and others at fair value. The model depends upon an instrument's classification into one of the four categories of financial assets or one of the two categories of financial liabilities discussed in chapter 5. For example, depending on the nature of the instrument and management's intentions, a fixed interest security intended to be held-to-maturity would be measured at amortised cost and not at fair value. Notwithstanding this, as explained in chapter 6, the standard gives entities the option to classify financial instruments that meet certain special criteria at fair value with all gains and losses taken to profit and loss. The ability for entities to use the fair value option simplifies the application of IAS 39 by mitigating some anomalies that result from the use of the mixed measurement model.

9.3 This chapter deals with IAS 39's basic measurement requirements and addresses the concepts of fair value and amortised cost, including the use of the effective interest method and the standard's impairment model. However, the special form of accounting that applies when a financial asset or liability is designated by management in a hedging relationship is covered in chapter 10.

9.3.1 In November 2009 the IASB issued the first part of IFRS 9, 'Financial Instruments', relating to classification and measurement of financial instruments. The new approach to classifying financial assets based on the entity's business model for managing the financial assets and the contractual cash flow characteristics of the financial asset and replaces the numerous categories of financial assets in IAS 39. Financial assets will be measured at amortised cost or fair value and the fair value option is retained but the presentation of gains and losses is changed. A separate exposure draft proposes a single impairment model that will apply to assets measured at amortised cost, thus replacing the numerous impairment methods in IAS 39 that arise from the different classification categories. It is the IASB's intention that IFRS 9 will ultimately replace IAS 39 in its entirety. IFRS 9 is dealt with in chapter 12.

Initial measurement

Initial fair value

9.4 When a financial asset or financial liability is recognised initially, IAS 39 requires the entity to measure it at its 'fair value' plus, in certain situations, transaction costs (see para 9.11 below). [IAS 39 para 43]. The standard defines fair value as the amount for which an asset could be exchanged, or a liability settled, between knowledgeable willing parties in an arm's length transaction. [IAS 39 para 9]. The concept of fair value and requirements for determining the fair value of financial instruments are discussed in detail from paragraph 9.72 below.

9.5 Given that fair value is the price that arm's length market participants would pay or receive in a routine transaction under the market conditions at the date at which the asset or liability is to be measured for accounting purposes (the measurement date), it follows that a financial instrument's initial fair value will normally be the transaction price, that is, the fair value of the consideration given or received. [IAS 39 para AG 64].

9.6 In some circumstances, however, the consideration given or received (say the face amount) is may not necessarily be the financial instrument's fair value. For example, the fair value of a long-term note receivable that carries no interest is not equal to its face amount and, therefore, part of the consideration received is something other than its fair value. As the note receivable would have to be recorded initially at its fair value, its fair value has to be estimated. The instrument's fair value may be evidenced by comparison with other observable current market transactions in the same instrument (that is, without modification or repackaging) or based on a valuation technique whose variables include only data from observable markets. [IAS 39 para AG 76]. For a long-term loan or receivable with no stated interest, the fair value is normally arrived at by using a discounted cash flow valuation method. Under this method, the fair value can be estimated as the present value of all future cash receipts discounted using the prevailing market rate of interest for a similar instrument (similar as to currency, term, type of interest rate and other factors) with a similar credit rating issued at the same time. Any additional amount lent is an expense or a reduction of income, unless it qualifies for recognition as some other type of asset. [IAS 39 para AG 64].

9.7 However, as a pragmatic measure, the standard permits short-term receivables and payables to be measured at the original invoice amount if the effect of discounting is immaterial. [IAS 39 para AG 79]. The IFRIC also considered the accounting for extended payment terms, such as six-month's interest-free credit, and concluded that the accounting treatment under IAS 39 was clear. In such circumstances, the effect of the time value of money should be reflected when this is material. [IFRIC Update July 2004].

Example 1 – Interest free loan to a company

Entity A lends C1,000 to entity B for 5 years and classifies the asset under loans and receivables. The loan carries no interest. Instead, entity A expects other future economic benefits, such as an implicit right to receive goods or services at favourable prices.

On initial recognition, the market rate of interest for a similar 5 year loan with payment of interest at maturity is 10% per year. The loan's initial fair value is the present value of the future payment of 1,000 discounted using the market rate of interest for a similar loan of 10% for 5 years, that is, C621.

In this example, the consideration given of C1,000 is for two things – the fair value of the loan of C621 and entity A's right to obtain other future economic benefits that have a fair value of C379 (the difference between the total consideration given of C1,000 and the consideration given for the loan of C621).

Entity A recognises the loan at its initial fair value of C621 that will accrete to C1,000 over the term of the loan using the effective interest method (see further para 9.51 below).

The difference of C379 is not a financial asset, since it is paid to obtain expected future economic benefits other than the right to receive payment on the loan asset. Entity A recognises that amount as an expense unless it qualifies for recognition as an asset under, say, IAS 38, 'Intangible assets', or as part of the cost of investment in subsidiary, if entity B is a subsidiary of entity A.

Example 2 – Interest free loan to an employee

An entity grants an interest free loan of C1,000 to an employee for a period of two years. The market rate of interest to this individual for a two year loan with payment of interest at maturity is 10%.

The consideration given to the employee consists of two assets:

- The fair value of the loan, that is $C1,000/(1.10)^2 = C826$.

- The difference of C174 that is accounted for as employee compensation in accordance with IAS 19, 'Employee benefits'.

Example 3 – Interest free loan received from a government agency

An entity is located in an enterprise zone and receives an interest free loan of C500,000 from a government agency. The loan carries no interest and is repayable at the end of year three.

In its annual improvements to IFRSs issued in May 2008, the IASB amended IAS 20 to require that loans received from a government that have a below-market rate of interest should be recognised and measured in accordance with IAS 39. The benefit of the below-market rate of interest should be measured as the difference between the initial carrying value of the loan determined in accordance with IAS 39 and the proceeds received. [IAS 20 para 10A].

So if the fair value is estimated at C450,000 under IAS 39, the loan would be recorded initially at its fair value of C450,000. The difference between the consideration received and the fair value of the loan, that is, C50,000, would fall to be accounted for as a government grant in accordance with IAS 20.

However, the IASB noted that applying IAS 39 to loans retrospectively may require entities to measure the fair value of loans at a past date. So the IASB decided that the amendment should be applied prospectively to government loans received in periods beginning on or after 1 January 2009. Earlier application is permitted. If an entity applies the amendments for an earlier period it should disclose that fact. [IAS 20 para 43].

9.8   In some circumstances, instead of originating an interest free loan, an entity may originate a loan that bears an off-market interest rate (for example, a loan that carries a higher or lower rate than the prevailing current market rate for a similar loan) and pays or receives an initial fee as compensation. In that situation, the entity still recognises the loan at its initial fair value, that is, net of the fee paid or received as illustrated below. The fee paid or received is amortised to profit or loss using the effective interest method. [IAS 39 para AG 65]. A similar requirement is included in IAS 18, 'Revenue', where fees that are an integral part of a financial instrument's effective interest rate are generally treated as an adjustment to the effective interest rate. [IAS 18 para IE 14(a)].

Example – Off-market loan with origination fee

An entity originates a loan for C1,000 that is repayable in 5 year's time. The loan carries interest at 6%, which is less than the market rate of 8% for a similar loan. The entity receives C80 as compensation for originating a below market loan.

The entity should recognise the loan at its initial fair value of C920 (net present value of C60 of interest for 5 years and principal repayment of C1,000 discounted at 8%). This is equal to the net cash received (loan of C1,000 less origination fee of C80). The net amount of the loan of C920 accretes to C1,000 over the 5 year term using an effective interest of 8%.

In this example, the upfront fee received of C80 exactly compensates the entity for interest short fall of C20 for each of the next 5 years discounted at the market rate of 8%. Hence, no gain or loss arises on initial recognition.

9.9   A further exception to the general rule that the transaction price is not necessarily the financial instrument's initial fair value is of particular relevance to banking and insurance entities. Such entities often originate structured transactions and use models to estimate their fair values. Such models may show a 'day 1' gain (that is, the fair value exceeds the transaction price). However, IFRS permits departure from the transaction price only if fair value is evidenced by observable current market transactions in the same instrument or a valuation technique whose variables include only data from observable markets. As a result, an immediate 'day 1' gain is rarely recognised on initial recognition. This issue is considered further in paragraph 9.107 below.

Transaction costs

9.10   Transaction costs are incremental costs that are directly attributable to the acquisition or issue or disposal of a financial asset or financial liability. An incremental cost is one that would not have been incurred if the entity had not acquired, issued or disposed of the financial instrument. [IAS 39 para 9].

9.11   Transaction costs include fees and commissions paid to agents (including employees acting as selling agents), advisers, brokers and dealers, levies by regulatory agencies and securities exchanges and transfer taxes and duties. Transaction costs do not include debt premiums or discounts, financing costs or internal administrative or holding costs. [IAS 39 para AG 13].

9.12   The standard defines transaction costs to include internal costs, provided they are incremental and directly attributable to the acquisition, issue or disposal of a financial asset or financial liability. [IAS 39 para BC222(d)]. However, in practice, other than payments made to employees acting as selling agents (common in insurance contracts that fall to be accounted for under IAS 39 as financial instruments), salary costs of employees that would be incurred irrespective of whether the loan was granted are not incremental, nor are allocated indirect administrative costs or overheads.

9.13   The appendix to IAS 18, 'Revenue', sets out a number of examples of financial services fees. IAS 18 distinguishes such fees between those that are an integral part of generating an involvement with the resulting financial instrument, those that are earned as services are provided and those that are earned on the execution of a significant act. Such fees may fall into two categories: fees associated with origination of a loan (loan origination fees) and fees associated with commitment to lend (commitment fees).

9.14   Loan origination fees may consist of:

- Fees that are charged to the borrower as 'pre-paid' interest or to reduce the loan's nominal interest rate (explicit yield adjustments).

- Fees to compensate the lender for origination activities such as evaluating the borrower's financial condition, evaluating and recording guarantees, collateral and other security arrangements, negotiating the instrument's terms, preparing and processing documents and closing the transaction.

- Other fees that relate directly to the loan origination process (for example, fees that are paid to the lender as compensation for granting a complex loan or agreeing to lend quickly).

9.15   Commitment fees are fees that are charged by the lender for entering into an agreement to make or acquire a loan. Sometimes they are referred to as facility fees for making a loan facility available to a borrower. The accounting treatment depends on whether or not it is probable that the entity will enter into a specific lending arrangement and whether the loan commitment is within IAS 39's scope.

If it is probable that the entity will enter into the lending agreement and the loan commitment is not within IAS 39's scope, the commitment fee received is regarded as compensation for an ongoing involvement with the acquisition of a financial instrument and, together with the transaction costs (as defined in IAS 39), is deferred and recognised as an adjustment to the effective interest rate. If the commitment expires without the entity making the loan, the fee is recognised as revenue on expiry. [IAS 18 App para 14(a)(ii)]. On the other hand, if it is unlikely that a specific lending arrangement will be entered into and the loan commitment is outside IAS 39's scope, the commitment fee is recognised as revenue on a time proportion basis over the commitment period. Loan commitments that are within IAS 39's scope are accounted for as derivatives and measured at fair value. [IAS 18 App para 14(b)(ii); IAS 39 para 9].

9.15.1   The borrower's accounting mirrors that of the lender as discussed above. Therefore, to the extent there is evidence that it is probable that some or all of the facility will be drawn down, the facility fee is accounted for as a transaction cost under IAS 39. Where this is the case, the facility fee is deferred and treated as a transaction cost when draw-down occurs; it is not amortised prior to the draw-down. For example, draw-down might be probable if there is a specific project for which there is an agreed business plan. If a facility is for C20 million and it is probable that only C5 million of the facility will be drawn down, a quarter of the facility fee represents a transaction cost of the C5 million loan and is deferred until draw-down occurs. To the extent there is no evidence that it is probable that some or all of the facility will be drawn down, the facility fee represents a payment for liquidity services – that is, to secure the availability of finance on pre-arranged terms over the facility period. As such, to the extent draw down is not probable, the facility fee is capitalised as a prepayment for services and amortised over the period of the facility to which it relates. The availability of finance on pre-arranged terms provides benefit to an entity in a similar way to an insurance policy. If finance is needed in the future due to unforeseen events, the facility in place ensures that an entity can obtain this finance on known terms regardless of the economic environment in the future.

9.16   Direct loan origination costs relate to costs incurred by the entity for undertaking activities set out in the second bullet point of paragraph 9.14 above. Internal costs directly related to those activities should include only that portion of employee cost directly related to time spent performing those activities (see para 9.14 above).

9.17   It is apparent from the nature of the above fees that they are an integral part of generating an involvement with the resulting financial instrument and together with the related direct origination costs, are accounted for in a financial instrument's initial measurement as follows:

■   When a financial asset or financial liability is recognised initially and not designated as at fair value through profit or loss, transaction costs (net of fees received) that are directly attributable to the acquisition or issue are added to the initial fair value. For financial assets, such costs are added to the amount originally recognised. For financial liabilities, such costs are deducted from the amount originally recognised. This applies to financial instruments carried at amortised cost and available-for-sale financial assets. [IAS 39 para 43].

■ For financial instruments that are measured at fair value through profit or loss, transaction costs (net of any fees received or paid) are not added to or deducted from the initial fair value, but are immediately recognised in profit or loss on initial recognition.

■ Transaction costs expected to be incurred on a financial instrument's transfer or disposal are not included in the financial instrument's measurement.

[IAS 39 para IG E1.1].

Example 1 – Initial measurement – transaction cost

An entity acquires an equity available-for-sale financial asset at its fair value of C100. Purchase commission of C2 is also payable. At the end of the entity's financial year, the asset's quoted market price is C105. If the asset were to be sold, a commission of C4 would be payable.

As the asset is not classified initially at fair value through profit or loss, the entity recognises the financial asset at its fair value that includes the purchase commission, that is, at C102. At the end of the entity's financial year, the asset is recorded at C105 without regard to the commission of C4 payable on sale. The change in fair value of C3 recognised in other comprehensive income includes the purchase commission of C2 payable at the acquisition date.

Example 2 – Allocation of transaction costs to a convertible instrument that contains a conversion option as an embedded derivative

An entity, with functional currency of C, issues a 5 year, euro-denominated convertible bond for C100. Transaction costs of C2 were incurred by the issuer. The host liability is to be accounted for at amortised cost. The fair value of the embedded derivative on initial recognition was C20.

Transaction costs relating to issuance of a convertible instrument for which the conversion feature is classified as an embedded derivative should be allocated to the host liability and the embedded conversion option in either of the following ways (that is, there is an accounting policy choice):

■ Approach 1 – The convertible bond represents a liability in its entirety, as the conversion feature fails the fixed-for-fixed requirement for equity classification (see chapter 7). On initial recognition, the financial liability (that is, the entire instrument) should be recognised at fair value less transactions costs that are directly attributable to its issuance since the instrument is not at fair value through profit or loss. As the embedded derivative's fair value at initial recognition is C20, the host liability is initially recognised at C78 (C100 – C20 – C2) and there is no impact on profit or loss.

■ Approach 2 – Under this approach, transaction costs are allocated to each component in proportion to the allocation of proceeds. Therefore, costs allocated to the embedded derivative are charged to profit or loss on initial recognition, and those allocated to the host contract are deducted from its initial carrying amount. Accordingly, the embedded derivative is recognised initially at C20, with (20/100) of the transaction costs (that is, C0.4) being recognised in profit or loss. The host liability is recognised initially at C78.4 (C100 – C20 – (80/100) × C2).

9.18   Entities may also receive fees for the provision of a service, such as loan servicing fee, or for the execution of a significant act such as placement fees for arranging a loan between two third parties and loan syndication fees. These fees are not integral to lending or borrowing and, therefore, cannot form part of the financial instrument's measurement.

9.19   The treatment of transaction costs on the subsequent measurement of available-for-sale financial assets is considered in paragraph 9.30 below and those carried at amortised cost are considered in paragraph 9.59 below.

Settlement date accounting for regular way transactions

9.20   When an entity uses settlement date accounting for an asset that is subsequently measured at cost or amortised cost, the asset is recognised initially at settlement date, but measured at the fair value on trade date. [IAS 39 para 44]. This is an exception to the general rule in paragraph 9.4 above that a financial asset should be recognised at its fair value on initial recognition. The accounting for regular way trades is considered in chapter 8.

Subsequent measurement of financial assets

General

9.21   As set out in chapter 6, financial assets are classified in one of four categories. Following their initial recognition, the classification determines how the financial asset is subsequently measured, including any profit or loss recognition. The following table summarises the requirements that are considered in detail in the remainder of this chapter.

Classification	Financial asset	Measurement basis	Changes in carrying amount	Impairment test (if objective evidence)
At fair value through profit or loss	Debt	Fair value	Profit or loss	No [5]
	Equity	Fair value	Profit or loss	No [5]
	Derivatives not designated as effective hedging instruments	Fair value	Profit or loss	–
Loans and receivables	Debt	Amortised cost	Profit or loss [3]	Yes
Held-to-maturity investments	Debt	Amortised cost	Profit or loss [3]	Yes
Available-for-sale financial assets	Debt	Fair value	OCI [2] Profit or loss [3]	Yes
	Equity	Fair value	OCI [2] Profit or loss [4]	Yes
	Equity [1]	Cost (fair value not reliably measurable)	Profit or loss [4]	Yes

1 Equity instruments that do not have any quoted market price in an active market and whose fair value cannot be reliably measured and derivative assets that are linked to and must be settled by delivery of such unquoted equity instruments.

2 Change in fair value other than those noted in note 3 or 4 below where relevant.

3 Interest calculated using the effective interest method, foreign exchange differences, impairment and reversal of impairment, where relevant, are taken to profit or loss.

4 Dividends and impairment are taken to profit or loss. Foreign exchange difference on (non-monetary) equity AFS investments taken to equity and recycled to profit or loss on disposal or impairment.

5 Any impairment will be taken though profit or loss as part of the change in fair value and so separate impairment testing is not necessary.

9.22 Financial assets that are designated as hedged items are subject to measurement under the hedge accounting requirements. These requirements apply in addition to, and may modify, the general accounting requirements that are discussed below. Hedge accounting is covered in chapter 10.

Financial assets at fair value through profit or loss

9.23 After initial recognition, financial assets falling within this category (including assets held-for-trading and derivative assets not designated as effective hedging instruments and assets designated on initial recognition at fair value through profit or loss) are measured at fair value, without the deduction of transaction costs that the entity may incur on sale or other disposal. [IAS 39 para 46]. Such transaction costs are future costs that relate to the sale or the disposal and have no relevance to determining fair value. Therefore, they are properly included in the period in which the sale or the disposal takes place.

9.24   The standard's requirements for determining the fair value of instruments that fall to be measured on this basis are considered from paragraph 9.72 below. Investments in equity instruments that do not have a quoted market price in an active market and whose fair value cannot be reliably measured and derivatives that are linked to and must be settled by delivery of such unquoted equity instruments, are measured at cost (see further para 9.104 below).[IAS 39 para 46(c)].

9.25   All gains and losses arising from changes in fair value of financial assets falling within this category are recognised, not surprisingly, in profit or loss. [IAS 39 para 55(a)]. This means that assets falling within this category are not subject to review for impairment as losses due to fall in value (including impairment) would automatically be reflected in profit or loss.

Loans and receivables

9.26   Loans and receivables, as defined in chapter 6, are measured at amortised cost using the effective interest method. [IAS 39 para 46(a)]. They are measured on this basis whether they are intended to be held-to-maturity or not. [IAS 39 para AG 68]. The amortised cost method of accounting is discussed from paragraph 9.51 below.

9.27   Gains and losses are recognised in profit or loss when loans and receivables are derecognised or impaired and throughout the amortisation process. Special rules apply for gain or loss recognition when loans and receivables are designated as hedged items. [IAS 39 para 56].

Held-to-maturity investments

9.28   Held-to-maturity investments are also measured at amortised cost using the effective interest method. Gains and losses are accounted for in the same way as loans and receivables. [IAS 39 para 46(b)].

Available-for-sale assets

9.29   Available-for-sale financial assets are measured at fair value. As with assets designated as at fair value through profit or loss, transaction costs that will be incurred on the sale or disposal of such assets are not deducted from the fair value. However, there is an exemption from measurement at fair value of an available-for-sale asset if its fair value cannot be measured reliably (see para 9.24 above). This exemption only applies to unquoted equity instruments and derivative contracts based on those instruments. These instruments are measured at cost. [IAS 39 para 46(c)].

9.30   As explained in paragraph 9.17 above, transaction costs that are directly attributable to the acquisition of an available-for-sale financial asset are added to the initial fair value. For available-for-sale financial assets, transaction costs are recognised in other comprehensive income as part of a change in fair value at the subsequent measurement. If an available-for-sale financial asset has fixed or determinable payments and does not have an indefinite life, the transaction costs are amortised to profit or loss using the effective interest method (see para 9.52 below). If an available-for-sale financial asset does not have fixed or determinable payments and has an indefinite life, the transaction costs are recognised in profit or loss when the asset is derecognised or becomes impaired and the cumulative gain or loss, including transaction costs, deferred in other comprehensive income is reclassified to profit or loss. [IAS 39 para AG 67].

9.31   All gains and losses arising from changes in fair value of available-for-sale financial assets are recognised directly in other comprehensive income except as follows:

■   Interest calculated using the effective interest method is recognised in profit or loss (see further para 9.51 below). Dividends on an available-for-sale equity instruments are recognised in profit or loss when the entity's right to receive payment is established. [IAS 18 para 30(c)].

■   Foreign exchange gains and losses on monetary financial assets are recognised in profit or loss (see further para 9.162 below).

■   Impairment losses are recognised in profit or loss (see further para 9.152 below). Reversals of impairment of a debt instrument are also recognised in profit or loss, but reversals of impairment on equity instruments are not (see further para 9.154 below).

[IAS 39 para 55(b)].

9.32   When an available-for-sale financial asset is derecognised as a result of sale or is impaired, the cumulative gain or loss previously recognised in other comprehensive income is reclassified to profit or loss. [IAS 39 paras 55(b), 67]. For example, assume that an entity acquires an equity security for C500 that has a fair value at the end of the year of C600. A gain of C100 is recognised in other comprehensive income. In the following year, the entity sells the security for C550. In the year of sale, a profit of C50, being the difference between proceeds of C550 and original cost of C500 is recognised. This represents the difference between proceeds of C550 and previous carrying value of C600 (C50 loss) and the recycling to profit or loss of C100 gain previously recognised in other comprehensive income.

9.33   In the above example, a single security is used to illustrate the accounting for recycling. In practice, the entity may have acquired the same security in tranches at different dates and at different prices over a period of time. IAS 39 does not specify whether such fungible assets (or indeed any other fungible financial assets) should be considered individually or in aggregate, and, if in aggregate, which measurement basis (weighted average, first in first out (FIFO), specific identification) is appropriate for calculating the gain or loss on a partial disposal. This is in contrast to IAS 2, 'Inventories', which specifies the use of weighted average or FIFO in most circumstances. In practice, entities may opt, as an accounting policy choice, for any one of the methods. The method used should be applied consistently for both impairment and disposal and disclosed.

9.33.1   It is conceivable that within a group, portfolios have a different nature – for example, an available-for-sale portfolio held for liquidity purposes *versus* an available-for-sale portfolio held for long-term strategic investment purposes. In this instance, it may be possible to justify using different cost formulae within an entity for the same securities. However, whatever cost formula is used, it should be used for both impairment and measurement of gains and losses on disposal.

9.34   The subsequent measurement of available-for-sale financial assets with fixed and determinable payments is complicated by the fact that fair value changes are recognised in other comprehensive income, but interest income is recognised in each period in profit or loss using the effective interest method. In order to ensure that the change in fair value is correctly calculated at the measurement date, it would be necessary to compare the instrument's clean price (the fair value of the instrument less accrued interest) with its amortised cost, also excluding accrued interest, at that date. Therefore, although the instrument is measured at fair value, the amortised cost must still be calculated using the effective interest method in order to determine interest income.

Example – Debt security classified as available-for-sale investment

On 1 January 20X5, an entity purchases 10% C10 million 5 year bonds with interest payable on 1 July and 1 January each year. The bond's purchase price is C10,811,100. The premium of C811,100 is due to market yield for similar bonds being 8%. Assuming there are no transaction costs, the effective interest rate is 8% (the effective interest method is discussed further in para 9.52 below).

The entity classifies the bond as available-for-sale. The entity prepares its financial statements at 31 March. On 31 March 20X5, the yield on bonds with similar maturity and credit risk is 7.75%. At that date, the fair value of this bond calculated by discounting 10 semi-annual cash flows of C500,000 and principal payment of C10 million at maturity at the market rate of 7.75% amounted to C11,127,710.

Since the bond is classified as available-for-sale, the bond will be measured at fair value with changes in fair value recognised in other comprehensive income.

At 1 January 20X5, the fair value of the bond is the consideration paid of C10,811,100 and the entry to record this is as follows:

	Dr C	Cr C
At 1 January 20X5		
Available-for-sale investment	10,811,100	
Cash		10,811,100

On 31 March 20X5, the entity will record interest income for the 3 months at the effective interest rate of 8%, that is, C10,811,100 × 8% × 3/12 = C216,222. Since the

next coupon of C500,000 is due on 1 July 20X5, the entity will record a half-year interest accrual of C250,000. The difference of C33,778 between the interest income accrued and that recognised in the profit or loss represents the amortisation of the premium. The entry to record the interest income on 31 March 20X6 is as follows:

	Dr C	Cr C
At 31 March 20X5		
Available-for-sale investment (accrued interest)	250,000	
Available-for-sale investment (premium)		33,778
Profit or loss – interest income		216,222

The bond's amortised cost at 31 March 20X5 is, therefore, C10,777,322 (10,811,100 – 33,778)

The fair value of the bond at 31 March 20X5 is C11,127,710. This includes the accrued interest of C250,000. To calculate the clean price of the bond, the accrued income is deducted from the fair value. Therefore, the clean price of the bond is C10,877,710.

A comparison of the clean price of the bond and its amortised cost at 31 March 20X5 results in a gain as follows:

	C
Fair value of bond at 31 March 20X5 – clean price	10,877,710
Amortised cost of bond at 31 March 20X5	10,777,322
Change in value – Unrealised gain	100,388

The entry to record the gain at 31 March 20X5 is as follows:

	Dr C	Cr C
At 31 March 20X5		
Available-for-sale investments	100,388	
Other comprehensive income		100,388

The movement in available-for-sale asset is shown below:

	C
At 1 Jan 20X5 – Fair value (inclusive of premium)	10,811,100
Accrued income (reflected in fair value)	250,000
Amortisation of premium	(33,778)
Fair value adjustment – gain	100,388
At 31 Mar 20X5 – Fair value	11,127,710

	C
Recognised in profit or loss – income	216,222
Recognised in other comprehensive income – gain	100,388
Total change in fair value	316,610

9.35 As stated in paragraph 9.31 above, dividends on an available-for-sale equity instrument are recognised in profit or loss when the entity's right to receive payment is established. The right to receive payment is established when the equity instrument's issuer declares a dividend or in the case of quoted equity securities, at the ex-dividend date. When a share goes ex-dividend shortly before the dividend payment is actually due, the price will drop (other things being equal) by the amount of the dividend. Therefore, depending upon the ex-dividend date (when the dividend income is recognised) and the payment date (when the receivable is settled), the realisation of part of the fair value through dividend payment will affect both profit or loss and equity as illustrated below.

Example – Dividend on available-for-sale investments

An entity acquires 1,000 quoted equity shares in another entity for C20,000. The shares are classified as available-for-sale. Just prior to the entity's year end of 31 December 20X5, the security goes ex-dividend following declaration of a dividend of C1.50 per share. At 31 December 20X5, the quoted ex-dividend price of the shares amounts to C21 per share. The entity receives payment of the dividend on 6 January 20X6.

At 31 December 20X5, the entity will recognise the dividend income in profit or loss and the change in the fair value of the shares in other comprehensive income as noted below:

	Dr C	Cr C
Dividend receivable	1,500	
Profit or loss – dividend income – 1,000 @ 1.50		1,500
Available-for-sale financial asset	1,000	
Other comprehensive income – 1,000 @ (21-20)		1,000

The shares' quoted price prior to the dividend adjustment would have been C22.50 giving a total fair value change of C2,500. However, as part of this change (C1,500) is realised as a result of the dividend income recognised in profit or loss; there is an equal and offsetting change in other comprehensive income.

Designation as hedged items

9.36 Financial assets that are designated as hedged items are subject to measurement under IAS 39's hedging accounting requirements. [IAS 39 para 46]. These special accounting rules generally override the normal accounting rules for financial assets. Hedge accounting is covered in chapter 10.

Reclassifications between categories

9.37 The amendment to IAS 39 issued in October 2008 allows reclassification of certain financial assets after initial recognition out of a category measured at fair value (that is, held-for-trading or available-for-sale) and into another category under limited circumstances (see chapter 6 and IAS 39 para 50 A-E). The tainting rules applicable to the held-to-maturity category remain unchanged.

9.37.1   When a financial asset is reclassified, the fair value at the date of reclassification becomes its new cost or amortised cost. [IAS 39 para 50 C and F]. Any gains or losses already recognised in profit or loss are not reversed. The new 'cost' is also used as the basis for assessing impairment in the future.

9.37.2   On reclassification, the effective interest rate is recalculated using the fair value at the date of reclassification. This new effective interest rate will be used to calculate interest income in future periods and considered as the original effective interest rate when measuring impairment.

9.37.3   For a financial asset denominated in a foreign currency that is reclassified to loans and receivables, the 'amortised cost' of the financial asset at the date of reclassification is calculated in the foreign currency and then translated at the spot rate to the functional currency at the date of reclassification. [IAS 39 para IG E3.4].

9.37.4   When an available-for-sale financial asset with fixed maturity is reclassified as held-to-maturity investment or loans and receivables, the fair value of the financial asset on that date becomes its new amortised cost. Any previous gain or loss on that asset that has been recognised directly in other comprehensive income is amortised to profit and loss over the investment's remaining life using the effective interest method. Any difference between the new amortised cost and the amount payable on maturity is also amortised in a similar manner, akin to the amortisation of a premium or a discount. If the financial asset is subsequently impaired, any gain or loss that has been recognised directly in other comprehensive income is recognised in profit or loss. [IAS 39 para 54(a)]. Essentially, interest income should not change as a result of reclassification and should continue to be based on the original amortisation schedule (that is, prior to reclassification). This is because the combination of the amortisation of the difference between the new amortised cost on the reclassified financial asset and the amount payable on maturity and the gain or loss to be amortised from other comprehensive income will result in the same net effective interest rate as originally determined prior to reclassification.

Example – Available-for-sale debt security reclassified to loans and receivables

On 1 January 20X9, an entity reclassifies a C9m bond from available-for-sale to loans and receivables. On the date of the reclassification, the bond's amortised cost is C9,198,571 and the original effective interest rate is 8.75%. The bond's fair value is C9,488,165, which becomes its new amortised cost. The excess of the new carrying amount over the amount receivable at maturity on 31 December 2X10 (that is C488,165) is amortised to profit or loss over the remaining term to give a new effective rate of 7% including interest coupons receivable, as shown below.

In addition, the cumulative gain of C289,594 in other comprehensive income as at 31 December 20X8 (that is, the difference between the fair value of C9,488,165 and the amortised cost of C9,198,571) is also amortised to profit or loss during the remaining two years to maturity. The effect in profit or loss is the same as if the bond was classified as loans and receivables, as illustrated below:

	Cash received C	Interest income @ 7% C	New amortised co C
1 Jan 20X9			9,488,165
31 Dec 20X9	900,000	664,172	9,252,337
31 Dec 2 X10	9,900,000	647,663	—
		1,311,835	
Amortisation of gain in other comprehensive income in 20X9 and 2X10		289,594	
Total amount recognised in profit or loss		1,601,429	

If the C9m bonds had not been reclassified as available-for-sale, the total amount recognised in profit or loss would have been as follows:

	Cash received C	Interest income @ 8.75% C	Amortised cost C
31 Dec 20X8			9,198,571
31 Dec 20X9	900,000	804,876	9,103,447
31 Dec 20X10	9,900,000	796,553	
Total income from date of reclassification to maturity		1,601,429	

9.38 When a held-to-maturity investment is reclassified as available-for-sale, it should be remeasured at fair value at the date of reclassification. The difference between its previous carrying amount and fair value should be recognised in other comprehensive income. [IAS 39 paras 51, 52].

Example – Held-to-maturity investment reclassified as available-for-sale financial asset

On 1 January 20X0, an entity purchases 10% C10m 10 year bonds with interest payable annually on 31 December each year. The bond's purchase price is C10,811,100. This results in a bond premium of C811,100 and an effective interest rate of 8.75%. The bonds were classified by the entity as held-to-maturity.

On 31 December 20X5, when the bonds amortised cost and fair value amounted to C10,407,192 and C10,749,395 respectively, the entity sells C1m bonds and realises a gain as shown below:

	C
Fair value of C1m bond (10% of C10,749,395)	1,074,940
Carrying value of C1m bond (10% of C10,407,192)	1,040,719
Profit on disposal recognised in profit or loss	34,221

Since the entity has sold more than an insignificant amount of its held-to-maturity investments, the portfolio is tainted. As a result, the entity has to reclassify the remaining C9m bonds as available-for-sale assets. The difference between the carrying value of C9m bonds and their fair value is recognised in other comprehensive income as shown below:

	C
Fair value of C9m bond (90% of C10,749,395)	9,674,455
Carrying value of C9m bonds (90% of C10,407,192)	9,366,473
Gain on reclassification recognised in other comprehensive income	307,982

Even though the remaining investment is classified as available-for-sale, the entity will continue to recognise the interest income and the amortisation of the premium using the effective interest method in profit or loss and fair value changes in other comprehensive income, as illustrated in the example in paragraph 9.34. After the tainting period is over, the entity may reinstate the bonds again to held-to-maturity. This will happen after 31 December 20X7 (two full financial years following the partial disposal).

[The next paragraph is 9.40.]

Settlement date accounting for regular way transactions

9.40 As stated in paragraph 9.20 above, when an entity uses settlement date accounting for an asset that is subsequently measured at cost or amortised cost, the asset is recognised initially at its fair value at trade date. Any subsequent change in fair value between trade date and settlement date is not recognised (other than impairment losses). For assets that are subsequently measured at fair value, any change in fair value between trade date and settlement date is recognised:

- In profit or loss for assets classified as at FVTPL.
- In other comprehensive income for assets classified as available-for-sale.

9.41 When assets measured at fair value are sold on a regular way basis, the change in fair value between trade date (the date the entity enters into the sales contract) and settlement date (the date proceeds are received) is not recorded because the seller's right to changes in fair value ceases on the trade date (see further chapter 6).

Negative fair values

9.42 The standard clarifies that if a financial instrument that was previously recognised as a financial asset is measured at fair value and its fair value falls below zero, it becomes a financial liability that should be measured as considered below. [IAS 39 para AG 66].

Subsequent measurement of financial liabilities

9.43 After initial recognition, an entity should measure financial liabilities, other than those described in paragraphs 9.45 to 9.50 below, at amortised cost using the effective interest method as discussed from paragraph 9.51 below. [IAS 39 para 47].

9.44 Where a financial liability is carried at amortised cost, a gain or loss is recognised in profit or loss when the financial liability is derecognised or through the amortisation process. [IAS 39 para 56].

Financial liabilities at fair value through profit or loss

9.45 After initial recognition, financial liabilities falling within this category (including liabilities held-for-trading and derivative liabilities not designated as hedging instruments) are measured at fair value. However, a derivative liability that is linked to and must be settled by delivery of an unquoted equity instrument whose fair value cannot be reliably measured should be measured at cost. [IAS 39 para 47(a)].

9.46 A change in a financial liability's fair value in this category that is not part of a hedging relationship should be recognised in the profit or loss for the period. [IAS 39 para 55]. The standard's requirements for determining the fair value of instruments that fall to be measured on this basis are considered from paragraph 9.72 below.

Financial liabilities arising on transfers of financial assets

9.47 Certain financial liabilities may arise when a transfer of a financial asset does not qualify for derecognition, or is accounted for using the continuing involvement approach. For example, a sale of an asset that is accompanied by the seller giving a guarantee of the asset's future worth may, depending on the substance, give rise to the asset's derecognition and recognition of a liability in respect of the guarantee or it may result in the asset not being derecognised and the proceeds being shown as a liability. Special rules apply for the measurement of the transferred asset and the associated liability so that these are measured on a basis that reflects the rights and obligations that the entity has retained. [IAS 39 paras 29, 31, 47(b)]. See further chapter 8.

Financial guarantee contracts

9.48 Financial guarantee contracts are defined in chapter 3. Financial guarantee contracts that are accounted for as financial liabilities under IAS 39 by the issuer are initially recognised at fair value. If the financial guarantee contract was issued to an unrelated party in a stand-alone arm's length transaction, its fair value at inception would likely be to equal the premium received, unless there was evidence to the contrary. [IAS 39 para AG4(a)].

9.48.1 In some circumstances, an issuer expects to receive recurring future premiums from an issued financial guarantee contract (for example, it issues a five year guarantee with annual premiums due at the start of each year). In that situation, an issue arises as to whether the issuer should recognise a receivable for the discounted value of the expected future premiums or should it recognise only the initial cash received (if any). As stated above, IAS 39 requires the financial guarantee contract to be initially recorded at fair value; that is likely to equal the premium received. By analogy with derivative contracts the fair value will take into account any future cash flows on the instrument including those relating to premiums receivable.

9.48.2 IAS 39 does not explicitly prohibit the recognition of a separate receivable for future premiums not yet due. This is evidenced by the basis for conclusions, paragraph BC 23D, which states that the IAS 39 requirement for initial recognition at fair value is consistent with US GAAP as represented by FIN 45 (FIN 45 requires recognition of a liability for the guarantee and a separate receivable for future premiums). Accordingly, entities are permitted to recognise a separate receivable. The entity should select a presentation policy and apply it consistently to all issued financial guarantee contracts.

9.48.3 Subsequent to initial recognition, an issuer accounts for financial guarantee contracts at the higher of:

■ the amount determined in accordance with IAS 37, 'Provisions, contingent liabilities and contingent assets'; and

■ the amount initially recognised (fair value) less, when appropriate, cumulative amortisation of the initial amount recognised in accordance with IAS 18, 'Revenue'.

[IAS 39 para 47(c)].

9.48.4 However, the above requirements do not apply:

■ if the financial guarantee contract was designated at fair value through profit or loss at inception. A contract designated at inception as at fair value through profit or loss is measured at fair value subsequently; or

■ if the financial guarantee contract was entered into or retained on transferring financial assets or financial liabilities to another party and prevented derecognition of the financial asset or resulted in continuing involvement (see chapter 8).

[IAS 39 para 47(a)(b), AG 4].

9.48.5   From the perspective of the holder who is also the lender the contract is outside IAS 39's scope. The holder's accounting treatment depends on whether it has purchased the guarantee contract for new debt instruments or for pre-existing debt instruments. In the first case the holder/lender, should amortise the cost of the guarantee using the effective interest rate method, unless the debt instrument is measured at fair value through profit and loss. In the second case the cost is recognised as a pre-payment asset and amortised over the shorter of the life of the guarantee and the expected life of the guaranteed debt instruments. The asset is tested for impairment under IAS 36 in circumstances where the guarantee is not invoked. The holder recognises the amortisation and impairment charges as a reduction of interest.

Intra-group financial guarantee contracts

9.48.6   As stated in chapter 3, intra-group financial guarantee contracts are not exempted from IAS 39's requirements and, on a stand-alone basis, will have to be measured in accordance with the standard. On a consolidation basis, the financial guarantee is not recognised as a separate contract, but is part of the group's liability to a third party (for example, a guarantee given by the parent to a subsidiary's bankers in the event the subsidiary fails to repay a loan to the bank when due). In the individual financial statements, the financial guarantee is recognised initially at fair value in accordance with IAS 39 (unless IFRS 4 applies).

9.48.7   Establishing such a fair value may be difficult if the financial guarantee contracts between related parties were not negotiated at arm's length and there are no comparable observable transactions with third parties. Given that intra-group guarantees are unlikely to be negotiated in a 'stand-alone arm's length transaction', fair value would have to be estimated. Paragraph 9.103.1 provides guidance on how to measure the fair value of intra-group financial guarantees.

9.48.8   As the fair value of an intra-group guarantee is unlikely to be equal to the fee charged, if any, the issuer would need to determine whether any difference should be treated as an expense or a capital contribution *via* an increase in investments in the subsidiary. This is an accounting policy choice. The method used should reflect the transaction's economic substance, be applied consistently to all similar transactions and be clearly disclosed in the financial statements. While each entity within a group can choose its own accounting policies, those policies must be aligned on consolidation.

Commitments to provide off-market loans

9.49   An entity may enter into a commitment to provide a loan at a below-market rate. After initial recognition at fair value, such a commitment is subsequently measured in the same way as a financial guarantee contract stated above. [IAS 39 para 47(d)].

Designation as hedged items

9.50   Financial liabilities that are designated as hedged items are subject to measurement under IAS 39's hedging accounting requirements. [IAS 39 para 47]. These special accounting rules generally override the normal accounting rules for financial liabilities. Hedge accounting is covered in chapter 10.

Amortised cost and the effective interest method

General

9.51   The amortised cost of a financial asset or financial liability is defined as the amount at which the financial asset or financial liability is measured at initial recognition minus principal repayments, plus or minus the cumulative amortisation using the 'effective interest method' of any difference between that initial amount and the amount payable at maturity and minus any reduction (directly or through the use of an allowance account) for impairment or uncollectibility. [IAS 39 para 9].

9.52   The effective interest method is a method of calculating the amortised cost of a financial asset or a financial liability (or group of financial assets or financial liabilities) and of allocating the interest income or interest expense over the relevant period. The method's principal features are as follows:

■   The effective interest rate is the rate that exactly discounts estimated future cash payments or receipts through the financial instrument's *expected life* or, when appropriate, a shorter period, to the net carrying amount of the financial asset or financial liability (see para 9.60 below). The effective interest rate is sometimes termed the level yield to maturity or to the next repricing date and is the internal rate of return of the financial asset or liability for that period. The internal rate of return can be calculated using a financial calculator, or the IRR function in a spreadsheet.

■   When calculating the effective interest rate, an entity should estimate cash flows considering all the financial instrument's contractual terms (for example, pre-payment, call and similar options), but should not consider future credit losses.

■   The calculation should include all fees and points paid or received between parties to the contract that are an integral part of the effective interest rate, transaction costs, and all other premiums or discounts.

[IAS 39 para 9].

9.53   The effective interest rate method is grounded in historical transaction values, because its determination is based on the initial carrying amount of the financial asset or liability. Therefore, once determined it is not recalculated to reflect fair value changes in financial assets, for example, interest bearing available-for-sale assets due to changes in market interest rates. The effective interest method produces a periodic interest income or expense equal to a constant percentage of the carrying value of the financial asset or liability as illustrated in the example given in paragraph 9.62.

Estimation of cash flows

9.54   As noted in paragraph 9.52 above, the effective interest method uses a set of *estimated* future cash flows through the expected life of the financial instrument using all the financial instrument's contractual terms, rather than *contractual* cash flows. However, the financial instrument's expected life cannot exceed its contracted life. This applies not only to individual financial instruments, but to groups of financial instruments as well to achieve consistency of application. As the cash flows are often outlined in a contract or linked in some other way to the financial asset or financial liability in question, there is a presumption that the future cash flows can be reliably estimated for most financial assets and financial liabilities, in particular for a group of similar financial assets and similar financial liabilities. [IAS 39 para 9]. For example, for a portfolio of pre-payable mortgage loans, financial institutions often estimate pre-payment patterns based on historical data and build the cash flows arising on early settlement (including any pre-payment penalty) into the effective interest rate calculation.

9.55   However, in some rare cases it might not be possible to estimate reliably the cash flows of a financial instrument (or group of financial instruments). In those rare cases, the entity should use the contractual cash flows over the full contractual term of the financial instrument (or group of financial instruments). [IAS 39 para 9].

9.56   The standard requires that in estimating the future cash flows all the instrument's contractual terms, including pre-payment, call and similar options should be considered. [IAS 39 para 9]. Such pre-payment, call and put options, which are often embedded in the debt instruments, are derivatives. Therefore, as explained, in chapter 5, the entity must first determine whether such options need to be separately accounted for as embedded derivatives. Separate accounting for the embedded derivative will not be necessary if the option's exercise price is approximately equal to the instrument's amortised cost on each exercise date, or the exercise price reimburses the lender for an amount up to the approximate present value of the lost interest for the remaining term of the host contract, because in that situation the embedded derivative is regarded as closely related to the debt host. [IAS 39 para AG 30(g)].

9.57   Where a pre-payment, call or put option falls to be separately accounted for, its impact on estimating the future cash flows for the purposes of determining the effective interest rate should be ignored. Although this is not explained in the standard, it is rather obvious as to do otherwise would result in double counting the effects of the embedded derivative in profit or loss – first through the option's fair value movement and, secondly, through its effect on the effective interest rate. In practice, this means that if the option is regarded as closely related and not separately accounted for, the entity, in determining the instrument's expected life, needs to assess whether the option is likely to be exercised in estimating the future cash flows at inception. Furthermore, this assessment should continue in subsequent periods until the debt instrument is settled, because the likelihood of the option being exercised will affect the timing and amount of the future cash flows and will have an immediate impact in profit or loss. On the other hand, if the option is accounted for as a separate derivative, such considerations are not necessary as the likelihood of the option being exercised will be reflected in its fair value. In that situation, the effective interest rate is based on the instrument's contractual term. See further paragraph 9.65 below.

9.58 The standard also makes it clear that expected or future credit losses (defaults) should not be included in estimates of cash flows, because this would be a departure from the incurred loss model for impairment recognition. However, in some cases, financial assets are acquired at a deep discount that reflects incurred losses (for example, purchase of impaired debt). As such losses are already reflected in the price, they should be included in the estimated cash flows when computing the effective interest rate. [IAS 39 para AG 5]. Accordingly, the effective interest rate of the acquired distressed loan would be the discount rate that equates the present value of the expected cash flows (this would be less than the contractual cash flows specified in the loan agreement because of incurred credit losses) with the purchase price of the loan. The alternative of not including such credit losses in the calculation of the effective interest rate means that the entity would recognise a higher interest income than that inherent in the price paid.

Transaction costs and fees

9.59 Transaction costs and fees are discussed from paragraph 9.11 above. To the extent that they are integral to generating an involvement with a financial instrument, such costs and fees are included in the financial instrument's initial measurement. For financial instruments that are carried at amortised cost, such as held-to-maturity investments, loans and receivables, and financial liabilities that are not at fair value through profit or loss, transaction costs and fees are, therefore, included in calculating amortised cost using the effective interest method. This means that, in effect, they are amortised through profit or loss over the instrument's life (see para 9.52 above).

Amortisation period

9.60 Consistent with the estimated cash flow approach outlined from paragraph 9.54 above, the standard requires fees, points paid or received, transaction costs and other premiums or discount that are integral to the effective interest rate to be amortised over the instrument's expected life or, when applicable, a shorter period. A shorter period is used when the variable (for example, interest rates) to which the fee, transaction costs, discount or premium relates is repriced to market rates before the instrument's expected maturity. In such a case, the appropriate amortisation period is the period to the next such repricing date. [IAS 39 AG6]. The application of this requirement in the context of a floating rate instrument is considered in paragraph 9.66 below.

9.61 There is a presumption that the expected life of a financial instrument (or group of similar financial instruments) can be estimated reliably. However, in those rare cases when it is not possible to estimate reliably the expected life, the entity should use the full contractual term of the financial instrument (or group of financial instruments) as the amortisation period. [IAS 39 para 9]. The expected life cannot exceed the contractual term.

Illustrations of the effective interest rate method of amortisation

Fixed interest instruments

9.62 The examples that follow illustrate the application of the effective interest rate method of amortisation to fixed interest loans. In example 1, the fixed rate loan asset is repayable only at maturity (a similar example is given in IAS 39 para IG B26). In example 2, the fixed rate loan asset is repayable in equal annual instalments. In example 3, the loan's pre-determined rate of interest increases over the instrument's term ('stepped interest').

Example 1 – Fixed interest loan asset repayable at maturity

On 1 January 20X5, entity A originates a 10 year 7% C1m loan. The loan carries an annual interest rate of 7% payable at the end of each year and is repayable at par at the end of year 10. Entity A charges a 1.25% (C12,500) non-refundable loan origination fee to the borrower and also incurs C25,000 in direct loan origination costs.

The contract specifies that the borrower has an option to pre-pay the instrument and that no penalty will be charged for pre-payment. At inception, the entity expects the borrower not to pre-pay.

The initial carrying amount of the loan asset is calculated as follows:

	C
Loan principal	1,000,000
Origination fees charged to borrower	(12,500)
Origination costs incurred by lender	25,000
Carrying amount of loan	1,012,500

As explained in paragraph 9.56 above, it is first necessary to determine whether the pre-payment option should be separately accounted for. In this example, as the loan's principal amount is likely to be approximately equal to the loan's amortised cost at each exercise date, the borrower's option to pre-pay is closely related and not separately accounted for.

As the entity expects the borrower not to pre-pay, the amortisation period is equal to the instrument's full term. In calculating the effective interest rate that will apply over the term of the loan at a constant rate on the carrying amount, the discount rate necessary to equate 10 annual payments of C70,000 and a final payment at maturity of C1 million to the initial carrying amount of C1,012,500 is approximately 6.823%.

The carrying amount of the loan over the period to maturity will, therefore, be as follows:

	Cash in flows (coupon)	Interest income @ 6.823%	Amortisation of net fees	Carrying amount
	C	C	C	C
1 Jan 20X5				1,012,500
31 Dec 20X5	70,000	69,083	917	1,011,588
31 Dec 20X6	70,000	69,025	975	1,010,613
31 Dec 20X7	70,000	68,959	1,041	1,009,572
31 Dec 20X8	70,000	68,888	1,112	1,008,460
31 Dec 20X9	70,000	68,812	1,188	1,007,272
31 Dec 20Y0	70,000	68,731	1,269	1,006,003
31 Dec 20Y1	70,000	68,644	1,356	1,004,647
31 Dec 20Y2	70,000	68,552	1,448	1,003,199
31 Dec 20Y3	70,000	68,453	1,547	1,001,652
31 Dec 20Y4	70,000	68,348	1,652	1,000,000
	700,000	687,500	12,500	
31 Dec 20Y4	Repayment of principal			(1,000,000)
31 Dec 20Y4	Carrying value of loan			Nil

As can be seen from the above, the effective interest income for the period is calculated by applying the effective interest rate of 6.823% to the loan's amortised cost at the end of the previous reporting period. The annual interest income decreases each year to reflect the decrease in the asset's carrying value as the initial net fee is amortised. Thus the difference between the calculated effective income for a given reporting period and the loan's coupon is the amortisation of the net fees during that reporting period. The loan's amortised cost at the end of the previous period plus amortisation in the current reporting period gives the loan's amortised cost at the end of the current period. By maturity date, the net fees received are fully amortised and the loan's carrying amount is equal to the face amount, which is then repaid in full.

Example 2 – Fixed interest loan asset repayable in equal annual instalments

On 1 January 20X5, entity A originates a 10 year 7% C1 million loan. The loan is repaid in equal annual payments of C142,378 through to maturity date at 31 December 20Y4. Entity A charges a 1.25% (C12,500) non-refundable loan origination fee to the borrower and also incurs C25,000 in direct loan origination costs.

The contract specifies that the borrower has an option to pre-pay the instrument and that no penalty will be charged for pre-payment. At inception, the entity expects the borrower not to pre-pay.

The initial carrying amount of the loan is calculated as follows:

	C
Loan principal	1,000,000
Origination fees charged to borrower	(12,500)
Origination costs incurred by lender	25,000
Carrying amount of loan	1,012,500

As in the previous example, the pre-payment option will not be separately accounted for. In calculating the effective interest rate that will apply over the term of the loan at a constant rate on the carrying amount, the discount rate necessary to equate 10 annual payments of C142,378 to the initial carrying amount of C1,012,500 is approximately 6.7322%. The carrying amount of the loan over the period to maturity will, therefore, be as follows:

	Cash in flows	Interest Income @ 6.7322%	Carrying amount
	C	C	C
1 Jan 20X5			1,012,500
31 Dec 20X5	142,378	68,164	916,958
31 Dec 20X6	142,378	61,732	842,716
31 Dec 20X7	142,378	56,733	762,629
31 Dec 20X8	142,378	51,342	676,335
31 Dec 20X9	142,378	45,532	583,435
31 Dec 20Y0	142,378	39,278	482,260
31 Dec 20Y1	142,378	32,467	373,640
31 Dec 20Y2	142,378	25,154	257,417
31 Dec 20Y3	142,378	17,330	133,059
31 Dec 20Y4	142,378	8,958	–
	1,423,780	411,280	

Example 3 – Fixed interest loan asset with interest step-up

On 1 January 20X5, entity A originates a 5 year debt instrument for C1million loan that is repayable at maturity. The contract provides for 5% interest in year 1 that increases by 2% in each of the following 4 years. Entity A also receives C25,000 in loan origination fees.

The loan's initial carrying amount is calculated as follows:

	C
Loan principal	1,000,000
Origination fees charged to borrower	(25,000)
Carrying amount of loan	975,000

In calculating the effective interest rate that will apply over the term of the loan at a constant rate on the carrying amount, the discount rate necessary to equate 5 annual step-up payments and a final payment at maturity of C1 million to the initial carrying amount of C925,000 is approximately 9.2934 %.

	Interest income @ 9.2934%	Cash in flows (coupon)	Carrying amount
	C	C	C
1 Jan 20X5			975,000
31 Dec 20X5	90,610	50,000	1,015,610
31 Dec 20X6	94,385	70,000	1,039,995
31 Dec 20X7	96,651	90,000	1,046,646
31 Dec 20X8	97,268	110,000	1,033,914
31 Dec 20X9	96,086	130,000	1,000,000
	475,000	450,000	

If the borrower were to repay the entire loan of C1 million early, say in 20X9, when the loan asset's carrying value is C1,033,914, the excess amount of C33,914 would have to be recognised in profit or loss. This effectively represents the excess income recognised in earlier periods that is now written back as shown below:

	C
Total income recognised to 31 Dec 20X8	378,914
Amortisation of fees	(25,000)
Cash received to 31 Dec 20X8	(320,000)
Excess income recognised prior to pre-payment by borrower in 20X9	33,914

Changes in estimated cash flows

9.63   As explained above, the cash flows that are discounted to arrive at the effective interest rate are estimated cash flows that are expected to occur over the instrument's expected life. However, in practice, actual cash flows rarely occur in line with expectations. There is usually variation in the amount, timing or both. Differences from the original estimates present a problem for the effective interest rate. If the variation is ignored, either the asset or liability will amortise before all of the cash flows occur, or a balance may remain after the last cash flow.

9.63.1   The standard, therefore, requires an entity to adjust the carrying amount of the financial asset or financial liability (or group of financial instruments) to reflect actual and revised estimated cash flows whenever it revises its cash flow estimates. The entity recalculates the carrying amount by computing the present value of estimated future cash flows at the financial instrument's original effective interest rate, or, when applicable, the revised effective interest calculated in accordance with IAS 39 paragraph 92 (see chapter 10). The adjustment is recognised in profit or loss as income or expense. [IAS 39 para AG 8].

> **Example – Changes in estimates of cash flows**
>
> The facts are the same as in example 1 in paragraph 9.62 above, except that on 1 January 20Y1, entity A revises its estimates of cash flows as it now expects that, because of a significant fall in interest rates during the previous period, the borrower is likely to exercise its option to pre-pay. Accordingly, entity A anticipates that 40% of the loan is likely to be repaid by the borrower in 20Y1, with the remaining 60% progressively at 20% in the following three years to maturity.
>
> The revised cash flows are shown below. In accordance with paragraph 9.64 above, the opening balance at 1 January 20Y1 is adjusted. The adjusted amount is calculated by discounting the amounts the entity expects to receive in 20Y1 and subsequent years using the original effective rate of 6.823%. This results in the adjustment shown below. The adjustment is recognised in profit or loss in 20Y1.
>
> | | | Carrying amount |
> | --- | --- | --- |
> | 1 Jan 20Y1 | Opening amortised carrying amount before revision | 1,006,003 |
> | | Adjustment for changes in estimate – profit or loss | 2,563 |
> | 1 Jan 20Y1 | Adjusted amortised carrying amount after revision | 1,003,440 |

	Opening amortised carrying amount	Interest income @ 6.823%	Cash in flows (coupon + repayment of principal)	Closing amortised carrying amount
	C	C	C	C
31 Dec 20Y1	1,003,440	68,465	70,000 + 400,000	601,905
31 Dec 20Y2	601,905	41,068	42,000 + 200,000	400,973
31 Dec 20Y3	400,973	27,358	28,000 + 200,000	200,331
31 Dec 20Y4	200,331	13,669	14,000 + 200,000	–

9.64 For financial assets reclassified in accordance with IAS 39 paragraphs 50B, D and E (see para 9.37.1), any increase in the estimates of expected future cash flows arising from recoveries is reflected by adjusting the effective interest rate prospectively, rather than as an adjustment to the carrying amount. Any increased recoverability of cash receipts is, therefore, spread over the debt instrument's remaining life. [IAS 39 para AG 8]. A decrease in the estimate of expected cash flows would be recorded as an impairment loss.

9.64.1 An increase in estimates of future cash receipts can be determined on a discounted or undiscounted basis. It is an accounting policy choice and should be applied consistently to all reclassified financial assets. Entities may determine whether there is a change in recoverable cash receipts on an undiscounted basis. In such a case, an entity adjusts effective interest rate for any increase in the total amount of undiscounted cash receipts it expects to recover, but not for a change in recoverable amount (that is, discounted) due only to changes in the timing or pattern of cash receipts. Entities may alternatively determine whether there is a change in recoverable cash receipts on a discounted basis. In such circumstances, an entity adjusts the effective interest rate if there is a change in the present value of the estimated cash receipts, thus taking into account timing and pattern of receipt as well as quantum. In both cases, the reference to 'recoverability' indicates that such cash receipts arise from a reversal of credit losses.

Example 1 – Increase in expected future cash flows arising from recoveries

An entity has reclassified a floating-rate financial asset to loans and receivables on 1 July 20X8. The loan was originally purchased for C100. At the date of reclassification, the fair value of the instrument had decreased substantially as a result of a decline in the creditworthiness of the counterparty to C80, and the entity expects to get undiscounted cash receipts of C90. At 31 December, the credit rating of the counterparty has increased (for example, because of government backing) and the entity now expects to get undiscounted cash receipts of C100. The entity should recalculate its effective interest rate prospectively to reflect those new cash receipts. The increase in expected future cash receipts should be reflected in a new effective interest rate.

Example 2 – Decrease in expected future cash flows arising from recoveries

An entity reclassified a fixed rate asset to loans and receivables on 1 July 20X8. The loan was originally purchased for C100. At the date of reclassification, the fair value of the instrument had decreased substantially as a result of a decline in the creditworthiness of the counterparty to C60, and the entity expects to get undiscounted cash receipts of C75. At 31 December 20X8, the recoverability of cash receipts has decreased further to C50. The amendment to paragraph AG 8 requires the effective interest rate to be adjusted only where there are increases in the estimates of future cash receipts. Decreases in estimates of future cash receipts do not result in a downwards adjustment to the effective interest rate. The reduction in estimated cash receipts at 31 December 20X8 will be reflected as an impairment loss in profit or loss measured in accordance with paragraph 63 of IAS 39 (see further para 9.126).

Example 3 – Increase in expected future cash flows arising from recoveries after impairment

An entity reclassified a fixed rate debt instrument to loans and receivables on 1 July 20X8. The loan was originally purchased for C100. At the date of reclassification, the instrument's fair value had decreased substantially as a result of a decline in the counterparty's creditworthiness to C60. At 31 December 20X8, the recoverability of cash receipts has decreased to C50, and the entity records an impairment loss. At 31 March 20X9, the recoverability of cash receipts has increased to C60. The entity should account for the increase in expected cash receipts as a reversal of the impairment recorded at 31 December 20X8 (see para 9.150).

9.64.2　When, subsequent to a reclassification, there is an increase in the cash flows expected to be recovered followed by a decrease in those expected cash flows, but the expected cash flows remain above the amount expected when the asset was reclassified (that is, there is not an impairment subsequent to reclassification), we consider that either of the following approaches would be acceptable:

■　Only increases in cash flows are dealt with by amending the effective interest rate prospectively. Any decreases, even those after an increase and still above the cash flows expected at the reclassification date, are accounted for by means of a cumulative catch up in accordance with IAS 39 paragraph AG8 (using, as the discount rate, the effective interest rate on the reclassified instrument that was determined after the prospective change in the effective interest rate due to an increase in the cash flows).

■　Increases and decreases above the level of cash flows expected on the reclassification date are dealt with prospectively by amending the effective interest rate. Any decreases below the cash flows expected on the reclassification date are accounted for by means of a cumulative catch-up in accordance with IAS 39 paragraph AG8, or as an impairment.

Issuer call option in debt instruments

9.65 The terms of a debt instrument may include an issuer call option, that is, a right of the issuer (but not the investor) to redeem the instrument early and pay a fixed price (generally at a premium over the par value). There may also be other pre-payment features that cause the whole or part of the outstanding principal to be repaid early. Adding call options and/or other pre-payment options should make the instrument less attractive to investors, since it reduces the potential upside on the bond. As market interest rates go down and the bond price increases (reflecting its above market interest rate), the bonds are likely to be called back. As explained in paragraph 9.56 above, such a call option embedded in the debt host is a derivative and would fall to be separately accounted for if its exercise price is not approximately equal to the debt host's amortised cost at each exercise date. Consider the example given below.

Example – Issuer call option in debt instrument

Entity A issues a fixed rate loan for C1m and incurs issue costs of C30,000 resulting in an initial carrying value of C970,000. The loan carries an interest rate of 8% per annum and is repayable at par at the end of year 10. However, under the contract, entity A can call the loan at any time after year 4 by paying a fixed premium of C50,000.

As explained in paragraph 9.56 above, it is first necessary to determine whether the call option is closely related to the host debt instrument. As the fixed premium is required to be paid whenever the call option is exercised after year 4, it may or may not be equal to the present value of any interest lost during the remaining term after exercise of the option. Furthermore, as the call option's exercise price is C1,050,000 (inclusive of the premium), it is unlikely to be approximately equal to the debt instrument's amortised cost in year 4, or at any time subsequently. Therefore, the call option has to be separated from the host debt contract and accounted for separately. This assumes that the expected life of the instrument is the full 10 year term. However, if the expected life is assumed to be 4 years, the 10 year loan with a call option after 4 years is economically equivalent to a 4 year loan with a 6 year extension option. Since there is no concurrent adjustment to the interest rate after 4 years, the term extension option would not be closely related and would need to be accounted for separately (see chapter 5). Therefore, in this case whichever way the loan and option are viewed, the embedded derivative is separated.

Even though the option is out of the money at inception, because the option's exercise price is greater than the debt instrument's carrying value, it has a time value. Suppose the option's fair value is C20,000 at inception. Since the value of a callable bond is equal to the value of a straight bond less the value of the option feature, the accounting entries at inception would be as follows:

	Dr C	Cr C
Embedded option (derivative asset)	20,000	
Cash	970,000	
Debt instrument (host)		990,000

Since the call option will be fair valued and accounted for separately with fair value movements taken to profit or loss, it has no impact on the entity's estimate of future cash flows as explained in paragraph 9.56 above and, accordingly, the amortisation period will be the debt host's period to original maturity. On this basis, the effective interest rate amounts to 8.15%. The amortisation schedule is shown below.

	Opening amortised cost	Interest expense @ 8.15%	Cash payments	Closing amortised cost
	C	C	C	C
Year 1	990,000	80,685	80,000	990,685
Year 2	990,685	80,741	80,000	991,427
Year 3	991,427	80,802	80,000	992,228
Year 4	992,228	80,867	80,000	993,095
Year 5	993,095	80,938	80,000	994,033
Year 6	994,033	81,014	80,000	995,047
Year 7	995,047	81,097	80,000	996,144
Year 8	996,144	81,186	80,000	997,330
Year 9	997,330	81,283	80,000	998,613
Year 10	998,613	81,387	1,080,000	–

The entity would recognise interest expense in profit or loss and the loan's amortised cost in the balance sheet each year in accordance with the above amortisation schedule.

In years 1 and 2, there is no change in interest rate since inception for an instrument of similar maturity and credit rating. The option's fair value (time value) at the end of year 2 is C10,000. The decrease in fair value of C10,000 since inception will be reported in profit and loss and the option will be recorded at C10,000 at the end of year 2.

At the end of year 3, interest rates have fallen and the option's fair value increases to C18,000. The increase in value of C8,000 will be recorded in profit or loss and the option will be recorded at its fair value of C18,000 at the end of year 3.

At the end of year 4, interest rates have fallen further. The option's fair value increases to C30,000 and the company decides to repay the loan at the end of year 4.

The accounting entries to reflect the change in the option's fair value and the loan's early repayment at the end of year 4 are as follows:

	Dr	Cr
	C	C
Embedded Option	12,000	
Profit or loss		12,000
Early repayment of loan		
Debt instrument (host)	993,095	
Embedded option (derivative asset)		30,000
Cash		1,050,000
Loss on derecognition of liability	86,905	

The loss of C86,905 in profit or loss reflects the fact that the fair value of the host contract has gone up in value as interest rates have fallen compared to its carrying value at amortised cost. The fair value of the host contract is actually C1,080,000, which is the option's fair value plus the fair value of the consideration given. The market rate of interest that discounts the interest payments of C80,000 for the next 6 years plus the principal repayment of C1,000,000 at maturity to the fair value of the host is 6.95%, indicating a significant fall in value compared to the instrument's stated interest rate of 8%.

Suppose that instead of an additional premium or penalty payable on early exercise, the option's exercise price is the fair value of the loan at each exercise date. In other words, the exercise price of the pre-payment option is a 'market adjusted value'. A market adjusted value is calculated by discounting the contractual guaranteed amount payable at the end of the specified term to present value using the current market rate that would be offered on a new loan with a similar credit rating and having a maturity period equal to the remaining maturity period of the current loan. As a result, the market adjusted value may be more or less than the loan principal, depending upon market interest rates at each option exercise date.

In that situation, the pre-payment option enables the issuer simply to pay off the loan at fair value at the pre-payment date. Since the holder receives only the market adjusted value, which is equal to the loan's fair value at the date of pre-payment, the pre-payment option (the embedded derivative) has a fair value of zero at all times. Since the pre-payment option, on a stand-alone basis, would not meet the definition of a derivative, it cannot be an embedded derivative, the loan is simply carried at its amortised cost as above, on the assumption that the loan is not going to be pre-paid. If, however, the entity expects to pre-pay the loan, the loan would be amortised over its expected life.

Floating rate instruments

9.66 As will be apparent from the above illustrations, the application of the effective interest rate method is relatively straight forward for fixed interest instruments with fixed terms. Indeed, it appears to be specifically designed for such instruments. However, the analysis is more complicated in the case of a financial instrument that provides for future cash flows that are determinable rather than fixed. Floating rate interest on a financial instrument that is linked to a reference rate such as LIBOR and a principal amount linked to a price index are examples of determinable cash flows. The apparent complication arises because, unlike fixed interest instruments where the effective interest rate generally stays constant over the instrument's term, for floating rate instruments, the periodic re-estimation of determinable cash flows to reflect movements in market rates of interest alters the instrument's effective yield.

9.67 However, although fluctuations in interest rates result in a change in the effective interest rate, there is usually no change in the instrument's fair value. Accordingly, where a floating rate instrument is acquired or issued and the amount at which it is recognised initially is equal to the principal receivable or payable at maturity, re-estimating the future interest payments normally has no significant effect on the carrying amount of the asset or liability. [IAS 39 para AG

7]. This means that the effective yield will always equal the rate under the interest rate formula (for example, LIBOR + 1%) in the instrument. The effect is that the carrying amount remains unchanged by the process, illustrated in paragraph 9.64 above, of re-estimating future cash flows and the effective interest rate. The result is that changes in LIBOR are reflected in the period in which the change occurs.

9.68   However, if a floating rate instrument is issued or acquired at a discount or premium, or the entity receives or incurs loan origination fees or costs, the question arises as to whether the premium or discount and other transaction fees or costs should be amortised over the period to the next repricing date, or over the instrument's expected life. The answer depends upon the nature of the premium or discount and its relationship with market rates.

■   An amortisation period to the next repricing date should be used if the premium or discount on a floating rate instrument reflects interest that has accrued on the instrument since interest was last paid, or changes in market interest rate since the floating interest rate was reset to market rates. This is because the premium or discount relates to the period to the next interest reset date as, at that date, the variable to which the premium or discount relates (that is interest rates) is reset to market rates. In this case, the loan's fair value at the next repricing date will be its par value. This is illustrated in example 1 below.

■   The instrument's expected life should be used as the amortisation period if the premium or discount results from changes in the credit spread over the floating rate specified in the instrument, or other variables that are not reset to market rates. In this situation, the date the interest rate is next reset is not a market-based repricing date of the entire instrument, since the variable rate is not adjusted for changes in the credit spread for the specific issue. This is illustrated in example 2 below.

[IAS 39 para AG 6].

Example 1 – Amortisation of discount over the period to the next repricing date

On 15 May 20X6, an entity acquires a C100 nominal 5 year floating rate bond that pays quarterly interest at 3 month LIBOR + 50 basis points for C99.25. LIBOR at the last reset date on 30 March 20X6 was 4.50% which determines the interest that would be paid on the bond on 30 June 20X6. On the purchase date, LIBOR was 4.75%. The discount of 0.75 (5.25% – 4.50%) is amortised to the next repricing date, that is, 30 June 20X6.

Example 2 – Amortisation of discount over the expected life of the instrument

A 20 year bond is issued at C100, has a principal amount of C100, and requires quarterly interest payments equal to current 3 month LIBOR plus 1% over the instrument's life. The interest rate reflects the market-based rate of return associated with the bond issue at issuance. Subsequent to issuance, the loan's credit quality deteriorates resulting in a rating downgrade. Therefore, the bond trades at a discount. Entity A purchases the bond for 95 and classifies it as held-to-maturity.

In this case, the discount of C5 is amortised to net profit or loss over the period to the bond's maturity and not to the next date interest rate payments are reset, as there is no adjustment to the variable rate as a result of the credit downgrade.

9.69   There is no specific guidance in the standard as to how transaction costs incurred in originating or acquiring a floating rate instrument should be amortised. Since such costs are sunk cost and are not subject to repricing, they will be amortised over the instrument's expected life. Any methodology that provides a reasonable basis of amortisation may be used. For example, entities may find it appropriate to amortise the fees and costs by reference to the interest rate at inception ignoring any subsequent changes in rates or to simply adopt a straight-line amortisation method.

Inflation linked bond

9.69.1   Entities sometimes issue or invest in debt instruments whose payments (principal and interest) are linked to the change in an inflation index of the period. Such an inflation-linked bond needs to be assessed to determine if the inflation-linking mechanism is a closely related embedded derivative that does not need to be recognised and measured separately under IAS 39. There are two possible approaches to account for changes in estimated future cash flows for an inflation-linked bond where the inflation linking mechanism has been found to be closely related.

■   Applying the guidance in IAS 39 paragraph AG7, under which the bond is treated as a floating-rate debt instrument with the inflation link being part of the floating-rate mechanism. The EIR at initial recognition is determined as the rate that sets the estimated future cash flows to be paid on the bond, based on the expected level of the inflation index over the expected term of the bond to equal the fair value of the bond (usually the issue proceeds). However, if in subsequent periods there is a change in inflation expectations, the entity reflects these changes by adjusting both the expected future cash flows on the debt and the EIR. It follows that such changes in the entity's expectations of future inflation result in no adjustment to the carrying amount of the debt and no gain or loss.

■   Applying the guidance in IAS 39 paragraph AG8 under which the EIR is determined at inception in the same way as above. However, if in subsequent periods there is a change in the level of the inflation expectations for the bond's remaining term, the entity revises its estimates of the future cash flows to be paid on the bond accordingly. It recalculates the bond's carrying amount by discounting the revised estimated cash flows using the original EIR. The resulting adjustment to the bond's carrying amount is recognised immediately in the income statement as a gain or loss. The result is that a gain or loss is recognised in the current period for changes in the entity's expectations of the future level of the inflation index.

9035

9.69.2   Given that the standard is not clear as to how the EIR method applies for instruments with variable cash flows, the IFRIC was asked to provide guidance on how to apply the effective interest rate method to a financial instrument whose cash flows are linked to changes in an inflation index. [IFRIC update July 2008]. The IFRIC noted that paragraphs AG6–AG8 of IAS 39 provide the relevant application guidance. Judgement is required to determine whether an instrument is a floating rate instrument within the scope of paragraph AG7 or an instrument within the scope of paragraph AG8. In view of the existing application guidance in IAS 39, the IFRIC decided not to add this issue to its agenda. However, since the application of the effective interest rate method has widespread application in practice, the IFRIC has decided to refer the matter to the IASB.

9.69.3   Until such time as the IASB provides clarification, we believe an entity should make an accounting policy choice as to which method is acceptable and apply this method to all similar instruments. The way in which the above guidance should be applied is illustrated in the example given below.

Example – Inflation-linked bond

On 1 January 20X5, an entity invests in an inflation-linked bond for C100,000. The term of the bond is 5 years. The bond pays a fixed coupon of 5% per annum (real) at the end of each year on principal that is adjusted annually by the applicable year's percentage change in the consumer price index. The principal repayable at the end of year 5 is similarly adjusted for inflation.

Terms of the bond	
Proceeds received on 1 Jan 20X5	100,000
Fixed coupon @ 5% per annum (real interest rate)	5,000
Term	5 years
Principal and real interest adjusted annually for changes in the consumer price index	

Following are data of actual inflation rates and annual expected inflation rates on various dates

Annual expected percentage change in consumer price index						
	1 Jan 20X5	1 Jan 20X6	1 Jan 20X7	1 Jan 20X8	1 Jan 20X9	Actual change
20X5	0.70%					1.20%
20X6	2.60%	1.40%				2.40%
20X7	2.80%	1.90%	1.70%			0%
20X8	2.80%	3.50%	2.10%	1.20%		3.40%
20X9	2.80%	3.50%	2.60%	1.60%	2.50%	2.50%

The expected inflation adjusted interest payments at the end of each year and the principal payment at the end of year 5 are shown below. The expected cash flows at the end of a year are calculated by multiplying the principal of C100,000 by the expected

Measurement of financial assets and liabilities

change in the consumer price index in that year. So at the beginning of 20X5, the principal at the end of 20X5 is expected to be C100,000 × 1.007 = C100,700. As the nominal coupon rate is 5%, the interest expected to be paid for 20X5 would be C5,035 (C100,700@5%). Similarly, at 1 Jan 20X6, the expected inflated adjusted principal at the end of year 20X6 would be C100,000 × 1.012 (the opening amount as adjusted by the actual increase in inflation during 20X5) × 1.014 (expected increase during 20X6) = C102,617 and the expected adjusted interest would be C5,131 (C102,617@5%).

Annual expected interest and principal cash flows						Actual inflation adjusted cash flows	
	1 Jan 20X5	1 Jan 20X6	1 Jan 20X7	1 Jan 20X8	1 Jan 20X9	Interest	Principal
20X5	5,035					5,060	
20X6	5,166	5,131				5,181	
20X7	5,311	5,228	5,270			5,181	
20X8	5,459	5,411	5,380	5,244		5,358	
20X9 – interest	5,612	5,601	5,520	5,328	5,492	5,492	
Principal	112,242	112,014	110,401	106,550	109,831		109,831
20X9	117,854	117,615	115,921	111,878	115,323	26,272	109,831

Note that the principal expected to be paid at the end of 20X9 is adjusted for expected changes in the index since 1 Jan 20X5. For example, the expected principal payable in 20X9 estimated at 1 Jan 20X5 = 100,000 × 1.007 × 1.026 × 1.028 × 1.028 × 1.028 = 112,242.

There are essentially two ways in which the bond could be amortised in accordance with the guidance provided in paragraph AG7 of IAS 39.

The first method views the EIR as a 'floating inflation adjusted rate' – similar to LIBOR. In this method, the finance cost recognised in profit or loss is the actual inflation adjusted interest paid during the year plus the actual increase in principal as adjusted for inflation during the year. So the carrying amount is equal to the inflation adjusted amount at the end of the period. This method is simple and is often used in practice.

Amortisation of bond based on AG7 – Method 1			
	Opening balance	Finance cost	Cash flow	Closing balance
31 Dec 20X5	100,000	6,260	5,060	101,200
31 Dec 20X6	101,200	7,610	5,181	103,629
31 Dec 20X7	103,629	5,181	5,181	103,629
31 Dec 20X8	103,629	8,881	5,358	107,152
31 Dec 20X9	107,152	8,171	115,323	0
		36,103	136,103	

The second method complies strictly with the guidance in paragraph AG7. In this method, the finance cost in each period is based on an adjusted EIR, calculated by discounting the expected cash flows to equal to the carrying amount at the beginning of each period. No further gain or loss arises.

Amortisation of bond based on AG7 – Method 2

	Opening balance	Finance cost @ adjusted EIR (see below)	Cash flow	Closing balance
31 Dec 20X5	100,000	7,408	5,060	102,348
31 Dec 20X6	102,348	7,496	5,181	104,662
31 Dec 20X7	104,662	7,172	5,181	106,653
31 Dec 20X8	106,653	5,235	5,358	106,530
31 Dec 20X9	106,530	8,793	115,323	0
		36,103	136,103	

Calculation of adjusted EIR based on expected cash flows

	EIR %	1 Jan 20X5	31 Dec 20X5	31 Dec 20X6	31 Dec 20X7	31 Dec 20X8	31 Dec 20X9
20X5	7.408	-100,000	5,035	5,166	5,311	5,459	117,854
20X6	7.324		-102,348	5,131	5,228	5,411	117,615
20X7	6.853			-104,662	5,270	5,380	115,921
20X8	4.908				-106,653	5,244	111,878
20X9	8.254					-106,530	115,323

The original effective interest rate at inception is 7.408%

The way in which the bond would be amortised in accordance with the guidance provided in paragraph AG8 of IAS 39 is shown below. As the finance cost in each period is based on the original EIR at inception, the carrying value at the end of each period is adjusted to the present value of the expected cash flows discounted at the original EIR. This gives rise to a further adjustment that is recognised as part of the finance cost in each period.

Amortisation of bond based on AG8

	Opening balance	Finance cost @ 7.408%	Cash flow	Closing balance	AG8 adjustment	Adjusted closing balance (see below)	Total finance cost
31 Dec 20X5	100,000	7,408	5,060	102,348	-297	102,050	7,110
31 Dec 20X6	102,050	7,559	5,181	104,428	-1,305	103,123	6,255
31 Dec 20X7	103,123	7,639	5,181	105,581	-3,720	101,860	3,919
31 Dec 20X8	101,860	7,545	5,358	104,048	3,321	107,369	10,866
31 Dec 20X9	107,369	7,953	115,323	0	0	0	7,953
		136,103					36,103

Present value of expected cash flows based on original discount rate

	31 Dec 20X6	31 Dec 20X7	31 Dec 20X8	31 Dec 20X9	PV @7.408%
31 Dec 20X5	5,131	5,228	5,411	117,615	102,050
31 Dec 20X6		5,270	5,380	115,921	103,123
31 Dec 20X7			5,244	111,878	101,860
31 Dec 20X8				115,323	107,369

Comparison between AG7 and AG8

	AG7 – Method 1		AG7 – Method 2		AG8	
	Finance cost	Loan balance	Finance cost	Loan balance	Finance cost	Loan balance
31 Dec 20X5	6,260	101,200	7,408	102,348	7,110	102,050
31 Dec 20X6	7,610	103,629	7,496	104,662	6,255	103,123
31 Dec 20X7	5,181	103,629	7,172	106,653	3,919	101,860
31 Dec 20X8	8,881	107,152	5,235	106,530	10,866	107,369
	8,171	0	8,793	0	7,953	0
	36,103		36,103		36,103	

The comparisons between the two methods indicate that the finance cost calculated in accordance with AG7 is consistent with the trend in the actual inflation rate.

Perpetual debt instruments

9.70   It is not uncommon for entities to issue debt instruments on terms with no redemption date, but on which interest payments are made, usually at a fixed rate or a variable market based rate (for example, a fixed margin over LIBOR) in perpetuity. At initial recognition, assuming there are no transaction costs, the debt instrument will be recorded at its fair value, which is the amount received. The difference between this initial amount and the maturity amount, which is zero if the interest rate at inception is the market rate for that instrument, will never be amortised, as there is no repayment of principal. This means that at each reporting date the debt instrument will be recorded at its principal amount, which is also its amortised cost. This is because the amortised cost, which is the present value of the stream of future cash payments discounted at the effective interest rate (fixed for fixed rate instruments or variable for floating rate instruments) equals the principal amount in each period. [IAS 39 para IG B24]. If, on the other hand, the entity incurs transaction costs, the debt instrument will be recorded in each reporting period at its initial amount, which is the amount received less transaction costs. The result is that the transaction costs are never amortised, but reflected in the carrying amount indefinitely.

9.71   Sometimes perpetual debt instruments are repackaged in such a way that the principal amount is effectively repaid. One way of achieving this is to pay a high rate of interest for a number of years (the primary period) which then falls to a negligible amount. If the interest were simply charged to profit or loss, the company would bear an artificially high interest expense during the primary period and little or no interest expense thereafter to perpetuity. Such treatment might reflect the form of the loan agreement, but not its substance. From an economic perspective, some or all of the interest payments are repayment of principal as illustrated in the example below. A similar example is included in IAS 39 paragraph IG B25.

Example – Perpetual debt instrument with decreasing interest

An entity issues a perpetual bond for C100,000 on which interest at 14% is paid annually for the first 10 years and thereafter at a nominal rate of 0.125%.

It is clear that at the end of the ten year period, the bond has little or no value. The principal amount is repaid, in effect, over the initial 10 year primary period. Consequently, the interest payments during the primary period represent a payment for interest and repayment of capital. The effective interest rate calculated on the basis of C14,000 for 10 years followed by C125 to perpetuity is 6.84%.

	Opening amortised cost	Interest expense @ 6.84%	Cash payments	Closing amortised cost
	C	C	C	C
Year 1	100,000	6,840	14,000	92,840
Year 2	92,840	6,350	14,000	85,190
Year 3	85,190	5,827	14,000	77,017
Year 4	77,017	5,268	14,000	68,285
Year 5	68,285	4,671	14,000	58,956
Year 6	58,956	4,033	14,000	48,989
Year 7	48,989	3,351	14,000	38,340
Year 8	38,340	2,622	14,000	26,962
Year 9	26,962	1,844	14,000	14,806
Year 10	14,806	1,013	14,000	1,819
		41,819	140,000	

Although the carrying value at the end of year 10 is small, an amount of C100,000 may fall to be repayable should the entity go into liquidation. In practice, however, there will usually be arrangements to enable the entity to repurchase the debt instrument for a nominal amount and, therefore, extinguish any liability on it.

Fair value measurement considerations

General

9.72 The IASB believes that fair value is the most relevant measure for financial instruments and is the only relevant measure for derivative assets and liabilities. As a result, IAS 39 gives entities an option to measure all financial assets and liabilities that meet certain qualifying criteria at fair value. The importance of fair value in the measurement process arises because it is a market-based notion that is unaffected by the history of the asset or liability, the specific entity that holds the asset or the liability and the future use of the asset or the liability. Thus, it represents an unbiased measure that is consistent from year to year, within an entity and between entities. As a result, if an investor knows a financial instrument's fair value and has information about its essential terms and risks, it has all the information it needs to make decisions about that instrument.

9.73 Consistent with other financial reporting standards, IAS 39 defines fair value as *"the amount for which an asset could be exchanged, or a liability settled, between knowledgeable, willing parties in an arm's length transaction"*. [IAS 39 para 9]. The price at which an asset could be exchanged is the price an entity would have received if it had sold the asset. Similarly, the price at which a liability is settled is the price an entity would have paid if it had been relieved of the liability. This implies that fair value is an estimate of the market 'exit' price that is determined by reference to a current hypothetical transaction between willing parties. Willing parties are presumed to be market-place participants representing unrelated buyers and sellers that are knowledgeable, having a common level of understanding about factors relevant to the asset or liability and the transaction and willing and able to transact in the same market(s) having the legal and financial ability to do so.

9.73.1 The IASB issued an exposure draft on fair value measurement in May 2009. The exposure draft does not require additional fair value measurements, but proposes a single source of guidance that explains how to measure fair value. The proposals more closely align IFRS and US GAAP in some areas, such as the application of a single three-level hierarchy to all fair value measurements.

9.74 Underlying the definition of fair value is a presumption that an entity is a going concern without any intention or need to liquidate, to curtail materially the scale of its operations or to undertake a transaction on adverse terms. Fair value is not, therefore, the amount that an entity would receive or pay in a forced transaction, involuntary liquidation or distress sale (see from para 9.77.2). However, fair value does reflect the instrument's credit quality. [IAS 39 para AG69]. This means that when a financial liability is measured at fair value, its credit quality must be reflected in the valuation process (see further para 9.112 below).

9.75 There is a general presumption that fair value can be reliably measured for all financial instruments. Nonetheless, the measurement process can be quite complex and gives rise to numerous issues. It is not surprising, therefore, that IAS 39 provides a significant amount of guidance about how to determine fair values, in particular for financial instruments for which no quoted market prices are available. Therefore, in looking for a reliable measure of fair value, the standard provides a hierarchy for determining an instrument's fair value as shown below:

9.76 As can be seen from the above, the hierarchy gives the highest priority to quoted prices in active markets. Unfortunately, for many of the financial assets for which fair values are required, there may be no active market. In the absence of an active market, fair value is established by using a valuation technique. Indeed, as financial instruments become more complex in nature, the ability to obtain a quoted market price diminishes and the requirement to derive a fair value using valuation techniques increases. Such valuation techniques include the use of recent market transactions in similar instruments between knowledgeable, willing parties in an arm's length transaction. Hence, recent market transactions and valuation techniques are given equal prominence in the hierarchy. However, as with any valuation, judgement will often be necessary. Only as a last resort, is an entity permitted to use cost and this is limited to unquoted equity instruments whose fair value cannot be measured reliably and derivatives that are linked to and must be settled in such instruments.

Quoted prices in an active market

9.77 The existence of published price quotations in an active market *is* the best evidence of fair value and, where available, they *must* be used to measure the financial instrument. The phrase 'quoted in an active market' means that quoted prices are readily and regularly available from an exchange, dealer, broker, industry group, pricing service or regulatory agency and those prices represent actual and regularly occurring market transactions on an arm's length basis. [IAS 39 para AG 71].

9.77.1 Readily available means that the pricing information is currently accessible and regularly available means that transactions occur with sufficient frequency to provide pricing information on an ongoing basis. For example, in an active market, such as the London Stock Exchange, quoted prices that represent actual (observable) transactions that are readily and regularly available.

9.77.2 What is meant in practice by the phrase 'regularly available' is a matter of judgement. An absence of transactions for a short period, or a lower than normal volume of transactions, does not necessarily mean that a market has ceased to be active or that observed transactions are distress sales, nor does it necessarily mean that transactions are motivated other than by normal business considerations. If transactions are occurring frequently enough for an entity to obtain reliable pricing information on an ongoing basis, the market is considered active.

9.77.3   Similar to the above, an imbalance between supply and demand (for example, fewer buyers than sellers) is not always a determinant of a forced transaction. A seller might be under financial pressure to sell but is still able to sell at a market price if there is more than one potential buyer in the market and a reasonable amount of time is available to market the instrument.

9.77.4   Indicators of a forced transaction include the following, as identified in the final report of the IASB's Expert Advisory Panel in October 2008:

- A legal requirement to transact, for example, a regulatory mandate.

- A necessity to dispose of an asset immediately and there is insufficient time to market the asset to be sold.

- The existence of a single potential buyer as a result of the legal or time restrictions imposed.

9.77.5   However, considering the first bullet above, if an entity sells assets to market participants to meet regulatory requirements, the regulator does not establish the transaction price and the entity has a reasonable amount of time to market the assets, the transaction price would still provide evidence of fair value. Similarly, transactions initiated during bankruptcy should not automatically be assumed to be forced. Determining whether a transaction is forced requires a thorough understanding of the facts and circumstances of the transaction.

9.78   In determining whether a market is active, the emphasis is on the level of activity for a particular asset or liability. [IAS 39 para AG 71]. For instance, if the market is not well established and only a small volume of a particular instrument is traded relative to the amount of the instrument in issue or trading is infrequent, quoted prices in those markets will not be suitable for determining fair value. In that situation, the entity will have to move down the hierarchy to determine a suitable fair value.

9.78.1   The IASB Expert Advisory Panel report mentioned above discusses the characteristics of an inactive market. It includes a significant decline in the volume and level of trading activity; significant variation in available prices over time or among market participants; and a lack of current prices. However, these factors alone do not necessarily mean that a market is no longer active.

9.79   It is not necessary for quoted prices to be obtained from regulated markets. Prices can be obtained from other sources although the available information may vary. For example, some industry groups or pricing services publish price information about certain instruments, while little or no information may be available about prices of other instruments. An entity is not generally required to perform an exhaustive search for price information, but should consider any information that is publicly available, or that can be obtained reasonably from brokers, industry groups, publications of regulatory agencies or similar sources, such as journals and web sites, It should be noted that these prices may be indicative prices only. It should not be assumed that these prices reflect the price in an active market (see para 9.102).

9.80   The objective of determining fair value for a financial instrument that is traded in an active market is to arrive at the price at which a transaction would occur at the balance sheet date in that instrument (that is, without modifying or repackaging the instrument) in the *most advantageous* active market to which the entity has immediate access. [IAS 39 para AG 71]. This means that if an entity has immediate access to different markets having different prices for essentially the same financial asset, the most advantageous market is the one with the price that maximizes the net amount that would be received in a current transaction for the financial asset. For example, if a trader that originates a derivative instrument with an entity in an active 'retail' market takes out an offsetting derivative in a more advantageously priced active dealers' 'wholesale' market, the trader records the derivative with the entity at the higher value and recognises a profit on initial recognition. However, the price in the more advantageous dealers' market should be adjusted for any differences in counterparty credit risk between the derivative instrument with the entity and that with the dealers' market. [IAS 39 para BC98]. It follows that price can be taken from the most favourable market readily available to the entity, even if that was not the market in which the transaction actually occurred.

9.81   For the purpose of determining the most advantageous market, costs to transact in the respective markets should be considered. If such costs are not taken into account, the entity will be unable to determine which market offers the most advantageous price. However, as explained in paragraph 9.17 above, the price used to estimate fair value, that is, the price in the most advantageous market, should not be adjusted for transaction costs that may be incurred on sale or disposals.

Example – Quoted prices in different markets

An entity holds financial assets that are traded in markets A and B. The entity has access to both markets. The price in market A is C25 and costs to transact in that market are C5 (the net amount that would be received for the asset in that market is C20). The price in market B is C35 and costs to transact in that market are C20 (the net amount that would be received for the asset in that market is C15). In that case, the most advantageous market is market A. The estimate of fair value would be determined using the price in market A (C25). That price would not be adjusted for costs to transact in that market.

Bid and ask prices

9.82   As stated in a paragraph 9.77 above, financial instruments may be traded on exchanges, in dealer markets, and in brokered transactions. Closing prices of financial instruments such as stocks, bonds, options, warrants etc, are readily and regularly available on exchange markets and these are used to value instruments identical to those being traded. However, many securities and financial instruments that are not traded on the organised exchanges are traded in dealer markets, such as AIM and NASDAQ. In such markets, dealers stand ready to trade (either buy or sell for their own account), thereby providing liquidity by using their capital to hold an inventory of the securities for which they make a market. Typically, bid and ask prices are more readily and regularly available than closing prices. Similarly, in a brokered market, brokers attempt to match buyers with sellers but do not stand ready to trade for their own account. The broker knows the prices bid and asked by the respective parties, but each party is typically unaware of another party's price requirements. Prices of completed transactions are sometimes available. Brokered markets include electronic communication networks (ECNs), in which buy and sell orders are matched.

9.83   In an active dealer market where bid and ask prices are more readily and regularly available than closing prices, fair value should be determined using these prices. However, the price that will normally be appropriate for valuation purposes will depend on whether the relevant financial instrument being valued is an asset or a liability, and whether it is already held or to be acquired. The standard specifies the appropriate quoted market prices that should be used as indicated in the table below. [IAS 39 para AG72].

	Instrument held	Instrument to be acquired
Financial asset	Bid	Ask
Financial liability	Ask	Bid

The bid price represents the price a dealer is willing to pay for the instrument and, therefore, the price the entity would receive if it sold the asset. The ask price represents the amount at which a dealer is willing to sell the instrument and, therefore, the price that the entity would have to pay to acquire the asset. The ask price (also known as the 'offer' price) will almost always be higher than the bid price. The difference represents the dealer's profit, which is called the 'spread'. The standard clarifies that the terms 'bid price' and 'asking (offer) price' should be used in the context of quoted market prices and the 'bid-ask' spread should be interpreted as including only transaction costs. [IAS 39 para AG70].

Example 1 – Treatment of bid-ask spread on initial recognition

An entity purchases an equity financial asset that it classifies as equity available-for-sale, paying the ask (offer) price of C102 and a brokerage commission of C3. At the balance sheet date, the entity uses the bid price to re-measure the financial asset and to recognise changes in fair value in other comprehensive income.

The following data is relevant:

	Acquisition	Balance sheet date
Reference price		
Bid price	C100	C110
Ask or offer price	C102	C113

Financial assets classified as available-for-sale should be initially recognised at fair value, plus transaction costs paid to acquire the asset.

As stated above, the ask price represents the amount at which a dealer is willing to sell and, therefore, the price that the entity would have to pay to acquire the asset. The difference between the bid price that represents the asset's fair value and the ask price (the bid-ask spread) is a transaction cost. The commission paid to the broker is also a transaction cost.

Given the asset is classified as available-for-sale (that is, not at fair value through profit or loss) the transaction costs are included in the initial carrying value of the asset. Therefore, the asset will be recorded at its fair value of C100 (bid price) plus the bid-ask spread (C2) plus commission (C3), a total of C105. At the balance sheet date, the asset will be valued at bid price (C110) at that date and any difference between this price and the amount recognised initially (C5) will be recorded in other comprehensive income.

Therefore, the appropriate accounting entries at initial recognition and at the balance sheet date are as follows:

	Dr C	Cr C
At acquisition		
Available-for-sale asset (bid price inclusive of transaction costs)	105	
Cash		105
At balance sheet date		
Available-for-sale asset	5	
Gain in other comprehensive income		5

If the asset is a debt instrument, the bid-ask spread, brokerage commission, and any premium, discount or other deferred fees and costs, are subsequently amortised and recognised as part of interest income over the asset's life using the effective interest method.

If the market price had not changed since the date of acquisition, the entity would report a loss of the difference between C105 and bid price of C100, that is a loss of C5.

Example 2 – Treatment of bid-ask spread not included in initial carrying value of a financial asset

The facts are the same as in example 1 above, except that the entity classifies the financial asset as at fair value through profit or loss.

Financial assets classified as at fair value through profit or loss should be recognised initially at fair value. As stated in paragraph 9.17 above, transaction costs arising on a financial asset classified as at fair value through profit or loss are immediately recognised in profit or loss and do not form part of the initial carrying value of the asset. Hence, the asset is measured on initial recognition using the bid price (C100). At the balance sheet date, the asset will be valued at bid price (C110) at that date and any difference between this price and the amount recognised initially (C10) will be recorded in profit or loss.

The appropriate accounting entries at initial recognition and at the balance sheet date are as follows:

	Dr C	Cr C
At acquisition		
Financial asset at fair value through profit or loss (bid price)	100	
Profit or loss (bid-ask spread of C2 + commission of C3)	5	
Cash		105
At balance sheet date		
Financial asset at fair value through profit or loss	10	
Gain		10

9.84   The standard does not permit the use of mid-market price (average of bid and ask prices) for valuation purposes when quoted bid and ask prices are available. This is because applying mid-market prices to an individual instrument would result in entities recognising up-front gains and losses for the difference between the bid-ask price and the mid-market price. [IAS 39 para BC99]. This makes sense as the mid-market price cannot be relied upon to represent the price at which a market transaction would occur. The IASB Expert Advisory Panel report issued in October 2008 clarifies that if a valuation technique is used to estimate fair value and the model calculates a mid-market price, fair value should be adjusted to take into account the relevant bid-offer spread. However, IAS 39 offers a concession in circumstances where an entity holds assets and liabilities with offsetting market risks. In those circumstances, the entity may use mid-market prices as a basis for establishing fair values for the offsetting risk positions and apply the bid or ask price to the net open position as appropriate. [IAS 39 para AG72]. The IASB believes that use of the mid-market price is appropriate because the entity has locked in its cash flows from the asset and liability and potentially could sell the matched position without incurring the bid-ask spread. It is presumed that such matching positions would be settled within a similar time period.

9.85   The rules applicable to some investment funds require net asset values to be reported to investors on the basis of mid-market prices. The existence of regulations that require a different measurement basis for specific purposes does not justify a departure from the general requirement to use the current bid price in the absence of a matching liability position. Therefore, in its financial statements, an investment fund should measure its assets at current bid prices. In reporting its net asset value to investors, an investment fund may wish to provide a reconciliation between the fair values recognised on its balance sheet and the prices used for the net asset value calculation. [IAS 39 para IG E2.1].

Unavailability of published prices

9.86   Where current prices of financial instruments are unavailable at the reporting date, the price of the most recent transaction should be used adjusted for any changes in conditions between the date of the transaction and the balance sheet date. [IAS 39 para AG 72]. This is essentially a valuation technique that is considered further from paragraph 9.89 below.

9.87   If a published price quotation in an active market does not exist for a financial instrument in its entirety, but active markets exist for its component parts, fair value is determined on the basis of the relevant market prices for the component parts. [IAS 39 para AG 72]. This is relevant for complex financial instruments, which by their nature are illiquid and prices cannot be obtained as an instrument in their own right. An example might be a commodity-linked debt instrument whose coupon is indexed to the price of crude oil, but where the coupon can never exceed ten per cent nor be less than nil per cent. In that situation, as active markets exist for the basic components (the debt instrument and derivatives linked to that commodity), but not for the whole instrument, an overall valuation can be obtained by combining the values of the component parts.

Large blocks of instruments

9.88   The fair value of a portfolio of financial instruments is the product of the number of units of the instrument and its quoted market price. [IAS 39 paras AG71 to AG73]. This definition precludes an entity from using a 'blockage' factor (that is, a premium or discount based on the relative size of the position held, such as a large proportion of the total trading units of an instrument) in determining the fair value of a large block of financial instruments. In other words, if an entity holds a large block of a particular instrument and the only available market exit prices come from transactions involving small blocks, no adjustment should be made for the expected effect of selling the large block in a single transaction as illustrated in the following example, taken from the implementation guidance to IAS 39.

Example – Valuation of large holding

Entity A holds 15% of entity B's share capital. The shares are publicly traded in an active market. The currently quoted price is C100. Daily trading volume is 0.1% of outstanding shares. Because entity A believes that the fair value of the entity B shares it owns, if sold as a block, is greater than the quoted market price, entity A obtains several independent estimates of the price it would obtain if it sells its holding. These estimates indicate that entity A would be able to obtain a price of C105, that is, a 5% premium above the quoted price.

The published price quotation in an active market is the best estimate of fair value. Therefore, entity A should use the published price quotation (C100). Entity A cannot depart from the quoted market price solely because independent estimates indicate that entity A would obtain a higher (or lower) price by selling the holding as a block. [IAS 39 IG para E2.2].

9.88.1 Although the converse situation is not dealt with in the standard, it follows that if an entity holds only a small number of instruments and the available market exit prices come from transactions involving large blocks, the entity should not adjust the available price for the potential effect of selling individual instruments.

Valuation techniques in the absence of an active market

9.89 The best evidence of fair value is the quoted price in an active market. If the market for a financial instrument is not active, fair value should be determined using a valuation technique. The objective of using a valuation technique is to establish what the transaction price would have been on the measurement date in an arm's length exchange motivated by normal business considerations. This is by no means an easy task and involves the exercise of a significant amount of judgement. Even at the end of the most careful and detailed valuation, there will be uncertainty about the final numbers, coloured by the assumptions of risks and returns and any resulting bias introduced in the process.

9.90 As the objective of the valuation process is to arrive at a reasonable estimate of a financial instrument's fair value, the technique used should reasonably reflect how the market could be expected to price the instrument. That expectation is likely to be met if the valuation technique makes maximum use of market inputs and relies as little as possible on entity-specific inputs. Also the inputs should reasonably represent market expectations and measures of the risk-return factors inherent in the financial instrument. In other words, an acceptable valuation technique should incorporate all factors that market participants would consider in setting a price, and be consistent with accepted economic methodologies for pricing financial instruments. [IAS 39 paras AG75 to AG76]. A valuation technique should, therefore, reflect how the market could be expected to price the instrument under the conditions that exist at the measurement date. Even where a market is considered to be inactive, the most recent transaction prices should be considered as an input to a valuation model, provided that these are not forced transactions. Current market conditions cannot be ignored.

9.91 Periodically, an entity should calibrate the valuation techniques it uses and test their validity using prices from any observable current market transactions in the same instrument (that is, without modification or repackaging) or based on any available observable market data. [IAS 39 para AG 76]. As market conditions change, it might be necessary either to change the models used or to make additional adjustments to model valuations. Valuation adjustments are appropriate if they result in a better estimate of the price at which an orderly transaction would take place between market participants on the measurement date. Valuation adjustments include, for example, model deficiencies highlighted through calibration of the model, liquidity adjustments and credit adjustments. Adjustments to valuation technique are not appropriate if they adjust the measurement away from fair value, for example, for conservatism. [IASB Expert Advisory Panel report, October 2008].This process is not only important but essential, as the benchmark for comparison in most valuations remains the market price. When a value from the use of a valuation technique is significantly different from market price, there are two possibilities: one is that the valuation is correct and the market is wrong; the other is that the valuation is wrong and the market is correct. The presumption should be that the market is correct.

9.92 Valuation techniques that are well established in financial markets include recent market transactions, reference to a transaction that is substantially the same and discounted cash flows and option pricing models. These techniques are considered below. If there is a valuation technique commonly used by market participants to price the instrument and that technique has been demonstrated to provide reliable estimates of prices obtained in actual market transactions, that technique should be used. [IAS 39 para AG 74]. For example, well established external proprietary software packages are available for pricing many types of financial options. An entity that holds or writes one of those options would use the model best suited for the type of option held or written.

9.93 Valuation techniques used to estimate fair value should be applied on a consistent basis. A change in the valuation techniques used is appropriate only if the change results in a more reliable estimate of fair value, for example, as new markets develop or as new and improved valuation techniques become available.

Inputs to valuation techniques

9.94 As explained above, an appropriate valuation technique should incorporate observable market data about the market conditions and other factors that are likely to affect the instrument's fair value. The technique would be only as robust as the inputs used. Market inputs should be determined based on information that is timely, originated from sources independent of the entity and used by market-place participants in making pricing decisions. Examples of market inputs that may be used, directly or indirectly, as a basis for determining a financial instrument's fair value include the following:

■   The time value of money (that is, interest at the basic or risk-free rate).

Basic interest rates can usually be derived from observable government bond prices and are often quoted in financial publications. These rates typically vary with the expected dates of the projected cash flows along a yield curve of interest rates for different time horizons.

For practical reasons, an entity may use a well-accepted and readily observable general rate, such as LIBOR or a swap rate, as the benchmark rate. However, as benchmark is not a risk free interest rate, the credit risk adjustment appropriate to the particular financial instrument is determined on the basis of its credit risk in relation to the credit risk in this benchmark rate.

In some countries, the central government's bonds may carry a significant credit risk and may not provide a stable benchmark basic interest rate for instruments denominated in that currency. Some entities in these countries may have a better credit standing and a lower borrowing rate than the central government. In such a case, basic interest rates may be more appropriately determined by reference to interest rates for the highest rated corporate bonds issued in the currency of that jurisdiction.

■   Credit risk.

The effect on fair value of credit risk (that is, the premium over the basic interest rate for credit risk) may be derived from observable market prices for traded instruments of different credit quality or from observable interest rates charged by lenders for loans of various credit ratings.

■   Foreign currency exchange prices.

Active currency exchange markets exist for most major currencies, and prices are quoted daily in financial publications.

■   Commodity prices.

There are observable market prices for many commodities.

■   Equity prices.

Prices (and indices of prices) of traded equity instruments are readily observable in some markets. Present value based techniques may be used to estimate the current market price of equity instruments for which there are no observable prices.

■   Volatility (that is, magnitude of future changes in price of the financial instrument or other item).

Measures of the volatility of actively traded items can normally be reasonably estimated on the basis of historical market data or by using volatilities implied in current market prices

■   Pre-payment risk and surrender risk.

This is the risk that a financial instrument may be pre-paid or surrendered earlier than its maturity date. Expected pre-payment patterns for financial assets and expected surrender patterns for financial liabilities can be estimated on the basis of historical data. However, the fair value of a financial liability that can be surrendered by the counterparty cannot be less than the present value of the surrender amount (see para 9.110 below).

■ Servicing costs for a financial asset or a financial liability.

Costs of servicing can be estimated using comparisons with current fees charged by other market participants. If the costs of servicing a financial asset or financial liability are significant and other market participants would face comparable costs, the issuer would consider them in determining the fair value of that financial asset or financial liability. It is likely that the fair value at inception of a contractual right to future fees equals the origination costs paid for them, unless future fees and related costs are out of line with market comparables.

[IAS 39 para AG 82].

Recent transaction prices

9.95 Where, current prices of financial instruments are unavailable at the reporting date, the price of the most recent transaction should be used. [IAS 39 para AG 72]. This is a fairly simple technique and provides a foundation for estimating fair value, as long as there has not been a significant change in economic circumstances since the relevant transaction occurred.

9.96 If, however, conditions have changed since the relevant transaction occurred, the fair value should reflect the change in conditions by reference to current prices or rates for similar financial instruments, as appropriate. That means, the most recent market-exit transaction price would be adjusted for changes due to passage of time as long as such an adjustment is capable of producing a reasonable estimate of fair value. It would also be adjusted if changes in market conditions indicate that transactions occurring at the balance sheet date probably would not have occurred at that price. An example would be a change in the risk-free interest rate following the most recent price quote for a corporate bond. That observable price would be adjusted to reflect the interest for the period between the transaction date and the measurement date (to take into account the time value of money), the effect on fair value of the changes in rates and any cash distribution in that period. Similarly, if the entity can demonstrate that the last transaction price is not fair value (for example, because it reflected the amount that an entity would receive or pay in a forced transaction, involuntary liquidation or distress sale), that price should be adjusted. [IAS 39 para AG 72].

9.97 However, it may not always be possible to make the adjustment referred to above, because not all the information may be available at each measurement date. For example, at the date that an entity makes (or acquires) a debt instrument that is not actively traded, the transaction price is also a market price.

At the next measurement date, although the general level of market interest rates are available, the entity may not have information from recent transactions to determine the appropriate credit spread over the basic interest rate that market participants would consider in pricing the instrument on that date. In that situation, in the absence of evidence to the contrary, it would be reasonable to assume that no changes have taken place in the spread that existed at the date the loan was made. However, the entity would be expected to make reasonable efforts to determine whether there is evidence that there has been a change in such factors. When evidence of a change exists, the entity would consider the effects of the change in determining the financial instrument's fair value. [IAS 39 para AG 78].

Using price information about similar financial instruments

9.98 Another market based valuation technique estimates a financial instrument's value by using quoted prices for similar financial instruments in active markets, adjusted as appropriate for differences, whenever that information is available. Instruments are considered to be similar if they have similar remaining maturity, cash flow pattern, currency, credit risk, collateral and interest basis. [IAS 39 para AG77]. Estimating a financial instrument's fair value based on the market price of a similar financial instrument is best explained by an example.

Example – Valuation based on market price of a similar financial instrument

On 1 January 20X5, entity A acquires a bond issued by entity B through a private placement. The consideration paid and, therefore, the bond's fair value at initial recognition is C1 million. The entity classifies the bond as at fair value through profit or loss. The bond has no observable market price. At 31 December 20X5, the entity is able to identify actively traded corporate bonds that are similar to its bond.

In carrying out the evaluation, the major elements of the two bonds that should be compared are as follows:

- The amount and timing of the contractual cash flows, including pre-payment expectations.

- The currency in which the bonds are payable.

- The credit risk rating and the factors on which changes in the credit risk rating are dependent. For example, the fair value of bonds issued by entities with different industry and geographical bases would be expected to respond differently to changes in the market factors.

- Any other term and conditions that could affect the bond's fair value.

9.99 By definition, similar financial instruments are not identical and some of the differences will cause the fair value to be different. Therefore, it is necessary to ensure that the effect on fair value of any such differences is reasonably determinable. In the above example, the initial net effects of differences may be discerned by comparing the fair values of the two instruments at the acquisition date of the non-traded bond, assuming that its fair value is equal to the consideration paid. It is likely that the private placement bond's fair value will be less than that of the market-traded bond, because it is less marketable. Therefore, it may be reasonable to assume that any premium for marketability differences between the effective interest rates of the two bonds at the date the entity acquired its bond remains unchanged from period to period, except if an observable event that could be expected to affect marketability takes place.

Other valuation techniques

9.100   Where it is not possible to estimate a financial instrument's fair value by reference to market prices, the entity uses other valuation techniques (pricing models and methodologies). Because they require more estimation and assumptions, they are necessarily more subjective than the market price approach. Two valuation techniques that are widely used are the discounted cash flow (present value) approach and option pricing models.

9.101   Present value is a technique used to link future amounts (cash flows) to the present through a discount rate. Present value concepts are central to the development of techniques for estimating the fair value of financial instruments because the market exit price of a financial instrument represents market participant's collective estimate of the present value of its expected cash flows. Therefore, cash flows and discount rate should reflect only factors that are specific to the financial instrument being measured and should reflect assumptions that market participants would use in their estimates of fair value. Also, as the cash flows used are estimates rather than known amounts, a fair value estimate, using present value, is made under conditions of uncertainty. As market participants generally seek compensation for bearing the uncertainty inherent in cash flows (risk premium), the effect of variability (risk) in the cash flows should be reflected either in the cash flows or in the discount rate.

9.101.1   In applying discounted cash flow analysis, an entity uses discount rates equal to the prevailing rates of return for financial instruments having substantially the same terms and characteristics, including the credit quality of the instrument, the remaining term over which the contractual interest rate is fixed, the remaining term to the principal's re-payment and the currency in which payments are to be made. Short-term receivables and payables with no stated interest rate may be measured at the original invoice amount if the effect of discounting is immaterial. [IAS 39 para AG 79].

9.101.2   Option pricing models, first developed by Black and Scholes, can be used to value any asset (not just financial instruments) that has the characteristics of an option, with some caveats. For example, an unquoted equity instrument can be valued as a call option on the entity's assets, the exercise price of the call being equal to the value of the entity's debt. Option pricing models are based on the premise that it is possible to create a replicating portfolio using a combination of the underlying asset and risk-free borrowing and lending to create the same cash flows as the option being valued. The principles of arbitrage then apply and the option's value is then equal to the value of the replicating portfolio. Although real markets do not always follow the idealised behaviour of financial models, these portfolios constructed in line with theoretical models have been found to be robust in practice, despite their imperfections.

Broker quotes and pricing services

9.102 An entity may not have its own valuation model and may instead rely on broker quotes, third-party pricing services or information from other financial institutions. The existence of such prices doesn't necessarily indicate an active market. In this case, the entity needs to understand how the third party has derived that valuation and whether it is in accordance with the requirements of IAS 39. Factors to consider include:

■ Whether and how the valuation incorporates current market events (for example, does it include 'stale' prices).

■ How frequently the valuation is updated to reflect changing market conditions.

■ The number of sources from which the valuation is derived (a valuation derived from many quotes or data sources generally being preferable to one based on a small number).

■ Whether it reflects actual transactions or merely indicative prices.

■ Whether it reflects a price at which the entity could be expected to transact (for example, a market to which the entity has access).

■ Whether it is consistent with available market information, including any current market transactions in the same or similar assets.

Application to intra-group financial guarantee contracts

9.103 The way in which the various valuation techniques discussed above can be applied to determine the fair value of an intra-group financial guarantee contract that is not negotiated in an arm's length transaction is considered in the paragraphs that follow (see from para 9.48 for accounting for financial guarantee contracts).

References to market prices of similar instruments

9.103.1 An entity may be unable to identify a market price for financial guarantees identical to those that either it or a member of its group has issued. However, it may be possible to identify market prices for similar guarantees, credit default swaps or credit insurance products, the price of which could be adjusted. For example, parent P has guaranteed C100 million of five year debt issued by subsidiary S. It may be possible to identify credit insurance products issued by a bank relating to debt of this amount, maturity and credit quality. However, an adjustment may still be necessary, for example, to reflect liquidity aspects and differences between P's credit rating and that of the bank.

Interest rate differentials

9.103.2   Under this method, the entity calculates the value of the difference between the interest charged on the guaranteed loan and what would have been charged had the loan not been guaranteed. The premise is that the interest that the bank is willing to forego represents a 'price' that it is willing to pay for the guarantee. For example, parent P has guaranteed C100 million of five year debt issued by subsidiary S. Subsidiary S pays interest of X per cent on the debt. In the absence of the guarantee, the bank would impose an interest rate of Y per cent. Hence, the fair value of the guarantee represents the difference in the present value of the interest payments over the period of the guarantee.

9.103.3   This model is simple in principle, but presents practical problems when attempting to measure Y per cent. It is unlikely that the bank would provide a reliable estimate. Determining Y per cent requires an estimate of the credit spread (for example, above a base index such as LIBOR) appropriate to subsidiary S in isolation. This may prove difficult as, even without the guarantee, subsidiary S's credit rating will benefit from the company being a member of parent P's group. Nevertheless, models based on determining a stand alone credit rating for subsidiary S do exist and these should enable a reliable estimate to be made.

Discounted cash flow analysis (expected value)

9.103.4   Instead of considering the 'price' that a bank would pay for a guarantee, it might be possible to consider the 'price' that the issuer would demand for accepting the guarantee obligation. This can be estimated using a probability-adjusted discounted cash flow analysis. For example, parent P has guaranteed C100 million of five year debt issued by subsidiary S. The probability of default by subsidiary S is estimated at 0.04 per cent (based on historical default rates amongst companies with the same credit rating as subsidiary S) and the loss in the event of default is estimated at 50 per cent (based on subsidiary S's asset base and other collateral available to the bank). The expected value of the liability (its fair value) would, therefore, be C20,000.

9.103.5   Similar to the interest rate differential approach described above, this model is simple in principle, but presents practical problems when attempting to estimate the probability of default and the loss given default. Although data on these points is available, they rely on determining subsidiary S's credit rating as in the interest rate differential approach.

Fair value of derivatives and credit risk

9.104   Paragraph AG69 of IAS 39 requires the fair value of a financial instrument to reflect its credit quality. Paragraph AG82(b) adds that where an entity uses a valuation technique to estimate fair value, credit risk would generally be built into the valuation model. Therefore, fair value should incorporate the impact of credit risk to the extent that credit risk affects the price for which a derivative could be exchanged between willing parties in an arm's length transaction.

9.104.1 Counterparty credit risk typically arises when a derivative is in an asset position at the reporting date. On the other hand, the entity's own credit risk will be incorporated when the derivative is in a liability position at the reporting date. IAS 39 is clear that financial assets measured at fair value need to be valued on an 'exit price' basis, but it is less clear how to estimate the fair value of liabilities. Paragraph BC89 of IAS 39's Basis for Conclusions indicates that credit risk affects the value at which liabilities could be repurchased or settled. In many cases, the only way an entity can settle a derivative liability at the reporting date is through paying the counterparty a 'close-out amount' that does not incorporate changes in the entity's credit risk since the inception of the contract. In other words, an entity often has no practical ability to realise gains by settling liabilities at a lower amount due to deterioration in its own credit risk.

9.104.2 The standard is unclear whether the practical ability to settle a liability in a way that enables the entity to realise gains and losses from changes in its own credit risk should be considered in determining fair value. In our view, either of the following approaches is acceptable for measuring the fair value of liabilities not traded in an active market:

- Fair value based on a presumption that an entity has the practical ability to settle the liability in a way that enables it to realise gains and losses from changes in its own credit risk ('the full own credit risk approach').

- Fair value based on a 'close-out amount' that would be paid to the counterparty. This reflects the amount the entity would pay to settle the liability with the counterparty at the reporting date ('the counterparty close-out approach')

9.104.3 The chosen accounting policy should be applied consistently in both measuring and disclosing fair value. The policy selected should be disclosed where it has a significant effect on either measurement or disclosure.

9.104.4 Depending on the accounting policy chosen, credit risk may have an impact on hedge effectiveness for both cash flow and fair value hedge relationships. When an entity determines fair value for financial liabilities based on the 'counterparty close-out approach', in many cases the entity's own credit risk would not have a significant impact on hedge effectiveness during the period that the derivative is in a liability position. On the other hand, when an entity determines fair value for financial liabilities based on the 'full own credit risk approach', hedge effectiveness would be impacted by changes in the entity's own credit risk. Hedge accounting is covered in chapter 10.

Unquoted equity instruments and related derivatives

9.105 Normally it is possible to estimate an equity instrument's fair value that does not have a quoted market price in an active market, as well as derivatives that are linked to and must be settled by delivery of such unquoted equity instruments with sufficient reliability by applying valuation techniques based on reasonable assumptions. The fair values of such instruments are deemed to be reliably measurable if:

■ the variability in the range of reasonable fair value estimates is not significant for that instrument; or

■ the probabilities of the various estimates within the range can be reasonably assessed and used in estimating fair value.

[IAS 39 para AG 80].

9.105.1 There are many situations in which the variability in the range of reasonable fair value estimates is likely not to be significant and, hence, the fair value is reasonably measurable. However, if the range of reasonable fair value estimates is significantly wide and the probabilities of the various estimates cannot be reasonably assessed, an entity is precluded from measuring the instrument at fair value. In that situation, such instruments are measured at cost, less impairment. [IAS 39 paras 46(c), AG81]. It is not permissible for the entity to measure the equity instrument at fair value, for instance, by judgementally picking a fair value estimate within a range.

9.106 A similar dispensation applies to derivative financial instruments that can only be settled by physical delivery of such unquoted equity instruments. It does not apply to derivative instruments in any other situations as illustrated in the following example.

> **Example – Reliability of fair value measurement**
>
> An entity acquires a complex stand alone derivative that is based on several underlying variables, including commodity prices, interest rates and credit indices. There is no active market or other price quotation for the derivative and no active markets for some of its underlying variables. The entity contends that the derivative's fair value cannot be reliably measured.
>
> Notwithstanding the entity's contention, there is a presumption that the fair value of derivatives can be determined reliably by reference to appropriate market prices, or prices of similar instruments, or discounted cash flow or other pricing models or by reference to prices/rates for components, with the exception only of derivatives that are linked to and must be settled by delivery of an unquoted equity instrument (see para 9.104 above). This is not the situation here and, therefore, the entity cannot measure the derivative at cost or amortised cost.

'Day 1' gain or loss

9.107 As noted in paragraph 9.77 above, the best evidence of the instrument's fair value on initial recognition is the transaction price. However, it is possible that the instrument's fair value may not be the transaction price. The only exception to using the transaction price is if the fair value is evidenced by comparison with other observable current market transactions in the *same* instrument, or is based on a valuation technique whose variables include *only* data from observable markets. [IAS 39 para AG 76]. In such situations, the entity is required to use this value. Consequently, the difference between the estimated fair value using a valuation technique and the transaction price results in immediate 'day 1' recognition of a gain or loss. The IASB concluded that these conditions were necessary and sufficient to provide reasonable assurance that this fair value was genuine for the purposes of recognising up-front gains or losses. In all other cases, the transaction price gives the best evidence of fair value and 'day 1' gain recognition is precluded, an approach that achieves convergence with US GAAP. [IAS 39 para BC104].

> **Example – Day '1' gain or loss recognition**
>
> Entity A acquires a financial asset for C110, which is not quoted in an active market. The asset's fair value based on the entity's own valuation technique amounted to C115. However, that valuation technique does not solely use observable market date, but relies on some entity-specific factors that market participants would not normally consider in setting a price.
>
> The entity cannot recognise a 'day 1' profit of C5 and record the asset at C115. The use of unobservable entity-specific inputs to calculate a fair value that is different from transaction price on 'day 1' is so subjective that its reliability is called into question. Hence, recognition of a 'day 1' gain or loss is not appropriate. Accordingly, the entity restricts its valuation to the transaction price and the asset is recorded at C110.

9.108 A question arises as to whether and how any gain or loss not recognised on 'day 1' should be recognised subsequently, or at all. An unrecognised 'day 1' gain or loss should be recognised after initial recognition only to the extent that it arises from a change in a factor (including time) that market participants would consider in setting a price. [IAS 39 para AG 76A]. It is not clear how the phrase *"a change in a factor (including time) that market participants would consider in setting a price"* should be interpreted. One interpretation is that a gain or loss should remain unrecognised until all market inputs become observable. Another interpretation is that it permits the recognition of 'day 1' gain or loss in profit or loss on a systematic basis over time, even in the absence of any observable transaction data to support such a treatment. Indeed, some constituents asked the Board to clarify whether straight-line amortisation was an appropriate method of recognising the difference. The Board decided not to do this. It concluded that although straight-line amortisation may be an appropriate method in some cases, it will not be appropriate in others. [IAS 39 para BC222(v)(ii)]. This would appear to suggest that an unrecognised 'day 1' gain or loss could be amortised either on a straight line basis or on another rational basis that reflects the nature of the financial instrument (for example, a non-linear amortisation for some option-based derivatives).

9.109 It should be noted that an unrecognised 'day 1' gain or loss is not separately identified in the balance sheet. However, IFRS 7 requires disclosure of the unrecognised amount, together with the change in the amount previously deferred, and the entity's accounting policy for determining when amounts deferred are recognised in profit or loss (see chapter 11).

Demand deposit liabilities

9.110   A demand deposit represents a promise by the deposit-taking institution to deliver cash either to the depositor or to third parties designated by the depositor. It imposes a contractual obligation that is a financial liability. A typical example is a current account in a bank. The current account holder can demand settlement at any time and the bank generally has the right to return the depositor's money at any time (even though that right is seldom exercised). It is often argued that the fair value of the financial liabilities with a demand feature is less than the demand amount, because not all depositors withdraw their money at the earliest opportunity. Often there is a core of deposits (withdrawals replaced by new deposits) that is left outstanding for long periods of time.

9.111   However, the IASB was not prepared to concede that demand financial liabilities could have a fair value different from face value until further work had been done, particularly, in respect of insurance contract liabilities. Consequently, IAS 39 makes it clear that the fair value of a financial liability with a demand feature is not less than the amount payable on demand, discounted from the first date that the amount could be required to be paid. [IAS 39 para 49]. This follows from the fact that the maturity date of an item with no contractual repayment terms cannot be later than the earliest date on which payment can be demanded. The Basis for Conclusion section in IAS 39 notes that recognising a financial liability with a demand feature at less than the demand amount would give rise to an immediate gain on the origination of such a deposit, which is not considered appropriate. In substance, the gain represents the benefits of future interest free or low interest use of funds expected to occur as a result of the deposit relationship. Such benefits are not considered to be directly attributable to the rights and obligations that constitute the demand deposit liabilities existing at a measurement date and accordingly should not enter into the estimate of their fair value. The future benefit of the deposit relationship may be recognised as an intangible asset in circumstances where customer relationships are acquired, together with the related portfolio of demand deposits, if the recognition criteria in IAS 38, 'Intangible assets', are met. However, the Basis for Conclusion section in IAS 39 notes that, absent such an acquisition, the market price observed for such financial liabilities is the price at which they are originated between the customer and the deposit-taker, that is, the demand amount. [IAS 39 para BC 94]. In the absence of an acquisition of a portfolio of demand deposits, this customer deposit intangible asset should not be recognised.

Credit risk of liabilities

9.112   When financial liabilities are measured at fair value, changes in their credit risk should be reflected in their fair value measurement. Many question whether a liability's credit risk or changes in its credit risk should enter into the measurement of its liabilities. They argue that it is not useful to report lower liabilities when an entity is in financial difficulty precisely because its debt levels are too high and that it would be difficult to explain to users of financial statements the reasons why income would be recognised when a liability's creditworthiness deteriorates. The IASB, however, takes the view that because financial statements are prepared on a going concern basis, credit risk affects the value at which liabilities could be repurchased or settled. Accordingly, a financial liability's fair value reflects the credit risk relating to that liability. Therefore, the IASB decided to include credit risk relating to a financial liability in the fair value measurement of that liability for the following reasons:

■ entities realise changes in fair value, including fair value attributable to the liability's credit risk, for example, by renegotiating or repurchasing liabilities or by using derivatives;

■ changes in credit risk affect the observed market price of a financial liability and hence its fair value;

■ it is difficult from a practical standpoint to exclude changes in credit risk from an observed market price; and

■ a financial liability's fair value (that is, the price of that liability in an exchange between a knowledgeable, willing buyer and a knowledgeable, willing seller) on initial recognition reflects its credit risk. Therefore, it is inappropriate to include credit risk in the initial fair value measurement of financial liabilities, but not subsequently.

[IAS 39 para BC89].

9.113 It should be noted that the issue relates to the financial liability's credit risk, rather than the entity's creditworthiness. Although the two are closely related, a deterioration of the entity creditworthiness may not, by itself, affect the credit risk of all the entity's liabilities in the same way. For example, the fair value of liabilities secured by valuable collateral, guaranteed by third parties or ranking ahead of virtually all other liabilities is generally unaffected by changes in the entity's creditworthiness. [IAS 39 para BC92]. If an entity designates a financial liability as at fair value through profit or loss, IFRS 7 requires it to disclose the amount of change in the fair value of the financial liability that is attributable to changes in the liability's credit risk (see further chapter 11). There is further discussion of how to reflect credit risk into measurement of fair value from paragraph 9.104.

9.113.1 In May 2010, the IASB issued an exposure draft proposing changes to IFRS 9, 'Financial instruments'. The expsoure draft proposes retaining the classification and measurement requirements of IAS 39 for financial liabilities, including bifurcation of embedded derivatives, except that the effects of changes in the credit risk of liabilities designated under the fair value option would not affect profit or loss. Changes in fair value of a liability due to an entity's own credit risk will be recognised as a component of 'other comprehensive income'. The proposal responds to the concern that recognising the effects of changes in the fair value of a liability attributable to the liability's credit risk in profit or loss is counter-intuitive and does not provide useful information unless the liability is held for trading.

Impairment of financial assets

9.114 A financial asset measured at amortised cost is impaired when its carrying value exceeds the present value of the future cash flows discounted at the financial asset's original effective interest rate. A financial asset that is carried at fair value through profit or loss does not give rise to any impairment issues as diminution in value due to impairment is already reflected in the fair value and, hence, in profit or loss. It follows that impairment issues are only relevant to financial assets that are carried at amortised cost and available-for-sale financial assets whose fair value changes are recognised in other comprehensive income.

9.115 IAS 39 deals with impairment of financial assets through a two-step process. First, an entity must carry out an impairment review of its financial assets at each balance sheet date. The aim of this review is to determine whether there is objective evidence that impairment exists for a financial asset. [IAS 39 para 58]. This is considered from paragraph 9.120 below.

9.116 Secondly, if there is objective evidence of impairment, the entity should measure and record the impairment loss in the reporting period. [IAS 39 para 58]. The measurement of impairment losses differs between financial assets carried at amortised cost (see para 9.126 below), financial assets carried at cost (see para 9.151 below) and available-for-sale financial assets (see para 9.152 below). There is also a difference on whether impairment losses can be reversed depending on whether the available-for-sale instrument is debt or equity (see para 9.154 below).

Incurred versus expected losses

9.117 Under IAS 39, a financial asset or a group of financial assets is impaired and impairment losses are incurred if, and only if, there is objective evidence of impairment as a result of one or more events that occurred after the asset's initial recognition (a 'loss event'). It may not be possible to identify a single, discrete event that caused the impairment. Rather the combined effect of several events may have caused the impairment. In addition, the loss event must have a reliably measurable effect on the present value of estimated future cash flows and be supported by current observable data. [IAS 39 para 59].

9.118 Losses expected as a result of future events, no matter how likely, are not recognised. Possible or expected future trends that may lead to a loss in the future (for example, an expectation that unemployment will rise or a recession will occur) are also not taken into account. The standard states that to recognise impairment on the basis of expected future transactions and events would not be consistent with an amortised cost model.

9.119   As the impairment model in IAS 39 is based on the 'incurred loss' model and not on an 'expected loss' model, an impairment loss is not recognised at the time an asset is originated, that is, before a loss event can have occurred as illustrated in the following example:

> **Example – Recognition of an impairment loss on origination**
>
> Entity A lends C1,000 to a group of customers. Based on historical experience, entity A expects that 1% of the principal amount of loans given to the customers will not be collected.
>
> Entity A is not permitted to reduce the carrying amount of a loan asset by C10 on initial recognition through the recognition of an immediate impairment loss.
>
> Under the incurred loss model of IAS 39, an impairment loss is recognised only if there is objective evidence of impairment as a result of a past event that occurred after initial recognition. Furthermore, recognition of an immediate impairment loss based on future expectation would be inconsistent with the general rule that a financial asset should be initially measured at fair value. For a loan asset, the fair value is the amount of cash lent adjusted for any fees and costs (unless a portion of the amount lent is compensation for other stated or implied rights or privileges). [IAS 39 para IGE4.2]. In practice, however, the expectation of loss is built in to the credit spread for the customer.

Objective evidence of impairment

9.120   IAS 39 provides examples of factors that may, either individually or taken together, provide sufficient objective evidence that an impairment loss has been incurred in a financial asset or group of financial assets. They include observable data that comes to the attention of the holder of the asset about the following loss events:

- Significant financial difficulty of the issuer or obligor.

- A breach of contract, such as a default or delinquency in interest or principal payments.

- The lender, for economic or legal reasons relating to the borrower's financial difficulty, granting to the borrower a concession that the lender would not otherwise consider.

- It becomes probable that the borrower will enter bankruptcy or other financial reorganisation.

- The disappearance of an active market for that financial asset because of financial difficulties.

- Observable data indicating that there is a measurable decrease in the estimated future cash flows from a group of financial assets since the initial recognition of those assets, although the decrease cannot yet be identified with the individual financial assets in the group, including:

- adverse changes in the payment status of borrowers in the group (for example, an increased number of delayed payments or an increased number of credit card borrowers who have reached their credit limit and are paying the minimum monthly amount); or

- national or local economic conditions that correlate with defaults on the assets in the group (for example, an increase in the unemployment rate in the geographical area of the borrowers, a decrease in property prices for mortgages in the relevant area, a decrease in oil prices for loan assets to oil producers, or adverse changes in industry conditions that affect the borrowers in the group).

[IAS 39 para 59].

9.121 A downgrade of an entity's credit rating is not, of itself, evidence of impairment, although it may be evidence of impairment when considered with other available information. Other factors that an entity considers in determining whether it has objective evidence that an impairment loss has been incurred include information about:

- The debtors' or issuers' liquidity.

- Solvency, business and financial risk exposures.

- Levels of and trends in delinquencies for similar financial assets.

- National and local economic trends and conditions.

- The fair value of collateral and guarantees.

These and other factors may, either individually or taken together, provide sufficient objective evidence that an impairment loss has been incurred in a financial asset or group of financial assets. [IAS 39 para 60, IG para E4.1].

9.122 A decline in the fair value of a financial asset below its cost or amortised cost is not necessarily evidence of impairment (for example, a decline in the fair value of an investment in a debt instrument that results from an increase in the risk-free interest rate). Also, in contrast with the fifth bullet point mentioned in paragraph 9.120 above, the disappearance of an active market because an entity's financial instruments are no longer publicly traded is not evidence of impairment. [IAS 39 para 60].

Evidence of impairment for equity instruments

9.123 The standard provides additional guidance about impairment indicators that are specific to investments in equity instruments. They apply in addition to the impairment indicators described above, which focus on the assessment of impairment in debt instruments.

9.124 The additional impairment indicators that may indicate that the equity investment's cost may not be recovered are:

- Significant adverse changes in the technological, market, economic or legal environment in which the issuer operates. For example, such changes include but are not limited to:

- Structural changes in the industry or industries in which the issuer operates, such as changes in production technology or the number of competitors.

- Changes in the level of demand for the goods or services sold by the issuer resulting from factors such as changing consumer tastes or product obsolescence.

- Changes in the political or legal environment affecting the issuer's business, such as enactment of new environment protection, tax or trade laws.

- Changes in the issuer's financial condition evidenced by changes in factors such as its liquidity, credit rating, profitability, cash flows, debt/equity ratio and level of dividend payments.

- A 'significant' or 'prolonged' decline in the fair value of an investment in an equity instrument below its cost.

[IAS 39 para 61].

9.125 In the context of the last bullet point above, the IFRIC confirmed that a significant decline in fair value should be evaluated against the original cost at initial recognition and 'prolonged' should be evaluated against the period in which the fair value of the investment has been below that original cost. In May 2009 the IFRIC tentatively decided, that a significant or prolonged decline cannot be considered only an indicator of possible impairment in determining whether there is objective evidence. When such a decline exists, recognition of an impairment loss is required. Furthermore, any further declines in value after an impairment loss has been recognised in profit or loss should be recognised immediately in profit or loss. [IAS 39 para IG E4.9]. IAS 39 refers to original cost on initial recognition of an equity instrument and does not permit a prior impairment to establish a new deemed cost against which subsequent declines in fair value are evaluated. [IFRIC Update April 2005]. However, no guidance is provided on what is a 'significant' or 'prolonged' decline in the fair value of an equity instrument. Consequently, judgement is required.

9.125.1 Whether a decline in fair value below cost is considered as 'significant' must be assessed on an instrument-by-instrument basis. In our view, the assessment of significant should be based on both qualitative and quantitative factors. An entity should develop an accounting policy for assessing a 'significant' decline in fair value.

9.125.2 The expected level of volatility for an instrument may also be a factor that entities should take into consideration when assessing what is 'significant'. Volatility is a tendency of a stock's value to fluctuate. Stocks with higher volatility are considered riskier because their value changes more from day to day. Stocks will a lower volatility are more stable and, therefore, viewed as less risky. For example, a company may hold listed shares in an established supermarket chain whose share price changes by 3 per cent over a period of time and listed shares in a speculative mining enterprise whose share price fluctuates by 10 per cent over the same period. In this case, a larger decline in the mining company's shares might be tolerated before an entity records an impairment loss, given its greater volatility compared with the supermarket chain. It is also important to note that where volatility is taken into account in a company's assessment of whether a decline is significant, the volatility is considered relative to the instrument's fair value at the date impairment is being considered, not its original cost. In addition, that volatility should be determined over a relatively long period. For example, a market downturn due to decline in the overall economy over a short period of time would not be considered adequate to establish an estimate of expected future volatility.

9.125.3   What is a 'prolonged' decline in fair value will also require judgement and a policy will need to be established. In general, a period of 12 months or greater below original cost is likely to be a 'prolonged' decline. However, the assessment of 'prolonged' should not be compared to the entire period that the investment has been or is expected to be held. For example, if a security's fair value has been below cost for 12 months, whether that security has been held or is intended to be held for two or 20 years is irrelevant. The assessment is whether the period of 12 months accords with the entity's chosen policy.

9.125.4   Following the amendment to IAS 39 described in paragraph 9.37, on reclassification of an equity instrument out of a category measured at fair value (that is, held-for-trading or available-for-sale) and into another category, the fair value at the date of reclassification becomes its new cost or amortised cost. [IAS 39 para 50C, F]. This new cost or amortised cost is the basis against which future 'significant' or 'prolonged' declines in fair value should be assessed.

9.125.5   In practice, an entity may have purchased securities in a company on multiple dates and at different prices. IAS 39 does not provide guidance on this point. By analogy to IAS 2, 'Inventories', in our view the basis for measuring the cost for calculating impairment could be a specific identification method, weighted average cost or FIFO method. The basis should be the same as the basis for calculating realised gains or losses upon disposal and should remain consistent across periods. This is an accounting policy choice and should be applied consistently.

Financial assets carried at amortised cost

General requirements

9.126   Financial assets carried at amortised cost are those that are classified as either loans and receivables or held-to-maturity. If there is objective evidence that an impairment loss on such an asset has been incurred, the amount of the loss should be measured as the difference between the asset's carrying amount and the present value of estimated future cash flows. The expected cash flows should exclude future credit losses that have not been incurred and should be discounted at the financial asset's original effective interest rate (that is, the effective interest rate computed at initial recognition). [IAS 39 para 63].

9.127   The standard allows the carrying amount of the asset to be reduced either directly by writing it down or through use of an allowance account such as a loan loss provision or provision for bad and doubtful debts. However, the amount of the loss should be recognised in profit or loss. [IAS 39 para 63]. The asset's carrying amount in the entity's balance sheet is stated net of any related allowance. [IAS 39 para AG 84].

9.128   In some circumstances, it may not be practicable to make a reasonably reliable direct estimate of the present value of future cash flows expected from an impaired financial asset measured at amortised cost. As a practical expedient, the carrying amount of the impaired asset may be determined in these circumstances on the basis of an instrument's fair value using an observable market price. [IAS 39 para AG 84].

9.129   A loan's observable market price is the loan's quoted price that can be obtained from reliable market sources. For example, loans with an active secondary market could be measured based on the observable market price. Similarly, an entity that has a viable plan to dispose of loans in a bulk sale could measure impairment by comparison to the net proceeds received on similar loan sales. However, it is likely that the use of the observable market price will be infrequent, because either there may not be a market for the loans or the market may be illiquid.

9.130   The expected future cash flows that are included in the calculation are the contractual cash of the instrument itself, reduced or delayed based on the current expectations of the amount and timing of these cash flows as a result of losses incurred at the balance sheet date. In circumstances where the amount outstanding is expected to be collected in full, but the collection period is delayed, an impairment loss must still be recognised, unless the creditor receives full compensation (for example, in the form of penalty interest) for the period of the delinquency, as illustrated in the example below.

Example – Impairment arising from changes in the amount and timing of cash flows

Entity A is concerned that, because of financial difficulties, customer B will not be able to make all principal and interest payments due on a loan in a timely manner. It negotiates a restructuring of the loan. Entity A expects that customer B will be able to meet its obligations under the restructured terms in any of the 5 scenarios indicated below.

- Customer B will pay the original loan's full principal amount 5 years after the original due date, but none of the interest due under the original terms.

- Customer B will pay the original loan's full principal amount on the original due date, but none of the interest due under the original terms.

- Customer B will pay the original loan's full principal amount on the original due date with interest only at a lower interest rate than the interest rate inherent in the original loan.

- Customer B will pay the original loan's full principal amount 5 years after the original due date and all interest accrued during the original loan term, but no interest for the extended term.

- Customer B will pay the original loan's full principal amount 5 years after the original due date and all interest, including interest for both the loan's original term and the extended term.

[IAS 39 para IG E4.3].

Given that customer B is in financial difficulties, an impairment loss has been incurred, as there is objective evidence of impairment. The amount of the impairment loss for a loan measured at amortised cost is the difference between the loan's carrying amount and the present value of future principal and interest payments discounted at the loan's original effective interest rate.

In the first four scenarios above, the present value of the future principal and interest payments discounted at the loan's original effective interest rate will be lower than the loan's carrying amount. Therefore, an impairment loss is recognised in those cases.

In the final scenario, even though the timing of payments has changed, the lender will receive interest on interest, and the present value of the future principal and interest payments discounted at the loan's original effective interest rate will equal the carrying amount of the loan. Therefore, there is no impairment loss. However, this fact pattern is unlikely given customer B's financial difficulties.

9.131   Where an impaired financial asset is secured by collateral, the calculation of the present value of the estimated future cash flows of the collateralised financial asset should reflect the cash flows that may result from foreclosure less costs for obtaining and selling the collateral, whether or not foreclosure is probable. [IAS 39 para AG 84]. As the measurement of the impaired financial asset reflects the collateral asset's fair value, the collateral is not recognised as an asset separately from the impaired financial asset, unless it meets the recognition criteria for an asset in another standard. [IAS 39 IG para E4.8].

9.131.1   For financial assets reclassified to another category following the amendment to IAS 39 in October 2008, see paragraph 9.37.4.

Appropriate discount rate

9.132   As stated above, impairment of a financial asset carried at amortised cost is measured by discounting the expected future cash flows using the financial instrument's original effective interest rate. Since impairment reflects a fall in the asset's carrying amount, which is evidenced by a decrease in the estimate of expected cash flows to be received from the financial asset, discounting at a rate of interest that reflects a current market rate of interest would impose fair value measurement on the financial asset. This would not be appropriate for assets that are measured at amortised cost. [IAS 39 para AG 84]. The historical effective rate should be used as the discount rate even where it is lower or higher than the rate on current loans originated by the entity. In other words, loan impairments are based solely on the reduction in estimated cash flows rather than on changes in interest rates. This approach ensures that a financial asset carried at amortised cost that becomes impaired continues to be carried at an amount that considers the present value of all expected future cash flows, in a manner consistent with the asset's measurement before it became impaired.

9.133   Even if the terms of a loan, receivable or held-to-maturity investment are renegotiated or otherwise modified because of financial difficulties of the borrower, impairment is measured using the original effective interest rate before the terms were modified. [IAS 39 para AG 84]. However, in some situations, significant modification of the terms may result in derecognition of the existing asset and recognition of a new asset.

9.134   There are, however, three specific instances where the original discount rate is not used to measure impairment losses.

- For variable rate loans and variable rate held-to-maturity investments, the discount rate for measuring any impairment loss is the current variable rate determined under the contract. [IAS 39 para AG 84].

- For financial assets reclassified out of held-for-trading or available-for-sale, the effective interest rate will be recalculated using the fair value at the date of reclassification (see para 9.37.2). This new effective interest rate will be used to calculate interest income in future periods and considered as the original effective interest rate when measuring impairment. Subsequent to reclassification, an increase in the recoverability of cash flows would also result in an adjusted effective interest rate (see para 9.64).

- For a fixed rate loan that is designated as a hedged item in a fair value hedge of interest rate risk, the loan's carrying amount is adjusted for any changes in its fair value attributable to interest rate movements. The loan's original effective interest rate before the hedge, therefore, becomes irrelevant and the effective interest rate is recalculated using the loan's adjusted carrying amount. The adjusted effective rate is used as the rate for discounting the estimated future cash flows for measuring the impairment loss on the hedged loan. [IAS 39 para IG E4.4]. Hedge accounting is considered in chapter 10.

Example – Impairment of fixed rate loan

The facts are the same as in example 2 in paragraph 9.62 above, except that at 31 December 20X9 it became clear that as a result of structural changes in the industry in which the borrower operates, the borrower was in financial difficulties and its credit rating had been downgraded. At that date, the loan's amortised carrying value, calculated at the original effective rate of 6.7322%, amounted to C583,435.

Faced with this objective evidence, the entity believes that the borrower will be unable to make all the remaining 5 annual scheduled repayments of C142,378. Accordingly, the entity restructures the loan under which the annual payment due on 31 December 20Y0 is waived followed by three annual payments of C175,000 until 31 December 20Y3. The interest on the outstanding loan under the revised payment schedule is reduced to 6.3071%.

The present value of the annual payments of C175,000 due on 31 Dec 20Y1, Y2 and Y3, discounted at the original effective interest rate of 6.7322% amounts to C432,402. Accordingly, the entity recognises an impairment loss of C151,033 (C583,435 − C432,402) in profit or loss on 31 December 20X9. Therefore, the carrying amount is written down by the amount of the impairment loss.

9.135 Consistent with the initial measurement requirements set out in paragraph 9.7 above, cash flows relating to short-term receivables are not discounted if the effect of discounting is immaterial. [IAS 39 para AG 84].

Evaluation of impairment on a portfolio basis

9.136 IAS 39 contains specific guidance for assessing and measuring the impairment losses of a group of financial assets that is carried at amortised cost. The assessment process is as follows:

■ First, financial assets that are considered to be individually significant are assessed for impairment individually based on whether objective evidence of impairment exists.

■ Secondly, all other assets that are not individually significant are assessed for impairment. They may be assessed either individually or collectively on a group basis as indicated below.

■ Thirdly, all assets that have been individually assessed for impairment, whether significant or not, but for which there is no objective evidence of impairment, are included within a group of assets with similar credit risk characteristics and collectively assessed for impairment.

■ Fourthly, assets that are individually assessed for impairment and for which an impairment loss is (or continues to be) recognised are not included in a collective assessment for impairment.

[IAS 39 para 64].

9.137 It seems perhaps illogical and superfluous to subject individual loans that have been reviewed individually for impairment and found not to be impaired to be included again in a portfolio of similar loans for collective assessment. The Basis for Conclusions sets out in extensive detail the arguments for and against this requirement and concludes that impairment that cannot be identified with an individual loan may be identifiable on a portfolio basis. [IAS 39 paras BC111 to BC117].

9.138 There is no guidance in the standard as to what is meant by 'individually significant'. What is significant for one entity may not be significant to another, so each entity should assess what is significant based on its own facts and circumstances.

> **Example – Individual versus collection assessment**
>
> An entity has a portfolio of similar receivables amounting to C100m. The entity considers that within this portfolio are C30m of loans that are individually significant. It assesses these loans for impairment on an individual basis and determines that C20m of loans are impaired. Of the remaining C70m loans that are not significant, the entity selects C15m for individual assessment and finds them all to be individually impaired. The rest of the portfolio is subject to an impairment review on a collective basis.
>
> The result of this assessment means that loans amounting to C35m that have been assessed for impairment on an individual basis, whether significant or not, and found to be impaired will not be included for collective assessment. The remaining C65m of loans (C10m of individually significant loans that are found not to be impaired) and C55m that were not assessed for impairment on an individual basis) are included in the collective assessment.
>
> However, loss probabilities and other loss statistics differ at a portfolio level between the C10m of individually evaluated loans that are found not to be impaired and the C55m of loans that were not individually evaluated for impairment. This means that a different amount of impairment may be required for these sub-portfolios. [IAS 39 AG 87].

9.139 For the purpose of a collective evaluation of impairment, financial assets should be grouped on the basis of similar credit risk characteristics that are indicative of the debtors' ability to pay all amounts due according to the contractual terms. This may be done on the basis of a credit risk evaluation or grading process that considers asset type, industry, geographical location, collateral type, past-due status and other relevant factors. If an entity does not have a group of assets with similar risk characteristics, it does not make the additional assessment. [IAS 39 para AG 87]. In that case, such assets are individually assessed for impairment.

9.140 It should be noted that as soon as information is available that specifically identifies losses on individually impaired assets in a group, those assets should be removed from the group. [IAS 39 para AG 88].

9.141 The Basis for Conclusions in IAS 39 provides detailed guidance on how to perform impairment assessments within groups of financial assets. Most of the detailed guidance will be highly relevant to banks and financial institutions that have large portfolios of loans and receivables. The following elements are critical to an adequate process:

■, Future cash flows in a group of financial assets should be estimated on the basis of historical loss experience for assets with credit risk characteristics similar to those in the group.

- Entities that have no entity-specific loss experience or insufficient experience should use peer group experience for comparable groups of financial assets.

- Historical loss experience should be adjusted on the basis of current observable data to reflect the effects of current conditions.

- Changes in estimates of future cash flows should be directionally consistent with changes in underlying observable data (such as changes in unemployment rates, property prices, payment status, or other factors indicative of changes in the probability of losses in the group and their magnitude).

- The methodology and assumptions used for estimating future cash flows should be reviewed regularly to reduce any differences between loss estimates and actual loss experience.

[IAS 39 para BC124].

9.142 Applying the above process ensures that the collective assessment of impairment for a group of financial assets is still an 'incurred' and not an 'expected' loss model that aims to reflect the loss events that have occurred with respect to individual assets in the group, but have not yet been identified on an individual asset basis. IAS 39 provides an example of an entity that determines, on the basis of historical experience, that one of the main causes of default on credit card loans is the death of the borrower. Although the death rate is unchanged from one year to the next, some of the borrowers in the group may have died in that year. This indicates that an impairment loss has occurred on those loans, even if, at the year-end, the entity is not yet aware which specific borrowers have died. It would be appropriate for an impairment loss to be recognised for these 'incurred but not reported' (IBNR) losses. However, it would not be appropriate to recognise an impairment loss for deaths that are expected to occur in a future period, because the necessary loss event (the death of the borrower) has not yet occurred. [IAS 39 para AG 90].

9.143 The standard allows the use of formula-based approaches or statistical methods to determine impairment losses in a group of financial assets as long as they:

- Do not give rise to an impairment loss on a financial asset's initial recognition.

- Are consistent with the general requirements outlined above.

- Incorporate the effect of the time value of money.

- Consider the cash flows for all of the remaining life of an asset (not only the next year).

- Consider the age of the loans within the portfolio.

[IAS 39 para AG 92].

Measurement difficulties in the absence of observable data

9.144   Making a reasonably reliable estimate of the amount and timing of future cash flows from an impaired financial asset is a matter of judgement. The best estimate is based on reasonable and supportable assumptions and observable data concerning the ability of a debtor to make payments in relation to circumstances existing at the impairment measurement date.

9.145   However, sometimes observable data required to estimate the amount of an impairment loss on a financial asset may be limited or no longer fully relevant to current circumstances. For example, this may be the case when a borrower is in financial difficulties and there is little available historical data relating to similar borrowers. In such cases, an entity should use its judgement to estimate the amount of any impairment loss and to adjust observable data for a group of financial assets to reflect current circumstances. The use of reasonable estimates is an essential part of the financial statement's preparation and does not undermine their reliability. [IAS 39 para 62].

General provisions for bad and doubtful debts

9.146   It has not been uncommon for entities under previous GAAPs to determine bad debt provisions for non-performing loans based on a provision matrix or similar formula that specifies fixed provision rates for the number of days a loan or a debt is overdue. For example, the provisioning rates could be zero per cent if less than 90 days overdue, 20 per cent if 90-180 days, 50 per cent if 181-365 days and 100 per cent if more than 365 days. Such a method of provisioning would not be acceptable under IAS 39, unless it produces a result that is sufficiently close to the one obtained by following a discounted cash flow methodology required by the standard, which is considered highly unlikely. [IAS 39 para IG E4.5].

9.147   Similarly, it was fairly common for entities under previous GAAPs to make a general provision for bad and doubtful debts on the grounds of prudence and set aside sums that are not specifically related to losses in a group of assets, but intended to cover unplanned and unexpected losses. Such provisioning methods are not allowed under IAS 39 as it results in impairment or bad debt losses that are in excess of those that can be attributed to incurred losses. Accordingly, amounts that an entity might want to set aside for additional possible impairment in financial assets, such as reserves that cannot be supported by objective evidence about impairment, are not recognised as impairment or bad debt losses under IAS 39. [IAS 39 para IG E4.6]. This does not prevent an entity designating part of its reserves in equity to cover such 'prudence' or related losses.

Recognition of interest on impaired assets

9.148   Once a financial asset or a group of similar financial assets has been written down as a result of an impairment loss, interest income is thereafter recognised using the rate of interest used to discount the future cash flows for the purpose of measuring the impairment loss. [IAS 39 para AG 93]. That is the discount in the carrying amount is unwound. This would be the original effective rate for fixed rate instruments carried at amortised cost and current interest rate for floating rate instruments.

9.149 An entity should not stop accruing interest on loans that are non-performing. When non-performing loans are reviewed for impairment, the collection or non-collection of the future interest payments would be taken into account in the estimation of future cash flows for the purposes of the impairment calculation. Interest income would be recognised as the discount unwinds.

Example – Income recognition on impaired loans

The facts are the same as in the example in paragraph 9.134 above. Following recognition of the impairment loss at 31 December 20X9, the amortised cost amounted to C432,402.

On the assumption that cash inflows will occur as restructured, the amortisation schedule based on the revised cash flows and the original discount rate is shown below. In accordance with paragraph 9.148 above, interest income is recognised at the rate of discount used to the measure the impairment.

	Cash in flows	Interest income @ 6.7322%	Carrying amount
1 Jan 20Y0			432,402
31 Dec 20Y0		29,110	461,512
31 Dec 20Y1	175,000	31,070	317,582
31 Dec 20Y2	175,000	21,380	163,962
31 Dec 20Y3	175,000	11,038	–
	525,000	92,598	

Reversal of impairment losses on assets held at amortised cost

9.150 As stated in paragraph 9.115 above, an impairment review should be carried out at each reporting date. If, in a subsequent period, the amount of the impairment loss decreases and the decrease can be related objectively to an event occurring after the impairment was recognised (such as an improvement in the debtor's credit rating), the previously recognised impairment loss should be reversed either directly or by adjusting an allowance account. The reversal should not result in a carrying amount of the financial asset that exceeds what the amortised cost would have been had the impairment not been recognised at the date the impairment is reversed. The amount of the reversal should be recognised in profit or loss. [IAS 39 para 65]. This is in contrast with an equity instrument where an impairment loss is specifically not reversed (see para 9.154).

9.150.1 If a financial asset has been reclassified out of a category measured at fair value (that is, held-for-trading or available-for-sale) and into a category measured at amortised cost, an increase in cash flows would be a reversal of impairment only if the impairment loss was recognised after the date of reclassification. Any other increase in cash flows will be a change in expected cash flows and adjusted cumulatively in accordance with paragraph AG 8 of IAS 39 (see para 9.64).

Financial assets carried at cost

9.151   As set out in paragraph 9.104 above, an unquoted equity instrument that is not carried at fair value because its fair value cannot be reliably measured, or on a derivative asset that is linked to and must be settled by delivery of such an unquoted equity instrument, are measured at cost. For such instruments, if there is objective evidence that an impairment loss has been incurred, the amount of the impairment loss is measured as the difference between the carrying amount of the financial asset and the present value of estimated future cash flows discounted at the current market rate of return for a similar financial asset. Such impairment losses are not permitted to be reversed. [IAS 39 para 66].

Available-for-sale financial assets

9.152   When a decline in the fair value of an available-for-sale financial asset has been recognised directly in other comprehensive income and there is objective evidence that the asset is impaired, the cumulative loss that had been recognised directly in other comprehensive income should be reclassified from equity and recognised in profit or loss even though the financial asset has not been derecognised. [IAS 39 para 67]. It is not appropriate to allocate part of the reduction below cost to impairment and part to a fair value movement through other comprehensive income.

9.153   The amount of cumulative loss that is recycled to profit or loss is the difference between the acquisition cost (net of any principal repayment and amortisation) and current fair value, less any impairment loss on that financial asset previously recognised in profit or loss. [IAS 39 para 68]. Any portion of the cumulative net loss that is attributable to foreign currency changes on that asset that had been recognised in equity is also recognised in profit or loss (see para 9.163 below). Subsequent losses, including any portion attributable to foreign currency changes, are also recognised in profit or loss until the asset is derecognised. [IAS 39 para IG E4.9].

9.153.1   For financial assets reclassified out of a category measured at fair value (that is, held-for-trading or available-for-sale) and into another category, see paragraph 9.37.4.

Example – Impairment of available-for-sale debt security

On 1 January 20X3, an entity purchased C10 million 5 year bond with semi-annual interest of 5% payable on 30 June and 31 December each year. The bond's purchase price was C10,811,100, which resulted in a bond premium of C811,100 and an effective interest rate of 8% (4% on a semi-annual basis). The entity classified the bond as available-for-sale.

The entity received all the interest due in 20X3 and 20X4 on a timely basis. At 31 December 20X4, the amortised cost of the loan amounted to C10,524,226. The cumulative amount recognised in equity to that date was a loss C266,322.

The entity did not receive the half-yearly interest due on 30 June 20X5 and it soon became clear that the issuer was in financial difficulties. At 31 December 20X5, the entity reviews the issuer's financial condition and prospects for repayment of the loan and determines that the bond is impaired. On the basis of the information available at the time, the entity's best estimate of future cash flows (on a yearly basis) is cash receipts of C2m on 31 December 20X6 and C7m on 31 December 20X7, the scheduled repayment date.

Although the bond is non-performing, the entity recognises the interest income for the period to 31 December 20X5 at the original effective interest rate. On this basis, the bond's amortised cost at 31 December 20X5 amounts to C11,383,002.

As the bond is classified as available-for-sale, it is necessary to determine the bond's fair value at 31 December 20X5. As there is no observable market price for the bond, the bond's fair value, can only be obtained by discounting the expected cash flows at the current market rate. As a market rate for a comparable bond may not exist, it would be necessary to derive a current market rate for the bond. One way of estimating the current rate for a comparable bond with terms and credit risk profiles similar to the existing bond is by reference to a benchmark rate or the risk-free rate, which is part of the bond's effective rate of interest of 8%, and amending that rate by the original credit risk premium of the existing bond.

Assume that when the bond was purchased on 1 January 20X3, the risk-free rate was 6% for a debt instrument with the same terms as the one purchased by the entity. Thus, the credit risk premium of the bond is 200 basis points. At 31 December 20X5, the risk-free rate for a similar type of instrument is 8%. Therefore, using the bond's credit risk premium of 200 basis points, the current interest rate for discounting the expected cash flows is 10% (8% + 200 basis point). Using this rate of 10%, the present value of the expected cash flow of C2m and C7m arising on 31 December 20X6 and 31 December 20X7 amounts to C7,603,305.

Therefore, the impairment loss recognised in profit or loss is as follows:

Amortised cost at 31 December 20X4	10,524,226
Accrual of half-yearly interest to 30 June 20X5 @ 4%	420,969
	10,945,195
Accrual of half-yearly interest to 31 December 20X5 @ 4%	437,808
Amortised cost at 31 December 20X5 before impairment	11,383,003
Fair value of bond at 31 December 20X5	(7,603,305)
Impairment arising during 20X5	3,779,698
Recycling of loss recognised in equity	266,322
Impairment recognised in profit or loss	4,046,020
Bond stated in the balance sheet at 31 December 20X5	7,603,305

On 31 December 20X6, the holder received the expected cash flow of C2m. The amortised cost of the bond at 31 December 20X6 amounts to:

Amortised cost at 31 Dec 20X5	7,603.305
Accrual of interest to 31 Dec 20X6 @10%	760,330
	8,363,635
Less cash received at 31 Dec 20X6	2,000,000
Amortised cost at 31 Dec 20X6	6,363,635

Note that once the bond has been written down as a result of an impairment loss, interest income is thereafter recognised using the rate of interest used to discount the future cash flows for the purpose of measuring the impairment loss. (See para 9.148.) This rate is 10% as stated above.

During the year to 31 December 20X6, interest rates increased and as a result the bond's fair value at 31 December 20X6 fell to C6.0m. There was no further change in the credit status/rating of the issuer and there is no evidence of any further credit-related impairment since the original assessment of impairment was made during 20X5. At 31 December 20X6, there is a difference between the bond's amortised cost and its fair value as shown below:

Amortised cost at 31 Dec 20X6 as above	6,363,635
Fair value at 31 Dec 20X6	6,000,000
Further reduction	363,635

The further reduction of C363,635 is also the difference between the fair value of C7,603, 305 at 31 December 20X5 after adjusting for interest income of 10% and the cash of £2m received and the fair value of C6,000,000 at 31 December 20X6.

The question arises as to whether the further decrease of C363,635 should be taken to the AFS reserve in equity or recognised as a further impairment loss in profit or loss for the period to 31 December 20X6.

There are two acceptable views. An entity makes an accounting policy choice as to which view it accepts and applies this view to all similar transactions. If material, an entity discloses this policy in its financial statements.

View A – AFS reserve in equity

Without any further objective evidence of impairment, no further impairment charge is recognised in profit or loss. Hence, the change in fair value is recognised in equity.

This view is consistent with paragraph 58 of IAS 39, which requires an entity to assess at each balance sheet date whether there is any objective evidence that a financial asset is impaired. If such evidence exists, the entity should apply the requirement for available-for-sale financial asset considered in paragraphs 9.152 and 9.153 above. In this situation, at 31 December 20X6, as there is no new evidence of a further credit impairment, the requirements of those paragraphs do not apply and the further decrease of C363,635 is recognised in equity. In addition, IAS 39 paragraph IG E4.10 acknowledges that the AFS reserve in equity can be negative – for example, because of a decline in the fair value of an investment in a debt instrument that results from an increase in the basic risk free interest rate.

Similarly, had interest rates decreased resulting in an increase in fair value, it would be appropriate to recognise that change in the AFS reserve in equity. This would not be considered a reversal of impairment as for a reversal to occur there should be an increase in fair value attributable to an improvement in the issuer's credit standing.

View B – impairment/reversal of impairment in profit or loss

This view is that, at the reporting date, there is still objective evidence of impairment since acquiring the asset and, therefore, a further decline in fair value is recognised in profit or loss as further impairment. Any changes in fair value (gains or losses) subsequent to impairment are reflected in profit or loss up to the asset's amortised cost and afterwards in equity.

This view interprets paragraph 58 of IAS 39 as referring to evidence of impairment since acquiring the asset. This view is also consistent with the treatment in a period in which objective evidence of impairment first arises on an asset where the entire change in fair value (IAS 39 para 68) is recognised in profit or loss, even if some of that change in fair value is market related (for example, due to an increase in interest rates). This is a broader reading of the term event in paragraph 70 of IAS 39 to mean any event rather than only a credit-related event.

This view is also consistent with paragraph IG E4.9 of IAS 39. It states that for non-monetary AFS financial assets that became impaired in a previous period, any subsequent losses including the portion attributable to foreign exchange losses (that are also not additional impairments) are also recognised in profit or loss until the asset is derecognised.

Similarly, had interest rates decreased resulting in an increase in fair value and the increase can be objectively related to an event occurring after the impairment loss was recognised in profit or loss, it would be appropriate to recognise the change in profit or loss as a reversal of the previous impairment in accordance with IAS 39 paragraph 70.

Reversal of impairment losses

9.154   It is possible that after an impairment loss has been recognised for an available-for-sale financial asset circumstances change in a subsequent period such that the fair value of the available-for-sale financial instrument increases. In those circumstances, the treatment required by the standard for reversals of impairment losses on available-for-sale debt instruments is different from those on available-for-sale equity instruments as noted below:

■   For available-for-sale debt instruments (monetary assets), past impairment losses should be reversed through the profit or loss when fair value increases and the increase can be objectively related to an event occurring after the impairment loss was recognised in profit or loss. [IAS 39 para 70].

■ For available-for-sale equity investments (non-monetary assets), past impairment losses recognised in profit or loss should not be reversed through profit or loss when fair value increases. [IAS 39 para 69]. This means that subsequent increases in fair value including those that have the effect of reversing earlier impairment losses are all recognised in equity. This is a significant change from the previous version of the standard.

9.155 The inability to reverse impairment losses recognised in profit or loss on available-for-sale equity instruments raises a particular issue for entities that have recognised such impairment losses in their interim reports. This is because, at the subsequent reporting or balance sheet date, conditions may have changed to such an extent that a loss would not have been recognised, or a smaller loss would have been recognised, if the impairment review were first carried out at that date.

9.156 The confusion arises because paragraph 28 of IAS 34, 'Interim financial reporting', requires an entity to apply the same accounting policies in its interim financial statements as are applied in its annual financial statements. This suggests that an impairment loss recognised in the interim period should not be reversed at the subsequent balance sheet date. On the other hand, the same paragraph states that 'the frequency of an entity's reporting (annual, half-yearly, or quarterly) should not affect the measurement of its annual results. To achieve this objective, measurement for interim reporting purposes should be made on a 'year-to-date' basis. This suggests that an impairment loss recognised in one interim period can be reversed at the subsequent balance sheet date.

9.157 The IFRIC considered the matter and issued IFRIC 10, 'Interim financial reporting and impairment', in July 2006. The IFRIC concluded that the prohibitions on reversals of recognised impairment losses on investments in equity instruments in IAS 39 should take precedence over the more general statement in IAS 34 regarding the frequency of an entity's reporting not affecting the measurement of its annual results.Therefore, any impairment losses that are recognised in a previous interim period in respect of an investment in an equity instrument may not be reversed in a later interim periods or when preparing the annual financial statements. [IFRIC 10 para 8]. The Interpretation applies to annual periods beginning on or after 1 November 2006. Earlier application is encouraged. If an entity applies the Interpretation for a period beginning before 1 November 2006, it should disclose that fact.

Foreign currency financial instruments

General

9.158 Financial instruments are often denominated in foreign currencies. The way in which changes in foreign exchange rates in foreign currency financial assets and liabilities should be dealt with is covered in IAS 21, 'The effects of changes in foreign exchange rates'. The measurement principles of IAS 39 generally do not override these rules, except in the area of hedge accounting which is considered in chapter 10.

9.159 Under IAS 21, all transactions in foreign currencies are initially recognised at the spot exchange rate at the date of the transaction. The spot exchange rate is the exchange rate for immediate delivery. It follows that on initial recognition, all foreign currency financial instruments are translated at the spot rate into the entity's functional currency, irrespective of whether the instrument is carried at cost, amortised cost or fair value.

9.160 Gains and losses associated with financial instruments, such as interest income and expense and impairment losses, are recognised at the spot exchange rate at the dates on which they arise. Dividends should be recognised in profit or loss when the shareholder's right to receive payment is established. [IAS 18 para 30(c)]. The exchange rate ruling at that date, which is normally the dividend declaration date, is used to record the income. Entities are permitted to use an average rate where it represents an approximation to the spot rate in that period.

Subsequent measurement

9.161 The subsequent measurement of foreign currency financial assets and liabilities will depend on whether the assets and liabilities are monetary or non-monetary in nature. Monetary items are units of currency held and assets and liabilities to be received or paid in a fixed or determinable number of units of currency. [IAS 21 para 8]. It follows that financial assets and liabilities that are debt instruments are monetary items. Derivative financial instruments are also monetary items as they are settled at a future date, even though the underlying may be non-monetary. Non-monetary items are all items other than monetary items. In other words, the right to receive (or an obligation to deliver) a fixed or determinable number of units of currency is absent in a non-monetary item. This is the case for financial assets that are equity instruments.

Monetary financial assets

9.162 IAS 21 requires that an entity should translate its foreign currency monetary items outstanding at the balance sheet date using the closing spot rate at that date. [IAS 21 para 23(a)]. Exchange differences arising on translating monetary items or on the settlement of monetary items at rates different from those at which they were translated on initial recognition during the period or in previous financial statements, are recognised in profit or loss in the period in which they arise. [IAS 21 para 28]. However, exchange differences on monetary items that are designated as hedging instruments in cash flow hedges or net investments in foreign entities are recognised in equity. [IAS 39 para AG 83].

9.163 For the purpose of recognising foreign exchange gains and losses under IAS 21, a foreign currency monetary available-for-sale financial asset is treated as if it were carried at amortised cost in the foreign currency. Accordingly, for such a financial asset, exchange differences arising from changes in amortised cost, such as interest calculated using the effective interest method and impairment losses are recognised in profit or loss. All other gains and losses are recognised in equity. [IAS 39 para 55(b)]. An example illustrating the above treatment is included as example E3.2 in the Implementation Guidance to IAS 39. A similar example is given below.

Example – Available-for-sale debt security denominated in foreign currency

On 1 January 20X1, an entity whose functional currency is the local currency (LC) purchases a foreign currency (FC) denominated bond for its fair value of FC1,000. The bond has 5 years remaining to maturity and a principal amount of FC1,250 million. Interest is payable annually at 4.7% (that is, FC59) on 31 December each year. Assuming there are no transaction costs, the effective interest rate is 10%. The entity classifies the bond as available-for-sale.

The relevant foreign exchange rates are as follows:

	Average rate FC =	Closing rate FC =
1 January 20X1		LC 1.50
31 December 20X1	LC 1.75	LC 2.00
31 December 20X2	LC 2.25	LC 2.50
31 December 20X3	LC 2.35	LC 2.20
31 December 20X4	LC 2.05	LC 1.90
31 December 20X5	LC 2.10	LC 2.30

For the purpose of this illustrative example, it is assumed that the use of the average exchange rate provides a reliable approximation of the spot rates applicable to the accrual of interest income during the year.

The cumulative gain or loss that is recognised in equity is the difference between the amortised cost (adjusted for impairment, if any) and the fair value of the available-for-sale financial asset in the entity's functional currency.

At 1 January 20X1, the fair value of the bond (FC1,000) translated in the entity's functional currency is LC1.5m and the entry to record this is as follows:

At 1 January 20X5	Dr LC	Cr LC
Available-for-sale financial asset	1,500	
Cash		1,500

The amortisation schedule in foreign currency (FC) is as follows:

Date	Interest income @ 10%	Cash inflow	Amortised cost
1 Jan 20X1			1,000
31 Dec 20X1	100	59	1,041
31 Dec 20X2	104	59	1,086
31 Dec 20X3	109	59	1,136
31 Dec 20X4	113	59	1,190
31 Dec 20X5	119	59	1,250

As the entity classifies the bond as an available-for-sale investment, the asset is treated as an asset measured at amortised cost in foreign currency for the purposes of applying IAS 21. Therefore, the amortisation schedule in the entity's functional currency (LC) shown below is calculated from the above amounts at the appropriate exchange rates as follows:

	Interest income @ 10% (average rate) LC	Cash inflow @ 4.7% (actual rate) LC	Amortised cost LC
1 Jan 20X1			1,500
31 Dec 20X1	175	118	1,557
31 Dec 20X2	234	148	1,643
31 Dec 20X3	256	130	1,769
31 Dec 20X4	232	112	1,889
31 Dec 20X5	250	136	2,003
	1,147	644	

	Amortised cost as above FC	Amortised cost translated at year end rate LC	Carrying amount as determined above LC	Cumulative exchange difference LC	Exchange difference recognised in profit or loss LC
31 Dec 20X1	1,041	2,082	1,557	525	525
31 Dec 20X2	1,086	2,715	1,643	1,072	547
31 Dec 20X3	1,136	2,498	1,769	729	(342)
31 Dec 20X4	1,190	2,261	1,889	372	(358)
31 Dec 20X5	1,250	2,875	2,003	872	500

As the debt instrument is classified as an available-for-sale investment, it is necessary to determine the bond's fair value at each balance sheet date. The bond's fair value at each balance sheet date is given below. The difference between the amortised cost and asset's fair value is the cumulative gain or loss that is recognised in equity. This difference will include exchange differences that would not be separated out from the overall movement recognised in equity. All other changes in foreign exchange rates are recognised in profit or loss as shown above.

	Fair value	Fair value at year end rate	Amortised cost at year end rate as above	Cumulative difference	Gain or loss recognised in equity
	FC	LC	LC	LC	LC
31 Dec 20X1	1,060	2,120	2,082	38	38
31 Dec 20X2	1,070	2,675	2,715	(40)	(78)
31 Dec 20X3	1,140	2,508	2,499	9	49
31 Dec 20X4	1,200	2,280	2,261	19	10
31 Dec 20X5	1,250	2,875	2,875	0	(19)

The movements in the fair value of the bond can be summarised as follows:

	Fair value at the beginning of the period	Interest income	Cash received	Exchange difference recognised in profit or loss	Gain or loss recognised in equity	Fair value at the end of the period
	LC	LC	LC	LC	LC	LC
31 Dec 20X1	1,500	175	(118)	525	38	2,120
31 Dec 20X2	2,120	234	(148)	547	(78)	2,675
31 Dec 20X3	2,675	256	(130)	(342)	49	2,508
31 Dec 20X4	2,508	232	(112)	(358)	10	2,280
31 Dec 20X5	2,280	250	(136)	500	(19)	2,875

Dual currency bond

9.163.1 Dual currency bonds are bonds that are denominated in one currency, but pay interest in another currency at a fixed exchange rate. For example, an entity with pound sterling as a functional currency may issue a debt instrument that provides for the annual payment of interest in euros and the repayment of principal in pound sterling. Sometimes both the interest payments and the principal repayments may be denominated in currencies that are different from the entity's functional currency. For example, an entity with pound sterling functional currency may issue a euro denominated bond that pays interest in US dollars. Such a foreign currency bond can be viewed as a host debt instrument with principal and interest payments denominated in pound sterling and two embedded swaps that convert the pound sterling interest payments into US dollars and the pound sterling principal payments into euros. However, as explained in paragraph 5.55, IAS 39 does not permit such embedded foreign currency derivatives to be separated from the host debt instrumen, because IAS 21 requires foreign currency gains and losses to be recognised in profit or loss. [IAS 39 para AG33(c)].

9.163.2 We believe the most appropriate accounting treatment would be to analyse the bond into its two components – the interest component that exposes the entity to US dollar exchange rate risk and the principal component that exposes the entity to euro exchange rate risk. Each component would be recognised at its fair value at initial recognition, being the present value of the future payments to be made on the respective components. This means that the entity would have an instalment bond with annual payments denominated in US dollars for the US dollar interest payments and a zero coupon bond denominated in euros for the euro principal payment. The carrying amount of each component would be translated to pound sterling at each period end using the closing exchange rate and the resulting exchange differences recognised in the income statement in accordance with paragraph 28 of IAS 21.

9.163.3 Analysing the dual currency bond into its two components for measurement purposes reports the foreign currency risk on the principal on a discounted basis, recognising that the euro payment is not due until redemption and also captures the foreign exchange risk associated with the dollar interest cash flows inherent in the bond. The analysis is consistent with the rationale given in paragraph AG 33(c) of IAS 39 for not separating the foreign currency embedded derivative.

Example – Dual currency bond

On 1 January 20X5, an entity with pound sterling functional currency issued a €5m bond repayable in 3 year's time. The bond pays fixed interest at 6% per annum in US dollars, calculated on a notional dollar equivalent of the proceeds raised in euros. There is no issue cost.

The following exchange rates are relevant:

	01 Jan 20X5	31 Dec 20X5	31 Dec 20X6	31 Dec 20X7
£1 = Spot rate	€1.4142	€1.4530	€1.4852	€1.3571
Average rate		€1.4627	€1.4673	€1.4621
£1 = Spot rate	$1.9187	$1.7208	$1.9591	$1.9973
Average rate		$1.8207	$1.8429	$2.0018
€1 = Spot rate	$1.3569			

In accordance with the treatment discussed above, the amounts that should be recognised in the income statement and the balance sheet at the end of each period are shown below:

	£	€	US$
Proceeds received		5,000,000	6,784,500
Interest payable @ 6% pa on USD amount			407,070
Zero Coupon Bond = PV of € principal			
repayment at the end of year 3 discounted 6%	2,968,531	4,198,096	
Instalment Bond = PV of 3 yearly USD			
interest payments discounted at 6%	567,104		1,088,103
Proceeds received for the single bond	3,535,635		

Note that the discounting is carried out at 6% assuming a flat yield curve. The actual proceeds of €5,000,000 translated at the spot rate at 1 January 20X5 are actually £3,535,568. The small difference of 67 is due to the effect of discounting and cross exchange rate and is ignored.

Amortisation of instalment bond

Balance carried forward	Balance brought forward	Finance cos @ 6%	Cash	Payments
	US$	US$	US$	
31/12/20X5	1,088,103	65,286	407,070	746,319
31/12/20X6	746,319	44,779	407,070	384,028
31/12/20X7	384,028	23,042	407,070	0

	Balance brought forward	Finance cost at average rate	Payment at spot rate	Balance carried forward	Retranslated US$ @ year end rate	Exchange difference
	£	£	£	£	£	£
31 Dec 20X5	567,104	35,858	236,559	366,403	433,705	67,301
31 Dec 20X6	433,705	24,298	207,784	250,219	196,023	-54,196
31 Dec20X7	196,023	11,510	203,810	3,723	0	-3,723
		71,666	648,153			9,382

Amortisation of zero coupon bond

	Balance brought forward	Finance cost@ 6%	Cash Payments	Balance carried forward
	€	€	€	€
31/12/20X5	4,198,096	251,886		4,449,982
31/12/20X6	4,449,982	266,999	0	4,716,981
31/12/20X7	4,716,981	283,019	5,000,000	0

	Balance brought forward	Finance cost at average rate	Payment at spot rate	Balance carried forward	Translated US$ @ year end rate	Exchange difference
	£	£	£	£	£	£
31/12/20X5	2,968,531	172,206		3,140,737	3,062,617	-78,120
31/12/20X6	3,062,617	181,966		3,244,583	3,175,991	-68,592
31/12/20X7	3,175,991	193,570	3,684,327	-314,766	0	314,766
		547,742	3,684,327			168,054

Amortisation of single bond

	Opening balance sheet	Income statement	Cash payments	Finance cost	Exchange gain/(loss)
	£	£	£	£	£
31/12/20X5	3,535,635	208,064	-10,819	236,559	3,496,322
31/12/20X6	3,496,322	206,264	-122,788	207,784	3,372,013
31/12/20X7	3,372,013	205,081	311,043	3,888,137	0
		619,409	177,436	4,332,480	

These amounts are calcultated by adding the bonds two components together.

Non-monetary financial assets

9.164 Translation of non-monetary items depends on whether they are recognised at historical cost or at fair value. Items recognised at historical cost are not retranslated at subsequent balance sheet dates. This would apply to foreign currency denominated unquoted equity instruments that are measured at cost, because their fair values cannot be reliably determined. However, most non-monetary financial instruments, such as equity instruments, are measured at fair value. Non-monetary assets that are measured at fair value in a foreign currency are translated using the exchange rates at the date when the fair value was determined. [IAS 21 para 23(c)]. When a gain or loss on a non-monetary item is recognised directly in equity, any exchange component of that gain or loss should also be recognised directly in equity. Therefore, for available-for-sale equity instruments remeasured through equity the entire change in fair value is recognised in equity. [IAS 39 para AG 83].

Impairment of foreign currency financial asset

9.165 Although not specifically dealt with in IAS 39, measuring impairment losses on financial assets that are denominated in foreign currency is, in principle, no different from those that are denominated in the entity's functional currency. Thus, for a foreign currency financial asset that is carried at amortised cost, the expected future cash flows denominated in the foreign currency are discounted at the financial asset's original effective interest rate. This amount is then translated into the entity's functional currency using the foreign exchange rate at the date when the impairment is recognised. The difference between the translated present value and the carrying amount in the entity's functional currency is the impairment loss that is recognised in profit or loss. Similarly, if in a subsequent period, circumstances change that result in a reversal of the impairment loss, in whole or in part, the reversal should be measured using the foreign exchange rate at the date when the reversal is recognised.

9.166   For foreign currency non-monetary assets that are held as available-for-sale with changes in fair value recognised in equity, the situation is different. In this case, the amount of the loss that is removed from equity and included in profit or loss is the difference between the asset's acquisition cost translated at the rate of exchange ruling at the acquisition's date and its current fair value translated at the rate of exchange ruling at the date of the impairment. [IAS 21 para 25]. This is because an impairment loss may be recognised in the foreign currency, but not in the entity's functional currency and *vice versa* as illustrated below.

Example – Foreign currency equity instrument designated as available-for-sale

On 1 January 20X3, an entity whose functional currency is the local currency (LC) purchases a foreign currency (FC) denominated equity instrument at its fair value of FC1,000. The entity classifies the equity as available-for-sale. The exchange rate at acquisition was FC = LC1.5. The asset's fair value at subsequent balance sheet dates in FC and the closing exchange rates are given below:

Date	Exchange rate	Fair value of asset FC	Fair value of asset LC	Change in fair value recognised in OCI Recognised in the period LC	Change in fair value recognised in OCI Cumulative LC
1 Jan 20X3	1.5	1,000	1,500		
31 Dec 20X3	1.7	900	1,530	30	30
31 Dec 20X4	1.6	800	1,280	-250	-220
31 Dec 20X4 Loss reclassified from equity and recognised in profit or loss					220
31 Dec 20X5	1.8	850	1,530	250	250

As can be seen from the above, even though the asset's fair value measured in FC at 31 December 20X3 is less than the original cost in FC, no impairment loss is recognised in that year because any impairment of an equity AFS asset is determined in terms of an entity's functional currency (as confirmed by an agenda decision published in the IFRIC in July 2009). An impairment loss is recognised in the following year when the fair value measured in the entity's functional currency (LC1,280) is lower than the asset's acquisition price (LC1,500). The impairment loss of C220 is reclassified from equity and recognised in profit or loss. Even if circumstances change, as happens in 31 Dec 20X5, the loss recognised in profit or loss is never reversed. Instead, the change in fair value during the year of LC250 is recognised in equity (see further para 9.154 above).

9.167 For foreign currency monetary assets that are held as available-for-sale, past impairment losses recognised in profit or loss can be reversed through profit or loss as explained in paragraph 9.154 above. Again the exchange rate at the date of the reversal should be used to measure the amount of the reversal. Since, for the purposes of recognising foreign exchange gains and losses under IAS 21, a monetary available-for-sale asset is treated as if it were carried at amortised cost in the foreign currency, all exchange differences arising on the reversal should be recognised in profit or loss.

Financial assets held in foreign operations

9.168 An entity may have both financial assets that are classified as at fair value through profit or loss and available-for-sale investments. When such an entity is a foreign operation that is a subsidiary, its financial statements are consolidated with those of its parent. In that situation, IAS 39 applies to the accounting for financial instruments in the financial statements of the foreign operation and IAS 21 applies in translating the financial statements of a foreign operation for incorporation in the reporting entity's consolidated financial statements. Under IAS 21, all exchange differences resulting from translating the financial statements of a foreign operation are recognised in equity until disposal of the net investment. This would include exchange differences arising from financial instruments carried at fair value, which would include both financial assets classified as at fair value through profit or loss and financial assets that are available-for-sale as illustrated in the example below.

> **Example – Financial instruments held in a foreign entity – Interaction of IAS 39 and IAS 21**
>
> Entity A is domiciled in the UK and its functional currency and presentation currency is pound sterling. Entity A has a foreign subsidiary, entity B, in France whose functional currency is the euro. Entity B is the owner of a debt instrument, which is held-for-trading and, therefore, carried at fair value under IAS 39. [IAS 39 para IE 3.3].
>
> In entity B's financial statements for year 20X5, the fair value and carrying amount of the debt instrument is €400. In entity A's consolidated financial statements, the asset is translated into pound sterling at the spot exchange rate applicable at the balance sheet date, say €1 = £0.50. Thus, the carrying amount in the consolidated financial statements is £200.
>
> At the end of year 20X5, the fair value of the debt instrument has increased to €440. Entity B recognises the trading asset at €440 in its balance sheet and recognises a fair value gain of €40 in its income statement. During the year, the spot exchange rate has increased from €1 = £0.50 to €1 = £0.75, resulting in an increase in the instrument's fair value from £200 to £330 (€440 @ 0.75). Therefore, entity A recognises the trading asset at £330 in its consolidated financial statements.
>
> Since entity B is a foreign entity, entity A translates the income statement of entity B in accordance with IAS 21 *"at the exchange rates at the dates of the transactions"*. Since the fair value gain has accrued through the year, entity A uses the average rate of €1

= £0.625 as a practical approximation. Therefore, while the fair value of the trading asset has increased by £130 (£330 – £200), entity A recognises only £25 (€40 @ 0.625) of this increase in consolidated profit or loss. The resulting exchange difference, that is, the remaining increase in the debt instrument's fair value £105 (£130 – £25) is classified as equity until the disposal of the net investment in the foreign operation.

Chapter 10

Hedge accounting

Chapter 10

Hedge accounting

Introduction

What is hedging?

10.1   Entities face many types of business risk. One of the most significant is financial risk. Different companies, however, are exposed to different risks. Some entities may be concerned about commodity prices, such as the price of copper or oil; others may be concerned about interest rates or exchange rates. Successful entities manage the types of risk described by deciding to which risk, and to what extent, they should be exposed, by monitoring the actual exposure and taking steps to reduce risks to within agreed limits, often through the use of derivatives. However, hedging one risk may magnify another. Management has to decide for example whether it is cash flow risk averse, which will mean that it is not concerned with fair value risk.

10.2   The process of entering into a derivative transaction with a counterparty in the expectation that the transaction will eliminate or reduce an entity's exposure to a particular risk is referred to as hedging. Risk reduction is obtained because the derivative's value or cash flows are expected, wholly or partly, to move inversely and, therefore, offset changes in the value or cash flows of the 'hedged position' or item. The hedged position/item can include recognised assets and liabilities, a firm commitment or a forecast transaction. Sometimes an entity can arrange its affairs so as to be naturally hedged. This would be the case, for example, if an entity's portfolio of fixed interest securities is financed by fixed rate borrowings of the same amount and duration. In this case, a rise in the general level of interest rates will decrease the value of both asset and liability positions by approximately the same amount, so that the entity has no net exposure to interest rate risk. Hedging in an economic sense, therefore, concerns the reduction or elimination of different financial risks such as price risk, interest rate risk, currency risk, etc, associated with the hedged position. It is a risk management activity that is now commonplace in many entities.

What is hedge accounting?

10.3   Once an entity has entered into a hedging transaction, it will be necessary to reflect the transaction in the financial statements of the entity. Accounting for the hedged position should be consistent with the objective of entering into the hedging transaction, which is to eliminate or reduce significantly specific risks that management considers can have an adverse effect on the entity's financial position and results, whilst acknowledging that such strategies can increase other risks with which management is less concerned. This consistency can be achieved if both the hedging instrument and the hedged position are recognised and measured on symmetrical bases and offsetting gains and losses are reported in profit or loss in the same periods. Unfortunately, mismatches occur under existing recognition and measurement standards and practices. Hedge accounting practices have been developed to correct or mitigate these mis-matches.

10.4 In simple terms 'hedge accounting' is a technique that modifies the normal basis for recognising gains and losses (or revenues and expenses) on associated hedging instruments and hedged items so that both are recognised in earnings in the same accounting period. Hedge accounting thus affords management the opportunity to eliminate or reduce the income statement volatility that otherwise would arise if the hedged items and hedging instruments were accounted for under GAAP separately, without regard to the hedge's business purpose.

[The next paragraph is 10.6.]

Hedge accounting under IAS 39

10.6 IAS 39 provides a set of strict criteria that must be met before hedge accounting can be used. These require that the hedge relationship is designated and formally documented at inception. There are also requirements to demonstrate both at inception and throughout the life of the hedge that the hedge is 'highly effective'. As a result, not all hedging activities undertaken by entities qualify for hedge accounting. Failure to meet any of the criteria whilst the hedge is in place would result in the discontinuance of hedge accounting.

10.7 The standard also specifies three methods of hedge accounting that were designed to reflect the standard's requirement to measure all derivatives at fair value. As a result, hedge accounting in IAS 39 can be applied to three types of hedging relationships as indicated below:

■ Where the hedged risk is that the hedged item's *fair value* will change in response to some variable, such as changes in interest rates, foreign exchange rates, or market prices, gains and losses on the hedging instrument and the offsetting losses and gains on the hedged item are both recognised in profit or loss. This is referred to as a fair value hedge.

■ Where the hedged risk is that the hedged item's future *cash flows* will change in response to such variables, the gain or loss on the hedging instrument is initially recognised in other comprehensive income and subsequently recycled from equity to profit or loss as the hedged item affects profit or loss. This is referred to as a cash flow hedge.

■ Where the hedge risk is that the carrying amount of a *net investment* in a foreign operation will change in response to exchange rate movements, the gain or loss on the hedging instrument is initially recognised in other comprehensive income and subsequently recycled to profit or loss from equity on disposal of that foreign operation. This is referred to as a hedge of a net investment in a foreign operation.

10.8 IAS 39 does not mandate the use of hedge accounting. It is a privilege not a right. Entities intending to use hedge accounting must have proper systems and procedures to monitor each hedging relationship. Many entities may find these requirements too onerous and decide not to try to hedge account. However, this approach generally comes at a cost – income statement volatility.

Hedged items

10.9 Before the hedge accounting principles and methods set out in the standard can be appreciated, it is first necessary to understand the basic definitions and concepts of hedged items and hedging instruments that underpin all hedging relationships.

Definition

10.10 A hedged item is an asset, liability, firm commitment, highly probable forecast transaction or net investment in a foreign operation that:

■ exposes the entity to risk of changes in fair value or future cash flows; and
■ is designated as being hedged.

[IAS 39 para 9].

10.11 In particular, the hedged item can be:

■ a single asset, liability, firm commitment, highly probable forecast transaction or net investment in a foreign operation;

■ a group of assets, liabilities, firm commitments, highly probable forecast transactions or net investments in foreign operations with similar risk characteristics; or

■ in a portfolio hedge of interest rate risk only, a portion of the portfolio of financial assets or financial liabilities that share the risk being hedged.

[IAS 39 para 78].

10.12 One of the key aspects of the above definition is that the hedged item must expose the entity to risk of changes in the fair value or future cash flows that could affect profit or loss. [IAS 39 para 86(a)-(b)]. This could be in the current or future periods. As a result, hedge accounting cannot apply to hedges of any items included in equity or transactions that directly affect equity (see further para 10.42 below).

10.13 The assets or liabilities referred to above are assets and liabilities that are recognised in the entity's balance sheet. It could be a financial item or a non-financial item such as inventory. Unrecognised assets cannot qualify as a hedged item except for firm commitments. For example, internally generated core deposit intangibles (for a bank) are not recognised as intangible assets under IAS 38. Because they are not recognised, they cannot be designated as hedged items. [IAS 39 para IG F2.3].

10.14   For hedge accounting purposes, only assets, liabilities, firm commitments or highly probable forecast transactions that involve a party external to the entity can be designated as hedged items. It follows that hedge accounting can be applied to transactions between entities in the same group only in the individual or separate financial statements of those entities and not in the consolidated financial statements of the group. [IAS 39 para 80]. However, there are exceptions to this general rule, which are considered from paragraph 10.36 below.

Designation of groups of items as hedged items

10.15   The definition of a hedged item in paragraph 10.11 above permits similar assets, or similar liabilities to be grouped together and designated as a hedged item. Designating a group/portfolio of items as a hedge requires that:

■   the individual assets or individual liabilities in the group share the risk exposure that is designated as being hedged; and

■   the change in the fair value attributable to the hedged risk for each individual item in the group is expected to be approximately proportional to the overall change in fair value attributable to the hedged risk of the group of items.

[IAS 39 para 83].

10.16   In grouping similar assets and liabilities in a portfolio, an entity should consider various factors, including:

■   The type of assets or liabilities.

■   The interest rate (fixed or variable) and, in the case of fixed rate assets or liabilities, the coupon rate.

■   The currency in which the assets or liabilities are denominated.

■   The scheduled maturity date and, in the case of prepayable assets, the prepayment terms, past prepayment history and expected future prepayment performance.

10.17   With respect to the first bullet point in paragraph 10.15 above, this means that the group or portfolio of items must share the same risk exposure with respect to the risk being hedged. It is not necessary that each item in the group shares all of the same risks, as long as they all share a common risk characteristic that is the subject of the hedge. Sharing the same risk exposure means not only that the hedged items have a common risk (for example, foreign currency risk), but also that the exposure moves in the same direction. For example, forecast foreign currency sales and purchases do not share the same risk exposure, because the risk to the entity from the purchase moves in the opposite direction to the risk exposure from the sale.

10.18 With respect to the second bullet point in paragraph 10.15 above, the standard does not provide any guidance on the meaning of 'approximately proportional'. It should be noted that FAS 133 provides some guidance in the context of US GAAP. It considers that a movement of the fair value of the individual items within a fairly narrow range, such as from 9 per cent to 11 per cent, when the fair value of the portfolio as a whole moves 10 per cent, would be consistent with this requirement, but a move such as from 7 per cent to 13 per cent would not be consistent.

Example 1 – Designating a portfolio of bonds as the hedged item

An entity has a portfolio of fixed rate corporate bonds with different coupons. All the bonds mature within a period of 4-5 years. The entity designates an interest rate swap to hedge the entire portfolio's risk-free interest rate.

The above group of bonds may be designated as the hedged item as the risk free rate that is being hedged is common to all the bonds. However, it is also necessary to ensure that the fair value movements of each individual bond that is attributable to the hedged interest-free rate are expected to be approximately proportional to the portfolio's fair value movements that is attributable to the hedged risk. The entity's management should, therefore, model the changes of fair value of the portfolio relative to fair values of individual bonds in response to the hedged risk.

Example 2 – Designating a portfolio of shares as the hedged item

Entity A acquires a portfolio of French CAC 40 shares, in the same proportions as are used to calculate the French CAC 40 index and classifies the investments as available-for-sale. At the same time, the entity purchases a put option on the CAC 40 index to hedge changes in the fair value of the portfolio. The option constitutes a near perfect hedge of decreases in the value of the portfolio, in economic terms. Any decline in the portfolio's fair value below the options' strike price will be offset by an increase in the put option's intrinsic value.

In the scenario above, the entity cannot designate the portfolio of shares as the hedged item in a hedge of equity price risk. The hedged risk is the total change in value of each share in the portfolio. Some share prices may increase and others may decrease. The relationship will not qualify for hedge accounting, because the change in the fair value attributable to the hedged risk for each individual item in the group (individual share prices) is not expected to be approximately proportional to the overall change in fair value attributable to the hedged risk of the group.

Hedging an overall net position

10.19 An entity cannot designate an overall net position as the hedged item. This is because hedging a common risk in portfolio of similar assets and liabilities would necessitate an allocation of the overall gain or loss on the hedging instrument to the individual items in the portfolio. Furthermore, if some of the items in the portfolio were producing gains and others losses, the entity would have to impute both gains and losses to the single hedging instrument to offset both the gains and the losses on the hedged items. As such an allocation would be inherently arbitrary and produce significant ineffectiveness, designating the hedged item as a net position is not permitted. [IAS 39 para 84]

10.20   However, almost the same effect on profit or loss can be achieved by designating some of the underlying gross items as the hedged item equal in amount to the net position. For example, an entity (C functional currency) with a firm commitment to make a purchase in a foreign currency of FC100 and a firm commitment to make a sale in the foreign currency of FC90 can hedge the net amount of FC10 by acquiring a derivative and designating it as a hedging instrument associated with FC10 of the firm purchase commitment of FC100. Similarly, an entity with C100 of fixed rate assets and C90 of fixed rate liabilities with terms of a similar nature could hedge the net C10 exposure by designating as the hedged item C10 of those assets. [IAS 39 para AG 101].

10.21   An entity's hedging strategy and risk management practices may assess cash flow risk on a net basis, but the net cash flow exposure cannot be designated as a hedged item for hedge accounting purposes. This is because, as explained above, it would not be possible to identify the net exposure arising from forecast sales and purchases as the exposure being hedged, because forecast sales and purchases are not similar items and the effectiveness test would fail. However, once again hedge accounting can be achieved by designating some of the forecast purchases or sales as the hedged item equal in amount to the net position, as illustrated in the example below.

Example 1 – Hedging a net FX position

Entity A, whose functional currency is the euro, has a global treasury centre that is responsible for collecting and assessing the group's foreign currency risks and offsetting the net position using derivative instruments with an external party. For example, it forecasts sales of US$2.5m and purchases of US$1m in June and has, therefore, entered into a forward contract to sell US$1.5m against euros in that month.

As stated in paragraph 10.19 above, the entity is prohibited from designating a net position as the hedged item. It is possible to achieve a similar effect by designating the hedged item as part of one of the gross positions that is equal in amount to the net position. Entity A can, therefore, designate the forward contract as a hedge of highly probable forecast sales of US$1.5m in June.

Example 2 – Hedging a net interest rate position

Entity B has a number of bank loans with different interest rates and terms. The entity also has loans receivable with different interest rates. Management proposes to hedge the net interest-rate risk position in a number of separate maturity bands through the use of interest-rate swaps for the net asset or liability in each maturity band.

Management may allocate the net exposure in each band to a specific asset or liability, so that the net position in each maturity band could qualify as a hedged item. This approach provides management with an interest-rate gap methodology to manage interest-rate risk. [IAS 39 para AG111]. Alternatively, management may choose to apply fair value hedge accounting (see paragraph 10.193 onwards for definition and examples of fair value hedge accounting) for a portfolio hedge of interest rate risk and designate an amount of assets or liabilities in given time buckets as hedged items. [IAS 39 para 81A].

Designation of financial items as hedged items

10.22   When the hedged item is a financial instrument or a forecast transaction involving a financial instrument, some examples of financial risk exposures that can be hedged are described in the non-exhaustive list below.

Examples of financial instrument risks that can be hedged

- Market risk – the risk that a financial instrument's fair value or cash flows will fluctuate because of changes in market prices. Market risk embodies not only the potential for loss but also the potential for gain. It comprises three types of risk as follows:

  - Interest rate risk – the risk that a financial instrument's fair value or future cash flows will fluctuate because of changes in market interest rates.

  - Currency risk – the risk that a financial instrument's fair value or future cash flows will fluctuate because of changes in foreign exchange rates.

  - Other price risk – the risk that a financial instrument's fair value or future cash flows will fluctuate because of changes in market prices (other than those arising from interest rate risk or currency risk), whether those changes are caused by factors specific to the individual financial instrument or its issuer, or factors affecting all similar financial instruments traded in the market.

- Credit risk – the risk that one party to a financial instrument will cause a financial loss for the other party by failing to discharge an obligation.

- Liquidity risk – the risk that an entity will encounter difficulty in meeting obligations associated with financial liabilities.

  Other examples of risks that can be hedges in financial items include:

  - Pre-payment risks in mortgages.

  - Credit spread.

  - Closely related embedded derivatives that were not separated from the host financial contract.

[IFRS 7 Appendix A]

Hedges of portions of financial items

10.23 For hedges of financial assets and financial liabilities, IAS 39 does not restrict hedge accounting to hedges of the entire risk of change in the fair value or all of the cash flows of a financial instrument, or the entire exposure to interest rate risk, currency risk, credit risk or other risks of changes in a financial instrument's fair value or cash flows. In June 2008 the IASB changed IAS 39 to clarify that provided that effectiveness can be measured, it is possible to designate the risks associated with only a portion of its cash flows or fair value, such as one or more selected contractual cash flows or portions of them or a percentage or a proportion of the fair value. For example:

(a)   all of the cash flows of a financial instrument may be designated for cash flow or fair value changes attributable to some (but not all) risks; or

(b)   some (but not all) of the cash flows of a financial instrument may be designated for cash flow or fair value changes attributable to all or only some risks (that is, a 'portion' of the cash flows of a financial instrument may be designated for changes attributable to all or only some risks).

10.23.1 To be eligible for hedge accounting, the designated risks and portions must be separately identifiable components of the financial instrument, and changes in the cash flows or fair value of the entire financial instrument arising from changes in the designated risks and portions must be reliably measurable. For example:

(a)   For a fixed rate financial instrument hedged for changes in fair value attributable to changes in a risk-free or benchmark interest rate, the risk-free or benchmark rate is normally regarded as both a separately identifiable component of the financial instrument and reliably measurable.

(b)   Inflation is not separately identifiable and reliably measurable and cannot be designated as a risk or a portion of a financial instrument unless the requirements in (c) are met.

(c)   A contractually specified inflation portion of the cash flows of a recognised inflation-linked bond (assuming there is no requirement to account for an embedded derivative separately) is separately identifiable and reliably measurable as long as other cash flows of the instrument are not affected by the inflation portion.

It should be noted that hedges of portions apply only to financial assets and liabilities and not to non-financial assets and liabilities (see para 10.31 below).

[IAS 39 para AG99E-AG99F].

Example – Hedges of portions

An entity acquires a fixed rate bond with a maturity of five years. The bond is classified as loans and receivables.

The entity could hedge a variety of risk exposures relating to a fixed rate debt including the following:

| | Risk exposure | | Contractual cash flows | |
	All	Specific component	Principal	Interest
Hedge the fair value of all the cash flows for all risks (100% of fair value of the debt).	√		√	√
Hedge the fair value of all the cash flows for a specific risk, for example, interest rate or credit risk (100% of fair value of the debt for a specific risk).		√	√	√
Hedge a proportion of the fair value of all the cash flows for all risks (90% of fair value of the debt).	√		90%	90%
Hedge a proportion of the fair value of all the cash flows for a specific risk, for example, interest or credit risk (90% of fair value of the debt for a specific risk).		√	90%	90%
Hedge the fair value of a specifically identified cash flow for all risk.	√		√ or	√
Hedge the fair value of a specifically identified cash flow for a specific risk (for example, interest rate or credit risk).		√	√ or	√
Hedge the fair value of a portion of a specifically identified cash flow for all risk.	√		90% or	90%
Hedge the fair value of a portion of a specifically identified cash flow for a specific risk, for example, interest rate or credit risk.		√	90% or	90%

Hedging a risk component of a financial instrument

10.24 Consistent with paragraph 10.23 above, financial assets or liabilities may be hedged with respect to a specific risk (a component of total risk), provided that the exposure to the specific risk component is identifiable and separately measurable, which is also a pre-requisite for measuring effectiveness. Some examples of situations where component of a risk may be hedged are given below. [IAS 39 para 81]. Other examples include: hedging the foreign currency exposure in a portfolio of foreign currency denominated listed equity securities, rather than hedging the full market price risk (see para 10.28 below) and hedging the fair value exposure to changes in credit spread in a floating rate debt instrument. [IAS 39 IG F.2.19].

Example – Hedging a risk component of a fixed rate debt instrument

An entity issues 8% fixed rate debt instrument for C100 that is repayable at par at the end of year 2. At the time of issue the market interest rate is 6%. Therefore, the credit spread on the new issue is 2%.

In this scenario, the entity can designate an identifiable and separately measurable portion of the interest rate exposure as the hedged risk. Such a portion may be a risk-free interest rate or benchmark interest rate component of the debt instrument's total interest rate exposure, that is, the entity's own credit spread of 2% may be excluded. This is subject to the *proviso* that effectiveness can be measured.

So if the entity intends to designate the benchmark LIBOR component of 6% as the hedged risk, it may take out a receive 6% fixed pay floating LIBOR interest rate swap to hedge the changes in the debt's fair value due to changes in LIBOR. The hedge will be expected to be highly effective as the credit spread is not included in the net cash flows relating to the swap.

Note that it is not necessary for the pay leg of the swap to be the same as LIBOR (receive 6% pay LIBOR). The entity could take out a receive 8% pay floating LIBOR + 2% interest rate swap and still designate the benchmark LIBOR component as the hedged risk. This is because the fair value of the swap comprises the net of the present values of both the fixed and the floating legs. Therefore, increasing both sides of the swap by 2% (from receive 6% pay LIBOR to receive 8% pay LIBOR + 2%) will not change the fair value for a given change in interest rates. However, this is only true when the payment frequency of both legs is identical. If the fixed leg pays yearly and the variable leg pays quarterly, there would be a difference.

10.25 If a portion of the cash flows of a financial asset or financial liability is designated as the hedged item, that designated portion must be less than the total cash flows of the asset or liability. As a designated portion of the cash flows cannot be greater than the whole, an entity that issues a debt instrument whose effective interest rate at issuance is below LIBOR (such an issuance of debt at below LIBOR rates may be possible by some entities with exceptionally strong credit rating), cannot designate the following components as hedges:

- a portion of the liability equal to the principal amount plus interest at LIBOR; and

- a negative residual portion.

[IAS 39 para AG 99C].

It should be noted, however, that the above prohibition does not feature in the EU carve-out version of IAS 39.

10.26 However, the entity may designate all of the cash flows of the entire financial asset or financial liability as the hedged item and hedge them for only one particular risk (for example, only for changes that are attributable to changes in LIBOR) as illustrated in the example below:

> **Example – Designating a benchmark interest rate as the hedged risk on a fixed rate debt instrument issued at sub-LIBOR rate**
>
> An entity issues a 5% fixed rate debt instrument for C100 that is repayable at par at the end of year 2. At the time of issue, the benchmark LIBOR rate is 6%.
>
> The entity can designate the entire financial liability as the hedged item (that is, principal + interest) and hedge the change in the fair value or cash flows of that entire liability that is attributable to changes in LIBOR. Some ineffectiveness will occur. However, the entity may choose a hedge ratio of other than one to one (a proportion of the total cash flow) in order to improve the effectiveness of the hedge. [IAS 39 para AG 99C].

10.27 It is also possible to hedge the benchmark interest rate risk portion of a fixed rate financial instrument some time after its origination, by which time interest rates may have changed since the instrument's origination. This is possible if the benchmark rate is higher than the contractual rate paid on the item as illustrated in the example below. [IAS 39 para AG 99D]. It should be noted that the restriction that the hedged benchmark rate is higher than the contractual rate does not feature in the EU carve-out version of IAS 39.

> **Example – Designating a benchmark interest rate as the hedged risk of a fixed rate debt instrument subsequent to its origination**
>
> On 1 April 20X1, an entity issues a 6% fixed rate debt instrument for C100 that is repayable at par at the end of year 5 (31 March 20X6). Interest is payable annually in arrears. At the time of issue, the benchmark LIBOR rate is 5%. On 1 July 20X2, the entity decides to hedge the interest rate risk on the debt instrument with an interest rate swap when LIBOR has increased to 7%. At that time, the fair value of the debt instrument is C93.
>
> The entity calculates that if it had issued the debt instrument on 1 July 20X2 when it first designates it as the hedged item for its fair value of C93, the effective yield on the instrument would have been 8.1%. Because LIBOR on 1 July 20X2 is 7% and is less than this effective yield, the entity can designate a LIBOR portion of 7% that consists partly of the contractual interest cash flows and partly of the discount that is included in the difference between the current fair value of C93 and the amount repayable on maturity of C100.

10.28 Under IAS 39, when a gain or loss on a non-monetary available-for-sale equity security is recognised in other comprehensive income, any exchange component of that gain or loss is also recognised directly in other comprehensive income. [IAS 39 para AG 83]. Normally, items taken to other comprehensive income/equity cannot be hedged, however, foreign currency exposure in such an equity security can be hedged provided there is a clear and identifiable exposure to changes in foreign exchange rates and all the other hedge accounting criteria are met. In the case of a fair value hedge, the changes in foreign currency exposure will be recognised in profit or loss. The implementation guidance explains that this would be possible only if:

- the equity instrument is not traded on an exchange (or in another established marketplace) where trades are denominated in the same currency as the entity's functional currency (investor); and

- dividends to the investor are not denominated in the investor's functional currency.

Thus, if a share is traded in multiple currencies and one of those currencies is the reporting entity's functional currency, hedge accounting for the foreign currency component of the share price is not permitted.

[IAS 39 para IG F2.19].

Example – Hedging foreign currency risk of an available-for-sale investment

On 1 April 20X5, entity A, a Swiss company with Swiss Francs as its functional currency, buys equity shares in entity B located in the US. The shares are listed on the New York Stock Exchange and pay dividends in US$. The acquisition cost is US$1m. On that date US$ = CHF1.3 resulting in an investment of CHF1.3m. Entity A classifies the investment as available-for-sale.

At the same time, to protect itself from the exposure to changes in the foreign exchange rate associated with the shares, entity A enters into a forward contract to sell US$1m and buy CHF. Entity A intends to roll over the forward exchange contract for as long as it retains the shares. It is assumed that the hedge is effective and the other conditions for hedge accounting are met.

Entity A could designate the currency exposure relating to the shares' fair value as the hedged risk, because it meets the two conditions set out in the above paragraph. Also, entity A could designate the forward contract as either a fair value hedge of the foreign exchange exposure of US$1m or as a cash flow hedge of a forecast sale of the shares, provided the future sale and its timing are highly probable. For the purposes of this example, it is assumed that the forward contract is designated as a fair value hedge.

At 31 March 20X6, the entity's financial year end, shares increased in value to US$2m. At that date, US$ = CHF1.20.

	CHF m
The change in fair value is calculated as follows:	
Value of investment at 31 March 20X6 – US$2m @ 1.2 =	2.4
Value of investment at 1 April 20X5 – US$1m @ 1.3 =	1.3
Fair value change	1.1
Exchange component of change – US 1m (@ 1.2 – @1.3)	(0.1)
Recognised in other comprehensive income – change in fair value US$1m @ 1.2	1.2

In this situation, the gain arising from the changes in the forward contract's fair value is recognised in the income statement. This includes both the spot component (which may be designated as part of the hedging relationship to improve effectiveness) and the forward points component (see further paragraph 10.56 below). The entity also recognises the exchange loss of CHF100,000 in profit or loss to offset the gain on the forward contract. [IAS 39 para 89(b)]. The remaining portion of the change in fair value of CHF1.2m is deferred in equity in accordance with the subsequent measurement rules for available-for-sale investments.

Partial term hedging

10.29 The ability to hedge a portion of one or more selected cash flows of a financial asset or liability means that an entity will be able to hedge exposures that have a term that is less than the hedged item's term – so called 'partial term' hedges. This is subject to the proviso that effectiveness can be measured and the other hedge accounting criteria are met. This will usually be so if the hedging derivative also has the same term as the selected cash flows, as illustrated in the example below. It should be noted that the notion of 'partial term' does not apply to a hedging instrument as stated in paragraph 10.61 below. Note, where a forecasted transaction is designated with a foreign currency derivative of shorter duration, if the hedging relationship is designated on a "forward" basis (i.e. as a hedge of changes in forward exchange rates), it will not be fully effective. This is because a time portion of a forecasted transaction is not an eligible portion of a non-financial item and the hypothetical derivative must be based on the full term until the forecasted transaction is expected to occur. However, such a relationship may be designated on a "spot" basis (i.e. as a hedge of changes in spot exchange rates) with minimal ineffectiveness.

Example – Partial term hedging

Entity A acquires a 10% fixed rate government bond with a remaining term to maturity of ten years. Entity A classifies the bond as available for sale. On the same date, to hedge against fair value exposure on the bond associated with the first five year interest payments, the entity acquires a 5 year pay-fixed, receive-floating swap. The swap has a fair value of zero at the inception of the hedge relationship.

The swap may be designated as hedging the fair value exposure of the interest rate payments on the government bond until year 5 and the change in value of the principal payment due at maturity to the extent affected by changes in the yield curve relating to the 5 years of the swap. [IAS 39 para IG F2.17].

The same principle applies if the hedged item had been a financial liability instead of a financial asset with the same terms. In that situation, the entity could designate the fair value exposure of the first 5 years interest payments due to changes in interest rate only and hedge that exposure using a 5 year receive-fixed, pay-floating interest rate swap.

The entity is also able to achieve effective partial term cash flow hedges. For instance, assume an entity issues a 10 year floating rate debt and wish to hedge the variability in the first three year of interest payments. This could be easily done by using a 3 year receive-floating, pay-fixed interest rate swap.

Loans and receivables

10.30 Under IAS 39, loans and receivables are carried at amortised cost. An entity may decide to hold such loans and receivables to maturity. Indeed, banking institutions in many countries hold the bulk of their loans and receivables until maturity. Therefore, it would appear that as changes in the fair value of such loans and receivables that are due to changes in market interest rates will not affect profit or loss, fair value hedge accounting for loans and receivables is precluded (see para 10.12 above). However, it is always possible that such instruments will be disposed of or extinguished before then, in which case the change in fair values would affect profit or loss. Accordingly, fair value hedge accounting is permitted as such loans and receivables are not designated as held-to-maturity. Financial assets designated as held to maturity can not be designated as hedged items for interest rate or pre-payment risk (see para 10.43). [IAS 39 IG para F2.13].

Designation of non-financial items as hedged items

10.31 If the hedged item is a non-financial asset or non-financial liability, it may only be designated as a hedged item:

■ for foreign currency risks; or

■ in its entirety for all risks.

[IAS 39 para 82].

Hedges of portions of non-financial items

10.32 The standard explains that changes in the price of an ingredient or component of a non-financial asset or non-financial liability generally do not have a predictable, separately measurable effect on the item's price that is comparable to the effect of, say, a change in market interest rates on a bond's price. Therefore, because of the difficulty of isolating and measuring the appropriate portion of the cash flows or fair value changes attributable to specific risks other than foreign currency risks, a non-financial asset or non-financial liability is a hedged item only in its entirety or for foreign exchange risk. [IAS 39 para AG 100]. Accordingly, when an entity chooses to hedge the fair value of inventory (a non-financial asset), the inventory cannot be separated into its commodity and other components, regardless of whether the inventory consists of a single commodity component and conversion or rework costs, or is a product comprised of multiple commodities. The standard makes no exception to this rule even though in some cases it may be possible to isolate the changes in cash flows or fair value attributable to a particular risk. In some cases, ineffectiveness can be minimized by designating multiple derivatives as a hedging instrument based on the expected ingredients of the non-financial item (for example, where a metal concentrate containing gold and copper is hedged using a combination of gold and copper forwards) or by designating the quantity of the hedged item expected to contain the quantity of the non-financial item contracted for in the hedging instrument.

Example 1 – Separation of risks in non-financial assets

An entity manufacturers aluminium cans from sheets of aluminium. The entity intends to use aluminium futures as a fair value hedge of the exposure to changes in the aluminium cans' fair value held in inventory.

The entity cannot designate aluminium's market price as the hedged risk, even though the price of aluminium is likely to account for a significant portion of the exposure to changes in the price of aluminium cans held in inventory. Permitting an entity to designate the market price of aluminium as the hedged risk would ignore other components of the price of the cans, such as protective coating materials, labour and production overheads.

However, provided the requirement for effectiveness and other hedge accounting criteria are met (see para 10.136 below), the derivative instrument (aluminium futures) could be designated as a hedge of the exposure to changes in the full fair value of the inventory. See also example in paragraph 10.97 below

Example 2 – Forecast purchase of a non-monetary asset in foreign currency

Entity A is planning to buy a large piece of machinery from a foreign supplier. The forecast purchase will be denominated in a foreign currency, so the company enters into a forward contract to hedge the risk of movements in the relevant foreign exchange rate.

The forecast purchase can be designated as a hedged item in a cash flow hedge of foreign currency risk, provided that the forecast purchase is highly probable, the requirements for effectiveness and the other conditions for hedge accounting are met. The hedged risk (movements in exchange rates) will affect the amount paid for the machine and will, therefore, affect profit or loss as the machine is depreciated.

10.33 As stated in paragraph 10.31 above, a non-monetary item can be hedged for foreign currency risk only if it is separately measurable. As the hedged item is remeasured in a fair value hedge (see para 10.93 below), a non-monetary financial asset that was purchased in a foreign currency and initially recorded, under IAS 21 in the purchaser's functional currency, at the exchange rate at the date of the transaction cannot be classified as a fair value hedge for foreign currency risk. This is because it is not subsequently remeasured under IAS 21 and, therefore, does not contain any separately measurable foreign currency risk. Nevertheless, if all the hedge accounting conditions are met, an entity could designate as a cash flow hedge the anticipated sale of the non-monetary asset in a foreign currency. This is because, in a cash flow hedge, the non-monetary item is not remeasured. However, in practice, it would be rare for such a hedge to meet all the hedging accounting criteria as illustrated in the example below.

Example – Foreign currency borrowings hedging a ship

A shipping entity in Denmark has a US subsidiary that has the same functional currency (the Danish Krone). In its consolidated financial statements shipping entity measures its ships at historical cost less depreciation. In accordance with IAS 21 graph 23(b), the ships are measured in Danish Krone using the historical exchange rate. To hedge, fully or partly, the potential currency risk on the ships at disposal in US dollars, the shipping entity normally finances its purchases of ships with loans denominated in US dollars.

US dollar borrowings cannot be classified as a fair value hedge of a ship, because ships do not contain any separately measurable foreign currency risk, even though the entity purchases and sells them in US dollars.

US dollar borrowing (or a portion of it) may, however, be designated as a cash flow hedge of the ship's anticipated sale proceeds in US dollars financed by the borrowing provided all the hedging criteria are met. Those conditions are likely to be met if the sale is highly probable because it is expected to occur in the immediate future, the amount of the sales proceeds designated as being hedged is equal to the amount of the foreign currency borrowing designated as the hedging instrument and the timing of the future cash flows on the debt coincides with the timing on the future cash flow from the disposal. [IAS 39 IG para F6.5].

Firm commitments

10.34   A firm commitment is a binding agreement for the exchange of a specified quantity of resources at a specified price on a specified future date or dates. [IAS 39 para 9]. Therefore, the key characteristic of a firm commitment is that it must have fixed terms, namely: fixed quantity, fixed price and fixed timing of the transaction. A firm commitment must be with a party that is external to the entity (see para 10.14 above). As the firm commitment is a binding agreement, it is usually legally enforceable. Firm commitments are discussed further in paragraph 10.93 below.

Forecast transactions

10.35   In many cases, entities will not be hedging risk exposures arising from firm commitments but rather those arising from forecast transactions that they expect to happen, but for which there is not a binding contract. Therefore, the definition of a hedged item also includes a forecast transaction. A forecast transaction is an uncommitted but highly probable, anticipated future transaction. [IAS 39 para 9]. Concluding that an uncommitted but anticipated transaction is highly probable and will happen is more difficult than for transactions arising from firm commitments. The qualifying conditions for getting hedge accounting for forecast transactions are considered further from paragraph 10.108 below.

Intra-group and intra-entity hedging transactions

10.36   It is fairly common for entities within a consolidated group to enter into transactions with other group members or segments. Often these transactions may expose the entities to various risks that they wish to hedge. The entity exposed to the risk can hedge it by entering into internal derivative contracts with, say, the group treasury, or through external derivative contracts. However, as stated in paragraph 10.14 above, only assets, liabilities, firm commitments or highly probable forecast transactions that involve a party external to the entity can be designated as hedged items. It follows that such intra group transactions can be designated as hedged items only in the individual or separate financial statements of those entities and not in the consolidated financial statements of the reporting group. This is because the intra-group transactions cancel out on consolidation and, therefore, do not expose the consolidated group to any risk that affects consolidated profit or loss. There are, however, two exceptions to this general rule involving foreign currency exposures and these are considered in the paragraphs that follow.

10.37   Under IAS 21, foreign exchange gains and losses on intra group monetary asset (or liability) between group entities with different functional currencies, whether short-term or long-term, do not fully eliminate in the consolidated profit or loss. This is because a foreign currency monetary item represents a commitment to convert one currency into another and exposes the reporting entity to a gain or loss through currency fluctuations. Accordingly, in the reporting entity's consolidated financial statements, such exchange differences continue to be recognised in profit or loss. For this reason, the foreign currency exposure on such an intra group monetary item can be designated as a hedged item on consolidation. [IAS 39 para 80].

Example – Hedging intra group monetary items

Subsidiary A, whose functional currency is the euro, has an intra group receivable from subsidiary B, whose functional currency is the Swiss franc. The receivable is denominated in Swiss francs and subsidiary A enters into a €/CHF forward contract with an external party to hedge the resulting foreign currency risk.

In its separate financial statements, subsidiary A translates the receivable into euros using the spot rate at the balance sheet date and recognises a foreign currency gain or loss in accordance with IAS 21. Subsidiary B, in its separate financial statements, records the payable to subsidiary A in its own functional currency and does not recognise any gain or loss. On consolidation, the gain or loss recognised by subsidiary A is translated into the group's presentation currency and is recognised in the group's income statement. There is no offsetting loss or gain arising from subsidiary B.

Subsidiary A uses the €/CHF forward contract to hedge the foreign currency exchange risk on the receivable from subsidiary B in its individual financial statements. As the receivable gives rise to an exposure to foreign currency gains or losses that is not fully eliminated on consolidation, the foreign currency exposure on the intra group receivable can be designated as the hedged item in the consolidated financial statements. The group can designate the €/CHF forward contract in subsidiary A as the hedging instrument. The hedge accounting achieved by subsidiary A is reversed on consolidation and replaced with hedge accounting achieved by the group.

For group purposes, it is not necessary for the subsidiary to take out the forward contract for the foreign exchange exposure on the intra group receivable to qualify as a hedged item on consolidation. The parent entity could have taken out the same forward contract hedging the €/CHF exchange risk instead.

Forecast intra-group transactions

10.38 IAS 39 permits the foreign currency risk of a highly probable forecast intra group transaction to be designated as a hedged item in the consolidated financial statements, provided the following two conditions are met:

■ the highly probable forecast intra group transaction is denominated in a currency other than the functional currency of the group member entering into that transaction; and

■ the foreign currency risk will affect the group's consolidated profit or loss.

[IAS 39 para 80].

10.39 The group member entering into the transaction can be a parent, subsidiary, associate, joint venture or branch. The first condition is necessary because, under IAS 21, a foreign currency exposure arises only when a transaction is denominated in a currency other than the functional currency of the entity entering into that transaction. The second condition is met if the forecast intra group transaction is related to an external transaction. An example is forecast sales or purchases of inventories between members of the same group if there is an onward sale of the inventory to a party external to the group (see example below). However, if there is no external related transaction, which will often be the case for royalty payments, interest payments or management charges between members of the same group, the foreign currency risk of those forecast intra group transactions would not affect consolidated profit or loss and, so, cannot qualify as hedged items. [IAS 39 para AG 99A]. Intra group foreign currency dividends can never qualify as hedged items (see para 10.42 below).

10.40 If a hedge of a forecast intra-group transaction qualifies for hedge accounting, any gain or loss that is recognised directly in equity should be reclassified into profit or loss in the same period or periods during which the foreign currency risk of the hedged transaction affects consolidated profit or loss (see further para 10.118 below).

> **Example – Hedging the foreign currency risk of an intra group forecast transaction**
>
> Group A (pound sterling presentation currency) includes entity B with euro functional currency and entity C with US dollar functional currency in the consolidation. Entity B manufactures tyres and incurs production costs in euros. It sells most of the tyres to entity C and those transactions are denominated in US dollars. Entity C markets and sells those tyres to external customers in the US, also in US dollars.
>
> In June 20X6 entity B forecasts that it will sell tyres to entity C in October 20X6 amounting to US$ 10m. These sales are highly probable and all the other conditions in IAS 39 for hedge accounting are met. Entity C expects to sell this inventory to external customers in early 20X7. At the same time in June 20X6, entity B enters into a euro/US$ derivative (buy €/sell US$) to hedge the foreign currency risk of the forecast sale of US$10m to entity C in October 20X6.

Group A intends to designate the forward contract as hedging the foreign currency risk of the forecast intra group sales of US$10m by entity B in a cash flow hedging relationship in the consolidated financial statements. It is able to do so because all the following conditions are met

- The intra group sales are highly probable and all the other conditions for using hedge accounting are met.

- The intra group sales are denominated in a currency (US$) other than entity B's functional currency (€).

- The existence of the expected onwards sale of the inventory in US dollars to third parties outside the group results in the hedged exposure affecting the pound sterling consolidated profit or loss. This is because the intra group profit on sale recognised in entity B is € number that is fixed according to the €/$ rate when the sale takes place in October 20X6. This profit is eliminated on consolidation against the carrying value of tyre inventory in entity C and released to consolidated profit or loss when the onward sale of inventory to third parties take place in 20X7.

Gains/losses on the €/US$ derivative are recognised initially in consolidated equity to the extent the hedge is effective. These amounts are reclassified to consolidated profit or loss in 20X7 when the external sales occur.

The standard notes the difficulty in demonstrating that there is a related external transaction for intra-group royalty and interest payments, but does not preclude the use of hedge accounting for such transactions where a clear link to an external transaction can be demonstrated.

Example – Linkage to an external transaction

A GBP parent obtains a GBP external loan and immediately lends the proceeds in USD to a subsidiary with a USD functional currency. The subsidiary uses the money to make external loans to customers in USD. In the consolidated financial statements including the parent and subsidiary the group proposes to hedge the GBP/USD risk of the loan to the subsidiary with a GBP/USD swap. In considering whether the hedge can be designated under IAS 39 it is necessary to evaluate the linkage between the loan by the parent and the external transaction by considering factors such as whether:

- the stated purpose of the parent lending is to allow the subsidiary to on-lend to external parties;

- there is a short time lag between lending by the parent an on-lending by the subsidiary (ideally simultaneous on-lending);

- similar terms exist between the loan to the parent and the subsidiary. If the loan with the parent is longer in duration than the external loan the parent should demonstrate an intention to rollover the external loans;

- if the loans were repaid early by the subsidiary's external borrowers, there is a requirement to repay the loan to the parent company.

Items that do not qualify as hedged items

10.41   There are a number of items that, for various reasons, cannot qualify as a hedged item in a hedging relationship. For such items the normal measurement and recognition rules will apply. These items are as considered below.

Own equity instruments

10.42   Hedge accounting cannot be applied for hedges of any items included in equity or transactions that directly affect equity. This is because the hedged item cannot create an exposure to risk that will affect profit or loss. Therefore, hedges of risks relating to the forecast sale, purchase or redemption of an entity's own equity shares cannot qualify as hedged items. Similarly, distributions to holders of an equity instrument are debited by the issuer directly to equity. [IAS 32 para 25]. Therefore, such distributions cannot be designated as a hedged item. However, a dividend that has been approved in a general meeting of members and has not yet been paid and is recognised as a financial liability may qualify as a hedged item, for example, for foreign currency risk if it is denominated in a foreign currency as illustrated in the example below. [IAS 39 IG para F2.7].

> **Example – Inter-company dividends denominated in foreign currency**
>
> Entity A, whose functional currency is the pound sterling, has a subsidiary in the US, whose functional currency is the US dollar. On 1 January 20X6, entity A forecasts that it will receive a US$100m dividend from its US subsidiary in six months. The inter company dividend was approved in general meeting of members (or equivalent) on 30 April 20X6, at which time both entity A and its subsidiary recognised the dividend as a receivable or payable in their respective financial statements.
>
> The foreign currency dividend receivable in entity A's balance sheet was retranslated at the reporting period end, 31 May 20X6, resulting in a foreign currency loss. The subsidiary paid the dividend on 30 June 20X6.
>
> Entity A wanted to designate the foreign currency risk on highly probable inter-company dividend as the hedged item in its group financial statements in a cash flow hedge from 1 January 20X6 to 30 June 20X6, in order to hedge the exposure to changes in the £/US$ exchange rate. However, inter-company dividends are not foreign currency transactions that can be hedged, because they do not affect the consolidated income statement. They are distributions of earnings.
>
> The foreign currency exposure arising from the receivable in US dollars recognised on 30 April 20X6 can be designated as a hedged item because it gives rise to foreign currency gains and losses that do not fully eliminate on consolidation and, therefore, affect the consolidated income statement (see para 10.37 above). Entity A can, therefore, apply hedge accounting from that date until 30 June 20X6 when the cash is received in its group financial statements.

Held-to-maturity investments

10.43   Unlike loans and receivables (see para 10.30 above), a held-to-maturity (HTM) investment (whether it pays fixed or floating interest) cannot be hedged for interest rate risk, because designation of an investment as held-to-maturity requires the holder's positive intent and ability to hold the instrument to maturity. Held-to-maturity classification implies that the net changes in fair value stemming from changes in market interest rates from inception to maturity will not have an impact on profit or loss as the entity has committed itself to retaining the investment to maturity. Similarly, a held-to-maturity investment cannot be hedged for pre-payment risk – risk that an investment will be paid earlier or later than expected. As interest rates fall below rates on existing loans, borrowers may, and commonly do, pre-pay their existing loans and refinance at lower rates. Therefore, as pre-payment risk is primarily a function of interest rates, it is more akin to interest rate risk and, accordingly, cannot be designated as a hedged risk. However, a held-to-maturity investment can be a hedged item with respect to risks from changes in foreign currency exchange rates and credit risk. [IAS 39 para 79].

10.44   Although hedge accounting is prohibited for hedging the interest rate risk of a held-to-maturity asset, the prohibition only applies to held-to-maturity assets that have already been recognised on the entity's balance sheet. The prohibition does not apply to a forecast purchase of a held-to-maturity asset as illustrated in the example in paragraph 10.44 below.

> **Example – Forecast purchase of held-to-maturity investment**
>
> An entity has a forecast transaction to purchase a financial asset that it intends to classify as held-to-maturity when the forecast transaction occurs. It enters into a derivative contract to lock in the current interest rate and designates the derivative as a hedge of the forecast purchase of the financial asset.
>
> Provided all the hedge accounting criteria are met, the entity can apply cash flow hedge accounting to the forecast purchase of a held-to-maturity security. This is because the investment is not classified as held-to-maturity until the transaction occurs. [IAS 39 IG para F2.10].

10.45   The standard also permits cash flow hedge accounting for future interest receipts from a debt instrument that originated from the re-investment of interest receipts from an held-to-maturity investment as illustrated in the example below.

> **Example – Hedging reinvestment risk of funds obtained from held-to-maturity investments**
>
> An entity owns a variable rate asset that it has classified as held-to-maturity. The cash from variable interest receipts is re-invested in debt instruments. The entity enters into a derivative contract to lock in the current interest rate on the reinvestment of variable rate cash flows and designates the derivative as a cash flow hedge of the forecast future interest receipts on debt instruments.

Provided all the hedge accounting criteria are met, the hedging relationship will qualify for cash flow hedge accounting even though the cash from the interest receipts that are being reinvested come from an asset that is classified as held-to-maturity. The source of the funds used to purchase the debt instrument is not relevant in determining whether the reinvestment risk can be hedged. This answer applies also if the source of the funds used to purchase the debt instrument had been a fixed rate held-to-maturity investment. [IAS 39 IG para F2.11].

Equity method investment and investment in consolidated subsidiaries

10.46   An equity method investment, such as an associate, cannot be a hedged item in a fair value hedge because the equity method recognises in profit or loss the investor's share of the associate's profit or loss, rather than changes in the investment's fair value. [IAS 39 para AG 99]. Although this applies to consolidated financial statements, an entity may be able to designate an investment in an associate as a fair value hedge in its separate financial statements, provided that its fair value can be measured reliably.

10.47   The ability of an entity to treat an associate as the hedged item in a cash flow hedge is considered in the following example.

Example – Forecast cash flows in associates

Entity A has a 25% investment in a foreign entity over which it has significant influence. It, therefore, accounts for the foreign entity as an associate using the equity method. The associate's functional currency, in which most of its sales and costs are denominated, differs from entity A's functional currency. In entity A's consolidated financial statements its share of the associate's net results will fluctuate with the changes in the exchange rate. The entity intends to designate a portion of the forecast cash flows in the associate as the hedged item in a hedge of foreign currency risk.

Under the functional currency concept in IAS 21, a cash flow that is denominated in an associate's functional currency does not give rise to a foreign currency (transaction) exposure for the associate in its separate financial statements. The variability in entity A's share of its associate's net results arises only in its consolidated financial statements and arises from the translation of the associate's financial statements into the group's presentation currency. This is a translation rather than a transaction exposure. IAS 39 permits an entity to apply hedge accounting to a hedge of the translation risk on its existing net investment, but this does not extend to the investee's forecast future cash flows or profits.

10.48   An investment in a consolidated subsidiary cannot be a hedged item in a fair value hedge, because consolidation recognises in profit or loss the subsidiary's profit or loss, rather than changes in the investment's fair value. If a subsidiary was allowed to be designated as a hedged item, it would result in double counting, as both the income from the investment as well as changes in the fair value would be reported in profit or loss. A hedge of a net investment in a foreign operation is different because it is a hedge of the foreign currency exposure, not a fair value hedge of the change in the investment's value. [IAS 39 para AG 99]. Another example of a transaction undertaken by a foreign subsidiary that cannot be hedged at the consolidation level is considered below

Example 1 – Forecast foreign currency transaction undertaken by a foreign subsidiary

Entity A's functional currency is the euro. It has a US subsidiary, subsidiary B, whose functional currency is the US dollar. Subsidiary B has highly probable forecast sales denominated in Japanese yen.

Entity A wishes to hedge subsidiary B's forecast Japanese yen inflows back into euros (entity A's functional currency) using external foreign currency forward contracts (¥/€). Entity A's management intends to designate, in the consolidated financial statements, the forward contracts as hedging instruments in a cash flow hedge of the forecast transactions denominated in Japanese yen.

The ¥/€ forward contracts taken out by entity A do not qualify for cash flow hedge accounting on consolidation. This is because there is no ¥/€ cash flow exposure that affects consolidated profit or loss. The consolidated income statement will be exposed to ¥/US$ movements, as subsidiary B will translate its ¥ sales into its own functional currency (US$). The exposure to movements in US/€ constitutes a translation risk rather than a cash flow exposure and, therefore, cannot be the subject of a cash flow hedge.

However, it is possible for the subsidiary B to use a ¥/US$ forward contract to designate a cash flow hedge of its ¥/US$ transaction exposure. Alternatively, entity A could use a ¥/US$ forward contract to hedge the exposure since IAS 39 does not require that the operating unit that is exposed to the risk being hedged be a party to the hedging instrument. [IAS 39 para IG F2.14].

Entity A could also hedge its net investment in subsidiary B using a €/US$ forward (see para 10.133 below). This would, however, not include the forecast transaction.

Example 2 – Parent hedging forecasted future revenues denominated in the functional currency of a subsidiary which is different from functional currency of the parent

Entity A, based in Germany, whose functional currency is euro, has a subsidiary in the UK, whose functional currency is GBP. The group's presentation currency is also euro. The UK subsidiary sells gas within the UK for GBP to British customers. At the group level, the group's treasury department enters into external GBP/euro forward contract to hedge against movements in GBP *versus* euro on behalf of the group. The group cannot obtain cash flow hedge accounting for the UK subsidiary sales. The sales of the UK subsidiary are made in its functional currency so it has no foreign currency exposure. The consolidated group has a foreign currency exposure, but it will not affect the group's reported net profit or loss. At the consolidated level the foreign currency exposure will be deferred as part of cumulative translation adjustment in equity when the UK subsidiary's financial statements are translated into the group's presentation currency for consolidation [IAS 21 para 39(c)]. Group management may, therefore, consider the possibility of net investment hedge accounting under paragraph 102 of IAS 39. However, the group will not be able to obtain hedge accounting for hedges of forecasted sales – see last sentence of the example 1 above.

Example 3 – Hedging of foreign currency sales of a foreign subsidiary denominated in group's presentation currency by the parent

A European parent entity whose functional currency is euro, has a Chinese subsidiary whose functional currency is RMB. The presentation currency of the group is euro. The Chinese entity has highly probable forecast sales in euro that its management has not hedged. The parent's management enters into EUR/RMB forward contracts and designates these as cash flow hedges of the Chinese subsidiary forecast sales.

The forecast euro sales give rise to a currency risk that will affect the subsidiary's profit or loss in its separate financial statements. This is because the RMB amount at which the sales are reported in the subsidiary's separate financial statements will be affected by the EUR/RMB exchange rate at the time the sales occur.

However, in the consolidated financial statements the sales will be translated into euro using the exchange rates at the dates of the transactions (or an average rate when this approximates the rates at the dates of the transactions) in accordance with paragraph 39(b) of IAS 21. Hence, the RMB amount at which the sales are reported in the group's consolidated financial statements will not be affected by the EUR/RMB exchange rate at the time the sales occur. Accordingly, the currency risk of these forecast sales will not affect the consolidated profit or loss when expressed in euro.

The forecast transaction meets the requirements of paragraph 88(c) of IAS 39. The reference in paragraph 88(c) of IAS 39 to 'profit or loss' refers to the subsidiary's profit or loss where the exposure is located and not to the profit or loss of the consolidated entity. This is consistent with the functional currency framework in IAS 21 under which a foreign exchange exposure arises whenever a transaction is denominated in a currency other than the functional currency of the entity entering into the transaction. Paragraph IG F.2.14 of IAS 39 also permits the hedging instrument to be entered into by the parent and states that it need not be entered into by the subsidiary that has the exposure. Hence, provided all the other criteria in paragraph 88 of IAS 39R are met, the group may obtain cash flow hedge accounting in its consolidated financial statements.

Future earnings

10.49   Future earnings or future results cannot be designated as hedged items because they are the net effect of various transactions that do not share the same risk characteristic. However, future revenue or future expenditure may be separately designated as hedged items if the underlying risk exposure can be specifically identified and measured (see example in para 10.108 below).

Derivative instruments

10.50   A derivative instrument (whether a stand-alone or separately recognised embedded derivative) cannot be designated as a hedged item, either individually or as part of a hedged group in a fair value or cash flow hedge. For instance, it is not possible to designate a pay-variable, receive-fixed forward rate agreement (FRA) as a cash flow hedge of a pay-fixed, receive-variable FRA. This is because derivative instruments are always deemed held for trading and measured at fair value with gains and losses recognised in profit or loss unless they are designated and effective hedging instruments. As an exception, IAS 39 permits the designation of a purchased option as the hedged item in a fair value hedge. [IAS 39 paras AG 94, IG F2.1]. A contract to buy or sell a non-financial asset that can be settled net in cash and that is accounted for as a derivative under IAS 39 cannot be a hedged item.

General business risk

10.51 To qualify for hedge accounting, the hedge must relate to a specific identified and designated risk and not merely to the entity's general business risks and must ultimately affect the entity's profit or loss. For example, a firm commitment to acquire a business in a business combination cannot be a hedged item, except for foreign exchange risk in respect of the purchase consideration, because the other risks being hedged cannot be specifically identified and measured. These other risks are general business risks. Similarly, a hedge of the risk of obsolescence of a physical asset or the risk of expropriation of property by a government is not eligible for hedge accounting; effectiveness cannot be measured because those risks are not measurable reliably. [IAS 39 paras AG 98, AG 110]. Similarly, the risk that a transaction will not occur such that it would result in less revenue than expected is an overall business risk that is not eligible as a hedged item. [IAS 39 para IG F2.8].

Hedging instruments

Definition

10.52 A hedging instrument is a designated derivative or, for a hedge of the risk of changes in foreign currency exchange rates, only a designated non-derivative financial asset or non-derivative financial liability, whose fair value or cash flows are expected to offset changes in the fair value or cash flows of a designated hedged item. [IAS 39 para 9].

10.53 For hedge accounting purposes, only instruments that involve a party external to the reporting entity (that is, external to the group, or individual entity that is being reported on) can be designated as hedging instruments. It follows that internal derivative contracts between members of a group (for example, a trading subsidiary entering into a derivative contract with group treasury) cannot be designated as a hedging instrument in the group's consolidated financial statements. Therefore, if an entity wishes to achieve hedge accounting in the consolidated financial statements, it must designate a hedging relationship between a qualifying external hedging instrument and a qualifying hedged item. However, internal derivative contracts may qualify for hedge accounting in the individual or separate financial statements of individual entities within the group provided that they are external to the individual entity being reported on (see para 10.79 below). [IAS 39 para 73].

Derivative financial instruments

10.54 IAS 39 does not restrict the circumstances in which a derivative may be designated as a hedging instrument provided the hedge accounting conditions are met (see para 10.138 below), except for some written options. This means that derivative instruments such as forward exchange contracts, futures contracts, interest rate swaps, cross-currency and commodity swaps and purchased options can all be designated as hedging instruments. An embedded derivative that is accounted for separately from its host contract can be used as a hedging instrument. Also, those contracts for purchases or sales of non-financial assets that are accounted for as derivatives under IAS 39 (that is, can be settled net or by exchanging another financial instrument and that are not for own use) may be used as hedging instruments.

Example 1 – Hedging with a sales commitment

Entity J's functional currency is the Japanese yen. It has issued a US$ fixed rate debt instrument with semi-annual interest payments that matures in 2 years with principal due at maturity of 5 million US dollars. It has also entered into a fixed price sales commitment for 5 million US dollars that matures in two years that is not accounted for as a derivative, because it meets the exemption for normal sales. Entity J intends to designate the sales commitment as a hedge of the fair value change of the maturity amount of the debt attributable to foreign currency risk.

In this scenario, the sales commitment is accounted for as a firm commitment and not as a derivative and, therefore, cannot be designated as a hedging instrument. However, if the foreign currency component of the sales commitment is required to be separated as an embedded derivative on the grounds that US dollar is not the customer's functional currency and otherwise not closely related under IAS 39, it could be designated as a hedging instrument in a hedge of the exposure to changes in the fair value of the debt's maturity amount attributable to foreign currency risk. [IAS 39 para IG F1.2]. However, as the exchange difference on the fixed rate debt would, in any event, be reported in profit or loss under IAS 21, a separate hedging relationship is not necessary.

Example 2 – Hedging with fixed to fixed cross currency swaps

Entity X, whose functional currency is the euro, has issued a US dollar fixed rate debt. Entity X's management intends to hedge the foreign exchange cash flow exposure on the debt's interest and principal by entering into a fixed to fixed euro/US dollar cross currency interest rate swap.

Entity X expects the cross currency interest rate swap to be a highly effective hedge of the cash flow exposure, since the critical terms of the hedging instrument and the hedged item match.

IAS 39 does not specify the methodology that should be used for effectiveness testing other than to require this to be consistent with the entity's risk management strategy. One possible method would be to apply dollar offset test comparing the following:

---

1   The cumulative gain or loss on the hedging instrument from inception of the hedge calculated as the difference between:

    (a)   the fair value of the swap at inception; and

    (b)   the fair value of the swap at the testing date.

2   The cumulative change in the fair value of the expected cash flows on the debt from the inception of the hedge calculated as the difference between:

    (a)   the present value of all fixed USD cash flows on the bond, determined using the forward USD/EUR rates for the respective maturities at inception of hedge accounting (that is, as if the USD/EUR exchange rates had been fixed at the forward USD/EUR rate on each coupon date) discounted using euro LIBOR at the testing date; and

    (b)   the periodic valuation of all fixed USD cash flows on the bond using the forward rate at the testing date and discounted using euro LIBOR at the testing date.

If all the critical terms of the swap exactly match the terms of the underlying bond, this test is likely to give rise to no ineffectiveness. If this is the case and, if all the remaining requirements of paragraph 88 of IAS 39 relating to documentation and designation are met, management could defer the entire change in the fair value of the swap in other comprehensive income.

At each reporting date, the underlying bond will be re-measured through profit or loss using the spot exchange rate in accordance with IAS 21. At the same time an equivalent offsetting portion of the fair value adjustment of the swap should be recycled to profit or loss. The remaining revaluation gain or loss deferred in equity relates to the forward points, that is, the difference between the spot rate and the forward rate. These forward points deferred in equity should be recognised in profit or loss over the period of the hedging relationship (this being the period(s) in which the hedged item affects profit or loss) using the effective interest rate method.

10.55   It is not necessary for an entity to enter into a new derivative contract every time it enters into a new hedging relationship. Provided the hedge accounting criteria are met, a pre-existing derivative instrument that has been held for some time and classified as held-for-trading can be designated as a hedging instrument in a new hedging relationship, as can a derivative that has been designated previously as a hedging instrument in a hedge relationship that no longer qualifies for hedge accounting. However, an existing derivative will have a non-zero fair value because of its 'off market terms'. Consequently, it cannot be assumed that the new relationship will be highly effective without performing the necessary analysis of the impact of the 'off market' nature of the derivative on the new relationship. The 'off market' nature of the derivative can be described as an 'embedded financing' within the derivative. For example, a derivative asset can be thought of as containing an 'embedded loan receivable' and a derivative liability as containing an 'embedded loan payable'. This 'embedded' financing can be a source of ineffectiveness. Changing the designation of a derivative from a trading instrument to a hedging instrument occurs at inception of the new hedging relationship.

Portions and proportions of a hedging instrument

10.56   There is normally a single fair value measure for a hedging instrument in its entirety and the factors that cause changes in fair value are co-dependent. Thus, a hedging relationship is designated by an entity for a hedging instrument in its entirety. It follows that a derivative instrument cannot be split into components representing different risks with each component designated as the hedging instrument. The only exceptions permitted are:

- separating the interest element and the spot price of a forward contract; and

- separating the intrinsic value and time value of an option contract and designating as the hedging instrument only the change in intrinsic value of an option.

These exceptions are permitted because the intrinsic value of the option and the premium or discount on the forward can generally be measured separately.

[IAS 39 para 74].

> **Example 1 – Definition of a forward contract**
>
> For hedging purposes, entity A enters into the following derivative instruments:
>
> - A fixed to fixed cross-currency swap.
> - A floating to floating cross-currency swap.
> - A floating to fixed cross-currency swap.
>
> Entity A's management wishes to designate only the spot element of these derivatives as hedging instruments in separate hedging relationships.
>
> Paragraph 74 of IAS 39 allows an entity to designate the spot element of a derivative as a hedging instrument provided the derivative is a forward contract. A simple forward contract is a contract to exchange a fixed amount of a financial or non-financial asset on a fixed future value date or dates beyond the spot value date. For the purposes of applying paragraph 74 of IAS 39, the term 'forward contract' should be interpreted as being any derivative instrument that is a simple forward contract or that may be constructed using only a series of simple forward contracts. Forward contracts may be settled by gross delivery of the financial asset in return for cash, or on a net basis at each settlement date.
>
> The fixed to fixed cross-currency swap entered into by entity A constitutes a forward contract under paragraph 74 of IAS 39 provided that the settlements on each leg of the swap occur on the same dates in the future (that is, there is no timing mismatch between the two legs of the swap).
>
> However, the other derivatives (the floating to floating cross-currency swap and the floating to fixed cross-currency swaps) are not forward contracts since they cannot be constructed using only simple forward contracts.

Example 2 – Splitting a written swaption into components

Entity A, whose functional currency is euro, issues 30-year fixed-rate debt. At the same time, entity A enters into an interest rate derivative with a third party with the following terms: entity A receives 7% fixed and pays 5% fixed for 7 years. After 7 years, the counterparty has the option to require entity A to enter into a pay fixed 5%, receive LIBOR interest rate swap with a maturity of 23 years. (Economically, entity A has sold the counterparty a swaption on a 23 year swap with 7 years until exercise date and with premium payments spread over 7 years).

Entity A proposes to split the derivative into separate components, one of which is an on-market receive fixed, pay variable interest rate swap. It would designate this component as a hedge of the first seven years of interest rate exposure under the fixed rate debt. The remaining component would be treated as a trading derivative.

Entity A must designate the entire derivative as a hedging instrument in the hedging relationship. This derivative may not be split into its components, because of the requirements of paragraph 74 of IAS 39 and paragraph IG F1.8 of IAS 39.

In addition the combined instrument is a written option and cannot be designated as a hedging instrument under paragraph AG94 of IAS 39 (see para 10.70).

10.57 The fair value of a foreign exchange forward contract is affected by changes in the spot rate and by changes in the forward points. The latter derives from the interest rate differential between the currencies specified in the forward contract. Changes in the forward points may give rise to ineffectiveness if the hedged item is not similarly affected by interest rate differentials unless only the spot component of the forward is designated as the hedging instrument (see para 10.186 below).

10.58 The fair value of an option can be divided into two portions: the intrinsic value, which is determined in terms of the difference between the strike price and the current market price of the underlying (as described in more detail below); and the time value, which is the option's remaining value and depends on the volatility of the price of the underlying, interest rates and the time remaining to maturity. When the option is used to hedge the one-sided risk on a non-optional position, changes in the option's time value will not be offset by an equivalent change in the value or cash flows of the hedged item (for more details about hedging of portions see para 10.23). IAS 39 does not specify how the intrinsic value of an option is determined. Intrinsic value can be defined based on the spot rate. For example, for an interest rate cap that is used to hedge exposure to interest rates on floating rate debt, the intrinsic value may be deferred by projecting all future cash flows on the cap at the current spot rate and discounting the result using the zero-coupon curve. If the current spot rate is below the market rate, the cap is 'out of the money' in all periods. Alternatively, the intrinsic value could be defined using the forward rate curve. The projected cash flows would be calculated using the forward rates. In that case the cap may be in the money in some periods, even when the current spot rate is below the strike price.

The intrinsic value of a European option (that is, an option which is settled at the end of its term) may be defined as discounted where the difference between:

– the strike price of the option's underlying specified in the option; and

– the market price of the underlying

is discounted to present value.

The intrinsic value may also be defined as undiscounted – that is, simply as the absolute difference between the strike price and market price of the underlying asset.

The intrinsic value of an American style option may be defined as the difference between the undiscounted spot price on the day when it is determined and the strike price specified in the option contract. This is because the American style option can be exercised at any time.

10.59   Generally, it may be advantageous to exclude the forward points and the time value of an option to improve effectiveness. However, this comes at a price as it will most probably increase the volatility in the income statement. This is because as the forward points or time value are not subject to hedge accounting, any changes in their fair value will be recognised as gains or losses in the income statement as they occur. If forward points were included in the hedge relationship then they could generate ineffectiveness for example if the timing of the hedged forecast transaction changed and change in fair value of the forward was higher in absolute terms than change in fair value of the hedged cash flow (see para 10.116). [IAS 39 para 96].

10.60   A proportion of the entire hedging instrument, such as 50 per cent of the notional amount, may be designated as the hedging instrument. [IAS 39 para 75]. The proportion that is not acting as a hedge is either treated as held-for-trading or designated as a hedging instrument in another hedge relationship.

Example – Proportions of derivatives as hedging instruments

Entity A, whose functional currency is the euro, enters into a US$10m forward contract on 1 June 20X1 to hedge forecast future US$-denominated sales in March 20X2. At the time of entering into the forward contract, only US$8m of forecast sales are considered to be highly probable of occurring in March 20X2.

In this situation, entity A can designated 80% of the forward contract as a hedge of the highly probable future sales of US$8m in March 20X2. The remaining US$2m of the forward contract (20%) may either be designated as trading or as a hedging instrument in another hedge relationship. In other words, 20% of the total change in the fair value of the forward contract would be reported in profit or loss, or used as an offset in another hedge relationship.

10.61 A hedging relationship may not be designated for only a portion of the time period during which a hedging instrument remains outstanding as illustrated in the example below. [IAS 39 para 75].

> **Example – Portion of the outstanding life of a derivative as a hedging instrument**
>
> An entity enters into a pay-fixed, receive-variable interest rate swap to hedge the cash flow exposure of a floating rate debt instrument. Both the swap and the debt instrument are entered into on the same date. The floating rate debt instrument has a term of 5 years and the swap has a term of 7 years.
>
> The entity cannot designate the cash flows arising in the first 5 years of the 7 year swap as a hedging instrument. The swap's fair value derives from the present value of the net settlements over the entire 7 year period, not the first 5 years. Furthermore, the fair value of the swap cannot be time apportioned using linear interpolation, as the change in the swap's fair value per unit of time is non-linear.
>
> However, the entity can designate the entire 7 year swap as a hedge of the 5 year debt, but ineffectiveness will arise because of timing mismatches and is likely to be so large (that is, outside the 80%-125% range, see para 10.146) as to prohibit hedge accounting.
>
> On the other hand, if the swap's terms and the debt are reversed so that they are 5 years and 7 years respectively, the 5 year swap can be designated as a hedge of the first 5 years of the debt instrument. This is referred to as 'partial-term' hedging and is discussed in paragraph 10.29 above.

Hedging more than one risk with a single instrument

10.62 A derivative, such as a forward contract, swap or an option, is used as a hedging instrument to hedge a single risk (foreign currency, interest rate or equity price risk). However, entities may often use a single derivative such as a cross-currency swap (combined interest rate and currency swap) to convert a variable rate position in a foreign currency to a fixed rate position in the entity's functional currency. IAS 39 permits a single hedging instrument to be designated as a hedge of more than one type of risk provided that:

■ The risks hedged can be identified clearly.

■ The effectiveness of the hedge can be demonstrated.

■ It is possible to ensure that there is specific designation of the hedging instrument and different risk positions.

[IAS 39 para 76].

10.63 If a single hedging instrument is used to hedge different risk exposures and each of these risk exposures are accounted for using different forms of hedge accounting (fair value hedge for one, cash flow hedge for the other), IFRS 7 requires separate disclosures for each type of hedge (see chapter 11). [IAS 39 IG para F1.12].

Example 1 – Dual foreign currency forward exchange contract to hedge currency risk

Entity A's functional currency is the Japanese yen. Entity A has a 5 year floating rate US dollar liability and a 10 year fixed rate pound sterling denominated bond (an asset). The principal amounts of the asset and liability when converted into the Japanese yen are the same. Entity A enters into a single foreign currency forward contract to hedge its foreign currency exposure on both instruments under which it receives US dollars and pays pound sterling at the end of 5 years.

Entity A designates the forward exchange contract as a hedging instrument in a cash flow hedge against the foreign currency exposure on the principal repayments of both instruments. Since entity A's functional currency is Yen, it is exposed to US$/¥ foreign currency risk on the floating rate liability and ¥/£ foreign exchange risk on the fixed rate asset.

IAS 39 permits a single hedging instrument to be designated as a hedge of multiple types of risk if three conditions stated in paragraph 10.62 above are met. In this example, the derivative hedging instrument satisfies all of these conditions, as follows:

- The risks hedged can be identified clearly. The risks are the exposures to changes in the forward exchange rates between US dollars and yen and yen and pounds, respectively.

- The effectiveness of the hedge can be demonstrated. For the pound sterling bond, the effectiveness is measured as the degree of offset between the fair value of the principal repayment in pounds sterling and the fair value of the pound sterling payment on the forward exchange contract. For the US dollar liability, the effectiveness is measured as the degree of offset between the fair value of the principal repayment in US dollars and the US dollar receipt on the forward exchange contract. Even though the receivable has a 10-year life and the forward protects it for only the first 5 years, hedge accounting is permitted for only a portion of the exposure as described in paragraph 10.29 above.

- It is possible to ensure that there is specific designation of the hedging instrument and different risk positions. The hedged exposures are identified as the principal amounts of the liability and the note receivable in their respective currency of denomination.

[IAS 39 para IG F1.13].

It should be noted that in respect of the second point above, the US $/£ forward is theoretically divided into two different derivatives. The Yen is imputed as the base currency for the two derivatives creating a synthetic US$/Yen (receive US dollar, pay Yen) foreign currency forward and a synthetic ¥/£ (receive Yen, pay sterling) foreign currency forward. The synthetic Yen leg is defined in such a manner that the fair value of each synthetic forward contract is nil at the hedge's inception. This can be pictorially represented as follows:

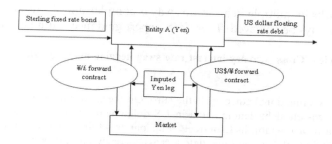

Furthermore, it should be noted that the hedge accounting criteria must be satisfied for both the designated hedged risks. For instance, if effectiveness of the hedge can be demonstrated for US$/¥ risk only and not ¥/£ risk, hedge accounting is not permitted.

Example 2 – Cross currency interest rate swap hedging multiple risks in a single hedged item

Entity A's functional currency is the euro. On 1 July 20X6, entity A issues a 10 year fixed-rate debt denominated in US dollar with an annual 5% coupon. Entity A's overall risk management policy is to borrow in its own functional currency. The entity determined, however, that its overall financing costs would be reduced if it were to issue foreign currency denominated debt and purchase a currency swap to convert the debt synthetically into a floating euro denominated debt. Accordingly, the entity hedges the transaction by entering into a cross currency interest rate swap (combined foreign currency and interest rate swap) under which it receives US$ fixed, pays euro floating. The swap's terms match those of the debt.

IAS 39 permits the cross currency swap to be designated as a hedging instrument as a hedge of more than one risk, provide the criteria described in paragraph 10.62 above are met. Therefore, the cross-currency swap can be designated either as a fair value hedge of both the interest rate risk and currency risk of the US$ debt, or as a fair value hedge of the interest rate risk and a cash flow hedge of the foreign currency risk.

If the entity had issued a US$ floating rate debt and synthetically converted it into a fixed euro debt by entering into a receive US$ floating, pay euro fixed cross-currency swap, the entity could have designated the swap as a cash flow hedge of interest rate risk and a cash flow hedge or fair value hedge of the currency risk.

In both cases, the risks being hedged are clearly identifiable, the effectiveness of the hedges can be demonstrated and it is possible to ensure that there is specific designation of the hedging instrument and different risk positions.

10.64   It is also possible to use a single derivative instrument to hedge more than one risk in more than one hedged item. In order to do this, the entity should be able to identify the hedged risks in each of the hedged items and split the single derivative into its components in order to allocate those components to each hedged risk identified. As a derivative has only a single fair value, care should be taken in splitting a derivative so that it does not result in the recognition of cash flows in the single hedging instrument that do not contractually exist. Hedging multiple risks in multiple items in this way is complex and the desired effectiveness may not always be achieved. Therefore, expert guidance should always be sought.

Example – Cross currency interest rate swap hedging multiple risks in multiple hedged items

Entity A's functional currency is the euro. On the same date, entity A has issued a 10 year fixed-rate debt denominated in US dollar with an annual 5% coupon and has made a 10 year 6 months LIBOR + 80bp loan to a third party in sterling. Entity A has also entered into on the same date a cross-currency interest rate (CCIR) US$ fixed/£ floating swap. Under the terms of the swap. Entity A will receive fixed interest in US dollar at 4% and will pay variable 6-month LIBOR interest in sterling. The entity wishes to obtain hedge accounting for the swap.

With regard to the loan asset, entity A is exposed to a £/€ exchange risk, because the loan is denominated in sterling which is not entity A's functional currency. It is also exposed to cash flow interest rate risk (sterling 6 months LIBOR) because entity A will pay variable coupon on the loan. Entity A is also exposed to a credit risk (change in the credit rating of the issuer of the loan).

With regard to the liability, entity A is exposed to a risk of changes in the fair value of the debt due to €/US$ exchange risk (both the notional amount and the interest on the loan are denominated in US dollars, which is not entity A's functional currency). Entity A is also exposed to fair value interest rate risk (US$ 6 months LIBOR is defined as the benchmark risk), because it will pay fixed coupon in US$ on the debt.

Two ways in which entity A could use the CCIR swap as a hedging instrument are described below. A single swap (receive US$ 4% fixed, pay floating £) may be analysed into its separate risk components for hedging purposes by imputing a notional leg denominated in the entity's functional currency. The additional leg may be either fixed or floating, provided the chosen alternative qualifies for hedge accounting for both of the exposures hedged and effectiveness can be reliably measured for both elements. Prospective and retrospective effectiveness testing must be performed on both elements of the hedge relationship. Both elements must be highly effective in order for the hedge relationship to qualify for hedge accounting.

Therefore, the entity could separate the swap by inserting a euro floating leg (6 month LIBOR) into the CCIR swap, creating a US$ fix/€ float swap and a € float/£ float swap. Entity A will end up with a fair value hedge of both the interest rate and currency risk on the US $ debt and a cash flow hedge of the foreign currency exposure on the sterling floating rate loan. This is shown in the diagram below.

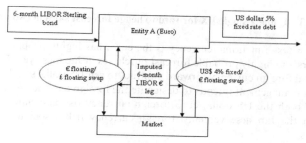

Alternatively, entity A could separate the swap by inserting a € fixed leg into the CCIR swap, creating a US $ fixed/€ fixed swap and a € fixed/£ floating swap. Entity A will end up with a cash flow hedge of the currency risk on the US$ debt and a cash flow hedge of the interest rate and foreign currency risk on the sterling floating rate loan. This is shown in the diagram below.

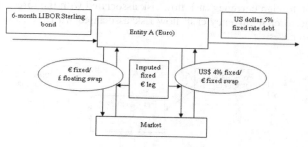

The risks hedged can be identified clearly.

Situation 1 (€ floating leg)

For the US$ denominated debt, the hedging relationship is a fair value hedge of the exposure to changes in the fair value attributable to both changes in the 6 months US LIBOR interest rate (benchmark rate) and US$/€ spot rate movements.

For the sterling floating loan, the hedging relationship is a cash flow hedge of the variability in cash flow attributable to the £/€ spot rate movements.

Situation 2 (€ fixed leg)

For the US$ denominated debt, the hedging relationship is a cash flow hedge of the variability in cash flow on the fixed rate US$-denominated debt attributable to the US$/€ spot rate movements.

For the sterling floating loan, the hedging relationship is a cash flow hedge of the variability in cash flow attributable to both the change in sterling 6 months LIBOR (benchmark rate) and £/€ spot rate movements.

Example 3 – Using a single FX forward to hedge forecast sales in two different currencies

Entity J, whose functional currency is the euro, has highly probable forecast sales in US dollars and highly probable forecast purchases in Japanese yen. Entity J enters into an external foreign currency forward contract to sell US dollars and buy Japanese yen. Entity J's management intends to designate the foreign currency forward contract as a hedge of both the US dollar/euro foreign currency risk associated with the forecast sales and the Japanese yen/euro foreign currency risk associated with the forecast purchases.

For hedge effectiveness testing the Japanese yen/US dollar forward contract is theoretically divided into two different derivatives. The euro is imputed as the base currency for the two derivatives creating a synthetic US dollar/euro foreign currency forward and a synthetic euro/Japanese yen foreign currency forward. The hedged item is designated as two risks:

- The foreign currency cash flow risk associated with the forecast US dollar sales.
- The foreign currency cash flow risk associated with the forecast Japanese yen purchases.

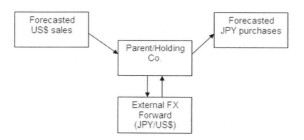

The Japanese yen/US dollar forward may be designated as a cash flow hedge of both the foreign currency cash flow risks associated with the forecast sales in US dollars and the forecasted purchases in Japanese yen, provided all of the conditions in paragraph 76 of IAS 39 are met.

This solution is consistent with paragraph IG F2.18 of IAS 39, which allows a Japenese yen functional currency entity to designate a US dollar/sterling swap as a hedge of both a US dollar liability and sterling asset. However, each hedging relationship must be tested for effectiveness separately and if one of the two hedging relationships becomes ineffective (either because an effectiveness test is failed or because one of the forecast transactions is no longer highly probable to occur), hedge accounting will be discontinued prospectively for both hedge relationships.

Combination of derivative instruments

10.65 A derivative may also be designated as the hedging instrument in combination with one or more other derivatives, or even, for a hedge of foreign exchange risk, in combination with groups of non-derivative assets or liabilities. Two or more derivatives or proportions of them may be viewed in combination and jointly designated as the hedging instrument, provided none of them is a written option or a net written option (see further para 10.70 below). For hedges of currency risk, two or more non-derivatives, or proportions of them, may be designated as the hedging instrument. [IAS 39 para 77].

10.66 Derivative instruments do not have to be similar to be combined, either together or with non-derivative instruments. Even when the risks arising from some derivatives offset(s) those arising from others, the combination can still be designated as a hedging instrument. [IAS 39 para 77].

10.67 Multiple derivatives need not be acquired at the same time to be designated as a hedge of the same item. They could be acquired at different times. For instance, an entity can designate two purchased options as a hedge of the same hedged item. Multiple derivatives can be used to hedge the same risk or different risks, provided that all of the other hedge criteria have been met and there is no 'duplicate' hedging of the same risk. For example, assume that two derivatives are designated as a hedge of the risk of a change in the fair value of a fixed-rate asset. One derivative hedges interest rate risk and the other hedges credit risk. In assessing an expectation of offsetting changes in fair value that are attributable to the type of risk that is being hedged, an entity would consider the two hedges separately, since the derivatives are hedging two separate risks.

Example – Combination of derivatives designated as a hedging instrument

Entity A's functional currency is pound sterling. On 1 January 20X5, the entity issues a 5 year 5% fixed-rate £100m debt with interest payable annually on 31 December. The debt is classified as other financial liabilities.

The risk management policy of entity A requires it to pay variable rate interest on debt except during the first 2 years. Accordingly, entity A enters into:

- A 5-year £100m notional receive fixed 5%, pay floating (3 month LIBOR) interest swap (swap 1).

- A 2-year £100m notional pay fixed 5%, receive floating (3 month LIBOR) interest swap (swap 2).

IAS 39 permits entity A to designate the combination of swap 1 and swap 2 as a hedge of the fair value exposure relating to interest rate movements in the debt instrument for the cash flows on the bond (principal plus interest) that will occur in period 1 January 20X7 to 31 December 20X9. This is because IAS 39 permits the designation of a portion of the fair value or cash flows of a financial instrument as a hedged item. Therefore, provided that all criteria for hedge accounting are met (in particular the hedge, as described, is expected to be highly effective and the new hedge relationship is consistent with entity A's risk management policies), fair value hedge accounting can be applied.

As a result of combining the two swaps entity A will achieve its objective of paying fixed interest in the first two years and achieve fair value hedge of the interest rate risk in the remaining 3 years as shown below:

		20X5	20X6	20X7	20X8	20X9
Debt instrument		-5%	-5%	-5%	-5%	-5%
Swap 1 – receive 5%		+5%	+5%	+5%	+5%	+5%
– pay 3 month Libor		Libor	Libor	Libor	Libor	Libor
Swap 2 – receive 3 month Libor		Libor	Libor			
– pay 5%		-5%	-5%			
Net interest		-5%	-5%	Libor	Libor	Libor
Hedging instrument						

Changes in the aggregate fair value of swap 1 and swap 2 will be recognised in profit or loss. Similarly changes in the fair value of the debt attributable to interest rate movements relating to the period 1 January 20X7 to 31 December 20X9 will be recognised in profit or loss (see para 10.94 below). Some ineffectiveness is likely to arise because of the variable rate leg of swap 1 that is not mirrored in the hedged item. Also, the fair value of swap 2 is based on a different section of the yield curve from the section of the yield curve used for determining swap 1's fair value of (2 year *versus* 5 years).

10.68   IAS 39 also permits derivative instruments to be combined with non-derivative instruments, or proportions of them and the combination designated as the hedging instrument, but only for hedges of foreign currency risk. For example, a Swedish kroner functional currency entity could hedge its net investment in Korea with debt denominated in US dollars combined with Korean won *versus* US dollar swap (excluding forward points) in its consolidated financial statements. Similarly, an entity could use a combination of foreign currency cash instrument and a derivative to hedge the foreign currency risk of a firm commitment, provided all the hedge accounting conditions are met. If the entity wanted to minimise ineffectiveness in the profit or loss account, the entity may impute two identical (but offsetting) Swedish kroner pay and receive legs and then designate resulting pay Swedish kroner *versus* receive US dollar swap as a hedge of US dollar debt and receive Swedish kroner *versus* pay Korean won swap as a hedge of a foreign net investment in Korean operation. Similarly, an entity could use a combination of foreign currency cash instrument and a derivative to hedge the foreign currency risk of a firm commitment, provided all the hedge accounting conditions are met.

Options as hedging instruments

10.69   Options, in contrast to forward and swaps, give the holder the right but not the obligation to exercise the instrument and exchange the underlyings. Generally, options that have the potential to reduce risk exposure can qualify as hedging instruments. For instance, a purchased option has potential gains equal to or greater than losses and, therefore, has the potential to reduce profit or loss exposure from changes in fair values or cash flows. Therefore, it can qualify as a hedging instrument. [IAS 39 para AG 94].

Example 1 – Purchased option as a hedging instrument in cash flow hedges

Entity A operates a mail-order business. Its functional currency is the euro, but it purchases approximately 20% of its merchandise from the USA.

Entity A issues the mail-order catalogue for the coming year, incorporating its price list, before entering into a firm purchase commitment with US suppliers. Entity A, therefore, sets the prices in the catalogue based on expected exchange rates of €1 = US$1.25. It is highly probable that the entity will make purchases of at least €500,000 from the US in the first six months.

The entity's documented risk management policy requires it to hedge the risk that exchange rates will be higher than expected by purchasing a call option to buy US dollars for euros with a strike price equal to the expected exchange rate. Entity A, therefore, purchased a call option at a rate of €1 = US$1.25, for a maximum of €500,000 in six months' time at a cost of €60,000.

The spot rate at the time of entering into the option contracts was €1 = US$1.1.

Entity A can designate the intrinsic value of the purchased option as a hedge against the movements in the €/$ exchange rate. The exposure being hedged is the variability in cash flows that would arise if the US dollar exchange rate exceeds the expected level of €1 = US$1.25.

Example 2 – Purchased option as a hedging instrument in fair value hedges

Entity A has issued a 5 year €100m debt that bears interest at a fixed rate of 3%. It wishes to hedge the risk of increases in the fair value of the debt if interest rates decrease. It enters into a €100m 5 year floor on 3 month EURIBOR with a strike rate of 3%.

The purchased option (the interest rate floor) can be designated as a hedging instrument in a hedge of changes in the fair value of the 5 year debt as a result of changes in interest rates. IAS 39 states that a financial item may be hedged with respect to the risks associated with only a portion of its cash flow or fair value, provided that effectiveness can be measured (see para 10.23 above). It is, therefore, possible to designate the hedge as the risk of changes in the fair value if interest rates fall below 3%. The effectiveness of the hedge will be improved if the entity designates only the intrinsic value of the floor as the hedging instrument. In this case, the floor's time value is excluded from the hedge relationship and changes in its value are recognised in the income statement as they occur.

10.69.1   In July 2008 the Board amended IAS 39 in order to clarify the exposures arising from a financial instrument that may be designated as hedged items. As part of that amendment, the Board explained that in a hedge of one-sided risk, entities are permitted to designate the hedged risk as the intrinsic value of a purchased option that has the same principal terms as the hedged item, but may not include the time value of the option. For example, an entity can designate the variability of future cash flow outcomes resulting from a price increase of a forecast commodity purchase. Only cash flow losses that result from an increase in the price above the specified level are designated. The Board prohibited the inclusion of option's time value in the designated one sided risk on a non-optional hedged item because time value is not a component of a forecast transaction that will affect profit or loss (paragraph 86(b)). Greater hedge effectiveness is, therefore, likely to be achieved if the hedging instrument is designated in the same way – that is, to exclude time value. Since hedging a one-sided risk is not a hedge of a portion, the Board also explained that this clarification covers financial as well as non-financial items.

10.69.2   This change was effective, retrospectively, for annual periods beginning on or after 1 July 2009 (this affects the first year end of 31 December 2010 or 31 March 2011 for entities with December and March year ends respectively). If an entity had previously applied hedge accounting for one-sided risk where the designated hedged item had included the time value as well as intrinsic value it would have had to de-designate this hedging relationship and re-designate a new hedge relationship that excluded the time value from the hedged item on or before the date it adopted the amendment. The deferred gains or losses recognised in other comprehensive income, which included the time value, would have remained in other comprehensive income, assuming that the underlying hedged item had still been expected to occur. Where the hedge documentation is not amended to exclude the time value from the hedged item, such hedge designation is no longer allowed by this amendment and hedge accounting should not be applied. If the error is material, the prior year comparatives would have to be re-stated as if hedge accounting had never been applied. Entities are not permitted to change hedge documentation retrospectively to say that they meant to designate only the intrinsic value of the options.

10.70   A *written* option (as opposed to a purchased option) exposes its writer to the possibility of unlimited loss but limits the gain to the amount of premium received. A written option serves only to reduce the potential for gain in the hedged item or hedged transaction. It leaves the potential for loss on the hedged item or hedged transaction unchanged, except for the amount of the premium received. As a result, a written option generally increase risk exposure because the potential loss on an option that an entity writes could be significantly greater than the potential gain in value of a related hedged item. In other words, a written option is not effective in reducing the profit or loss exposure of a hedged item. Therefore, a written option does not qualify as a hedging instrument, either on its own or in combination with other derivatives, unless it is designated as an offset to a purchased option. In addition, a written option can be designated as an offset to a purchase option that is embedded in another financial instrument. For example, in a callable debt, a written option can be used as a hedging instrument to hedge the callable liability where the issuer can call the debt early. [IAS 39 para AG 94].

10.71   An entity may enter into a hedging strategy that involves a written put option and a purchased call option combining to form a collar. The objective of such a hedging strategy is to protect the entity from loss below a certain value (the floor/written put) and also limit the upside potential for gain above a certain value (the cap/purchased call) so as to reduce the cost of the hedging strategy. A typical example is an interest rate collar. Therefore, such an interest rate collar or other derivative instrument that combines a written option and a purchased option does not qualify as a hedging instrument if it is, in effect, a net written option (for which a net premium is received). [IAS 39 para 77].

10.72   However, an interest rate collar or other derivative instrument that includes a written option may be designated as a hedging instrument, if the combination is a net purchased option or zero cost collar (that is, it is neither a net written or a net purchased option). Such a combination is not a net written option and, therefore, can be designated as a hedging instrument provided all the following conditions are met:

- No net premium is received either at inception or over the life of the combination of options. The distinguishing feature of a written option is the receipt of a premium to compensate the writer for the risk incurred.

- Except for the strike prices, the critical terms and conditions of the written option component and the purchased option component are the same (including underlying variable or variables, currency denomination and maturity date).

- The notional amount of the written option component is not greater than the notional amount of the purchased option component.

[IAS 39 para IG F1.3].

10.72.1   Where a collar whose fair value was zero at inception is designated as a hedging instrument some time into its life, it may have some fair value on the date of designation. If its fair value on the date of designation is negative then the first criteria above would be failed and such a collar would not be allowed for designation as a hedging instrument. If the collar's fair value is zero or positive then, subject to compliance with the criteria two and three it would be allowed for designation as a hedging instrument.

10.72.2   It should be noted that since a collar combines two options, it is subject to the amendment described in paragraph 10.69.1. Hence, it will not be fully effective if the net time value of the written and purchased options is included in the designation of the hedging instrument. That is, ineffectiveness is minimised where the collar is designated on an intrinsic value basis (see para 10.185 onwards).

10.73   If a combination of a written option and a purchased option (such as an interest rate collar) is transacted as a single instrument with one counterparty, an entity cannot split the derivative instrument into its written option component and purchased option component and designate the purchased option component as a hedging instrument. This is because a hedging relationship is designated by an entity for a hedging instrument in its entirety. The only exceptions permitted are splitting the time value and intrinsic value of an option and splitting the interest element and spot price on a forward (see para 10.56 above). [IAS 39 para IG F1.8].

Example 1 – Combination of written and purchased options

Entity A purchases a call option from bank X and sells a put option to bank Y. Bank X and bank Y are not related. The contracts are entered into on the same day, with the purpose of creating a collar. The premium paid on the purchased call equals the premium received on the sold put; no net premium is, therefore, received.

The combination of these two instruments cannot be designated as a hedging instrument, as one of the options is a sold (written) option for which a premium is received. A collar can only be designated as a hedging instrument if the purchased and written option are combined in a single instrument and the collar is not a net written option (that is, no net premium is received).

If the two instruments have the same counterparty and are entered into simultaneously and in contemplation of one another with the intent of creating a collar, the two instruments should be viewed as one transaction.

Example 2 – Combination of written and purchased options

Entity A holds a variable interest rate debt and wishes to hedge the risk of the interest rate increasing above 3%. Entity A's assessment of the risk of the interest rate increasing above 4% is remote and it is prepared to bear that excess risk. It, therefore, enters into a 'cap spread' structure, which is a single instrument, consisting of:

■ the purchase of an interest rate cap whose strike rate is 3% (purchased option); and

■ the sale of an interest rate cap whose strike rate is 4% (written option).

The cap spread is structured as a single contract entered into with the same counterparty.

Entity A can designate the hedged risk as the risk that the interest rate rises to between 3% and 4%, provided that the cap spread does not constitute a net written option (that is, the entity does not receive a net premium for the cap spread). In this case, the entity is permitted to apply hedge accounting if the strategy is in line with the company's risk management strategy and all other conditions for hedge accounting are met.

If the entity had entered into two separate options (a purchased interest rate cap and a written interest rate cap), it could not designate both options as the hedging instrument. This is because two or more derivatives may be jointly designated as the hedging instrument only when none of them is a written option.

Example 3 – Designating a combination of several derivatives as a hedging instrument in a fair value hedge

Entity A has issued a 7%, 5 year fixed rate bond and at the same time entered into a receive-fixed (7%), pay-floating (LIBOR) 5 year interest rate swap to hedge the bond against changes in fair values resulting from changes in interest rates. The entity has also entered into a zero cost collar (a combination of written floor at 5% and purchased cap at 10%) to limit variability in cash flows arising from the combination of the fixed rate debt and interest rate swap. There is no net premium received for the cap and floor, therefore, there is no net written option.

Entity A's management can designate the combination of the interest rate swap and the zero cost collar as a hedging instrument to hedge the changes in the bond's fair value arising from changes in the risk-free rate, provided all other hedge accounting criteria required by paragraph 88 of IAS 39 are met. Although the zero cost collar contains a written option component, this is written as a single instrument and the combination is not a net written option as no premium is received by entity A at inception or over the contract's life. The hedging documentation could specify that the hedged risk is the risk of changes in the bond's fair value arising from changes in the risk-free rate within the range from 5% to 10%. Specifying the hedge in this way would improve hedge effectiveness.

Dynamic hedging strategies

10.74 IAS 39 states that a dynamic hedging strategy that assesses both an optional contract's intrinsic value and time value can qualify for hedge accounting. [IAS 39 para 74]. This allows an entity to apply hedge accounting for a 'delta neutral' hedging strategy and other dynamic hedging strategies under which the quantity of the hedging instrument is constantly adjusted in order to maintain a desired hedge ratio (for example, to achieve a delta neutral position insensitive to changes in the hedged item's fair value). For example, a portfolio insurance strategy that seeks to ensure that the hedged item's fair value item does not drop below a certain level, while allowing the fair value to increase, may qualify for hedge accounting. [IAS 39 para IG F1.9].

10.75 To qualify for hedge accounting, the entity must document how it will monitor and update the hedge and measure hedge effectiveness, be able to track properly all terminations and redesignations of the hedging instrument and demonstrate that all other criteria for hedge accounting in IAS 39 are met. Also, it must be able to demonstrate an expectation that the hedge will be highly effective for a specified short period of time during which the hedge is not expected to be adjusted. [IAS 39 para IG F1.9].

Example – Dynamic hedging strategy

Entity A whose functional currency is the euro has an investment in listed equity security denominated in US dollars. The fair value at acquisition was US$ 70 and entity A hedged it by entering into sell US$ 70 buy €44 foreign currency forward. Entity A periodically re-assesses the fair value of the equity security and FX revaluation of it is based on such fair value. Entity A also re-assesses the amount of the exposure that should be hedged in accordance with its strategy. For instance, the fair value of the security reduces from US$ 70 to US$ 40 then the nominal amount of the forward should be adjusted from sell US$ 70 to US$ 40.

When changing the amount of hedged exposure in US$, entity A first:

■ de-designates the existing hedge relationship between US$ 70 security vs. sell US$70/buy €44 forward;

10043

■ enters into a new foreign currency forward contract (being buy US$ 30 sell €20) with the same maturity date to modify its position; and

■ re-designates the new combination of derivative instruments (the previous hedging instrument being buy US$ 70/sell €44 plus the new forward being sell US$ 30 / buy €20) as the hedging instrument.

Entity A is permitted to periodically de-designate and re-designate the cash flow hedge relationship. However the mechanism of de-designation and re-designation must be properly documented and consistent with its risk management policy. Assuming that the other hedge accounting criteria are met, the accounting treatment at the date of de-designation and re-designation is as follows:

■ Hedge accounting may be applied to the original hedge relationship until the date of its de-designation.

■ Hedge accounting may be applied to the second hedge relationship starting from the date of re-designation.

The strategy described will require a significant amount of documentation to support the de-designation/re-designation process and a detailed monitoring of the accounting entries. Entity A will have to disclose in its financial statements the objective of this hedging strategy and the corresponding policies, together with a discussion of the associated risks and the business objectives pursued.

10.76 It follows from the above that there is no prohibition in IAS 39 against terminating one hedge and initiating another with the same hedging instrument. Furthermore, there is no limitations on the frequency of such terminations/ designations and re-designations. Provided an entity can properly track all of the terminations and re-designations and demonstrate that all other qualifying criteria, such as high effectiveness, have been met, hedge accounting using the same instrument on a recurring basis is not prohibited. However, initiating new hedging relationships with existing derivatives may not qualify for hedge accounting if the ineffectiveness caused by the derivatives' 'non-zero' fair value is too great to satisfy the 80 per cent – 125 per cent range for effectiveness.

All-in-one hedges

10.77 Under IAS 39, a derivative can be an instrument which is settled gross by delivery of the underlying asset and the payment of the price specified in the contract rather than by net settlement of the difference between the two legs. The implementation guidance states that such an instrument can be designated as a hedging instrument in a cash flow hedge of the variability of the consideration to be paid or received in the future transaction that will occur on gross settlement of the derivative contract itself, assuming the other cash flow hedge accounting criteria are met. Without the derivative, there would be an exposure to variability in the purchase or sale price. As the derivative eliminates the exposure, it qualifies as a hedging instrument. This applies to all fixed price contracts that are accounted for as derivatives under IAS 39.

Example – Gross settled derivative designated as an 'all-in-one hedge'

An entity enters into a forward contract to purchase a bond that will be settled by delivery. The forward contract is a derivative, because its term exceeds the regular way delivery period in the marketplace.

The entity may designate the forward as a cash flow hedge of the variability of the consideration to be paid to acquire the bond (a future transaction), even though the derivative is the contract under which the bond will be acquired. [IAS 39 para IG F2.5].

10.78   Such 'all-in-one hedge' accounting strategy can be beneficial to entities. For instance, if an entity enters into a fixed price contract to buy a commodity that falls to be accounted for as a derivative under IAS 39, the contract would be recognised at fair value with gains and losses recognised in profit or loss. By applying an all-in-one hedge accounting strategy, the entity is able to defer gains and losses on the hedging instrument in equity under cash flow hedge accounting until the hedged transaction occurs. In other words, the entity is able to keep gains and losses from being recognised in profit or loss on what is effectively a fixed price purchase or sale commitment.

Internal hedging instruments

10.79   Entities with sophisticated central treasury functions often use internal hedging transactions to 'transfer' interest rate and currency risk to the group treasury. For instance, central treasury may enter into internal derivative contracts such as forward contracts and swaps with subsidiaries and various divisions of a consolidated group with the objective of 'converting' all financial assets and liabilities of those operating units to variable rate instruments in the reporting currency. Central treasury will assess its exposure to various currencies and to interest rate risk and enter into external forward contracts and swaps to manage those risks on a centralised basis, thereby generating economies of scale and pricing efficiency.

10.80   Consistent with paragraph 10.36 above, internal derivative contracts used to transfer risk exposures between different companies within a group or divisions within a single legal entity cannot be designated as hedging instruments if the derivative contracts are *internal* to the entity being reported on. It follows that internal derivative contracts cannot be designated as hedging instruments in the consolidated financial statements. Nor can they be designated as hedging instruments in the individual or separate financial statements of a legal entity for hedging transactions between divisions in the entity. IAS 39 makes it clear that only instruments that involve a party external to the reporting entity (that is, a group, or an individual entity that is being reported on) can qualify as designated hedging instruments.

10.81   However, if an internal contract is offset with an external party, the external contract may be regarded as the hedging instrument and the hedging relationship may qualify for hedge accounting. [IAS 39 para IG F1.4]. In such situations, the hedging relationship consists of the external instrument and the item that was the subject of the internal hedge. The internal derivative is often used as a tracking mechanism to relate the external derivative to the hedged item. Indeed, many entities take advantage of this provision in IAS 39 that allows them to net risk through a central treasury centre and thereafter hedge the net exposure by entering into external contracts with third parties. This avoids the cost of each subsidiary entering into contracts with third parties, some of which may duplicate each other. The following example illustrates the situations described above.

> **Example – Internal derivative contracts**
>
> The banking division of Entity A enters into an internal interest rate swap with the trading division of the same entity. The purpose is to hedge the interest rate risk exposure of a loan (or group of similar loans) in the loan portfolio. Under the swap, the banking division pays fixed interest payments to the trading division and receives variable interest rate payments in return.
>
> If a hedging instrument is not acquired from an external party, IAS 39 does not allow hedge accounting treatment for the hedging transaction undertaken by the banking and trading divisions. This is because only derivatives that involve a party external to the entity can be designated as hedging instruments. [IAS 39 para 73]. Furthermore, any gains or losses on intra-group or intra-entity transactions are eliminated on consolidation. Therefore, transactions between different divisions within entity A do not qualify for hedge accounting treatment in entity A's financial statements. Similarly, transactions between different entities within a group do not qualify for hedge accounting treatment in entity A's consolidated financial statements.
>
> However, if in addition to the internal swap in the above example the trading division enters into an interest rate swap or other contract with an external party that offsets the exposure hedged in the internal swap, hedge accounting is permitted under IAS 39. For the purposes of IAS 39, the hedged item is the loan (or group of similar loans) in the banking division and the hedging instrument is the external interest rate swap or other contract.
>
> The trading division may aggregate several internal swaps or portions of them that are not offsetting each other and enter into a single third party derivative contract that offsets the aggregate exposure. Under IAS 39, such external hedging transactions may qualify for hedge accounting treatment provided that the hedged items in the banking division are identified and the other conditions for hedge accounting are met. It should be noted, however, that hedge accounting is not permitted where the hedged items are held-to-maturity investments and the hedged risk is the exposure to interest rate changes. [IAS 39 para IG F1.4].

10.82 IAS 39 provides a very useful summary of its application to internal hedging transactions that is reproduced below.

■ The standard does not preclude an entity from using internal derivative contracts for risk management purposes and it does not preclude internal derivatives from being accumulated at the treasury level or some other central location so that risk can be managed on an entity-wide basis or at some higher level than the separate legal entity or division.

- Internal derivative contracts between two *separate entities* within a consolidated group can qualify for hedge accounting by those entities in their individual or separate financial statements, even though the internal contracts are not offset by derivative contracts with a party external to the consolidated group.

- Internal derivative contracts between two *separate divisions* within the same legal entity can qualify for hedge accounting in that legal entity's individual or separate financial statements only if those contracts are offset by derivative contracts with a party external to the legal entity.

- Internal derivative contracts between separate divisions within the same legal entity and between separate entities within the consolidated group can qualify for hedge accounting in the consolidated financial statements only if the internal contracts are offset by derivative contracts with a party external to the consolidated group.

- If the internal derivative contracts are not offset by derivative contracts with external parties, the use of hedge accounting by group entities and divisions using internal contracts must be reversed on consolidation.

[IAS 39 para IG F1.4].

For segment reporting purposes entities may present financial information including the effects of hedging as reported to management; for that purpose entities do not have to meet the IAS 39 criteria for hedge accounting. This was the subject of an amendment published in 2008 that removed reference to segments from paragraph 73 of IAS 39. Hence, internal derivatives between segments may be freely accounted for as hedges for the purpose of segment reporting if this is the information presented to the chief operating decision maker. Disclosure of intra-group hedging policies may be required.

Offsetting internal hedging instruments

10.83   As noted in the example in paragraph 10.79 above, central treasury often, before laying off the risk, first nets off internal derivative contracts against each other and then enters into a single third party derivative contract that offsets the net exposure. The circumstances in which such a single external contract can be treated as a hedging instrument on consolidation is considered below in the context of interest rate risk and foreign currency risk management.

Example 1 – Offsetting internal derivative contracts used to manage interest rate risk

Entity A has a number of subsidiaries. All treasury activities of the group are undertaken by entity A. Individual subsidiaries intending to hedge their exposure to interest rate risk are required to enter into separate derivative contracts with entity A.

Entity A then aggregates the internal derivative contracts and enters into a single external derivative contract that offsets the internal derivative contracts on a net basis. For instance, Entity A may enter into three internal receive-fixed, pay-variable interest rate swaps (total notional amount of say C100m) that lay off the exposure to variable interest cash flows on variable rate liabilities in the three subsidiaries and one internal receive-variable, pay-fixed interest rate swap (notional amount of C80m) that lays off the exposure to variable interest cash flows on variable rate assets in another subsidiary. It then enters into receive-variable, pay-fixed interest rate swap (notional amount of C20m) with an external counterparty that exactly offsets the four internal swaps. It is assumed that the hedge accounting criteria are met.

In entity A's consolidated financial statements, the single offsetting external derivative would not qualify as a hedging instrument in a hedge of an overall net position, that is, it cannot be used to hedge all of the items that the four internal derivatives are hedging, as explained in paragraph 10.28 above.

However, as explained in paragraph 10.29 above, designating a part of the underlying items as the hedged position on a gross basis is permitted, that is, the external derivative can hedge C20m of variable rate liabilities totalling C100m. Therefore, even though the purpose of entering into the external derivative was to offset internal derivative contracts on a net basis, hedge accounting is permitted if the hedging relationship is defined and documented as a hedge of a part of the underlying cash inflows or cash outflows on a gross basis. [IAS 39 Para IG F2.15].

Example 2 – Offsetting internal derivative contracts hedging foreign currency fair value risk

An entity has a number of subsidiaries. Subsidiary A has trade receivables in foreign currency (FC) of 100, due in 60 days, which it hedges using a forward contract with the treasury centre (TC) subsidiary. Subsidiary B has payables of FC50, also due in 60 days, which it hedges using a forward contact with TC. TC nets the two internal derivatives and enters into a net external forward contract to pay FC50 and receive LC in 60 days.

At the end of month 1, FC weakens against LC. Subsidiary A incurs a foreign exchange loss of LC10 on its receivables, offset by a gain of LC10 on its forward contract with TC. Subsidiary B makes a foreign exchange gain of LC5 on its payables offset by a loss of LC5 on its forward contract with TC. TC makes a loss of LC10 on its internal forward contract with subsidiary A, a gain of LC5 on its internal forward contract with subsidiary B, and a gain of LC5 on its external forward contract. At the end of month 1, the following entries are made in the individual or separate financial statements of subsidiary A, subsidiary B and TC.

Accounting entries		Dr (Cr)		
	Receivable	Payable	Derivative	P &L
Subsidiary A				
Recognition of loss on receivable	(10)			10
Recognition of gain on internal derivative			10	(10)
Subsidiary B				
Recognition of gain on payable		5		(5)
Recognition of loss on internal derivative			(5)	5
Central Treasury (TC)				
Recognition of loss on internal derivative with A			(10)	10
Recognition of gain on internal derivative with B			5	(5)
Recognition of gain on external derivative			5*	(5)

* External derivative

The above entries are recorded in the individual financial statements of the three entities. In this case, no hedge accounting is required because gains and losses on the internal derivatives and the offsetting losses and gains on the hedged receivables and payables are recognised immediately in the income statements of entity A and entity B without hedge accounting.

In the consolidated financial statements, the internal derivative transactions are eliminated. In economic terms, the payable in B hedges FC50 of the receivables in A. The external forward contract in TC hedges the remaining FC50 of the receivable in A. Hedge accounting is not necessary in the consolidated financial statements, because monetary items are measured at spot foreign exchange rates under IAS 21 irrespective of whether hedge accounting is applied.

The net balances before and after eliminating the accounting entries relating to the internal derivatives are the same, as set out below. Accordingly, there is no need to make any further accounting entries on consolidation to meet the requirements of IAS 39.

		Dr (Cr)		
	Receivable	Payable	Derivative	P &L
Consolidation				
Receivable in A	(10)			
Payable in B		5		
External derivative			5	

[IAS 39 para IG F1.7].

Example 3 – Offsetting internal derivative contracts hedging foreign currency cash flow risk

An entity has a number of subsidiaries. Subsidiary A has a highly probable future revenues of FC200 on which it expects to receive cash in 90 days. B has highly probable future expenses of FC500 (advertising cost), also to be paid for in 90 days. Entity A and entity B enter into separate forward contracts with TC to hedge these exposures and TC enters into an external forward contract to receive FC300 in 90 days.

FC weakens at the end of month 1.

A incurs a 'loss' of LC20 on its anticipated revenues because the LC value of these revenues decreases. This is offset by a 'gain' of LC20 on its forward contract with TC.

B incurs a 'gain' of LC50 on its anticipated advertising cost because the LC value of the expense decreases. This is offset by a 'loss' of LC50 on its transaction with TC.

TC incurs a 'gain' of LC50 on its internal transaction with B, a 'loss' of LC20 on its internal transaction with A and a loss of LC30 on its external forward contract.

Entity A and entity B complete the necessary documentation, the hedges are effective, and both entity A and entity B qualify for hedge accounting in their individual financial statements. A defers the gain of LC20 on its internal derivative transaction in a hedging reserve in equity and B defers the loss of LC50 in its hedging reserve in equity. TC does not claim hedge accounting, but measures both its internal and external derivative positions at fair value, which net to zero. At the end of month 1, the following entries are made in the individual or separate financial statements of A, B and TC.

Hedge accounting entries at end of month 1	Dr (Cr) Derivative	Equity	P&L
Subsidiary A			
Recognition of gain on internal derivative with TC	20	(20)	
Subsidiary B			
Recognition of loss on internal derivative with TC	(50)	50	
Subsidiary TC			
Recognition of loss on internal derivative with A	(20)		20
Recognition of gain on internal derivative with B	50		(50)
Recognition of loss on external derivative	(30)*		30

* External derivative

For the consolidated financial statements, TC's external forward contract on FC300 is designated, at the beginning of month 1, as a hedging instrument of the first FC300 of B's highly probable future expenses. IAS 39 requires that in the consolidated financial statements at the end of month 1, the accounting effects of the internal derivative transactions must be eliminated. However, the net balances before and after elimination of the accounting entries relating to the internal derivatives are the same, as set out below. Accordingly, there is no need to make any further accounting entries in order for the requirements of IAS 39 to be met.

Note that only FC300 in costs that were designated in hedge relationships are effectively reported at the hedged foreign currency rate in profit or loss. The revenue and cost of sales that were not designated in hedge relationships are reported at the currency rate ruling on the date of the respective transactions.

Consolidation	Derivative	Equity	P&L
Recognition of loss on external derivative	(30)	30	

[IAS 39 para IG F1.7].

Example 4 – Offsetting internal derivative contracts hedging fair value and cash flow risks

Assume that the exposures and the internal derivative transactions are a combination of the transactions is in examples 2 and 3 above. However, instead of entering into two external derivatives to hedge separately the fair value and cash flow exposures, TC enters into a single net external derivative to receive FC250 in exchange for LC in 90 days.

TC has four internal derivatives, two maturing in 60 days and two maturing in 90 days. These are offset by a net external derivative maturing in 90 days. The interest rate differential between FC and LC is minimal and, therefore, the ineffectiveness resulting from the mismatch in maturities is expected to have a minimal effect on profit or loss in TC.

As in examples 2 and 3, subsidiary A and subsidiary B apply hedge accounting for their cash flow hedges and TC measures its derivatives at fair value. Subsidiary A defers a gain of LC20 on its internal derivative transaction in equity and subsidiary B defers a loss of LC50 on its internal derivative transaction in equity.

At the end of month 1, the following entries are made in the individual or separate financial statements of subsidiary A, subsidiary B and TC.

			Dr (Cr)		
Hedge accounting entries	Receivable	Payable	Derivative	Equity	P&L
Subsidiary A					
Loss on receivable	(10)				10
Gain on internal derivative with TC (FV)			10		(10)
Gain on internal derivative with TC (CF)			20	(20)	
	(10)		30	(20)	–
Subsidiary B					
Gain on payable		5			(5)
Loss on internal derivative with TC (FV)			(5)		5
Loss on internal derivative with TC (CF)			(50)	50	
		5	**(55)**	**50**	–

Subsidiary TC

	Dr (Cr)	
Loss on internal derivative with A (FV)	(10)	10
Loss on internal derivative with A (FV)	(20)	20
Gain on internal derivative with B (CF)	5	(5)
Gain on internal derivative with B (CF)	50	(50)
Loss on external contract (Net)	(25)*	25

* External derivative

The gross amounts relating to fair value of monetary assets and liabilities and the forecast transactions in subsidiary A and subsidiary B are as follows:

	Dr (Cr) Monetary items	Dr (Cr) Forecast transactions	
Subsidiary A	100		200
Subsidiary B	50	500	

For the consolidated financial statements, the following designations are made at the beginning of month 1:

■ The payable of FC50 in entity B is designated as a hedge of the first FC50 of the highly probable future revenues in entity A (non-monetary item designated as a hedging instrument hedging foreign exchange risk). Therefore, at the end of month 1, the following entries are made in the consolidated financial statements: Dr Payable LC5; Cr Other comprehensive income LC5.

■ The receivable of FC100 in entity A is designated as a hedge of the first FC100 of the highly probable future expenses in entity B (non-monetary item designated as a hedging instrument in hedging foreign exchange risk). Therefore, at the end of month 1, the following entries are made in the consolidated financial statements: Dr Equity LC10, Cr Receivable LC10.

■ The external forward contract on FC250 in TC is designated as a hedge of the next FC250 of highly probable future expenses in entity B. Therefore, at the end of month 1, the following entries are made in the consolidated financial statements: Dr Other comprehensive income LC25; Cr External forward contract LC25.

In the consolidated financial statements at the end of month 1, IAS 39 requires the accounting effects of the internal derivative transactions to be eliminated. The effect of the above entries are summarised below:

Consolidation	Receivable	Payable	External derivative	Other comprehensive income/equity
Hedge accounting entries	(10)	5	(25)	30

As can be seen, the total net balances before and after elimination of the accounting entries relating to the internal derivatives are the same, as set out above. Accordingly, there is no need to make any further accounting entries to meet the requirements of IAS 39. [IAS 39 para IG F1.7].

10.84 An entity's risk management objectives and strategies may require an entity to enter into a master netting agreement with a counterparty under which the entity is required to settle all external derivative contracts with that counterparty on a net basis. Although netting arrangements imply that an entity is able to set off profitable and loss making contracts against each other, this, in itself, would not preclude the external derivative contracts from being designated as hedging instruments.

Example 1 – External derivative contracts that are settled net

Entity A has a number of subsidiaries. All the group's treasury activities are undertaken by entity A. Individual subsidiaries intending to hedge their exposure to interest rate risk are required to enter into separate derivative contracts with entity A, which in turn enters into a separate offsetting matching derivative contract with a single external counterparty B. For instance, if entity A enters into an intra-group receive 5% fixed, pay LIBOR or interest rate swap, then entity A would also enter into a separate offsetting pay 5% fixed, receive LIBOR interest swap with counterparty B.

Although each of the external derivative contracts is formally documented as a separate contract, only the net of the payments on all of the external derivative contracts is settled by entity A, as there is a netting agreement with the external counterparty B.

The individual external derivative contracts, such as the pay 5% fixed, receive-LIBOR interest rate swap above, can be designated as hedging instruments of underlying gross exposures, such as the exposure to changes in variable interest payments on the pay-LIBOR borrowing above, in the group's consolidated financial statements, even though the external derivatives are settled on a net basis.

External derivative contracts that are legally separate contracts and serve a valid business purpose, such as laying off risk exposures on a gross basis, qualify as hedging instruments even if those external contracts are settled on a net basis with the same external counterparty, provided the hedge accounting criteria in IAS 39 are met. [IAS 39 para IG F2.16] Note that it would not be considered a valid business purpose if the entity entered into the two transactions only to achieve hedge accounting for one of them (that is, if accounting treatment for one of them was the only reason for entering into two transactions and not one).

It may well be that by entering into the external offsetting contracts and including them in the centralised portfolio, entity A is no longer able to evaluate the exposures on a net basis. As a result, it may decide to manage the portfolio of offsetting external derivatives separately from the entity's other exposures. Thus, it enters into an additional, single derivative to offset the portfolio's risk.

In this situation, the individual external derivative contracts in the portfolio can still be designated as hedging instruments of underlying gross exposures. This is so even if the final external derivative is affected with the same counterparty under the same netting arrangement and, as a result, may net to zero.

The purpose of structuring the external derivative contracts in the above manner, which is consistent with the entity's risk management objectives and strategies, constitutes a substantive business purpose. Therefore, external derivative contracts that are legally separate contracts and serve a valid business purpose qualify as hedging instruments. In other words, hedge accounting is not precluded simply because the entity has entered into a swap that mirrors exactly the terms of another swap with the same counterparty if there is a substantive business purpose for structuring the transactions separately. [IAS 39 paras IG F2.16, IG F1.14].

Non-derivative financial instruments

10.85 As stated in paragraph 10.52 above, a non-derivative financial asset or liability may not be designated as a hedging instrument, except as a hedge of foreign currency risk. Therefore, an entity can use foreign currency denominated monetary assets and liabilities as hedging instruments in hedges of foreign currency risk. This means that foreign currency cash deposits, loans and receivables, available-for-sale monetary items and held-to-maturity investments carried at amortised cost may be designated as a hedging instrument in a hedge of foreign currency risk. The following examples illustrate the type of situations in which a non-derivative financial instrument can be designated as a hedging instrument.

Example 1 – Hedging with a non-derivative the fair value exposure of an available-for-sale bond

Entity J, whose functional currency is the Japanese yen, has issued US$5m 5 year fixed rate debt. It also owns a US$5m 5 year fixed rate bond that it has classified as available-for-sale. Entity J intends to designate its US dollar liability as a hedging instrument in a fair value hedge of the entire fair value exposure of its US dollar bond.

The total change in bond's fair value is a function of interest rate risk, currency risk and credit risk. The debt instrument is a non-derivative that cannot be used to hedge the entire fair value exposure of the bond. However, the debt instrument can be designated as a hedge of the foreign currency component of the bond in either a fair value or cash flow hedge.

In this situation, hedge accounting is unnecessary since the amortised cost of the hedging instrument and the hedged item are both remeasured using closing rates with any differences arising in the period recognised in profit or loss in accordance with IAS 21. In other words, there is a natural offset regardless of whether entity J designates the relationship as a cash flow hedge or a fair value hedge. Any gain or loss on the non-derivative hedging instrument designated as a cash flow hedge is immediately recognised in profit or loss in accordance with IAS 39 paragraph 100 to correspond with the recognition of the change in spot rate on the hedged item in profit or loss. [IAS 39 para IG F1.1].

Example 2 – Hedging a firm commitment with a non-derivative financial instrument

Entity J's functional currency is the Japanese yen. It has issued a fixed rate debt instrument with semi-annual interest payments that matures in 2 years with principal due at maturity of US$5 million. It has also entered into a fixed price sales commitment for US$5 million that matures in 2 years and is not accounted for as a derivative because it meets the exemption for normal sales. Entity J intends to designate the fixed rate debt instrument as a hedge of the entire fair value change of the firm sales commitment.

The US dollar liability cannot be designated as a fair value hedge of the *entire* fair value exposure of its fixed price sales commitment and qualify for hedge accounting, because it is a non-derivative. However, as IAS 39 permits the designation of a non-derivative asset or liability as a hedging instrument in either a cash flow hedge or a fair value hedge of foreign exchange risk, entity J can designate its US dollar liability as a cash flow hedge of the foreign currency exposure associated with the future receipt of US dollars on the fixed price sales commitment.

Any gain or loss on the non-derivative hedging instrument that is recognised in equity during the period preceding the future sale is recognised in profit or loss when the sale takes place (see further para 10.121 below). [IAS 39 para IG F1.2].

Example 3 – Hedging a foreign currency exposure in a net investment with a hedging instrument denominated in a different currency

An entity with a Sing$ functional currency has an investment in a subsidiary in Hong Kong with a HK$ functional currency. Since the HK$ is linked to the US$, management decides to designate a US dollar borrowing as the hedging instrument in a hedge of its net investment.

Management may use a US$ borrowing to hedge a net investment denominated in HK$ if it is highly correlated to that currency, there is qualitative evidence to support the relationship and actual results are in the range of 80-125%. It is possible to designate a borrowing in one foreign currency as a hedge of a net investment in another currency with any ineffectiveness recognised in profit or loss. However, the requirements of paragraph AG105 of IAS 39 – that the hedging instrument is expected to be highly effective – is likely to prevent the use of hedge accounting for most currency pairs. A high degree of correlation between the two currencies would be achieved if one of the currencies was formally pegged to the other, as in this case, but for hedge accounting to be possible, it must be reasonable to assume that this correlation will continue. Some ineffectiveness will arise as a result of inefficiencies in the linking mechanism.

10.86 Consistent with paragraph 10.60 above, a proportion of a non-derivative financial instrument, such as 50 per cent of the carrying amount of a foreign currency liability, may be designated as the hedging instrument. However, as stated in paragraph 10.61 above, an entity cannot treat the cash flows of only a proportion of the period during which a non-derivative instrument designated as a hedge against foreign currency risk remains outstanding and exclude the other cash flows from the designated hedging relationship. For example, the cash flows during the first three years of a ten – year borrowing denominated in a foreign currency cannot qualify as a hedging instrument in a cash flow hedge of the first three years of revenue in the same foreign currency.

Items that do not qualify as hedging instruments

10.87 Generally, financial assets and financial liabilities whose fair value cannot be reliably measured cannot be hedging instruments. This means that an investment in an unquoted equity instrument that is not carried at fair value because its fair value cannot be reliably measured, or a derivative that is linked to and must be settled by, delivery of such an unquoted equity instrument cannot be designated as a hedging instrument. [IAS 39 para AG 96].

10.88 An entity's own equity instruments are not financial assets or financial liabilities of the entity and, therefore, cannot be designated as hedging instruments. [IAS 39 para AG 97]. Similarly, minority interests in consolidated financial statements are treated as part of equity and, hence, cannot be designated as hedging instruments in the consolidated financial statements.

10.88.1 Firm commitments and forecast transactions can not be designated as hedging instruments since they are not normally recognised in the financial statements. However, if the foreign currency component of the sales commitment is required to be separated as an embedded derivative under paragraph 11 of IAS 39 and paragraph AG33(d) of IAS 39, it could be designated as a hedging instrument in a hedge of the exposure to changes in the fair value of the maturity amount of the debt attributable to foreign currency risk. [IAS 39 para IG F1.2].

10.88.2 IFRS 3 'Business combinations', requires an acquirer entity to re-asses *"designation of a derivative instrument as a hedging instrument in accordance with IAS 39...on the basis of the pertinent conditions as they exist at the acquisition date"*. [IFRS 3 para 16]. In other words the acquirer is required to re-designate all hedge relationships of the acquired entity as if they started at the date of acquisition.

10.88.3 Corporates that are using derivatives for hedging normally take them out at market rate. If the derivatives do not contain option provisions they are expected, therefore, to have fair value of zero at inception. If such derivatives are designated as hedges at inception the underlying hedged risk (modelled as a hypothetical derivative – see para 10.170) would be almost a mirror of the actual derivative and such hedge relationships are often highly effective.

10.88.4 As market rates would be likely to have changed from the inception of acquiree's hedges until the date of the business combination the requirement to re-assess designation of derivatives as hedges means that the underlying hypothetical derivative would have to be 're-set' to the market rates current at the time of business combination and, hence, their fair value would then also be 're-set' to zero.

10.88.5 The 'off-market' nature of the hedging derivative at the date of acquisition could be described as an embedded financing within the derivative, representing the amount that would have to be paid to settle a derivative liability (or the amount that would be received to settle a derivative asset) at the date that the entity decides to re-designate the derivative in a new hedge relationship. This embedded financing does not necessarily keep the new hedge relationship from being within the required range of effectiveness (80-125 per cent), but it could be a source of ineffectiveness. Specifically, it is the change in fair value of the financing element that represents the hedge ineffectiveness, not the eventual settlements of the embedded financing element. As a result more hedge relationships will be likely to fail, or at least there will be more ineffectiveness.

10.88.6 IFRS 3 is applied prospectively to business combinations for which the acquisition date is on or after the beginning of the first annual reporting period beginning on or after 1 July 2009; earlier application is permitted (see also chapter 25 of the PricewaterhouseCoopers IFRS Manual of Accounting).

The hedge accounting models

10.89 Hedge accounting recognises the offsetting effects on profit or loss of changes in the fair values of the hedging instrument and the hedged item. Hedge accounting may be applied to three types of hedging relationships:

- Fair value hedges (see para 10.91 below).

- Cash flow hedges (see para 10.106 below).

- Hedges of a net investment in a foreign operation (see para 10.124 below).

[IAS 39 para 86].

Risk reduction and hedge accounting

10.90 IAS 39 does not require risk reduction on an entity-wide basis as a condition for hedge accounting. Exposure is assessed on a transaction basis. IAS 39 focuses on the risks inherent in an individual item, without requiring an entity-wide risk reduction test. For example, an entity may have a fixed rate asset and a fixed rate liability, each having the same principal amount. Under the instrument's terms, interest payments on the asset and liability occur in the same period and the net cash flow is always positive, because the interest rate on the asset exceeds the interest rate on the liability. The entity may decide to enter into an interest rate swap to receive a floating interest rate and pay a fixed interest rate on a notional amount equal to the asset's principal and designate the interest rate swap as a fair value hedge of the fixed rate asset. Although the effect of the interest rate swap on an entity-wide basis is to create an exposure to interest rate changes that did not previously exist, hedge accounting may be applied to this hedge relationship provided that the relevant hedge accounting criteria are met. [IAS 39 para IG F2.6].

Fair value hedges

Definition

10.91 A 'fair value hedge' is a hedge of the exposure to changes in fair value of a recognised asset, liability or unrecognised firm commitment, or portion thereof, that is attributable to a particular risk and could affect profit or loss. [IAS 39 para 86(a)].

10.92 Examples of some fair value hedges that often occur in practice are shown below:

Hedges of market price risk exposure An entity fixes the value of its commodity inventory by entering into a commodity futures contract.	**Fair value exposure** The entity is hedging the risk of changes in the inventory's overall fair value.
An entity purchases a put option to protect the fall in value of its quoted equity investments.	The entity is hedging the risk of fall in the fair value of the equity securities below the option's strike price.
Hedges of interest rate exposures An entity with fixed rate debt converts the debt into a floating rate using an interest rate swap.	The entity is hedging the risk of changes in the fair value of the debt due to changes in interest rate.
Hedges of foreign currency exposures An entity enters into a binding contract to purchase machinery for a fixed amount in foreign currency at a future date and hedges the amount in its functional currency by entering into a forward foreign exchange contract.	The entity is hedging the risk of changes in the purchase price of machinery due to changes in foreign exchange rate.
An entity enters into a forward contract to hedge a foreign currency receivable or a payable due for settlement in six months' time.	The entity is hedging the risk of changes in the carrying amount of the receivable or payable due to changes in foreign exchange rate.

Fair value hedge accounting

10.93 Under IAS 39, if a fair value hedge meets the hedge accounting conditions discussed in paragraph 10.137 below during the period, it should be accounted for as follows:

■ the gain or loss from re-measuring the hedging instrument at fair value (for a derivative hedging instrument) or the foreign currency component of its carrying amount measured in accordance with IAS 21 (for a non-derivative hedging instrument) should be recognised in profit or loss; and

■ the gain or loss on the hedged item attributable to the hedged risk adjusts the carrying amount of the hedged item and is recognised in profit or loss. This applies even if the hedged item is an available-for-sale financial asset or if it is otherwise measured at cost.

[IAS 39 para 89].

10.94 As stated in the second bullet point above, where the hedged item is an available-for-sale financial asset, the gain or loss attributable to the risk being hedged is recognised in profit or loss, rather than other comprehensive income, although the remainder of any fair value change is still recognised in other comprehensive income

10.95   The standard explains that if only particular risks attributable to a hedged item are hedged, recognised changes in the hedged item's fair value unrelated to the hedged risk are recognised in accordance with paragraph 55 of IAS 39 (see chapter 9). This means that changes in fair value of a hedged financial asset or financial liability that is not part of the hedging relationship would generally be accounted as follows:

■   For instruments measured at amortised cost, such changes would not be recognised.

■   For instruments measured at fair value through profit or loss, such changes would be recognised in profit or loss in any event.

■   For available-for-sale financial assets, such changes would be recognised in other comprehensive income as explained above. However, exceptions to this would include foreign currency gains and losses on monetary items and impairment losses, which would be recognised in profit or loss in any event.

10.96   If the fair value hedge is fully effective, the gain or loss on the hedging instrument would exactly offset the loss or gain on the hedged item attributable to the risk being hedged and there would be no net effect in profit or loss. However, this would rarely be the case and often some difference would arise. The recognition of this difference in profit or loss is commonly referred to as hedge ineffectiveness. Hedge ineffectiveness is considered further from paragraph 10.184 below.

10.97   An in-depth application of fair value hedge accounting for a hedge of interest rate risk of a fixed rate debt instrument using an interest rate swap (including full prospective and retrospective hedge effectiveness testing) is illustrated in the comprehensive examples included at the end of this chapter.

Example – Fair value hedge of inventory (commodity)

On 1 October 20X5, a metal refining entity has 1m troy ounces of silver in its inventory. The silver is recorded at an average historical cost of C5.00 per ounce (C5m total value). To protect the inventory from a decline in silver prices, the entity hedges its position by selling 200 silver futures contracts on a specified commodity exchange. Each contract is for 5,000 troy ounces of silver priced at C5.55 per ounce. The futures contracts mature on 31 March 20X6, which is the date that the entity has scheduled delivery of the entire silver inventory to its customer at the spot price at that date.

The entity designates the futures contract as a fair value hedge of its silver inventory (that is, it is hedging changes in the inventory's fair value). Based on historical data, the entity determines and documents that changes in the fair value of the silver futures contracts will be highly effective in offsetting all changes in the fair value of the silver inventory.

On 31 December 20X5 (the entity's financial year end) and on 31 March 20X6, the entity determines that the fair value of its silver inventory has declined cumulatively by C160,000 and C320,000 respectively. The fair value of the silver inventory has declined by more than the spot price of silver, because the fair value of the inventory is influenced by other factors such as changes in expected labour and transport costs.

On 31 March 20X6, the entity closes out its futures. On the same day it also sells the entire silver inventory at the spot price of C5.25 per ounce.

The following data is relevant:

Date	Spot price	Futures price (for delivery on 31 March 20X6)	Fair value of futures contract assuming yield curve is flat at 6% per year*
	C	C	C
1 Oct 20X5	5.40	5.55	–
31 Dec 20X5	5.30	5.40	147,830
31 Mar 20X6	5.25	5.25	300,000

*Fair value = (1m ounces × (5.55 – 5.40))/$1.06^{1/4}$ = C147,830
*Fair value = (1m ounces × (5.55 – 5.25)) = C300,000

The entity assesses hedge effectiveness by comparing the entire change in the fair value of the futures contract to the entire change in the fair value of the silver inventory, based on futures prices. A summary of the hedge's effectiveness, calculated using the dollar offset method discussed in paragraph 10.164, is shown below.

Date	Change in full fair value of future contracts Gain (loss)	Change in full fair value of inventory Gain (loss)	Effectiveness ratio for the period
	C	C	C
31 Dec 20X5	147,830	160,000	92.39
31 Mar 20X6	152,170	160,000	95.11

Ignoring any margin payments on the futures contract, the accounting entries from inception of the hedge to its termination following closure of the future contracts (which is settled daily) and delivery of inventory are as follows:

Date	Transaction	Dr (Cr) Cash	Futures contract	Inventory	Profit or loss
	C	C	C	C	
31 Dec 20X5	Change in fair value of futures contract	147,830	(147.830)		
31 Dec 20X5	Change in fair value of silver stock		(160,000)	160,000	
31 Dec 20X5	Cumulative cash settlement for period*	147,830	(147,830)	–	–
	Entity A's year end	147,830	–	(160,000)	12,170
		152,170	(152,170)		

31 Mar 20X6	Change in fair value of futures contract				
31 Mar 20X6	Change in fair value of silver stock	(160,000)	160,000		
31 Mar 20X6	Sale of silver @ 5.25	5,250,000	(5,250,000)		
31 Mar 20X6	Cost of sale	(4,680,000)	4,680,000		
31 Mar 20X6	Cumulative cash settlement for period*	152,170	(152,170)	–	–
		5,550,000	–	(5,000,000)	(550,000)

* Futures contracts are settled daily. The entries summarises the daily journals for each day throughout the quarter.

The fair value hedge example illustrates that if the entity had not hedged the change in fair value of the silver stock, it would have made a gain of C250,000 (revenue of C5,250,000 less cost of sales of C5,000,000). By entering into the hedge the company has 'locked in' a net profit of C550,000, that is, gross profit of C570,000 (revenue of C5,250,000 less cost of sales of C4,680,000) less loss of C20,000 on the hedging activity. In this example, the hedge was not 100% effective, which lead to some ineffectiveness being recognised in profit or loss.

At the entity's year end, the derivative asset and the carrying value of the inventory amounted to C147,830 and C4,840,000. The carrying value of C4,840,000 is neither cost nor realisable value nor fair value. It is cost less a hedging adjustment. The gain on the derivative offsets the loss on the inventory in profit or loss, except for ineffectiveness of C12,170. This matching is achieved by accelerating the recognition in the profit or loss of part of the gain or loss on the silver inventory. In other words part of the gain or loss that would normally be recognised only on the sale of the inventory is recorded earlier. Therefore, in the case of a fair value hedge, hedge accounting accelerates income recognition on the hedged item to match the profit or loss effect of the hedging instrument.

Adjustments to hedged items

10.98   The adjustment to the carrying amount of a hedged asset or liability that are made to the hedged item due to fair value changes that are attributable to a specific hedged risk, as stated in the second bullet point in paragraph 10.93 above, are dealt with in accordance with the normal accounting treatment for that item. The adjustment is often referred to as a 'basis adjustment', because the hedging gain or loss adjusts the carrying value of the hedged item resulting in an amount that is neither cost nor fair value. Thus, in the above example, changes in fair value of silver are adjusted against the carrying value of silver inventory and the adjusted carrying amount becomes the cost basis for the purposes of applying the lower of cost and net realisable value test under IAS 2, 'Inventories'. In other words, the basis adjustment remains part of the carrying value of inventory and enters into the determination of earnings when the inventory is sold.

10.99   When the hedged item is an interest bearing financial instrument for which the effective interest rate method of accounting is used, any adjustment to the carrying amount of the hedged financial instrument should be amortised to profit or loss. The adjustment should be based on a recalculated effective interest rate at the date the amortisation begins and should be fully amortised by maturity. Amortisation may begin as soon as an adjustment exists and should begin no later than when the hedged item ceases to be adjusted for changes in its fair value attributable to the risk being hedged.

10.100   The IASB decided to permit entities to defer amortisation of a basis adjustment until the hedged interest bearing financial instrument ceases to be basis adjusted in order to simplify the accounting and record keeping that an entity might otherwise have to undertake to track and properly account for such adjustments, as explained in the example below.

Example – Deferral of amortisation of basis adjustment

Entity A enters into an interest rate swap contract to hedge changes in the fair value of a fixed rate borrowing of C100m due for settlement in 5 years. The terms of the borrowing and the swap exactly match. Interest rates rise so that the borrowing's fair value falls to C90m and the swap's fair value changes from zero to – C10m.

Under fair value hedge accounting, the swap is carried as a liability of C10m (less any settlement paid). The carrying amount of the borrowing is reduced to C90m. Both the loss and the gain are recognised in the profit or loss. Under the amortised cost method, the C90m carrying amount of the liability would be amortised back up to C100m, giving rise to additional finance cost over the remaining period to maturity.

As explained above, the standard allows amortisation to be deferred until hedge accounting is discontinued. If the swap is in place until the borrowing's maturity date, the debt's carrying amount will be adjusted back to C100m through further hedge accounting adjustments. In other words, any fair value adjustments to the debt's carrying value would be reversed by maturity as the fair value of the liability immediately before settlement must be C100m. Therefore, no amortisation will be necessary.

However, if only the first 2 years of the debt instrument is hedged for interest rate risk and the entity chooses to defer amortisation until end of year 2 when hedge accounting ceases, a significant income statement impact could result in later periods. This is because the entity would need to 'catch up' the basis of the hedged item to its settlement amount of C100m over the remaining 3 years.

Hedges of firm commitments

10.101   Hedges of firm commitments are generally treated as fair value hedges except in one situation. If a firm commitment has a price fixed in foreign currency, the standard allows the hedge of the foreign currency risk in the firm commitment to be accounted for as a cash flow hedge of the foreign currency risk. [IAS 39 para 87]. If a firm commitment has a fixed price in the functional currency of the entity rather than a price fixed in a foreign currency, there would be no cash flow variability in the entity's functional currency in the anticipated transaction and cash flow hedging would not be possible. For this reason, hedges of firm commitments, other than those denominated in a foreign currency, are accounted for as fair value hedges because the entity is exposed to changes in fair value of that commitment.

10.102   When an unrecognised firm commitment to acquire an asset or assume a liability is designated as a hedged item in a fair value hedge, the accounting treatment is as follows:

■   The subsequent cumulative change in the fair value of the firm commitment attributable to the hedged risk since inception of the hedge is recognised as an asset or a liability with a corresponding gain or loss recognised in profit or loss.

■   The changes in the fair value of the hedging instrument are also recognised in profit or loss.

■   When the firm commitment is fulfilled, the initial carrying amount of the asset or liability is adjusted to include the cumulative change in the firm commitment that was recognised in the balance sheet under point one above.

[IAS 39 paras 93, 94].

Example – Measurement of the fair value of a firm commitment

On 1 January 20X6 entity A enters into a firm commitment to purchase 100,000 widgets for C5 each in 6 month's time. On 31 March 20X6, the entity's year end, the market price of the widgets has increased to C6.

The fair value of a firm commitment represents the amount that an entity would have to pay, or the amount that it would receive, upon terminating the commitment. On 1 January 20X6, the company has an obligation to pay C500,000 in 6 month's time and a right to receive 100,000 widgets in 6 months. The initial value of the obligation and the right are generally equal, resulting in a net fair value of zero.

At 31 March 20X6 when the widget's market price increases to C6, the right's value to receive widgets increases. This is because the widget's value received in six months would be C600,000, while the obligation to pay C500,000 in six months would remain the same, resulting in a fair value that reflects the C100,000 difference adjusted for the discount that is appropriate for the remaining three month duration of the commitment. The present value of the C100,000 represents the amount that the entity could reasonably expect to receive if the counterparty to the commitment were to terminate the commitment at 31 March 20X6.

Firm commitments represent rights and obligations that are assets and liabilities, even though they are generally not recorded. If entity A designates the firm commitment as a hedged item, it would account for the changes in the fair value of the hedged commitment due to changes in the market price of widgets in a manner similar to how that entity would account for any hedged asset or liability that it records. That is, changes in fair value (that are attributable to the risk that is being hedged) would be recognised in profit or loss and, on the balance sheet, recognised as an adjustment of the hedged item's carrying amount.

Because firm commitments normally are not recorded, accounting for the initial change in the fair value of the firm commitment would result in the entity recognising the firm commitment on the balance sheet. Therefore, in this example, the entity would record the present value of C100,000 as an asset on the balance sheet with a corresponding gain in profit or loss. A recognition of subsequent changes in fair value would adjust that recognised firm-commitment amount.

Discontinuing fair value hedge accounting

10.103 Fair value hedge accounting should be discontinued prospectively if any of the following occurs:

■ The hedging instrument expires or is sold, terminated or exercised. For this purpose, the replacement or rollover of a hedging instrument into another hedging instrument is not an expiration or termination if such replacement or rollover is part of the entity's documented hedging strategy.

■ The hedge no longer meets the criteria for hedge accounting discussed in paragraph 10.137 below.

■ The entity revokes the designation.

[IAS 39 para 91].

10.104 When an entity ceases to apply hedge accounting because the hedge does not meet hedge effectiveness criteria, it should discontinue hedge accounting from the last date on which compliance with hedge effectiveness was demonstrated. However, if the event or change in circumstances that caused the hedging relationship to fail the effectiveness criteria can be identified and it can be demonstrated that the hedge was effective before the event or change in circumstances occurred, the entity should discontinue hedge accounting from the date of the event or change in circumstances. [IAS 39 para AG 113].

10.105 The table below sets out the accounting treatment to be applied when fair value hedge accounting is discontinued.

Discontinuance of fair value hedges (including firm commitments)

Hedge termination events	Hedging instrument		Hedged item	
	Continue mark-to-market accounting Note 1	Derecognise from the balance sheet	Derecognise from the balance sheet Note 2	Freeze basis adjustments Note 3
Hedging instrument no longer exists (that is, sold, terminated, extinguished, exercised or expired)		√		√
The hedge no longer meets the criteria for hedge accounting (effectiveness)	√			√
The entity revokes the hedge designation	√			√
The hedged item is sold or extinguished	√		√	

Note 1 – The hedging instrument will continue to be marked to market, unless it is re-designated as a hedging instrument in a new hedge.

Note 2 – The derecognition of the hedged item occurs through profit or loss (for example, the firm commitment asset or liability or the gain or loss on sale or extinguishment of the hedged item (inclusive of fair value basis adjustments) is recognised in profit or loss).

Note 3 – The hedged item ceases to be adjusted for changes in its fair value attributable to the risk being hedged and continues to be accounted for in a manner that was applicable prior to it being hedged. Once the basis adjustment on the hedged item is frozen, it either:

- Continues as part of the carrying amount of the asset up to the date the carrying value is recovered through use or sale or the asset becomes impaired.

- Is amortised through profit or loss (for interest bearing financial instruments). Amortisation should begin no later than when the hedged item ceases to be adjusted for changes in its fair value attributable to the risk being hedged (see para 10.101 above).

Example 1 – Discontinuance of a fair value hedge of a bond

Two years ago, entity A issued at par a C4m, 5 year fixed interest rate bond. At the same time, it entered into a 5-year fixed-to-floating interest rate swap that it designated as a fair value hedge of the bond. After 2 years, the hedge fails a retrospective test and the entity determines it is no longer expected to be highly effective for the remaining 3 years of the hedge. At the date the hedge last passed an effectiveness test, the bond's carrying value included a cumulative adjustment of C0.2m, reflecting the change in the fair value of the hedged risk.

Entity A discontinues hedge accounting prospectively (that is, previous accounting entries are not reversed). If the reason for discontinuance is that the hedge failed an effectiveness test, hedge accounting is discontinued from the last date when the hedge was demonstrated to be effective.

The adjustments to the carrying amount of the hedged item to reflect the changes in fair value that are attributable to the hedged risk remain as part of the item's carrying value, but no further adjustments are made in future periods. When the hedged item is carried at amortised cost, these previous hedging adjustments are amortised over the item's remaining life by recalculating its effective interest rate, or on a straight-line basis if this is not practicable.

The adjusted carrying value of C4.2m will be the basis for calculating a new effective interest rate, starting from the last date the hedge passed an effectiveness test. The hedging adjustment of C0.2m is, therefore, recognised in profit or loss over the bond's remaining life.

Example 2 – Discontinuance of a fair value hedge of an available-for-sale investment

Entity A is a Swiss entity whose functional currency is the Swiss franc (CHF). Entity A buys an equity investment in entity X, which is classified as available-for-sale. Entity X's shares are listed only in the US in US dollars and it pays dividends in US dollars. The fair value at the date of purchase including transaction costs is US$10m.

Entity A does not want to be exposed to the risk of future losses if the US$ weakens against the CHF. It intends to hold the investment for 2 years and enters into a forward contract to sell US$ and receive CHF in 2 years, with a notional amount of US$9m to hedge US$9m of the fair value of the investment in entity X.

Entity A designates the forward contract as a fair value hedge of the currency risk on US$9m of its investment in entity X. This designation allows entity A to take the foreign exchange movements on US$9m of the investment to the income statement to offset the fair value changes in the derivative. The rest of the fair value movements in CHF for the instrument are retained in equity until the instrument is sold.

One year later, entity A believes that the US dollar is not likely to decline further and decides to discontinue the hedge and revoke the hedge designation. The hedge is demonstrated to have been highly effective up to the time it is discontinued.

Entity A discontinues hedge accounting prospectively (that is, previous accounting entries are not reversed). When the hedged item is an equity instrument classified as available-for-sale, all future changes in the instrument's fair value, including all changes related to exchange rate movements, are deferred in equity until the instrument is sold or impaired.

Cash flow hedges

Definition

10.106 A 'cash flow hedge' is a hedge of the exposure to variability in cash flows that is attributable to a particular risk associated with a recognised asset or liability or a highly probable forecast transaction and could affect profit or loss. [IAS 39 para 86(b)].

10.107 Examples of some cash flow hedges that often occur in practice are shown below:

Hedges of market price risk exposure	Cash flow exposure
An entity that has a highly probable sales of a commodity in the future at the then prevailing market price 'fixes' the selling price of the goods by entering into a futures contract.	The entity is hedging the risk of variability in the cash flows to be received on the sale due to changes in the good's market price.
Hedges of interest rate exposures	
An entity with floating rate debt converts the rate on the debt to a fixed rate using an interest rate swap.	The entity is hedging the risk of variability in interest payments due to changes in the interest rate specified for the debt.

An entity that has a highly probable issuance of fixed rate debt in the future at the then coupon rate enters into a forward starting interest rate swap to protect itself from the effects of changes in a specified interest rate that may occur before the debt is issued.	The entity is hedging the variability in the expected interest payments from the issuance of a debt due to changes in a specified interest rate on a debt expected to be issued within a specified period.

Hedges of foreign currency exposures

An entity that has a highly probable sale of goods in foreign currency takes out a forward exchange contract to 'fix' the local (functional) currency price of the goods.	The entity is hedging the risk of changes in local (functional) currency amount of the sale due to changes in foreign exchange rates.
An entity enters into a forward contract to hedge a foreign currency receivable or a payable due to be settled in six months' time.	The entity is hedging the risk of changes in the amount receivable or payable on settlement in six month's time due to changes in the foreign exchange rates.

Forecast transactions

10.108 A forecast transaction is an uncommitted but anticipated future transaction. [IAS 39 para 9]. To qualify for cash flow hedge accounting, the forecasted transaction should be specifically identifiable as a single transaction or a group of individual transactions. If the hedged transaction is a group of individual transactions, those individual transactions must share the same risk exposure for which they are designated as being hedged. Thus, a forecast purchase and a forecast sale cannot both be included in the same group of individual transactions that constitute the hedged transaction (see para 10.21 above).

10.109 The key criterion for hedge accounting purposes is that the forecast transaction that is the subject of a cash flow hedge must be 'highly probable'. In IFRS terminology, probable means 'more likely than not'. Therefore, in the context of forecast transaction, the term 'highly probable' is taken to indicate a much greater likelihood of happening than the term 'more likely than not'. This is consistent with the IASB's use of highly probable in IFRS 5, 'Non-current asset held for sale and discontinued operations', where 'highly probable' is regarded as implying a significantly higher probability than 'more likely than not'. [IFRS 5 para BC81]. The other conditions are that the forecast transaction must be with a party that is external to the entity (see para 10.14 above) and it presents an exposure to variations in cash flows for the hedged risk that could affect profit or loss (see para 10.12 above).

10.110 IAS 39's implementation guidance explains that a transaction's probability should be supported by observable facts and the attendant circumstances and should not be based solely on management's intentions, because intentions are not verifiable. In assessing the likelihood that a transaction will occur, an entity should consider the following circumstances:

- The frequency of similar past transactions.

- The financial and operational ability of the entity to carry out the transaction.

- Substantial commitments of resources to a particular activity (for example, a manufacturing facility that can be used in the short run only to process a particular type of commodity).

- The extent of loss or disruption of operations that could result if the transaction does not occur.

- The likelihood that transactions with substantially different characteristics might be used to achieve the same business purpose (for example, an entity that intends to raise cash may have several ways of doing so, ranging from a short-term bank loan to an offering of ordinary shares).

- The entity's business plan.

[IAS 39 para IG F3.7].

10.111 The length of time until a forecast transaction is projected to occur is also a factor in determining probability. Other factors being equal, the more distant a forecast transaction is, the less likely it is that the transaction would be regarded as highly probable and the stronger the evidence that would be needed to support an assertion that it is highly probable. For example, a transaction forecast to occur in five years may be less likely to occur than a transaction forecast to occur in one year. However, forecast interest payments for the next 20 years on a plain vanilla variable rate debt would typically be highly probable if supported by an existing contractual obligation and it is expected that the debt will not be paid early.

10.112 In addition, other factors being equal, the greater a forecast transaction's physical quantity or future value in proportion to the entity's transactions of the same nature, the less likely it is that the transaction would be regarded as highly probable and the stronger the evidence that would be required to support an assertion that it is highly probable. For example, less evidence generally would be needed to support forecast sales of 100,000 units in the next month than 950,000 units in that month when recent sales have averaged 800,000 units per month for the past three months. [IAS 39 para IG F3.7].

10.113 A history of having designated hedges of forecast transactions and then determining that the forecast transactions are no longer expected to occur would call into question both an entity's ability to predict forecast transactions accurately and the propriety of using hedge accounting in the future for similar forecast transactions. [IAS 39 para IG F3.7].

10.114 The documentation that needs to be put in place before a forecast transaction can be designated as a hedged item is considered further from paragraph 10.139 below.

Cash flow hedge accounting

10.115 Under IAS 39, if a cash flow hedge meets the hedge accounting conditions discussed in paragraph 10.137 below during the period, it should be accounted for as follows:

■ the portion of the gain or loss on the hedging instrument that is determined to be an effective hedge should be recognised directly in other comprehensive income; and

■ the ineffective portion of the gain or loss on the hedging instrument should be recognised in profit or loss.

[IAS 39 para 95].

10.116 In particular:

■ the separate component of equity associated with the hedged item is adjusted to the *lesser* of the following (in absolute amounts):

■ the cumulative gain or loss on the hedging instrument from inception of the hedge; and

■ the cumulative change in fair value (present value) of the expected future cash flows on the hedged item from inception of the hedge;

■ any remaining gain or loss on the hedging instrument or designated component of it (that is not an effective hedge) is recognised in profit or loss; and

■ if an entity's documented risk management strategy for a particular hedging relationship excludes from the assessment of hedge effectiveness a specific component of the gain or loss or related cash flows on the hedging instrument, that excluded component of gain or loss is recognised in accordance with the instrument's normal classification. If the hedging instrument is a derivative, the excluded components can include the time value of an option or the interest element of a forward (see para 10.56 above) or a proportion, such as 50 per cent of a derivative (or non-derivative financial instrument for hedges of foreign currency risk) (see para 10.60 above). Changes in the value of those excluded components are recognised in profit or loss (unless, in the case a proportion of a derivative, the remaining portion is designated as the hedging instrument in a different cash flow hedge or a net investment hedge).

[IAS 39 para 96].

10.117 The way in which an entity accounts for cash flow hedges is illustrated in the examples below. In addition, another more in-depth application of cash flow hedge accounting for a hedge of a highly probable foreign currency purchase of raw materials using a forward contract (including full prospective and retrospective hedge effectiveness testing) is given in illustration 2 at the end of this chapter.

Example 1 – Cash flow hedge of commodity sale

The facts are the same as in the example in paragraph 10.97 above, except that the entity decides to designate a silver forward contract as a cash flow hedge of the forecast sale of 1million troy ounces of silver to a customer that is expected to occur on 31 March 20X6. It is highly probable that the sale will occur based on its sales history with the customer. The entity is hedging it's exposure to change in cash flows from the highly probable sales. The futures contract entered into on 1 October 20X5 on a specified commodity exchange for 1 million troy ounces of silver at a forward price of C5.55 per ounce matures on 31 March 20X6 and will be settled net in cash. This is the date the entity expects to deliver 1 million troy ounces of silver to its customer at the forward price.

The hedging relationship qualifies for cash flow hedge accounting. The entity determines and documents the entire change in the full fair value of the forward contract will be highly effective in offsetting all the variability in cash flow from the expected sale based on the forward prices.

The entity prepares its financial statements to 31 December each year. The accounting entries from inception of the hedge to its termination following closure of the forward contract (which is settled daily) and the inventory's delivery are as follows:

Date	Transaction	Cash C000	Forward contract C000	Equity C000	Silver stock C000	Dr Cr Profit and loss C000
31 Dec 20X5	Change in fair value of fwd contract		147,830	(147,830)		
31 Mar 20X6	Change in fair value of fwd contract		152,170	(152,170)		
31 Mar 20X6	Sale of silver inventory	5,250,000				(5,250,000)
31 Mar 20X6	Cost of sale				(5,000,000)	5,000,000
31 Mar 20X6	Recycle of hedging gain from equity			300,000		(300,000)
31 Mar 20X6	Settlement of fwd contract	300,000	(300,000)			
		5,550,000	–	–	(5,000,000)	(550,000)

As can be seen from the above, through the hedge transaction, the entity has locked in a cash flow of C5.55 per troy ounce of silver, that is, C5,500,000. This is equivalent to the sale at spot rate plus the gain on the derivative.

Example 2 – Cash flow hedge of a variable rate debt

Entity A has a floating rate liability of C10m with 5 years remaining to maturity. It enters into a 5 year pay-fixed, receive-floating interest rate swap in the same currency and with the same principal terms as the liability to hedge the exposure to variable cash flow payments on the floating rate liability attributable to interest rate risk.

At inception, the swap's fair value is zero. Subsequently, there is an increase of C490,000 in the swap's fair value. This increase consists of a change of C500,000 resulting from an increase in market interest rates and a change of minus C10,000 resulting from an increase in the credit risk of the swap counterparty. There is no change in the fair value of the floating rate liability, but the fair value (present value) of the future cash flows needed to offset the exposure to variable interest cash flows on the liability increases by C500,000.

Entity A determines that although the hedge is not fully effective, because part of the change in the derivative's fair value is attributable to the counterparty's credit risk that is not reflected in the floating rate liability, the hedge is still highly effective. Therefore, entity A credits the effective portion of the change in fair value of the swap, that is, the net change in fair value of C490,000 to other comprehensive income. There is no debit to profit or loss for the change in fair value of the swap attributable to the deterioration in the credit quality of the swap counterparty, because the cumulative change in the present value of the future cash flows needed to offset the exposure to variable interest cash flows on the hedged item, C500,000, exceeds the cumulative change in value of the hedging instrument, C490,000 (see para 10.117 above). If entity A concludes that the hedge is no longer highly effective, it discontinues hedge accounting prospectively as from the date the hedge ceased to be highly effective (see para 10.122 below).

Alternatively, if the change in the fair value of the swap increased to C510,000 of which C500,000 results from the increase in market interest rates and C10,000 from a decrease in the credit risk of the swap counterparty, there would be a credit to profit or loss of C10,000 for the change in the swap's fair value attributable to the improvement in the swap counterparty's credit quality. This is because the cumulative change in the value of the hedging instrument, C510,000 exceeds the cumulative change in the present value of the future cash flows needed to offset the exposure to variable interest cash flows on the hedged item, C500,000. The difference of C10,000 represents the ineffectiveness attributable to the derivative hedging instrument, the swap and is recognised in profit or loss. [IAS 39 para IG F5.2].

Reclassifying gains and losses from equity

10.118 If a hedge of a forecast transaction subsequently results in the recognition of a financial asset or liability, the associated gains or losses that were recognised directly in equity (see para 10.116 above) should be reclassified into profit or loss in the same period or periods during which the asset acquired or liability assumed affects profit or loss (such as in the periods when interest expense or income is recognised). However, if an entity expects that all or a portion of a loss recognised in other comprehensive income will not be recovered in one or more future periods, it should reclassify into profit or loss the amount that is not expected to be recovered. [IAS 39 para 97]. In addition, in the April 2009

'Improvements to IFRSs', the IASB amended paragraph 97 of IAS 39 to clarify the case when an entity hedges some, but not all, of the cash flows of a forecast transaction that would result in the recognition of a financial asset or liability, for example, the first three years of a highly probable forecast five year fixed debt issuance in six months time. In such a case the associated gains or losses deferred in other comprehensive income should be reclassified from equity to profit or loss as a reclassification adjustment in the same period or periods during which the hedged forecast cash flows affect profit or loss (that is, over the first three years of the debt in the above example). The amendment was effective for annual periods beginning on or after 1 January 2010.

10.119   If a hedge of a forecast transaction subsequently results in recognising a *non-financial* asset or liability (or a forecast transaction for a *non-financial* asset or liability becomes a firm commitment for which fair value hedge accounting is applied), then the entity should adopt either of the following approaches as its accounting policy and apply that policy consistently:

■   It should reclassify the associated gains and losses that were recognised directly in equity into profit or loss in the same period or periods during which the asset acquired or liability assumed affects profit or loss (such as in the periods that depreciation or cost of sales is recognised). However, if an entity expects that all or a portion of a loss recognised directly in equity will not be recovered in one or more future periods, it should reclassify into profit or loss the amount that is not expected to be recovered.

■   It should remove the associated gains and losses that were recognised directly in equity and include them in the initial cost or other carrying amount of the asset or liability (often referred to as 'basis adjustment').

[IAS 39 paras 98–99].

10.120   For cash flow hedges other than those covered by paragraphs 10.118 and 10.119 above, amounts that had been recognised directly in equity should be recognised in profit or loss in the same period or periods during which the hedged forecast transaction affects profit or loss (for example, when a forecast sale occurs). [IAS 39 para 100].

Example 1 – Reclassification of derivative loss recorded in equity

Entity A regularly purchases inventory from a foreign supplier and designates a forecast purchase of particular inventory as the hedged item in a cash-flow hedge. At the date the inventory is purchased, a loss on the hedging instrument of C30 has accumulated in equity. In a subsequent period, the purchased inventory has a carrying amount of C100 (without any basis adjustment) and a fair value of C110. The entity expects to sell the inventory at a price equivalent to its fair value.

In this example, the entity determines that the combined value of the loss deferred in equity and the carrying amount of the inventory (that is, C130) exceeds the inventory's fair value of C110, such that a net loss of C20 on the hedged transaction will be recognised in a future period. Therefore, in accordance with the first bullet point in paragraph 10.119 above, the loss of C20 should immediately be reclassified into profit or loss since the entity determines that the loss cannot be recovered.

The same effect in profit or loss would result had the entity chosen to adjust the inventory's carrying value by the amount of the loss deferred in equity of C30 as noted in the last bullet point in paragraph 10.119 above. In that case, the carrying value of the inventory of C130 would be greater than fair value of C110 resulting in the recognition of an immediate loss of C20 in profit or loss in accordance with IAS 2, 'Inventory'.

Example 2 – Reclassification of derivative gain recorded in equity

Entity A regularly purchases inventory from a foreign supplier and designates a forecast future purchase of particular inventory as the hedged item in a cash-flow hedge. At the date that the inventory is purchased, a gain on the hedging instrument of C30 has accumulated in equity. In a subsequent period, the fair value of the purchased inventory, which has a carrying amount of C100 (no basis adjustment), declines to C80.

In accordance with IAS 2, the entity writes down the inventory to its net realisable value of C80 and recognises an impairment loss of C20. The entity should also reclassify from equity an equivalent amount of gain of C20 (that is, part of the total gain of C30 deferred in equity) to profit or loss. The effect of the above adjustments is that inventory is recorded at its net realisable value of C80, the gain deferred in equity is C10 and there is no net impact in profit or loss. The gain in equity of C10 would continue to be deferred until the hedged forecast transaction impacts profit or loss when the inventory is sold or there is a further reduction in fair value.

The same effect in profit or loss would result had the entity chosen to adjust the inventory's carrying value by the amount of the gain deferred in equity of C30. In that situation, the carrying value of the inventory of C70 would be less than fair value of C80 and there will be no immediate impact on profit or loss. The hedging gain of C10 included in the carrying value will affect profit or loss when the inventory is sold.

Example 3 – Reclassification of derivative gains/losses hedging partial term of forecast debt issuance

Entity A took out a 5 year (pay fix, receive float) forward starting swap 6 months ago to hedge the first 5 years of cashflows on its highly probable forecast issuance of 15 year fixed rate debt. It is assumed that appropriate documentation was in place, that entity A demonstrated the issuance of debt was highly probable and effectiveness tests were passed prospectively and retrospectively. As anticipated at inception, on issuance of the debt, the forward starting swap is terminated. Interest rates have increased since the forward starting swap was transacted, which has resulted in a gain on the swap, but the debt being issued at a higher interest rate. In accordance with the amendment to paragraph 97 referred to in paragraph 10.118 above, this gain will be released to the income statement over the first 5 years of the debt as the hedged cash flows affect the income statement.

Discontinuing cash flow hedge accounting

10.121 Cash flow hedge accounting should be discontinued prospectively if any of the following occurs:

- The hedging instrument expires or is sold, terminated or exercised.

  For this purpose, the replacement or rollover of a hedging instrument into another hedging instrument is not an expiration or termination if such replacement or rollover is part of the entity's documented hedging strategy.

  In this case, the cumulative gain or loss on the hedging instrument that remains recognised directly in equity from the period when the hedge was effective should remain in equity until the forecast transaction occurs. Thereafter, it should be dealt with in accordance with paragraphs 10.118 to 10.120 above.

- The hedge no longer meets the criteria for hedge accounting discussed in paragraph 10.137 below.

  In this case, unless the next bullet point is also met, the cumulative gain or loss on the hedging instrument that remains recognised directly in equity from the period when the hedge was effective should remain in equity until the forecast transaction occurs. Thereafter, it should be dealt with in accordance with paragraphs 10.118 to 10.120 above.

- The forecast transaction is no longer expected to occur.

  In this case, the cumulative gain or loss on the hedging instrument that remains recognised directly in equity from the period when the hedge was effective should be recognised in profit or loss. However, a forecast transaction that is no longer highly probable (and, therefore, the hedge no longer meets the criteria for hedge accounting discussed in para 10.136 below) may still be expected to occur, in which case, the cumulative gain or loss is treated in the same way as set out in the previous bullet point.

- The entity revokes the designation.

  In this case, the cumulative gain or loss on the hedging instrument that remains recognised directly in equity from the period when the hedge was effective should remain in equity until the forecast transaction occurs. Thereafter, it should be dealt with in accordance with paragraphs 10.118 to 10.120 above. However, if the transaction is no longer expected to occur, the cumulative gain or loss in equity is dealt with in accordance with the third bullet point above.

[IAS 39 para 101].

10.122 The above rules are summarised in the table below:

Discontinuance of cash flow hedges

| | Hedging instrument | | Amount accumulated in equity | |
Hedge termination events	Continue mark-to-market accounting Note 1	Derecognise from the balance sheet	Reclassify to profit or loss	Retain amounts in equity Note 2
Hedging instrument no longer exists (that is, sold, terminated, extinguished, exercised, or expired)		√		√
The hedge no longer meets the effectiveness criteria for hedge accounting	√			√
The entity revokes the hedge designation	√			√
The forecast transaction is no longer highly probable, but is still expected to occur	√			√
The forecast transaction is no longer expected to occur	√		√	
Variability of cash flow ceases (for example, the forecast transaction becomes a fixed price firm commitment)	√			√

Note 1 – The hedging instrument will continue to be marked to market, unless it is re-designated as a hedging instrument in a new hedge.

Note 2 – The cumulative gain or loss on the hedging instrument previously recognised directly in other comprehensive income from the period when the hedge was effective remains recognised in equity and is reclassified to profit or loss when profit or loss is impacted by the hedged item.

10.123   When an entity ceases to apply hedge accounting because the hedge does not meet hedge effectiveness criteria, it should discontinue hedge accounting from the last date on which compliance with hedge effectiveness was demonstrated. However, if the event or change in circumstances that caused the hedging relationship to fail the effectiveness criteria can be identified and it can be demonstrated that the hedge was effective before the event or change in circumstances occurred, the entity should discontinue hedge accounting from the date of the event or change in circumstances. [IAS 39 para AG113].

Example – Discontinuance of cash flow hedge

On 1 January 20X6, entity A has a highly probable sale that is expected to occur on 31 May 20X6. Entity A expects to collect the cash on 30 June 20X6. Entity A's functional currency is pound sterling and the sale is denominated in US dollars. At the same time on 1 January 20X6, entity A takes out a £/US$ forward contract to hedge the future sale. This forward contract matures on 30 June 20X6. Entity A has put in place all the documentation required to achieve cash flow hedge accounting.

On 1 March 20X6, the transaction is no longer considered to be highly probable, but is still expected to occur. On 1 April 20X6, the transaction is no longer expected to occur. The entity does not close out the forward contract earlier than maturity.

The fair value of the forward contract at each date is as follows:

	Fair value of forward (maturity 30 June 20X6) £'000
31 January 20X6	35,000
28 February 20X6	30,000
31 March 20X6	25,000
30 April 20X6	27,000
31 May 20X6	28,000
30 June 20X6	32,000

The accounting entries from the inception of the hedge to settlement of the forward contract, assuming perfect effectiveness (that is, the hedged risk is the forward rate and no other mismatches occur), are as follows:

Date	Transaction	Cash £000	Forward contract £000	Equity £000	Debit (Credit) Profit or loss £000
31 Jan 20X6	Change in fair value of forward		35	(35)	
28 Feb 20X6	Change in fair value of forward		(5)	5	
	Hedge accounting ceases prospectively from 1 March 20X6. Gain deferred in equity remains in equity but the forward is now marked to market through profit or loss				
31 Mar 20X6	Change in fair value of forward		(5)		5
30 Apr 20X6	Change in fair value of forward		2		(2)
30 Apr 20X6	Recycling of gain as hedged transaction is no longer expected to occur			30	(30)
31 May 20X6	Change in fair value of forward		1		(1)
30 Jun 20X6	Change in fair value of forward		4		(4)
30 Jun 20X6	Settlement of forward	32	(32)	–	–
		32	–	–	(32)

Had the transaction continued to be highly probable, the movements on the forward contract to the extent that the hedge was effective would continue to be taken to equity until the sale occurred in May at which date the gain would be recycled from equity to the income statement. Management would then de-designate the forward contract as a hedge and the fair value movements would be recorded through the income statement between May and June and this should offset the gain or loss on the receivable (settlement due on 30 June 20X6) caused by currency fluctuations. There would be some ineffectiveness as the interest element (forward points) included in the forward contract's fair value is not present in the undiscounted trade receivable.

Net investment hedges

Background

10.124 A net investment in a foreign operation is defined as *"the amount of the reporting entity's interest in the net assets of that operation"*. [IAS 21 para 8]. Such foreign operations may be subsidiaries, associates, joint ventures or branches. An entity may decide to hedge against the effects of changes in exchange rates in its net investment in a foreign operation. This may be done with non-derivative financial liabilities or with derivatives. Because the foreign operation's net assets are reported in the reporting entity's consolidated financial statements, hedging a net investment in a foreign operation can only be carried out at the consolidation level. Under IAS 21, 'The effect of changes in foreign currencies', the reporting entity's share of the net assets of a foreign operation is translated into the group's presentation currency at the closing exchange rate, and all resulting exchange differences are recognised as a separate component in equity until it disposes of the foreign operation. The hedge of a net investment in a foreign operation at the consolidated level is, therefore, a hedge of the translation foreign currency risk arising on the foreign operation, which is included in the reporting entity.

10.125 The IFRIC recognised that IAS 39 and IAS 21 provided limited guidance on the application of their requirements for hedges of net investments in foreign operations and therefore issued IFRIC 16, 'Hedges of a net investment in a foreign operation, on 3 July 2008. IFRIC 16 applies only to hedges of net investments in foreign operations; it should not be applied by analogy to other types of hedge accounting such as fair value or cash flow hedge accounting.

Hedged items

10.126 In a hedge of the foreign currency risks arising from a net investment in a foreign operation, the hedged item can be an amount of net assets equal to or less than the carrying amount of the net assets of the foreign operation in the consolidated financial statements of the parent entity. The amount of the net assets that may be designated as the hedged item in the consolidated financial statements of a parent depends on whether any lower level parent of the foreign operation has applied hedge accounting for all or part of the net assets of that foreign operation and that accounting has been maintained in the parent's consolidated financial statements. The hedged risk may be designated as the foreign currency exposure arising between the functional currency of the foreign operation and the functional currency of any parent entity (the immediate, intermediate or ultimate parent entity) of that foreign operation. The fact that the net investment is held through an intermediate parent does not affect the nature of the economic risk arising from the foreign currency exposure to the ultimate parent entity.

10.127   However, the hedged risk must relate to the functional currencies of the entities involved (that is, the foreign operation and any of its parents). IFRIC 16 does not permit an entity to hedge a foreign operation to the group's presentation currency. This is because IAS 21 places no restrictions on what presentation currency a group can select, and therefore presentation currency risk is not viewed as a true economic exposure. In practice, this limitation is likely to have little effect as most entities either only hedge functional currency risk or choose a presentation currency that is also the functional currency of a relevant parent.

10.128   If the same net assets of a foreign operation are hedged by more than one parent entity within the group (for example, both a direct and an indirect parent entity) for the same risk, only one hedging relationship will qualify for hedge accounting in the consolidated financial statements of the ultimate parent. A hedging relationship designated by one parent entity in its consolidated financial statements need not be maintained by another higher level parent entity. However, if it is not maintained by the higher level parent entity, the hedge accounting applied by the lower level parent should be reversed before the higher level parent's hedge accounting is recognised.

Example

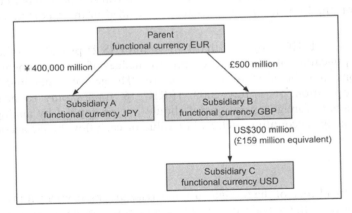

For example, in the group depicted above the parent can hedge its net investment in each of subsidiaries A, B and C for the foreign exchange risk between their respective functional currencies (Japanese yen (JPY), pounds sterling and US dollars) and euro. In addition, parent can hedge the USD/GBP foreign exchange risk between the functional currencies of subsidiary B and subsidiary C. In its consolidated financial statements, subsidiary B can hedge its net investment in subsidiary C for the foreign exchange risk between their functional currencies of US dollars and pounds sterling.

Parent wishes to hedge the foreign exchange risk from its net investment in subsidiary C. Assume that subsidiary A has an external borrowing of US$300m. The net assets of subsidiary A at the start of the reporting period are ¥400,000m including the proceeds of the external borrowing of US$300m. The hedged item can be an amount of net assets equal to or less than the carrying amount of parent's net investment in subsidiary C (US$300m) in its consolidated financial statements. In its consolidated financial statements parent can designate the US$300m external borrowing in subsidiary A as a hedge of the EUR/USD spot foreign exchange risk associated with its net investment in the US$300m net assets of subsidiary C. In this case, both the EUR/USD foreign exchange difference on the US$300m external borrowing in subsidiary A and the EUR/USD foreign exchange difference on the US$300m net investment in subsidiary C are included in the foreign currency translation reserve in parent's consolidated financial statements after the application of hedge accounting. In the absence of hedge accounting, the total USD/EUR foreign exchange difference on the US$300m external borrowing in subsidiary A is recognised in parent's consolidated financial statements as follows:

■ USD/JPY spot foreign exchange rate change, translated to euro, in profit or loss, and

■ JPY/EUR spot foreign exchange rate change in equity.

Instead of such designation, in its consolidated financial statements parent can designate the US$300m external borrowing in subsidiary A as a hedge of the GBP/USD spot foreign exchange risk between subsidiary C and subsidiary B. In this case, the total USD/EUR foreign exchange difference on the US$300m external borrowing in subsidiary A is instead recognised in parent's consolidated financial statements as follows:

■ the GBP/USD spot foreign exchange rate change in the foreign currency translation reserve relating to subsidiary C,

■ GBP/JPY spot foreign exchange rate change, translated to euro, in profit or loss, and

■ JPY/EUR spot foreign exchange rate change in equity.

Parent cannot designate the US$300m external borrowing in subsidiary A as a hedge of both the EUR/USD spot foreign exchange risk and the GBP/USD spot foreign exchange risk in its consolidated financial statements. A single hedging instrument can hedge the same designated risk only once. Subsidiary B cannot apply hedge accounting in its consolidated financial statements because the hedging instrument is held outside the group comprising subsidiary B and subsidiary C.

Hedging instruments

10.129 A derivative or a non-derivative instrument (or a combination of derivative and non-derivative instruments) may be designated as a hedging instrument in a hedge of a net investment in a foreign operation. The hedging instrument(s) may be held by any entity or entities within the group, as long as the designation, documentation and effectiveness requirements of IAS 39 paragraph 88 that relate to a net investment hedge are satisfied. In particular, the hedging strategy of the group should be clearly documented because of the possibility of different designations at different levels of the group.

10.130   The designated risk may be spot foreign exchange risk if the hedging instruments are not derivatives (for example, a debt instrument). If the hedging instruments are forward contracts, an entity can designate either the spot or the forward foreign exchange risk as the hedged risk.

[IFRIC 16 para 14, AG2].

Effectiveness testing

10.131   When determining the effectiveness of a hedging instrument in the hedge of a net investment, an entity calculates the gain or loss on the hedging instrument by reference to the functional currency of the parent entity against whose functional currency the hedged risk is measured, in accordance with the hedge documentation. This is the same regardless of the type of hedging instrument used. This ensures that the effectiveness of the instrument is determined on the basis of changes in fair value or cash flows of the hedging instrument, compared with the changes in the net investment as documented. Any effectiveness test is not therefore dependent on the functional currency of the entity holding the instrument. In other words, the fact that some of the change in the hedging instrument is recognised in profit or loss by one entity within the group and some is recognised in other comprehensive income by another does not affect the assessment of hedge effectiveness.

10.131.1   In our example above, the total change in value in respect of foreign exchange risk of the US$300 million external borrowing in subsidiary A is recorded in both profit or loss (USD/JPY spot risk) and equity (EUR/JPY spot risk) in parent's consolidated financial statements in the absence of hedge accounting. Both amounts are included for the purpose of assessing the effectiveness of the hedge because the change in value of both the hedging instrument and the hedged item are calculated by reference to the euro functional currency of parent against the US dollar functional currency of subsidiary C, in accordance with the hedge documentation. The method of consolidation (that is, direct method or step-by-step method) does not affect the assessment of the effectiveness of the hedge. However, as explained in paragraph 10.131.4 below, it may affect the amounts that are recycled when the hedged foreign operation is disposed of.

Recycling on disposal of foreign operation

10.131.2   When a foreign operation that was hedged is entirely disposed of, the amount reclassified or 'recycled' to profit or loss from the foreign currency translation reserve in respect of the hedging instrument is the effective portion of the revaluation of the hedging instrument calculated in accordance with IAS 39 paragraph 102. The amount reclassified to profit or loss from the foreign currency translation reserve in respect of the net investment in that foreign operation is the amount included in that parent's foreign currency translation reserve in respect of that foreign operation. [IAS 21 para 48]. This latter amount may vary depending on what consolidation method (direct or step-by-step) the entity has chosen.

10.131.3   The direct method of consolidation is the method of consolidation in which the financial statements of the foreign operation are translated directly into the functional currency of the ultimate parent. The step-by-step method is the method of consolidation in which the financial statements of the foreign operation are first translated into the functional currency of any intermediate parent(s) and then translated into the functional currency of the ultimate parent (or the presentation currency if different). IAS 21 does not prescribe which method of consolidation entities should use. In the ultimate parent's consolidated financial statements, the aggregate net amount recognised in the foreign currency translation reserve in respect of all foreign operations is not affected by the consolidation method. However, whether the ultimate parent uses the direct or the step-by-step method of consolidation (see para 10.128 above) may affect the amount included in its foreign currency translation reserve in respect of an individual foreign operation. The amount of foreign currency translation reserve for an individual foreign operation determined by the direct method of consolidation reflects the economic risk between the functional currency of the foreign operation and that of the ultimate parent (if the parent's functional and presentation currencies are the same). The use of the step-by-step method of consolidation may result in the reclassification to profit or loss of an amount different from that used to determine hedge effectiveness. This difference may be eliminated by determining the amount relating to that foreign operation that would have been posted if the direct method of consolidation had been used. However, IAS 21 does not require this adjustment. It is, therefore, an accounting policy choice that should be followed consistently for all net investments. Entities with foreign currency net investments will have to disclose their choice of accounting policy for revaluation of the net investments in foreign operations.

10.131.4   The IFRIC noted that this issue arises also when the net investment disposed of was not hedged and, therefore, is not strictly within the scope of the interpretation. However, because it was a topic of considerable confusion and debate, the IFRIC decided to include a brief example illustrating its conclusions, which are discussed below.

[IFRIC 16 para 16, 17, BC38, BC39].

Example – choice of consolidation method and effect on recycling

Using the same facts as in the example of the group in paragraph 10.128 above, parent used a USD borrowing in subsidiary A to hedge the EUR/USD risk of the net investment in subsidiary C in Parent's consolidated financial statements. Parent uses the step-by-step method of consolidation. Assume the hedge was fully effective and the full USD/EUR accumulated change in the value of the hedging instrument before disposal of subsidiary C is €24m (gain). This is matched exactly by the fall in value of the net investment in subsidiary C, when measured against the functional currency of Parent (euro). If the direct method of consolidation is used, the fall in the value of

10081

parent's net investment in subsidiary C of €24m is reflected totally in the foreign currency translation reserve relating to subsidiary C in parent's consolidated financial statements. However, because parent uses the step-by-step method, this fall in the net investment value in subsidiary C of €24m is reflected both in subsidiary B's foreign currency translation reserve relating to subsidiary C and in parent's foreign currency translation reserve relating to subsidiary B. The aggregate amount recognised in the foreign currency translation reserve in respect of subsidiaries B and C is not affected by the consolidation method. Assume that using the direct method of consolidation, the foreign currency translation reserves for subsidiaries B and C in parent's consolidated financial statements are €62m gain and €24m loss respectively; using the step-by-step method of consolidation those amounts are €49m gain and €11m loss respectively.

IAS 39 requires the full €24m gain on the hedging instrument to be reclassified to profit or loss when the investment in subsidiary C is disposed of. Using the step-by-step method, the amount to be reclassified to profit or loss in respect of the net investment in subsidiary C is only €11m loss. The parent could adjust the foreign currency translation reserves of both subsidiaries B and C by €13m in order to match the amounts reclassified in respect of the hedging instrument and the net investment as would have been the case if the direct method of consolidation had been used, if that was its accounting policy. An entity that had not hedged its net investment could make the same reclassification.

IAS 39 requires the full €24m gain on the hedging instrument to be reclassified to profit or loss when the investment in subsidiary C is disposed of. Using the step-by-step method, the amount to be reclassified to profit or loss in respect of the net investment in subsidiary C is only €11m loss. The parent could adjust the foreign currency translation reserves of both subsidiaries B and C by €13m in order to match the amounts reclassified in respect of the hedging instrument and the net investment as would have been the case if the direct method of consolidation had been used, if that was its accounting policy. An entity that had not hedged its net investment could make the same reclassification.

Where a foreign operation is partially disposed of, the amount of the hedging reserves to reclassify to the income statement has changed under IAS 27 as compared to IAS 27 (superseded). In the table below hedging reserves refer to the cash flow hedge reserve in the subsidiary itself and the net investment hedge reserve in the consolidated financial statements. The table below illustrates common situations and the effect on hedging reserves:

Relationship of foreign operation before disposal	Relationship of foreign operation after disposal	Reclassification of hedging reserves
Subsidiary	Subsidiary (with new NCI recognised)	Reattribute share of hedging reserves to non-controlling interest(s). No amount reclassified to profit and loss.
Subsidiary	Associate	Reclassify 100% of hedging reserves related to foreign operation to profit and loss as part of gain or loss on disposal of subsidiary.

Associate	Associate	Reclassify proportionate amount of share of hedging reserves to profit and loss as part of gain or loss on partial disposal of an associate.
Associate or subsidiary	Financial asset (IAS 39)	Reclassify 100% of share of hedging reserve related to foreign operation to profit and loss as above

If a foreign operation that is a subsidiary is contributed to a joint venture, the question of whether to recycle is based on the policy choice. See chapter 26 of the IFRS Manual of Accounting.

It should be noted that reductions of the net investment in a foreign operation through payment of non-liquidating distributions or repayment of quasi-equity loans may no longer trigger reclassification of CTA. Whether such reductions trigger a reclassification of CTA is, in our view, an accounting policy choice as discussed in chapter 7 of the IFRS Manual of Accounting. Where such a payment is made and a policy of reclassifying CTA adopted, then this would also trigger the reclassification of the net investment hedge reserve related to that foreign operation.

Hedging with derivatives

10.132   It is also possible to hedge a net investment with derivatives. A derivative that is commonly used is a forward contract. However, in this situation, it would be necessary for the entity to designate at inception whether effectiveness would be measured by reference to changes in spot exchange rates or changes in forward exchange rates. If the spot rate method is used, only the change in the fair value of the forward contract due to changes in spot rates would be reported in other comprehensive income and the balance of the fair value of the forward (due to the forward points) would be included in profit or loss. On the other hand, if the forward rate method is used, the full change in the fair value of the forward would be reported in other comprehensive income. This is explained further in paragraph 10.186 below. If the notional amount of a currency forward that swaps the functional currency of the hedged net investment into the investor's functional currency matches the portion of the net investment hedged, it is likely to be an effective hedging instrument.

10.133   It is possible to designate a cross-currency interest rate swap as a hedge of a net investment in a foreign operation. However, such cross-currency interest rate swaps (CCIRS), having foreign exchange and interest rates as underlyings may not be effective hedging instruments since the hedged net investment is not affected by changes in interest rates. Nevertheless, cross-currency swaps could be designated as hedging instruments in a net investment hedge, provided both legs of the swap are either floating rates or fixed rates. This is because a cross-currency interest rate swap that has two floating legs has a fair value that is primarily driven by changes in foreign exchange rates rather than changes in interest rates.

However, a cross-currency swap interest rate swap with one fixed-leg and one floating-rate leg is unlikely to be effective as a hedging instrument in a net investment hedge.

10.133.1 To designate a fixed-fixed CCIRS as a hedge of net investment, management should bear in mind that hedges of a net investment in a foreign operation are accounted similarly to cash flow hedges. [IAS 39 para 102]. There is no other guidance within IAS 39, or the Basis for Conclusions, regarding the basis for this similarity. One interpretation of this statement could be that a net investment hedge is capable of being viewed as analogous to a cash flow hedge of the foreign currency cash flows that would arise from a sale of the net investment at a (or several) future date(s) for the cash flow variability arising due to foreign currency risk. This interpretation would give a rationale for accounting for net investment hedges in a similar manner to cash flow hedges.

Example

An entity A, with Swiss francs as its functional currency, which has a net investment of US$ 120m. Entity A wishes to eliminate foreign exchange risk associated with the retranslation of part of this net investment into its functional currency and enters into a fixed-fixed CCIRS. The swap has a CHF 100m receive leg receiving interest at 3 per cent and US$80m pay leg paying interest at five per cent (assume that CHF100m and US$80m are equivalent based on the spot rate at inception). The swap has annual interest settlements, a five year maturity and has a zero fair value at inception.

In applying paragraph 102 of IAS 39, the cash flow hedge method may be applied to the US dollar net investment by viewing the hedged net investment as a series of cash flows on various 'deemed disposal' dates in the future. In other words, the net investment hedge would be treated in a manner similar to a cash flow hedge of cash flows arising on a deemed sale of US$4m (that is, US$80m × 5%) of the net investment at the end of each of the next 4 years, and a deemed sale of US$84m at the end of year 5. The total net investment of US$ 120m exceeds the aggregate of the deemed disposals (US$4 + US$4 + US$4 + US$4 + US$84 = US$100m) and, hence, this designation is acceptable.

This net investment (series of deemed cash flows) is identical to the profile of cash flows in a US$80m foreign currency debt (which is an asset of entity A) that pays interest annually at 5%, and hence effectiveness may be measured in a manner similar to that used for a cash flow hedge of a fixed rate foreign currency debt.

In a cash flow hedge of a recognised foreign currency fixed rate liability, a fixed-fixed CCIRS can be used to hedge the foreign currency exposure. The most appropriate hypothetical derivative to test effectiveness is a fixed to fixed CCIRS which would ensure little-to-no ineffectiveness.

As hedges of a net investment in a foreign operation are accounted similarly to cash flow hedges, an at-market fixed-fixed CCIRS may be used as a hypothetical derivative to test effectiveness in a net investment hedge. This hypothetical derivative is a CCIRS that is equivalent (and opposite) to the actual hedging instrument. Ineffectiveness is likely to be minimal as the fair value changes in the hedging instrument and hypothetical derivative will offset.

However, this designation requires the net investment to equal or exceed the aggregate of notional principal and interest flows on the CCIRS, in this case US$100m. This approach cannot be adopted where the notional principal in the CCIRS is equal to the net investment balance.

Hedging in individual or separate financial statements

10.134   IAS 27, 'Consolidated and separate financial statements', states that in a parent's separate financial statements, investments in subsidiaries, jointly controlled entities and associates that are included in the consolidated financial statements should be carried at cost or accounted for in accordance with IAS 39. This means that the equity investment can be designated as 'available-for-sale' or 'at fair value through profit or loss' (if permitted by IAS 39). However, in some jurisdictions, entities normally record their investments in subsidiaries, associates and joint ventures at cost in their separate financial statements. A question, therefore, arises as to whether a foreign currency borrowing can be designated as a hedge of the entity's foreign equity investment in its separate financial statements where the foreign equity investment is recorded at historical cost.

10.135   The answer is that it may be possible to construct a hedging relationship to achieve hedge accounting despite the apparent contradictions with IAS 21 and IAS 39. The rationale for achieving hedge accounting is set out in IG E3.4 of the implementation guidance of IAS 39. In summary, IG E3.4 states that, as an exception, if the financial asset or financial liability is designated as a hedged item in a fair value hedge of the exposure to changes in foreign currency rates under IAS 39, the hedged item is re-measured for changes in foreign currency rates even if it would otherwise have been recognised using a historical rate under IAS 21. This exception applies to non-monetary items that are carried in terms of historical cost in the foreign currency (such as equity investments in foreign subsidiaries) and are hedged against exposure to foreign currency rates. In effect, this exception allows an entity to hedge the change in the historical foreign currency cost of the foreign equity investment due to the movement in the relevant foreign currency rates. In these circumstances, the historical foreign currency cost of the foreign currency investment would be retranslated at each balance sheet date at the closing rate and the exchange difference arising on the retranslation will be recognised in profit or loss to offset the exchange difference recognised in profit or loss arising on the retranslation of the foreign currency borrowings (where these are used as the hedging instrument) or the change in the fair value of the foreign currency derivative, that is used as the hedging instrument. Although this treatment is an exception, nevertheless it is still classified as a fair value hedge. Accordingly, the hedging criteria set out in paragraph 10.136 below must still be met in order to achieve fair value hedge accounting in the reporting entity's separate financial statements. Whether, in practice, a parent entity would apply hedge accounting in its separate financial statements is a moot point that may well depend on the tax treatment of undertaking such hedging activities.

> **Example – Hedge of a foreign subsidiary in entity's separate financial statements**
>
> Entity A whose functional currency is the pound sterling acquired a subsidiary B in France for €300m in 20X0 when the £/€ exchange rate on the day of the transaction was £1 = €1.50. Entity A, therefore, measures its investment on initial recognition at £200m (€300/1.50). Entity A borrowed €300m to make the purchase and designates the euro borrowing as a hedge of the exposure to the change in £/€ spot rate.
>
> Assuming that the hedging criteria in paragraph 10.136 below are met and using the exception discussed above, entity A will retranslate its investment in its French subsidiary at each balance sheet date using the closing £/€ spot rate. Therefore, if at the first balance sheet reporting date following the acquisition, the spot rate has moved to £1 = €1.75, entity A will re-measure the historical euro cost of its investment into £171.43m. The exchange difference of £28.57m is recognised as an exchange loss in profit or loss for the period. At the same time the €300m borrowing is retranslated at the closing rate and the exchange gain of £28.57m is also recognised in profit or loss. Therefore, in this case the net effect as a result of hedge accounting is £nil on profit or loss. This example ignores any tax consequences of such a strategy.

Criteria for obtaining hedge accounting

10.136 Hedge accounting is an exception to the normal accounting principles for financial instruments (and sometimes non-financial instruments). IAS 39, therefore, requires hedge relationships to meet certain criteria in order to qualifying for hedge accounting. The three types of hedging relationship set out in paragraph 10.89 qualify for hedge accounting only if all of the following conditions are met:

- At the inception of the hedge there is formal designation and documentation of the hedging relationship and the entity's risk management objective and strategy for undertaking the hedge.

- The hedge is expected to be highly effective in achieving offsetting changes in fair value or cash flows attributable to the hedged risk, consistently with the originally documented risk management strategy for that particular hedging relationship.

- A forecast transaction that is the subject of a cash flow hedge must be highly probable and must present an exposure to variations in cash flows that could ultimately affect profit or loss.

- The effectiveness of the hedge can be reliably measured, that is, the hedged item's fair value or cash flows that are attributable to the hedged risk and the hedged instrument's fair value can be reliably measured.

- The hedge is assessed on an ongoing basis and determined actually to have been highly effective throughout the financial reporting periods for which the hedge was designated.

[IAS 39 para 88(a)-(e)].

10.137 The criteria for hedge accounting are onerous and have systems implications for all entities. Hedge accounting is optional and management should consider the costs and benefits when deciding whether to use it. Much of the burden and cost associated with hedge accounting arises from the effectiveness testing requirement. These requirements are considered from paragraph 10.145 below.

Documentation and designation

10.138 Formal hedge documentation in support of the hedge must be prepared at the inception of the hedge and should include the following:

■ The entity's risk management objective and strategy for undertaking the hedge.

■ The nature of the risk being hedged.

■ The hedged item.

■ The hedging instrument.

■ How the entity will assess the hedging instrument's effectiveness in offsetting the exposure to changes in the hedged item's fair value or cash flows attributable to the hedged risk.

[IAS 39 para 88(a)].

10.139 Since there must be formal designation and documentation of the hedging relationship at the inception of the hedge, a hedge relationship cannot be designated retrospectively. However, IAS 39 does not require a hedging relationship to be established at the time the hedging instrument is acquired. For instance, an entity is permitted to designate and formally document a derivative contract as a hedging instrument after entering into the derivative contract. Hedge accounting will apply prospectively from the date all hedge accounting criteria in paragraph 10.136 above are met. [IAS 39 paras IG F3.8, F3.9].

10.139.1 Risks associated with assets previously designated at fair value through profit and loss that were not previously designated as a hedged risk can be so designated from the date they are reclassified in accordance with 'Reclassification of financial assets' amendment.

Documentation relating to forecast transaction

10.140 When the entity is hedging a forecast transaction, the hedge relationship documentation should also identify the date on, or time period in, which the forecast transaction is expected to occur. This is because to qualify for hedge accounting:

■ the hedge must relate to a specific identified and designated risk;

- it must be possible to measure its effectiveness reliably; and

- the hedged forecast transaction must be highly probable.

[IAS 39 para IG F3.11].

10.141 To meet the above criteria, the hedged forecast transaction must be identified and documented with sufficient specificity so that when the transaction occurs, it is clear whether the transaction is or is not the hedged transaction. Therefore, a forecast transaction may be identified as the sale of the first 15,000 units of a specific product during a specified three-month period, but it could not be identified as the last 15,000 units of that product sold during a three-month period, because the last 15,000 units cannot be identified when they are sold. For the same reason, a forecast transaction cannot be specified solely as a percentage of sales or purchases during a period. [IAS 39 para IG F3.10].

10.142 An entity is not required to predict and document the exact date a forecast transaction is expected to occur. However, it is required to identify and document the time period during which the forecast transaction is expected to occur within a reasonably specific and generally narrow range, as a basis for assessing hedge effectiveness. To determine that the hedge will be highly effective, it is necessary to ensure that changes in the expected cash flow's fair value are offset by changes in the hedging instrument's fair value and this test may be met only if the cash flows occur within close proximity of each other. [IAS 39 para IG F3.11].

10.143 The change in timing of the forecast transaction within the specific and narrow time range does not affect the validity of the designation. For instance, if, subsequent to designating a derivative as a hedging instrument in a cash flow hedge of a forecast transaction such as a commodity sale, the entity expects the forecast sale to occur in an earlier period than originally anticipated, the original designation is not invalidated. Provided the hedging relationship met all the hedge accounting conditions, including the requirement to identify and document the period in which the sale was expected to occur within a reasonably specific and narrow range of time as explained above, the entity can conclude that this transaction is the same as the one that was designated as being hedged. However, this may well affect the assessment of the effectiveness of the hedging relationship since the derivative would need to be designated as a hedging instrument for the whole remaining period of its existence, which will include a period after the forecast sale. [IAS 39 para IG F 5.4].

Example – Hedging cash flows in specific time periods

Entity A manufactures and sells ice cream. Its functional currency is the euro, but 30% of its sales are made in the UK and denominated in pounds sterling. Entity A forecasts highly probable sales in the UK for the next summer season on a monthly basis. Using these forecasts, it enters into forward contracts to sell pounds sterling in exchange for Euros. Due to the nature of its business, entity A is not able to forecast or track individual sales transactions.

Although the forecast transaction should be specifically identifiable as a single transaction or a group of individual transactions in order to qualify for cash flow hedge accounting, Entity A can designate the forecast sales of ice cream as the hedged item. It should do this by designating the hedged item as the first £Xm of highly probable cash flows in specific time periods (for example, in each month). To qualify for hedge accounting, the designation must be sufficiently specific to ensure that when a forecast transaction occurs, it is possible to determine objectively whether that transaction is or is not the one that is hedged. If the forecasted cash flows are no longer expected to occur in the designated time period, management cannot continue with hedge accounting for the related hedging instruments. It should reclassify the amounts previously deferred in equity to profit or loss at that point.

Example documentation

10.144 IAS 39 does not mandate any standard format for documenting the hedging relationship and, therefore, in practice, the nature and style of the documentation may vary from entity to entity. The important thing to note is that the documentation must include all of the basic contents required by IAS 39 paragraph 88 (see para 10.138 above) and must be in place at inception of the hedge. Examples of hedge designation and documentation are included in the three comprehensive examples illustrated from paragraph 10.202 below.

Hedge effectiveness

10.145 The requirement to assess hedge effectiveness is critical for a hedge transaction to qualify for hedge accounting. But this requirement is also the most onerous of the hedge accounting criteria because of the time, cost and effort that it entails. Hedge effectiveness is defined as *'the degree to which changes in the fair value or cash flows of the hedged item that are attributable to a hedged risk are offset by changes in the fair value or cash flows of the hedging instrument'*. [IAS 39 para 9]. Assessing the degree or the extent to which such offset will be effective for hedge accounting purposes is by no means an easy task. The difficulty is also exacerbated by the lack of practical guidance in the standard for undertaking the effectiveness exercise. Often, it will require the use of complex statistical techniques whose output will require careful interpretations. As a result, the approach taken by entities may vary: from electing not to adopt hedge accounting and managing the resulting volatility in the income statement through communications with the market, to putting hedge accounting systems and processes in place and thereby obtaining the benefits of hedge accounting. In practice, most entities are likely to adopt a mixed approach, undertaking hedge accounting only for large material hedges and not electing to adopt hedge accounting for immaterial ones.

Requirements for assessing effectiveness

10.146 To qualify for hedge accounting, IAS 39 requires a hedge to be highly effective. A hedge is regarded as highly effective if both of the following two conditions are met:

- At the inception of the hedge and in subsequent periods, the hedge is expected to be highly effective in achieving offsetting changes in fair value or cash flows attributable to the hedged risk during the period for which the hedge is designated.

- The actual results of the hedge are within a range of 80-125 per cent.

[IAS 39 para AG 105].

10.147   In order to comply with the first condition above, an entity needs to perform a *prospective hedge effectiveness assessment*. This is a forward looking test that assesses whether the entity expects the hedging relationship to be highly effective in achieving offset in the future. An expectation that the hedging relationship will be highly effective can be demonstrated in various ways, including a comparison of the critical terms of the hedging instrument with those of the hedged item (see para 10.160 below), or a comparison of past changes in the fair value or cash flows of the hedged item that are attributable to the hedged risk with past changes in the fair value or cash flows of the hedging instrument (see para 10.164 below), or by demonstrating a high statistical correlation between the fair value or cash flows of the hedged item and those of the hedging instrument (see para 10.182 below). The entity may choose a hedge ratio of other than one to one in order to improve the effectiveness of the hedge as described in paragraph 10.184 below. [IAS 39 para AG 105(a)].

10.148   In order to comply with the second condition above, an entity needs to perform a *retrospective hedge effectiveness assessment*. This is a backward looking test that assesses whether the hedging relationship actually has been highly effective in achieving offset. The objective is to demonstrate that the hedging relationship has been highly effective by showing that actual results of the hedge are within a range of 80-125 per cent. For example, if actual results are such that the loss on the hedging instrument is C120 and the gain on the hedged item is C100, offset can be measured by 120/100, which is 120 per cent, or by 100/120, which is 83 per cent. In this example, assuming the hedge meets the first condition above, the entity would conclude that the hedge has been highly effective. [IAS 39 para AG 105(b)].

10.149   An entity is required to perform the prospective test at the inception of the hedging relationship *and* at the beginning of each assessment period to demonstrate that the hedge is expected to be highly effective in the future. If, at any point, the prospective consideration indicates that the hedging instrument is not expected to be highly effective in the future, hedge accounting must be discontinued from that point forward. An entity must also perform the retrospective test at the end of every period to demonstrate that the hedge has been highly effective through the date of the periodic assessment. If the retrospective test indicates that the hedging instrument has not been highly effective, hedge accounting must be discontinued from the point the hedging relationship ceased to be highly effective. Both tests must be met for a particular period of the hedge relationship for hedge accounting to be available. The requirements are illustrated as follows:

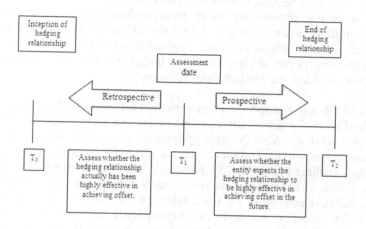

Prospective and Retrospective Assessment

Note: The diagram refers to tests being carried out at time T, (the assessment date). It is assumed that the prospective test at inception of hedge at time T_o has been met.

10.150 Given the nature of the two assessments, it is possible for an entity to pass the prospective test at the beginning of the period but fail the retrospective test at the end of the period (for example, due to unexpected market factors). In that situation, hedge accounting would be precluded for the current period in question. However, a new hedge relationship could be designated and hedge accounting applied in future periods for the same hedging instrument and hedged item, provided the prospective test is met for those periods. Similarly, if the entity passes the retrospective test at the end of one period, but fails the prospective test at the beginning of the next period, hedge accounting would be permitted for the period just ended, but could not be applied in the next period. To some degree, these results will be impacted by the manner in which an entity elects to assess hedge effectiveness, because the entity is not required to use the same method for both the prospective and the retrospective assessments.

Example – Failed retrospective test with a successful prospective test

A hedge relationship designated by entity A fails the retrospective test for a given period. Accordingly, entity A ceases to apply hedge accounting from the last date on which it demonstrated effectiveness. Entity A performs a successful prospective effectiveness test with the same hedging instrument and the same hedged item at the start of the following period. It should be noted that this prospective effectiveness testing will need to take account of the fact that the derivative now has a non-zero fair value as discussed in paragraph 10.55 above.

In this scenario, entity A can designate a new hedge relationship for the remaining life of the instrument following a successful prospective effectiveness test. IAS 39 does not preclude an entity from designating the same derivative as a hedge of the same item in a subsequent period, provided the hedge relationship meets the criteria for hedge accounting (including effectiveness) in that subsequent period. [IFRIC Update April 2005].

10.151 Effectiveness is assessed, at a minimum, at the time an entity prepares its annual or interim financial statements. [IAS 39 para AG 106]. However, the standard does not prevent an entity from undertaking an assessment more frequently. Indeed, an entity may wish to assess effectiveness more frequently say, at the end of each month or other applicable reporting period, in order to minimise the time period during which the hedge may fail due to ineffectiveness and to better manage the hedged risk exposure.

10.152 IAS 39 does not specify a single method for assessing hedge effectiveness. The method an entity adopts for assessing hedge effectiveness depends on its risk management strategy. Also the appropriateness of a given method of assessing hedge effectiveness will depend on the nature of the risk being hedged and the type of hedging instrument used. IAS 39, however, does require an entity to document at the inception of the hedge how effectiveness will be assessed. The method of assessing effectiveness must be reasonable and consistent with other similar hedges, unless different methods can be explicitly justified. The defined and documented method should be used on a consistent basis throughout the hedge's duration. [IAS 39 paras 80, IG F4.4]. There is nothing in the standard to prevent an entity from using one method for prospective testing and another different method for retrospective testing as long as the chosen methods are reasonable and properly documented upfront and used on a consistent basis throughout the hedge's duration. Methods normally used for testing hedge effectiveness are considered in paragraph 10.159 below.

10.153 There is nothing in the standard to prevent an entity from changing its method of assessing hedge effectiveness. If an entity wishes to change its method of assessing hedge effectiveness, this will result in a new hedging relationship. Hence, the entity should de-designate the old hedging relationship and then immediately designate a new hedging relationship using the new method of assessing hedge effectiveness. As a result, new documentation would need to be prepared. It should be noted, however, that there is a danger in de-designating and re-designating the hedge relationship. This is because the hedging instrument will have a non-zero fair value and this may well impact the assessment of hedge ineffectiveness due to ineffectiveness caused by the non-zero fair values.

Assessment on a cumulative or a period-by-period basis

10.154 IAS 39 permits an entity to assess hedge effectiveness using either a period-by-period approach or a cumulative approach, provided the chosen approach is incorporated into the hedging documentation at inception of the hedge. [IAS 39 para IG F4.2]. The period-by-period approach involves comparing the changes in the hedging instrument's fair values (or cash flows) that have occurred during the period being assessed to the changes in the hedged item's fair value (or hedged transaction's cash flows) attributable to the risk hedged that have occurred during the same period. The cumulative approach involves comparing the cumulative changes (to date from inception of the hedge) in the hedging instrument's fair values (or cash flows) to the cumulative changes in the hedged item's fair value (or hedged transaction's cash flows) attributable to the risk hedged. The two methods can produce significantly different results as illustrated below:

| Assessment period | Cumulative basis | | | Period-by-period basis | | |
	Hedging instrument	Hedged item	Ratio (%)	Hedging instrument	Hedged item	Ratio (%)
Quarter 1	50	(50)	100%	50	(50)	100%
Quarter 2	105	(107)	98%	55	(57)	96%
Quarter 3	129	(120)	108%	24	(13)	184%
Quarter 4	115	(116)	99%	(14)	4	350%

10.155 It is clear from the above table that the period-by-period approach of retrospective assessment results in the disqualification of hedge accounting in quarters 3 and 4. By contrast, had the cumulative method of retrospective assessment been applied, all periods would have been considered highly effective and qualified for hedge accounting. It is, therefore, important to ensure that the chosen method of assessment, in this instance, the cumulative method, is documented at the inception of the hedging relationship. Indeed, in most situations, the cumulative method would be adopted in practice as it results in less ineffectiveness. Another example of assessing expected hedge effectiveness on a cumulative basis is given below.

> **Example – Hedge effectiveness assessment on a cumulative basis**
>
> An entity designates a LIBOR-based interest rate swap as a hedge of a borrowing whose interest rate is a UK base rate plus a margin. The UK base rate changes, perhaps, once each quarter or less, in increments of 25-50 basis points, while LIBOR changes daily. Over a period of 1-2 years, the hedge is expected to be almost perfect. However, there will be quarters when the UK base rate does not change at all, while LIBOR has changed significantly.
>
> Expected hedge effectiveness may be assessed on a cumulative basis if the hedge is so designated and that condition is incorporated into the appropriate hedging documentation. Therefore, even if a hedge is not expected to be highly effective in a particular period, hedge accounting is not precluded if effectiveness is expected to remain sufficiently high over the life of the hedging relationship. However, any ineffectiveness is required to be recognised in profit or loss as it occurs. [IAS 39 para IG F4.2].

Counterparty credit risk

10.156 An entity must consider the likelihood of default by the counterparty to the hedging instrument in assessing hedge effectiveness. This is because an entity cannot ignore whether it will be able to collect all amounts due under the contractual provisions of the hedging instrument. When assessing hedge effectiveness, both at the inception of the hedge and on an ongoing basis, the entity should consider the risk that the counterparty to the hedging instrument will default by failing to make any contractual payments to the entity when due (see section 9 'Measurement of financial assets and liabilities' of this chapter for further guidance). For a cash flow hedge, the fair value of the underlying cash flow (hypothetical derivative) will not be affected by change in credit risk of the hedge counterparty. However, the fair value of the actual hedging instrument will be affected. This will lead to ineffectiveness and may even cause hedge relationship to fail if the effectiveness test result falls outside of the 80% –125% range. Furthermore if it becomes probable that the derivative counterparty bank will default, an entity would be unable to conclude that the hedging relationship is expected to be highly effective in achieving offsetting cash flows. As a result, hedge accounting would be discontinued. For a fair value hedge, if there is a change in the counterparty's creditworthiness, the fair value of the hedging instrument will change, which affects the assessment of whether the hedge relationship is effective and whether it qualifies for continued hedge accounting. [IAS 39 para IG F4.3].

Transaction costs

10.156.1 Transaction costs are never part of a fair value movement under IAS 39 and, therefore, they should be excluded from hedge effectiveness tests.

> **Example – transaction costs**
>
> Entity A, whose functional currency is the pound sterling, granted a US$ denominated loan to entity B. Entity A measures the loan at amortised cost, which at initial recognition is the amount lent of US$1m plus transaction costs of US$ 5,000. Entity A designates the loan as a hedging instrument for the foreign exchange risk of a forecast purchase of US$1m. The repayment of the loan and the forecast purchase occur on the same date and all other requirements for hedge accounting are met. Since transaction costs of US$5,000 would not be included in the loan's fair value if it had been carried at fair value, entity A's management should exclude transaction costs of US$5,000 from the effectiveness test.

Pre-payment risk

10.157 Pre-payment risk will impact the effectiveness of fair value hedges of pre-payable assets, such as mortgage loans and, therefore, should be taken into account when an entity designates the hedge relationship. The hedged mortgage loans' contractual terms include the pre-payment option (for the borrower), which cannot be ignored. Furthermore, pre-payment rates are primarily a function of interest rates and, hence, IAS 39 specifies that pre-payment risk is a component of interest rate risk. Therefore, if an entity intends to hedge a portfolio of mortgage loans for interest rate risk, pre-payment risk cannot be excluded. For instance, an entity may have a portfolio of C500 million of mortgage loans that may be pre-paid at par. The entity may wish to hedge the changes in fair value of this portfolio attributable to interest rate movements by entering into a simple receive-variable, pay-fixed interest rate swap. Such a swap, however, would not be a highly effective hedging instrument, because the hedged item contains a pre-payment option that is not present in the swap. However, if the entity can demonstrate (based on historical data) that C100 million of the portfolio would not pre-pay if interest rate were to decline, it could designate that specific portion of the mortgage portfolio as the hedged item.

10.158 Cash flows after the pre-payment date may be designated as the hedged item to the extent it can be demonstrated that they are 'highly probable'. For example, cash flows after the pre-payment date may qualify as highly probable if they result from a group or pool of similar assets (for example, mortgage loans) for which pre-payments can be estimated with a high degree of accuracy or if the pre-payment option is significantly out of the money. In addition, the cash flows after the pre-payment date may be designated as the hedged item if a comparable option exists in the hedging instrument. [IAS 39 para IG F2.12].

Methods used to assess hedge effectiveness

10.159 IAS 39 does not specify a single method for assessing hedge effectiveness prospectively or retrospectively. The method an entity adopts for assessing hedge effectiveness depends on its risk management strategy and should be included in the documentation at the inception of the hedge. There are a number of methods that are used in practice ranging from the most simple (qualitative) to the more complex (highly quantitative). Although the particular method selected would depend on the nature and type of the hedging relationship, all of the methods attempt to gauge the relative change in value of the hedged item and the hedging instrument. The methods that are commonly used in practice to assess hedge effectiveness are described in the paragraphs that follow. It should be noted, however, that whatever method is used test the effectiveness of a hedge, a quantitative retrospective test must be performed to determine the amount of ineffectiveness that has occurred and that must be recognised in profit or loss (see para 10.189 below).

Critical terms comparison

10.160 This method consists of comparing the principal terms of the hedging instrument with those of the hedged item. If the principal terms of the hedging instrument and of the hedged item are the same, the changes in fair value and cash flows attributable to the risk being hedged may be likely to offset each other fully, both when the hedge is entered into and afterwards. [IAS 39 para AG 108]. The principal terms of the hedging instrument and hedged items are those that are critical to the assessment of hedge effectiveness. Further, critical terms are the same if and only if the terms are exactly the same and there are no features (such as optionality) that would invalidate an assumption of perfect effectiveness. Therefore, this method may only be used in limited circumstances, but in such cases it is the simplest way to demonstrate that a hedge is expected to be highly effective on a prospective basis. This method does not require any calculation. For instance, an interest rate swap is likely to be an effective hedge if the notional and principal amounts, term, re-pricing dates, dates of interest and principal receipts and payments and basis for measuring interest rates are the *same* for the hedging instrument and the hedged item. [IAS 39 para AG 108]. A separate assessment is required for the retrospective effectiveness test, as ineffectiveness may arise even when critical terms match; for example, because of a change in the liquidity of a hedging derivative or in the creditworthiness of the derivative counterparty.

10.161   Similarly, a hedge of a highly probable forecast purchase of a commodity with a forward contract is likely to be highly effective if:

■   the forward contract is for the purchase of the same quantity of the same commodity at the same time and location as the hedged forecast purchase;

■   the fair value of the forward contract at inception is zero; and

■   either the change in the discount or premium on the forward contract is excluded from the assessment of effectiveness and recognised in profit or loss or the change in expected cash flows on the highly probable forecast transaction is based on the commodity's forward price. [IAS 39 para AG 108].

In these circumstances, the change in the derivative's fair value can be viewed as a proxy for the present value of the change in cash flows attributable to the risk being hedged. The documentation that the critical terms of the hedging instrument and hedged item match must be performed at the inception of the hedging relationship and on an ongoing basis throughout the hedging period.

10.162   It should be noted that that the critical terms of the hedged item and hedging instrument listed in the above example all pertain to factors that could produce ineffectiveness in a hedging relationship. The fair value of the forward must be zero at the inception of the hedging relationship because forward contracts with a value of other than zero include a 'financing' element that is a source of ineffectiveness (see para 10.55 above). Accordingly, the use of this method should be restricted to situations where an entity enters into the derivative at or very close to the same time it establishes the hedging relationship.

10.163   Even if all of the critical terms of a hedging relationship match, an entity *cannot assume perfect hedge effectiveness throughout the life of the hedge without further effectiveness testing*. An entity still must assess retrospectively the effectiveness of the relationship, at a minimum, at the time it prepares its annual or interim financial statements. A separate quantitative assessment is required for the retrospective effectiveness test, as ineffectiveness may arise even when critical terms match as illustrated in the following example. [IAS 39 para IG F4.7].

> **Example – Testing effectiveness retrospectively when critical terms match**
>
> Entity A enters into a 5 year fixed-rate borrowing. On the same date, it enters into a receive-fixed/pay-floating interest rate swap on which the floating leg is reset every 3 months. The principal terms of the swap and the debt match (start date, end date, fixed payment dates, calendar basis, principal amount, fixed interest rate) and there are no features or conditions (such as optionality) that would invalidate an assumption of perfect effectiveness.

In this section, as the principal terms of the debt and the fixed leg of the swap match and entity A is able to demonstrate and document that the change in the fair value of the floating leg of the swap will not give rise to material ineffectiveness, this is sufficient that the hedge is expected to be highly effective on a prospective basis. Thus, a numerical test is not required to demonstrate prospective effectiveness.

However, even though the critical terms of the fixed rate borrowing and the swap match, hedge effectiveness cannot be assumed throughout the life of the hedge and a retrospective test must be performed. The objective of the retrospective effectiveness test is to determine that the hedge actually has been highly effective throughout the financial reporting period for which it was designated. If the principal terms of the hedging instrument match those of the hedged item, ineffectiveness may still arise, for example if:

■   in the case of a fair value hedge;

■   there is a change in the swap's liquidity;

■   there is a change in the swap counterparty's creditworthiness; or

■   the floating rate leg is not reset on the testing date.

Dollar offset method

10.164   This is a quantitative method that consists of comparing the change in fair value or cash flows of the hedging instrument with the change in fair value or cash flows of the hedged item attributable to the hedged risk. If this ratio falls within the range of 80-125 per cent as explained in paragraph 10.150, the hedge is regarded as highly effective. Depending on the entity's risk management policies, this test can be performed either on a cumulative basis or on a period-by-period basis as explained in paragraph 10.155 above. The formula for assessing hedge effectiveness on cumulative basis under the dollar-offset method can be expressed as follows:

$$0.8 \leq \left| - \left| \frac{\sum\limits_{i=1}^{n} X_i}{\sum\limits_{i=1}^{n} Y_i} \right| \right| \leq 1.25$$

where $\sum\limits_{i=1}^{n} X_i$ is the cumulative sum of the periodic changes in the values of the

hedging instrument and $\sum\limits_{i=1}^{n} Y_i$ is the cumulative sum of the periodic changes in

the values of the hedged item and n = number of periods since inception of the hedge. Since X_i and Y_i are variables that offset each other the minus sign has been introduced to ensure that the ratio is an absolute number.

For a perfect hedge, the change in the value of the hedging instrument exactly offsets the change in the value of the hedged item. Therefore, the above ratio of the cumulative sum of the periodic changes in value of the hedging instrument and the hedged item would equal one in a perfect hedge.

Example – Dollar-offset method

Entity A has a C1,000 debt at 10% fixed rate with a 2 year term. Interest payments are made annually In order to hedge against future changes in interest rates it enters into a 2 year C1,000 notional interest rate swap requiring interest payments at one year LIBOR in exchange for the receipt of fixed interest at 10% (fair value hedge of interest rate risk).

At inception, LIBOR is expected to be 10% for the following 2 years, but at the end of year 1 LIBOR is expected to be 5% for the second year.

At the end of year 1, the retrospective test would be performed as follows:

		C
Hedged item (debt)	Fair value at inception =	1,000
	Fair value at end of year 1 = C1,000 × 1.10/1.05	1,048
	Change in fair value	(48)
Hedging instrument	Fair value at inception	0
	Fair value at end of year 1 = C50 */1.05	48
	Change in fair value	48

* Difference in anticipated swap cash flows = C1,000 × (10% – 5%)

Dollar offset test at end of year 1

$$\frac{\text{Change in fair value of hedging instrument}}{\text{Change in fair value of hedged item}} = \frac{48}{(48)} = 1$$

This hedge is, therefore, currently 100% effective.

If there had been a contractual difference or delay in the timing of the cash flows either on the debt or the swap, or if effectiveness is tested at a date other than the swap re-pricing date, then some ineffectiveness would most likely result. Also no account has been taken here of the credit risk in the swap payments, which could have introduced some ineffectiveness. Note that any credit risk on the debt was not designated as part of the hedging relationship and any impact of this would be booked to the income statement anyway over time, though not on a fair value basis.

Consider the example above, but the cash flows on the debt are anticipated to slip by one month at the end of year 2. The end of year 1 retrospective test would show:

		C
Hedged item (debt)	Fair value at inception =	1,000
	Fair value at end of year 1 = C1,000 × $1.10/(1.05)^{13/12}$	1,043
	Change in fair value	(43)
Hedging instrument	Fair value at inception	0
	Fair value at end of year 1 = C50 */1.05	48
	Change in fair value	48

* Difference in anticipated swap cash flows = Clm × (10% – 5%)

Dollar offset test at end of year 1

$$\frac{\text{Change in fair value of hedging instrument}}{\text{Change in fair value of hedged item}} = \frac{48}{(43)} = 1.12$$

Due to the cash flow slippage on the debt ineffectiveness of C5 has been introduced. This is still within the 80-125 % range so hedge accounting is still permitted, however, the C5 will need to be recognised in profit or loss as explained further in paragraph 10.186 below.

10.165 The above examples illustrate that the dollar-offset method has the advantage that the calculation is straightforward and does not rely on maintaining a large population of valuation data. When applied retrospectively to an assessment of actual effectiveness, the dollar-offset method can be applied either on a period-by-period basis or cumulatively from the date of the inception of the hedge as explained in paragraph 10.154 above. However, the example in that paragraph also indicated that even though on a cumulative basis the hedge was highly effective, two test ratios were outside the critical range on a period-by-period basis. This is an unfortunate consequence of the 80/125 rule that during periods of market stability virtually any hedge is likely to fail as small changes in the values of either the hedged item or the hedging instrument can produce extreme ratios. This is a general shortcoming of the dollar-offset method and is likely to occur when there are short testing intervals. As a result, the dollar offset method can be unreliable, causing hedges that are, by other reasonable standards, highly effective, to fail the effectiveness test. In practice, however, this short coming is often overcome by performing a cumulative dollar-offset test.

10.166 Notwithstanding the above, when the dollar offset method is used for assessing retrospectively the effectiveness of a hedge, it has the advantage of determining the amount of ineffectiveness that has occurred and of generating the numbers required for the accounting entries. For instance, to the extent that the sum of the changes in the value of the hedged item and the hedging instrument is not zero, there is an element of ineffectiveness in the hedge that is included in profit or loss. Thus, even when a hedge is determined to be highly effective, there is an impact on profit or loss when there is not an exact offset of the hedged risk as illustrated in the example in paragraph 10.165 above.

10.167   The dollar offset method can be performed using different approaches. Three approaches that are generally used in practice are:

■   The hypothetical derivative method (see para 10.168 below).

■   The benchmark rate method (see para 10.171 below).

■   The sensitivity analysis method (see para 10.172 below).

Hypothetical derivative method

10.168   The hypothetical derivative method is used under dollar offset method to measure the effectiveness of cash flow hedges. Under the hypothetical derivative method, the hedged risk is modelled as a derivative called a 'hypothetical derivative' (as it does not exist). The hypothetical derivative approach compares the change in the fair value or cash flows of the hedging instrument with the change in the fair value or cash flows of the hypothetical derivative. The hypothetical derivative method is referred to as 'method B' in IAS 39 paragraph IGF5.5. The measurement of hedge ineffectiveness is based on a comparison of the change in fair value of the actual derivative designated as the hedging instrument and the change in fair value of a hypothetical derivative. That hypothetical derivative would have terms that identically match the critical terms of the hedged item. For example, for a cash flow hedge that involves either a variable rate asset or a liability, the hypothetical derivative would be a swap that must have the same notional amount and the same re-pricing dates. Also, the index on which the hypothetical swap's variable rate is based should match the index on which the asset or liability's variable rate is based, and must mirror any caps, floors or any other non-separated embedded derivative features of the hedged item. Thus, the hypothetical swap would be expected to perfectly offset the hedged cash flows. The change in fair value of the 'perfect' hypothetical swap is regarded as a proxy for the present value of the cumulative change in expected future cash flows on the hedged transaction.

10.169   Accordingly, once an entity has determined the change in fair value of the hypothetical swap and the change in the fair value of the actual swap for particular periods, it would use this data to assess the hedging relationship's effectiveness. The actual swap would be recorded at fair value on the balance sheet and the amount reported in equity would be adjusted to a balance that reflects the lesser of either the cumulative change in the actual swap's fair value or the cumulative change in the 'perfect' hypothetical swap's fair value. Determining of the fair value of both the 'perfect' hypothetical swap and the actual swap should use discount rates based on the relevant swap curves. Thus, for the hypothetical swap the discount rates used are the spot rates implied by the current yield curve for hypothetical zero coupon bonds due on the date of each future net settlement of the swap. The amount of ineffectiveness, if any, recorded in profit or loss would then be equal to the excess of the cumulative change in the fair value of the actual swap over the cumulative change in the fair value of the 'perfect' hypothetical swap.

10.170 The hypothetical derivative method often is useful in evaluating the effectiveness of cash flow hedging relationships involving other derivatives, such as cross-currency swaps, commodity swaps and forward exchange contracts.

> **Example – Hypothetical derivative method**
>
> Entity A hedges the foreign currency risk of highly probable forecast transactions using forward contracts. Entity A intends to measure the effectiveness of the hedge by modelling the hedged risk of the forecast transaction as a hypothetical derivative.
>
> As explained above, this method is specifically mentioned in IAS 39. Entity A would construct a hypothetical derivative whose terms reflect the relevant terms of the hedged item. Since entity A hedges the foreign currency risk of highly probable sales, the relevant hypothetical derivative is a forward foreign currency contract for the hedged amount maturing at the date on which the cash flows are anticipated, at the relevant forward rate at inception of the hedge. The change in the fair value of the hypothetical derivative is then compared with the change in the fair value of the hedging instrument to determine effectiveness.

The benchmark rate method

10.171 The benchmark rate approach is used under the dollar offset method to measure the effectiveness of cash flow hedges. Although not specifically mentioned in IAS 39, it is a variant of the hypothetical derivative method that is permitted by the standard and discussed in paragraph 10.170 above. Under this method, a 'target' rate is established as the benchmark rate for the hedge. For example, in an interest rate hedge of a variable rate debt instrument using an interest rate swap, the benchmark rate is usually the swap's fixed rate at the inception of the hedge. The benchmark rate method first identifies the difference between the hedging item's actual cash flows and the benchmark rate. It then compares the change in the amount or value of this difference with the change in the cash flow or fair value of the hedging instrument as illustrated in the example below.

> **Example – Cash flow hedge effectiveness testing – 'fixed benchmark method'**
>
> Entity A issues a variable rate bond. On the same date, it enters into an interest rate swap under which it will receive variable and pay a fixed rate of interest. An equivalent fixed rate debt instrument with the same maturity could have been issued at 8%. Entity A designates the swap as a cash flow hedge of the bond. All the criteria for hedge accounting in paragraph 10.136 are met.
>
> Entity A proposes to test effectiveness both prospectively and retrospectively by comparing:
>
> ■ the present value of the cumulative change in expected future cash flows on the swap; with

- the present value of the cumulative change in the expected future interest cash flows on the variable leg less the fixed rate (8%).

In this situation, entity A can use the 'fixed benchmark method' in a cash flow hedge relationship for both prospective and retrospective effectiveness testing. This method reflects the risk management objective of the hedging relationship – that is, to swap a series of future variable cash flows to a fixed rate and is consistent with the requirements in IAS 39 that the method an entity adopts for assessing hedge effectiveness depends on its risk management strategy. [IAS 39 para AG 107].

Entity A should define the hedged risk as the change in the fair value of the variable cash flows, less the change in the fair value of a fixed rate of interest that could have been achieved at the inception of the underlying debt instrument (8%). It, therefore, measures the variability against a specified fixed rate. Effectiveness testing should be performed based on the ability of the hedging instrument to deliver that specified set of cash flows and should, therefore, measure variability from that fixed rate.

Example – Hedge effectiveness testing – 'Change in variable cash flow method'

Using the facts as set out in the example 1 above, the entity's management proposes to test effectiveness both prospectively and retrospectively by comparing the present value of the cumulative change in expected future cash flows on the swap's floating rate leg and the present value of the cumulative change in the expected future interest cash flows on the floating rate liability.

This method is sometimes referred to as the 'change in variable cash flow' method. This method is an acceptable method for performing prospective effectiveness testing, but not for retrospective effectiveness testing.

The justification for using this approach for prospective effectiveness testing is that the change in variable cash flows method is consistent with the cash flow hedge objective of effectively offsetting the changes in the hedged cash flows attributable to the hedged risk and that only the floating rate leg of the swap provides the cash flow hedge protection.

With regards to retrospective effectiveness testing, the change in variable cash flow method is not permitted for retrospective effectiveness testing since only a portion of the derivative (the floating rate leg only) is used for the test. Paragraph 74 of IAS 39 states that a hedging relationship is designated by an entity for a hedging instrument in its entirety and that the only exceptions are for the split between time value and intrinsic value of an option and the spot and forward points on a foreign exchange forward. Neither of these exceptions applies when the hedging instrument is an interest rate swap. The entire fair value of the hedging instrument must be used in performing retrospective hedge effectiveness testing.

The last paragraph of IAS 39 IG F5.5 explicitly states that this method is not acceptable, as it has the effect of measuring ineffectiveness on only a portion of the derivative. IAS 39 does not permit the bifurcation of a derivative for the purposes of assessing effectiveness.

Sensitivity analysis method

10.172 This method is applied to assess the effectiveness of a hedge prospectively. The method consists of measuring the effect of a hypothetical shift in the underlying hedged risk (for example, a 10 per cent shift in the foreign currency exchange rate being hedged) on both the hedging instrument and the hedged item.

Regression analysis

10.173 Regression analysis is a statistical technique used to analyse the relationship between one variable (the dependent variable) and one or more other variables (known as independent variables). A common application of regression analysis is to build a model using past information that can be used to predict, say, the value of the dependent variable (for example, current year revenue of a particular retail outlet) for a new observation of the independent variable (for example, local employment). However, in the context of hedge effectiveness test, the method investigates the extent to which changes in the hedged item (the independent variable) and the hedging instrument (the dependent variable) are highly and negatively correlated and, thus, supportive of the assertion that there will be a high degree of offset in fair values or cash flows achieved by the hedge.

10.174 For purposes of the hedge accounting effectiveness test, the analysis usually involves a *simple* linear regression that involves determining a 'line of best fit' and then assessing the 'goodness of fit' of this line. *Multiple* linear regression analysis examines the relationship between a dependent variable and two or more independent variables. The linear equation estimated in a simple regression is commonly expressed as:

$$Y = a + bX + e$$

Y: The dependent variable
X: The independent variable
a: The intercept, where the line crosses the Y axis
b: The gradient of the line
e: The random error term

The values of the X and Y variables are plotted and a 'best fit' line is drawn as illustrated below.

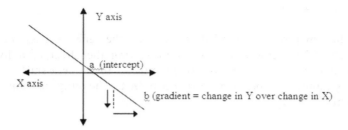

10.175 There are three critical test statistics to determine an effective hedge relationship when using regression analysis. These are as follows:

■ Gradient of the line (b) must be negative and in the range -0.8 < b < -1.25.

The gradient that the regression analysis determines 'best fits' the data, is the ratio of the change in Y value over the change in X value (assuming the model is developed using the hedging derivative as Y or the dependent variable and the hedged item as X or the independent variable). The gradient is a very important component when developing a highly effective hedging relationship and represents the variance-minimising hedge ratio. A gradient of -1 means that for a C1 increase (decrease) in the hedged item, the derivative will generally decrease (increase) by C1, which represents a perfect hedge. The gradient should be negative because the derivative is expected to offset changes in the hedged item. Therefore, if the regression analysis is performed using equal units of the hedging instrument and the hedged item, the gradient b can be used to determine the optimal hedge ratio (that is, the optimal volume of derivative that should be transacted to maximise expected effectiveness). This ratio can then be used by the entity to determine how many units of the hedging instrument it should transact to best mitigate the risk for the particular position being hedged. For example, if the gradient = -0.95, a hedge ratio based on 95 units of the hedging instrument to 100 units of the hedged item will maximise expected effectiveness.

Once the hedge ratio has been determined and the hedge transacted, the regression analysis is re-performed using the actual quantities of the hedging instrument and the hedged item. The gradient is used when assessing the effectiveness of the actual hedge relationship. The gradient must be negative and fall within the range of -0.8 to -1.25. If the gradient is positive, there is no hedge relationship (that is, the hedging instrument does not mitigate the hedged risk). If the gradient is negative but outside of the range of -0.8 to -1.25, there is some hedge relationship, but it is not strong enough to pass the effectiveness test. Hedge accounting is not permitted in either case.

■ The co-efficient of determination (R^2) > 0.96

The co-efficient of determination (R^2) measures the degree of explanatory power or correlation between the dependent and independent variable. Best practice is that it should have a value greater than 0.96, since this is equivalent to a dollar offset of between 80% and 125%. R^2 represents the proportion of variability in the hedging derivative (the dependent variable) that can be explained by variation in the hedged item (the independent variable). By way of illustration, an R^2 of .98 indicates that 98 per cent of the movement in the hedging instrument is 'explained' by variation in the hedged item. R^2 values will always be positive (as it is a squared number) and can never exceed 1 (that is, it is not possible to explain more than 100 per cent of the movement in the dependent variable). The square root of R^2 or 'r' is called the co-efficient of correlation. The co-efficient of correlation can be either positive or negative depending on the underlying relationship between the dependent and independent variables. Whereas values of R^2 are easily interpreted, 'r' does not have a clear-cut operational interpretation. It should be noted that although it is best practice to have a value of $R^2 > 0.96$, a value of 0.8 (used under US GAAP) maybe acceptable, provided the other regression statistics are also met. In other words, $R^2 > 0.8$ is not, on its own, sufficient.

- The statistical validity of the overall regression model (the F-statistic) must be significant.

  The F-statistic is a standard output from the statistical model. It is a measure of the statistical significance of the relationship between the dependent variable and the independent variable (that is, whether the derivative relationship, relative to the hedged risk, is a statistically valid relationship). A non-significant F-statistic indicates there is no statistically significant relationship between the dependent and independent variables. The F-statistic varies with the number of data points used. It can be obtained from statistical tables. To be significant, the result of the F-statistic should be less than 5 per cent (sometimes expressed as a whole number, for example, 4.96) at a 95 per cent or greater confidence level.

10.176 It is important to note that in order to be deemed highly effective, a regression analysis of a hedging relationship must yield acceptable levels for all three factors as noted above. For example, a regression analysis may produce an $R^2 = 0.96$, but an F-statistic that is not significant at the 95 per cent threshold. In this situation, it is not possible to conclude that there is a statistically significant relationship between the hedged item and the hedging derivative and, therefore, the hedging relationship is not considered effective. Another example is where an entity establishes a 1 for 1 hedge and the regression analysis results in an $R^2 = 0.96$, an F-statistic that is significant at the 95 per cent threshold, but a gradient of only -0.7. In this situation, the hedge relationship would be ineffective, because, on average, it would achieve a dollar offset of only 70 per cent of the hedged item. However, if the entity adjusted its hedge ratio from 1 to 1 to reflect the gradient of -0.7 in order to achieve a higher dollar offset, hedge accounting would be permitted.

10.177 When using regression analysis to test the effectiveness of a hedge, it is important to use a sufficient number of matched paired data points to ensure a statistically valid analysis. Generally speaking, the higher the sample size, the more robust will be the analysis and more reliable the conclusion drawn from the model's output. For statistically reliable results, hedge effectiveness should be based on more than 30 observations. However, as a rule of thumb, no less than 12 observations should be used.

10.178   In using regression or other statistical analysis, it also will be necessary for an entity to determine the interval between data points – for example, whether to use daily, weekly, monthly, or quarterly changes in prices in assessing effectiveness. Generally, the selection frequency would depend on:

■   The nature of the hedged item.

■   The nature of the hedging derivative.

■   Whether certain data points will most appropriately represent the interaction of the hedged item versus the hedging instrument.

■   The availability of the data.

Ideally, the entity should try to incorporate as much *relevant* information as possible. Determining what is relevant requires considerable judgment. For instance, it would not be appropriate to use past data that is no longer representative of the current or future market conditions. In those circumstances, it may be appropriate to use a shorter more recent data set consisting of say, daily or weekly frequency period that more faithfully represents the current hedging relationship. On the other hand, too short a period might be equally problematic. If, say, interest rates remained stable over the past few months, a regression analysis based over this short time span would provide a poor indication of how the hedge will perform when interest rates become more volatile.

10.179   When a regression analysis is first performed (at the inception of the hedging relationship), an entity may need to determine that the hedging relationship will be highly effective on a prospective basis. This analysis may use historical data to determine valuations for the proposed derivative and the hedged item. The historical data observation would *typically* (but not necessarily) cover the same period as the length of the hedging relationship. For example, assume an entity issues a three-year fixed rate debt instrument today and enters into an interest rate swap to hedge the fair value exposure to changes in interest rate. The entity should use last three year's data as input for a regression analysis to test whether, at inception, given the terms of the loan and the swap, the hedge is likely to be highly effective on a prospective basis. Conversely, if the last three years' data were not representative of the next three years', use of regression analysis would not be appropriate.

10.180   As the standard requires that effectiveness should be assessed at a minimum at the time an entity prepares its annual or interim financial statements, the entity would carry out both prospective and retrospective hedge effectiveness testing at the subsequent measurement date. If one method is being used for both prospective and retrospective analyses, the same number of data points should be used in the subsequent assessment. Assuming that the entity has chosen monthly data points, the regression analysis at the next annual reporting date would also include 36 data points (12 monthly actual data after inception and the 24 monthly data before inception). As such, 12 months of the oldest data is excluded from the regression analysis. Accordingly, the regression analysis will always contain the same number of data points. It should be noted that the method outlined is not the only acceptable method to determine inputs for regression analysis. Instead of using discrete monthly data, the entity could use a cumulative retrospective evaluation as long as the same number of data points is included in the analysis.

10.181   From an accounting perspective, regression analysis proves whether or not the relationship is sufficiently effective to qualify for hedge accounting. It does not calculate the amount of any ineffectiveness, nor does it provide the numbers necessary for the accounting entries where the analysis demonstrates that the 'highly effective' test has been passed. The accounting entries are based on the dollar-offset method of measuring the changes in the fair values of the derivative and in the hedged risk of the hedged item, both calculated using actual rates at the test date as explained in paragraph 10.189 below.

Comparison between regression analysis and dollar offset method

10.182   There may be circumstances where the results from regression analysis support the use of hedge accounting, but the dollar offset measurement indicate that the hedge would not be highly effective if the dollar offset method had been used. Indeed, it would not be unusual for this to happen, as the two methods are very different. Therefore, in a period where the dollar offset accounting measurement indicates that the accounting results are slightly outside of the 80 to 125 per cent range, hedge accounting would still be appropriate assuming that there was a sound statistical regression analysis supporting the use of hedge accounting for that period. However, if the dollar offset accounting measurements indicate that the hedging relationship was significantly outside of the 80 to 125 per cent range, then the validity and soundness of the regression analysis would be called into question. In that situation, the entity should seek to ascertain the causes for such differences. It may be that small changes in the values of either the hedged item or the hedging instrument cause the dollar offset method to be outside the range based on current hedge designation. In that situation, continuation of hedge accounting may be appropriate. However, continual failure to achieve high effectiveness under the dollar offset method for reasons other than small dollar differences may invalidate the use of regression analysis for the hedging relationship. In that situation, hedge accounting should be discontinued prospectively unless the entity is able to correct any known deficiencies in the prior model and demonstrate that the new model produces a sound statistical regression result that is representative of the hedging relationship.

Hedge ineffectiveness

Sources of hedge ineffectiveness

10.183   Hedge relationships are seldom perfect. Therefore, ineffectiveness will almost always arise with the result that changes in the fair value or cash flows of the hedged item that are attributable to a hedged risk and the hedging instrument do not offset within a period. Examples of differences that can produce ineffectiveness include:

■ Basis differences – the fair value or cash flows of the hedged item depend on a variable that is different from the variable that causes the fair value or cash flows of the hedging instrument to change. For example, an entity designates the benchmark interest rate as the hedged risk when the hedged item uses a different index, such as the prime base rate. The basis difference between those indices would affect the assessment and measurement of hedge ineffectiveness.

■ Location differences – the fair value or cash flows of the hedged item and hedging instrument both depend on the price of the same commodity, but are based on the price at different locations. The price of a commodity will be different in different locations, because of factors such as regional supply and demand and transportation costs.

■ Timing differences – the hedged item and hedging instrument occur or are settled at different dates. For example, an entity hedges the forecast purchase of a commodity with a derivative that settles at an earlier or later date than the date of the forecast purchase. Another example is a floating rate debt whose variability is hedged with an interest rate swap where the interest rate reset dates on the two instruments are different.

■ Quantity or notional amount differences – the hedged item and hedging instrument are based on a different quantities or notional amounts.

■ Changes in the fair value or cash flows of a derivative hedging instrument relating to risks other than the specific risk being hedged. For example, an entity hedges the variability in the price of a forecast purchase of a commodity with a derivative whose cash flows are based on the price of a different commodity and this is the only source of ineffectiveness in the relationship.

■ Use of off market derivatives – an off market derivative is an existing derivative that has a non-zero fair value. Hedge ineffectiveness can arise when using an off market derivative in a number of common place scenarios such as: documentation of a hedge not completed at inception, attempting to restart hedge accounting following a documentation deficiency, temporary interruption of a hedging strategy, change of method of assessing hedge effectiveness in the middle of a hedge period, hedges acquired in a business combination and renegotiation of terms of the derivative.

Minimising hedge ineffectiveness

10.184 The key to minimising hedge ineffectiveness lies in the hedge designation. In many cases, it will be possible to minimise the ineffectiveness in a hedging relationship by the way an entity designates the risk being hedged. This is because under IAS 39 financial assets or liabilities can be hedged with respect to specific risk only (a component of total risk), provided that the exposure to the specific risk component is identifiable and separately measurable (see para 10.24 above). Also, it is possible to designate a hedged financial asset or a financial liability with respect to the risks associated with only a portion of its cash flows or fair value (see para 10.23 above). For non-financial items only certain risks can be hedged and this is discussed from paragraph 10.31. Therefore, considerable ineffectiveness can be eliminated when the risk designated as being hedged matches the risk of the hedging instrument. Consider the following example.

> **Example – Exclusion of credit risk from interest rate risk**
>
> On 1 October 20X5, entity A issues a fixed-interest note at 8% for C1,000. On the same day, entity A enters into an interest rate swap to pay LIBOR and receive interest at 7% based on the same payment terms and with a notional principal of C1,000. At inception entity A designates the swap as a hedge of the variability in fair value of the issued note.
>
> | | **Fair values** | | |
> | | 1 October 20X5 | 30 September 20X6 | Change |
> | --- | --- | --- | --- |
> | Fixed interest note | (1,000) | (1,048) | (48) |
> | Interest rate swap | – | 102 | 102 |
> | Difference | | | 54 |
>
> | | | | |
> | --- | --- | --- | --- |
> | The effectiveness of the hedging relationship | = | – 102/48 = | 213% |
>
> Hedge accounting is not permitted, as the results of the effectiveness test are significantly below the minimum required effectiveness of 125%. The main reason for the difference in fair value movements leading to the ineffectiveness is entity A's deteriorating creditworthiness.
>
> IAS 39 permits an entity to designate any portion of risk in a financial asset or liability as the hedged item. Hedge effectiveness is generally significantly easier to achieve if the designated hedged risk matches the hedging instrument as closely as possible. In this case, entity A should re-designate the risk being hedged in order to improve the hedge effectiveness for future periods. As the entity's deteriorating creditworthiness is the major cause of the hedge ineffectiveness, it should exclude this risk going forward and hedge only the changes in the bond's fair value attributable to changes in the risk-free interest rate. The new designation to exclude the bond's credit risk from the hedge relationship will improve hedge effectiveness, because the bond's credit risk is not reflected in the hedge.

10.185 There is normally a single fair value measure for a hedging derivative in its entirety. Therefore, a derivative cannot be split into components representing different risks and designating such components as the hedging instruments. However, as stated in paragraph 10.56 above, the interest element of a forward contract and the time value of an option may be excluded from the fair value measurement of the hedging derivative. These exclusions can often improve the hedge's effectiveness as they allow the hedging derivative's risk to match that of the hedged item. In that case, changes in the excluded component, for example, interest element portion of the fair value of the forward exchange contract are recognised in profit or loss. The interest element of a forward contract is never amortised to profit or loss under IAS 39. [IAS 39 para IG F6.4].

10.186 Similarly, when the hedging instrument is an option rather than a forward contract, the option's time value can be excluded from the option's fair value and hedge effectiveness assessed based on the changes in the option's intrinsic value. However, in such situations, the excluded time value, which is not of the hedge relationship, will be recognised in profit or loss as explained in paragraph 10.59 above and illustrated in the example below.

Example – Exclusion of time value of option from hedge effectiveness assessment

Entity A owns 100,000 equity shares in a quoted entity B, which it has classified as available-for-sale. The current price of the security is C25. To give itself partial protection against decreases in the share price of entity B, Entity A acquires an at-the-money put option on 100,000 shares of entity B at a strike price of C25 for C10,000. Entity A designates the change in the intrinsic value of the put as a hedging instrument in a fair value hedge of changes in the fair value of its share in entity B.

In this situation, IAS 39 permits entity A to designate changes in the intrinsic value of the put option as a hedge of its equity investment that is consistent with entity A's hedging strategy. The hedge relationship is designated only for the price range when the put option is in-the-money (current market price = strike price), that is, the option provides protection against the risk of variability in the fair value of entity B's 100,000 shares below or equal to the strike price of the put of C25.

Effectiveness is measured by comparing the change in the investment's fair value below the strike price of C25 with changes in the option's intrinsic value. Therefore, when the option is out-of-the-money, no effectiveness measurement is necessary, but prospective assessment is still required. This means that gains and losses on entity B's 100,000 shares for prices above C25 are not attributable to the hedged risk for the purposes of assessing hedge effectiveness and for recognising gains and losses on the hedged item. Therefore, entity A reports changes in the shares' fair value in other comprehensive income if it is associated with variation in its price above C25. [IAS 39 paras 55, 90]. Changes in the fair value of the shares associated with price declines below C25 form part of the designated fair value hedge and are recognised in profit or loss. [IAS 39 para 89(b)]. Assuming the hedge is effective, those changes are offset by changes in the intrinsic value of the put, which are also recognised in profit or loss. [IAS 39 para 89(a)].

Since the option is at-the-money at inception, the premium paid of C10,000 is all attributable to the option's time value. Changes in the put option's time value are not included in the assessment of hedge effectiveness and are recognised in profit or loss. [IAS 39 para 55(a)]. The option's fair value may change due to factors such as volatility of the share price, the passage of time and risk free rate. As such factors do not affect the option's intrinsic value (current price – strike price), they form part of the time value component.

10.187   Another issue in connection with ineffectiveness arises when assessing the effectiveness of hedging instruments such as interest rate swaps. In an interest rate swap, the payments are usually set at the beginning of a period and paid at the next interest reset date. Where hedge effectiveness assessments are undertaken between two re-pricing dates, the effect of interest accrual will affect the swap's fair value. Accordingly, the corresponding changes in the swap's fair value will not fully offset changes in the bond's fair value. However, it is possible to improve the hedge's effectiveness by using the swap's 'clean' fair value rather than the 'dirty' fair value that includes the accrued interest. Using the clean fair value in effectiveness testing often decreases the ineffectiveness, as it excludes the accrued interest on the swap's variable leg that will not have any offsetting component in the bond.

Measuring hedge ineffectiveness

10.188   High effectiveness must be achieved initially and on an ongoing basis in order for a hedging relationship to qualify for hedge accounting. High effectiveness does not guarantee, however, that there will be no earnings volatility resulting from hedge ineffectiveness. Where the hedge is highly effective but not perfectly effective (that is, if a dollar-offset test is used the hedge is between 80 and 125 per cent effective, but it is not 100 per cent effective), there will be some volatility in earnings due to the ineffective portion of the hedge. Equally, the designation of the hedge may be very precise and thus achieves hedge accounting but volatility will be caused by that which has been excluded from the hedge relationship, although this is not 'hedge ineffectiveness'.

10.189   Regardless of whether dollar-offset or regression analysis is used to assess prospective and/or retrospective hedge effectiveness, the dollar offset measurements are used to determine the amount of ineffectiveness that has occurred and that must be recognised in profit or loss in each reporting period. Similarly, where hedge effectiveness is assessed using clean prices of an interest rate swap, the spot component of a forward contract, or the intrinsic value of an option to improve hedge effectiveness, the measurement of the hedging instrument for accounting purposes must still be based on the entire fair value of the derivative that will include accrued interest, forward points or intrinsic value.

10.190   The extent to which hedge ineffectiveness is recognised in profit or loss will depend on whether the hedge is a fair value hedge or a cash flow hedge. In a fair value hedge, any hedge ineffectiveness directly affects profit or loss. This is because the entire change in the fair value of the hedged item (attributable to the hedged risk) and the entire change in the fair value of the hedging instrument are both reflected in profit or loss in each reporting period and the two changes may not perfectly offset each other.

10.191 For cash flow hedges, the measurement of hedge effectiveness is different from a fair value hedge. As explained in paragraph 10.116 above, the amount recognised in equity for a cash flow hedge is the lower of the cumulative gain or loss on the hedging instrument from inception of the hedge and the cumulative change in fair value (present value) of the expected future cash flows on the hedged item from inception of the hedge. To the extent that the cumulative gain or loss on the hedging instrument exceeds the cumulative change in fair value of the expected cash flows on the hedged item, the excess is recognised in profit or loss. However, if there is a shortfall, there will be no ineffectiveness recognised in profit or loss.

10.192 The implementation guidance to IAS 39 provides a very comprehensive example of the dollar offset method for cash flow hedges. [IAS 39 IGF5.5]. The example sets out two practical methods for assessing effectiveness and measuring ineffectiveness for cash flow hedge of a forecast issuance of fixed rate debt. These two methods are known as 'the hypothetical derivative method' and the 'change in fair value method'. Although the example is not reproduced here, the way in which the hypothetical derivative and the change in fair value methods work in practice is explained in paragraphs 10.168 and 10.193 respectively. Regardless of which method is used for the measurement of cash flow hedge effectiveness, an entity must meet the requirements of paragraph 10.136 above for designation of a cash flow hedging relationship. That is, in designating a cash flow hedging relationship, an entity must have the expectation, both at inception of the hedge and ongoing, that the relationship will be highly effective at achieving offsetting changes in cash flows.

Change in fair value method

10.193 The change in fair value method is referred to as 'method A' in IAS 39 graph IG F5.5. This method is applicable for determining hedge effectiveness for variable rate financial assets and liabilities and forecast issuance of fixed rate debt. Under this method, the measurement of hedge ineffectiveness is based on a calculation that compares the present value of the cumulative change in expected variable future interest cash flows that are designated as the hedged transactions and the cumulative change in the fair value of the swap designated as the hedging instrument. The discount rates applicable to determining the fair value of the swap designated as the hedging instrument should also be applied to the computation of present values of the cumulative changes in the hedged cash flows. This method will result in ineffectiveness.

Change in variable cash flow method

10.194 The 'change in variable cash flow method' is sometimes proposed as a method to test the effectiveness of a cash flow hedge. For example, an entity may under IAS 39 use a receive-variable, pay-fixed interest rate swap as a cash flow hedge of a variable rate bond. Under the method, the entity would test effectiveness by comparing the present value of the cumulative change in expected future cash flows on the floating rate leg of the swap with the present value of the cumulative change in the expected future interest cash flows on the floating rate liability.

10.195 Although this method is not mentioned in IAS 39, it is an acceptable method for performing prospective, but not for retrospective effectiveness testing. The justification for using this method for prospective effectiveness testing is that it is consistent with the cash flow hedge objective of effectively offsetting the changes in cash flows attributable to the hedged risk. It is the floating rate leg of the swap that achieves this offset. However, the method is not permitted under IAS 39 for retrospective testing, because it has the effect of measuring ineffectiveness on only a portion of the derivative (that is, only the floating rate leg). IAS 39 does not permit effectiveness to be assessed retrospectively using only a portion of a derivative as discussed in para 10.56 above.

Portfolio (or macro) hedging

10.196 Portfolio or macro hedging is a technique used to reduce or eliminate the risk of a portfolio of assets and liabilities. Banks and similar financial institutions often use this technique to manage the interest rate risk of a portfolio of assets and liabilities. They did this by hedging the net position (for example, net of fixed rate assets and fixed rate liabilities).

10.197 Prior to the issue of the amended version of IAS 39 (see below), the hedging techniques used by banks were not in accordance with the underlying core principles of IAS 39 of not permitting hedges of a net position of assets and liabilities to qualify for hedge accounting. In addition, many of the assets included in a portfolio are typically pre-payable fixed rate assets, that is, the counterparty has the right to pre-pay the item before its contractual maturity. When interest rates change, the resulting change in the fair value of the pre-payable asset differs from the change in fair value of the hedging derivative (which is not pre-payable), with the result that the hedge would often fail the IAS 39 hedge effectiveness test. Furthermore, many of the liabilities included in a portfolio are repayable on demand or after a notice period (often referred to as core deposits). Including them in a portfolio implies that their fair values change with movements in interest rates, which is against the notion in IAS 39 that the fair value of a demand deposit is not less than the amount repayable on demand, because that amount does not change with movements in interest rates.

10.198 Therefore, when the exposure draft of proposed improvements to IAS 39 was published in June 2002, it did not contain any substantial changes to the requirements for hedge accounting as they applied to a portfolio hedge of interest rate risk. Banks were concerned that portfolio hedging strategies that they regarded as effective hedges would not qualify for fair value hedge accounting under IAS 39. They would either:

- not qualify for hedge accounting at all, with the result that profit or loss would be volatile; or

■ qualify only for cash flow hedge accounting with the result that equity would be volatile. This is could potentially give rise to genuine problems for some banks because of capital adequacy requirements imposed by prudential regulators.

10.199   The banks' concerns found considerable political sympathy and the IASB was strongly encouraged to come to an agreement with them. As a result, after much deliberation, in March 2004, the IASB published an amendment to IAS 39, 'Fair value hedge accounting for portfolio hedge of interest rate risk'. Unfortunately, not all of the banks' concerns were addressed. In particular, significant restrictions for hedging deposits with a demand feature still remained. As a result, the version of IAS 39 that was endorsed by the EU had a carve-out that primarily allows banks to apply fair value hedge accounting to hedges of the interest rate risk in their portfolio of demand or core deposits for interest rate risk, which is prohibited by the full IAS 39 as noted in paragraph 10.197 above. It also removed the need for banks to recognise ineffectiveness in the income statement as a result of under hedging that may arise in certain circumstances in fair value hedge accounting for a portfolio hedge of interest rate risk.

10.200   IAS 39 sets out in paragraphs AG114-AG132 a series of procedures that an entity would need to comply with for achieving hedge accounting for a fair value hedge of interest rate risk associated with a portfolio of financial assets or financial liabilities. It should be noted, however, that in the EU carve-out version some of the above paragraphs were amended and some deleted. The implementation guidance to IAS 39 also sets out a series of issues that an entity should consider when applying cash flow hedge accounting to a portfolio hedge of interest rate risk. [IAS 39 IG F6.2]. A very comprehensive example of applying the approach discussed in IG F6.2 is also included [IAS 39 IG F6.3]. As the topic of macro hedging is of little interest to entities other than banks and other financial institutions, it is not dealt with in this chapter.

Comprehensive examples

10.201   Three detailed illustrations of how hedge accounting can be applied in practice are given below. The objective is to present the mechanics of applying IAS 39 requirements, starting with the entity's risk management and effectiveness testing policies, working through the necessary designation and effectiveness testing and culminating with the accounting entries.

10.202   The three examples illustrate some of the most common hedging strategies used in practice. They cover the three types of hedges recognised for accounting purposes by IAS 39 (fair value hedges, cash flow hedges and net investment hedges). The issues addressed are summarised in the table below:

	Type of hedge and hedged risk	Hedged item and hedging instrument	Effectiveness testing		Other key points of the illustration
			Prospective	Retrospective	
Illustration 1					
'Conversion' of fixed rate debt into variable rate debt using an interest rate swap	Fair value hedge – Interest rate risk	Fixed rate debt – Interest rate swap	Dollar offset using clean market values, sensitivity analysis approach	Dollar offset on a cumulative basis using clean market values, benchmark approach	Credit risk not hedged
Illustration 2					
Hedge of highly probable foreign currency forecast purchases	Cash flow hedge – Foreign exchange risk	Highly probable forecast transaction – Forward contract	Dollar offset, sensitivity analysis approach	Dollar offset on a cumulative basis, hypothetical derivative approach	Spot/spot rate designation – Change in timing of cash flows – Basis adjustment
Illustration 3					
Foreign currency hedge of a net investment in a foreign operation	Net investment hedge – Foreign exchange risk	Net investment – Borrowing	Dollar offset using dirty market values, sensitivity analysis approach	Dollar offset on a cumulative basis using dirty market values, benchmark approach	Credit risk in borrowing excluded – Effect of losses

10.203   Despite the range of approaches covered, these illustrations do not set out all of the ways of complying with IAS 39's hedging requirements. Other approaches to hedge accounting may meet IAS 39's requirements. One issue not covered in the illustrations is the discontinuance of hedge accounting. This is covered earlier in the chapter. The underlying calculations in some of the illustrations have been performed using more decimal places for interest rates and discount factors than are presented. If the calculations are reperformed using the data presented, some minor differences in the numbers may arise. Finally, at various points 'helpful hint' boxes have been included. These highlight important issues, give additional guidance and contain tips relating to the illustrations.

Fair value hedge of fixed rate debt

Company A is a UK company with a £ functional currency. Company A's reporting dates are 30 June and 31 December.

On 15 March 20X5, company A issues at par a £10m four year debt with the following characteristics:

Type	Issued debt
Principal amount	£10m
Start date	15 March 20X5
Maturity date	15 March 20X9
Interest rate	7%
Settlement date	15 March, 15 June, 15 September and 15 December each year

No transaction costs are incurred relating to the debt issuance. On the date on which the debt was issued, consistent with its risk management policies, company A enters into a four year pay three month £ LIBOR receive five per cent interest rate swap. The variable leg of the swap is pre-fixed/post-paid on 15 March, 15 June, 15 September and 15 December each year. The fixing of the variable leg for the first three-month period is 4.641 per cent.

> **Helpful hint**
>
> A pre-fixed/post-paid interest rate swap is an interest rate swap in which the variable coupon is determined based on the market interest rate at the beginning of each period and is paid at the end. The variable coupon on the interest rate swap determined on 15 March is paid on 15 June, and so on.
>
>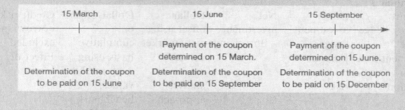

The cash flows on the debt and the swap can be represented as follows:

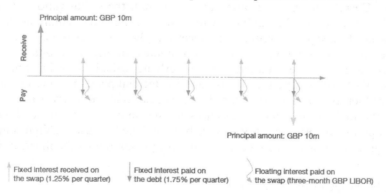

Three-month £ LIBOR rate at various dates when the swap is reset is as follows:

15 Mar 20X5	4.562%
15 Jun 20X5	5.080%
15 Sep 20X5	5.280%
15 Dec 20X5	5.790%

The forward rates derived from the £ LIBOR swap yield curve and the implied zero coupon rates at the dates of testing effectiveness are as follows:

	Forward rates for testing dates			Zero coupon rates for testing dates		
	15 Mar 20X5 (YC1)	30 Jun 20X5 (YC2)	31 Dec 20X5 (YC3)	15 Mar 20X5 (ZC1)	30 Jun 20X5 (ZC2)	31 Dec 20X5 (ZC3)
15 Jun 20X5	4.562%	–	–	4.641%	–	–
15 Sep 20X5	4.623%	5.069%	–	4.672%	5.172%	–
15 Dec 20X5	4.684%	5.130%	–	4.704%	5.204%	–
15 Mar 20X6	4.744%	5.191%	5.705%	4.735%	5.235%	5.835%
15 Jun 20X6	4.805%	5.251%	5.767%	4.766%	5.266%	5.866%
15 Sep 20X6	4.865%	5.311%	5.827%	4.798%	5.298%	5.898%
15 Dec 20X6	4.926%	5.371%	5.887%	4.829%	5.329%	5.929%
15 Mar 20X7	4.986%	5.432%	5.947%	4.860%	5.360%	5.960%
15 Jun 20X7	5.046%	5.492%	6.007%	4.892%	5.392%	5.992%
15 Sep 20X7	5.107%	5.552%	6.067%	4.923%	5.423%	6.023%
15 Dec 20X7	5.167%	5.612%	6.127%	4.954%	5.454%	6.054%
15 Mar 20X8	5.228%	5.673%	6.187%	4.986%	5.486%	6.086%
15 Jun 20X8	5.288%	5.733%	6.246%	5.017%	5.517%	6.117%
15 Sep 20X8	5.348%	5.793%	6.306%	5.048%	5.548%	6.148%
15 Dec 20X8	5.409%	5.853%	6.366%	5.080%	5.580%	6.180%
15 Mar 20X9	5.469%	5.913%	6.426%	5.111%	5.611%	6.211%

> **Helpful hint**
>
> The forward rates are used to calculate the projected cash flows. The zero-coupon rates are used to discount the projected cash flows to the testing date.

Extracts of risk management policies for interest rate risk

Company A is exposed to market risk, primarily related to foreign exchange, interest rates and the market value of the investments of liquid funds.

Company A manages its exposure to interest rate risk through the proportion of fixed and variable rate net debt in its total net debt portfolio. Such a proportion is determined twice a year by company A's financial risk committee and approved by the board of directors. The benchmark duration for net debt is 12 months.

To manage this mix, company A may enter into a variety of derivative financial instruments, such as interest rate swap contracts.

Extracts of hedge effectiveness testing policies

Strategy 1A Hedges of interest rate risk using interest rate swaps for fair value hedges

Prospective effectiveness testing

Prospective effectiveness testing should be performed at the inception of the hedge and at each reporting date. The hedge relationship is highly effective if the changes in fair value or cash flow of the hedged item that are attributable to the hedged risk are expected to be offset by the changes in fair value or cash flows of the hedging instrument.

Prospective effectiveness testing should be performed by comparing the numerical effects of a shift in the hedged interest rate (£ LIBOR zero coupon curve) on both the fair value of the hedging instrument and the fair value of the hedged item.

This comparison should normally be based on at least three interest rate scenarios. However, for hedges where the critical terms of the hedging instrument perfectly match the critical terms, including reset dates of the hedged item, one scenario is sufficient.

$$\text{Effectiveness} = \frac{\text{Change in clean fair value of hedging instrument when zero coupon curve is shifted}}{\text{Change in clean fair value of hedged item when zero coupon curve is shifted}}$$

Change in the clean fair value of a swap is the difference between the clean fair value of the projected cash flows of the swap discounted using the zero coupon curve derived from the swap yield curve at the date of testing, and the clean fair value of the projected shifted cash flows discounted using the shifted zero-coupon rates.

Change in the clean fair value of a bond is the difference between the clean fair value of the cash flows on the bond excluding the credit spread discounted using the zero coupon curve derived from the swap yield curve at the date of testing, and the clean fair value of the same cash flows discounted using the shifted zero coupon rates.

The scenarios that should be used in the effectiveness test are:

(1)   a parallel shift (upwards) of 100 basis points of the zero coupon curve;

(2)   a change in the slope of the zero coupon curve of a 5% increase in the rate for one year cash flows, a 10% increase in the rate for two year cash flows, and a 15% increase in the rate for three and more year cash flows; and

(3)   a change to a flat zero coupon curve at present three-month LIBOR.

> **Helpful hint**
>
> The number of scenarios needed to assess prospectively the effectiveness of a hedge when using the dollar offset method will vary depending on the terms

of the hedge. When the critical terms of the hedging instrument (start date, end date, currency, fixed payment date, interest rate re-set date, fixed interest rate, principal amount) do not match those of the hedged item, or the hedged item contains a feature – such as optionality – that is likely to cause ineffectiveness, several scenarios should be used, including scenarios that reflect the mismatch in terms or optionality.

The pre-fixed/post-paid feature of the swap that is not present in the bond prevents the use of the critical terms method, as there will be some ineffectiveness. Three scenarios should be used to test effectiveness prospectively, consistent with the entity's policy. The example below shows only the first of these three scenarios.

The dirty fair value is the fair value including accrued interest. The clean fair value excludes accrued interest. Using the clean fair value in effectiveness testing often decreases the ineffectiveness, as it excludes the accrued interest on the variable leg of the swap that will not have any offsetting component in the bond.

Retrospective effectiveness testing

Retrospective effectiveness testing should be performed at each reporting date using the dollar offset method on a cumulative basis. Hedge effectiveness is demonstrated by comparing the cumulative change in the clean fair value of the hedging instrument with the cumulative change in the clean fair value of the hedged item attributable to the hedged risk and showing that it falls within the required range of 80%-125%.

$$\text{Effectiveness} = \frac{\text{Cumulative change in clean fair value of hedging instrument}}{\text{Cumulative change in clean fair value of hedged item}}$$

Change in the clean fair value of a swap is the difference between:

(a) the clean fair value of the projected cash flows of the swap based on the original yield curve discounted using the zero coupon curve derived from the yield curve at the beginning of the hedge; and

(b) the clean fair value of the projected cash flows of the swap based on the yield curve at the date of testing discounted using the zero coupon curve derived from the yield curve at the date of testing.

Change in the clean fair value of a bond is the difference between:

(a) the clean fair value of the cash flows on the bond, excluding the credit spread discounted using the zero coupon curve derived from the yield curve at the beginning of the hedge; and

(b) the clean fair value of the same cash flows discounted using the zero coupon curve derived from the yield curve at the date of testing.

> **Helpful hint**
>
> In a fair value hedge, the carrying amount of the hedged item, in this case the debt, is adjusted for changes in value attributable to the hedged risk only. This might not be the same as the total changes in the fair value of the debt. Fair value changes attributable to credit or other risks that are not hedged are not included in the adjustment of the carrying amount of the hedged item.

Hedge designation

Company A's hedge documentation is shown below.

1 Risk management objective and strategy

For the current period, company A's approved strategy in accordance with its risk management policies is to maintain a ratio of fixed:floating rate net debt of between 40:60 and 50:50. In order to achieve this ratio, management has selected this debt to be swapped from fixed to floating.

2 Type of hedging relationship

Fair value hedge: swap of fixed to floating interest rates.

3 Nature of risk being hedged

Interest rate risk: change in the fair value of debt number C426 million attributable to movements in the £ LIBOR zero coupon curve. Credit risk on the debt is not designated as being hedged.

4 Identification of hedged item

Transaction number: reference number C426 million in the treasury management system.

The hedged item is a four-year, £10m, 7% fixed rate debt, which pays interest quarterly.

5 Identification of hedging instrument

Transaction number: reference number L1815E in the treasury management system.

The hedging instrument is a four-year interest rate swap, notional value £10m, under which fixed interest of 5% is received quarterly and actual three-month LIBOR is paid with a three-month reset.

Hedge designation: the fair value movements on the full notional £10m of the swap L1815E is designated as a hedge of fair value movements in the debt C426 million attributable to movements in £ LIBOR zero coupon curve (see point 3 above).

6 Effectiveness testing

Testing shall be performed using hedging effectiveness testing strategy 1A in the effectiveness testing policy.

Description of prospective test

Dollar offset method, being the ratio of the change in the clean fair value of the swap L1815E, divided by the change in clean fair value of the bond C426 million attributable to changes in £ LIBOR zero coupon curve.

The critical terms of the swap do not perfectly match the critical terms of the hedged debt. The prospective tests will therefore, as required by the risk management policies, be performed based on three scenarios. (Only scenario 1, the 100 basis point increase, is illustrated below; all three would be performed in practice.)

Frequency of testing: at inception of the hedge and at each reporting date (30 June and 31 December).

Description of retrospective test

Dollar offset method, being the ratio of the change in the clean fair value of swap L1815E, divided by the change in the clean fair value of the bond C426 million attributable to changes in the £ LIBOR zero coupon curve on a cumulative basis.

Frequency of testing: at every reporting date (30 June and 31 December) after inception of the hedge.

Effectiveness tests and accounting entries

1 Prospective effectiveness test on 15 March 20X5

Company A's management should assess prospectively the effectiveness of the hedge, as required by IAS 39.

Based on the hedge documentation, the prospective effectiveness test consists of comparing the effects of a 100 basis points shift upwards of the zero coupon curve on the clean fair value of the swap and the clean fair value of the hedged item.

A coupon of 7% per annum is paid on the debt (that is, £175,000 per quarter), which can be split into an AA interest rate of 5% and a credit spread of 2%. For effectiveness testing purposes, only the cash flows relating to the AA interest rate (that is, £125,000 per quarter) are taken into account. The credit risk associated with the debt is not part of the hedge relationship; the credit spread of 2% in the coupon is, therefore, excluded from the tests.

Prospective effectiveness test on 15 March 20X5

	15 Jun 20X5	15 Sep 20X5	15 Dec 20X5 ...	15 Dec 20X8	15 Mar 20X9	Total
Cash flows on the swap						
Fixed leg	125,000	125,000	125,000 ...	125,000	125,000	
Variable leg*	(114,059)	(115,573)	(117,088) ...	(135,221)	(136,729)	
Net cash flows	10,941	9,427	7,912 ...	(10,221)	(11,729)	
Discounted CF @ ZC1	10,818	9,214	7,644 ...	(8,488)	(9,609)	0
Shifted zero coupon curve						
Fixed leg	125,000	125,000	125,000 ...	125,000	125,000	
Variable leg + 1%	(114,059)	(139,640)	(141,144) ...	(159,148)	(160,646)	
Net cash flows	10,941	(14,640)	(16,144) ...	(34,148)	(35,646)	
Discounted CF @ ZC1 + 1%	10,792	(14,242)	(15,486) ...	(27,368)	(28,117)	**(315,574)**
						(315,574)
Cash flows on the debt						
Cash flows	(125,000)	(125,000)	(125,000) ...	(125,000)	(10,125,000)	
Discounted CF at ZC1**	(123,590)	(122,178)	(120,764) ...	(103,804)	(8,294,694)	**(10,000,000)**
Discounted CF @ ZC1 + 1%	(123,297)	(121,599)	(119,906) ...	(100,182)	(7,986,407)	**(9,660,676)**
						339,324
Effectiveness						-93.0%

* The variable leg of the swap is the projected cash flow according to forward rates derived from the swap yield curve. As an example, the 15 Sep 20X5 projected cash flow is calculated as 10 million £* 4.623%/4 = 115,573, as the swap has quarterly reset and settlement.

** The discounted cash flows are calculated using the zero coupon rate for the relevant point on the implied zero coupon curve using the normal discounting formula $cf/(1 + r)^{\hat{}}(d/360)$, where cf is the undiscounted cash flow, r is the relevant zero coupon rate and d is the number of days remaining to the cash flow (on 360 day basis). As an example, the discounted cash flow on 15 Sep 20X5 is calculated as $125,000/(1.0467)^{\hat{}}(180/360) = 122,178$.

Conclusion: The hedge is expected to be highly effective.

Helpful hint

The ineffectiveness in the prospective test comes from the change in the fair value of the variable leg of the swap that occurs when projected cash flows are changed. The change in fair value of the fixed leg of the swap perfectly offsets changes in the fair value of the bond.

---

2 Accounting entries on 15 March 20X5

The debt is recognised at the proceeds received by company A, which represents its fair value on the issuance date. The debt is classified as other financial liabilities and will subsequently be measured at amortised cost.

	Dr	Cr
Cash	10,000,000	
Other financial liabilities – debt		10,000,000

Issuance at par of a £10m four-year debt with a fixed coupon of 7%

The swap entered into by company A is recognised at fair value on the balance sheet. The fair value of the swap is nil at inception, as it is issued at market rate. The floating rate for the first period is set to 4.562%, which is the three-month swap rate.

	Dr	Cr
Derivative instruments	nil	
Cash		nil

Recognition of the interest rate swap at fair value (nil)

3 Accounting entries on 15 June 20X5

On 15 June, the first coupon on the loan is paid and the first period of the swap is settled.

Recognition of interest on the debt

	Dr	Cr
Finance costs – interest expense	175,000	
Cash		175,000

Interest on the debt at 7% for three months

Cash settlement of the swap

	Dr	CR
Finance costs – interest expense	114,059	
Finance costs – interest expense		125,000
Cash	10,941	

Settlement of the swap: receive 5% and pay 4.562% for three months

These two transactions result in a total charge of £164,059 to finance cost, which is equivalent to 6.562% interest for the period (that is, the rate on the variable leg of the swap of 4.562% + 2% credit spread). The variable rate on the swap for the following quarter is set at the three-month swap rate of 5.080%.

10123

> **Helpful hint**
>
> In order to increase clarity, we have chosen to show the entry gross (that is, with the effects of the pay and receive legs of the swap shown separately). This entry is often made on a net basis.
>
> The charge to interest expense has been made without performing an effectiveness test, as no effectiveness test is required until 30 June. In the event that the next effectiveness test is failed, the entries will have to be reversed out of interest expense, as hedge accounting is not permitted for the period after the last successful test. The entries could be to 'other operating income and expense'.

4 Retrospective effectiveness test on 30 June 20X5

IAS 39 requires the effectiveness of a hedging relationship to be assessed retrospectively as a minimum at each reporting date. Based on company A's risk management policies, the effectiveness of the hedge must be assessed using the dollar offset method.

The dollar offset method consists of comparing the effects of the change in £ LIBOR swap yield curve between 15 March and 30 June (in this case, a parallel shift of 0.5%) on the clean fair values of the hedged item and the hedging instrument.

Retrospective effectiveness test on 30 June 20X5

	15 Sep 20X5	15 Dec 20X5	15 Mar 20X6	...	15 Dec 20X8	15 Mar 20X9	Total
Cash flows on the swap							
Fixed leg	104,167	125,000	125,000	...	125,000	125,000	
Variable leg at YC2	(105,833)*	(128,257)	(129,765)	...	(146,327)	(147,830)	
Net cash flows	(1,667)	(3,257)	(4,765)	...	(21,327)	(22,830)	
Discounted CF at ZC2	(1,649)	(3,182)	(4,596)	...	(17,676)	(18,646)	**(161,184)**
Clean fair value at original yield curve							**0**
Change in clean fair value (cumulative)							**(161,184)**
Cash flows on the debt							

Cash flows	(104,167)**	(125,000)	(125,000)	...	(125,000)	(10,125,000)	
Discounted CF at ZC2	(103,078)		(122,127)	(120,563) ...	(103,600)	(8,269,357)	**(9,839,030)**
Clean fair value at original yield curve							**(10,000,000)**
							160,970
Effectiveness							**-100.1%**

* The variable rate for the first period is set to 5.08%. The rest of the variable cash flows are projected according to the forward rates derived from the current swap yield curve (YC2), as they have not yet been set.

** The effect of accruals needs to be removed, as the test is based on the clean fair value. 75 days of the next coupon have not yet been accrued; the amount of the first coupon included in the test is, therefore, the cash flow 125,000*75/90.

Conclusion: The hedge has been highly effective for the period ended 30 June 20X5.

> **Helpful hint**
>
> Based on company A's risk management policies, the retrospective effectiveness test above uses the clean fair values of the swap and the debt. Accrued interest for the current period as well as the fair value changes due to the passage of time on the original swap yield curve are excluded from the tests.
>
> The relationship is ineffective because the variable leg of the swap is pre-fixed/post-paid. As the interest on the variable leg of the swap is determined at the beginning of the period (15 June) it is fixed until the next re-pricing date and, therefore, has an exposure to changes in its fair value. If the variable leg of the swap had been post-fixed/post-paid, then the ineffectiveness would have been lower.

5 Accounting entries on 30 June 20X5

Recognition of accrued interest on the bond

Accrued interest for 15 days on the loan is recognised.

	Dr	Cr
Finance costs – interest expense	29,167	
Accrued interest		29,167

Interest on the debt at 7% for 15 days

Recognition of fair value changes of the swap

The recorded change in dirty fair value of the swap can be reconciled to the clean fair value of the swap as follows:

Clean fair value on 30 Jun 20X5	(161,184)
Accrued interest on receive fixed 5% for 15 days (discounted)	20,617
Accrued interest on pay variable 5.080% for 15 days (discounted)	(20,947)
Dirty fair value	**(161,514)**

The swap is recorded at the dirty fair value (that is, including the accrued interest).

	Dr	Cr
Other operating income and expense – ineffectiveness	161,184	
Finance costs – interest expense	330	
Derivative instruments		161,514

Fair value hedge – change in fair value of the swap including accrued interest

Fair value adjustment to the hedged item

All the criteria for hedge accounting are met for the period ended 30 June 20X5, and fair value hedge accounting can be applied. The carrying amount of the debt is adjusted for the fair value change of the hedged risk (that is, the changes in the clean fair value of the debt attributable to changes in the zero coupon curve). The entry is as follows:

	Dr	Cr
Other operating income and expense – ineffectiveness		160,970
Other financial liabilities – debt	160,970	

Fair value hedge – change in fair value of the debt attributable to the hedged risk

As the hedge is not 100% effective, the ineffectiveness of £214 (£161,184 – £160,970) is recognised in profit or loss. Best practice is to present the ineffectiveness in 'other operating income and expense', as illustrated above.

6 Prospective effectiveness test on 30 June 20X5

The same method is used as at the inception of the hedge.

Prospective effectiveness test on 30 June 20X5

	15 Sep 20X5	15 Dec 20X5	15 Mar 20X6	...	15 Dec 20X8	15 Mar 20X9	Total
Cash flows on the swap							
Fixed leg	104,167	125,000	125,000	...	125,000	125,000	
Variable leg @	(105,833)						
YC2		(128,257)	(129,765)	...	(146,327)	(147,830)	
Net cash flows	(1,667)	(3,257)	(4,765)	...	(21,327)	(22,830)	
Discounted CF	(1,649)						
@ ZC2		(3,182)	(4,596)	...	(17,676)	(18,646)	**(161,184)**

Shifted zero coupon curve						
Fixed leg	104,167	125,000	125,000 ...	125,000	125,000	
Variable leg @ YC2+1%	(105,833)	(152,234)	(153,731) ...	(170,177)	(171,669)	
Net cash flows	(1,667)	(27,234)	(28,731) ...	(45,177)	(46,669)	
Discounted CF @ ZC2+1%	(1,646)	(26,493)	(27,526) ...	(36,241)	(36,807)	**(451,850)**
						(290,666)

Cash flows on the debt

Cash flows	(104,167)	(125,000)	(125,000) ...	(125,000)	(10,125,000)	
Discounted CF @ ZC2	(103,078)	(122,127)	(120,563) ...	(103,600)	(8,269,357)	**(9,839,030)**
Discounted CF @ ZC2+1%	(102,875)	(121,599)	(119,758) ...	(100,277)	(7,985,352)	**(9,528,668)**

Effectiveness						310,362
						-93.7%

Conclusion: The hedge is expected to be highly effective.

7 Accounting entries on 1 July 20X5

The accrual of the interest on the debt is reversed.

	Dr	Cr
Finance costs – interest expense		29,167
Accrued interest	29,167	

Interest on the debt reversed at 7% for 15 days

The accrual on the swap is reversed.

	Dr	Cr
Finance costs – interest expense		330
Other operating income and expense – ineffectiveness	330	

Accrued interest on the swap reversed for 15 days

8 Accounting entries on 15 September 20X5

On 15 September the coupon on the loan is paid and the second period of the swap is settled.

Recognition of interest on the debt

	Dr	Cr
Finance costs – interest expense	175,000	
Cash		175,000

Interest on the debt at 7% for three months

Cash settlement of the swap

	Dr	Cr
Finance costs – interest expense	127,000	
Finance costs – interest expense		125,000
Cash		2,000

Settlement of the swap: receive 5% and pay 5.080% for three months

These two transactions result in a total charge of £177,000 to finance cost, which is equivalent to 7.08% interest for the period (that is, the variable rate of 5.08% plus 2% credit spread).

The floating rate on the swap for the following quarter is set at the three-month swap rate of 5.28%.

9 Accounting entries on 15 December 20X5

On 15 December the coupon on the loan is paid and the third period of the swap is settled.

Recognition of interest on the debt

	Dr	Cr
Finance costs – interest expense	175,000	
Cash		175,000

Interest on the debt at 7% for three months

Cash settlement of the swap

	Dr	Cr
Finance costs – interest expense	132,000	
Finance costs – interest expense		125,000
Cash		7,000

Settlement of the swap: receive 5% and pay 5.28% for three months

These two transactions result in a total charge of £182,000 to finance cost, which is equivalent to 7.28% interest for the period (that is, the variable rate of 5.28% plus 2% credit spread).

The floating rate on the swap for the following quarter is set at the three-month swap rate of 5.79%.

10 Retrospective effectiveness test on 31 December 20X5

The same method for retrospective testing is used as on 30 June 20X5. As required in company A's risk management policies, the effectiveness test is done using the dollar offset method on a cumulative basis.

Retrospective effectiveness test on 31 December 20X5

	15 Mar 20X6	15 Jun 20X6	15 Sep 20X6	...	15 Dec 20X8	15 Mar 20X9	Total
Cash flows on the swap							
Fixed leg	104,167	125,000	125,000	...	125,000	125,000	
Variable leg at YC3	(120,625)	(144,165)	(145,666)	...	(159,157)	(160,654)	
Net cash flows	(16,458)	(19,165)	(20,666)	...	(34,157)	(35,654)	
Discounted CF at ZC3	(16,265)	(18,671)	(19,844)	...	(28,605)	(29,386)	**(308,922)**
Clean fair value at original yield curve							
Change in clean fair value (cumulative)							**0**
							(308,922)
Cash flows on the debt							
Cash flows	(104,167)	(125,000)	(125,000)	...	(125,000)	(10,125,000)	
Discounted CF at ZC3	(102,943)	(121,776)	(120,028)	...	(104,681)	(8,345,128)	**(9,692,833)**
Clean fair value at original yield curve							
							(10,000,000)
Change in clean fair value (cumulative)							
Effectiveness							**307,167**
							-100.6%

Conclusion: The hedge has been highly effective for the period ended 31 December 20X5.

11 Accounting entries on 31 December 20X5

Recognition of accrued interest on the bond

Accrued interest for 15 days on the loan is recognised.

	Dr	Cr
Finance costs – interest expense	29,167	
Accrued interest		29,167

Interest on the debt at 7% for 15 days

Recognition of fair value changes of the swap

Clean fair value of the swap	(308,922)
Accrued interest on receive fix 5% for 15 days	20,589
Accrued interest on pay variable 5.79% for 15 days	(23,842)
Dirty fair value of the swap on 31 December 20X5	(312,175)
Dirty fair value of the swap on 30 June 20X5	(161,514)
Change in fair value to be recognised on 31 December 20X5	**(150,661)**

The swap is recorded at the dirty fair value (that is, including the accrued interest).

	Dr	Cr
Other operating income and expense – ineffectiveness	147,408	
Finance costs – interest expense	3,253	
Derivative instruments		150,661
Fair value hedge – change in fair value of the swap		

Fair value adjustment to the hedged item

All the criteria for hedge accounting are met for the period ended 31 December 20X5, and fair value hedge accounting can be applied.

Fair value adjustment on debt on 30 June 20X5	160,970
Fair value adjustment on debt on 31 December 20X5	307,167
Change in the clean fair value of the debt	**146,197**

As the hedge is not 100% effective, the ineffectiveness of £1,211 (£147,408 – £146,197) is recognised in profit or loss. Best practice is to present the ineffectiveness in 'other operating income and expense', as illustrated above.

12 Prospective effectiveness test on 31 December 20X5

The same method is used as at the inception of the hedge.

Prospective effectiveness test on 31 December 20X5

	15 Mar 20X6	15 Jun 20X6	15 Sep 20X6	...	15 Dec 20X8	15 Mar 20X9	Total
Cash flows on the swap							
Fixed leg	104,167	125,000	125,000	...	125,000	125,000	
Variable leg at YC3	(120,625)	(144,165)	(145,666)	...	(159,157)	(160,654)	
Net cash flows	(16,458)	(19,165)	(20,666)	...	(34,157)	(35,654)	
Discounted CF at ZC3	(16,265)	(18,671)	(19,844)	...	(28,605)	(29,386)	**(308,922)**

Shifted zero coupon curve					
Fixed leg	104,167	125,000	125,000 ...	125,000	125,000
Variable leg at YC3 + 1%	(120,625)	(168,030)	(169,520) ...	(182,917)	(184,403)
Net cash flows	(16,458)	(43,030)	(44,520) ...	(57,917)	(59,403)
Discounted CF at ZC3 + 1%	(16,233)	(41,740)	(42,466) ...	(47,176)	(47,511)	**(556,044)**

(247,122)

Cash flows on the debt

Cash flows	(104,167)	(125,000)	(125,000) ...	(125,000)	(10,125,000)	
Discounted CF at ZC3	(102,943)	(121,776)	(120,028) ...	(104,681)	(8,345,128)	**(9,692,833)**
Discounted CF at ZC3 + 1%	(102,742)	(121,253)	(119,231) ...	(101,818)	(8,097,959)	**(9,426,135)**

266,698

Effectiveness   **-92.7%**

Conclusion: The hedge is expected to be highly effective.

The testing and accounting entries are carried out in the same manner throughout the remaining life of the hedge relationship.

	Balance sheet				Income statement	
						Other operating income and expense – ineffectiveness
					Finance cost – interest expense	
	Derivative instruments	Accrued interest	Other financial liabilities – debt	Cash		
15 Mar 20X5						
Debt			(10,000,000)	10,000,000		
Swap						
15 Jun 20X5						
Interest on debt				(175,000)	175,000	
Settlement of swap				10,941	114,059	
					(125,000)	
30 Jun 20X5						
Accrued interest on debt		(29,167)			29,167	
Fair value change of swap	(161,514)				330	161,184
Hedge adjustment to debt			160,970			(160,970)
01 Jul 20X5						
Accruals reversed on debt		29,167			(29,167)	
Accruals reversed on swap					(330)	330

   10131

Hedge accounting

15 Sep 20X5				
Interest		(175,000)	175,000	
Settlement of swap		(2,000)	127,000	
			(125,000)	
15 Dec 20X5				
Interest		(175,000)	175,000	
Settlement of swap		(7,000)	132,000	
			(125,000)	
31 Dec 20X5				
Accrued interest on debt	(29,167)		29,167	
Fair value change of swap	(150,661)		3,253	147,408
Hedge adjustment to debt		146,197		(146,197)

Cash flow hedge of a highly probable forecast purchase in foreign currency

Background and assumptions

Company C is a Swedish company with a SEK functional currency. Its reporting dates are 30 June and 31 December.

Company C produces and sells electronic components for the automotive industry and is planning to launch a new electronic component that it expects to be more reliable and cheaper than the existing alternatives.

Production is scheduled to start in June 20X6. Company C's management expects to purchase a significant amount of raw material in May 20X6 for the start of production. An external company based in Spain will supply the raw material. Based on C's production plans and the prices that the supplier is currently charging, Company C's management forecasts that 500,000 units of raw material will be received and invoiced on 1 May 20X6 at a price of EUR 50 per unit. The invoice is expected to be paid on 31 August 20X6.

On 1 January 20X5, Company C's management decides to hedge the foreign currency risk arising from its highly probable forecast purchase. C enters into a forward contract to buy EUR against SEK. On that date, the forecast purchase is considered as highly probable, as the board of directors has approved the purchase, and negotiations with the Spanish supplier are far advanced.

The foreign currency forward contract entered into as a hedge of the highly probable forecast purchase is as follows:

Type	European forward contract
Amount purchased	EUR 25,000,000
Amount sold	SEK 192,687,500
Forward rate	EUR 1 = SEK 7.7075
Start date	1 January 20X5
Maturity date	31 August 20X6

Exchange rates on various dates during the hedge are as follows:

	1 Jan 20X5	30 Jun 20X5	31/12/20X5	30 Jun 20X6	31 Jul 20X6	31 Aug 20X6	31/10/20X6
SEK/EUR spot rate	7.6900	7.6500	7.7500	7.8100	7.9000	8.1500	8.0500
SEK/EUR forward rate*	7.7075	7.6622	7.7574	7.8118	7.9008	8.1500	
Forward points	0.0175	0.0122	0.0074	0.0018	0.0008	0.0000	

* For a forward maturing on 31 August 20X6.

Annualised interest rates applicable for discounting a cash flow on 31 August 20X6 at various dates during the hedge are as follows:

	1 Jan 20X5	30 Jun 20X5	31/12/20X5	30 Jun 20X6	31 Jul 20X6	31 Aug 20X6
SEK interest rate	1.3550%	1.3850%	1.3670%	1.3850%	1.4240%	1.4030%
EUR interest rate	1.4916%	1.5213%	1.5100%	1.5200%	1.5470%	1.5170%

Extracts of risk management policies for foreign currency risk

Foreign currency risk

Company C's functional and presentation currencies are the SEK (Swedish krona). Company C is exposed to foreign exchange risk because some of its purchases and sales are denominated in currencies other than SEK. It is therefore exposed to the risk that movements in exchange rates will affect both its net income and financial position, as expressed in SEK.

Company C's foreign currency exposure arises from:

- highly probable forecast transactions (sales/purchases) denominated in foreign currencies;

- firm commitments denominated in foreign currencies; and

- monetary items (mainly trade receivables, trade payables and borrowings) denominated in foreign currencies.

Company C is mainly exposed to EUR/SEK and GBP/SEK risks. Transactions denominated in foreign currencies other than EUR and GBP are not material.

Company C's policy is to hedge all material foreign exchange risk associated with highly probable forecast transactions, firm commitments and monetary items denominated in foreign currencies.

Company C's policy is to hedge the risk of changes in the relevant spot exchange rate.

Hedging instruments

Company C uses only forward contracts to hedge foreign exchange risk. All derivatives must be entered into with counterparties with a credit rating of AA or higher.

Extracts of effectiveness testing policies for interest rate risk

Strategy 2A: Cash flow hedges of foreign currency exposure in highly probable forecast transactions

Prospective effectiveness testing for cash flow hedges

Prospective effectiveness testing should be performed at the inception of the hedge and at each reporting date. The hedge relationship is highly effective if the changes in fair value or cash flow of the hedged item that are attributable to the hedged risk are expected to be offset by the changes in fair value or cash flows of the hedging instrument.

Prospective effectiveness testing should be performed by comparing the numerical effects of a shift in the exchange rate (for example, EUR/SEK rate) on: the fair value of the hedged cash flows measured using a hypothetical derivative; and the fair value of the hedging instrument. Consistent with Company C's risk management policy, the hedged risk is defined as the risk of changes in the spot exchange rate. Changes in interest rates are excluded from the hedge relationship (for both the hedging instrument and the hedged forecast transaction) and do not affect the calculations of effectiveness. Only the spot component of the forward contract is included in the hedge relationship (that is, the forward points are excluded).

At least three scenarios should be assessed unless the critical terms of the hedging instrument perfectly match the critical terms of the hedged item, in which case one scenario is sufficient.

Retrospective effectiveness testing for cash flow hedges

Retrospective effectiveness testing must be performed at each reporting date using the dollar offset method on a cumulative basis. The hedge is demonstrated to be effective by comparing the cumulative change in the fair value of the hedged cash flows measured using a hypothetical derivative; and the fair value of the hedging instrument. A hedge is considered to be highly effective if the results of the retrospective effectiveness tests are within the range 80%-125%.

$$\text{Effectiveness} = \frac{\text{Cumulative change in fair value of hedging instrument}}{\substack{\text{Cumulative change in fair value of hedged item} \\ \text{(hypothetical derivative)}}}$$

Change in the fair value of the spot component of the hedging instrument (the forward contract) is the difference between the fair value of the spot component at the inception of the hedge, and the end of the testing period based on translating the foreign exchange leg of the forward contract at the current spot rate and discounting the net cash flows on the derivative using the zero-coupon rates curve derived from the swap yield curve.

Change in fair value of the hedged cash flows of the hedged item (hypothetical derivative) is the difference between the value of the hypothetical derivative at the inception of the hedge, and the end of the testing period based on translating the foreign exchange leg of the hypothetical derivative at the current spot rate and discounting the net cash flows on the hypothetical derivative using the zero-coupon rates curve derived from the swap yield curve.

> **Helpful hint**
>
> The fair value of a foreign exchange forward contract is affected by changes in the spot rate and by changes in the forward points. The latter derives from the interest rate differential between the currencies specified in the forward contract. Changes in the forward points may give rise to ineffectiveness if the hedged item is not similarly affected by interest rate differentials.

Hedge designation

Company C's hedge documentation is as follows:

1   Risk management objective and strategy

In order to comply with Company C's foreign exchange risk management strategy, the foreign exchange risk arising from the highly probable forecast purchase detailed in 5 below is hedged.

2   Type of hedging relationship

Cash flow hedge: hedge of the foreign currency risk arising from highly probable forecast purchases.

3   Nature of risk being hedged

EUR/SEK spot exchange rate risk arising from a highly probable forecast purchase denominated in EUR that is expected to occur on 1 May 20X6 and to be settled on 31 August 20X6.

4   Identification of hedged item

Purchase of 500,000 units of raw material for EUR 50 per unit.

5   Forecast transactions

Hedged amount: EUR 25,000,000

Nature of forecast transaction: purchase of 500,000 units of raw material

Expected timescale for forecast transaction to take place:

- delivery: 1 May 20X6

- cash payment: 31 August 20X6

Expected price: EUR 50 per unit.

Rationale for forecast transaction being highly probable to occur:

- production of electronic component is scheduled to start in June 20X6;

- purchase has been approved by the board of directors; and

- negotiations with supplier are far advanced.

Method of reclassifying into profit and loss amounts deferred through equity: in accordance with Company C's chosen accounting policy, the gains or losses recognised in other comprehensive income will be included in the carrying amount of the inventory acquired (that is, basis adjustment).

6   Identification of hedging instrument

Transaction number: reference number K1121W in the treasury management system.

The hedging instrument is a forward contract to buy EUR 25,000,000 with the following characteristics:

Type	European forward contract
Amount purchased	EUR 25,000,000
Amount sold	SEK 192,687,500
Forward rate	EUR 1 = SEK 7.7075
Spot rate at inception	EUR 1 = SEK 7.6900
Spot component of notional amount	SEK 192,250,000
Start date	1 January 20X5
Maturity date	31 August 20X6

Hedge designation: the spot component of forward contract K1121W is designated as a hedge of the change in the present value of the cash flows on the forecast purchase identified in 5 above that is attributable to movements in the EUR/SEK spot rate, measured as a hypothetical derivative.

7   Effectiveness testing

Hedge accounting strategy 2A should be applied (see hedge effectiveness testing policy). The hypothetical derivative that models the hedged cash flows is a forward contract to pay EUR 25,000,000 on 31 August 20X6 in return for SEK.

The spot component of this hypothetical derivative is SEK 192,250,000 (that is, EUR 25,000,000 at the spot rate on 1 January 20X5 of 7.6900).

Description of prospective testing

Dollar offset method, being the ratio of the change in the fair value of the spot component of forward contract K1121W, divided by the change in present value of the hedged cash flows (hypothetical derivative) attributable to changes in spot EUR/SEK rate.

Frequency of testing: at inception of the hedge and then at each reporting date (30 June and 31 December).

Description of retrospective testing

Dollar offset method, being the ratio of the change in fair value of the spot component of the forward contract, divided by the change in present value of the hedged cash flows (hypothetical derivative) attributable to changes in spot EUR/SEK rate, on a cumulative basis.

Frequency of testing: at every reporting date (30 June and 31 December) after inception of the hedge.

Effectiveness tests and accounting entries

1   Prospective effectiveness test on 1 January 20X5

On 1 January 20X5, the forward EUR/SEK exchange rate is 7.7075. On that date, the spot EUR/SEK exchange rate is 7.6900. Company C's management should assess prospectively the effectiveness of the hedge, as required in IAS 39.

Based on the hedge documentation, the prospective effectiveness test consists of comparing the effects of a 10% shift of the spot EUR/SEK exchange rate on both the fair value of the spot component of the hedging instrument and on the hedged cash flows (hypothetical derivative).

Hedged item and hedging instrument (spot components)

The EUR leg of both the hypothetical derivative (hedged item) and the forward contract (hedging instrument) are translated into SEK using the shifted spot exchange rate (8.459), then discounted back using the current SEK interest rate (1.3550%) for a cash flow due on 31 August 20X6. The SEK leg is discounted back using the current SEK interest rate. The difference between the present values of each leg represents the fair value of the spot component. As the fair value of this spot component is nil at inception, the change in fair value is equal to its fair value.

Hedged item Hypothetical derivative – spot component			Hedging instrument Spot component	
Notional amount	(25,000,000)	EUR	25,000,000	EUR Notional amount
Spot rate + 10%	8.4590		8.4590	Spot rate + 10%
Notional amount in SEK	(211,475,000)	SEK	211,475,000	SEK Notional amount in SEK
Discount factor*	0.9776		0.9776	Discount factor
FV of the EUR leg (spot) (A)	(206,729,957)	EUR	206,729,957	SEK FV of the EUR leg (spot) (A)
Spot component of notional	192,250,000	SEK	(192,250,000)	Spot component of notional
Discount factor	0.9776		0.9776	Discount factor
FV of SEK leg (spot) (B)	187,936,324	SEK	(187,936,324)	SEK FV of SEK leg (spot) (B)
(A-B) FV of the hypothetical derivative (spot)	**(18,793,632)**	**SEK**	**18,793,632**	**SEK (A-B) FV of the derivative (spot)**
Effectiveness	**-100%**			

* The discount factor has been derived from the annualised SEK interest rate on 1 January for cash flows on 31 August 20X6 and has been calculated as $1/(1.01355)^\wedge(607\text{days}/360)$.

Conclusion: the hedge is expected to be highly effective.

> **Helpful hint**
>
> As the critical terms of the forward perfectly match the critical terms of the forecast purchase, a quantitative test is not necessarily required. A qualitative test consisting of a comparison of the critical terms of the hedging instrument and the hedged item may be used as long as it is consistent with Company C's risk management policies.

2   Accounting entries on 1 January 20X5

No entry, as the fair value of the forward contract is nil, as shown below:

Derivative

Notional amount in EUR	25,000,000	EUR
Forward rate	7.7075	
Notional amount in SEK	192,687,500	SEK
Discount factor	0.9776	
FV of the EUR leg	188,364,007	SEK

Notional amount in SEK	(192,687,500) SEK
Discount factor	0.9776
FV of the SEK leg	(188,364,007) SEK
FV of the derivative	0 SEK

3 Retrospective effectiveness test on 30 June 20X5

IAS 39 requires the effectiveness of a hedging relationship to be assessed retrospectively as a minimum at each reporting date. Based on Company C's risk management policies, the effectiveness of the hedge is assessed using the dollar offset method on a cumulative basis.

The dollar offset method consists of comparing the effects of the change in spot EUR/SEK exchange rate (from 7.69 to 7.65) on the fair value of the spot component of the hedging instrument and the hypothetical derivative (hedged cash flows).

	Hedged item Hypothetical derivative – spot component			Hedging instrument Spot component	
Notional amount	(25,000,000)	EUR	25,000,000	EUR	Notional amount
Spot rate at test date	7.6500		7.6500		Spot rate at test date
Notional amount in SEK	(191,250,000)	SEK	191,250,000	SEK	Notional amount in SEK
Discount factor	0.9838		0.9838		Discount factor
FV of the EUR leg (spot) (A)	(188,155,087)	EUR	188,155,087	SEK	(1/(1.01385)^(427days/360)) FV of the EUR leg (spot) (A)
Spot comp of notional at inception	192,250,000	SEK	(192,250,000)		Spot comp of notional at inception
Discount factor	0.9838		0.9838		Discount factor
FV of SEK leg (spot) (B)	189,138,905	SEK	(189,138,905)	SEK	FV of SEK leg (spot) (B)
(A-B) FV of the derivative (spot)	983,818	SEK	(983,818)	SEK	(B-A) FV of the derivative (spot)
Effectiveness	-100%				

Conclusion: the hedge has been highly effective for the period ended 30 June 20X5.

> **Helpful hint**
>
> Ineffectiveness can arise from a number of causes, including changes in the date of the forecast transaction and changes in the credit risk or liquidity of the forward contract.

4   Accounting entries on 30 June 20X5

All the criteria for hedge accounting are met for the period ended 30 June 20X5. Cash flow hedge accounting can therefore be applied. The hedge is 100% effective; the change in the fair value of the spot component of the hedging instrument is, therefore, recognised in other comprehensive income. The full fair value of the hedging instrument includes the forward points. The change in the fair value of the forward points component is recognised in the income statement.

Derivative

Notional amount in EUR	25,000,000	EUR
Forward rate	7.6622	
Notional amount in SEK	191,554,154	SEK
Discount factor	0.9838	
FV of the EUR leg	188,454,319	SEK
Notional amount in SEK	(192,687,500)	SEK
Discount factor	0.9838	
FV of the SEK leg	(189,565,963)	SEK
FV of the derivative	**(1,111,644)**	**SEK**

The entry is as follows:

	Dr	Cr
Derivative (financial liability)		1,111,644
Cash flow hedge reserve (equity)	983,818	
Interest expense (income statement)	127,826	
Cash flow hedge – change in fair value of the forward contract		

> **Helpful hint**
>
> The forward points represent the interest rate differential between the currencies of the forward contract. It is common to recognise fair value movements on the forward points component as interest income or expense, although they could also be recognised as 'operating income and expense'.

5   Prospective effectiveness test on 30 June 20X5

The same method is used as at the inception of the hedge.

Hedged item Hypothetical derivative – spot component			**Hedging instrument** Spot component	
Notional amount	(25,000,000)	EUR	25,000,000	EUR Notional amount
Spot rate + 10%	8.4150		8.4150	Spot rate + 10%
Notional amount in SEK	(211,475,000)	SEK	210,375,000	SEK Notional amount in SEK
Discount factor	0.9838		0.9838	Discount factor
FV of the EUR leg (spot) (A)	(206,970,596)	EUR	206,970,596	SEK FV of the EUR leg (spot) (A)
Spot component of notional	191,250,000	SEK	(191,250,000)	Spot component of notional
Discount factor	0.9838		0.9838	Discount factor
FV of SEK leg (spot) (B)	188,155,087	SEK	(188,155,087)	SEK FV of SEK leg (spot) (B)
(A-B) FV of the hypothetical derivative (spot)	**(18,815,509)**	**SEK**	**18,815,509**	**SEK (A-B) FV of the derivative (spot)**
Effectiveness	-100%			

Conclusion: the hedge is expected to be highly effective.

6 Retrospective effectiveness test on 31 December 20X5

Change in timing of expected cash flow

In December 20X5, management decides to delay the start of production by two months, due to the late delivery of an essential machine. The production will now start in August 20X6, and the raw materials will be purchased in July. The invoice for the raw materials is expected to be paid on 31 October 20X6.

Annualised interest rates applicable for discounting a cash flow on 31 October 20X6 at various dates during the hedge are as follows:

	31/12/20X5	30 Jun 20X6	31 Jul 20X6	31 Aug 20X6
SEK interest rate	1.3920%	1.4060%	1.4420%	1.4030%

The dollar offset method consists of comparing the effects of the cumulative change in spot EUR/SEK exchange rate (from 7.69 to 7.75) on the fair value of the spot component of the hedging instrument and the hedged cash flow (hypothetical derivative). As the hedged cash flow has been delayed, it is discounted from the revised payment date. The payment date on the hedging instrument and the associated discount factor remain unchanged.

	Hedged item Hypothetical derivative – spot component		Hedging instrument Spot component		
Notional amount	(25,000,000)	EUR	25,000,000	EUR	Notional amount
Spot rate at test date	7.7500		7.7500		Spot rate at test date
Notional amount in SEK	(193,750,000)	SEK	193,750,000	SEK	Notional amount in SEK
Discount factor*	0.9884		0.9909		Discount factor**
FV of the EUR leg (spot) (A)	(191,501,389)	EUR	191,982,442	SEK	FV of the EUR leg (spot) (A)
Spot comp of notional at inception	192,250,000	SEK	(192,250,000)	SEK	Spot component of notional at inception
Discount factor*	0.9884		0.9909		Discount factor**
FV of SEK leg (spot) (B)	190,018,798	SEK	(190,496,126)	SEK	FV of SEK leg (spot) (B)
(A-B) FV of the derivative (spot)	**(1,482,591)**	**SEK**	**1,486,316**	**SEK**	**(A-B) FV of the derivative (spot)**
Effectiveness	**-100.25%**				

* Discount factor calculated based on changed timing of cash flows – $(1/(1.01392)^{\wedge}(304\text{days}/360))$.

** Discount factor calculated based on original timing of cash flows – $(1/(1.01367)^{\wedge}(243\text{days}/360))$.

Conclusion: the hedge has been highly effective for the period ended 31 December 20X5.

7 Accounting entries on 31 December 20X5

The full fair value of the hedging instrument is as follows:

Derivative

Notional amount in EUR	25,000,000	EUR
Forward rate	7.7574	
Notional amount in SEK	193,935,000	SEK
Discount factor	0.9909	
FV of the EUR leg	192,165,754	SEK
Notional amount in SEK	(192,687,500)	SEK
Discount factor	0.9909	
FV of the SEK leg	(190,929,635)	SEK
FV of the derivative	**1,236,119**	**SEK**

All the criteria for hedge accounting are met for the period ended 31 December 20X5. Cash flow hedge accounting can therefore be applied. The hedge is not, however, 100% effective and, therefore, the amount recognised in other comprehensive income is adjusted to the lesser of (a) the cumulative change in the fair value of the spot component of the hedging instrument, and (b) the cumulative change in the fair value of the spot component of the hypothetical derivative.

	Derivative (full fair value)	Hedging instrument (spot component)	Hedged item hypothetical derivative (spot component)	Effective portion	Ineffective portion
30 Jun 20X5	(1,111,644)	(983,818)	983,818	(983,818)	–
31/12/20X5	1,236,119	1,486,316	(1,482,591)	1,482,591	3,725
Change	2,347,763	2,470,134	(2,466,409)	2,466,409	3,725

The difference between the full fair value of the forward contract and the amount deferred in other comprehensive income is charged to the income statement. The portion relating to the forward points is recognised in 'interest expense' and the ineffectiveness (SEK 1,486,316 – SEK 1,482,591 = SEK 3,725) is recognised in 'other operating income and expense'.

> **Helpful hint**
>
> The forward points reflect an interest element and can therefore be included in interest income and expense. Alternatively all fair value movements in excess of the effective portion may be recognised in 'other operating income and expense'.

The entry is as follows:

	Dr	Cr
Derivative (financial asset)	2,347,763	
Cash flow hedge reserve (equity)		2,466,409
Interest expense (income statement)	122,371	
Other operating income and expense		3,725

Cash flow hedge – change in fair value of the forward contract

8 Prospective effectiveness test on 31 December 20X5

The same method is used as at the inception of the hedge.

Hedged item Hypothetical derivative – spot component				Hedging instrument Spot component
Notional amount	(25,000,000)	EUR	25,000,000	EUR Notional amount
Spot rate + 10%	8.5250		8.5250	Spot rate + 10%
Notional amount in SEK	(213,125,000)	SEK	213,125,000	SEK Notional amount in SEK
Discount factor	0.9884		0.9909	Discount factor
FV of the EUR leg (spot) (A)	(210,651,528)	EUR	211,180,686	SEK FV of the EUR leg (spot) (A)
Spot comp of notional at inception	193,750,000	SEK	(193,750,000)	SEK Spot component of notional
Discount factor	0.9884		0.9909	Discount factor**
FV of SEK leg (spot) (B)	191,501,389	SEK	(191,982,442)	SEK FV of SEK leg (spot) (B)
(A-B) FV of the derivative (spot)	**(19,150,139)**	**SEK**	**19,198,244**	**SEK (A-B) FV of the derivative (spot)**
Effectiveness	-100.25%			

Conclusion: the hedge is expected to be highly effective.

9   Retrospective effectiveness test on 30 June 20X6

The dollar offset method consists of comparing the effects of the change in spot EUR/SEK exchange rate (from 7.69 to 7.81) on the fair value of the spot component of the hedging instrument, and the hypothetical derivative (hedged cash flows). As the hedged cash flow has been delayed, it is discounted from the revised payment date. The payment date on the hedging instrument and the associated discount factor remain unchanged.

Hedged item Hypothetical derivative – spot component				Hedging instrument Spot component
Notional amount	(25,000,000)	EUR	25,000,000	EUR Notional amount
Spot rate at test date	7.8100		7.8100	Spot rate at test date
Notional amount in SEK	(195,250,000)	SEK	195,250,000	SEK Notional amount in SEK
Discount factor*	0.9952		0.9976	Discount factor**
FV of the EUR leg (spot) (A)	(194,320,802)	EUR	194,788,017	SEK FV of the EUR leg (spot) (A)

Spot comp of notional at inception	192,250,000	SEK	(192,250,000)	SEK Spot component of notional at inception
Discount factor	0.9952		0.9976	Discount factor
FV of SEK leg (spot) (B)	191,335,079	SEK	(191,795,116)	SEK FV of SEK leg (spot) (B)
(A-B) FV of the derivative (spot)	(2,985,723)	SEK	2,992,901	SEK (A-B) FV of the derivative (spot)
Effectiveness	-100.24%			

* Discount factor calculated based on changed timing of cash flows – (1/(1.014060)^(123days/360)).
** Discount factor calculated based on original timing of cash flows – (1/(1.01385)^(62days/360)).

Conclusion: the hedge has been highly effective for the period ended 30 June 20X6.

10 Accounting entries on 30 June 20X6

The full fair value of the hedging instrument is as follows:

Derivative

Notional amount in EUR	25,000,000	EUR
Forward rate	7.8118	
Notional amount in SEK	195,293,907	SEK
Discount factor	0.9976	
FV of the EUR leg	194,831,821	SEK
Notional amount in SEK	192,687,500	SEK
Discount factor	0.9976	
FV of the SEK leg	(192,231,581)	SEK
FV of the derivative	**2,601,240**	**SEK**

All the criteria for hedge accounting are met for the year ended 30 June 20X6. Cash flow hedge accounting can therefore be applied. The hedge is not however 100% effective; the amount recognised in other comprehensive income is, therefore, adjusted to the lesser of (a) the cumulative change in the fair value of the spot component of the hedging instrument, and (b) the cumulative change in the fair value of the spot component of the hypothetical derivative.

	Derivative (full fair value)	Hedging instrument (spot component)	Hedged item hypothetical derivative (spot component)	Effective portion	Ineffective portion
31/12/20X5	1,236,119	1,486,316	(1,482,591)	1,482,591	3,725
30 Jun 20X6	2,601,240	2,992,901	(2,985,723)	2,985,723	7,178
Change	1,365,121	1,506,585	(1,503,132)	1,503,132	3,453

The difference between the full fair value of the forward contract and the amount deferred in equity is charged to the income statement. The portion relating to the forward points is recognised in 'interest income' and the ineffectiveness is recognised in 'other operating income and expense'.

The entry is as follows:

	Dr	Cr
Derivative (financial asset)	1,365,121	
Cash flow hedge reserve (equity)		1,503,132
Interest expense (income statement)	141,464	
Other operating income and expense		3,453

Cash flow hedge – change in fair value of the forward contract

11 Prospective effectiveness test on 30 June 20X6

The same method is used as at the inception of the hedge.

Hedged item Hypothetical derivative – spot component			Hedging instrument Spot component		
Notional amount	(25,000,000)	EUR	25,000,000	EUR	Notional amount
Spot rate + 10%	8.5910		8.5910		Spot rate + 10%
Notional amount in SEK	(214,775,000)	SEK	214,775,000	SEK	Notional amount in SEK
Discount factor	0.9952		0.9976		Discount factor
FV of the EUR leg (spot) (A)	(213,752,882)	EUR	214,266,819	SEK	FV of the EUR leg (spot) (A)
Spot comp of notional at inception	195,250,000	SEK	(195,250,000)	SEK	Spot component of notional
Discount factor	0.9952		0.9976		Discount factor
FV of SEK leg (spot) (B)	191,335,079	SEK	(191,795,116)	SEK	FV of SEK leg (spot) (B)
(A-B) FV of the derivative (spot)	**(22,417,803)**	**SEK**	**22,471,703**	**SEK**	**(A-B) FV of the derivative (spot)**
Effectiveness	**-100.24%**				

Conclusion: the hedge is expected to be highly effective.

12 Retrospective effectiveness test on 31 July 20X6

The dollar offset method consists of comparing the effects of the change in spot EUR/SEK exchange rate (from 7.69 to 7.90) on the fair value of the spot component of the hedging instrument, and the hedged cash flows (hypothetical derivative). As the hedged cash flow has been delayed, it is discounted from the revised payment date. The payment date on the hedging instrument and the associated discount factor remain unchanged.

Hedged item Hypothetical derivative – spot component			Hedging instrument Spot component	
Notional amount	(25,000,000)	EUR	25,000,000	EUR Notional amount
Spot rate at test date	7.9000		7.9000	Spot rate at test date
Notional amount in SEK	(197,500,000)	SEK	197,500,000	SEK Notional amount in SEK
Discount factor*	0.9963		0.9988	Discount factor**
FV of the EUR leg (spot) (A)	(196,778,708)	EUR	197,259,676	SEK FV of the EUR leg (spot) (A)
Spot comp of notional at inception	192,250,000	SEK	(192,250,000)	SEK Spot component of notional
Discount factor	0.9963		0.9988	Discount factor
FV of SEK leg (spot) (B)	191,547,882	SEK	(192,016,064)	SEK FV of SEK leg (spot) (B)
(A-B) FV of the derivative (spot)	(5,230,826)	SEK	5,243,612	SEK (A-B) FV of the derivative (spot)
Effectiveness	-100.24%			

* Discount factor calculated based on changed timing of cash flows – (1/(1.01442)^(92days/360)).
** Discount factor calculated based on original timing of cash flows – (1/(1.01424^(31days/360)).

Conclusion: the hedge has been highly effective for the period ended 31 July 20X6.

Helpful hint

Although IAS 39 does not explicitly require it, an effectiveness test is performed when the hedged highly probable forecast transaction occurs in order to determine the amount to be reclassified into the carrying amount of the hedged item.

---

13   Accounting entries on 31 July 20X6

Recognition of the purchase

	Dr	Cr
Inventory	197,500,000	
Trade payable		197,500,000

Purchase of EUR 25m at spot rate of 7.90

As the trade payable is short-term and EUR interest rates are low, Company C has determined that the effect of discounting is not material. The trade payable is therefore recognised at its face value, as permitted in IAS 39.

Recognition of the change in the fair value of the derivative

The full fair value of the hedging instrument is as follows:

Derivative

Notional amount in EUR	25,000,000	EUR
Forward rate	7.9008	
Notional amount in SEK	197,520,232	SEK
Discount factor	0.99878	
FV of the EUR leg	197,279,883	SEK
Notional amount in SEK	(192,687,500)	SEK
Discount factor	0.99878	
FV of the SEK leg	(192,453,032)	SEK
FV of the derivative	**4,826,851**	**SEK**

All the criteria for hedge accounting are met as at 31 July 20X6. Cash flow hedge accounting can therefore be applied. The hedge is not however 100% effective; the amount recognised in other comprehensive income is, therefore, adjusted to the lesser of (a) the cumulative change in the fair value of the spot component of the hedging item, and (b) the cumulative change in the fair value of the spot component of the hypothetical derivative.

	Derivative (full fair value)	Hedging instrument (spot component)	Hedged item hypothetical derivative (spot component)	Effective portion	Ineffective portion
30 Jun 20X6	2,601,240	2,992,901	(2,985,723)	2,985,723	7,178
31 Jul 20X6	4,826,851	5,243,612	(5,230,826)	5,230,826	12,786
Change	2,225,611	2,250,711	(2,245,103)	2,245,103	5,608

The difference between the full fair value of the forward contract and the amount deferred in equity is charged to the income statement. The portion relating to the forward points is recognised in 'interest expense' and the ineffectiveness is recognised in 'other operating income and expense'.

The entry is as follows:

	Dr	Cr
Derivative (financial asset)	2,225,611	
Cash flow hedge reserve (equity)		2,245,103
Interest expense (income statement)	25,100	
Other operating income and expense		5,608

Cash flow hedge – change in fair value of the forward contract

Basis adjustment

Company C's accounting policy is that the gain on the hedging derivative is included in the carrying amount of the inventory acquired. The gain is reclassified to profit or loss when the inventory affects profit or loss (that is, on sale of the goods containing the hedged components or impairment of the inventory).

	DR	CR
Cash flow hedge reserve (equity)	5,230,826	
Inventory		5,230,826

Reclassification of gains recognised in equity into the carrying amount of the inventory acquired by Company C

Helpful hint

The 'basis adjustment' approach is not required. It can be used only if the hedged item is non-financial (for example, a forecast purchase of inventory) and only if its use is consistent with the Company's chosen accounting policy. If Company C's management had chosen not to adjust the carrying amount of the inventory acquired, the amount accumulated in the cash flow hedge reserve would have remained in equity until the inventory affects the income statement (for example, when it is sold or impaired).

---

14   Retrospective effectiveness test on 31 August 20X6

The spot EUR/SEK exchange rate is 8.15. Company C's management assesses the effectiveness of the hedge retrospectively. The same method is used as at 30 June 20X6. As required in Company C's risk management policies, the effectiveness test uses the dollar offset method on a cumulative basis.

Hedged item			**Hedging instrument**		
Hypothetical derivative – spot component			Spot component		
Notional amount	(25,000,000)	EUR	25,000,000	EUR	Notional amount
Spot rate at test date	8.1500		8.1500		Spot rate at test date
Notional amount in SEK	(203,750,000)	SEK	203,750,000	SEK	Notional amount in SEK

	0.9976		1.0000		
Discount factor	0.9976		1.0000		Discount factor
					$(1/(1.0403)^\wedge$ $(61\text{days}/360))$
FV of the EUR leg (spot) (A)	(203,269,558)	EUR	203,750,000	SEK	FV of the EUR leg (spot) (A)
Spot comp of notional at inception	192,250,000	SEK	(192,250,000)	SEK	Spot component of notional
Discount factor	0.9976		1.0000		Discount factor
FV of SEK leg (spot) (B)	191,796,675	SEK	(192,250,000)	SEK	FV of SEK leg (spot) (B)
(A-B) FV of the derivative (spot)	**(11,472,883)**	**SEK**	**11,500,000**	**SEK**	**(A-B) FV of the derivative (spot)**
Effectiveness	**-100.24%**				

Conclusion: the hedge has been highly effective for the period ended 31 August 20X6.

15   Accounting entries on 31 August 20X6

Translation of the trade payable at the spot rate

The trade payable is a monetary item denominated in a foreign currency that must be retranslated at the spot rate under IAS 21, with the resulting currency gain or loss recognised in profit or loss.

The calculation of the gain or loss is as follows:

Trade payable translated at 31 July at 7.90	197,500,000
Trade payable translated at 31 August at 8.15	203,750,000
Foreign exchange loss to be recognised in profit or loss	**6,250,000**

The accounting entry is as follows:

	Dr	Cr
Other operating income and expenses – foreign exchange loss	6,250,000	
Trade payable		6,250,000

To recognise the foreign exchange loss on retranslating the trade payable

All the criteria for hedge accounting are met as at 31 August 20X6. Cash flow hedge accounting can, therefore, be applied. The hedge is not however 100% effective; the amount recognised in other comprehensive income is therefore adjusted to the lesser of:

(a) the cumulative change in the fair value of the spot component of the hedging instrument less the basis adjustment recognised in the previous period; and

(b) the cumulative change in the fair value of the spot component of the hypothetical derivative (hedged item) less the basis adjustment recognised in the previous period.

	Derivative (full fair value)	Hedging instrument (spot component)	Hedged item hypothetical derivative (spot component)	Effective portion (recognised as basis adjustment)	Ineffective portion
31 Jul 20X6	4,826,851	5,243,612	(5,230,826)	5,230,826	12,786
31 Aug 20X6	11,062,500	11,500,000	(11,472,883)	11,472,883	27,117
Change	6,235,649	6,256,388	(6,242,057)	6,242,057	14,331

The difference between the full fair value of the forward contract and the amount deferred in equity is charged to the income statement.

The entry is as follows:

	Dr	Cr
Derivative (financial asset)	6,235,649	
Cash flow hedge reserve (equity)		6,242,057
Interest expense (income statement)	20,739	
Other operating income and expense		14,331

Cash flow hedge – change in fair value of the forward contract

Settlement of derivative

Under the terms of the forward contract, Company C receives EUR 25m (at 8.15 – SEK 203,750,000) and pays SEK 192,687,500. The difference is the fair value of the derivative (SEK 11,062,842).

The accounting entry is as follows:

	DR	CR
Cash in EUR	203,750,000	
Cash in SEK		192,687,500
Derivative (financial asset)	11,062,500	

Settlement of the derivative in cash

Reclassification of gains and losses from equity to profit or loss

The amount deferred in equity is recycled to the income statement

	DR	CR
Other operating income and expenses – foreign exchange gain		6,242,057
Cash flow hedge reserve (equity)	6,242,057	
Reclassification of gains recognised in equity to profit or loss		

Company C decides to keep the euro amount received in a euro account until payment of the invoice.

Helpful hint

Hedge accounting is not always necessary when a company is hedging the foreign currency risk arising from short-term monetary items such as foreign currency payables and receivables.

A similar result to that achieved under hedge accounting would have been achieved had Company C de-designated the hedge relationship when the purchase was recognised, as:

1　the derivative, not being designated as a hedging instrument, would have been measured at fair value through profit or loss; and

2　the receivable, which is a monetary item, would have been revalued using the spot exchange rate at the balance sheet date.

16　Accounting entries on 31 October 20X6

The trade payable and the euro bank account are revalued using the closing rate (8.05).

	Dr	Cr
Trade payable	2,500,000	
Other operating income and expenses – foreign exchange gain		2,500,000
Euro bank account		2,500,000
Other operating income and expenses – foreign exchange gain	2,500,000	
Revaluation of trade payable and bank account (both EUR 25m)		

Finally the trade payable is settled.

	Dr	Cr
Trade payable	201,250,000	
Euro bank account		201,250,000
Reclassification of gains recognised in equity to profit or loss		

Summary of accounting entries

| | | Balance sheet | | | Income statement | | |
	Derivative instrument	Equity	Payable	Inventory	Bank account (SEK and EUR)	Interest expense	Other operating income and expense – foreign exchange gains and losses
1 Jan 20X5 No entry							
30 Jun 20X5 CFH accounting	(1,111,644)	983,818				127,826	
31/12/20X5 CFH accounting	2,347,763	(2,466,409)				122,371	(3,725)
30 Jun 20X6 CFH accounting	1,365,121	(1,503,132)				141,464	(3,453)
31 Jul 20X6 Purchase of inventory			(197,500,000)	197,500,000			
CFH accounting	2,225,611	(2,245,103)				25,100	(5,608)
Basis adjustment		5,230,826		(5,230,826)			
31 Aug 20X6 Foreign currency reval. of payable			(6,250,000)				6,250,000
CFH accounting	6,235,649	(6,242,057)				20,739	(14,331)
Reclassification		6,242,057					(6,242,057)
Settlement of derivative	(11,062,500)				11,062,500		
31/10/20X6 Revaluation			2,500,000		(2,500,000)		
Settlement of payable			201,250,000		(201,250,000)		

Net investment hedge in a foreign operation

Background and assumptions

Company K, a Swiss company with a CHF functional currency, has an Italian subsidiary, Company D, whose functional currency is EUR. Company K's reporting dates for its consolidated financial statements are 30 June and 31 December. The group's presentation currency is CHF.

On 1 January 20x5, Company K issues a two-year floating rate debt with the following characteristics:

Type	Issued debt
Principal amount	EUR 100m
Start date	1 January 20X5
Maturity date	31 December 20X6
Interest rate	Six-month EURIBOR

Settlement dates   30 June 20X5, 31 December 20X5, 30 June 20X6, 31 December 20X6

No transaction costs are incurred relating to the debt issuance. K's management has chosen to issue euro-denominated debt to hedge K's net investment in Company D. It wishes to reduce the consolidated balance sheet volatility arising from EUR/CHF fluctuations by designating the debt as a hedge of the net investment. On 1 January 20X5, the net investment in Company D is EUR 100m. It is not expected to fall below EUR 100m, as Company D has been a profitable company for many years and its forecasts for the next two years, as approved by Company K's board of directors, show it continuing to make material profits.

Exchange rates on various dates during the hedge relationship are as follows:

> **Helpful hint**
>
> A net investment in a foreign operation is the amount of the reporting entity's interest in the net assets of the operation, including goodwill. If the entity is financed through an inter-company loan that will not be repaid in the foreseeable future (quasi-equity), this loan is included in the net investment.
>
> A hedge of a net investment is a hedge of an accounting exposure (that is, the variability in equity arising from translating the net investment at different exchange rates).

Average exchange rates for the six-month periods during the hedge are as follows:

	1 Jan 20X5	30 Jun 20X5	31 Dec 20X5	30 Jun 20X6	31 Dec 20X6
EUR/CHF spot rate	1.5000	1.5800	1.6000	1.6200	1.6500
EUR/CHF forward rate	1.5667	1.6343	1.6364	1.6383	1.6500
Forward points	**0.0667**	**0.0543**	**0.0364**	**0.0183**	**0.0000**

	30 Jun 20X5	31 Dec 20X5	30 Jun 20X6	31 Dec 20X6
EUR/CHF average rate	1.5400	1.5900	1.6100	1.6400

Annual interest rates on various dates during the hedge are as follows:

	1 Jan 20X5	30 Jun 20X5	31 Dec 20X5	30 Jun 20X6	31 Dec 20X6
CHF interest rate	3.5500%	3.6200%	3.6500%	3.5750%	3.6450%
EUR interest rate	1.3505%	1.3500%	1.3750%	1.3250%	1.3550%

For the purpose of this illustration, the yield curve (that is, interest rate) at each reporting period end is assumed to remain the same through the term of the hedge designation (that is, the yield curve is flat at all times). This simplification does not have any impact on the effectiveness test in this example, as the reset dates of the loan coincide with the effectiveness testing date. With a non-flat yield curve, the calculation of the fair value of the variable rate debt will still give a fair value equal to the face value, as the variable coupons will be at market rate.

Extracts of the risk management policies for foreign currency risk

Background to the group

The group is an international retailer operating around the world, particularly in Western Europe (Switzerland, Italy and the UK) and the US. The biggest subsidiary is based in Italy.

Foreign currency risk

The group's presentation currency is CHF. Foreign currency risk arises from transactions denominated in foreign currencies and net investments in foreign operations.

Investments in foreign operations (translation foreign currency risk)

A foreign currency exposure arises from net investments in group entities whose functional currency differs from the group's presentation currency (CHF). The risk is defined as the risk of fluctuation in spot exchange rates between the functional currency of the net investments and the group's presentation currency. This will cause the amount of the net investment to vary. Such a risk may have a significant impact on the group's financial statements.

This translation risk does not give rise to a cash flow exposure. Its impact arises only from the translation of the net investment into the group's presentation currency. This procedure is required in preparing the group's consolidated financial statements.

Hedging instruments

The group uses derivatives (such as forward contracts and purchased options) and cash instruments (non-derivatives such as foreign currency borrowings) to hedge foreign currency risk. All derivatives must be entered into with counterparties with a credit rating of AA or higher.

Extracts of hedge effectiveness testing policies

Strategy 2C: Hedge of a net investment for foreign currency risk with a debt instrument.

Prospective effectiveness testing for net investment hedges

Prospective effectiveness testing should be performed at the inception of the hedge and at each reporting date. For hedges where the hedging instrument is a cash instrument, the hedge relationship is highly effective if the foreign currency gains and losses on the hedged item (net investment) that are attributable to the hedged risk (changes in spot exchange rates) are expected to be offset by the foreign currency gains and losses on the hedging instrument (cash instrument).

Prospective effectiveness testing must be performed by comparing the numerical effects of an upward shift in the benchmark exchange rate (EUR/CHF spot exchange rate) on both the value of the hedging instrument and the value of the hedged item.

■ **The value of the hedging instrument:** when the hedging instrument is a cash instrument (for example, a debt instrument), this value is determined by discounting the future cash flows, including interest payments, on the debt and translating the result at the spot exchange rate. Accrued interest (if any) is excluded from the calculation.

■ **The value of the net investment being hedged:** this is determined by translating the amount of the net investment into the group's presentation currency using the spot exchange rate.

This test should normally be performed using at least three currency scenarios. However, for hedges where the critical terms of the hedging instrument perfectly match the critical terms of the hedged item, one scenario is sufficient.

Retrospective effectiveness testing for net investment hedges

Retrospective effectiveness testing should be performed at each reporting date using the dollar offset method on a cumulative basis. The hedge is demonstrated to be effective under this method by comparing the cumulative foreign currency gains and losses on the hedging instrument with the cumulative foreign currency gains and losses on the net investment being hedged, and showing that it falls within the required range of 80%-125%.

■ **Foreign currency gains and losses on the hedging instrument:** when the hedging instrument is a cash instrument (for example, a debt instrument), such foreign currency gains and losses are determined by discounting the future cash flows (using the current euro interest rate) on the debt and translating the result at the spot exchange rate. Accrued interest (if any) is excluded from the calculation.

■ **Foreign currency gains and losses on the net investment being hedged:** such gains and losses are determined by translating the amount of the net investment into the group's presentation currency using the spot exchange rate.

Hedge designation

Company K's hedge documentation is as follows:

1   Risk management objective and strategy

In order to comply with Company K's foreign currency risk management strategy, the foreign currency translation risk arising on the net investment in Company D is hedged.

2   Type of hedging relationship

Net investment hedge.

3   Nature of risk being hedged

In accordance with the group's risk management policies, the hedged risk is the risk of changes in the EUR/CHF spot exchange rate that will result in changes in the value of the group's net investment in Company D when translated into CHF. The risk is hedged from 1 January 20X5 to 31 December 20X7.

4   Identification of hedged item

The group's net investment in EUR in Company D on 1 January 20x5 is EUR 100m. EUR 100m of the net investment is designated as the hedged item.

(5)   Identification of hedging instrument

Transaction number: reference number G0901Z in the treasury management system.

The hedging instrument is a two-year floating rate debt with the following characteristics:

Type	Issued debt
Principal amount	EUR 100m
Start date	1 January 20X5
Maturity date	31 December 20X6
Interest rate	Six-month EURIBOR
Settlement dates	30 June 20X5, 31 December 20X5, 30 June 20X6, 31 December 20X6

Hedge designation: the foreign currency exposure of debt G0901Z is designated as a hedge of the change in the value of the net investment identified in 4 above that is attributable to movements in the CHF/EUR spot rate.

6   Effectiveness testing

Effectiveness testing strategy 2C will be applied.

Description of prospective effectiveness testing

Dollar offset method, being the comparison of the numerical effects of a shift in the benchmark exchange rate (EUR/CHF spot exchange rate) on both the value of the hedging instrument and the value of the hedged item.

As permitted in the risk management policies, one scenario is used for assessing prospectively the effectiveness of the hedge relationship (a 10% upward shift of the EUR/CHF spot exchange rate), as the critical terms of the hedging instrument perfectly match the critical terms of the hedged item.

Frequency of testing: at inception of the hedge and then at each reporting date (30 June and 31 December).

Description of retrospective effectiveness testing

Dollar offset method, being the ratio of the cumulative foreign currency gains and losses on the debt (G0901Z), divided by the foreign currency gains and losses on the net investment being hedged.

Foreign currency gains and losses on the debt are the change in the present value of cash flows of the debt (interest and principal repayment) attributable to change in the EUR/CHF spot exchange rate.

Foreign currency gains and losses on the net investment being hedged are the change in the value of the net investment being hedged using the EUR/CHF spot exchange rate.

Frequency of testing: at every reporting date (30 June and 31 December) after inception of the hedge.

Effectiveness tests and accounting entries

1   Prospective effectiveness test on 1 January 20X5

At inception of the hedge, the forward EUR/CHF exchange rate is 1.5667 and the six-month EURIBOR is at 1.3505%. On that date, the spot EUR/CHF exchange rate is 1.5000.

Company K's management assesses the effectiveness of the hedge prospectively, as required by IAS 39. Based on the hedge documentation, the prospective effectiveness test consists of comparing the effects of a 10% shift of the EUR/CHF spot exchange rate on the net investment and the debt instrument.

Prospective effectiveness test on 1 January 20X5

	30 Jun 20X5	31 Dec 20X5	30 Jun 20X6	31 Dec 20X6	Total
Cash flows on the debt					
Expected cash flows at 1.3505% (EUR)	(675,250)	(675,250)	(675,250)	(100,675,250)	
Discount factor	0.99332	0.98653	0.97990	0.97344	
Discounted cash flows (EUR)	(670,736)	(666,153)	(661,675)	(98,001,436)	
EUR/CHF spot exchange rate	1.5000	1.5000	1.5000	1.5000	

Discounted cash flows (CHF)	**(1,006,104)**	**(999,229)**	**(992,513)**	**(147,002,154)**	**(150,000,000)**
Expected cash flows at 1.3505% (EUR)	(675,250)	(675,250)	(675,250)	(100,675,250)	
Discount factor	0.99332	0.98653	0.97990	0.97344	
Discounted cash flows (EUR)	(670,736)	(666,153)	(661,675)	(98,001,436)	
10% shift in EUR/CHF spot exchange rate	1.6500	1.6500	1.6500	1.6500	
Discounted cash flows (CHF)	**(1,106,714)**	**(1,099,152)**	**(1,091,764)**	**(161,702,370)**	**(165,000,000)**
				Change	**(15,000,000)**

Net investment		
Net investment in EUR	100,000,000	
EUR/CHF spot exchange rate	1.5000	
Net investment in CHF	150,000,000	**150,000,000**
Net investment in EUR	100,000,000	
10% shift in EUR/CHF spot exchange rate	1.6500	
Net investment in CHF	165,000,000	**165,000,000**
	Change	**15,000,000**
	Effectiveness	**100%**

Conclusion: the hedge is expected to be highly effective.

2 Entries on 1 January 20X5

The debt is recognised at the proceeds received by Company K, which represents its fair value on the issuance date. The debt is classified as other financial liabilities and will subsequently be measured at amortised cost.

	Dr	Cr
Cash	100,000,000	
Other financial liabilities – debt		100,000,000

Issuance at par of a EUR 100m two-year debt

3 Retrospective effectiveness test on 30 June 20X5

IAS 39 requires the effectiveness of a hedging relationship to be assessed retrospectively as a minimum at each reporting date. Based on Company K's risk management policies, the effectiveness of the hedge is assessed using the dollar offset method. The dollar offset method consists of comparing the effects of the change in EUR/CHF spot exchange rate on the hedged item (net investment) and the hedging instrument (cash instrument).

Retrospective effectiveness test on 30 June 20X5

	30 Jun 20X5	31 Dec 20X5	30 Jun 20X6	31 Dec 20X6	Total
Cash flows on the debt					
Expected cash flows at 1.3505% (EUR)	(675,250)	(675,250)	(675,250)	(100,675,250)	
Discount factor	0.99332	0.98653	0.97990	0.97344	
Discounted cash flows (EUR)	(670,736)	(666,153)	(661,675)	(98,001,436)	
EUR/CHF spot exchange rate at inception	1.5000	1.5000	1.5000	1.5000	
Discounted cash flows (CHF)	(1,006,104)	(999,229)	(992,513)	(147,002,154)	**(150,000,000)**
Expected cash flows at 1.3500% (EUR)		(675,000)	(675,000)	(100,675,000)	
Discount factor		0.99317	0.98650	0.98002	
Discounted cash flows (EUR)		(670,389)	(665,885)	(98,663,726)	
EUR/CHF spot exchange rate at testing date		1.5800	1.5800	1.5800	
Discounted cash flows (CHF)		(1,059,215)	(1,052,098)	(155,888,687)	**(158,000,000)**
				Change	**(8,000,000)**

Net investment

Net investment in EUR	100,000,000	
EUR/CHF spot exchange rate at inception	1.5000	
Net investment in CHF at inception	150,000,000	**150,000,000**
Net investment in EUR	100,000,000	
EUR/CHF spot exchange rate at testing date	1.5800	
Net investment in CHF at testing date	158,000,000	**158,000,000**
	Change	**8,000,000**
	Effectiveness	**100%**

Conclusion: the hedge has been highly effective for the period ended 30 June 20X5.

> **Helpful hint**
>
> In practice, both the prospective and retrospective effectiveness tests may be performed by:
>
> 1 translating the principal amount of the debt into CHF using the relevant EUR/CHF spot exchange rates (for the retrospective test, the rates at the beginning and end of the period); and
>
> 2 comparing the difference with the foreign currency gains and losses on the net investment.
>
> This 'short cut' gives the same results, as shown below.
>
> | | |
> |---|---|
> | Principal amount of the debt (in EUR) | EUR 100,000,000 |
> | EUR/CHF spot exchange rate at inception | 1.5000 |
> | | CHF 150,000,000 |
> | Principal amount of the debt (in EUR) | EUR 100,000,000 |
> | EUR/CHF spot exchange rate at testing date | 1.5800 |
> | | CHF 158,000,000 |
> | **Difference (+gain/-loss):** | **CHF (8,000,000)** |
> | Foreign currency gain on the net investment (see table above) | **CHF 8,000,000** |
> | **Effectiveness** | **100%** |

10161

3   Accounting entries on 30 June 20X5

Recognition of interest on the debt

Interest for the first six months (EUR 675,000) is paid on 30 June. The payment is translated using the spot rate on 30 June. The interest expense is translated at the average rate for the six month period as interest accrues over time. The difference in translation rates gives rise to a loss that is recorded as 'other operating income and expense'.

	Dr	Cr
Finance costs – interest expense	1,039,500	
Other operating income and expense	27,000	
Cash		1,066,500

Payment of interest on the debt at 1.35% for six months

Net investment hedge accounting

As the hedge has been fully effective for the period, the entire foreign currency loss on the debt is recognised in other comprehensive income, and there is no ineffectiveness to recognise in profit or loss.

	Dr	Cr
Translation reserve (equity)	8,000,000	
Debt instrument		8,000,000

Net investment hedge

> **Helpful hint**
>
> A gain of CHF 8 million will also be recognised in the translation reserve from the translation of the hedged net investment in the Italian subsidiary. As a result, the net change in the translation reserve for the six months ended 30 June 20X5 is nil.

4   Prospective effectiveness test on 30 June 20X5

The same method is used as at the inception of the hedge.

Prospective effectiveness test on 30 June 20X5

	30 Jun 20X5	31 Dec 20X5	30 Jun 20X6	31 Dec 20X6	Total
Cash flows on the debt					
Expected cash flows at 1.3505% (EUR)	(675,250)	(675,250)	(675,250)	(100,675,250)	
Discount factor	0.99332	0.98653	0.97990	0.97344	
Discounted cash flows (EUR)	(670,736)	(666,153)	(661,675)	(98,001,436)	

EUR/CHF spot exchange rate	1.5800	1.5800	1.5800	1.5800	
Discounted cash flows (CHF)	(1,059,763)	(1,052,522)	(1,045,447)	(154,842,269)	**(158,000,000)**
Expected cash flows at 1.3500% (EUR)		(675,000)	(675,000)	(100,675,000)	
Discount factor		0.99317	0.98650	0.98002	
Discounted cash flows (EUR)		(670,389)	(665,885)	(98,663,726)	
10% shift in EUR/ CHF spot exchange rate		1.7380	1.7380	1.7380	
Discounted cash flows (CHF)		(1,165,137)	(1,157,308)	(171,477,556)	**(173,800,000)**
				Change	**(15,800,000)**

Net investment		
Net investment in EUR	100,000,000	
EUR/CHF spot exchange rate	1.5800	
Net investment in CHF	158,000,000	**158,000,000**
Net investment in EUR	100,000,000	
10% shift in EUR/ CHF spot exchange rate	1.7380	
Net investment in CHF	173,800,000	**173,800,000**
	Change	**15,800,000**
	Effectiveness	**100%**

Conclusion: the hedge is expected to be highly effective.

5 Retrospective effectiveness test on 31 December 20X5

The forward EUR/CHF exchange rate is 1.6364 and the six-month EURIBOR is at 1.3750%. On that date, the spot EUR/CHF exchange rate is 1.6000. The method used is the same as at 1 January 20X5.

Retrospective effectiveness test on 31 December 20X5

	30 Jun 20X5	31 Dec 20X5	30 Jun 20X6	31 Dec 20X6	Total
Cash flows on the debt					
Expected cash flows at 1.3505% (EUR)	(675,250)	(675,250)	(675,250)	(100,675,250)	
Discount factor	0.99332	0.98653	0.97990	0.97344	
Discounted cash flows (EUR)	(670,736)	(666,153)	(661,675)	(98,001,436)	
EUR/CHF spot exchange rate at inception	1.5000	1.5000	1.5000	1.5000	
Discounted cash flows clean (CHF)	(1,006,104)	(999,229)	(992,513)	(147,002,154)	**(150,000,000)**
Expected cash flows at 1.3750%			(687,500)	(100,687,500)	
Discount factor			0.99316	0.98639	
Discounted cash flows (EUR)			(682,796)	(99,317,205)	
EUR/CHF spot exchange rate at testing date			1.6000	1.6000	
Discounted cash flows clean (CHF)			(1,092,473)	(158,907,527)	**(160,000,000)**
				Change	**(10,000,000)**
Net investment					
Net investment in EUR				100,000,000	
EUR/CHF spot exchange rate at inception				1.5000	
Net investment in CHF at inception				150,000,000	**150,000,000**
Net investment in EUR				100,000,000	
EUR/CHF spot exchange rate at testing date				1.6000	
Net investment in CHF at testing date				160,000,000	**160,000,000**
				Change	**10,000,000**
				Effectiveness	**100%**

Conclusion: the hedge has been highly effective for the period ended 31 December 20X5.

6 Accounting entries on 31 December 20X5

Recognition of interest on the debt

Interest for six months (EUR 687,500) is paid on 31 December. The payment is translated using the spot rate on 31 December. The interest expense is translated at the average rate for the six-month period as interest accrues over time. The difference in translation rates gives rise to a loss that is recorded as 'other operating income and expense'.

	Dr	Cr
Finance costs – interest expense	1,093,125	
Other operating income and expense	6,875	
Cash		1,100,000

Payment of interest on the debt at 1.375% for six months

Net investment hedge accounting

As the hedge has been fully effective for the period, the entire foreign exchange loss on the debt is recognised in other comprehensive income and there is no ineffectiveness to recognise in profit or loss.

	Dr	Cr
Translation reserve (equity)	2,000,000	
Debt instrument		2,000,000

Net investment hedge

Cumulative foreign exchange loss on the debt on 31 December 20X5	(10,000,000)
Cumulative foreign exchange loss on the debt on 30 June 20X5	(8,000,000)
Foreign exchange loss to be recognised in translation reserve	**(2,000,000)**

7 Prospective effectiveness test on 31 December 20X5

The same method is used as at the inception of the hedge.

Prospective effectiveness test on 31 December 20X5

	30 Jun 20X5	31 Dec 20X5	30 Jun 20X6	31 Dec 20X6	Total
Cash flows on the debt					
Expected cash flows at 1.3505% (EUR)	(675,250)	(675,250)	(675,250)	(100,675,250)	
Discount factor	0.99332	0.98653	0.97990	0.97344	
Discounted cash flows (EUR)	(670,736)	(666,153)	(661,675)	(98,001,436)	
EUR/CHF spot exchange rate	1.6000	1.6000	1.6000	1.6000	
Discounted cash flows (CHF)	(1,073,178)	(1,065,845)	(1,058,680)	(156,802,298)	**(160,000,000)**
Expected cash flows at 1.3750% (EUR)			(687,500)	(100,687,500)	
Discount factor			0.99316	0.98639	
Discounted cash flows (EUR)			(682,796)	(99,317,205)	
10% shift in EUR/CHF spot exchange rate			1.7600	1.7600	
Discounted cash flows (CHF)			(1,201,720)	(174,798,280)	**(176,000,000)**
				Change	**(16,000,000)**
Net investment					
Net investment in EUR				100,000,000	
EUR/CHF spot exchange rate				1.6000	
Net investment in CHF				160,000,000	**160,000,000**
Net investment in EUR				100,000,000	
10% shift in EUR/CHF spot exchange rate				1.7600	
Net investment in CHF				176,000,000	**176,000,000**
				Change	**16,000,000**
				Effectiveness	**100%**

Conclusion: the hedge is expected to be highly effective.

8 Retrospective effectiveness test on 30 June 20X6

On 30 June 20X6, Company K's net investment has decreased to EUR 98.5m because Company D made unexpected losses. The spot EUR/CHF exchange rate on 30 June 20X6 is 1.6200 and the six-month EURIBOR is 1.3250%. Effectiveness is tested using the same method as is described on 31 December 20X5.

Retrospective effectiveness test on 30 June 20X6

Cash flows on the debt	30 Jun 20X5	31 Dec 20X5	30 Jun 20X6	31 Dec 20X6	Total
Expected cash flows at 1.3505% (EUR)	(675,250)	(675,250)	(675,250)	(100,675,250)	
Discount factor	0.99332	0.98653	0.97990	0.97344	
Discounted cash flows (EUR)	(670,736)	(666,153)	(661,675)	(98,001,436)	
EUR/CHF spot exchange rate at inception	1.5000	1.5000	1.5000	1.5000	
Discounted cash flows clean (CHF)	(1,006,104)	(999,229)	(992,513)	(147,002,154)	**(150,000,000)**
Expected cash flows at 1.3250%				(100,662,500)	
Discount factor				0.99342	
Discounted cash flows (EUR)				(100,000,000)	
EUR/CHF spot exchange rate at testing date				1.6200	
Discounted cash flows clean (CHF)				(162,000,000)	**(162,000,000)**
				Change	**(12,000,000)**
Net investment					
Net investment in EUR				98,500,000	
EUR/CHF spot exchange rate at inception				1.5000	
Net investment in CHF at inception				147,750,000	**147,750,000**
Net investment in EUR				98,500,000	
EUR/CHF spot exchange rate at testing date				1.6200	

Net investment in CHF	159,570,000	**159,570,000**
	Change	**11,820,000**
	Effectiveness	**101.5%**

As illustrated above, the hedge is no longer fully effective because the carrying value of the hedged net investment is lower than the principal amount of the hedging debt instrument. However, the hedge remains highly effective.

Conclusion: the hedge has been highly effective for the period ended 30 June 20X6.

9   Accounting entries on 30 June 20X6

Recognition of interest on the debt

Interest for six months (EUR 662,500) is paid on 30 June. The payment is translated using the spot rate on 30 June. The interest expense is translated at the average rate for the six month period as interest accrues over time. The difference in translation rates gives rise to a loss that is recorded as 'other operating income and expense'.

	Dr	Cr
Finance costs – interest expense	1,066,625	
Other operating income and expense	6,625	
Cash		1,073,250

Payment of interest on the debt at 1.325% for six months

Net investment hedge accounting

As the hedge has not been fully effective for the period, ineffectiveness must be recognised in profit or loss.

Cumulative foreign exchange loss on the debt on 30 June 20X6	(12,000,000)
Cumulative foreign exchange loss on the debt on 31 December 20X5	(10,000,000)
Foreign exchange loss on the debt for the period (A)	**(2,000,000)**
Translation reserve balance on 30 June 20X6	11,820,000
Translation reserve balance on 31 December 20X5	10,000,000
Difference (B)	**1,820,000**

As the change in the hedging instrument (the debt) is greater than the change in the hedged item (the net investment), it is not fully absorbed by the hedged item.

The difference must therefore be recognised in the income statement as ineffectiveness.

	Dr	Cr
Other operating income and expense (A + B)	180,000	
Translation reserve (equity)	1,820,000	
Debt instrument		2,000,000

Net investment hedge

10 Prospective effectiveness test on 30 June 20X6

The same method is used as at the inception of the hedge. In addition, Company K's management does not expect its Italian subsidiary to make further losses for the remaining life of the hedge (until 31 December 20X6).

Prospective effectiveness test on 30 June 20X6

	30 Jun 20X5	31 Dec 20X5	30 Jun 20X6	31 Dec 20X6	Total
Cash flows on the debt					
Expected cash flows at 1.3505% (EUR)	(675,250)	(675,250)	(675,250)	(100,675,250)	
Discount factor	0.99332	0.98653	0.97990	0.97344	
Discounted cash flows (EUR)	(670,736)	(666,153)	(661,675)	(98,001,436)	
EUR/CHF spot exchange rate	1.6200	1.6200	1.6200	1.6200	
Discounted cash flows (CHF)	(1,086,592)	(1,079,168)	(1,071,914)	(158,762,326)	**(162,000,000)**
Expected cash flows at 1.3250% (EUR)				(100,662,500)	
Discount factor				0.99342	
Discounted cash flows (EUR)				(100,000,000)	
10% shift in EUR/CHF spot exchange rate				1.7820	
Discounted cash flows (CHF)				(178,200,000)	**(178,200,000)**
				Change	**(16,200,000)**
Net investment					
Net investment in EUR				98,500,000	
EUR/CHF spot exchange rate				1.6200	
Net investment in CHF				159,570,000	**159,570,000**

Net investment in EUR	98,500,000	
10% shift in EUR/ CHF spot exchange rate	1.7820	
Net investment in CHF	175,527,000	**175,527,000**
	Change	**15,957,000**
	Effectiveness	**101.5%**

Conclusion: the hedge is expected to be highly effective, although some ineffectiveness is expected because the carrying value of the hedged net investment is smaller than the principal amount of the hedging debt instrument.

> **Helpful hint**
>
> This ineffectiveness could be avoided by re-designating the hedge, so that the hedging instrument is designated as 98.5% of the debt instrument (that is, an amount that matches the reduced net investment). In this example, in which the losses are relatively small, such re-designation would make no difference to the accounting entries, as the hedge remains highly effective. However, had the losses been so big as to cause the hedge to fail the effectiveness test, re-designating the hedge in this way may allow the company to apply hedge accounting for future periods.

> **Helpful hint**
>
> What will happen if the hedged net investment is sold? If Company D is sold or otherwise disposed of, the hedging gains or losses on the debt previously accumulated in the translation reserve (equity) will be transferred to profit or loss as part of the gain or loss on disposal.

Summary of accounting entities

	Balance sheet		Income statement		
				Other	
			Translation	operating	
			reserve	income &	
	Debt instrument	Cash	(equity)	expense	Finance cost
01 Jan 20X5					
Recognition of the debt	(100,000,000)	100,000,000			
30 Jun 20X5					
Interest on the debt		(1,066,500)		27,000	1,039,500
Debt re-translation	(8,000,000)		8,000,000		
31 Dec 20X5					
Interest on the debt		(1,100,000)		6,875	1,093,125
Debt re-translation	(2,000,000)		2,000,000		
30 Jun 20X6					
Interest on the debt		(1,073,250)		6,625	1,066,625
Debt re-translation	(2,000,000)		1,820,000	180,000	

Chapter 11

Presentation and disclosure

Chapter 11

Presentation and disclosure

Presentation of financial instruments

11.1   The principles for presenting financial and other assets and liabilities, and any related income and expense, are set out in IAS 1, 'Presentation of financial statements'. This standard's requirements are considered in chapter 4 of the Manual of Accounting – IFRS. The paragraphs that follow consider only the presentation of financial assets and liabilities as current or non-current.

Presentation as current or non-current

11.2   IAS 1 states that an entity should present current and non-current assets, and current and non-current liabilities, as separate classifications on the face of the balance sheet, except when a presentation based on liquidity provides information that is reliable and is more relevant. When that exception applies, all assets and liabilities should be presented broadly in order of liquidity. [IAS 1 para 60].

Current and non-current assets

11.3   Where an entity presents assets and liabilities as either current or non-current, it should classify an asset as current when:

- it expects to realise the asset, or intends to sell or consume it in its normal operating cycle;

- it holds the asset primarily for the purpose of trading;

- it expects to realise the asset within 12 months after the reporting period; or

- the asset is cash or a cash equivalent (as defined in IAS 7, 'Cash flow statements'), unless it is restricted from being exchanged or used to settle a liability for at least 12 months after the reporting period.

[IAS 1 para 66].

11.4   Applying the above definition, it could be argued that financial assets classified as held for trading should be presented as current assets. [IAS 1 para 65]. Similarly, trading derivative assets should also be presented as current assets.

11.4.1   IAS 1 sets out the requirements for the presentation of an asset or a liability as current or non-current in the balance sheet and paragraph 56 specifically states that the presentation should be in such a format that it provides useful information about the liquidity and solvency of an entity.

11.4.2 Paragraph 68 of IAS 1 clarifies that some rather than all financial assets and liabilities classified as held for trading in accordance with IAS 39 are examples of current assets and liabilities respectively. Non-hedging derivatives are not required to be classified as current simply because they fall within the 'held for trading' category in IAS 39. Rather, the requirements of IAS 1 referred to above should be applied in determining classification. This means that financial assets, including portions of financial assets expected to be realised within 12 months of the balance sheet date, should only be presented as current assets if realisation within 12 months is expected. Otherwise they should be classified as non-current. Financial liabilities should be presented as current if they meet the criteria in paragraph 11.6.

11.4.3 The treatment of hedging derivatives will be similar. Where a portion of a financial asset is expected to be realised within 12 months of the balance sheet date, that portion should be presented as a current asset; the remainder of the financial asset should be shown as a non-current asset. This suggests that hedging derivatives should be split into current and non-current portions. However, as an alternative, the full fair value of hedging derivatives could be classified as current if the hedge relationships are for less than 12 months and as non-current if those relationships are for more than 12 months.

[The next paragraph is 11.6.]

Current and non-current liabilities

11.6 Where an entity presents assets and liabilities as either current or non-current, the entity should classify a liability as current when:

■　it expects to settle the liability in its normal operating cycle;

■　it holds the liability primarily for the purpose of trading;

■　the liability is due to be settled within twelve months after the reporting period; or

■　the entity does not have an unconditional right to defer settlement of the liability for at least twelve months after the reporting period.

[IAS 1 para 68].

11.6.1 Under IAS 32, the equity and liability components of financial instruments must be classified separately as financial liabilities, financial assets or equity instruments. [IAS 32 para 28]. The liability component of financial instruments should be classified as current or non-current, depending on the terms of the contract. Similar to financial assets, where a portion of a financial liability (including a hedging derivative) is expected to be settled within 12 months of the balance sheet date, or settlement cannot be deferred for at least 12 months after the balance sheet date, that portion should be presented as a current liability; the remainder should be presented as a non-current liability.

11.6.2   The question arises whether the liability component of a convertible financial instrument should be presented as current or non-current, when the instrument is convertible to equity at any time within the next 12 months, but if not converted, is repayable in cash only beyond 12 months. Such instruments would have an equity component, being the holders' right to convert the instrument into a fixed number of equity instruments of the issuer any time before the maturity date; and a liability component, being the entity's obligation to deliver cash to holders at the maturity date, which is more than one year after the balance sheet date.

11.6.3   The 2009 annual improvements clarified that conversion features that are at the holder's discretion do not impact the classification of the liability component of a convertible instrument. [IAS 1 para 69 (d)]. The liability component of the convertible debt should be classified as non-current when repayable in more than 12 months and the components of an instrument that are classified as equity should be ignored. In the case of a convertible instrument, ignoring the conversion option leaves a debt component that is not re-payable within 12 months. Ignoring any equity components when classifying the liability component reflects that the equity components are not part of the liability for accounting purposes. Any equity components are accounted for in the same way as if they had been issued as separate instruments. It follows that the presentation should be the same as if they had been issued as separate instruments.

11.6.4   In contrast, consider puttable debt that is puttable by the holder within the next 12 months but, if not put, is repayable only beyond 12 months. In this case, the puttable debt should be classified in its entirety as current, irrespective of whether IAS 39 requires the put option to be accounted for as a separated embedded derivative and, if it does, of whether the host debt contract is reported in a separate balance sheet line item from the embedded derivative. This reflects that the put option could cause the entire instrument to be settled in a manner that is regarded as a liability under IAS 32.

11.7   The presentation of financial liabilities as current or non-current would take account of similar considerations to financial assets (see para 11.4 above). However, IAS 1 provides additional guidance for financial liabilities that have been renegotiated or refinanced. Specifically, the standard requires that a financial liability should be presented as current when it is due to be settled within 12 months after the balance sheet date, even if:

- the original term was for a period longer than 12 months; and

- an agreement to refinance, or to reschedule payments, on a long-term basis is completed after the balance sheet date and before the financial statements are authorised for issue.

[IAS 1 para 72].

11.8   The current or non-current classification of financial liabilities is governed by the condition of those liabilities at the balance sheet date. Where rescheduling or refinancing is at the lender's discretion, and it occurs after the balance sheet date, it does not alter the liability's condition at that date. Accordingly, it is regarded as a non-adjusting post balance sheet event and it is not taken into account in determining the current/non-current classification of the debt. On the other hand where the refinancing or rescheduling is at the entity's discretion and the entity can elect to roll over an obligation for at least one year after the balance sheet date, the obligation must be classified as non-current, even if it would otherwise be due within a shorter period. However, if the entity expects to settle the obligation within 12 months, despite having the discretion to refinance for a longer period, then the debt should be classified as current. [IAS 1 para 73].

Example – rolling over bank facilities

A company has entered into a facility arrangement with a bank. It has a committed facility that the bank cannot cancel unilaterally and the scheduled maturity of this facility is 3 years from the balance sheet date. The company has drawn down funds on this facility and these funds are due to be repaid 6 months after the balance sheet date. The company intends to roll over this debt through the three year facility arrangement. How should this borrowing be shown in the company's balance sheet?

Would the answer be different if the facility and existing loan were with different banks?

The borrowing should be shown as non-current. Although the loan is due for repayment within six months of the balance sheet date, the company is entitled to 'rollover' this borrowing into a 'new loan'. The substance is, therefore, that the debt is not repayable until 3 years after the balance sheet date when the committed facility expires. In addition, the entity expects to rollover the debt, so does not expect to repay it within 12 months.

The position would be different if the facility was with a different bank or if the loan was in the form of commercial paper. In the first case, the company would have a loan repayable in six months, but would be entitled to take out a new loan to settle its existing debt. These two loans are separate and the new loan is not, either in substance or in fact, an extension of the existing. Similarly if the loan was in the form of commercial paper, which typically has a maturity of 90 to 180 days, it would be classified as a current liability as it is likely that the back up facility would be provided by a different bank.

11.9 It is common practice for financial institutions to include borrowing covenants in the terms of loans. Under these borrowing covenants a loan which would otherwise be long-term in nature becomes immediately repayable if certain items related to the borrower's financial condition are breached. Typically, these items are measures of liquidity or solvency based on ratios derived from the entity's financial statements. Where the borrower has breached the borrowing covenant by the balance sheet date, or ends less than 12 months from the balance sheet date but the lender agrees, after the balance sheet date but before authorisation of the financial statements, not to require immediate repayment of the loan, the agreement of the lender is regarded as a non-adjusting post balance sheet event. Since, at the year end, the agreement of the lender had not been obtained, the condition of the borrowing at the balance sheet date was that it was immediately repayable and should, therefore, be shown as a current liability. [IAS 1 para 74]. An example of disclosure of a breach of covenant disclosed in an interim report and events subsequent to the interim reporting date is given in Table 11.1.

Table 11.1 – Breach of covenant resulting in loans restated as current at period end, post the balance sheet refinancing

First Technology plc – Interim report – 31 October 2005

14. Bank overdrafts and loans

	Six months ended 31st October 2005	Six months ended 31st October 2004	Year ended 30th April 2005
	£'m	£'m	£'m
Bank overdrafts	0.3	2.8	1.0
Bank loans	112.4	111.4	105.3
	112.7	114.2	106.3
Repayable:			
On demand or within one year	112.7	7.9	6.2
In the second year	–	48.9	47.0
In the third year	–	8.1	7.8
In the forth year	–	8.1	7.8
In the fifth year	–	41.2	37.5
	112.7	114.2	106.3
Less: Amount due for settlement within 12 months (shown under current liabilities)	(112.7)	(7.9)	(6.2)
Amounts due for settlement after more than 12 months	–	106.3	100.1

The Group's principal source of debt at 31st October 2005 was a multi-currency syndicated bank loan ('the Facilities') entered into with a group of seven banks in May 2004 in connection with the Group's offer for BWT. The Facilities comprised three tranches: a US$75 million revolving credit facility; a term loan of up to US$75 million and a US$100 million revolving credit facility. The Facilities were repayable between May 2006 and May 2009. The Facilities were unsecured and initially carried interest at a margin of 1.5% over LIBOR (or EURIBOR for amounts advanced in Euros), plus mandatory costs. The applicable margin was variable (ranging from a minimum of 0.875% up to a maximum of 1.75%) according to the ratio of consolidated net borrowings to EBITDA.

The Facilities were subject to three financial covenants, which were tested quarterly. On 17th August 2005, First Technology PLC informed its bankers that it had failed to meet one of these covenants with respect to the test for the period ended 26th July 2005. As a result of the covenant breach, the Facilities technically became repayable on demand.

On 12th December 2005, the Group signed an agreement for a new bank loan ('the new Facility') with its two principal bankers, HSBC Bank plc and The Royal Bank of Scotland plc, the proceeds of which are being used to repay the existing Facilities. The new Facility comprises two tranches: a US$80 million revolving credit facility and a US$140 million term loan, each available until December 2006. Both tranches, under certain circumstances, can be extended at the Company's option for a further twelve months to December 2007. The new Facility carries interest at a margin of 1.5% over LIBOR, plus mandatory costs. The new Facility is unsecured, although certain of First Technology PLC's wholly-owned subsidiaries have given guarantees with respect to First Technology PLC's obligations under the agreement. However, in the event that the offer announced on 19th December, or any other offer, for the entire issued share capital of the Company does not become wholly unconditional or that the Company has not completed an equity issue raising proceeds of at least £40 million and used such amount to repay the new Facility, the Company will be required to give security by 30th September 2006. Any net proceeds of an equity issue must be applied to repay the new Facility. If the amount prepaid is more than £40 million, the Company has the option to extend the new Facility for an additional one year term. Under all circumstances, the Company retains the flexibility to re-finance this new Facility.

In July 2004, First Technology PLC entered into an interest rate swap to fix the rate of interest that it would pay under the US$75 million term loan tranche of the syndicated loan. The interest rate swap fixed for the whole term the rate of interest at 3.605% plus the applicable margin for this element of the Group's debt. This swap is now being used to fix the rate of interest payable under a proportion of the new Facility.

11.10   However, following a breach of a borrowing covenant, lenders often agree to a period of grace during which the borrower agrees to rectify the breach. The lender agrees not to demand repayment during this time but, if the breach is not rectified, the debt would become immediately repayable at the end of the period of grace. If, before the balance sheet date, the lender has agreed to such a period of grace and that period ends at least 12 months after the balance sheet date, then the liability should be shown as non-current. [IAS 1 para 75]. If the breach of the borrowing covenant occurs after the balance date, then the liability would still be shown as non-current, unless the breach was so serious that the financial statements could no longer be prepared on a going concern basis. However, if the breach occurred before the balance sheet date, but the period of grace was not granted until after the balance sheet date, then the liability would be classified as current. The key to this approach is that the loan's presentation is dictated by the loan's condition as at the balance sheet date. Events after the balance sheet date may give evidence of that condition but they do not change it. This is consistent with IAS 10, 'Events after the balance sheet date'.

11.11   The standard's approach to breaches of borrowing covenants focuses on the legal rights of the entity rather than on the intentions of either of the parties to the loan. In dealing with situations where the entity has the discretion to roll over or refinance loans, the entity's expectations on the timing of settlement play a part in deciding the liability's classification. The liability's classification is, however, unaffected by the entity's intentions in the case of a breach of a loan agreement. If the entity breaches the loan agreement before the balance sheet date and the lender grants a period of grace of more than 12 months from the balance sheet date, then the loan is classified as non-current even if it is the entity's intention to repay the loan within 12 months of the balance sheet date. In many cases, however, the period of grace will be a matter of negotiation between the borrower and the lender and will match the borrower's intentions in any event. In addition, breaches of loan agreements occur most often in entities that are experiencing financial difficulties and these entities are unlikely to wish to repay the loan earlier than required by the lender.

11.12 Although post balance sheet events may not alter the liability's classification, they may require disclosure as a non-adjusting event. IAS 1 paragraph 76 states that, in respect of loans classified as current liabilities, the following events must be disclosed as non-adjusting events in accordance with IAS 10, if they occur between the balance sheet date and the date of authorisation of the financial statements:

- Refinancing on a long-term basis.

- Rectification of a breach of a long-term loan agreement.

- The receipt from the lender of a period of grace to rectify a breach of a long-term loan agreement ending at least 12 months after the balance sheet date.

11.13 IAS 1 does not specify any disclosures for non-adjusting post balance sheet events in respect of loans classified as non-current liabilities. However, IAS 10 requires that an entity should disclose the following for each material category of non-adjusting event after the balance sheet date:

- The nature of the event.

- An estimate of its financial effect, or a statement that such an estimate cannot be made.

[IAS 10 para 21].

11.14 Further disclosure of defaults and breaches of loan agreements is required by IFRS 7 (see para 11.61 below).

Offsetting a financial asset and a financial liability

General principle

11.15 A financial asset and a financial liability should be offset when, and only when, both of the following conditions are satisfied:

- The entity currently has a legally enforceable right to set off the recognised amounts.

- The entity intends either to settle on a net basis, or to realise the asset and settle the liability simultaneously.

[IAS 32 para 42].

11.16 Where the above offset conditions are satisfied, the entity has the right to receive or pay a single net amount and intends to do so, it has, in effect, only a single financial asset or financial liability. In that situation, the financial asset and the financial liability are presented on the balance sheet on a net basis. Where the offset conditions are not satisfied, the financial asset and the financial liability are presented separately from each other, consistently with their characteristics as the entity's resources or obligations. [IAS 32 para 43].

11.17 There can be situations where there are transfers of financial assets that do not qualify for derecognition and in such case the entity has to recognise an associated liability (see chapter 8). Such assets and liabilities can not be offset because offsetting a recognised financial asset and a recognised financial liability and presenting the net amount is different from derecognising that financial asset or financial liability. Derecognising a financial instrument not only results in the removal of the previously recognised item from the balance sheet, but also may result in recognising of a gain or loss. Offsetting does not give rise to recognising a gain or loss. [IAS 32 paras 42, 44]. In other words, in considering presentation of particular items, recognition, derecognition and measurement need to be considered first.

Legal right of set-off

11.18 IAS 32 defines a right of offset as *"a debtor's legal right, by contract or otherwise, to settle or otherwise eliminate all or a portion of an amount due to a creditor by applying against that amount an amount due from the creditor"*. Because the right of offset is essentially a legal right, the conditions supporting the right may vary from one legal jurisdiction to another and, therefore, the laws applicable to the relationships between the parties would need to be considered carefully. [IAS 32 para 45]. It follows that instruments such as receivables and payables with the same counterparty would fall to be offset if a legal right of offset is agreed between the parties (and the entity intends to settle net or simultaneously).

11.19 In unusual circumstances, a debtor may have a legal right to apply an amount due from a third party against the amount due to a creditor provided that there is an agreement between the three parties that clearly establishes the debtor's right of set-off. [IAS 32 para 45].

Intention to settle on a net basis

11.20 It is clear from the general principle in paragraph 11.15 above that, in order to achieve offset, an entity must have both the right and the intention to do so. It is not sufficient to have one and not the other. Although the existence of an enforceable legal right of offset affects the entity's rights and obligations associated with a financial asset and a financial liability and may affect its exposure to credit and liquidity risk, it is, by itself, not a sufficient basis for offsetting. This is because, in the absence of an intention to exercise the right or to settle simultaneously, the amount and timing of the entity's future cash flows are not affected. However, if, in addition to the legal right, the entity clearly intends to exercise the right or to settle simultaneously, it is, in effect, exposed to a net amount, which reflects the timing of the expected future cash flows and the risks to which those cash flows are exposed. Similarly, an intention by one or both parties to settle on a net basis without the legal right to do so is not sufficient to justify offsetting because the rights and obligations associated with the individual financial asset and financial liability remain unaltered. [IAS 32 para 46].

11.21 An entity's intentions with respect to settlement of particular assets and liabilities may be influenced by its normal business practices, the requirements of the financial markets and other circumstances that may limit the ability to settle net or to settle simultaneously. When an entity has a right of offset, but does not intend to settle net or to realise the asset and settle the liability simultaneously, the effect of the right on the entity's credit risk exposure is disclosed in accordance with paragraph 11.83 below.

Simultaneous settlement

11.22 IAS 32 states that realisation of a financial asset and settlement of a financial liability are treated as simultaneous only when the transactions occur at the same moment. For example, the operation of a clearing house in an organised financial market or a face-to-face exchange will facilitate simultaneous settlement of two financial instruments. In these circumstances the cash flows are, in effect, equivalent to a single net amount and there is no exposure to credit or liquidity risk. In other circumstances, an entity may settle two instruments by receiving and paying separate amounts, becoming exposed to credit risk for the full amount of the asset or liquidity risk for the full amount of the liability. Such risk exposures, though brief, may be significant and therefore, net presentation is not appropriate. [IAS 32 para 48].

Situations where offset is usually inappropriate

11.23 IAS 32 sets out the following specific situations where the offset criteria in paragraph 11.15 above are not met.

- Several different financial instruments are used to emulate the features of a single financial instrument (a 'synthetic instrument'). For example, a floating rate long-term debt combined with an interest rate swap that involves receiving floating payments and making fixed payments synthesises a fixed rate long-term debt. Each of the individual financial instruments that together constitute a 'synthetic instrument':

  - represents a contractual right or obligation with its own terms and conditions;

  - may be transferred or settled separately;

  - is exposed to risks that may differ from the risks to which other financial instruments are exposed.

  Accordingly, when one financial instrument in a 'synthetic instrument' is an asset and another is a liability, they are not offset and presented on an entity's balance sheet on a net basis unless they meet the criteria for offsetting in paragraph 11.15 above.

- Financial assets and financial liabilities arise from financial instruments having the same primary risk exposure (for example, assets and liabilities within a portfolio of forward contracts or other derivative instruments), but involve different counterparties.

■ Financial or other assets are pledged as collateral for non-recourse financial liabilities.

■ Financial assets are set aside in trust by a debtor for the purpose of discharging an obligation without those assets having been accepted by the creditor in settlement of the obligation (for example, a sinking fund arrangement).

■ Obligations incurred as a result of events giving rise to losses are expected to be recovered from a third party by virtue of a claim made under an insurance contract.

[IAS 32 para 49].

Master netting agreements

11.24   An entity that undertakes a number of financial instrument transactions with a single counterparty may enter into a 'master netting arrangement' with that counterparty. Such an arrangement creates a right of set-off that becomes enforceable and affects the realisation or settlement of individual financial assets and financial liabilities only following a specified event of default or in other circumstances not expected to arise in the normal course of business. These arrangements are commonly used by financial institutions to provide protection against loss in the event of bankruptcy or other circumstances that result in a counterparty being unable to meet its obligations. In the event of default on, or termination of, any one contract, the agreement provides for a single net settlement of all financial instruments covered by the agreement. [IAS 32 para 50].

11.25   Where an entity has entered into such an agreement, the agreement does not provide a basis for offsetting unless both of the criteria in paragraph 11.15 above are satisfied. This is because the entity's right of set off under such an agreement is conditional and enforceable only on the occurrence of some future event, usually a default of the counterparty. To offset a financial asset and a financial liability, an entity must have a currently legally enforceable right to set off the recognised amounts. Thus, such an arrangement does not meet the conditions for offsetting. [IAS 32 para 50].

> **Example – Various arrangements in a group for cash management purposes**
>
> Group X comprises various subsidiaries, each of which has a separate bank account with bank B. At any time, some of these accounts have a positive cash balance and others a negative (overdraft) balance. Group X operates the following arrangements for cash management purposes:
>
> ■ Zero balancing (sometimes referred to as a cash sweep), under which the balances on a number of designated accounts are transferred to a single netting account on a regular basis, including at the balance sheet date. In some cases,

the amounts transferred are repaid to the relevant subsidiaries shortly afterwards. This may be agreed contractually or at the choice of group management.

■ Notional pooling, under which bank B calculates the net balance on a number of designated accounts with interest being earned or paid on the net amount. There may be a transfer of balances into a netting account, but this is not always at the balance sheet date.

Is Group X able to offset cash and overdraft balances and hence present net balances in its consolidated balance sheet?

If balances are to be presented net, both of the criteria set out in paragraph 11.15 should be satisfied. Group X should have a currently legally enforceable right to set-off, which means that it is enforceable at anytime and not just in stipulated circumstances, such as an event of default or bankruptcy. Also, Group X should demonstrate a clear prospect that there will be future settlement of cash flows with the same counterparty. A notional pooling for the purpose of calculating interest that does not involve settlement of the associated balances will not meet the requirements described in paragraph 11.20 above.

Assuming the agreement with bank B gives group X the necessary legally enforceable right to set off, its position will be as follows:

■ Where there is zero balancing at the balance sheet date and no repayment of funding (reversal of cash flows) takes place, either on the following day or any day thereafter, Group X has a single cash balance or overdraft at the balance sheet date and it is presented as such.

■ Where there is zero balancing at the balance sheet date, but the amounts transferred are repaid to the relevant subsidiaries shortly afterwards, Group X will not be able to demonstrate 'the intention to settle net' and therefore will not be able to present net balances in its consolidated balance sheet.

■ Where there is notional pooling, but no physical transfer of balances to one account, group X will not be able to demonstrate 'the intention to settle net', as the arrangement does not actually involve net cash settlement. Accordingly, the balances should be presented gross.

■ Where there is notional pooling and there is regular net cash settlement of the accounts, net presentation is appropriate. This will not be affected by the fact that actual settlement of the net position may not coincide with the balance sheet date, as long as group X can clearly demonstrate the intention to settle net through a regular practice of net cash settlement throughout the year.

Note that arrangements such as those described above can be complex; each arrangement should be viewed in light of its specific facts and circumstances.

11.26 When financial assets and financial liabilities subject to a master netting arrangement are not offset, the effect of the arrangement on an entity's exposure to credit risk is disclosed in accordance with paragraph 11.83 below.

Disclosure of financial instruments

11.27 There have been significant developments in risk management concepts and practices in recent years. New techniques have evolved for measuring and managing exposures to risks arising from financial instruments. This, coupled with the credit and liquidity crisis experienced recently in the financial markets, has increased the need for more relevant information and greater transparency about an entity's exposures arising from financial instruments and how those risks are managed. In response, the IASB published an amendment to IFRS 7 in March 2009 to enhance the disclosure requirements on fair value measurement (see para 11.78) and liquidity risk (see para 11.97). Financial statement users and other investors need such information to make more informed judgements about the risk that entities run from the use of financial instruments and their associated returns. IFRS 7 sets out the disclosure requirements for financial instruments.

[The next paragraph is 11.30]

Scope of IFRS 7

11.30 IFRS 7 applies to all types of financial instruments, except those that are specifically covered by another standard such as interests in subsidiaries, associates and joint ventures, acquirer's interest in contracts for contingent consideration in a business combination, employers' rights and obligations arising from employee benefit plans, share based payments and insurance contracts. IFRS 7's scope is similar to IAS 39. Chapter 3 discusses in detail which instruments are in the scope of IAS 39 and therefore also in IFRS 7's scope. However, although finance leases are mostly outside the scope of IAS 39, they remain within the scope of IFRS 7. Operating leases are not regarded as financial instruments and are not therefore in the scope of either IAS 39 or IFRS 7, except for those individual payments that are currently due and payable. [IAS 32 para AG 9].

11.30.1 Applying IFRS 7 can be challenging for entities that enter into contracts for the purchase, sale or usage of commodities. Commodity contracts that are settled net in cash or through other financial instruments are in IFRS 7's scope; those contracts that meet the 'own use exemption' would be outside IFRS 7's scope, because they are not financial instruments. [IAS 39 para 6]. These terms are discussed in detail in Chapter 3. It is likely for internal reporting purposes that management may exclude 'own use' contracts when assessing the company's exposure to financial risks, such as liquidity risk, credit risk and market risk, or they may treat all commodity contracts in the same way. The onus therefore falls on management to determine how to provide disclosures that capture the complete exposure of the risks faced by the reporting entity in connection with its commodity contracts. IFRS 7 does not preclude management from providing additional explanations or details to assist users of the financial statements in interpreting the disclosures or in providing a complete picture.

11.30.2 Receivables and payables arising from application of IAS 11, 'Construction contracts', need to be considered carefully in order to determine whether these items are in IFRS 7's scope or not. The amount due from/to customers is generally the net amount of cost incurred plus recognised profits less progress billings and recognised losses. This amount is 'billable' to customers. It, therefore, represents a contractual right to receive cash and is a financial asset in IFRS 7's scope. Progress billings to customers are also receivables in the IFRS 7's scope. On the other hand, advances received from customers are non-financial liabilities (obligation to perform work) and hence are not in the scope of IFRS 7.

11.30.3 In a similar manner, accruals representing a right to receive cash or an obligation to deliver cash are in IFRS 7's scope. For example, an accrual for goods received but not yet invoiced is within the IFRS 7's scope. On the other hand, a pre-paid expense, which is settled by the future delivery of goods or services, is not a financial instrument and is excluded from IFRS 7's scope.

11.30.4 Provisions as defined in IAS 37, 'Provisions, contingent liabilities and contingent assets', are scoped out of IFRS 7 because they are not financial instruments. [IAS 37 para 2; IFRS 7 paras 3-4; IAS 39 para 2(j)]. Financial guarantee contracts may be measured in accordance with IAS 37's principles if the provision is higher than the unamortised premium amount, but they are financial instruments within IAS 39's scope and so are within IFRS 7's scope. Financial guarantee contracts that are considered insurance contracts and measured in accordance with IFRS 4 are outside the scope of IFRS 7. [IFRS 4 para 4(d)].

11.30.5 IFRS 7 applies to both recognised and unrecognised financial instruments, even if the financial instrument may not be recognised under IAS 39. [IFRS 7 para 4, 5]. For example, some loan commitments are outside IAS 39's scope but within IFRS 7's scope because they expose an entity to financial risks, such as credit and liquidity risk. However, the same is not necessarily true for a firm commitment that is designated as a hedged item in a fair value hedge. The subsequent cumulative change in the fair value of the firm commitment attributable to the hedged risk is recognised as an asset or liability under IAS 39's hedge accounting rules. [IAS 39 para 93]. However, this 'firm commitment' asset or liability does not expose the entity to credit or liquidity risk until it becomes a financial asset or liability. The fact that hedge accounting is applied does not mean that the 'firm commitment' asset or liability is a financial instrument or that IFRS 7's disclosure requirements would apply.

11.30.6 There is no scope exemption in IFRS 7 for financial assets and liabilities within the scope of IFRS 5, 'Non-current assets held for sale and discontinued operations'. However, IFRS 5 specifies the disclosures required in respect of non-current assets (or disposal groups) classified as held for sale and discontinued operations. Paragraph 2 of the standard states that the classification and presentation requirements of IFRS 5 apply to all recognised non current assets and to all disposal groups of an entity and paragraph 5(c) specifies that the measurement provisions do not apply to financial assets within IAS 39's scope. A question arises as to whether IFRS 7 disclosures are also required for financial assets and financial liabilities classified as held-for-sale or part of disposal groups. This question was addressed by the IASB in an amendment to IFRS 5 issued in April 2009 and effective for accounting periods starting on or after 1 January 2010. The amendment clarifies that disclosures required by other standards do not apply to non-current assets or disposal groups held for sale unless they are outside the scope of IFRS 5's measurement requirements. [IFRS 5 para 5B(b)]. As financial instruments measured in accordance with IAS 39 are outside the scope of IFRS 5's measurement requirements, IFRS 7 should be applied. See chapter 26 of the IFRS Manual of Accounting.

11.31   Consistent with IAS 32 and IAS 39, the standard applies to all entities, not just those in the financial services sector. This means that it applies to a manufacturing entity whose only financial instruments may be cash, bank loans and overdrafts, trade debtors and creditors as well as to a bank with many and complex financial instruments. It also applies to subsidiaries of a consolidated group, even though in most large groups risks are managed at the consolidated level.

11.31.1   There is no scope exemption for the financial statements of subsidiaries or, as yet, for small and medium-sized companies. The application of IFRS 7 to subsidiaries may present a challenge, as financial risk is often managed at a consolidated or group level.

11.31.2   The 2010 IFRS annual improvements project made several changes to IFRS 7, mostly around the simplification of credit risk and collateral disclosures. The 2010 annual improvements are applicable for periods beginning on or after 1 January 2011, with early application permitted. See paragraph 11.90 onwards.

Objectives of IFRS 7

11.32   IFRS 7's objective is to provide information to users of financial statements about an entity's exposure to risks and how the entity manages those risks. To this end, the standard requires an entity to provide disclosures in its financial statements that enable users to evaluate:

■   the significance of financial instruments for the entity's financial position and performance; and

■   the nature and extent of risks arising from financial instruments to which the entity is exposed (quantitative disclosure) and how the entity manages those risks (qualitative disclosures).

[IFRS 7 paras 1, 7, 31].

11.33   The first bullet point above covers disclosures about the figures in the balance sheet and the income statement. IFRS 7 requires disclosures of categories of financial instruments and hedging activities. In addition, it requires various disclosures by 'class' of financial instruments (see para 11.39).

11.34 The second bullet point covers disclosure of qualitative and quantitative information about an entity's exposure to risks arising from financial instruments. IFRS 7 expands the qualitative disclosure to include information on the process that an entity uses to manage and measure risk. IFRS 7 introduces new quantitative risk disclosures that should be given 'through the eyes of management', that is, based on information provided internally to key management personnel. Certain minimum disclosures are also required to the extent they are not already covered by the 'through the eyes of management' information. Entities are required to communicate to the market how they perceive, manage and measure risk.

11.34.1 The 'through the eyes of management' approach brings financial reporting more closely into line with the way management run their businesses. As management's internal measures may not have previously been provided under IFRS or local accounting principles, they could enhance a company's ability to demonstrate the strengths of its control environment, but equally they could expose any flaws. They may also enable the market to better evaluate the strength (or otherwise) of an entity's risk management activities.

11.35 IFRS 7 includes mandatory application guidance that explains how to apply the standard's requirements. It is also accompanied by non-mandatory implementation guidance that describes how an entity might provide the necessary disclosures.

[The next paragraph is 11.39.]

General matters

Classes of financial instruments

11.39 IFRS 7 requires certain disclosures to be given by class of financial instruments, including the following:

- Financial assets not qualifying for derecognition (see para 11.55).

- The reconciliation of an allowance account (see para 11.59).

- The amount of impairment loss for financial assets (see para 11.64).

- Fair values and the methods or assumptions applied in determining those values.

- Specific disclosures relating to credit risk (see para 11.91).

The standard itself does not provide a prescriptive list of classes of financial instruments. However, IFRS 7 states that an entity should take into account the characteristics of financial instruments and that the classes selected should be appropriate to the nature of information disclosed. [IFRS 7 para 6].

11.40 A 'class' of financial instruments is not the same as a 'category' of financial instruments. Categories are defined in paragraph 9 of IAS 39 as financial assets at fair value through profit or loss (held for trading or designated at initial recognition), held-to-maturity investments, loans and receivables, available-for-sale financial assets, financial liabilities at fair value through profit or loss (held for trading or designated at initial recognition) and financial liabilities measured at amortised cost. [IFRS 7 para 8]. Classes should be determined at a lower level than the measurement categories and reconciled back to the balance sheet. [IFRS 7 para 6]. The level of detail for a class should be determined on an entity specific basis and may be defined for each individual disclosure in a different way. In determining classes of financial instrument, an entity should, at a minimum:

- Distinguish instruments measured at amortised cost from those measured at fair value.

- Treat as a separate class or classes those financial instruments outside IFRS 7's scope. IFRS 7's disclosure requirements would not apply to this class.

[IFRS 7 App B para 2].

11.41 For example, in the case of banks, the category 'loans and receivables' comprises more than one class, unless the loans have similar characteristics. In this situation, it may be appropriate to group financial instruments into the following classes:

- types of customers – for example, commercial loans and loans to individuals; or

- types of loans – for example, mortgages, credit cards, unsecured loans and overdrafts.

However, in some cases, 'loans to clients' can be one class if all the loans have similar characteristics (for example, a savings bank providing only one type of loan to individuals).

11.41.1 'Available-for-sale' assets could be split into bond and equity investment classes. The equity investments could be further subdivided into those that are listed and those that are unlisted.

Location, level of disclosure and aggregation

11.42 An entity is permitted to disclose some of the information required by the standard (specifically, the information on the nature and extent of risks arising from financial instruments required by paragraphs 31 to 42) either in the notes or on the face of the balance sheet or on the income statement. [IFRS 7 paras 8, 20]. Some entities might present some of the information required by IFRS 7, such as the nature and extent of risks arising from financial instruments and the entity's approach to managing those risks, alongside the financial statements in a separate management commentary or business review. This is only permissible where the information is incorporated by cross-reference from the financial statements and is made available to users of the financial statements on the same terms as the financial statements and at the same time. [IFRS 7 App B para 6].

11.43   An entity should decide, in the light of its own circumstances, how much detail it should provide, how much emphasis it should place on different aspects of the disclosure requirements and how much aggregation it should undertake to satisfy the standard's requirements. Obviously, a significant amount of judgement is required to display the overall picture without combining information with different characteristics. A balance should be maintained between providing excessive detail that may not assist users of financial statements and obscuring important information as a result of too much aggregation. For example, an entity should not obscure important information by including it amongst a large amount of insignificant detail. Similarly, an entity should not disclose information that is so aggregated that it obscures important differences between individual transactions or associated risks. [IFRS 7 App B para 3].

Risks arising from financial instruments

11.44   IFRS 7 requires a significant amount of qualitative and quantitative disclosure about risks associated with financial instruments. In the context of financial instruments, risk arises from the uncertainty in cash flows, which in turn affects the future cash flows and fair values of financial assets and liabilities. The following are the types of financial risk that are related to financial instruments:

- Market risk – the risk that the fair value or cash flows of a financial instrument will fluctuate, because of changes in market prices. Market risk embodies not only the potential for loss, but also the potential for gain. It comprises three types of risk as follows:

    - Interest rate risk – the risk that the fair value or future cash flows of a financial instrument will fluctuate because of changes in market interest rates.

    - Currency risk – the risk that the fair value or future cash flows of a financial instrument will fluctuate because of changes in foreign exchange rates.

    - Other price risk – the risk that the fair value or future cash flows of a financial instrument will fluctuate because of changes in market prices (other than those arising from interest rate risk or currency risk), whether those changes are caused by factors specific to the individual financial instrument or its issuer, or factors affecting all similar financial instruments traded in the market.

- Credit risk – the risk that one party to a financial instrument will cause a financial loss for the other party by failing to discharge an obligation.

- Liquidity risk – the risk that an entity will encounter difficulty in meeting obligations associated with financial liabilities.

[IFRS 7 App A].

11.44.1 Operational risk disclosures, on the other hand, are not within IFRS 7's scope.

Balance sheet disclosures

11.45 The carrying amounts of each of the following categories should be disclosed, either on the face of the balance sheet or in the notes:

- Financial assets at fair value through profit or loss, showing separately:
  - those designated as such upon initial recognition; and
  - those classified as held for trading in accordance with IAS 39.
- Held-to-maturity investments.
- Loans and receivables.
- Available-for-sale financial assets.
- Financial liabilities at fair value through profit or loss, showing separately:
  - those designated as such upon initial recognition; and
  - those classified as held for trading in accordance with IAS 39.
- Financial liabilities measured at amortised cost.

[IFRS 7 para 8].

11.46 Table 11.2 shows the analysis of financial assets and financial liabilities by category.

Table 11.2 – Analysis of financial assets and financial liabilities by class and by categories

Amer Sports Corporation – Annual Report – 31 December 2008

27 Balance sheet values of financial assets and liabilities by measurement categories December 31 2008

EUR million	Financial assets/ liabilities fair value through income statement	Derivative financial instruments used in hedge accounting	Loans and other receivables	Available-for-sale financial assets	Financial liabilities measured at amortized cost	Carrying amount by balance sheet item	Fair value
Non-current financial assets							
Other non-current financial assts			2.7	0.8		3.5	3.5
Derivative financial instruments							
Interest rate derivatives		0.2				0.2	0.2
Current financial assets							
Accounts receivables			523.4			523.4	523.4
Loan receivables			0.2			0.2	0.2
Other non-interest yielding receivables			49.5			49.5	49.5
Foreign exchange derivatives	3.6	1.5				5.1	5.1
Liquid funds			68.0			68.0	68.0
Balance sheet values by category	3.6	1.7	643.8	0.8	0.0	649.9	649.9
Long-term financial liabilities							
Long-term interest bearing liabilities					218.6	218.6	218.6
Other long-term liabilities					6.5	6.5	6.5
Derivative financial instruments							
Interest rate derivatives		1.8				1.8	1.8
Current financial liabilities							
Current interest-bearing liabilities					437.6	437.6	437.6
Accounts payable					164.8	164.8	164.8
Other current liabilities					172.5	172.5	172.5
Derivative financial instruments							
Foreign exchange derivatives	1.0	3.6				4.6	4.6
Balance sheet values by category	1.0	5.4	0.0	0.0	1,000.0	1,006.4	1,006.4

Presentation and disclosure

Financial assets or liabilities at fair value through profit or loss

11.47 If the entity has designated a loan or receivable (or group of loans or receivables) as at fair value through profit or loss, it should disclose:

- The maximum exposure to credit risk of the loan or receivable (or group of loans or receivables) at the reporting date (see para 11.88 below).

- The amount by which any related credit derivatives or similar instruments mitigate that maximum exposure to credit risk, for example financial guarantees and credit insurance.

- The amount of change, during the period and cumulatively, in the fair value of the loan or receivable (or group of loans or receivables) that is attributable to changes in the financial asset's credit risk, determined either

  - as the amount of change in its fair value that is not attributable to changes in market conditions that give rise to market risk; or

  - using an alternative method the entity believes more faithfully represents the amount of change in its fair value that is attributable to changes in the asset's credit risk.

  Changes in market conditions that give rise to market risk include changes in an observed (benchmark) interest rate, commodity price, foreign exchange rate or index of prices or rates (see para 11.49 below).

- The amount of the change in the fair value of any related credit derivatives or similar instruments that has occurred during the period and cumulatively since the loan or receivable was designated as at fair value through profit or loss.

[IFRS 7 para 9].

11.48 The disclosures described above apply only to those loans and receivables (or groups of loans and receivables) that have been designated at fair value through profit and loss ('FVTPL'). They do not apply to all loans and receivables or to all assets designated as FVTPL assets. For example, a listed bond asset is not classified as 'loans and receivables', as it is quoted. Therefore, in this case the above disclosures are not required.

11.49 Where an entity discloses the information required by the third bullet point in paragraph 11.47, it should also disclose the methods used to comply with the disclosure requirements. However, where the entity believes that this disclosure does not faithfully represent the change in the financial asset's fair value attributable to changes in its credit risk, it should disclose the reasons and the factors it believes are relevant in reaching that conclusion. [IFRS 7 para 11].

11.50 If the entity has designated a financial liability as at fair value through profit or loss, it should disclose:

- The amount of change, during the period and cumulatively, in the financial liability's fair value that is attributable to changes in the credit risk of that liability determined either:

  - as the amount of change in its fair value that is not attributable to changes in market conditions that give rise to market risk; or

  - using an alternative method the entity believes more faithfully represents the amount of change in its fair value that is attributable to changes in the asset's credit risk.

  Changes in market conditions that give rise to market risk include changes in an observed (benchmark) interest rate, the price of another entity's financial instrument, a commodity price, a foreign exchange rate or an index of prices or rates. For contracts that include a unit-linking feature, changes in market conditions include changes in the performance of the related internal or external investment fund (see para 11.52 below).

- The difference between the financial liability's carrying amount and the amount the entity would be contractually required to pay at maturity to the holder of the obligation.

[IFRS 7 para 10].

11.51 As stated in the first bullet point in paragraph 11.50 above, an entity is required to disclose the amount of change in a liability's fair value that is attributable to changes in the liability's credit risk. Although quantifying such changes might be difficult in practice, the IASB concluded that disclosure of such information would be useful to users and would help alleviate concerns that users may misinterpret the profit or loss changes in credit risk, especially in the absence of disclosures. Consequently, the standard provides a relatively easy method of computing the amount to be disclosed, as illustrated in the example below. The method assumes that the only relevant change in market condition for the liability is a change in the observed benchmark interest rate. Changes in fair value arising from factors other than changes in the instrument's credit risk or changes in interest rates are assumed not to be significant.

Example – Fair value change attributable to changes in a liability's credit risk

On 1 January 20X1, an entity issues a 10 year bond with a par value of C150,000 and an annual fixed coupon rate of 8%, which is consistent with market rates for bonds with similar characteristics. The entity uses LIBOR as its observable (benchmark) interest rate.

The entity assumes a flat yield curve, all changes in interest rates result from a parallel shift in the yield curve, and the changes in LIBOR are the only relevant changes in market conditions. It is also assumed that changes in the fair value arising from factors other than changes in the bond's credit risk or changes in interest rate are not significant.

At the date of inception of the bond, LIBOR was 5%. At the end of the first year, LIBOR has decreased to 4.75%. The bond's fair value is C153,811, consistent with a market interest rate of 7.6% for the bond. The market rate reflects the bond's credit rating at the end of the first year (see below).

The entity estimates the amount of change in the bond's fair value that is not attributable to changes in market conditions that give rise to market risk as follows:

- Calculate the instrument-specific component of the bond's internal rate of return:

  At inception, the internal rate of return for the 10 year bond is 8%. Since LIBOR at inception was 5%, the instrument-specific component of the internal rate of return is 3% (8% − 5%).

- Determine the discount rate to be used to calculate the present value of the bond at the end of year 1 using the bond's contractual cash flows:

  Since the only relevant change in the market conditions is that LIBOR has decreased to 4.75% at the end of the year, the discount rate for the present value calculation is 7.75% (4.75% + 3%).

- Calculate the present value at the end of year 1 using the above discount rate and the bond's contractual cash flows as follows:

		C
PV of C12,000 interest payable for 9 years (year 2 -10) =	$\frac{12,000 \times [1 - (1 + 0.0775)^{-9}]}{0.0775}$	75,748
PV of C150,000 payable in year 10 =	$150,000 \times (1+0.0775)^{-9}$	76,619
Total PV		152,367

- Calculate the present value at the end of year 1 using the market rate and the bonds contractual cash flows as follows:

		C
PV of C12,000 interest payable for 9 years (year 2 -10) =	$\frac{12,000 \times [1 - (1 + 0.076)^{-9}]}{0.076}$	76,226
PV of C150,000 payable in year 10 =	$150,000 \times (1 + 0.076)^{-9}$	77,585
Observed market value of liability		153,811

- Calculate change in fair value that is not attributable to the change in the benchmark interest rate

	C
Observed market value of bond	153,811
PV of bond as calculated above	152,367
Change in fair value not attributable to changes in the observed benchmark rate	1,444

The change in fair value not attributable to changes in the observed benchmark rate is a reasonably proxy for the change in fair value that is attributable to changes in the liability's credit risk, since the difference in present values calculated at 7.75% and 7.6% is assumed to reflect changes in the instrument's credit risk. Thus, the amount to be disclosed is C1,444. [IFRS 7 para IG 11].

11.52 Where an entity discloses the information required by the first bullet point in paragraph 11.50 above, it should also disclose the methods used to comply with the disclosure requirements. However, where the entity believes that the disclosure it has given to comply with the requirements does not faithfully represent the change in the fair value of the financial asset attributable to changes in its credit risk, it should disclose the reasons and the factors it believes are relevant are relevant in reaching that conclusion. [IFRS 7 para 11]. Table 11.5 shows an example of these disclosures.

[The next paragraph is 11.54.]

Other sundry balance sheet disclosure

Re-classification

11.54 If the entity has re-classified a financial asset (in accordance with paras 51-54 of IAS 39) as one measured:

■ at cost or amortised cost, rather than at fair value; or

■ at fair value, rather than at cost or amortised cost,

it should disclose the amount re-classified into and out of each category and the reason for that re-classification (see chapter 6). [IFRS 7 para 12].

11.54.1 In addition to the disclosure required by the previous paragraph, if the entity has taken advantage of the amendment to IAS 39 issued in October 2008 (see chapter 6) and has reclassified a financial asset out of the fair value through profit or loss category (in accordance with paras 50B or 50D of IAS 39) or out of the available-for-sale category (in accordance with para 50E of IAS 39), it should disclose the following:

■ The amount reclassified into and out of each category.

■ For each reporting period until derecognition, the carrying amounts and fair values of all financial assets that have been reclassified in the current and previous reporting periods.

■ If a financial asset was reclassified in accordance with paragraph 50B of IAS 39, the rare situation, and the facts and circumstances indicating that the situation was rare.

■ For the reporting period when the financial asset was reclassified, the fair value gain or loss on the financial asset recognised in profit or loss or other comprehensive income in that reporting period and in the previous reporting period.

■ For each reporting period following the reclassification (including the reporting period in which the financial asset was reclassified) until derecognition of the financial asset, the fair value gain or loss that would have been recognised in profit or loss or other comprehensive income if the financial asset had not been reclassified, and the gain, loss, income and expense recognised in profit or loss.

■ The effective interest rate and estimated amounts of cash flows the entity expects to recover, as at the date of reclassification of the financial asset.

[IFRS 7 para 12A].

11.54.2   An example of some of this disclosure is provided in the following table.

Table 11.3.1 – Financial assets reclassified from held for trading category in rare circumstances

Royal Bank of Scotland Plc – 2008 annual report Note 11 – Page 208

As discussed in accounting policies, during 2008 the Group reclassified financial assets from the held-for-trading and available-for-sale categories into the loans and receivables category (as permitted by paragraph 50D of IAS 39 as amended) and from the held-for-trading category into the available-for-sale category (as permitted by paragraph 50B of IAS 39 as amended).

The turbulence in the financial markets during the second half of 2008 was regarded by management as rare circumstances in the context of paragraph 50B of IAS 39 as amended.

The balance sheet values of these assets, the effect of the reclassification on the income statement for the period from the date of reclassification to 31 December 2008 and the gains and losses relating to these assets recorded in the income statement for the years ended 31 December 2008, 2007 and 2006 were as follows:

	2008 – on reclassification			31 December 2008		After reclassification					2007	2006
	Carrying value £m	Effective interest rate %	Expected cash flows £m	Carrying value £m	Fair value £m	Gains/ (losses) up to the date of reclassi- fication £m	Income £m	Impair- ment losses £m	Gains/ (losses) in AFS reserves £m	Amount that would have been recognised £m	Gains/(losses) recognised in the income statement in prior periods £m	£m
Reclassified from HFT to LAR:												
Loans:												
Leveraged finance	3,602	10.15	6,083	4,304	2,523	(457)	454	–		(1,206)	(155)	–
Corporate loans	5,040	6.19	7,582	5,827	4,940	(76)	198	–		(681)	(50)	3
	8,642		13,665	10,131	7,463	(533)	652	–		(1,887)	(205)	3
Debt securities:												
CDO of RMBS	215	4.92	259	236	221	4	5	–		(11)	5	6
RMBS	1,765	6.05	2,136	2,011	1,536	(115)	157	–		(302)	(12)	–
CMBS	1	11.11	4	1	1	1	–	–		–	–	–
CLOs	835	6.34	1,141	952	717	(22)	104	–		(130)	(14)	(2)

Other ABS	2,203	5.07	3,202	2,514	2,028	(67)	129		–	(338)	3	(1)
Other	2,538	2.62	2,764	2,602	2,388	72	3			(166)	94	476
	7,557		9,506	8,316	6,891	(127)	398		–	(947)	76	479
Total	16,199		23,171	18,447	14,354	(660)	1,050		–	(2,834)	(129)	482
Reclassified from HFT to AFS: Debt securities:												
CDO of RMBS	6,228	8.14	8,822	5,695	5,695	(1,330)	1,147	(464)	(1,069)	(280)	(400)	–
RMBS	5,205	8.03	8,890	5,171	5,171	(530)	24	–	(162)	(122)	(4)	73
CMBS	32	6.81	85	31	31	(5)	5	–	(3)	2	(4)	–
CLOs	1,457	5.02	1,804	1,288	1,288	(168)	421	–	(383)	58	(36)	1
Other ABS	2,199	6.02	3,183	1,847	1,847	(356)	(10)	–	(354)	(311)	(42)	72
Other	614	12.55	1,311	698	698	–	130	–	(166)	(5)	(1)	–
	15,735		24,095	14,730	14,730	(2,389)	1,717	(464)	(2,137)	(658)	(487)	146
Reclassified from AFS to LAR: Debt securities	704	1.38	772	1,028	968	(12)[1]	6	–	–	(37)[1]	–	–
Total	32,638		48,038	34,205	30,052	(3,061)	2,773	(464)	(2,137)	(3,529)	(616)	628

Note:

[1] Gains/(losses) recognised in the available-for-sale reserve

Amounts included in the consolidated income statement:

	Group		
	2008 £m	2007 £m	2006 £m
Gains on financial assets/liabilities designated as at fair value through profit or loss	(901)	1,074	573
Gains on disposal or settlement of loans and receivables	4	3	21

On the initial recognition of financial assets and liabilities valued using valuation techniques incorporating information other than observable market data, any difference between the transaction price and that derived from the valuation technique is deferred. Such amounts are recognised in profit or loss over the life of the transaction; when market data become observable; or when the transaction matures or is closed out as appropriate. At 31 December 2008, net gains of £102 million (2007 – £72 million) were carried forward in the balance sheet. During the year net gains of £89 million (2007 – £67 million) were deferred and £65 million (2007 – £10 million) released to profit or loss.

Derecognition

11.55 An entity may have transferred financial assets in such a way that part or all of the financial assets do not qualify for derecognition (see chapter 8). In that situation, the entity should disclose for each class of such financial assets:

- The nature of the assets.

- The nature of the risks and rewards of ownership to which the entity remains exposed.

- When the entity continues to recognise all of the assets, the carrying amounts of the assets and of the associated liabilities.

- When the entity continues to recognise the assets to the extent of its continuing involvement, the total carrying amount of the original assets, the amount of the assets that the entity continues to recognise and the carrying amount of the associated liabilities.

[IFRS 7 para 13].

Table 11.3.2 – Disclosure in respect of assets transferred but not derecognised

Daimler AG – Annual report – 31 December 2009

13. Receivables from financial services (extract)

Sale of receivables. Based on market conditions and liquidity needs, Daimler may sell portfolios of retail and wholesale receivables to third parties (i.e. special purpose entities). At the time of the sale, Daimler determines whether the legally transferred receivables meet the criteria for derecognition in conformity with the appropriate provisions. If the criteria are not met, the receivables continue to be recognized in the Group's consolidated statement of financial position.

As of December 31, 2009, the carrying amount of receivables from financial services sold but not derecognized for accounting purposes amounted to €1,006 million (2008: €697 million). The associated risks and rewards are similar to those with respect to receivables from financial services that have not been transferred. For information on the related total liabilities associated with these receivables sold but not derecognized, see Note 23.

17. Trade receivables (extract)

Sale of receivables. Based on market conditions and liquidity needs, Daimler may sell portfolios of trade receivables to third parties. At the time of the sale, Daimler determines whether the legally transferred receivables meet the criteria for derecognition in conformity with the appropriate provisions. If the criteria are not met, the receivables continue to be recognized in the Group's consolidated statement of financial position.

As of December 31, 2009, the carrying amount of trade receivables sold, but not derecognized for accounting purposes amounted to €38 million (2008: €67 million). For information on the liabilities related to sold but not derecognized receivables, see Note 23.

23. Financing liabilities (extract)

Based on market conditions and liquidity needs, Daimler may sell certain receivables and future lease payments resulting from equipment on operating leases to third parties. As of December 31, 2009, relating to these transactions, liabilities of €1,330 million (2008: €764 million) are accounted for as secured borrowings. The respective liabilities are reported under liabilities from ABS transactions in the amount of €1,292 million (2008: €697 million) and under liabilities to financial institutions in the amount of €38 million (2008: €66 million). In 2008, €1 million was reported under loans, other financing liabilities.

Collateral

11.56   An entity should disclose:

■   The carrying amount of financial assets it has pledged as collateral for liabilities or contingent liabilities, including amounts that have been re-classified in circumstances where the transferee has the right to sell or pledge the transferred asset. [IAS 39 para 37(a)].

■   The terms and conditions relating to its pledge. [IFRS 7 para 14].

11.57   When an entity holds collateral (of financial or non-financial assets) and is permitted to sell or repledge it in the absence of default by the owner of the collateral, it should disclose:

■   The fair value of the collateral held.

■   The fair value of any such collateral sold or repledged, and whether the entity has an obligation to return it.

■   The terms and conditions associated with its use of the collateral.

[IFRS 7 para 15].

11.58   An example of how an entity has disclosed the necessary information about assets pledged and held as collateral is given in Table 11.3.3 below.

Table 11.3.3 – Assets pledged and held as collateral

Deutsche Bank AG – Annual Report – 31 December 2009

[20] Assets Pledged and Received as Collateral

The Group pledges assets primarily for repurchase agreements and securities borrowing agreements which are generally conducted under terms that are usual and customary to standard securitized borrowing contracts. In addition the Group pledges collateral against other borrowing arrangements and for margining purposes on OTC derivative liabilities. The carrying value of the Group's assets pledged as collateral for liabilities or contingent liabilities is as follows.

in € m.	Dec 31, 2009	Dec 31, 2008[1]
Interest-earning deposits with banks	59	69
Financial assets at fair value through profit or loss	88,663	81,555
Financial assets available for sale	558	517
Loans	19,537	22,534
Other[2]	56	24
Total	**108,873**	**104,699**

[1] Prior year amounts have been adjusted.

[2] Includes Property and equipment pledged as collateral in 2007.

Assets transferred where the transferee has the right to sell or repledge are disclosed on the face of the balance sheet. As of December 31, 2009, and December 31, 2008, these amounts were € 80 billion and € 69 billion, respectively.

As of December 31, 2009, and December 31, 2008, the Group had received collateral with a fair value of € 225 billion and € 255 billion, respectively, arising from securities purchased under reverse repurchase agreements, securities borrowed, derivatives transactions, customer margin loans and other transactions. These transactions were generally conducted under terms that are usual and customary for standard secured lending activities and the other transactions described. The Group, as the secured party, has the right to sell or repledge such collateral, subject to the Group returning equivalent securities upon completion of the transaction. As of December 31, 2009, and 2008, the Group had resold or repledged € 200 billion and € 232 billion, respectively. This was primarily to cover short sales, securities loaned and securities sold under repurchase agreements.

Allowance amount for credit losses

11.59 When financial assets are impaired by credit losses and the entity records the impairment in a separate account (for example, an allowance account used to record individual impairments or a similar account used to record a collective impairment of assets) rather than directly reducing the asset's carrying amount, it should disclose a reconciliation of changes in that account during the period for each class of financial assets. [IFRS 7 para 16].

Compound financial instruments with multiple embedded derivatives

11.60 If an entity has issued an instrument that contains both a liability and an equity component (see chapter 6) and the instrument has multiple embedded derivatives whose values are interdependent (such as a callable convertible debt instrument), it should disclose the existence of those features. [IFRS 7 para 17].

Defaults and breaches

11.61 An entity is required to disclose information on defaults and breaches of loans payable (that is, financial liabilities other than short-term trade payables on normal credit terms) and other loan agreements. Such disclosures provide relevant information about the entity's creditworthiness and its prospects for obtaining future loans. Any defaults or breaches may affect the liability's classification as current or non-current in accordance with IAS 1 (see para 11.9 above) and may also require disclosure if the liability is considered as capital by the entity's management. [IAS 1 para 135(e)].

11.62 For loans payable recognised at the reporting date, an entity should disclose:

- Details of any defaults during the period of principal, interest, sinking fund, or redemption terms of those loans payable.

- The carrying amount of the loans payable in default at the reporting date.

- Whether the default was remedied, or the terms of the loans payable were renegotiated, before the financial statements were authorised for issue.

[IFRS 7 para 18].

11.63   If, during the period, there were breaches of loan agreement terms other than those described in the above paragraph, an entity should disclose the same information as above if those breaches permitted the lender to demand accelerated repayment, unless the breaches were remedied, or the loan's terms were renegotiated, on or before the reporting date. [IFRS 7 para 19].

11.63.1   The above requirements would apply if the terms were renegotiated after the balance sheet date but before the signing of the financial statements. However, the disclosure need not include short-term trade payables on normal credit terms as these do not meet the definition in the standard of loans payable. [IFRS 7 App A].

Income statement and equity disclosures

Items of income, expense, gains or losses

11.64   An entity should disclose the following items of income, expense, gains or losses, either on the face of the financial statements or in the notes:

- Net gains or net losses on:
  - Financial assets or financial liabilities at fair value through profit or loss, showing separately those on financial assets or financial liabilities designated as such upon initial recognition and those on financial assets or financial liabilities that are classified as held-for-trading in accordance with IAS 39. Where these financial instruments accrue interest income or expense, the standard allows an accounting policy choice on how to disclose these. The interest income, interest expense and dividend income can be reported as part of net gains or net losses on these financial instruments or can be disclosed separately as part of interest income and expenses. [IFRS 7 App B5(e)]. In addition, it is possible to adopt one treatment for interest income and expense and a different treatment for dividend income as no such prohibition exists in IFRS 7. However, different treatments cannot be adopted for interest income and interest expense.

    Note that if the dividend income is significant, regardless of how it is disclosed here, it will also need to be disclosed separately in the notes. [IAS 18 para 35(b)(v)].
  - Available-for-sale financial assets, showing separately the amount of gain or loss recognised directly in other comprehensive income during the period and the amount reclassified from equity and recognised in profit or loss for the period.
  - Held-to-maturity investments.
  - Loans and receivables.
  - Financial liabilities measured at amortised cost.

- Total interest income and total interest expense (calculated using the effective interest method) for financial assets or financial liabilities that are not at fair value through profit or loss.

- Fee income and expense (other than amounts included in determining the effective interest rate) arising from:

  - Financial assets or financial liabilities that are not at fair value through profit or loss.

  - Trust and other fiduciary activities that result in the holding or investing of assets on behalf of individuals, trusts, retirement benefit plans and other institutions.

- Interest income on impaired financial assets accrued in accordance with paragraph AG93 of IAS 39, which requires an entity to continue to recognise interest income using the rate of interest used to discount the future cash flows for the purposes of measuring the impairment loss (see chapter 9).

- The amount of any impairment loss for each class of financial asset.

[IFRS 7 para 20].

11.65   Certain of the disclosure requirements described above are illustrated in Table 11.4.

Table 11.4 – Items of income, expense, gains or losses

EADS N.V. – Annual Report – 31 December 2009

35. Information about financial instruments (extract)

E) NET GAINS OR LOSSES

EADS net gains or (losses) recognised in profit or loss in 2009 and 2008 respectively are as follows:

(in €m)	2009	2008
Financial assets or financial liabilities at fair value through profit or loss:		
> Held for trading	(100)	(149)
> Designated on initial recognition	12	64
Available-for-sale-financial assets:		
> Result before taxes removed from OCI and recognised in profit or loss	0	6
Net income from equity securities	133	313
Loans and receivables	(179)	(160)
Financial liabilities measured at amortised cost	83	79

Interest income from financial assets or financial liabilities through profit or loss is included in net gains and losses.

Net gains and losses of loans and receivables contain among others results from currency adjustments from foreign operations and impairment losses.

The following net gains and (losses) are recognised directly in equity in 2009 and 2008:

(in €m)	2009	2008
Available-for-sale-financial assets:		
> Unrealised net gains and (losses) recognised directly in OCI	162	6

F) TOTAL INTEREST INCOME AND TOTAL INTEREST EXPENSES

In 2009, the total interest income amounts to € 344 million for financial assets which are not measured at fair value through profit or loss. For financial liabilities which are not measured at fair value through profit or loss € -503 million are recognised as total interest expenses. Both amounts are calculated by using the effective interest method.

G) IMPAIRMENT LOSSES

The following impairment losses on financial assets are recognised in profit or loss in 2009 and 2008 respectively:

(in €m)	2009	2008
Available-for-sale financial assets	(12)	(23)
Loans and receivables	(76)	(114)
Other[1]	(3)	(36)
Total	(91)	(173)

[1] Concerns finance lease receivables.

Other disclosures

Accounting policies

11.66 IAS 1 requires an entity to disclose, in the summary of significant accounting policies, the measurement basis (or bases) used in preparing the financial statements and the other accounting policies used that are relevant to an understanding of the financial statements. [IAS 1 para 108; IFRS 7 para 21]. For financial instruments such disclosure may include:

- For financial assets or financial liabilities designated as at fair value through profit or loss:

    - The nature of the financial assets or financial liabilities the entity has designated as at fair value through profit or loss.

    - The criteria for so designating such financial assets or financial liabilities on initial recognition.

    - How the entity has satisfied the conditions for such designation, including, where appropriate, a narrative description of the circumstances underlying the measurement or recognition inconsistency that would otherwise arise, or how designation at fair value through profit or loss is consistent with the entity's documented risk management or investment strategy.

- The criteria for designating financial assets as available for sale.

- Whether regular way purchases and sales of financial assets are accounted for at trade date or at settlement date (see chapter 9).

- When an allowance account is used to reduce the carrying amount of financial assets impaired by credit losses:

  - The criteria for determining when the carrying amount of impaired financial assets is reduced directly (or, in the case of a reversal of a write-down, increased directly) and when the allowance account is used.

  - The criteria for writing off amounts charged to the allowance account against the carrying amount of impaired financial assets.

- How net gains or net losses on each category of financial instrument are determined, for example, whether the net gains or net losses on items at fair value through profit or loss include interest or dividend income.

- The criteria the entity uses to determine that there is objective evidence that an impairment loss has occurred.

- When the terms of financial assets that would otherwise be past due or impaired have been renegotiated, the accounting policy for financial assets that are the subject of renegotiated terms.

[IFRS 7 App B para 5].

11.67   IAS 1 also requires entities to disclose, in the summary of significant accounting policies or other notes, the judgements, apart from those involving estimations, that management has made in the process of applying the entity's accounting policies and that have the most significant effect on the amounts recognised in the financial statements. [IAS 1 para 113].

Hedge accounting

11.68   An entity should disclose the following separately for each type of hedge described in IAS 39 (that is, fair value hedges, cash flow hedges and hedges of net investments in foreign operations).

- A description of each type of hedge.

- A description of the financial instruments designated as hedging instruments and their fair values at the reporting date.

- The nature of the risks being hedged.

[IFRS 7 para 22].

11.69   In addition, for cash flow hedges, an entity should disclose:

- The periods when the cash flows are expected to occur and when they are expected to affect profit or loss.

■ A description of any forecast transaction for which hedge accounting had previously been used, but which is no longer expected to occur.

■ The amount that was recognised in other comprehensive income during the period.

■ The amount that was reclassified from equity and included in profit or loss for the period, showing the amount included in each line item in the income statement. This would also apply to hedging instruments with a short maturity that have been acquired and have matured within the same accounting period. As a practical expedient it is common for entities to recognise the gains and losses on such instruments directly in the income statement rather than to recognise the gains and losses initially in the hedging reserve and then recycle to the income statement. Although the accounting entries net off in the same accounting period, there should still be disclosure of the amounts that would have been recycled.

■ The amount that was reclassified from equity during the period and included in the initial cost or other carrying amount of a non-financial asset or non-financial liability whose acquisition or incurrence was a hedged highly probable forecast transaction.

[IFRS 7 para 23].

11.70 An entity should disclose separately:

■ In fair value hedges, gains or losses on:

　■ The hedging instrument.

　■ The hedged item attributable to the hedged risk.

The requirement here relates to the current reporting period only and not to a disclosure on a cumulative basis (since the inception of the hedge designation).

■ The ineffectiveness recognised in profit or loss that arises from cash flow hedges.

■ The ineffectiveness recognised in profit or loss that arises from hedges of net investments in foreign operations.

[IFRS 7 para 24].

11.71 Disclosure of information on fair value hedges, cash flow hedges and hedges of net investments is given in Table 11.5 below.

Table 11.5 – Income statement, hedge ineffectiveness, fair value hedges, amounts recycled from equity, interest

National Grid Plc – Annual Report – 31 March 2010

5. Finance income and costs

	2010 £m	2009 £m	2008 £m
Interest income and similar income			
Expected return on pension and other post-retirement benefit plan assets	981	1,236	1,064
Interest income on financial instruments:			
Interest income from bank deposits and other financial assets	18	60	209
Interest receivable on finance leases	–	1	2
Gains transferred from equity on disposal of available-for-sale investments	6	18	–
Interest income and similar income	**1,005**	**1,315**	**1,275**
Interest expense and other finance costs			
Interest on pension and other post-retirement benefit plan obligations	(1,193)	(1,250)	(1,001)
Interest expense on financial liabilities held at amortised cost:			
Interest on bank loans and overdrafts	(80)	(136)	(71)
Interest on other borrowings	(938)	(1,135)	(990)
Interest on finance leases	–	(14)	(11)
Interest on derivatives	22	5	(46)
Unwinding of discounts on provisions	(70)	(68)	(45)
Less: Interest capitalised [(i)]	99	133	119
Interest expense and other finance costs before exceptional items and remeasurements	**(2,160)**	**(2,465)**	**(2,045)**
Exceptional items			
Exceptional debt redemption costs	(33)	–	–
Remeasurements			
Net gains/(losses) on derivative financial instruments included in remeasurements [(ii)]:			
Ineffectiveness on derivatives designated as fair value hedges [(iii)]	67	(34)	1
Ineffectiveness on derivatives designated as cash flow hedges	(5)	(18)	13
Ineffectiveness on derivatives designated as net investment hedges	(19)	(2)	14
On undesignated forward rate risk relating to derivatives designated as net investment hedges	51	112	(53)
On derivatives not designated as hedges or ineligible for hedge accounting	(13)	(140)	18
Financial element of remeasurements on commodity contracts	(1)	(2)	(9)
	80	(84)	(16)
Interest expense and other finance costs	**(2,113)**	**(2,549)**	**(2,061)**
Net finance costs	**(1,108)**	**(1,234)**	**(786)**
Comprising:			
Interest income and similar income	1,005	1,315	1,275
Interest expense and other finance costs:			
Before exceptional items and remeasurements	(2,160)	(2,465)	(2,045)

Exceptional items and remeasurements	47	(84)	(16)
After exceptional items and remeasurements	(2,113)	(2,549)	(2,061)
	(1,108)	(1,234)	(786)

(i) Interest on funding attributable to assets in the course of construction was capitalised during the year at a rate of 2.8% (2009: 5.7%; 2008: 6.3%).

(ii) Includes a net foreign exchange gain on financing activities of £334m (2009: £1,500m loss; 2008: £885m loss) offset by foreign exchange gains and losses on derivative financial instruments measured at fair value.

(iii) Includes a net loss on instruments designated as fair value hedges of £90m (2009: £382m gain; 2008: £87m gain) offset by a net gain of £157m (2009: £416m loss; 2008: £86m loss) arising from fair value adjustments to the carrying value of debt.

Fair value

11.72 Except as set out in paragraph 11.76 below, for each class of financial assets and financial liabilities (see para 11.39 above), an entity should disclose the fair value of that class of assets and liabilities in a way that permits it to be compared with its carrying amount. [IFRS 7 para 25].

11.72.1 Where an entity has issued a convertible bond and has under IAS 32 accounted for it as a compound instrument, the equity component will not need to be fair valued. This is because the above requirement is only for financial assets and financial liabilities and the equity component does not meet the definition of a financial asset or a financial liability.

11.73 In disclosing fair values, an entity should group financial assets and financial liabilities into classes, but should offset them only to the extent that their carrying amounts are offset in the balance sheet. [IFRS 7 para 26].

11.74 An entity should disclose, for each class of financial instruments measured at fair value, the methods and, when a valuation technique is used, the assumptions applied in determining fair values of each class of financial asset or financial liability. For example, if applicable, an entity should disclose information about the assumptions relating to pre-payment rates, rates of estimated credit losses and interest rates or discount rates. If there has been a change in valuation technique, the entity should disclose that change and the reasons for making it. [IFRS 7 para 27].

11.75 If the market for a financial instrument is not active, its fair value is established using a valuation technique. [IAS 39 paras AG 74-79]. The best evidence of fair value at initial recognition is the transaction price (that is, the fair value of the consideration given or received), unless the fair value of that instrument is evidenced by comparison with other observable current market transactions in the same instrument (that is, without modification or repackaging) or based on a valuation technique whose variables include only data from observable markets as described in paragraph AG 76 of IAS 39. There could be a difference between the fair value at initial recognition and the amount that would be determined at that date using the valuation technique. If such a difference exists, an entity should disclose, by class of financial instrument:

■ Its accounting policy for recognising that difference in profit or loss to reflect a change in factors (including time) that market participants would consider in setting a price. [IAS 39 para AG 76A].

■ The aggregate difference yet to be recognised in profit or loss at the beginning and end of the period, and a reconciliation of changes in the balance of this difference.

[IFRS 7 para 28].

11.76   Disclosure of fair values is not required:

■ When the carrying amount is a reasonable approximation of fair value – for example, for financial instruments such as short-term trade receivables and payables.

■ For an investment in equity instruments that do not have a quoted market price in an active market, or derivatives linked to such equity instruments, that are measured at cost in accordance with IAS 39, because their fair value cannot be measured reliably.

■ For a contract containing a discretionary participation feature (as described in IFRS 4) if the fair value of that feature cannot be measured reliably.

[IFRS 7 para 29].

11.77   In the cases described in the second and third bullet points above, an entity should disclose information to help users of the financial statements make their own judgements about the extent of possible differences between the carrying amount of those financial assets or financial liabilities and their fair value, including:

■ The fact that fair value information has not been disclosed for these instruments because their fair value cannot be measured reliably.

■ A description of the financial instruments, their carrying amount and an explanation of why fair value cannot be measured reliably.

■ Information about the market for the instruments.

■ Information about whether and how the entity intends to dispose of the financial instruments.

■ If financial instruments whose fair value previously could not be reliably measured are derecognised, that fact, their carrying amount at the time of derecognition and the amount of gain or loss recognised.

[IFRS 7 para 30].

Fair value hierarchy

11.78   The IASB amended IFRS 7 in March 2009 to enhance the disclosure requirements regarding financial instruments measured at fair value. In order to increase comparability between entities and take one further step towards IFRS and US GAAP convergence, the IASB introduced a requirement to make disclosures according to a 'fair value hierarchy' similar to that required under US GAAP by SFAS 157, 'Fair value measurements'. This is different from the current fair value measurement hierarchy implicitly included in IAS 39. The amendment to IFRS 7 does not change these requirements.

11.78.1   As noted above, the amendment to IFRS 7 enhances the disclosure requirements regarding financial instruments measured at fair value. Unlike SFAS 157, it does not apply to items measured at fair value that are not financial instruments. Also, it does not apply to financial instruments measured at amortised cost (for example, held-to-maturity investments, or loans and receivables).

11.78.2   The hierarchy has three levels that reflect the significance of the inputs used in measuring fair value. These are as follows:

■   Quoted prices (unadjusted) in active markets for identical assets or liabilities (Level 1).

■   Inputs other than quoted prices included within level 1 that are observable for the asset or liability, either directly (that is, as prices) or indirectly (that is, derived from prices) (Level 2).

■   Inputs for the asset or liability that are not based on observable market data (unobservable inputs) (Level 3).

[IFRS 7 para 27A].

11.78.3   The level in the fair value hierarchy within which a financial instrument is categorised in its entirety is determined on the basis of the lowest level input that is significant to the fair value measurement. For this purpose, the significance of an input is assessed against the fair value measurement in its entirety. [IFRS 7 para 27A].

11.78.4   Assessing the significance of a particular input to the fair value measurement in its entirety requires judgement, considering factors specific to the asset or liability. In assessing the significance of unobservable inputs to a financial instrument's fair value, an entity should:

■   consider the sensitivity of the instrument's overall value to changes in the data; and

■   re-assess the likelihood of variability in the data over the instrument's life.

For example, if an interest rate swap with a ten-year life has an observable yield curve for nine years, provided that the extrapolation of the yield curve to ten years is not significant to the fair value measurement of the swap in its entirety, the fair value measurement is considered to be at level 2 in the hierarchy.

11.78.5   Only instruments traded on an exchange or an active index/market can fall within level 1 of the hierarchy. Generally, for a price to qualify as level 1, reporting entities should be able to obtain the price from multiple sources. A market is active for a financial instrument if quotes are regularly available and do not represent forced transactions (see chapter 9). The price quote may be a level 2 or level 3 input where there are few transactions for the instrument, where the price is not current, or where price quotations vary substantially either over time or among market makers, or for which little information is released publicly.

11.78.5.1   Whether or not an instrument is considered to have a 'price quoted in an active market' for the purposes of the fair value hierarchy is a different assessment from whether it is considered 'quoted in an active market' for the purposes of IAS 39 and the assessment of whether it can be classified as a loan or receivable. In writing the basis of conclusions to IFRS 7 the board acknowledged that some financial instruments that for measurement purposes are considered to have an active market in accordance with paragraphs AG 71 – AG73 of IAS 39 might be in level 2 for disclosure purposes in the fair value hierarchy. [IFRS 7 BC para 39D].

11.78.6   Many reporting entities obtain information from pricing services, broker pricing information and similar sources, for use as inputs in their fair value measurements. The information provided by these sources could be at any level in the fair value hierarchy, depending on the source of the information for a particular security. However, if the information forms an input to a valuation technique that would preclude classification at level 1, the level is determined on the basis of the valuation inputs, not on the methodology or complexity of the model – that is, the use of a model does not automatically result in a level 3 fair value measurement. For example, a standard valuation model using only observable inputs is likely to result in a measurement that is classified as level 2. However, to the extent that adjustments or interpolations are made by management to level 2 inputs in an otherwise standard model, the measurement may fall into level 3, depending on whether the adjusted inputs are significant to the measurement. Furthermore, if a reporting entity uses a valuation model that is proprietary and relies on unobservable inputs, the resulting fair value measurement is likely to be categorised as level 3.

11.78.7   The US standard (SFAS 157) provides examples of inputs and where they would typically lie in the hierarchy. In view of the similarity between SFAS 157 and the amended IFRS 7, the following examples from the former may be relevant.

■   As noted in paragraph 11.78.2, level 2 inputs are inputs other than quoted prices included within level 1 that are observable for the asset or liability, either directly (that is, as prices) or indirectly (that is, derived from prices). Examples of level 2 inputs for particular assets and liabilities include the following:

■ Receive-fixed, pay-variable interest rate swap based on the LIBOR swap rate. A level 2 input would include the LIBOR swap rate if that rate is observable at commonly quoted intervals for the swap's full term. However, other inputs will also need to be considered. For example, if credit is a component of the valuation for the pay and receive leg of the swap, its observability and significance to the measurement will need to be evaluated.

■ Three-year option on exchange-traded shares. A level 2 input would include the implied volatility for the shares derived through extrapolation to year three if prices for one- and two-year options on the shares are observable, and the extrapolated implied volatility of a three-year option is corroborated by observable market data for substantially the option's full term. In that case, the implied volatility could be derived by extrapolating from the implied volatility of the one- and two-year options on the shares and corroborated by the implied volatility for three-year options on comparable entities' shares, provided that correlation with the one- and two-year implied volatilities is established.

■ Equity investment. A level 2 input would include a valuation multiple (for example, a multiple of earnings or revenue or a similar performance measure) derived from observable market data, for example, multiples derived from prices in observed transactions involving comparable businesses, considering operational, market, financial, and non-financial factors.

■ As noted in paragraph 11.78.2, level 3 inputs are inputs that are not based on observable market data. They are inputs that reflect the reporting entity's own views about the assumptions market participants would use in pricing the asset or liability (including assumptions about risk), developed based on the best information available in the circumstances. Assumptions about risk include the risk inherent in a particular valuation technique used to measure fair value (such as a pricing model) and/or the risk inherent in the inputs to the valuation technique. Examples of level 3 inputs for particular assets and liabilities include the following:

■ Long-dated currency swap. A level 3 input would include interest rates in a specified currency that are not observable and cannot be corroborated by observable market data at commonly quoted intervals or otherwise for substantially the full term of the currency swap. The interest rates in a currency swap are the swap rates calculated from the respective countries' yield curves.

■ Three-year option on exchange-traded shares. A level 3 input would include historical volatility, that is, the volatility for the shares derived from the shares' historical prices. Historical volatility typically does not represent current market participant expectations about future volatility, even if it is the only information available to price an option.

- Equity investment. A level 3 input would include a financial forecast (for example, of cash flows or earnings) developed using the reporting entity's own data if there is no information that indicates that market participants would use different assumptions.

11.78.8 For each class of financial instruments measured at fair value, an entity should disclose the following (the quantitative disclosures should be presented in tabular format, unless another format is more appropriate):

- The level in the fair value hierarchy into which the fair value measurements are categorised in their entirety, segregating fair value measurements in accordance with the levels defined in paragraph 11.78.2 above.

- Any significant transfers between level 1 and level 2 of the fair value hierarchy and the reasons for those transfers. Transfers into each level should be disclosed and discussed separately from transfers out of each level. Significance should be judged with respect to profit or loss and total assets or total liabilities.

- For fair value measurements in level 3 of the fair value hierarchy, a reconciliation from the beginning balances to the ending balances, disclosing separately changes during the period attributable to the following:

  - Total gains or losses for the period recognised in profit or loss and a description of where they are presented in the statement of comprehensive income or the separate income statement (if presented).

  - Total gains or losses recognised in other comprehensive income.

  - Purchases, sales, issues and settlements (each type of movement disclosed separately).

  - Transfers into or out of level 3 (for example, transfers attributable to changes in the observability of market data) and the reasons for those transfers. For significant transfers, transfers into level 3 should be disclosed and discussed separately from transfers out of level 3.

- The amount of total gains or losses for the period included in profit or loss resulting from level 3 financial instruments that are attributable to those assets and liabilities held at the end of the reporting period and a description of where those gains or losses are presented in the statement of comprehensive income or the separate income statement (if presented).

- For fair value measurements in level 3, if changing one or more of the inputs to reasonably possible alternative assumptions would change fair value significantly, the entity should state that fact and disclose the effect of those changes. The entity should disclose how the effect of a change to a reasonably possible alternative assumption was calculated. Significance should be judged with respect to profit or loss, and total assets or total liabilities, or, when changes in fair value are recognised in other comprehensive income, total equity.

11.78.9 The disclosures described in the previous paragraph are required in financial statements for annual periods beginning on or after 1 January 2009. However, in the first year of application, an entity need not provide comparative information. [IFRS 7 para 44G].

11.78.10 In June 2010 the IASB released an exposure draft on 'Measurement uncertainty analysis disclosure for fair value measurements'. This exposure draft is a limited expansion of previous disclosure proposals around Level 3 fair value measurements which were included in the 'Fair value measurement' exposure draft issued in May 2009. The new exposure draft proposes that disclosures of measurement uncertainty of Level 3 fair values should reflect the interdependencies between unobservable inputs into the valuations.

11.78.11 Examples of the fair value hierarchy are provided in Tables 11.6.1 and 11.6.2. Table 11.6.1 also gives the Level 3 reconciliations and sensitivity analysis required by IFRS 7. It should be noted that the example does not reproduce the company's description of the control framework for financial instruments carried at fair value, its detailed description of valuation techniques used, details of risk related adjustments, model related adjustments and credit risk adjustment methodology.

Table 11.6.1 – Fair value disclosures relating to financial assets and liabilities

HSBC Holdings plc – Annual report – 31 December 2009

Fair values of financial instruments (extract)

(Audited)

Fair value valuation bases

The table below provides an analysis of the various bases described above which have been deployed for valuing financial assets and financial liabilities measured at fair value in the consolidated financial statements.

The movement in the balances of assets and liabilities measured at fair value with significant unobservable inputs was mainly attributable to a decrease in the fair value of derivative assets, loans held for securitisation and the disposal of securities in other portfolios. At 31 December 2009, financial instruments measured at fair value using a valuation technique with significant unobservable inputs represented 2 per cent of total assets and liabilities measured at fair value (2008: 2 per cent).

Bases of valuing financial assets and liabilities measured at fair value

	Quoted market price	Using observable inputs	With significant unobservable inputs	
	Level 1	Level 2	Level 3	Total
At 31 December 2009				
Assets				
Trading assets	272,509	142,452	6,420	421,381
Financial assets designated at fair value	24,184	11,773	1,224	37,181
Derivatives	1,961	244,472	4,453	250,886
Financial investments: available for sale	163,149	178,168	10,214	351,531
Liabilities				
Trading liabilities	119,544	139,812	8,774	268,130
Financial liabilities designated at fair value	27,553	52,032	507	80,092
Derivatives	1,843	240,611	5,192	247,646
At 31 December 2008				
Assets				
Trading assets	234,399	185,369	7,561	427,329
Financial assets designated at fair value	14,590	13,483	460	28,533
Derivatives	8,495	476,498	9,883	494,876
Financial investments: available for sale	103,949	173,157	9,116	286,222
Liabilities				
Trading liabilities	105,584	135,559	6,509	247,652
Financial liabilities designated at fair value	23,311	51,276	–	74,587
Derivatives	9,896	473,359	3,805	487,060

Financial instruments measured at fair value using a valuation technique with significant unobservable inputs – Level 3

	Assets				Liabilities		
	Available for sale US$m	Held for trading US$m	Designated at fair value through profit and loss US$m	Derivatives US$m	Held for trading US$m	Designated at fair value through profit and loss US$m	Derivatives US$m
At 31 December 2009							
Private equity investments	2,949	197	345	–	–	–	–
Asset-backed securities	4,270	944	–	–	–	–	–
Leveraged finance	–	73	–	–	–	–	25
Loans held for securitisation	–	1,395	–	–	–	–	–
Structured notes	–	196	–	–	5,055	–	–
Derivatives with monolines	–	–	–	1,305	–	–	–

Other derivatives	–	–	–	3,148	–	–	5,167
Other portfolios	2,995	3,615	879	–	3,719	507	–
	10,214	**6,420**	**1,224**	**4,453**	**8,774**	**507**	**5,192**
At 31 December 2008							
Private equity investments	2,689	54	225	–	–	–	–
Asset-backed securities	4,264	882	–	95	–	–	565
Leveraged finance	–	266	–	–	–	–	33
Loans held for securitisation	–	2,133	–	–	–	–	–
Structured notes	–	87	–	–	5,294	–	–
Derivatives with monolines	–	–	–	2,441	–	–	–
Other derivatives	–	–	–	7,347	–	–	3,207
Other portfolios	2,163	4,139	235	–	1,215	–	–
	9,116	**7,561**	**460**	**9,883**	**6,509**	**–**	**3,805**

At 31 December 2009, available-for-sale ABSs valued using a valuation technique with significant unobservable inputs principally comprised commercial property-related securities, leveraged finance-related securities and Alt-A securities with no particular concentration in any one category. Assets in other portfolios valued using a valuation technique with significant unobservable inputs were principally holdings in an Asian bond portfolio where the credit spreads are not directly observable.

Trading assets valued using a valuation technique with significant unobservable inputs principally comprised ABSs, loans held for securitisation and other portfolios. The ABSs are classified in Level 3 as a result of the unobservability of the underlying price of the assets. Loans held for securitisations are valued using a proprietary model which utilises inputs relating to the credit spread of the obligor. Other portfolios include holdings in various bonds, preference shares and debentures where the unobservability relates to the prices of the underlying securities. The decrease during the year was due to a reduction in the fair value of loans held for securitisation and disposals of positions within other portfolios.

Derivative products with monolines valued using techniques with unobservable inputs decreased during the year as a result of a decrease in exposure to the monoline counterparties, primarily as a result of decreasing credit spreads and from commutations undertaken. The primary unobservable input relates to the probability of default of the counterparty. Further details of the transactions with monocline counterparties are shown on page 163.

Derivative products valued using valuation techniques with significant unobservable inputs included certain correlation products, such as foreign exchange basket options, equity basket options, foreign exchange-interest rate hybrid transactions and long-dated option transactions. Examples of the latter are equity options, interest rate and foreign exchange options and certain credit derivatives. Credit derivatives include certain tranched CDS transactions. The decrease in Level 3 derivative assets during the year was mainly due to a decrease in the fair value of structured credit transactions.

Trading liabilities valued using a valuation technique with significant unobservable inputs principally comprised equity-linked structured notes which are issued by HSBC and provide the counterparty with a return that is linked to the performance of certain equity securities, and other portfolios. The notes are classified as Level 3 due to the unobservability of parameters such as long-dated equity volatilities and correlations between equity prices, between equity prices and interest rates and between interest rates and foreign exchange rates. The movement in Level 3 trading liabilities during the year was primarily due to the issue of new equity derivative linked structures classified in other portfolios, partially offset by transfers out of Level 3 as a result of increased observability of long-dated volatilities.

The increase in derivative liabilities valued using a valuation technique with significant unobservable inputs was primarily attributable to the transfer into Level 3 of swaps linked to securitisation structures whose valuation utilises inputs relating to the prepayment rates for the underlying asset pools which are unobservable. This was partially offset by transfers out of structured interest rate and equity derivatives due to increased observability of longdated swaptions and equity volatilities.

Reconciliation of fair value measurements in Level 3 of the fair value hierarchy

The following table provides a reconciliation of the movement between opening and closing balances of Level 3 financial instruments, measured at fair value using a valuation technique with significant unobservable inputs:

Movement in Level 3 financial instruments

| | Assets | | | | Liabilities | | |
	Available for sale US$m	Held for trading US$m	Designated at fair value through profit and loss US$m	Derivatives US$m	Held for trading US$m	Designated at fair value through profit and loss US$m	Derivatives US$m
At 1 January 2009	9,116	7,561	460	9,883	6,509	–	3,805
Total gains/ (losses) recognised in profit or loss	(260)	(730)	97	(5,275)	(107)	(3)	(1,372)
Total gains recognised in other comprehensive income	617	85	–	119	301	10	94
Purchases	1,785	1,598	260	–	22	–	–
New issuances	–	–	–	–	2,522	500	–
Sales	(806)	(2,166)	(13)	–	–	–	–
Settlements	(1,059)	(295)	(6)	(104)	(1,266)	–	(206)
Transfers out	(3,043)	(1,077)	–	(1,057)	(537)	–	(620)
Transfers in	3,864	1,444	426	887	1,330	–	3,491
At 31 December 2009	10,214	6,420	1,224	4,453	8,774	507	5,192
Total gains/ (losses) recognised in profit or loss relating to those assets and liabilities held on 31 December 2009	(371)	(596)	98	(3,753)	(136)	(3)	(135)

For available-for-sale securities, the unobservability of valuations of asset-backed (particularly Alt-A and leveraged finance-related) securities and the Asian bond portfolio discussed on page 173 resulted in assets in these categories being transferred or purchased into Level 3 during 2009.

Transfers out of Level 3 were primarily in respect of commercial property related ABSs due to certain valuations in these asset categories becoming observable during 2009.

For trading assets, transfers into Level 3 arose principally on ABSs, fixed income securities and a syndicated loan position where valuations for the specific instruments were not observable. Transfers out also related principally to ABSs and fixed income securities as valuations for specific instruments became observable. Purchases relate primarily to the unwind of certain ABS total return swap funding transactions, in which HSBC's market risk position did not change, but securities were purchased in place of the derivative transactions.

For derivative assets, transfers out of Level 3 were driven by decreases in residual maturity of longer-dated equity options to below the observability boundary, movement in equity prices leading to previously out-of-the money or in-the-money options becoming closer to at-the-money options, and some increased observability of long-dated swaption and foreign exchange volatilities. Transfers in were largely driven by the unobservability of prepayment rates on swaps linked to third-party securitisations.

For held-for-trading liabilities, transfers into Level 3 were primarily due to a reduction in the observability of volatilities and gap risk parameters on embedded derivatives within issued structured notes. Transfers out of Level 3 were driven by similar factors as derivative assets, also relating to embedded derivatives within issued structured notes.

For derivative liabilities, the unobservability of prepayment rates on securitisation swaps was the main reason for transfers into Level 3. Transfers out of Level 3 were driven by similar factors as derivative assets.

During 2009, there were no significant transfers between Levels 1 and 2.

For assets and liabilities classified as held for trading, realised and unrealised gains and losses are presented in the income statement under 'Trading income excluding net interest income'.

Fair value changes on long term debt designated at fair value and related derivatives are presented in the income statement under 'Changes in fair value of long-term debt issued and related derivatives'. The income statement line item 'Net income/(expense) from other financial instruments designated at fair value' captures fair value movements on all other financial instruments designated at fair value and related derivatives.

Realised gains and losses from available-for-sale securities are presented under 'Gains less losses of financial investments' in the income statement while unrealised gains and losses are presented in 'Fair value gains/(losses)' within 'Available-for-sale investments' in other comprehensive income/ (expense).

Effect of changes in significant unobservable assumptions to reasonably possible alternatives

As discussed above, the fair value of financial instruments are, in certain circumstances, measured using valuation techniques that incorporate assumptions that are not evidenced by prices from observable current market transactions in the same instrument and are not based on observable market data. The following table shows the sensitivity of these fair values to reasonably possible alternative assumptions:

Sensitivity of fair values to reasonably possible alternative assumptions

	Reflected in profit or loss		Reflected in equity	
	Favourable changes US$m	Unfavourable changes US$m	Favourable changes US$m	Unfavourable changes US$m
At 31 December 2009				
Derivatives, trading assets and trading liabilities[23]	**984**	**(577)**	–	–
Financial assets and liabilities designated at fair value	**102**	**(98)**	–	–
Financial investments: available for sale	–	–	**1,161**	**(1,157)**
At 31 December 2008				
Derivatives, trading assets and trading liabilities[23]	1,266	(703)	–	–
Financial assets and liabilities designated at fair value	30	(30)	–	–
Financial investments: available for sale	–	–	984	(1,005)

For footnote, see page 195.

The decrease in the effect of changes in significant unobservable inputs in relation to derivatives, trading assets and trading liabilities during the year primarily reflected the decreased sensitivity to the assumptions for the derivative portfolios. The increase in the effect of changes in significant unobservable inputs for available-for-sale assets arose from the increase in private equity holdings in Level 3 and from increased sensitivity to the assumptions for ABSs.

Sensitivity of fair values to reasonably possible alternative assumptions by Level 3 instrument type

	Reflected in profit or loss		Reflected in equity	
	Favourable changes US$m	Unfavourable changes US$m	Favourable changes US$m	Unfavourable changes US$m
At 31 December 2009				
Private equity investments	**54**	**(54)**	**302**	**(299)**
Asset-backed securities	**41**	**(41)**	**734**	**(735)**
Leveraged finance	**1**	**(1)**	–	–
Loans held for securitisation	**16**	**(16)**	–	–
Structured notes	**3**	**(3)**	–	–
Derivatives with monolines	**333**	**(25)**	–	–
Other derivatives	**309**	**(332)**	–	–
Other portfolios	**329**	**(203)**	**125**	**(123)**
At 31 December 2008				
Private equity investments	28	(28)	234	(261)
Asset-backed securities	90	(91)	667	(660)
Leveraged finance	2	(2)	–	–
Loans held for securitisation	41	(41)	–	–
Structured notes	8	(8)	–	–

Derivatives with monolines	341	(250)	–	–
Other derivatives	652	(224)	–	–
Other portfolios	134	(89)	83	(84)

Favourable and unfavourable changes are determined on the basis of changes in the value of the instrument as a result of varying the levels of the unobservable parameters using statistical techniques. When parameters are not amenable to statistical analysis, quantification of uncertainty is judgemental.

When the fair value of a financial instrument is affected by more than one unobservable assumption, the above table reflects the most favourable or most unfavourable change from varying the assumptions individually.

In respect of private equity investments, the valuations are assessed on an asset by asset basis using a valuation methodology appropriate to the specific investment, in line with industry guidelines. In many of the methodologies, the principal assumption is the valuation multiple to be applied to the main financial indicators. This may be determined with reference to multiples for comparable listed companies and includes discounts for marketability.

For ABSs whose prices are unobservable, models are used to generate the expected value of the asset. The principal assumptions in these models are based on benchmark information about prepayment speeds, default rates, loss severities and the historical performance of the underlying assets. The models used are calibrated by using securities for which external market information is available.

For leveraged finance, loans held for securitisation and derivatives with monolines the principal assumption concerns the appropriate value to be attributed to the counterparty credit risk. This requires estimation of exposure at default, probability of default and recovery in the event of default. For loan transactions, assessment of exposure at default is straightforward. For derivative transactions, a future exposure profile is generated on the basis of current market data. Probabilities of default and recovery levels are estimated using market evidence, which may include financial information, historical experience, CDS spreads and consensus recovery levels. In the absence of such evidence, management's best estimate is used.

For structured notes and other derivatives, principal assumptions concern the value to be attributed to future volatility of asset values and the future correlation between asset values. These principal assumptions include credit volatilities and correlations used in the valuation of structured credit derivatives (including leveraged credit derivatives). For such unobservable assumptions, estimates are based on available market data, which may include the use of a proxy method to derive a volatility or a correlation from comparable assets for which market

Table 11.6.2 – Fair value hierarchy

Centrica plc – Annual report – 31 December 2009

(Note: comparatives have not been included in this example)

9. Fair value of financial instruments (extract)

Fair value hierarchy

Financial assets and financial liabilities measured at fair value are classified into one of three categories:

Level 1

Fair value is determined using observable inputs that reflect unadjusted quoted market prices for identical assets and liabilities, for example exchange-traded commodity contracts valued using close-of-day settlement prices. The adjusted market price used for financial assets held by the Group is the current bid price.

Level 2
Fair value is determined using significant inputs that may be either directly observable inputs or unobservable inputs that are corroborated by market data, for example over-the-counter energy contracts within the active period valued using broker quotes or third-party pricing services and foreign exchange or interest rate derivatives valued using quotes corroborated with market data.

Level 3
Fair value is determined using significant unobservable inputs that are not corroborated by market data and may be used with internally-developed methodologies that result in management's best estimate of fair value, for example energy contracts within the inactive period valued using in-house valuation techniques.

The fair value hierarchy of financial assets and liabilities measured at fair value as at 31 December 2009 was as follows:

	Level 1 £m	Level 2 £m	Level 3 £m	Total £m
Financial assets				
Derivative financial instruments:				
Energy derivatives	46	550	64	660
Interest rate derivatives	–	72	–	72
Foreign exchange derivatives	2	74	–	76
Treasury gilts designated at fair value through profit and loss	104	–	–	104
Debt instruments	62	56	–	118
Equity instruments	17	–	11	28
Total financial assets	231	752	75	1,058
Financial liabilities				
Derivative financial instruments:				
Energy derivatives	(198)	(1,954)	(490)	(2,642)
Interest rate derivatives	–	(15)	–	(15)
Foreign exchange derivatives	–	(93)	–	(93)
Total financial liabilities	(198)	(2,062)	(490)	(2,750)

There were no significant transfers out of Level 1 into Level 2 and out of Level 2 into Level 1 during 2009.

The reconciliation of the Level 3 fair value measurements during the period is as follows:

	Equity instruments £m	Energy derivatives £m	2009 £m
Level 3 financial assets 1 January	3	399	402
Total realised and unrealised losses recognised in profit or loss	–	(247)	(247)
Transfers from Level 3 to Level 2	–	(88)	(88)
Acquisitions	8	–	8
31 December	11	64	75
Total gains for the period for Level 3 financial assets held at the end of the reporting period	–	64	64

Gains or losses for the period (above) are presented in the Income Statement and Statement of Other Comprehensive Income as follows:

	Exceptional items and certain re-measurements £m	Other comprehensive income £m	Total £m
Total losses for the period	(247)	–	(247)
Total gains for the period for assets held at the end of the reporting period	64	–	64

Losses for the period (above) are presented in the Income Statement and Statement of Other Comprehensive Income as follows:

	Energy derivatives £m	2009 £m
Level 3 financial liabilities		
1 January	(568)	(568)
Total realised and unrealised losses:		
Recognised in profit or loss	(54)	(54)
Recognised in other comprehensive income	(9)	(9)
Transfers from Level 3 to Level 2	141	141
31 December	(490)	(490)
Total losses for the period for Level 3 financial liabilities held at the end of the reporting period	(490)	(490)

Losses for the period (above) are presented in the Income Statement and Statement of Other Comprehensive Income as follows:

	Exceptional items and certain re-measurements £m	Other comprehensive income £m	Total £m
Total losses for the period	(247)	–	(247)
Total gains for the period for assets held at the end of the reporting period	64	–	64

The impacts of reasonably possible changes to assumed gas, power, coal, emissions and oil prices on the net fair value of the Group's fair value measurements categorised as Level 3 are as follows:

Energy price	2009 Reasonably possible change in variable
UK gas (p/therm)	+/-10
UK power (£/MWh)	+/-5
UK coal (US$/tonne)	+/-20
UK emissions (€/tonne)	+/-3
UK oil (US$/bbl)	+/-19

Increase/(decrease) in fair value	2009 £m
UK energy prices – increase/(decrease)	17/(17)

The impacts disclosed above result from changing the assumptions used for fair valuing energy contracts in relation to gas, power, emissions, coal and oil prices to reasonably possible alternative assumptions at the balance sheet date. The fair value impacts only concern those contracts entered into which are within the scope of IAS 39 and are marked-to-market based on valuation models using assumptions that are not currently observable in an active market. The sensitivity analysis provided is hypothetical only and should be used with caution, as the impacts provided are not necessarily indicative of the actual impacts that would be experienced because the Group's actual exposure to market rates is constantly changing as the Group's portfolio of energy contracts changes. Changes in fair values based on a variation in a market variable cannot be extrapolated as the relationship between the change in market variable and the change in fair value may not be linear.

Financial instrument risk disclosures

11.79   An entity should disclose information that enables users of its financial statements to evaluate the nature and extent of risks arising from financial instruments to which the entity is exposed at the reporting date. [IFRS 7 para 31].

11.80   The disclosures described from paragraph 11.83 onwards focus on the risks that arise from financial instruments and how they have been managed. These risks typically include, but are not limited to, credit risk, liquidity risk and market risk as discussed in paragraph 11.44 above. [IFRS 7 para 32].

11.81   When an entity uses several methods to manage a risk exposure, it should disclose information using the method or methods that provide the most relevant and reliable information. [IFRS 7 App B para 7].

11.82   The disclosures should be given either in the financial statements or incorporated by cross-reference from the financial statements to some other statement, such as a management commentary or risk report, that is available to users of the financial statements on the same terms as the financial statements and at the same time. Without the information incorporated by cross-reference, the financial statements are incomplete. [IFRS 7 App B para 6].

Qualitative disclosures

11.83   For each type of risk arising from financial instruments, an entity should disclose:

■   The exposures to risk and how they arise.

Information about risk exposures might describe exposures both gross and net of risk transfer and other risk-mitigating transactions.

■   Its objectives, policies and processes for managing the risk and the methods used to measure the risk. This might include, but is not limited to:

  ■   The structure and organisation of the entity's risk management functions, including a discussion of independence and accountability.

  ■   The scope and nature of the entity's risk reporting or measurement systems.

  ■   The entity's policies for hedging or mitigating risk, including its policies and procedures for taking collateral.

- The entity's processes for monitoring the continuing effectiveness of such hedges or mitigating devices.

- The entity's policies and procedures for avoiding excessive concentrations of risk.

■ Any changes in the above for the period.
Entities should disclose the reasons for the change. Such changes may result from changes in exposure to risk or from changes in the way those exposures are managed.

[IFRS 7 paras 33, IG 15-16].

11.84 An example of a company that has included the above disclosure requirements in its risk management policy is given in Table 11.8 below. Note that the disclosures precede the effective date of the revised IAS 1 and thus the titles of the performance statements referred to are before the new titles introduced by IAS 1.

Table 11.8 – Risk management policy

Diageo plc – Annual Report – 30 June 2009

Risk Management

This section on risk management forms part of the audited financial statements.

The group's funding, liquidity and exposure to interest rate and foreign exchange rate risks are managed by the group's treasury department. The treasury department uses a combination of derivative and conventional financial instruments to manage these underlying risks.

Treasury operations are conducted within a framework of board-approved policies and guidelines, which are recommended and subsequently monitored by the finance committee. This committee is described in the corporate governance report. These policies and guidelines include benchmark exposure and/or hedge cover levels for key areas of treasury risk. The benchmarks, hedge cover and overall appropriateness of Diageo's risk management policies are reviewed by the board following, for example, significant business, strategic or accounting changes. The framework provides for limited defined levels of flexibility in execution to allow for the optimal application of the board-approved strategies. Transactions giving rise to exposures away from the defined benchmark levels arising on the application of this flexibility are separately monitored on a daily basis using value at risk analysis. These derivative financial instruments are carried at fair value and gains or losses are taken to the income statement as they arise. At 30 June 2009 gains and losses on these transactions were not material.

The finance committee receives monthly reports on the activities of the treasury department, including any exposures away from the defined benchmarks.

Currency risk
The group publishes its consolidated financial statements in sterling and conducts business in many foreign currencies. As a result, it is subject to foreign currency exchange risk due to exchange rate movements, which will affect the group's transaction costs and the translation of the results and underlying net assets of its foreign operations. Where hedge accounting is applied, hedges are documented and tested for hedge effectiveness on an ongoing basis. Diageo expects hedges entered into to continue to be effective and therefore does not expect the impact of ineffectiveness on the income statement to be material.

Hedge of net investment in foreign operations

The group hedges a substantial portion of its exposure to fluctuations on the translation into sterling of its foreign operations by designating net borrowings held in foreign currencies and by using foreign currency swaps and forwards. Where a liquid foreign exchange market exists, the group's policy approved by the board is to seek to hedge currency exposure on its net investment in foreign operations within the following percentage bands: 80% to 100% for US dollars, 80% to 100% for euros and 50% to 100% for other significant currencies.

Exchange differences arising on the retranslation of foreign currency borrowings (including foreign currency swaps and forwards), to the extent that they are in an effective hedge relationship, are recognised in the statement of recognised income and expense to match exchange differences on net investments in foreign operations. Exchange differences on foreign currency borrowings not in a hedge relationship and any ineffectiveness are taken to the income statement.

Transaction exposure hedging

For currencies in which there is an active market, the group's policy approved by the board is to seek to hedge between 60% and 100% of forecast transactional foreign exchange rate risk, for up to a maximum of 21 months forward, using forward foreign currency exchange contracts with coverage levels increasing nearer to the forecast transaction date. The effective portion of the gain or loss on the hedge is recognised in the statement of recognised income and expense and recycled into the income statement at the same time as the underlying hedged transaction affects the income statement. Any ineffectiveness is taken to the income statement.

Hedge of foreign currency debt

The group uses cross currency interest rate swaps to hedge the forward foreign currency risk associated with certain foreign currency denominated bonds. The effective portion of the gain or loss on the hedge is recognised in the statement of recognised income and expense and recycled into the income statement at the same time as the underlying hedged transaction affects the income statement. Any ineffectiveness is taken to the income statement.

Interest rate risk

The group has an exposure to interest rate risk, arising principally on changes in US dollar, euro and sterling interest rates. To manage interest rate risk, the group manages its proportion of fixed to floating rate borrowings within limits approved by the board, primarily through issuing fixed and floating rate term debt and commercial paper, and by utilising interest rate derivatives. These practices serve to reduce the volatility of the group's reported financial performance. To facilitate operational efficiency and effective hedge accounting, the group's policy is to maintain fixed rate borrowings within a band of 40% to 60% of projected net borrowings, and the overall net borrowings portfolio is managed according to a duration measure. The board approved template specifies different duration guidelines and fixed/floating amortisation periods (time taken for the fixed element of debt to reduce to zero) depending on different interest rate environments. The majority of Diageo's existing interest rate hedges are designated as hedges. Designated hedges are expected to be effective.

Liquidity risk

Liquidity risk is the risk that an entity will encounter difficulty in meeting obligations associated with financial liabilities that are settled by delivering cash or other financial assets. The group's policy with regard to the expected maturity profile of borrowings of group financing companies is to limit the amount of such borrowings maturing within 12 months to 50% of gross borrowings less money market demand deposits, and the level of commercial paper to 30% of gross borrowings less money market demand deposits. In addition, it is group policy to maintain backstop facility terms from relationship banks to support commercial paper obligations.

Quantitative disclosures

11.85 For each type of risk arising from financial instruments, an entity should disclose:

- Summary quantitative data about its exposure to that risk at the reporting date. This disclosure should be based on the information provided internally to the entity's key management personnel (as defined in IAS 24, 'Related party disclosures'), for example, the entity's board of directors or chief executive officer. An entity with two distinct operations (for example, a retail division and a manufacturing division) may be monitored by management separately as two divisions. All disclosures should normally be provided on a consolidated basis. However, those disclosures that are based on management reporting could be presented separately for both the divisions as that is the way management monitors the financial risks, unless there were material transactions between the divisions, in which case separate disclosures could be misleading.

- The disclosures described in paragraphs 11.86 to 11.118, to the extent not provided in the previous bullet point, unless the risk is not material. [IFRS 7 para 34(b)]. These, in other words, are IFRS 7's minimum disclosure requirements, regardless of whether management uses this information to manage the entity's risks. In terms of determining whether a risk is material consider the following example. An entity invests in a foreign currency bond maturing in one year and simultaneously enters into an foreign currency forward contract with a corresponding maturity to offset the foreign currency risk. In this case, the materiality of the foreign currency risk on the bond is assessed without the foreign currency forward contract. The bond and the forward are dissimilar items and, therefore, the materiality assessment of the foreign currency risk is performed without considering the forward contract. If it is established that the foreign currency risk is material, the disclosure required in the sensitivity analysis (see para 11.106) is based on the net foreign currency exposure; that after offsetting the foreign currency bond against the forward contract. The same approach would apply for the assessment of credit risk, liquidity risk and other market risk.

- Concentrations of risk if not apparent from the previous two bullet points (see para 11.86 below).

[IFRS 7 para 34].

11.86 Concentrations of risk arise from financial instruments that have similar characteristics and are affected similarly by changes in economic or other conditions. The identification of concentrations of risk requires judgement taking into account the entity's circumstances. Disclosure of concentrations of risk should include:

- A description of how management determines concentrations (see para 11.87 below).

- A description of the shared characteristic that identifies each concentration (for example, counterparty, geographical area, currency or market).

- The amount of the risk exposure associated with all financial instruments sharing that characteristic.

[IFRS 7 App B para 8].

11.87 Concentrations of credit risk may arise from:

- Industry sectors.

  Thus, if an entity's counterparties are concentrated in one or more industry sectors (such as retail or wholesale), it would disclose separately exposure to risks arising from each concentration of counterparties.

- Credit rating or other measure of credit quality.

  Thus, if an entity's counterparties are concentrated in one or more credit qualities (such as secured loans or unsecured loans) or in one or more credit ratings (such as investment grade or speculative grade), it would disclose separately exposure to risks arising from each concentration of counterparties.

- Geographical distribution.

  Thus, if an entity's counterparties are concentrated in one or more geographical markets (such as Asia or Europe) it would disclose separately exposure to risks arising from each concentration of counterparties.

- A limited number of individual counterparties or groups of closely related counterparties.

[IFRS 7 para IG18].

11.88 Similar principles apply to identifying concentrations of other risks, including liquidity risk and market risk. For example, concentrations of liquidity risk may arise from the repayment terms of financial liabilities, sources of borrowing facilities or reliance on a particular market in which to realise liquid assets. Concentrations of foreign exchange risk may arise if an entity has a significant net open position in a single foreign currency, or aggregate net open positions in several currencies that tend to move together. [IFRS 7 para IG18].

11.89 If the quantitative data disclosed as at the reporting date are unrepresentative of an entity's exposure to risk during the period, an entity should provide further information that is representative. [IFRS 7 para 35]. To meet this requirement, an entity might disclose the highest, lowest and average amount of risk to which it was exposed during the period. For example, if an entity typically has a large exposure to a particular currency, but at year-end unwinds the position, the entity might disclose a graph showing the exposure at various times during the period, or disclose the highest, lowest and average exposures. [IFRS 7 para IG20]. In addition consider the following examples:

Example 1 – Year end credit risk exposure unrepresentative due to seasonal fluctuations

Entity Y is producing seeds for the agricultural industry. The main season for planting is the spring. 75% of entity Y's markets are in the northern hemisphere; 25% are in the southern hemisphere. Entity Y's account receivables are approximately C400 million in June and C100 million in December. Entity Y has a December year end. Does entity Y have to disclose additional information about its exposure to credit risk on the receivables that is representative of its exposure to risk during the year?

In this case, the December year end exposure to credit risk is unrepresentative of the entity's exposure during the period. Entity Y should provide further information that is representative, such as a description (with amounts) of how the exposures vary during the year, or the average (or highest) exposure to credit risk during the year.

Example 2 – Year end credit risk exposure unrepresentative due to a major acquisition

On 30 November 20X6, entity A (€ functional currency) acquires a major competitor. Due to the acquisition, the US$ denominated receivables increased from $100 million to $300 million and variable interest rate debt doubled from €200 million to €400 million compared to the balances as at 30 June 20X6. Entity A has a December year end. The balances as of 31 December 20X6 are considered to be representative of the next year(s). Does entity A have to disclose additional information that is representative of its exposure to risk during the year?

In this scenario, entity A should disclose additional information because the quantitative data as at 31 December 20X6 is not representative of the financial period 20X6. A mere statement that the data is not representative is not sufficient. To meet IFRS 7's requirement the entity might disclose the highest, lowest and average amount of risk to which it was exposed during the period. However, a full high/low/average analysis might not be required if the exposure at the year end is representative for future periods and if sufficient explanations of the facts and circumstances are provided.

Credit risk

11.90   Activities that give rise to credit risk include, but are not limited to:

■   Granting loans and receivables to customers and placing deposits with other entities. In these cases, the maximum exposure to credit risk is the carrying amount of the related financial assets.

■   Entering into derivative contracts (for example, foreign exchange contracts, interest rate swaps and credit derivatives). When the resulting asset is measured at fair value, the maximum exposure to credit risk at the reporting date will equal the carrying amount.

■   Granting financial guarantees. In this case, the maximum exposure to credit risk is the maximum amount the entity could have to pay if the guarantee is called on, which may be significantly greater than the amount recognised as a liability.

■ Making a loan commitment that is irrevocable over the life of the facility or is revocable only in response to a material adverse change. If the issuer cannot settle the loan commitment net in cash or another financial instrument, the maximum credit exposure is the commitment's full amount. This is because it is uncertain whether the amount of any undrawn portion may be drawn upon in the future. This may be significantly greater than the amount recognised as a liability.

[IFRS 7 App B para 10].

11.91   IFRS 7 requires an entity to disclose information about its exposure to credit risk by class of financial instrument. Financial instruments in the same class share economic characteristics with respect to the risk being disclosed (in this case, credit risk). For example, an entity might determine that residential mortgages, unsecured consumer loans, and commercial loans each have different economic characteristics. The information an entity should disclose by class of financial instrument is as follows:

■ The amount that best represents its maximum exposure to credit risk at the reporting date without taking account of any collateral held or other credit enhancements (for example, netting agreements that do not qualify for offset in accordance with IAS 32 – see para 11.26 above). The 2010 annual improvements clarified that this disclosure is not required for financial instruments whose carrying amount best represents the maximum exposure to credit risk. This amendment applies to annual periods beginning on or after 1 January 2011 and early application is permitted.

■ In respect of the amount disclosed above, a description of collateral held as security and other credit enhancements (see para 11.93 below).

■ Information about the credit quality of financial assets that are neither past due nor impaired (see para 11.95 below).

■ The carrying amount of financial assets that would otherwise be past due or impaired whose terms have been renegotiated. This disclosure should be given only in the year when the renegotiation took place, that is, in the year in which the asset's contractual terms were changed. In subsequent years the asset is considered based on the new (renegotiated) terms and disclosure would only be required if renegotiated again. The disclosure of the carrying amount of financial assets which would have otherwise been past due but have been renegotiated has been removed by the changes to IFRS 7 as part of the 2010 annual improvements. These amendments apply to annual periods beginning on or after 1 January 2011 and early application is permitted.

[IFRS 7 para 36].

11.91.1 The above disclosures do not apply to an entity's holdings of equity investments. This is because the definition of equity in IAS 32 requires that the issuer has no obligation to pay cash or transfer other assets. Therefore, such equity investments are subject to price risk, not credit risk. The only exception is where such financial assets have been impaired. They will then require the disclosure discussed in second bullet of paragraph 11.96.

11.91.2 In respect of the first bullet point in paragraph 11.91 above, the amount that best represents the entity's maximum exposure to credit risk relating to financial assets is typically the gross carrying amount, net of:

■ any amounts offset in accordance with IAS 32 (see para 11.15 above); and

■ any impairment losses recognised in accordance with IAS 39.

[IFRS 7 App B para 9].

[The next paragraph is 11.93.]

Collateral and other credit enhancements

11.93 In respect of the second bullet point in paragraph 11.91 above, an entity's description about collateral held as security and other credit enhancements might include:

■ The policies and processes for valuing and managing collateral and other credit enhancements obtained.

■ A description of the main types of collateral and other credit enhancements (examples of the latter being guarantees, credit derivatives and netting agreements that do not qualify for offset in accordance with IAS 32).

■ The main types of counterparties to collateral and other credit enhancements and their creditworthiness.

■ Information about risk concentrations within the collateral or other credit enhancements.

[IFRS 7 para IG22].

11.94 When an entity obtains financial or non-financial assets during the period by taking possession of collateral it holds as security or calling on other credit enhancements, and such assets meet the recognition criteria in other IFRSs, an entity should disclose:

■ The nature and carrying amount of the assets obtained.

■ When the assets are not readily convertible into cash, its policies for disposing of such assets or for using them in its operations.

[IFRS 7 para 38].

The 2010 annual improvements to IFRS 7 clarified that these disclosures are required only for foreclosed collateral at the balance sheet date. This amendment applies to annual periods beginning on or after 1 January 2011 and early application is permitted.

Credit quality of financial assets that are neither past due nor impaired

11.95   In respect of the third bullet point in paragraph 11.91, information about credit quality of financial assets that are neither past due nor impaired might include:

■   An analysis of credit exposures using an external or internal credit rating system.

Where an entity manages its credit exposures using an external credit rating system, an entity might disclose information about:

   ■   The carrying amounts of credit exposures for each external credit rating.

   ■   The rating agencies used.

   ■   The amount of an entity's rated and unrated credit exposures.

   ■   The relationship between internal and external ratings.

Where an entity manages its credit exposures using an internal credit rating system, an entity might disclose information about:

   ■   The internal credit ratings process.

   ■   The amounts of credit exposures for each internal credit rating.

   ■   The relationship between internal and external ratings.

■   The nature of the counterparty.

■   Historical information about counterparty default rates.

■   Any other information used to assess credit quality.

[IFRS 7 paras IG23-25].

Financial assets that are either past due or impaired

11.96   A financial asset is past due when the counterparty has failed to make a payment when contractually due. As an example, an entity enters into a lending agreement that requires interest to be paid every month. On the first day of the next month, if interest has not been paid, the whole loan is past due, not just the interest. Past due does not mean that a counterparty will never pay, but it can trigger various actions such as renegotiation, enforcement of covenants, or legal proceedings. [IFRS 7 para IG26]. An entity should disclose by class of financial asset:

- An analysis of the age of financial assets that are past due as at the reporting date but not impaired. The purpose of this disclosure is to provide users of the financial statements with information about those financial assets that are more likely to become impaired and to help users to estimate the level of future impairment losses. Thus, the entire balance which relates to the amount past due should be disclosed, rather than only the amount that is past due, as this is the amount that would be disclosed as the amount of the impaired financial assets if impairment crystallises.

Other associated balances due from the same debtor are not included if the debtor has not yet failed to make a payment on these balances when contractually due.

In preparing such an age analysis of financial assets, an entity uses its judgement to determine an appropriate number of time bands. For example, an entity might determine that the following time bands are appropriate:

- Not more than three months.

- More than three months and not more than six months.

- More than six months and not more than one year.

- More than one year.

- An analysis of financial assets that are individually determined to be impaired as at the reporting date, including the factors the entity considered in determining that they are impaired. These disclosures are not only given in the year of impairment, but also in each subsequent reporting period during which the fair value of a financial asset is below its historical cost and, therefore, considered 'impaired'. Such an analysis might include:

- The carrying amount, before deducting any impairment loss.

- The amount of any related impairment loss.

- The nature and fair value of collateral available and other credit enhancements obtained. The collateral disclosure requirement has been removed as part of the 2010 annual improvements to IFRS 7. These are applicable for periods starting on or after 1 January 2011, with early application permitted.

This is the only disclosure relating to credit risk that must be made in respect of an entity's equity investments (see para 11.91.1).

Example – Assessment of receivables individually determined to be impaired

Entity M has C300m of receivables which it has analysed as follows:

- C120m has been assessed individually for impairment and are considered to be impaired.

- C40m represents a collection of insignificant receivables that are individually determined to be impaired, but the impairment calculation is performed on the whole C40m amount for efficiency purposes.

- C140m represents a portfolio of receivables for which there is observable data indicating that there is a measurable decrease in the estimated future cash flows, although the decrease cannot be identified with individual balances.

Of these, only the first two amounts have been individually assessed for impairment and so would require disclosure under IFRS 7. [IFRS 7 para 36(b)]. Disclosure would not be required in respect of the third bullet, as the receivables have been assessed on a portfolio basis rather than individually. In respect of each of the amounts disclosed above, a description of collateral held by the entity as security and other credit enhancements and unless impracticable, an estimate of their fair value (see para 11.93 above).

[IFRS 7 paras 37, IG28-29].

11.97 An example of a company that has given credit risk disclosures (qualitative and quantitative) for a class of its financial assets (trade receivables) is given in Table 11.9.

Table 11.9 – Trade and other receivables

Adidas AG – Annual report – 31 December 2009

Financial Risks (extract)
Credit risks

A credit risk arises if a customer or other counterparty to a financial instrument fails to meet its contractual obligations. The adidas Group is exposed to credit risk from its operating activities and from certain financing activities. Credit risks arise principally from accounts receivable and to a lesser extent from other contractual financial obligations such as other financial assets, short-term bank deposits and derivative financial instruments see Note 28. Without taking into account any collateral or other credit enhancements, the carrying amount of financial assets represents the maximum exposure to credit risk.

At the end of 2009, there was no relevant concentration of credit risk by type of customer or geography. Instead, our credit risk exposure is mainly influenced by individual customer characteristics. Under the Group's credit policy, new customers are analysed for creditworthiness before standard payment and delivery terms and conditions are offered. This review utilises external ratings from credit agencies. Tolerance limits for accounts receivable are also established for each customer. Then both creditworthiness and accounts receivable limits are monitored on an ongoing basis. Customers that fail to meet the Group's minimum creditworthiness are in general allowed to purchase products only on a prepayment basis. Other activities to mitigate credit risks, which are employed on a selective basis only, include credit insurances, accounts receivable sales without recourse and bank guarantees as well as retention of title clauses.

The Group utilises allowance accounts for impairments that represent our estimate of incurred credit losses with respect to accounts receivable. The allowance consists of two components:

(1) an allowance based on historical experience of unexpected losses established for all receivables dependent on the ageing structure of receivables past due date, and
(2) a specific allowance that relates to individually assessed risk for each specific customer – irrespective of ageing.

At the end of 2009, no Group customer accounted for more than 10% of accounts receivable. Nevertheless, the negative impact of the deterioration of the global economy on consumer confidence and spending is not expected to be reversed significantly in 2010 in view of the still very challenging economic environment. As a consequence, we believe that our overall credit risk level from customers, particularly smaller retailers, remains high in several markets see Economic and Sector Development. Therefore, our estimate of the likelihood and potential financial impact of credit risks from customers remains medium.

Credit risks from other financial contractual relationships include items such as other financial assets, short-term bank deposits and derivative financial instruments. The adidas Group Treasury department arranges currency and interest rate hedges, and invests cash, with major banks of a high credit standing throughout the world. adidas Group companies are authorised to work with banks rated "BBB+" or higher.

Only in exceptional cases are subsidiaries authorised to work with banks rated lower than "BBB+". To limit risk in these cases, restrictions are clearly stipulated such as maximum cash deposit levels. In addition, the credit default swap premiums of our partner banks are monitored on a weekly basis. In the event that the defined threshold is exceeded, credit balances are shifted to banks compliant with the limit. During 2009, the credit default swap premiums for many banks declined from their highs in the aftermath of the financial turmoil in 2008, mainly as a result of governmental intervention worldwide. This development indicates a slight decrease of the associated risks.

Although financial market conditions stabilised in 2009, we continue to believe that the likelihood and potential financial impact of credit risks from these assets is medium. Nevertheless, we believe our risk concentration is limited due to the broad distribution of our investment business with more than 24 banks. At December 31, 2009, no bank accounted for more than 19% of our investment business and the average concentration, including subsidiaries' short-term deposits in local banks, was 1%. This leads to a maximum exposure of € 158 million in the event of default of any single bank. Furthermore, we held derivatives with a positive fair market value in the amount of € 55 million. The maximum exposure to any single bank resulting from these assets amounted to € 4 million and the average concentration was 3%.

07 Accounts receivable

Accounts receivable consist mainly of the currencies US dollar, euro and Japanese yen and are as follows:

ACCOUNTS RECEIVABLE
€ in millions

	Dec. 31, 2009	Dec. 31, 2008
Accounts receivable, gross	1,553	1,743
Less: allowance for doubtful accounts	124	119
Accounts receivable, net	**1,429**	**1,624**

Movement in allowances for doubtful accounts
€ in millions

	2009	2008
Allowances at January 1	119	111
Additions	68	49
Additions – Ashworth, Inc. acquisition	–	4
Reversals	(29)	(22)
Write-offs charged against the allowance accounts	(34)	(21)
Currency translation differences	0	(2)
Other changes	0	0

Allowances at December 31				**124**	**119**

Accounts receivable past due but not impaired

€ in million	past due 1 – 30 days	past due 31 – 60 days	past due 61 – 90 days	past due 91 – 180 days	past due more than 180 days
Dec. 31, 2009	**115**	**57**	**10**	**6**	**5**
Dec. 31, 2008	163	77	20	10	10

With respect to accounts receivable past due but not impaired, based on credit history and current credit ratings, there are no indications that customers will not be able to meet their obligations.

Further, no indications of default are recognisable for accounts receivable that are neither past due nor impaired.

Liquidity risk

11.98 Summary quantitative data about an entity's exposure to liquidity risk should be disclosed on the basis of the information provided internally to key management personnel. An entity should explain how those data are determined. If the outflows of cash (or another financial asset) included in those data could either:

■ occur significantly earlier than indicated in the data; or

■ be for significantly different amounts from those indicated in the data (for example, for a derivative that is included in the data on a net settlement basis, but for which the counterparty has the option to require gross settlement),

the entity should state that fact and provide quantitative information that enables users of its financial statements to evaluate the extent of liquidity risk, unless that information is included in the maturity analyses described in paragraph 11.99 below. [IFRS 7 App B para 10A]. An example of a cash outflow that could occur significantly earlier than indicated in the data could be a bond that is callable by the issuer in, say, two years but has a remaining contractual maturity of, say, ten years.

11.98.1 The amendment to IFRS 7 modified the minimum disclosure requirements related to liquidity risk. An entity should disclose:

■ A maturity analysis for non-derivative financial liabilities (including issued financial guarantee contracts) that shows the remaining contractual maturities.

■ A maturity analysis for derivative financial liabilities. The maturity analysis should include the remaining contractual maturities for those derivative financial liabilities for which contractual maturities are essential for an understanding of the timing of the cash flows.

■ A description of how it manages the liquidity risk inherent in the above. [IFRS 7 para 39].

11.98.2 This information can be summarised in one or several maturity analysis tables. It should be clear for the users of the financial statements whether the disclosure is based on contractual maturities or expected maturities and whether the financial liabilities are derivatives or non-derivatives.

11.99 In preparing the contractual maturity analyses described in paragraph 11.99, an entity uses its judgement to determine an appropriate number of time bands. For example, an entity might determine that the following time bands are appropriate:

■ Not later than one month.

■ Later than one month and not later than three months.

■ Later than three months and not later than one year.

■ Later than one year and not later than five years.

[IFRS 7 App B para 11].

11.100 For the maturity analyses based on contractual cash flows, when a counterparty has a choice of when an amount is paid, the liability is included on the basis of the earliest date on which the entity can be required to pay. For example, financial liabilities that an entity can be required to repay on demand (for example, demand deposits) are included in the earliest time band. [IFRS 7 App B para 11C(a)].

11.101 When an entity is committed to make amounts available in instalments, each instalment is allocated to the earliest period in which the entity can be required to pay. For example, an undrawn loan commitment is included in the time band containing the earliest date it can be drawn down. [IFRS 7 App B para 11C(b)].

11.101.1 When an entity has issued a financial guarantee contract, the maximum amount of the guarantee is allocated to the earliest period in which the guarantee could be called. [IFRS 7 App B para 11C(c)].

11.101.2 The maximum amount of an undrawn loan commitment should also be included in the maturity analysis, allocated to the earliest period in which the commitment could be called. Once a loan is drawn down, it will be included in the maturity analysis as a non-derivative financial liability.

11.102 The amounts disclosed in the maturity analyses on a contractual basis (see para 11.97) are the contractual undiscounted cash flows (including principal and interest payments). For example:

■ Gross finance lease obligations (before deducting finance charges).

- Prices specified in forward agreements to purchase financial assets for cash.

- Net amounts for pay-floating receive-fixed interest rate swaps for which net cash flows are exchanged.

- Contractual amounts to be exchanged in a derivative financial instrument (for example, a currency swap) for which gross cash flows are exchanged.

- Gross loan commitments.

[IFRS 7 App B para 11D].

11.102.1 The undiscounted cash flows described above differ from the amounts included in the balance sheet, which are based on discounted cash flows. There is no specific requirement to reconcile the amounts disclosed in the maturity analysis to the amounts included in the balance sheet.

11.103 When the amount payable is not fixed, the amount disclosed in the maturity analyses is determined by reference to the conditions existing at the end of the reporting period. For example, when the amount payable varies with changes in an index, the amount disclosed may be based on the level of the index at the end of the period. [IFRS 7 App B para 11D]. For floating rate financial liabilities and foreign currency denominated instruments, the use of forward interest rates and forward foreign exchange rates may be conceptually preferable, but the use of a spot rate at the end of the period is also acceptable. Whichever approach is adopted (that is, current/spot rate or forward rate at the reporting date), it should be applied consistently.

11.104 As noted in paragraph 11.99, the contractual cash flows of derivative financial liabilities for which contractual maturities are essential for an understanding of the cash flows should be included in maturity analysis. For example, this would be the case for the following:

- An interest rate swap with a remaining maturity of five years in a cash flow hedge of a variable rate financial asset or liability.

- All loan commitments.

[IFRS 7 App B para 11B].

11.104.1 Other derivatives are included in a separate maturity analysis on the basis on which they are managed. It may be expected that contractual maturities are essential for an understanding of the timing of cash flows for derivatives, unless the facts and circumstances indicate another basis is appropriate. For example, contractual maturities would not be essential for an understanding of the derivatives in a trading portfolio that are expected to be settled before contractual maturity on a net basis. Disclosure of fair values of such derivatives on an expected maturity basis would, therefore, be appropriate.

11.104.1.1 An entity should disclosure a maturity analysis of financial assets it holds for managing liquidity risk (for example, financial assets that are readily saleable or expected to generate cash inflows to meet cash outflows on financial liabilities), if that information is necessary to enable users of its financial statements to evaluate the nature and extent of liquidity risk. [IFRS 7 App B para 11E].

11.104.1.2   IFRS 7 gives as an example of an amount included in the maturity analysis on a contractual undiscounted basis the amounts exchanged in a gross-settled derivative contract). The standard refers only to a maturity analysis for derivative financial liabilities, so it would appear that only disclosure of gross cash outflows (that is, the pay leg) in respect of derivative financial liabilities is required. However, it may be more helpful to also disclose the cash inflows (that is, the receive leg). As explained in paragraph 11.104.1.1, IFRS 7 requires disclosure of a maturity analysis for financial assets where that information is necessary to enable users of financial statements to evaluate the nature and extent of liquidity risk. By analogy, we consider that disclosure of the receive leg in a gross-settled derivative financial liability will also often be necessary for an understanding of liquidity risk. A maturity analysis of derivative financial assets may also be required.

11.104.1.3   A similar analysis to the previous paragraph applies in the case of gross-settled commodity contracts. Where such a contract falls within IAS 39's scope, the associated cash outflows should be included in the maturity analysis where the contract is a financial liability at the reporting date (that is, it has a negative fair value) and where it will result in a cash outflow (rather than physical outflows of commodities). It may be helpful to disclose the contractual cash outflows of all commodity contracts, including those with both positive and negative fair values at the balance sheet date. Alternatively, it may be more meaningful to disclose gross-settled commodity contracts in a separate table showing both the cash inflows/outflows and the associated commodity outflows/inflows for all contracts. If this additional disclosure is given, an entity might cross-reference the cash outflows to the maturity analysis. Whichever of these alternative methods of presentation is adopted, the basis of preparation and measurement should be explained.

11.104.1.3.1   The liquidity risk disclosures for derivative financial liabilities can be summarised as follows:

	Gross settled deriviatives	Net settled derivatives
Contractual maturity is essential to understanding	• Disclose pay leg based on contractual maturity. • Disclose receive leg	• Disclose net cash flows based on contractual maturity.
Contractual maturity is not essential to understanding	Disclose how the risk is managed. For example, an entity might disclose: • Cash flows based on contractual maturities – pay and receive leg. • Fair value in the relevant time band (based on expected maturity (i.e. expected settlement date); contractual maturity or in the on demand category).	Disclose how risk is managed. For example, an entity might disclose: • Net cash flows based on contractual maturity. • Fair value in the relevant time band (based on expected maturity (i.e. expected settlement date); contractual maturity or in the on demand category).

11.104.1.4   For the purpose of the maturity analysis, embedded derivatives included in hybrid (combined) financial instruments should not be separated. A hybrid instrument should be included in the maturity analysis for non-derivative financial liabilities. [IFRS 7 App B para 11A].

11.104.1.5   Contracts settled in own shares that are not equity instruments of the issuer (for example, a contract that requires an entity to issue a fixed number of its own shares for a variable amount of cash upon the holder's request) are not in the scope of the maturity analysis, as the entity will issue own shares to meet the above obligation and does not, therefore, have an obligation to deliver cash or another financial asset. An obligation to deliver own shares does not give rise to liquidity risk as defined by IFRS 7. [IFRS 7 para BC58A(a)].

11.104.1.6   The factors that an entity might consider in providing a description of how it manages liquidity risk include, but are not limited to, whether the entity:

■   Has committed borrowing facilities (for example, commercial paper facilities) or other lines of credit (for example, stand-by credit facilities) that it can access to meet liquidity needs.

■   Holds deposits at central banks to meet liquidity needs.

■   Has very diverse funding sources.

■   Has significant concentrations of liquidity risk in either its assets or its funding sources.

■   Has internal control processes and contingency plans for managing liquidity risk.

■   Has instruments that include accelerated repayment terms (for example, on the downgrade of the entity's credit rating).

■   Has instruments that could require the posting of collateral (for example, margin calls for derivatives).

- Has instruments that allow the entity to choose whether it settles its financial liabilities by delivering cash (or another financial asset) or by delivering its own shares.

- Has instruments that are subject to master netting agreements.

[IFRS 7 App B para 11F].

11.104.1.7 Collateral requirements on financial instruments can pose a significant liquidity risk. For example, an entity with a derivative liability may be required to post cash collateral on the derivative should the liability exceed certain limits. As a result, if collateral calls pose significant liquidity risk, entities should provide quantitative disclosures of their collateral arrangements as those cash flows could occur earlier than the contractual maturity (see also para 11.98).

11.104.1.8 The description of how an entity manages its liquidity risk should also include a maturity analysis of financial assets it holds for managing liquidity risk (for example, financial assets that are readily saleable or expected to generate cash inflows to meet cash outflows on financial liabilities), if that information is necessary to enable users of its financial statements to evaluate the nature and extent of liquidity risk. [IFRS 7 App B para 11E].

11.104.1.9 Financial institutions typically use financial assets to manage their liquidity risk. A maturity analysis of financial assets is likely to be necessary to enable users of financial statements to evaluate the nature and extent of liquidity risk. However, the disclosure requirements are not only relevant for financial institutions. Certain other types of entities with significant trading activities (such as energy companies) may hold financial assets to manage liquidity risk. Where such activities are a significant part of the entity's business, a maturity analysis of financial assets may be required.

11.104.1.10 Where an entity presents a maturity analysis of financial assets, it should be prepared on the basis of information provided internally to key management personnel. It may be based either on contractual or expected maturity dates, depending on how the risk is managed. Alternatively, the analysis could be presented on a net basis (that is, fair value).

[The next paragraph is 11.104.3.]

11.104.3 The examples that follow illustrate how a maturity analysis may be prepared on a contractual basis for some typical financial instruments.

Example 1 – Floating rate notes

On 1 January 20X6 entity A issued two-year, US$30m floating rate notes that pay interest of 6m LIBOR plus 2%. The notes mature on 31 December 20X8.

Principal is redeemable at maturity. The carrying amount at the balance sheet date is US$30m (C21.6m).

The functional currency of the entity is C (currency units).

The spot rate at the balance sheet date is US$ = C0.72

The 6 month LIBOR at the balance sheet date is 5% per annum.

Scenario 1 – Contractual cash flows of the notes (using spot rates at the balance sheet date)

	30 Jun 20X7	31 Dec 20X7	30 Jun 20X8	31 Dec 20X8	Total
Principal (US$)	–	–	–	30,000	30,000
Interest payments (LIBOR + 2%)	1,050	1,050	1,050	1,050	4,200
Total (in US$)	1,050	1,050	1,050	31,050	34,200
US/C spot rate as at 31 Dec 20X6	0.72	0.72	0.72	0.72	0.72
Total cash flows (in C)	756	756	756	22,356	24,624

Scenario 2 – Contractual cash flows of the notes (using forward rates available at the balance sheet date)

6m LIBOR yield curve	5.25%	5.50%	5.75%	5.40%
6m LIBOR yield curve + 2% per annum	7.25%	7.50%	7.75%	7.40%

	30 Jun 20X7	31 Dec 20X7	30 Jun 20X8	31 Dec 20X8	Total
Principal (US$)	–	–	–	30,000	30,000
Interest payments (LIBOR + 2%)	1,088	1,125	1,163	1,110	4,486
Total (in US$)	1,088	1,125	1,163	31,110	34,486
US/C forward rate as at 31 Dec 20X6	0.75	0.78	0.79	0.76	
Total cash flows (in C)	816	878	919	23,644	26,257

Liquidity analysis

Solution 1 (based on spot rates)

Financial liabilities as at 31 Dec 20X6	Less than 1 month	Between 1 and 3M	Between 3M and 1Y	Between 1 and 5Y	Over 5Y	Balance sheet amounts
Floating rate notes	–	–	1.512	23,112	–	21,600

Alternative answer based on forward rates

Financial liabilities as at 31 Dec 20X6	Less than 1 month	Between 1 and 3 months	Between 3 months and 1 year	Between 1 and 5 years	Over 5 years	Balance sheet amounts
Floating rate notes	–	–	1,694	24,563	–	21,600

Either the spot rate or the forward rate could be used for the interest rate cash outflow calculation. The forward rate would be based on a yield curve (which will show by how much LIBOR is expected to move each quarter/six months).

Both alternatives are acceptable provided they are properly disclosed and applied consistently.

The sum of all the amounts in the maturity analysis does not reconcile to the balance sheet amount. This is because the liquidity analysis is based on the undiscounted cash flows.

Example 2 – Interest rate swap

Entity A entered into a two-year interest rate swap, notional value C10m, under which fixed interest of 5% per annum is received quarterly and actual 3 month LIBOR is paid. The contract is settled on a net basis. The swap has a negative fair value of C0.071m at the balance sheet date.

Estimated cash flows on the swap (C'000)

	31 Mar 20X7	30 Jun 20X7	30 Sept 20X7	31 Dec 20X7	31 Mar 20X8	30 Jun 20X8	30 Sept 20X8	31 Dec 20X8	Total
Fixed leg (receives fixed)	125	125	125	125	125	125	125	125	
Variable leg (pays 3 month LIBOR)	-110	-122	-136	-150	-155	-160	-172	-186	
Undiscounted net cash flows	15	3	-11	-25	-30	-35	-47	-61	-191
Discounted cashflows	13	2	-7	-14	-14	-15	-17	-19	-71

Only derivatives with a negative fair value (financial liabilities) at the balance sheet date should be included in the liquidity analysis. The cash flows to be included are those undiscounted cash flows that result in an outflow for the entity at each reporting date. While the standard only requires the gross cash outflows (that is, the pay leg) to be included in the maturity analysis, separate disclosure of the corresponding inflows (that is, the receive leg) might make the information more meaningful in the case of gross settled derivatives.

Liquidity analysis (based on forward rates)

Financial liabilities as of 31 Dec 20X6

	Less than 1 month	Between 1 and 3 months	Between 3 months and 1 year	Between 1 and 5 years	Over 5 years	Balance sheet amounts
Interest rate swaps		15	-33	-173		-71

11.104.4 For some instruments, such as perpetual bonds and written put options, it is difficult to determine how, if at all, to include amounts in the maturity analysis. In the case of perpetual bonds, where the debtor/issuer has a call option to redeem the bond, the debtor/issuer has discretion over the repayment of the principal. Until the option is exercised, the bond's contractual terms are that it is a non-redeemable perpetual bond. Once the call option is exercised, the bond's contractual terms are changed and the bond has a maturity date. If the call option was not exercised, then the undiscounted cash flows would be paid in perpetuity. This raises the question of what amount should be shown in the last time band. The standard does not deal explicitly with such a situation so a number of alternative approaches could be applied. One would be to include the principal amount in the last time band. Another option would be not to include any cash flows in the last time band, but disclose the principal amount in time band entitled 'no maturity'. Whatever form of disclosure is chosen, this is an area where it will be important to provide a clear narrative description of the instrument's terms.

[The next paragraph is 11.104.6.]

11.104.6 The inclusion of an 'out of the money' written put option (financial liability) in the maturity analysis will depend on whether the option is settled net or gross. If the option is out of the money and net settled, no liability is required to be disclosed in the maturity table, because there is no obligation to make a payment based on the conditions existing at the balance sheet date. [IFRS 7 App B para 11D]. However, for gross settled derivatives where the counterparty can force the issuer to make a payment, the pay leg is disclosed in the liquidity table in the earliest time bucket irrespective of whether the instrument is in or out of the money. An American style option should be disclosed in the earliest time band, a European style option depending on the exercise date.

11.104.7 A narrative disclosure should explain that written options have been included based on their intrinsic value and that the amount actually payable in the future may vary if the conditions change. This is supported by paragraph 10A(b) of appendix B to IFRS 7, which states that an explanation is required if the outflows of cash included in the maturity analysis could be significantly different from those disclosed in the contractual maturity table.

11.105 An entity that has provided a disclosure of its liquidity risk is shown in Table 11.10. This company does not have financial guarantees or loan commitments. Such features are more common in banks, although certain industrial companies, particularly in the construction industry do issue financial guarantees and companies in the motor industry often have lending facilities for customers. Note that the examples below include only certain of the potentially extensive disclosures that IFRS 7 requires.

Table 11.10 – Liquidity risk

Givaudan Plc – Annual report – 31 December 2009

4.2.6 Liquidity risk

Prudent liquidity risk management implies maintaining sufficient cash and marketable securities, the availability of funds through an adequate amount of committed credit facilities and the ability to close out market positions. Due to the dynamic nature of the underlying businesses, Group Treasury maintains flexibility in funding by maintaining availability under committed and uncommitted credit lines.

Group Treasury monitors and manages cash at the Group level and defines the maximum cash level at affiliate level. If necessary, inter-company loans within the Group provide for short-term cash needs; excess local cash is repatriated in the most appropriate manner.

The following table analyses the Group's remaining contractual maturity for financial liabilities and derivative financial instruments. The table has been drawn up based on the undiscounted cash flows of financial liabilities based on the earliest date on which the Group is obliged to pay. The table includes both interest and principal cash flows:

2009 in millions of Swiss francs	Up to 6 months	6 – 12 months	1 – 5 years	Over 5 years	Total
Short-term debt (excluding bank overdraft)	(74)				(74)
Accounts payable – trade and others	(294)				(294)
Net settled derivative financial instruments	(11)	(9)	(35)	1	(54)
Gross settled derivative financial instruments – outflows	(1,372)				(1,372)
Gross settled derivative financial instruments – inflows	1,377				1,377
Long-term debt	(32)	(27)	(2,337)	(115)	(2,511)
Balance as at 31 December	**(406)**	**(36)**	**(2,372)**	**(114)**	**(2,928)**
2008 in millions of Swiss francs	Up to 6 months	6 – 12 months	1 – 5 years	Over 5 years	Total
Short-term debt (excluding bank overdraft)	(245)				(245)
Accounts payable – trade and others	(314)				(314)
Net settled derivative financial instruments	(11)	(12)	(37)		(60)
Gross settled derivative financial instruments – outflows	(981)				(981)
Gross settled derivative financial instruments – inflows	1,012				1,012
Long-term debt	(67)	(31)	(2,571)	(258)	(2,927)
Balance as at 31 December	**(606)**	**(43)**	**(2,608)**	**(258)**	**(3,515)**

Market risk

Sensitivity analysis

11.106 Unless an entity complies with paragraph 11.114 below, it should disclose:

■ A sensitivity analysis for each type of market risk to which the entity is exposed at the reporting date, showing how profit or loss and equity would have been affected by changes in the relevant risk variable that were reasonably possible at that date. The sensitivity analysis should show the effect of changes over the period until the entity next presents these disclosures, which usually is its next annual report. [IFRS 7 App B para 19(b)]. Note that the standard requires this disclosure based on reasonably possible changes and not on a 'worst case scenario' or 'stress test'. Risk variables that are relevant to disclosing market risk include, but are not limited to:

- The yield curve of market interest rates. It may be necessary to consider both parallel and non-parallel shifts in the yield curve.

- Foreign exchange rates.

- Prices of equity instruments.

- Market prices of commodities.

- The methods and assumptions used in preparing the sensitivity analysis.

- Changes from the previous period in the methods and assumptions used and the reasons for such changes.

[IFRS 7 para 40].

11.107 In providing the sensitivity analysis for each type of market risk, an entity should decide how it aggregates information to display the overall picture without combining information with different characteristics about exposures to risks from significantly different economic environments. Entities are not required to disclose the effect for each change within a range of reasonably possible changes of the relevant risk variable. Disclosure of the effects of the changes at the limits of the reasonably possible range would be sufficient. [IFRS 7 App B paras 18 to 19]. For example, an entity that trades financial instruments might disclose this information separately for financial instruments held for trading and those not held for trading. Similarly, an entity would not aggregate its exposure to market risks from areas of hyperinflation with its exposure to the same market risks from areas of very low inflation. Conversely, if an entity has exposure to only one type of market risk in only one economic environment, it would not show disaggregated information. [IFRS 7 App B para 17].

11.107.1 In addition, where there are changes in volatility, an entity should not restate the prior year disclosures. For example, where the reasonable possible change in an exchange rate changes from 5 per cent in the prior year to 8 per cent in the current year, the prior year disclosures should not be restated. An entity could, however, present additional sensitivity information for the comparative period.

11.108 For the purposes of disclosing the effect on profit or loss and equity of reasonably possible changes in the relevant risk variable, for example interest rate risk, as required by the first bullet point of paragraph 11.106 above, an entity might show separately the effect of a change in market rates on:

- Interest income and expense.

- Other line items of profit or loss (such as trading gains and losses).

- When applicable, equity.

[IFRS 7 para IG34].

11.109 An entity might disclose a sensitivity analysis for interest rate risk for each currency in which the entity has material exposures to interest rate risk. Similarly, a sensitivity analysis is disclosed for each currency to which an entity has significant exposure. [IFRS 7 paras IG34, App B para 24].

11.109.1 This disclosure would also be relevant to those instruments where an entity has effectively hedged the interest rate risk, as illustrated in the following example.

Example – A bond hedged for variable interest rate risk

An entity hedges its exposure to variable interest rate risk on an issued bond. The hedge is designated as a cash flow hedge. The bond and the hedging instrument (interest rate swap) have a five-year remaining life. The variable leg of the swap exactly matches the variable interest of the bond (causing no ineffectiveness).

The high effectiveness of the hedge does not necessarily mean that there would be no impact on equity or profit or loss due to changes in interest rate risk. The accounting for a cash flow hedge means that the fair value movement related to the effective part of the hedging instrument is included in other comprehensive income. Amounts deferred in other comprehensive income are recycled in profit or loss when the hedged transaction occurs. Hence, reasonably possible movements in the interest rate risk exposure have an impact on both profit or loss and equity.

At the same time, reasonably possible movements in the interest rate risk exposure on the outstanding bond would impact profit or loss, as the bond was a recognised financial liability at the balance sheet date.

If the effects of recycling and ineffectiveness are not material, the entity could consider the following disclosure as an approximation for the sensitivity analysis: *"The movements related to the bond and the swap's variable leg are not reflected as they offset each other. The movements related to the remaining fair value exposure on the swap's fixed leg are shown in the equity part of the analysis".*

11.110 It should be noted that for the purposes of disclosing a sensitivity analysis for foreign currency risk, translation related risk is not taken into account. This is because foreign currency risk can only arise on financial instruments that are denominated in a currency other than the functional currency in which they are measured. [IFRS 7 App B para 23]. Translation exposures arise from financial and non-financial items held by an entity (for example, a subsidiary) with a functional currency different from the group's presentation currency. Therefore, translation-related risks are not taken into consideration for the purpose of the sensitivity analysis for foreign currency risks. This also includes quasi-equity loans (foreign currency inter-company loans that are part of the net investment in a foreign operation). On the other hand, any loans or derivatives used as hedges of translation risk should be included within the sensitivity analysis. Also, foreign currency denominated inter-company receivables and payables would be included because, even though they cancel in the consolidated balance sheet, the effect on profit or loss of their revaluation under IAS 21 is not fully eliminated. Although they cannot be included within the analysis of foreign currency risks, additional translation risks can, however, be separately disclosed. This may be appropriate where an entity manages its translation risks together with its foreign currency transaction risks (for example, where a forward contract hedges movements in the retranslation of a foreign operation).

11.110.1   In the same way that translation exposures may have an impact on equity but are not included in the sensitivity analysis, there are other items that may be exposed to market price risk, but which are not necessarily included. For example, consider instruments that expose an entity to changes in its own share price. These include entities that have issued warrants with a foreign currency exercise price, those that have issued convertible debt that fails the 'fixed for fixed' requirement in IAS 32 and those that have issued share based compensation awards that are classified as liabilities. In the first two cases, the entity should disclose information about the effect of reasonably possible changes in its share price on its profit or loss and equity. This is because the first two instruments are in the scope of IAS 39 and, therefore, in the scope of IFRS 7. The third instrument, although classified as a liability, is outside the scope of IAS 39 as it is accounted for under IFRS 2. It, therefore, also falls outside the IFRS 7's scope.

11.111   Because the factors affecting market risk vary depending on the specific circumstances of each entity, the appropriate range to be considered in providing a sensitivity analysis of market risk varies for each entity and for each type of market risk. [IFRS 7 para IG35].

11.112   However, an entity is not required to determine what the profit or loss for the period would have been if relevant risk variables had been different. Instead, it should disclose the effect on profit or loss and equity at the balance sheet date, assuming that a reasonably possible change in the relevant risk variable had occurred at the balance sheet date and had been applied to the risk exposures in existence at that date. For example, if an entity has a floating rate liability at the end of the year, the entity would disclose the effect on profit or loss (that is, interest expense) for the current year if interest rates had varied by reasonably possible amounts. [IFRS 7 App B para 18(a)].

11.113   Furthermore, an entity is not required to disclose the effect on profit or loss and equity for each change within a range of reasonably possible changes of the relevant risk variable. Disclosure of the effects of the changes at the limits of the reasonably possible range would be sufficient. [IFRS 7 App B para 18(b)].

11.114   If an entity prepares a sensitivity analysis, such as value-at-risk (VaR), that reflects interdependencies between risk variables (for example, interest rates and exchange rates) and uses it to manage financial risks, it may use that sensitivity analysis in place of the analysis described above. However, a precondition for disclosing sensitivity in such a format (VaR) is that the company uses VaR in managing its financial risks. It cannot choose just to apply VaR for disclosures purposes but continue to manage each risk variable separately. In addition, it is likely that outstanding intercompany foreign currency receivables and payables at the year end are not considered in the VaR model. If this is the case, the entity will need to prepare additional sensitivity disclosures for these amounts (see para 11.110 above). The entity should also disclose:

- an explanation of the method used in preparing such a sensitivity analysis, and of the main parameters and assumptions underlying the data provided; and

- an explanation of the objective of the method used and of limitations that may result in the information not fully reflecting the fair value of the assets and liabilities involved.

[IFRS 7 para 41].

11.114.1 In view of the requirement for VaR to be used in managing financial risk, IFRS 7 recognises that the measure used may not reflect the full potential risk over the next reporting period. [IFRS 7 App B para 20]. For example, an entity may use a 10 day VaR, or a measure that recognises only the potential for loss and not the potential for gain.

11.115 An example of a company that has provided an analysis of market risk sensitivity and how it manages its market risk is provided in Table 11.11.1 (Note the company had no equity investments and, therefore, price risk sensitivity has not been disclosed.) An example of a company providing a price risk sensitivity is provided in Table 11.11.2.

Table 11.11.1 – Disclosure of market risk management and sensitivity

Glaxosmithkline plc – Annual report – 31 December 2008

Interest rate risk management

The policy on interest rate risk management requires the minimum amount of net borrowings at fixed rates to increase with the ratio of forecast interest payable to trading profit. The fixed to floating ratio is reviewed monthly by the TMG.

We use an interest rate swap to redenominate one of our external borrowings into the interest rate coupon required by GSK. The duration of this swap matches the duration of the principal instrument. Interest rate derivative instruments are accounted for as fair value or cash flow hedges of the relevant assets or liabilities.

Foreign exchange risk management

Foreign currency transaction exposure arising on internal and external trade flows is not hedged. The exposure of overseas operating subsidiaries to transaction risk is minimised by matching local currency income with local currency costs. For this purpose, our internal trading transactions are matched centrally and we manage intercompany payment terms to reduce risk.

Exceptional foreign currency cash flows are hedged selectively under the management of Corporate Treasury.

We manage the short-term cash surpluses or borrowing requirements of subsidiary companies centrally using forward contracts to hedge future repayments back into the originating currency.

We seek to denominate borrowings in the currencies of our principal assets and cash flows. These are primarily denominated in US dollars, Euros and Sterling. Certain borrowings are swapped into other currencies as required.

Borrowings denominated in, or swapped into, foreign currencies that match investments in overseas Group assets are treated as a hedge against the relevant assets. Forward contracts are also used in major currencies to reduce our exposure to our investment in overseas Group assets (see 'Net Investment Hedges' section of this note for further details). The TMG review the ratio of borrowings to assets for major currencies monthly.

Sensitivity analysis
The sensitivity analysis has been prepared on the assumption that the amount of net debt, the ratio of fixed to floating interest rates of the debt and derivatives portfolio and the proportion of financial instruments in foreign currencies are all constant and on the basis of the hedge designations in place at 31st December. Financial instruments affected by market risk include borrowings, deposits and derivative financial instruments. The following analyses are intended to illustrate the sensitivity of such financial instruments to changes in relevant foreign exchange and interest rates.

Foreign exchange sensitivity
The table below shows the Group's sensitivity to foreign exchange rates on its US dollar, Euro and Yen financial instruments excluding obligations under finance leases and certain non-derivative financial instruments not in net debt and which do not present a material exposure. These three currencies are the major currencies in which GSK's financial instruments are denominated. GSK has considered movements in these currencies over the last three years and has concluded that a 20% movement in rates is a reasonable benchmark. In this table, financial instruments are only considered sensitive to foreign exchange rates where they are not in the functional currency of the entity that holds them. Intercompany loans which are fully hedged to maturity with a currency swap have been excluded from this analysis.

	2008		2007	
	Increase/ (decrease) in income £m	Reduction in equity £m	Increase/ (decrease) in income £m	Reduction in equity £m
20% appreciation (2007 – 10% appreciation) of the US dollar	210	991	38	580
20% appreciation (2007 – 10% appreciation) of the Euro	(20)	1,760	(10)	709
20% appreciation (2007 – 10% appreciation) of the Yen	1	52	–	15

A 20% (2007 – 10%) depreciation of the stated currencies would have an equal and opposite effect. The movements in the income statement relate primarily to hedging instruments for US dollar legal provisions, trade payables and trade receivables. Whilst these are economic hedges, the provisions are not financial instruments and therefore are not included in the table above. The sensitivity of these hedging instruments would be insignificant if the provisions were included. The movements in equity relate to foreign exchange positions used to hedge Group assets denominated in US dollar, Euro and Yen. Therefore, a depreciation on the currency swap would give rise to a corresponding appreciation on the Group asset. Foreign exchange sensitivity on Group assets other than financial instruments is not included above.

The table below shows the Group's sensitivity to interest rates on its floating rate Sterling, US dollar and Euro financial instruments, being the currencies in which GSK has historically issued debt and held investments. GSK has considered movements in these interest rates over the last three years and has concluded that a 2% increase is a reasonable benchmark. Debt with a maturity of less than one year is floating rate for this calculation. A 2% movement in interest rates is not deemed to have a material effect on equity.

	2008 Increase/ (decrease) in income	2007 Increase/ (decrease) in income
2% increase (2007 – 1% increase) in Sterling interest rates	16	1
2% increase (2007 – 1% increase) in US dollar interest rates	13	(16)
2% increase (2007 – 1% increase) in Euro interest rates	4	3

A 2% (2007 – 1%) decrease in these interest rates would have an equal and opposite effect, with the exception of US dollar, where interest rates could not be decreased by 2% as they are currently less than 0.5%. The maximum decrease in income would therefore be limited to £1 million. Interest rate movements on obligations under finance leases, foreign currency and interest rate derivatives, trade payables, trade receivables and other financial instruments not in net debt do not present a material exposure to the Group's balance sheet based on a 2% increase or decrease in these interest rates.

Table 11.11.2 – Disclosure of price risk management and sensitivity

Henderson Group plc – Annual report – 31 December 2009

28. Financial risk management (extract)

Financial risk management objectives and policies

Financial assets principally comprise investments in equity securities, short-term investments, trade and other receivables, and cash and cash equivalents. Financial liabilities comprise borrowings for financing purposes, certain provisions and trade and other payables. The main risks arising from financial instruments are price risk, interest rate risk, liquidity risk, foreign currency risk and credit risk. Each of these risks is discussed in detail below. The Group monitors financial risks on a consolidated basis and intra-Group balances are settled when it is deemed appropriate for both parties to the transaction. The Company is not exposed to material financial risk and separate disclosures for the Company have not been included.

The Group has designed a framework to manage the risks of its business and to ensure that the Directors have in place risk management practices appropriate for a listed company. The management of risk within the Group is governed by the Board and overseen by the Audit Committee.

28.1 Price risk

Price risk is the risk that a decline in the value of assets adversely impacts on the profitability of the Group.

The Group is exposed to price risk in respect of seed capital investments in Henderson funds (available-for-sale financial assets). Seed capital investments vary in duration, depending on the nature of the investment, with a typical range of less than one year for Listed Asset products and between three and five years for Private Equity and Property funds. The total market value of seed capital investments at 31 December 2009 was £41.7m (2008: £57.2m). In 2008, the Group also had a corporate investment in BP of £18.7m which has been disposed of in full during 2009.

Management monitors exposures to price risk on an ongoing basis. Significant movements in investment values are monitored on a daily basis. Where appropriate, management will hedge price risk, but there were no such hedges in place at 31 December 2009.

A fall in the value of an investment which is significant or prolonged is considered to be objective evidence of impairment under IAS 39. In such an event, an investment is written down to its fair value and cumulative amounts previously recognised in equity, in respect of market value and unhedged foreign exchange movements on the investment, are recognised in the consolidated income statement as an impairment charge.

Price risk sensitivities	2009		2008	
	Consolidated income statement £m	Other comprehensive income £m	Consolidated income statement £m	Other comprehensive income £m
Market value movement + /- 10%	–	4.2	–	7.6

Other market risk disclosures

11.116   When the sensitivity analyses disclosed in accordance with paragraph 11.106 above are unrepresentative of a risk inherent in a financial instrument (for example because the year-end exposure does not reflect the exposure during the year), the entity should disclose that fact and the reason it believes the sensitivity analyses are unrepresentative. [IFRS 7 para 42].

11.117   As noted above, the sensitivity analysis might be unrepresentative of a risk inherent in a financial instrument where the year end exposure does not reflect the exposure during the year. Other circumstances include the following:

■ A financial instrument contains terms and conditions whose effects are not apparent from the sensitivity analysis, for example options that remain out of (or in) the money for the chosen change in the risk variable. In such a situation, additional disclosure might include:

■ the terms and conditions of the financial instrument (for example, the options);

■ the effect on profit or loss if the term or condition were met (that is, if the options were exercised); and

■ a description of how the risk is hedged.

■ Financial assets are illiquid, for example, when there is a low volume of transactions in similar assets and an entity finds it difficult to find a counterparty. In such a situation, additional disclosure might include the reasons for the lack of liquidity and how the entity hedges the risk.

■ An entity has a large holding of a financial assets that, if sold in its entirety, would be sold at a discount or premium to the quoted market price for a smaller holding. In such a situation, additional disclosure might include:

■ The nature of the security (for example, entity name).

■ The extent of holding (for example, 15 per cent of the issued shares).

- The effect on profit or loss.

- How the entity hedges the risk.

[IFRS 7 para IG37-40].

11.118 An entity should provide sensitivity analyses for the whole of its business, but may provide different types of sensitivity analysis for different classes of financial instruments. [IFRS 7 App B para 21].

11.119 The sensitivity of profit or loss (that arises, for example, from instruments classified as at fair value through profit or loss and impairments of available-for-sale financial assets) is disclosed separately from the sensitivity of equity (that arises, for example, from instruments classified as available for sale). [IFRS 7 App B para 27]. For example, where the fair value of a non-monetary available-for-sale asset is close to the impairment threshold, an entity should distinguish between profit or loss and equity effects, taking into consideration its impairment policy. In cases where the asset is already impaired, the downward shift (due to the impairment) should be shown as affecting the profit or loss while the upward shift should be shown as affecting equity.

11.120 Financial instruments that an entity classifies as equity instruments are not remeasured. Neither profit or loss nor equity will be affected by the equity price risk of those instruments. Accordingly, no sensitivity analysis is required. [IFRS 7 App B para 28].

Chapter 12

IFRS 9, 'Financial instruments'

IFRS 9, 'Financial instruments'

Introduction

12.1   The IASB has been reviewing accounting issues that have emerged as a result of the recent global financial crisis, including those identified by the G20 and other international bodies such as the Financial Stability Board. The IASB is working closely with the FASB with the aim of ensuring a globally consistent and appropriate response to the crisis. As part of this, the IASB has accelerated its project to replace IAS 39, 'Financial instruments: Recognition and measurement', and sub-divided it into three main phases (see table below). The IASB completed part of the first phase of this project on financial assets and issued IFRS 9. 'Financial instruments', in November 2009. This chapter explains the requirements on accounting for financial assets as set out in IFRS 9. The phases and status of the project is shown in the table below.

Phase	Status
Classification and measurement	Financial assets – IFRS 9 published November 2009. Financial liabilities – Exposure draft published Q2 2010; final standard due Q4 2010.
Impairment	Exposure draft published Q4 2009; final standard due H1 2011.
Hedge accounting	Exposure draft expected Q4 2010; final standard due H1 2011.

12.2   IFRS 9 does not yet address the accounting for financial liabilities or impairment or hedge accounting as these are currently under discussion by the Boards. However, we expect these to be incorporated into IFRS 9 once the Board has finalised its new guidance in those areas.

Executive summary

12.3   IFRS 9 replaces the multiple classification and measurement models for financial assets in IAS 39 with a model that has only two classification categories: amortised cost and fair value. Classification under IFRS 9 is driven by the entity's business model for managing the financial assets and the contractual cash flow characteristics of the financial assets.

12.4 A financial asset is measured at amortised cost if two criteria are met:

■ The objective of the business model is to hold the financial asset for the collection of the contractual cash flows.

■ The contractual asset's cash flows solely represent payments of principal and interest.

12.5 IFRS 9 removes existing IAS 39 categories, notably the held-to-maturity and available-for-sale categories and the tainting rules associated with the former.

12.6 The standard also removes the requirement to separate embedded derivatives from financial asset hosts. It requires a hybrid contract to be classified in its entirety at either amortised cost or fair value.

12.7 Two of the existing three fair value option criteria become obsolete under IFRS 9, as a fair value driven business model requires fair value accounting, and most hybrid contracts are classified in their entirety at fair value. The remaining fair value option condition in IAS 39 is carried forward to the standard – that is, management may still designate a financial asset as at fair value through profit or loss on initial recognition if this significantly reduces an accounting mismatch. The designation at fair value through profit or loss continues to be irrevocable.

12.8 IFRS 9 prohibits reclassifications between amortised cost and fair value through profit or loss except when the entity's business model changes.

12.9 There is specific guidance for contractually linked instruments that create concentrations of credit risk, which is often the case with investment tranches in a securitisation.

12.10 IFRS 9's classification principles require all equity investments to be measured at fair value. However, management has an irrevocable option to present in other comprehensive income unrealised and realised fair value gains and losses on equity investments that are not held-for-trading. The election is available at initial recognition on an instrument-by-instrument basis, with no recycling to profit or loss.

12.11 IFRS 9 removes the cost exemption for unquoted equities and derivatives on unquoted equities, but provides guidance on when cost may be an appropriate estimate of fair value.

12.12 IFRS 9 is effective for annual periods beginning on or after 1 January 2013. Early application is permitted, although IFRS 9 has not yet been endorsed for use in the EU.

Objective

12.13 IFRS 9's objective is to establish principles for the financial reporting of financial assets that will present relevant and useful information to users of financial statements for their assessment of amounts, timing and uncertainty of the entity's future cash flows. [IFRS para 9.1.1].

Scope

12.14 IFRS 9 generally has to be applied by all entities preparing their financial statements in accordance with IFRS and to all types of financial assets within the scope of IAS 39, including derivatives. The scope of IAS 39 is broad and is addressed in chapter 3.

12.15 Essentially any financial assets that are currently accounted for under IAS 39 will fall within the IFRS 9's scope.

Initial recognition

12.16 Consistent with IAS 39, all financial assets in IFRS 9 are to be initially recognised at fair value, plus, in the case of a financial asset that is not at fair value through profit or loss, transaction costs that are directly attributable to the acquisition of the financial asset. [IFRS 9 para 5.1.1].

Classification and measurement

12.17 IFRS 9 has two measurement categories: amortised cost and fair value. In order to determine the financial assets that fall into each measurement category, it may be helpful for management to consider whether the financial asset is an investment in an equity instrument as defined in IAS 32, 'Financial instruments: Presentation'. Chapter 7 provides further details on this determination. If the financial asset is not an investment in an equity instrument, management should consider the guidance for debt instruments below.

Debt instruments

12.18 If the financial asset is a debt instrument (or does not meet the definition of an equity instrument in its entirety), management should consider whether both the following tests are met:

- The objective of the entity's business model is to hold the asset to collect the contractual cash flows.

- The asset's contractual cash flows represent only payments of principal and interest. Interest is consideration for the time value of money and the credit risk associated with the principal amount outstanding during a particular period of time.

[IFRS 9 paras 4.2-4.3].

12.19   If both these tests are met, the financial asset falls into the amortised cost measurement category. If the financial asset does not pass either of the above tests, or only one of the above tests, it is measured at fair value through profit or loss. [IFRS 9 para 4.4].

12.20   Even if both tests are met, management also has the ability to designate a financial asset as at fair value through profit or loss if doing so reduces or eliminates a measurement or recognition inconsistency ('accounting mismatch'). [IFRS 9 para 4.5]. IFRS 9 retains only one of the three conditions in IAS 39 to qualify for using the fair value option. It removes the conditions regarding being part of a group of financial assets that is managed and its performance evaluated on a fair value basis and where the financial asset contains one or more embedded derivatives, as they are no longer necessary under the classification model in IFRS 9.

Business model

12.21   Financial assets are subsequently measured at amortised cost or fair value based on the entity's business model for managing the financial assets. An entity assesses whether its financial assets meet this condition based on its business model as determined by the entity's key management personnel (as defined in IAS 24, 'Related party disclosures'). [IFRS 9 para App B4.1].

12.22   Management will need to apply judgement to determine at what level the business model condition is applied. That determination is made on the basis of how an entity manages its business; it is not made at the level of an individual asset. Therefore, the entity's business model is not a choice and does not depend on management's intentions for an individual instrument; it is a matter of fact that can be observed by the way an entity is managed and information is provided to its management.

12.23   Although the objective of an entity's business model may be to hold financial assets in order to collect contractual cash flows, some sales or transfers of financial instruments before maturity would not be inconsistent with such a business model.

12.24   The following are examples of sales before maturity that would not be inconsistent with a business model of holding financial assets to collect contractual cash flows:

■   an entity may sell a financial asset if it no longer meets the entity's investment policy, because its credit rating has declined below that required by that policy;

■   when an insurer adjusts its investment portfolio to reflect a change in the expected duration (that is, payout) for its insurance policies; or

■   when an entity needs to fund capital expenditure.

[IFRS 9 para App B4.3].

12.25 However, if more than an infrequent number of sales are made out of a portfolio, management should assess whether and how such sales are consistent with an objective of collecting contractual cash flows. There is no set rule for how many sales constitutes 'infrequent'; management will need to use judgement based on the facts and circumstances to make its assessment.

12.26 An entity's business model is not to hold instruments to collect the contractual cash flows – for example, where an entity manages the portfolio of financial assets with the objective of realising cash flows through sale of the assets. Another example is when an entity actively manages a portfolio of assets in order to realise fair value changes arising from changes in credit spreads and yield curves, which results in active buying and selling of the portfolio.

Example 1 – Factoring

An entity has a past practice of factoring its receivables. If the significant risks and rewards have transferred from the entity, resulting in the original receivable being derecognised from the balance sheet, the entity is not holding these receivables to collect its cash flows but to sell them.

However, if the significant risks and rewards of these receivables are not transferred from the entity, and the receivables do not, therefore, qualify for derecognition, the client's business objective may still be to hold the assets in order to collect the contractual cash flows.

Example 2 – Syndicated loans

An entity's business model is to lend to customers and hold the resulting loans for the collection of contractual cash flows. However, sometimes the entity syndicates out portions of loans that exceed their credit approval limits. This means that, at inception, part of such loans will be held to collect contractual cash flows and part will be held-for-sale. The entity, therefore, has two business models to apply to the respective portions of the loans.

Example 3 – Portfolio of sub-prime loans

An entity that operates in the sub-prime lending market purchases a portfolio of sub-prime loans from a competitor that has gone out of business. The loans are purchased at a substantial discount from their face value, as most of the loans are not currently performing (that is, no payments are being received, in many cases because the borrower has failed to make payments when due). The entity has a good record of collecting sub-prime loan arrears. It plans to hold the purchased loan balances to recover the outstanding cash amounts relating to the loans that have been purchased. As the business model is to hold the acquired loans and not to sell them, the business model test is met.

Contractual cash flows that are solely payments of principal and interest

12.27 The other condition that must be met in order for a financial asset to be eligible for amortised cost accounting is that the contractual terms of the financial asset give rise on specified dates to cash flows that are *"solely payments of principal and interest on the principal amount outstanding"*. In this case, interest is defined as consideration for the time value of money and for the credit risk associated with the principal amount outstanding during a particular period of time. [IFRS 9 para 4.3].

12.28 In order to meet this condition, there can be no leverage of the contractual cash flows. Leverage increases the variability of the contractual cash flows with the result that they do not have the economic characteristics of interest. Leverage is generally viewed as any multiple above one.

12.29 However, unlike leverage, certain contractual provisions will not cause the 'solely payments of principal and interest' test to be failed. For example, contractual provisions that permit the issuer to pre-pay a debt instrument or permit the holder to put a debt instrument, back to the issuer before maturity result in contractual cash flows that are solely payments of principal and interest as long as the following certain conditions are met:

- The pre-payment amount substantially represents unpaid amounts of principal and interest on the principal amount outstanding (which may include reasonable additional compensation for the early termination of the contract).

- The pre-payment amount is not contingent on future events (other than to protect the holder against the issuer's credit deterioration , or a change of control of the issuer or against changes in tax or law).

[IFRS 9 para App B4.10]

12.30 Contractual provisions that permit the issuer or holder to extend the contractual term of a debt instrument are also regarded as being solely payments of principal and interest, provided during the term of the extension the contractual cash flows are solely payments of principal and interest as well (for example, the interest rate does not step up to some leveraged multiple of LIBOR) and the provision is not contingent on future events. [IFRS 9 para App B4.11]

12.31 The following are examples of contractual cash flows that are not solely payments of principal and interest:

- Bonds where the amount of interest varies inversely to a market rate of interest (inverse floaters).

- Links to equity index, borrower's net income or other non-financial variables.

- Deferrals of interest payments where additional interest does not accrue on those deferred amounts.

- Variable rate loan where at each reset date, the borrower can choose to pay one month LIBOR for a three month term and one month LIBOR is not reset each month.

- Five year constant maturity bond at variable rate, which is reset periodically but always reflects a five year maturity (that is, disconnected with the term of the instrument except at origination).

- Convertible bond (from the holder's perspective).

12.32 If a contractual cash flow characteristic is not genuine, it does not affect the financial asset's classification. In this context, 'not genuine' means the occurrence of an event that is extremely rare, highly abnormal and very unlikely to occur. [IFRS 9 para App B4.18].

Example 1 – Changing credit spread

An entity has a loan agreement that specifies that the interest rate will change depending on the borrower's credit rating, EBITDA or gearing ratio. Such a feature will not fail the 'solely payments of principal and interest' test provided the adjustment is considered to reasonably approximate the credit risk of an instrument with that level of EBITDA, gearing or credit rating. That is, if such a covenant compensates the lender with higher interest when the borrower's credit risk increases then this is consistent with interest being defined as the consideration for the credit risk and the time value of money. However, if the covenant results in more than just compensation for credit or provides for some level of interest based on the entity's profitability, that will not meet the test.

Example 2 – Average rates

An entity has a loan agreement where interest is based on an average LIBOR rate over a period. That is, the loan has no defined maturity, but rolls every two years with reference to the two year LIBOR rate. The interest rate is reset every two years to equal the average two year LIBOR rate over the last two years. The economic rationale is to allow borrowers to benefit from a floating rate, but with an averaging mechanism to protect them from short-term volatility. Such a feature will not fail the 'solely payments of principal and interest' test provided the average rate represents compensation for only the time value of money and credit risk.

Non-recourse

12.33 A non-recourse provision is an agreement that, should the debtor default on a secured obligation, the creditor can look only to the securing assets (whether financial or non-financial) to recover its claim. Should the debtor fail to pay and the specific assets fail to satisfy the full claim, the creditor has no legal recourse against the debtor's other assets. The fact that a financial asset is non-recourse does not necessarily preclude the financial asset from meeting the condition to be classified at amortised cost. [IFRS 9 para App B4.17].

12.34 If a non-recourse provision exists, the creditor is required to assess (to 'look through to') the particular underlying assets or cash flows to determine whether the financial asset's contractual cash flows are solely payments of principal and interest. If the instrument's terms give rise to any other cash flows or limit the cash flows in a manner inconsistent with 'solely payments of principal and interest', the instrument will be measured in its entirety at fair value through profit or loss. [IFRS 9 para App B.17].

12.35　There is limited guidance as to how the existence of a non-recourse feature may impact the classification of non-recourse loans at amortised cost. Judgement will, therefore, be needed to assess these types of lending relationships.

Contractually linked instruments (tranches)

12.36　The payments on some financial assets are contractually linked to the payments received on a pool of other instruments. These are referred to as contractually linked instruments. They are often issued by special purpose entities (SPEs) in various tranches, with the more senior tranches being repaid in priority to the more junior ones. The classification criteria for the holder of such contractually linked instruments (tranches) should be assessed based on the conditions at the date the entity initially recognised the investment using a 'look through' approach. This approach looks at the terms of the instrument itself as well as through to the pool of underlying instruments to assess both the characteristics of these underlying instruments and the tranche's exposure to credit risk relative to the pool of underlying instruments. [IFRS 9 App B4.20-25].

12.37　To measure an individual tranche at amortised cost, the tranche itself (without looking through to the pool of underlying instruments) must give rise to cash flows that are solely payments of principal and interest and the underlying pool must contain one or more instruments that have contractual cash flows that are solely payments of principal and interest on the principal outstanding.

12.38　In this context, the underlying pool is that which creates (rather than passes through) the cash flows. [IFRS 9 App B4.22]

12.39　The underlying pool of instruments may also include instruments that:

■　Reduce the variability of the instruments in the underlying pool (for example, an interest rate cap or floor or a contract that reduces the credit risk of the underlying pool of instruments).

■　Align the cash flows of the tranches with the cash flows of the pool of underlying instruments to address differences in and only in:

■　whether the interest rate is fixed or floating,

■　the currency in which the cash flows are denominated, or

■　the timing of the cash flows.

[IFRS 9 App B4.24].

12.40　Any derivatives in the SPE structure should, therefore, reflect a risk that is present in either the assets or the liabilities or both to achieve amortised cost accounting for the tranche.

12.41   In addition, the credit risk of the tranche must be equal to or lower than the weighted average credit risk of the underlying pool of financial instruments. [IFRS 9 App B4.21c].

12.42   The standard does not explicitly address how the weighted average credit risk test should be performed. A simple way might involve comparing the credit rating of the tranche to the average credit rating of the underlying pool of assets if that gives a clear answer. If not, a more complex quantitative assessment may be required that compares the relative variability of the tranche held with that of the underlying assets.

12.43   Fair value measurement is required if any instrument in the pool does not meet the conditions outlined above, or if the composition of the underlying pool might change after the initial recognition such that it would no longer meet the qualifying conditions, or if it is impracticable to look through. [IFRS 9 App B4.26].

Example 1 – Investments in units issued by close-ended fund

An entity invests in units issued by a close-ended fund. The fund holds only debt instruments that themselves would qualify for amortised cost classification under IFRS 9 had these instruments been directly held by the unit holder. The objective of the fund is to hold the assets to maturity rather than to realise fair value changes. Payments made by this fund to the holder may, therefore, represent solely payments of principal and interest. The holder may, therefore, be able to measure its investment at amortised cost. However, if the fund does not hold debt instruments, the investor will not be able to measure its investment at amortised cost.

Example 2 – Derivatives in underlying pool of assets

An SPE holds floating rate EUR assets and issued fixed rate GBP notes contractually linked to the assets. The SPE has entered into one swap that is a pay EUR floating and receive GBP floating, and a second swap that is a pay GBP floating and receive GBP fixed. Both these swaps would meet the requirements in paragraph B4.24(b) of IFRS 9 of aligning the cash flows of the tranches with the cash flows of the pool of underlying instruments. The holder may, therefore, be able to measure its investment at amortised cost. However, if the SPE were to have a derivative that introduced a third currency – say USD – this would not align the cash flows, and the tranche would have to be measured at fair value through profit or loss.

Example 3 – Derivative with optionality in underlying pool of assets

An SPE holds a fixed-for-floating swap that also hedges pre-payment risk such that if the underlying pool of fixed rate assets pays down early, the derivative is cancelled with no further amounts to pay. This is to ensure there is no excess derivatives and no fair value gains/losses on settlement, as when the assets pre-pay, the notes pre-pay. This feature would not fail the requirements of paragraph B4.24 of IFRS 9; the holder may, therefore, be able to measure its investment at amortised cost.

Example 4 – Investments in collateralised debt obligations (CDOs)

An entity has an investment in a cash CDO where the issuing SPE holds the underlying referenced assets. Cash CDOs may qualify for amortised cost accounting as long as the underlying assets qualify for amortised cost accounting and the other requirements of IFRS 9 are met for contractually linked instruments. However, investments in synthetic CDOs (where the SPE has a credit derivative that references particular exposures) would not qualify, as the derivatives on the reference exposures do not have cash flows that are solely payments of principal or interest, nor do they align the cash flows permitted by IFRS 9.

Equity instruments

12.44   Investments in equity instruments (as defined in IAS 32 by considering the perspective of the issuer) are always measured at fair value. Equity instruments that are held for trading are required to be classified as at fair value through profit or loss. [IFRS 9 para 5.4.4]. For all other equities, management has the ability to make an irrevocable election on initial recognition, on an instrument-by-instrument basis, to present changes in fair value in other comprehensive income (OCI) rather than profit or loss. [IFRS 9 para 5.4.4]. If this election is made, all fair value changes, excluding dividends that are a return on investment, will be reported in OCI. There is no recycling of amounts from OCI to profit and loss – for example, on sale of an equity investment – nor are there any impairment requirements. However, the entity may transfer the cumulative gain or loss within equity. [IFRS 9 App B5.12]

Example 1 – Investment in perpetual note

An entity (the holder) invests in a subordinated perpetual note, redeemable at the issuer's option, with a fixed coupon that can be deferred indefinitely if the issuer does not pay a dividend on its ordinary shares. The issuer classifies this instrument as equity under IAS 32. The holder has the option to classify this investment at fair value through OCI under IFRS 9, as it is an equity instrument as defined in IAS 32.

Example 2 – Investment in a puttable share

An entity (the holder) invests in a fund that has puttable shares in issue – that is, the holder has the right to put the shares back to the fund in exchange for its *pro rata* share of the net assets. The puttable shares may meet the requirements to be classified as equity from the fund's perspective, but this in an exception, as they do not meet the definition of equity in IAS 32. However, the holder does not have the ability to classify this investment as fair value through OCI, as paragraph 96C of IAS 32 states that puttables should not be considered an equity instrument under other guidance. Investments in puttable shares are, therefore, required to be classified as fair value through profit or loss, as they cannot be regarded as equity instruments for IFRS 9.

Example 3 – Dividend return on investment

An entity invests in shares at a cost of C12 and designates these at fair value through OCI. The fair value then increases to C22, giving rise to an unrealised gain of C10 in OCI. The issuer then pays a special dividend of C10. This dividend is recorded in profit or loss in accordance with IAS 18, 'Revenue', as such a dividend does not represent a recovery of part of the cost of the investment.

Example 4 – Dividend return of investment

An entity invests in shares at a cost of C12 and designates these at fair value through OCI. The issuer then pays a special dividend of C10. This dividend is not recorded in profit or loss in accordance with IAS 18, as such a dividend represents a recovery of part of the cost of the investment, which is required to remain in OCI.

Example 5 – Hybrid equity instrument

An entity invests in preference shares that have a maturity date for the repayment of principal, but that also pay discretionary dividends based on the profits of the issuing entity and give a right to share in the net assets on liquidation. These shares are considered a compound instrument by the issuer and are treated as part liability and part equity. Under paragraph 4.7 of IFRS 9, a hybrid financial asset is to be classified in its entirety. This investment in its entirety does not meet the definition of an equity instrument in IAS 32; it is not, therefore, eligible to use the fair value through OCI classification. The contractual cash flows of this investment would need to be assessed. As it is not solely receiving payments of principal and interest, it would be measured at fair value through profit or loss.

Example 6 – Investments in associates

A venture capital organisation has an investment in an associate that it has previously designated at fair value through profit or loss in accordance with IAS 39, as is permitted by the scope exclusion in IAS 28, 'Investments in associates'. This investment is not permitted to be accounted for at fair value through OCI under IFRS 9, as IAS 28, 'Investments in associates', has not been amended to permit such accounting.

12.45 The standard removes the requirement in IAS 39 to measure unquoted equity investments at cost when the fair value cannot be determined reliably. However, it indicates that in limited circumstances, cost may be an appropriate estimate of fair value – for example, when insufficient more recent information is available from which to determine fair value; or when there is a wide range of possible fair value measurements and cost represents the best estimate of fair value within that range. However, IFRS 9 includes indicators of when cost might not be representative of fair value. These are:

- A significant change in the investee's performance compared with budgets, plans or milestones.

- Changes in expectation that the investee's technical product milestones will be achieved.

- A significant change in the market for the investee's equity or its products or potential products.

- A significant change in the global economy or the economic environment in which the investee operates.

- A significant change in the performance of comparable entities or in the valuations implied by the overall market.

- Internal matters of the investee such as fraud, commercial disputes, litigation, or changes in management or strategy.

- Evidence from external transactions in the investee's equity, either by the investee (such as a fresh issue of equity) or by transfers of equity instruments between third parties.

[IFRS 9 App B5.5-6].

12.46   Given the indicators above, it is not expected that cost will be representative of fair value for an extended period of time.

Embedded derivatives

12.47   The accounting for embedded derivatives in host contracts that are financial assets is simplified by removing the requirement to consider whether or not they are closely related and should, therefore, be separated. The classification approach in the new standard applies to all financial assets, including those with embedded derivatives.

12.48   Many embedded derivatives introduce variability to cash flows. This is not consistent with the notion that the instrument's contractual cash flows solely represent the payment of principal and interest. If an embedded derivative was not considered closely related under the existing requirements, this does not automatically mean the instrument will not qualify for amortised cost treatment under the new standard. However, most hybrid contracts with financial asset hosts will be measured at fair value in their entirety.

12.49   The accounting for embedded derivatives in non-financial host contracts and financial liabilities currently remains unchanged.

Reclassifications

12.50   An instrument's classification is made at initial recognition and is not changed subsequently, with one exception. Reclassifications between fair value and amortised cost (and *vice versa*) are required only when the entity changes how it manages its financial instruments (that is, changes its business model). [IFRS 9 para 4.9]. Such changes are expected to be infrequent. The reclassification must be significant to the entity's operations and demonstrable to external parties. Any reclassification should be accounted for prospectively. Entities are not, therefore, allowed to restate any previously recognised gains or losses. The asset should be remeasured at fair value at the date of a reclassification of a financial asset from amortised cost to fair value; this value will be the new carrying amount. Any difference between the previous carrying amount and the fair value would be recognised in a separate line item in the income statement. At the date of a reclassification of a financial asset from fair value to amortised cost, its fair value at that reclassification date becomes its new carrying amount. [IFRS 9 paras 5.3.1-5.3.3].

12.51 Examples of change in the business model that would require reclassification include:

- An entity has a portfolio of commercial loans that it holds to sell in the short-term. Following an acquisition of an entity whose business model is to hold commercial loans to collect the contractual cash flows, that portfolio is managed together with the acquired portfolio to collect the contractual cash flows.

- An entity decides to close its retail mortgage business and is actively marketing its mortgage loan portfolio.

[IFRS 9 App B5.9].

12.52 The following are not changes in business model:

- A change in intention related to particular financial assets.

- A temporary disappearance of a particular market for financial assets.

- A transfer of financial assets between parts of the entity with different business models.

[IFRS 9 App B5.11].

All other reclassifications are prohibited.

> **Example – Leverage feature in an instrument lapses**
>
> An entity holds a convertible bond where the conversion feature lapses after a certain period of time. The lapse of the term does not constitute a reclassification event. Classification is determined on initial recognition. It is only when an entity changes its business model that instruments can be reclassified.

Transition and effective date

12.53 The requirements in IFRS 9 are generally applied retrospectively to assets held at the date of initial application with some exceptions. For example, if it is impracticable to retrospectively apply the effective interest method or impairment requirements, the entity should determine the instrument's amortised cost, or any impairment on the financial asset, in each period, by using its fair value at the end of each comparative period. [IFRS 9 para 8.2.10].

12.54 The effective date of IFRS 9 is 1 January 2013, with early application permitted. However, the standard has not yet been endorsed for use in the EU.

12.55 Additional disclosures are required by IFRS 7, 'Financial instruments: Disclosures', when the entity adopts the standard. See paragraph 12.63 below. The standard provides transition relief from restating comparative information for entities that adopt IFRS 9 for reporting periods before 1 January 2012. [IFRS 9 para 8.2.12]. IFRS 9 introduces the concept of a 'date of initial application'. This date is important for:

- identifying the assets to which IFRS 9 should be applied (the standard is not applied to assets derecognised by the date of initial application);

- assessing the business model;

- designations or de-designations for using the fair value option; and

- designations of non-trading equity investments as at FV through other comprehensive income.

12.56 For example, at the date of initial application an entity assesses the business model for holding a particular asset on the basis of the facts and circumstances that exist at that date. The resulting classification is then applied retrospectively, irrespective of the entity's business model in prior reporting periods. Similarly, at the date of initial application, an entity may designate a financial asset at fair value through profit or loss or an investment in an equity instrument as at fair value through other comprehensive income on the basis of the facts and circumstances that exist at that date. That classification is then applied retrospectively.

12.57 The date of initial application may be any date between the issue of the new standard (November 2009) and 31 December 2010 for entities adopting the new IFRS before 1 January 2011. For entities adopting this IFRS on or after 1 January 2011, the date of initial application is the beginning of the first reporting period in which the entity adopts this IFRS. [IFRS 9 para 8.2.2].

Example 1 – From AFS to amortised cost under IFRS 9

Management has decided to apply IFRS 9 on 15 December 2009 (the date of initial application) and not restate its comparatives as is permitted under IFRS 9. The entity has a debt instrument that is accounted for as AFS under IAS 39. On the date of initial application of IFRS 9, it is determined that the asset is held to collect the contractual cash flows and those cash flows solely represent payments of principal and interest. It will, therefore, be measured at amortised cost under IFRS 9. This will require on transition the debt instrument to be measured at amortised cost at 1 January 2009 (as if it had always been measured at amortised cost since it was initially recognised by the entity). Any existing AFS reserve is reclassified against opening retained earnings at 1 January 2009.

Example 2 – From AFS to FV through profit and loss for equities

Management has decided to apply IFRS 9 on 15 December 2009 (the date of initial application) and not restate its comparatives as is permitted under IFRS 9. On the date of initial application, management decides that its holding of equity investments will be classified as FV through profit and loss. The original cost of these equities was C100. At 31 December 2008, fair value was C30, so the AFS reserve was negative C70. It was determined at that date that those equities were impaired; C70 was, therefore, reflected in the income statement. At 31 December 2009, the fair value of the equities is C55. The entity is not restating its comparatives for 2008. Therefore, in 2009, when it first applies IFRS 9 and measures the equities at FV through profit and loss, the increase of C25 in fair value would be reflected in profit or loss for the 2009 year end.

Example 3 – FV through profit and loss to amortised cost

Management has decided to apply IFRS 9 on 15 December 2009 (the date of initial application) and not restate its comparatives as is permitted under IFRS 9. The entity has a debt instrument that was held at FV through profit and loss under IAS 39. On the date of initial application of IFRS 9, it is determined that the asset is held to collect its cash flows and that its cash flows solely represent payments of principal and interest. On transition, the debt instrument is measured at amortised cost (as if it had always been measured at amortised cost since it was initially recognised by the entity). Any difference between that and its fair value under IAS 39 will be reflected in opening retained earnings at 1 January 2009.

Example 4 – FV through profit and loss to FV through OCI

Management has decided to apply IFRS 9 on 15 December 2009 (the date of initial application) and not restate its comparatives as is permitted under IFRS 9. The entity has an equity investment that it currently classifies as FV through profit and loss under IAS 39. On the date of initial application of IFRS 9, management decides that it will classify the equity investment as FV through OCI, as it is not held-for-trading. On transition, as this measurement has to be applied retrospectively, a reserve will be created (that is, reclassified from opening retained earnings at 1 January 2009) in OCI, based on the difference between the instrument's original cost and its fair value at the opening balance sheet date.

Example 5 – AFS instruments disposed of during period of adoption

Management has decided to apply IFRS 9 on 15 December 2009 (the date of initial application). On 30 June 2009, the entity disposed of an AFS debt security (original cost C100, and FV on date of disposal of C110) and recognised a gain of C10 as a result of reclassifying the AFS reserve to profit and loss. There are no adjustments to be made for that AFS investment when the entity adopts IFRS 9 in its 2009 financial statements, as IFRS 9 is not applied to financial assets that have already been derecognised by the date of initial application. The entity would apply the same AFS accounting to that debt security as it had under IAS 39 in its 2009 financial statements.

Example 6 – 2008 IAS 39 reclassification amendment

The transition provisions in IFRS 9 require an entity to apply it retrospectively with a few exceptions. The reclassification amendment of October 2008 allowed certain instruments to be reclassified out of held-for-trading and AFS; upon reclassification, the fair value at the date of reclassification becomes the new amortised cost of reclassified assets. Upon initial application of IFRS 9, assuming these reclassified assets will continue to be measured at amortised cost, management is required to go back to the asset's initial recognition and then measure it as if it had always been measured at amortised cost under IFRS 9. Its amortised cost for IFRS 9 will not, therefore, be the same amortised cost that was determined when these assets were reclassified under IAS 39.

Example 7 – Date of initial application determined retrospectively

On 30 June 2010, management set its date of initial application as 1 March 2010. Setting the date of initial application retrospectively is supported by the ability to select any date between the issue of the new standard and 31 December 2010. After 1 January 2011, the date of initial application must be the beginning of the reporting period when the standard is first adopted.

Presentation and disclosure

12.58   IFRS 9 made some consequential amendments to IFRS 7. The majority of the changes were to align the disclosure requirements with the new measurement categories; however, some new additional disclosures are also required.

12.59   Entities that have designated a financial asset at fair value through profit or loss that would otherwise be measured at amortised cost are required to disclose:

- The the financial asset's maximum exposure to credit risk at the end of the reporting period.

- The amount by which any related credit derivatives or similar instruments mitigate that credit risk and their fair value.

- The amount of change during the period and cumulatively in the financial asset's fair value that is attributable to changes in its credit risk.

12.60   Entities that apply IFRS 9 are required to disclose the following in relation to financial assets measured at fair value through OCI:

- Which investments in equity instruments have been designated to be measured at fair value through OCI.

- The reasons for using this presentation alternative.

- The fair value of each such investment at the end of the reporting period.

- Dividends recognised during the period, showing separately those related to investments derecognised during the reporting period and those related to investments held at the end of the reporting period.

- Any transfers of the cumulative gain or loss within equity during the period and the reason for such transfers.

- For any equity investments that were derecognised during the period, the reason for disposing of the investments, the fair value of the investments at the date of derecognition and the cumulative gain or loss on disposal.

[IFRS 7 para 11A-11B].

12.61   In addition, there are new disclosure requirements for assets that are required to be reclassified under IFRS 9 because of the change in business model, as follows:

- The date of reclassification.

- A detailed explanation of the change in business model and a qualitative description of its effect on the entity's financial statements.

- The amount reclassified into and out of each category.

- For each reporting period following reclassification until derecognition, the effective interest rate determined on the date of reclassification and the interest income or expense recognised.

- If the entity has reclassified financial assets so that they are measured at amortised cost since its last annual reporting date, the financial assets' fair value at the end of the reporting period and the fair value gain or loss that would have been recognised in profit or loss during the reporting period if the financial assets had not been reclassified.

[IFRS 7 paras 12B-12D].

12.62   An entity is required to disclose an analysis of the gain or loss recognised in the statement of comprehensive income arising from derecognising the financial assets measured at amortised cost showing separately gains and losses arising from derecognition of those financial assets. This disclosure must also include the reasons for derecognising those financial assets. [IFRS 7 para 20A].

12.63   When an entity first applies IFRS 9, there are additional disclosures required for each class of financial assets on the date of initial application, as follows:

- The original measurement category and carrying amount determined in accordance with IAS 39.

- The new measurement category and carrying amount determined in accordance with IFRS 9.

- The amount of any financial assets in the statement of financial position that were previously designated as measured at fair value through profit or loss but that are no longer so designated, distinguishing between those that IFRS 9 requires an entity to reclassify and those that an entity elects to reclassify.

- Qualitative information about how it applied the classification requirements in IFRS 9 to those financial assets whose classification has changed as a result of applying IFRS 9.

- Qualitative information about the reasons for any designation or de-designation of financial assets or financial liabilities as measured at fair value through profit or loss.

[IFRS 7 paras 44I-44J].

The quantitative disclosures should be presented in a tabular format.

Index

Locators are:
paragraph numbers: 11.149, for Chapter 11, paragraph 149

Entries are in word-by-word alphabetical order, where a group of letters followed by a space is filed before the same group of letters followed by a letter, eg 'capital structure and treasury policy' will appear before 'capitalisation'. In determining alphabetical arrangement, initial articles, conjunctions and small prepositions are ignored.

Index

embedded derivatives in equity host contracts, and, 5.58—5.61
deeply in-the-money, and, 8.98.11

Caps, floors and collars
embedded derivatives in debt host contracts, and, 5.38—5.42
embedded derivatives in executory contracts, and, 5.83

Cash flow hedges
accounting, 10.115—10.117
definition, 10.106
discontinuing accounting, 10.121—10.123
examples, 10.107
forecast transactions, 10.108—10.114
reclassifying equity gains and losses, 10.118—10.120

Changes in estimated cash flows
amortised cost (effective interest method), and, 9.63—9.64.2

Changes in tax laws
held-to-maturity investments, and, 6.49

Characteristics of financial instruments
conditional rights and obligations, 4.13—4.15
contingent rights and obligations, 4.13—4.15
contractual basis, 4.8—4.12
definitions
  equity instrument, 4.6
  financial asset, 4.4
  financial instrument, 4.3
  financial liability, 4.5—4.5.2
  introduction, 4.2
  key features, 4.7
derivatives
  accounting, 4.42
  contracts to buy or sell non-financial items, 4.39
  definition, 4.25
  examples, 4.38
  initial net investment, 4.33—4.34
  introduction, 4.23—4.24
  key features, 4.26—4.37
  notional amounts, 4.31—4.32
  payment provisions, 4.31—4.32
  regular way contracts, 4.41
  settlement at future date, 4.35—4.37
  underlying', 4.27—4.30
exchange under potentially favourable or unfavourable terms, 4.16
identification, 4.22
introduction, 4.1
non-derivative transactions, 4.40
non-financial assets and liabilities, and, 4.17—4.21
overview, 1.8—1.13

Classification of financial assets
available-for-sale financial assets (AFS)
  generally, 6.66—6.68
  reclassification into, 6.73
  reclassification out of, 6.74—6.74.2
categories
  available-for-sale financial assets, 6.66—6.68
  fair value through profit or loss, 6.3—6.25
  held-to-maturity investments, 6.26—6.57
  introduction, 6.2
  loans and receivables, 6.58—6.65
fair value through profit or loss (FVTPL)
  accounting mismatch, 6.8—6.16
  definition, 6.3—6.4
  designation, 6.5—6.20
  exception, 6.21
  group of financial assets and liabilities, 6.17—6.20
  held for trading, 6.22—6.25
  reclassification, 6.70—6.712
generally, 6.2

held-to-maturity investments (HTM)
  ability to hold to maturity, 6.35—6.36
  assessment of classification, 6.37
  business combination, 6.50—6.51
  changes in tax laws, 6.49
  decision tree, 6.57
  definition, 6.26—6.27
  determinable payments, 6.28—6.29
  fixed maturity, 6.28—6.29
  fixed payments, 6.28—6.29
  intent to hold to maturity, 6.30—6.34
  reclassification into, 6.74—6.74.2
  reclassification out of, 6.73
  regulatory changes, 6.53—6.56
  significant deterioration in issuer's creditworthiness, 6.46—6.48
  statutory changes, 6.53—6.56
  tainting rules, 6.38—6.45
introduction, 6.1—6.1.1
loans and receivables
  debt instruments quoted in active market, 6.65
  introduction, 6.58—6.62
  purchased loans, 6.65
  reclassification, 6.72
overview, 1.16—1.19
reclassification between categories
  available-for-sale financial assets, 6.73—6.74.2
  fair value through profit or loss, 6.70
  held-for-trading, 6.71—6.71.4
  held-to-maturity investments, 6.73—6.74.2
  introduction, 6.69
  loans and receivables, 6.71.5—6.72.1
  summary, 6.74.3
tainting rules
  exceptions, 6.41—6.45
  group situation, 6.40
  introduction, 6.38—6.39

Classification of financial instruments
available-for-sale financial assets, 6.66—6.68
disclosure, and, 11.39—11.41.1
financial assets
  See also **Classification of financial assets**
  available-for-sale financial assets, 6.66—6.68
  fair value through profit or loss, 6.3—6.25
  held-to-maturity investments, 6.26—6.57
  introduction, 6.2
  loans and receivables, 6.58—6.65
  reclassification between categories, 6.69—6.74.3
financial guarantee contracts, 6.84
financial liabilities
  fair value through profit or loss, 6.77—6.81
  introduction, 6.75—6.76
  other liabilities, 6.82
  reclassification between categories, 6.83
held-to-maturity investments, 6.26—6.57
IFRS 9, and, 6.1.1
introduction, 6.1—6.1.1
loans and receivables, 6.58—6.65
overview, 1.16—1.19
reclassification between categories
  available-for-sale financial assets, 6.73—6.74.2
  fair value through profit or loss, 6.70
  held-for-trading, 6.71—6.71.4
  held-to-maturity investments, 6.73—6.74.2
  introduction, 6.69
  loans and receivables, 6.71.5—6.72.1
  summary, 6.74.3

Closely related'
application of criteria to different hosts
  debt host contracts, 5.23—5.56
  equity host contracts, 5.57—5.61

Index